The Capital Budgeting Decision

Economic Analysis of Investment Projects

Harold Bierman, Jr.
*The Nicholas H. Noyes Professor
of Business Administration*

Seymour Smidt
*The Nicholas H. Noyes Professor
of Economics and Finance*

*Johnson Graduate School of Management
Cornell University*

The Capital Budgeting Decision

Economic Analysis of Investment Projects

SEVENTH EDITION

Macmillan Publishing Company
New York
Collier Macmillan Publishers
London

Macmillan Publishing Company
866 Third Avenue, New York, New York 10022

Collier Macmillan Canada, Inc.

Library of Congress Cataloging-in-Publication Data

Bierman, Harold.
  The capital budgeting decision.

  Includes index.
  1. Capital investments—Evaluation.   2. Capital
budget.   I. Smidt, Seymour.   II. Title.
HG4028.C4B54   1988   658.1′52   87–15257
ISBN 0-02-309941-0

Printing: 1 2 3 4 5 6 7 8   Year: 8 9 0 1 2 3 4 5 6 7

Preface to the Seventh Edition

Recalls one former head of an office-equipment company controlled by Exxon: "Their MBA's came in and said, 'Give us your five-year plan.' Our long-range plan was where we'd have lunch tomorrow."

> *Laurie P. Cohen*, The Wall Street Journal, *Monday, September 10, 1984*

This edition follows the direction of its predecessors. When the first edition was published in 1960, we were convinced that the net present value method was superior to other methods of making investment decisions. We still believe this. In the important area of uncertainty, however, our attitudes have undergone some changes that were first incorporated in the second edition. The greatest changes from the first edition will be found in the general method of incorporating uncertainty in the investment decision process and in the introduction of the strategic net present value concept.

We continue to advocate the net present value method. In practice, most projects are analyzed using an estimate of the expected cash flows. A risk adjustment is necessary. The risk adjustment should reflect all of the strategic aspects of the project. The most common procedure is to use a risk-adjusted discount rate. We attempt to point out the advantages and disadvantages of this approach. Even when using a risk-adjusted discount rate, it may not be appropriate to require all projects to earn a rate equal to the firm's average cost of capital. Some investments with internal rates of return greater than the firm's weighted average cost of capital may be acceptable. The average cost of capital is a useful concept in handling capital structure questions, but it is less useful in evaluating investment alternatives. However, it is simple to apply; thus, it is widely used in investment analysis.

Our preference is to use a default-free rate of interest to take the time value of money into consideration and to take risk into account separately, preferably by subtracting a dollar risk adjustment from the cash flows. This permits a more flexible approach. Some cash-flow components (such as tax shields) of an investment can be less uncertain than others (such as contribution margins).

Part I of the book has been extensively rewritten and rearranged. A new Chapter 2, "The Time Value of Money," has been inserted. Previously we relegated the basic elements of the time-value calculation to an appendix, but now those who want the calculations explained more fully can use Chapter 2 for that purpose. The new Chapter 3 is a consolidation of the old Chapters 2 and 4, with some material contained in Chapter 4. We now explain the net present value method in one chapter with fewer distractions. Chapter 4 now introduces the internal rate of return as well as the widely used payback and return on investment. The material was previously contained in Chapters 2 and 3.

Chapter 5 considers mutually exclusive investments, which were previously covered in Chapter 3. Chapter 6 deals with the determination and uses of cash flows and the impact of income taxes. This material was previously covered in Chapters 6 and 7. All these changes were made at the suggestion of more than one reviewer, and having made the changes, we agree that it is a more logical sequence than the one contained in the sixth edition. It is useful to first explain time-value calculations, then the net present value method, compare net present value and other available capital budgeting methods, deal with the complexity of mutually exclusive investments, and then define and explain cash flows.

This edition differs from previous editions in the arrangement of material. All of the basic material is in Part I. Part II deals with various special aspects of capital budgeting, such as replacement decisions, leasing, and timing. Part III covers uncertainty. Some of the material on uncertainty is no more difficult than other parts of the book, but a few chapters in this section are more complex. The material has been designed so that a professor who wishes to deal with fundamentals of uncertainty early in the course can assign Part III immediately following Part I. Part IV contains cases. Suggestions for using the cases are contained in the solutions manual, which is available from the publisher to instructors who adopt the text. If students have used our *Financial Management for Decision Making* in a previous course, the instructor who does not want to review the basic elements of capital budgeting can begin with Part II of this text.

In this edition we introduce the term *strategic net present value (S-NPV)* to call attention to adjustments that need to be made to a basic present value calculation so that the net present value will more accurately reflect the value of the project. Some of these adjustments were not traditionally considered to be part of capital budgeting or were not given adequate emphasis.

The value of a project must take into consideration the flexibility that it provides management. One project may commit management to a definite course of action; another may provide flexibility by giving management the option of making decisions in the future when more information is available. Chapter 18 emphasizes the need to assign a value to this flexibility. We point out that option pricing theory (also known as contingent claims analysis) sometimes provides a method for valuing flexibility.[1] But even though any knowledgeable, careful manager already incorporates the basic concepts of S-NPV, it is very

---

[1] See S. P. Mason and R. C. Merton, "The Role of Contingent Claims Analysis in Corporate Finance," in *Recent Advances in Corporate Finance*, ed. E. I. Altman and M. G. Subrahmanyam, (Homewood: Irwin, 1985), pp. 7–54; and F. Black and M. Scholes, "The Pricing of Options and Corporate Liabilities," *Journal of Political Economy*, May 1973, pp. 637–659.

useful to acknowledge formally the necessity of considering all decision alternatives and of using option theory where appropriate and feasible.

Project evaluation must also take into account the competitive position of the firm undertaking the project. Forecasting future cash flows requires estimates of the future prices of inputs and outputs. The accuracy of such forecasts can be increased if the project analyst gives careful consideration to the nature of competition in the input and output markets and to the firm's position in that competitive picture. Frequently, firms develop a strategic plan designed to encourage expansion in favorable areas and discourage it in product lines that are considered to be unfavorable. The interrelations between strategic planning and project analysis need consideration.

The concept of strategic net present value is intended to emphasize the need to consider the value of flexibility and the value of competitive position, as well as the extent to which the firm can accurately forecast the cash flows from a project.

We present intuitive solutions to capital budgeting decisions in the early chapters. An understanding of this basic material will avoid certain types of errors in evaluating investments. Even though it will not give exact answers to all the types of complex problems that managers must solve, it will help improve decision making.

Professors who adopt the book are eligible to receive a disk containing Lotus 123 spreadsheets and a site license allowing them to distribute the material to their students. The disk includes problem assignments and suggests various ways in which the use of personal computers can be integrated with the teaching of capital budgeting. The spreadsheet assignments can be used to help the student develop skills in programming spreadsheets, or can be used by students with a minimal knowledge of Lotus to reduce the burden of calculations traditionally associated with studying capital budgeting. One spreadsheet is a sophisticated financial calculator, which includes the capability of producing present value profile graphs.

We wish to thank the many persons in government, academic, and business areas, as well as our colleagues Jerry Hass, Vithala Rao, and John McClain, who have raised questions and made suggestions that have advanced our thinking. In addition, we want to thank Rita Smidt for helping program the spreadsheets, and Philomena Curley and Barbara Guile for their cheerful assistance.

Extracts from
Preface to the First Edition

Businessmen and economists have been concerned with the problem of how financial resources available to a firm should be allocated to the many possible investment projects. Should a new plant be built? Equipment replaced? Bonds refunded? A new product introduced? These are all to some extent capital budgeting decisions to which there are theoretically sound solutions. The purpose of this book is to express the solution of the economist in the language of the business manager.

Decades ago, economists such as Böhm-Bawerk, Wicksell, and Irving Fisher laid the theoretical foundation for a sound economic approach to capital budgeting. In recent years the technical literature has contained articles (such as those by Dean, Solomon, Lorie, Savage, and Hirshleifer) that have significantly increased our understanding of what is required for sound capital budgeting decisions. However, these works have not been directed toward business managers and, until recently, the work of these men has had no perceptible influence on the way businessmen actually made capital investment decisions. Businessmen have tended to make capital budgeting decisions using their intuition, rules of thumb, or investment criteria with faulty theoretical foundations and thus have been likely to give incorrect answers in a large percentage of the decisions.

The purpose of this book is to present for an audience that may be completely unfamiliar with the technical literature on economic theory or capital budgeting a clear conception of how to evaluate investment proposals.

The authors are convinced that the "present-value" method is superior to other methods of evaluating the economic worth of investments that have been discussed in the business literature. They recognize that considerations other than that of economic worth are also important in making investment decisions. The early pages of the book show that "cash payback" and "return on investment" may give incorrect results. The "yield" or "investor's method" is shown to be inferior to the present-value method, especially where there are several alternative investments available. The explanation of the reasons for the inferiority of yield to present value is particularly timely, since popular business magazines have carried many articles praising the yield method without mentioning its important drawbacks.

The first four chapters present an over-all picture of the method of analysis advocated in this book that would be a suitable introduction for management at any level who need to be informed about the ideas involved in evaluating capital investments, but who are not directly involved in preparing investment evaluations. The remainder of the book elaborates on the basic description of the first four chapters and gives material that will assist a person in actually preparing the analysis of investments.

Ithaca, New York

HAROLD BIERMAN, JR.
SEYMOUR SMIDT

Contents

PART II
Capital Budgeting Applications and Some Operational Problems

PART III

Capital Budgeting with Uncertainty

21 Valuing Flexibility: An Application of Option Valuation Techniques   448

PART IV

Cases

APPENDIX TABLES

The Capital Budgeting Decision

Economic Analysis of Investment Projects

PART I

Capital Budgeting
with Certainty

Sirs: The Indian who sold Manhattan for $24.00 was a sharp salesman. If he had put his $24 away at 6% compounded semiannually, it would now be $9.5 billion and could buy most of the now-improved land back.
S. Branch Walker, Stamford, CT. Life, August 31, 1959

In the first six chapters of this book we present a theoretically correct and easily applied approach to decisions involving benefits and outlays through time, that is, capital budgeting decisions. Essentially, the procedure consists of choosing a rate of discount that represents the time value of money and applying this rate of discount to future cash flows to compute their net present value. The sum of all the present values associated with an investment (including immediate outlays) is the net present value of the investment.

In these six chapters it is assumed that the case flows associated with an investment are known with certainty, that there are markets to borrow or lend funds at the rate of interest used in the time discounting, and that there are no constraints preventing the firm from using these markets. The objective of the discounting process is to take the time value of money into consideration, but it includes no adjustment for risk.

We advocate the use of the net present value method to evaluate investments both because of its simplicity and for its theoretical soundness. For many decisions, however, the internal rate of return method is equally effective.

1

CHAPTER 1

Capital Budgeting

The New York Times *on January 17, 1964, reported the following exchange between Alfred P. Sloan, former Chairman of General Motors, and a reporter:*

One questioner asked Mr. Sloan if he had made any mistakes in 40 years as a top executive of General Motors and added: "Think of one." "I don't want to keep you up all night," Mr. Sloan snapped. "The executive who makes an average of 50–50 is doing pretty good."

The controller points to the ancient, gray, six-story structure and says with pride, "This is one reason we can keep our costs down. Our plant is fully depreciated, so we don't have the large depreciation charges our competitors have."

Another company in the same industry sells a relatively new plant because it is not large enough for a three-shift operation. Rather than operate what is considered to be an inefficient production line (the production line had been completely overhauled within the last twelve months), a new plant is being constructed in another state.

The investment philosophies of the two companies making these decisions were vastly different. One was reluctant to invest money in plant and equipment. The other wanted to operate only the latest in plant and equipment. Which of the two companies was right? Maybe each company was following a policy that was correct for it, or perhaps they were both making faulty decisions. We cannot decide here because the necessary facts are not available to us. But the facts should be available to the responsible executives in both these companies, and these facts should be arranged in a useful manner and then interpreted correctly.

Consider the statement of a steel company executive that Japanese steelmakers were lucky in having their obsolete plants destroyed in World War II. It enabled them to start fresh with efficient plants and equipment. Were the Japanese really "lucky" to have had their productive capacity destroyed? We think not. Good decision making is more effective (and humane) than bombs.

Investment decisions may be tactical or strategic. A tactical investment

3

decision generally involves a relatively small amount of funds and does not constitute a major departure from what the firm has been doing in the past. The consideration of a new machine tool by Ford Motor Company is a tactical decision, as is a buy-or-lease decision made by Mobil Oil Company.

Strategic investment decisions may involve large sums of money and may also result in a major departure from what the company has been doing in the past. Acceptance of a large strategic investment will involve a significant change in the company's expected profits and in the risks to which these profits will be subject. These changes are likely to lead stockholders and creditors to revise their evaluation of the company. If a private corporation undertook the development of a supersonic commercial transport (costing over $4 billion), this would be a strategic decision. If the company failed in its attempt to develop the commercial plane, the very existence of the company would be jeopardized. Frequently, strategic decisions are based on intuition rather than on detailed quantitative analysis.

The future success of a business depends on the investment decisions made today. That business managers are generally aware of this is indicatd by the requirement that important investment decisions must be approved by the chief operating executive or the board of directors. In spite of this fact, the procedures used to help management make investment decisions are often inadequate and misleading. Few manufacturing concerns would sign a long-term contract for supplies of an important raw material without carefully investigating the various sources of supply and considering the relative advantages of each in terms of price, service, and quality. Yet occasionally management groups approve investments without a careful consideration of available alternatives. Even when there is an investigation of alternatives, the information obtained sometimes does not lead to effective decisions, because managements may not organize the information in a way that will help them make better decisions.

Business organizations are continually faced with the problem of deciding whether the commitments of resources—time or money—are worthwhile in terms of the expected benefits. If the benefits are likely to accrue reasonably soon after the expenditure is made, and if both the expenditure and the benefits can be measured in dollars, the solution to such a problem is relatively simple. If the expected benefits are likely to accrue over a long time period, the solution is more complex.

We shall use the term *investment* to refer to commitments of resources made in the hope of realizing benefits that are expected to occur over a reasonably long period of time in the future. Capital budgeting is a many-sided activity that includes searching for new and more profitable investment proposals, investigating engineering and marketing considerations to predict the consequences of accepting the investment, and making economic analyses to determine the profit potential of each investment proposal. The primary purpose of this book is to help business management analyze the profit potential of investments in plant and equipment, marketing programs, research projects, and the like.

The Role of Strategy in Investment Decision Making

The investment strategy of a firm is a statement of the formal criteria it applies in searching for and evaluating investment opportunities. Strategic planning guides the search for projects by identifying promising product lines or geographic areas in which to search for good investment projects. One firm's strategy may be to seek opportunities for rapid growth in emerging high-technology businesses; another may seek opportunities to become the low-cost producer of commodities with well-established technologies and no unusual market problems; a third firm may look for opportunities to exploit its special knowledge of a particular family of chemicals. A strategy should reflect both the special skill and abilities of the firm (its comparative advantage) and the opportunities that are available as a result of dynamic changes in the world economy.

Strategic planning leads to a choice of the forest; project analysis studies individual trees. The two activities should complement and reinforce each other. Project analysis may provide a feedback loop to verify the accuracy of the strategic plan. If there are good opportunities (high net present value projects) where the strategic plan says they should be found, and few promising opportunities in lines of business which the strategy identifies as unattractive, confidence in the strategic plan increases. Alternatively, if attractive projects are not found where the plan had expected them, or if desirable projects appear in lines of business that the strategic plan had identified as unattractive, a reassessment of both the project studies and the strategic plan may be in order.

Net Present Value and Productivity

Productivity is defined as a ratio of output to input. There are many productivity indices, since there are many ways to measure output or input. By any reasonable measure, productivity increases were an important source of economic growth for the United States for at least the first three-quarters of the twentieth century. However, since the late 1960s, there has been a significant drop in the rate of increase of productivity. This has been a source of concern to policy makers in the business and public sectors. Many attempts have been made to explain this change in the rate of growth of productivity. Scholars who are experts in the subject can account for some of the factors that appear to be causing the decline in the rate of growth productivity; one such explanation is the rapid rate of growth of the labor force during this period. But a substantial portion cannot be explained. According to the 1982 *Economic Report of the President*:

> There have been concerted efforts to explain the measured slowdown. These efforts have met with only limited success. While there are a number of possible explanatory

variables, available studies suggest that none separately nor in combination is capable of explaining more than half of the decline.[1]

While scholars cannot explain fully the surprising decline in productivity increases, some authors have offered ad hoc explanations. Among the suggested explanations is the idea that the extensive use of net present value techniques is responsible for a decline in capital expenditures, which in turn has caused the decline in productivity. The following quotation represents this point of view.

> As these techniques have gained ever wider use in investment decision making, the growth of capital investment and R&D spending in this country has slowed. We believe this to be more than a simple coincidence. We submit that the discounting approach has contributed to a decreased willingness to invest for two reasons: (1) it is often based on misperceptions of the past and present economic environment, and (2) it is biased against investment because of critical errors in the way the theory is applied. Bluntly stated, the willingness of managers to view the future through the reversed telescope of discounted cash flow is seriously shortchanging the futures of their companies.[2]

In fairness to the authors just quoted, a careful reading of the quotation, and of the article in which it appears, indicates that it is the "misuse" of net present value (NPV) that results in the undesirable effects, not the "use." Unfortunately, the last sentence of the quotation, and the subtitle of the article in which it appears, give the impression that there are some inherent flaws in the NPV or discounted cash flow (DCF) method that inevitably bias against investment.

Our position is summarized in the following propositions.

1. The DCF or present value framework is the best available framework for analyzing investment cash flows. But it is only a tool, and any tool can be misused. There is no inherent bias in the tool. It can be misused to produce bias against investments that are desirable or to cause bias in favor of investments that are undesirable. It is not a substitute for good judgment or for effective business strategic planning, but it is an aid to implementing these processes. The main objective of this book is to explain how to use this tool in an effective manner.

2. We do not claim to be able to explain the substantial drop in productivity, though we doubt that it is caused by the widespread adoption of present value techniques. Certainly there is no substantial evidence to support this proposition: Decision makers in Japan and West Germany have been using present value techniques as long as their American counterparts.

We think it is at least as plausible to argue that the decline in the competitive

---

[1] *Economic Report of the President.* Washington: Government Printing Office, February 1982, p. 114.

[2] Robert H. Hayes and David A. Garvin, "Managing as if Tomorrow Mattered: Investment Decisions that Discount the Future May Result in High Present Values but Bleak Tomorrows," *Harvard Business Review*, May–June 1982, pp. 17–72.

position of the economy in the United States is due to the more effective use of DCF methods by our international competitors. Previous editions of this book have been translated into at least five foreign languages, and more copies have been sold overseas, in English and in translation, than have been sold in the United States. The first foreign language in which the book was published was Japanese.

Is there any connection between the rate of productivity increase and the use of DCF technology at an industry level? There certainly could be. Lacking concrete evidence, we cannot give DCF the credit for preventing an even larger decline in productivity increase. Nor can the DCF method receive the blame for the decline that has actually occurred. We do argue that the DCF method is the best decision tool available. Managers should learn to use it effectively. That is what this book is about.

Investments as Cash Flows

To focus attention on the problems of economic analysis, we begin by assuming that we have investment proposals worthy of preliminary consideration and that for each investment proposal the necessary engineering and marketing research has been completed. We assume that these studies will enable us to measure the dollar value of the resources expended and the benefits received from the investment during each future interval of time. In the early chapters of this book we assume that these dollar values can be estimated in advance with certainty. Later we relax this assumption and consider the additional complications that arise when decision makers are uncertain about the amounts and timing of the cash flows that will result from an investment.

Many investments cannot be described in terms of the certain (or uncertain) cash flows they will generate in each interval of time. We exclude these investments from exact analysis. Even business organizations, which carry further than most other organizations the attempt to measure all costs and benefits in dollar terms, find that the costs or benefits of many investments cannot be completely described in terms of dollars. Consider an advertising program designed to build up the prestige associated with the name of a corporation. This is an investment, because the expenditures are made in the hope of realizing benefits that will continue long after the advertising expenditures have been made. But it is difficult to estimate in dollar terms the exact value of the benefits that will accrue from the advertising program.

In nonprofit organizations, whether private or public, investments whose costs and benefits cannot be measured reasonably well in dollar terms are made even more frequently than in business. Nevertheless, investment proposals for which both the cost and benefits can be measured in dollar terms do arise in all these organizations, and the quantity of resources involved in such investments is considerable. In designing a building, for example, the architect or engineer is frequently faced with alternative means of accomplishing the same objective.

The design of the heating or lighting systems are but two examples. Frequently, one alternative will have a high initial cost but low maintenance or operating expenses, whereas another alternative will have low initial costs but high operating or maintenance expenses. A choice between the two alternatives is in essence an investment decision.

Thus, although not all the investment decisions in an organization can be described in terms of the dollar value of the expenditures or benefits, important decisions that can be described in these terms seem to occur in all organizations in modern society. As we increase our ability to forecast the consequences of our decisions, the number of investments that can be described reasonably well in dollar terms will also increase.

In this book we shall be mainly concerned with the economic analysis of investments from the point of view of a profit-seeking enterprise. Nevertheless, many of the methods of analysis described apply to investment decisions arising in private nonprofit organizations or in local or national governments, if the investment can be described in terms of cash flows. In these latter organizations, the appropriate definition of the cash flow may be different. For example, in considering whether an investment was worthwhile, a private business would not try to take into account the additional profits that might be earned by other businesses as a result of its investment. A government engaged in economic planning would normally try to consider such profits. We shall consider these questions briefly in Chapter 16. Also, the costs and methods of finance available to business enterprises are often significantly different from those available to governments or private nonprofit institutions. A government cannot sell common stock; a business firm cannot levy taxes to finance the investments it would like to undertake. In other respects, the methods of analysis that apply in business organizations are usually applicable in governments as well.

Frequently, an investment proposal will involve both benefits and expenditures during one or more time periods. When this occurs, it will be convenient to combine the dollar estimates of the benefits and expenditures for each period of time. If, during a specific period of time, the benefits exceed the expenditures, we may speak of the net benefits or positive cash flows; if the expenditures exceed the benefits, we may refer to the net expenditures or cash outlays. We shall adopt the convention of referring to cash in flows or outlays during a given period of time by using positive or negative dollar amounts, respectively. We shall refer to the entire series of net cash flows associated with an investment as the cash flow stream of the investment.

If some of the cash flows are subject to taxation, we shall measure the cash flows after taxes. A business corporation is subject to taxes on its income, and this income in turn depends on the amount of depreciation charges that can be used to offset revenues in computing taxable income. The amount of cash flows resulting from an investment in any future year will depend upon the regulations or laws established by the tax authority. These laws or regulations will determine the kinds of expenditures that can be charged immediately to expense and those that must be capitalized and written off in subsequent years by depreciating the asset. Nonprofit organizations and governments are not subject to income taxes, and therefore the proceeds they receive from an investment do not depend upon their depreciation accounting method.

It should be stressed that the definition of net benefits or cash flows just given is *not* identical with the income concept used in corporate accounting. The major difference is that, in estimating cash flows, depreciation charges and other amortization charges of fixed assets are not subtracted from gross revenues because no cash expenditures are required. The cash outlays associated with the investment are subtracted at the time of investment, and these substitute for the depreciation expenses. Corporate accounting computes the income of each year and thus must allocate the cost of the investment over its life. For decision purposes we are interested in the overall effect of the investment on the wellbeing of the firm and its investors and do not have to measure its effect on the income of any one year.

Estimate of Cash Flows

It is frequently stated that refinements in capital budgeting techniques are a waste of effort because the basic information being used is so unreliable. It is claimed that the estimates of cash flows are only guesses and that to use anything except the simplest capital budgeting procedures is as futile as using racing forms to pick winners at the track or complicated formulas to determine whch way the stock market is going to move next.

It is true that in many situations reliable estimates of cash flows are difficult to make. Fortunately, there are a large number of investment decisions in which cash flows can be predicted with a fair degree of certainty. But even with an accurate, reliable estimate of cash flows, the wrong decision is frequently made because incorrect methods are used in evaluating this information.

When it is not possible to make a single estimate of cash flows that are certain to occur, it does not follow that incorrect methods of analysis are justified. If it is difficult to predict the outcome of an investment with certainty, and if the investment is large, the use of a careful and comprehensive analysis is justified, even if this means that the analysis will be more complicated and costly. With small tactical investments, somewhat less involved methods might be used because a more complex analysis would not be necessary, but again there is no need to use inferior methods that decrease the likelihood of making correct investment decisions.

Strategic Net Present Value (SNPV)

Strategic net present value (SNPV) is a variation of net present value. It differs by formally incorporating three types of considerations that may be omitted for the conventional NPV analysis.

1. Valuation of flexibility arising from the decision alternatives associated with
   a. The timing of the initial investment construction process and the rate at which construction takes place.
   b. The possibilities of extending the scope of the investment within the expected life of the investment.
   c. The possibilities of this investment affecting the firm's subsequent investments after the investment has ceased operations.
2. Valuation of the effects on the decision of the firm's competitive market position for the product that is affected by the decision.
3. Valuation of risk, using market measures where feasible.

Notice that SNPV is a process of formally extending the scope of analysis and recognizing the flexibility available to management.

Application of Capital Budgeting Techniques

Many different decisions may be thought of as investment and hence incorporated into the capital budgeting process. We shall illustrate in this section some of the situations of this nature.

Replacement Decision

A company is currently using three pieces of equipment that cost $10,000 each and are 70 percent depreciated. They can be replaced with one unit of equipment that would cost $200,000. It is expected that at normal activity the new machine would save $40,000 a year in labor, maintenance, and so on for a period of five years. Should the machines be replaced?

Size of Plant

A company must choose between a small plant that would cost $10 million and a larger plant that would cost $25 million. The earnings of both plants are computed, and it is found that the small plant would yield a return of 20 percent and the large plant, a return of 17 percent. Which plant should be chosen?

Lease or Buy

A company can either buy data-processing equipment or rent it. The cost of the equipment is $300,000, and the rental fee is $10,000 per month. It is estimated that improvements will make this equipment obsolete within five years. Should the company lease or buy?

Refunding of Debt

A company currently has a $10 million debt outstanding, bearing a coupon rate of 10 percent. The debt was issued at a discount, which is still unamortized to the extent of $500,000. The company can currently issue bonds to yield 9 percent. The costs of issuing the new bonds would be $200,000, and there would be a call premium on the old bonds of $300,000. The old bonds have twenty years remaining until they become due. Should the bonds be refunded?

Make or Buy

A company can buy a component at $50 per unit with a long-term contract or spend $10,000,000 on equipment to make it. It needs 1,000,000 units per year. Should it make or buy?

A Real Estate Investment

Miss Jones can invest in a real estate project. There is an initial investment of $100,000; then rentals and tax benefits will occur for a number of years. Finally, the debt must be repaid and the project sold. Is the investment desirable?

With some investments, alternatives can be screened with little or no detailed analysis. The passage of a law might lead to the necessity of making capital expenditures where the only other feasible alternative to consider is shutdown of the facility. In some cases, the desirability of making the mandated expenditures will be readily apparent with no analysis. Other projects might be rejected because they take the firm in directions that top management has rejected.

Although none of the preceding examples contains all the facts that would be necessary for a decision, they illustrate well the kind of problem that will be considered. The analytical methods that will be suggested in this book are applicable for all these examples.

Criteria for Evaluation Measures of Investment Worth

In the case of business organizations, the measures of investment worth that have been proposed and that are developed in this book concentrate on a form of the profit-maximization goal but attempt to include equally important conditions, such as the risks associated with the investments undertaken and the future structure of assets and liabilities that will be determined in part by the investment decisions currently being made.

To be a reasonable criterion, profit maximization has to consider the size of the investment employed and the alternative uses of the funds invested (including the possibility of returning these funds to the stockholders). One way of stating the objective of the investment decision procedure is to describe it as tending to maximize the current market value of the stockholders' holdings in the firm. Although not an exact criterion (for example, it does not help decide between an option that elevates the value of a stock now but depresses it later and one that depresses the stock now and elevates it later), maximization of the value of the stockholders' holdings is a reasonable description of what we would like our measure of investment worth to accomplish.

It is recognized that a complete statement of the organizational goals of a business enterprise would embrace a much wider range of considerations, including such things as the prestige, income, security, freedom, and power of the management group and the contribution of the corporation to the overall social environment in which it exists and to the welfare of the labor force that it employs. Insofar as the attainment of profits, without unnecessary risks or an unduly awkward financial structure, does not conflict with the other goals mentioned, the assumption that the pecuniary objectives are the proximate goals of a business organization is tenable.

The measure of investment worth that best describes the profit potential of a proposed investment is the net present value of the cash flows associated with the proposed investment. It is more consistent with furthering the stockholders' interests than straight maximization of income, because the accounting measures of income do not take into consideration alternative uses of the funds that would be tied up in investments. The net present value method, however, does not necessarily provide a useful measure of the additional risks to which the owners of a business will be exposed as a result of accepting an investment. Methods of incorporating such risks into the analysis are discussed in Chapter 18 and subsequent chapters.

Budget Process and Planning

Frequently, we think of the budget of a firm as being part of the cost-control apparatus and forget that it is an important tool for planning. The capital budget for the coming period will affect the cash budget and will be affected in turn by sales forecasts; thus the capital budget must be incorporated into the budgetary process.

The timing of cash flows resulting from capital expenditures is extremely important to the corporate officer attempting to plan the cash needs of the firm. Information is needed on the specific days the bills will have to be paid and at the time that cash will begin to be generated by the investment. It will not be possible to predict these events with certainty, but it should be possible to make reasonable estimates that will be useful.

If an attempt is being made to project other financial data over one or more years, the composition of the capital budget will affect the nature of the other planning budgets. For example, if an automobile company is planning to enter the steel industry, this would be disclosed in the capital budget and would certainly affect all other budgets.

The capital budget should be an integral part of the budget and planning process. The officer in charge of the capital budget must be in effective communication with the budget officer of the firm (if the positions are separate), because the decisions they make will result in a considerable amount of interaction.

Conclusions

In the first part of this book there is an assumption that the cash flows are known with certainty. This assumption may be somewhat difficult to accept, since it is well known that there are few cash flows associated with real investments that are actually known with certainty. There are two reasons for proceeding in this manner. First, we have to "walk through our plays" before starting to run. There are sufficient difficulties in just taking the time value of money into consideration without also incorporating risk factors. Second, when the cash flows are finally allowed to be uncertain, we shall suggest the use of procedures that are based on the initial recommendations made with the certainty assumption, so nothing is lost by initially making the assumption of certainty.

DISCUSSION QUESTIONS

1.A The ABC Company has to make a choice between two strategies:
Strategy 1 is expected to result in a market price now of $100 per share of common stock and a price of $120 five years from now.
Strategy 2 is expected to result in a market price now of $80 and a price of $140 five years from now.
What would you recommend? Assume that all other things are unaffected by the decision being considered.

1.B It has been said that few stockholders would think favorably of a project that promised its first cash flow in 100 years, no matter how large this return.
Comment on this position.

1.C Each of the following is sometime listed as a reasonable objective for a firm: (a) maximize profit (accounting income); (b) maximize sales (or share of the market); (c) maximize the value of a share of common stock t time periods from now; (d) ensure continuity of existence; (e) maximize the rate of growth; (f) maximize future dividends.
Discuss each item and the extent of its relevance to the making of investment decisions.

1.D   Prepare an example or an explanation that indicates why each of the following is an insufficient description of the goals of a profit-seeking organization: (a) maximize profits or earnings per share; (b) maximize the price per share of the common stock now; (c) maximize the price share of the common stock in the future; (d) maximize sales (or percentage of the market).

REFERENCES*

Journals: **Specific papers that may be of interest follow.**

Bacon, Peter W., "The Evaluation of Mutually Exclusive Investments," *Financial Management*, Summer 1977, pp. 55–58.

Beedles, William L., "A Note on Evaluating Non-Simple Investments," *Journal of Financial and Quantitative Analysis*, March 1978, pp. 173–176.

Bernhard, Richard H., "Mathematical Programming Models for Capital Budgeting—A Survey, Generalization, and Critique," *Journal of Financial and Quantitative Analysis*, June 1969, pp. 111–158.

Brigham, Eugene F., and Richard H. Pettway, "Capital Budgeting by Utilities," *Financial Management*, Autumn 1973, pp. 11–22.

Carter, E. Eugene, "Designing the Capital Budgeting Process," *TIMS Studies in the Management*, 1977, pp. 25–22.

Corr, Arthur V., "Capital Investment Planning," *Financial Executive*, April 1982, pp. 12–15.

Dean, J., "Measuring the Productivity of Capital," *Harvard Business Review*, January–February 1954, pp. 120–130.

Dorfman, Robert, "The Meaning of the Internal Rate of Return," *Journal of Finance*, December 1981, pp. 1010–1023.

Fogler, H. Russell, "Ranking Techniques and Capital Rationing," *Accounting Review*, January 1972, pp. 134–143.

Gittman, Lawrence J., and John R. Forrester, Jr., "Forecasting and Evaluation Practices and Performance: A Survey of Capital Budgeting," *Financial Management*, Fall 1977, pp. 66–71.

Hirschleifer, J., "On the Theory of Optimal Investment Decisions," *Journal of Political Economics*, August 1958, pp. 329–352.

Hoskins, Colin G., and Glen A. Mumey, "Payback: A Maligned Method of Asset Ranking?" *Engineering Economist*, Fall 1979, pp. 53–65.

---

* *Financial Management*, the *Engineering Economist*, and the *Journal of Business Finance & Accounting* carry a large number of relatively readable papers on capital budgeting. The *Journal of Finance* also frequently deals with the subject, but is somewhat less readable. The *Harvard Business Review* has occasional papers.

Keane, Simon M., "The Internal Rate of Return and the Reinvestment Fallacy," *Journal of Accounting and Business Studies*, June 1979, pp. 48–55.

Lewellen, Wilbur G., H. P. Lanser, and J. J. McConnell, "Payback Substitutes for Discounted Cash Flow," *Financial Management*, Summer 1973, 17–25.

Lorie, J. H., and L. J. Savage, "Three Problems in Rationing Capital," *Journal of Business*, October 1955, pp. 229–239.

Mao, James C. T., "Survey of Capital Budgeting: Theory and Practice," *Journal of Finance*, May 1970, pp. 349–360.

Rappaport, Alfred, and Robert A. Taggart, Jr., "Evaluation of Capital Expenditure Proposals Under Inflation," *Financial Management*, Spring 1982, pp. 5–13.

Sarnat, Marshall, and Haim Levy, "The Relationship of Rules of Thumb to the Internal Rate of Return: A Restatement and Generalization," *Journal of Finance*, June 1969, pp. 479–489.

Schwab, Bernhard, and Peter Lusztig, "A Comparative Analysis of the Net Present Value and the Benefit–Cost Ratios as Measures of the Economic Desirability of Investments," *Journal of Finance*, June 1969, pp. 507–516.

Weaver, James B., "Organizing and Maintaining a Capital Expenditure Program," *Engineering Economist*, Fall 1974, pp. 1–36.

Weingartner, H. Martin, "Capital Budgeting of Interrelated Projects: Survey and Synthesis," *Management Science*, March 1966, pp. 485–516.

——, "Some New Views on the Payback Period and Capital Budgeting Decisions," *Management Science*, August 1969, pp. 594–607.

Books

Archer, S. H., and C. A. D'Ambrosio, *The Theory of Business Finance, A Book of Readings*, 2nd ed. (New York: Macmillan Publishing Company, 1976).

Boness, A. J., *Capital Budgeting* (New York: Praeger Publishers, 1972).

Brigham, E. F., and R. E. Johnson, *Issues in Managerial Finance*, 2nd ed. (Hinsdale, IL: The Dryden Press, Division of CBS College Publishing, 1980).

Crum, R. L., and F. G. J. Derkinderen (Eds.), *Capital Budgeting Under Conditions of Uncertainty* (Boston: Martinus Nijhoff, 1981).

Dean, J., *Capital Budgeting* (New York: Columbia University Press, 1951).

Fisher, I. *The Theory of Interest* (New York: Macmillan Publishing Company, 1930).

Grant, E. L., W. G. Ireson, and R. S. Leavenworth,. *Principles of Engineering Economy*, 6th ed. (New York: Ronald Press, 1976).

Levy, H., and M. Sarnat, *Capital Investment and Financial Decisions*, 2nd ed. (Englewood Cliffs, NJ: Prentice-Hall, 1983).

Lind, R. C., *Discounting for Time and Risk in Energy Policy,* (Baltimore: The Johns Hopkins University Press, 1982).

Lutz, F., and V. Lutz, *The Theory of Investment of the Firm* (Princeton, NJ: Princeton University Press, 1951).

Masse, P., *Optimal Investment Decisions: Rules for Action and Criteria for Choices* (Englewood Cliffs, NJ: Prentice-Hall, 1962).

Merrett, A. J., and A. Sykes, *The Finance and Analysis of Capital Projects* (New York: John Wiley & Sons, 1963).

——. *Capital Budgeting & Company Finance* (New York: Longman, 1966).

Quirin, G. D., and J. C. Wiginton, *Analyzing Capital Expenditures* Homewood, IL: Richard D. Irwin, 1981).

Solomon, E., *The Management of Corporate Capital* (New York: Free Press, 1959).

Wilkes, F. M., *Capital Budgeting Techniques* (New York: John Wiley & Sons, 1977).

CHAPTER 2

The Time Value of Money

Implementing capital budgeting techniques depends on judgment and foresight of those looking into the future. Sophisticated analysis seldom compensates for bad judgment.

Vice President of Finance, a Fortune 500 firm

Time Discounting

One of the basic concepts of business economics and managerial decision making is that the value of an amount of money is a function of the time of receipt or disbursement of the cash. A dollar received today is more valuable than a dollar to be received in some future time period. The only requirement for this concept to be valid is that there be a positive rate of interest at which funds can be invested.

The time value of money affects a wide range of business decisions, and a knowledge of how to incorporate time value considerations systematically into a decision is essential to an understanding of finance. The objective of this chapter is to develop skills in finding the present equivalent of a future amount or future amounts and the future equivalent of a present amount. This framework is than applied to a variety of business decisions.

Symbols Used

C Cash flow

C_t Cash flow at end of period t

t Time index as in $\sum_{t=1}^{n} C_t$

$B(n, r)$ Present value of an annuity with first payment at the end of period 1. The number of periods is n, and the discount rate is r.

$(1 + r)^{-t}$ Present value of a dollar to be received at the end of period t using an r rate of discount.

PV   Present value of a cash flow stream where

$$PV = \sum_{t=1}^{n} (1 + r)^{-t} C_t$$

FV   Future value of a cash flow stream at the end of period n where

$$FV = \sum_{t=1}^{n} (1 + r)^{n - t} C_t \qquad \text{or} \qquad FV = PV(1 + r)^n$$

m Number of interest compoundings in a period.

j Nominal interest rate.

r Annual discount rate where

$$r = \left(1 + \frac{j}{m}\right)^m - 1$$

e^{-jt} Continuous present value factor using j rate of discount and t periods.

APR   Annual percentage rate; equal to the annual discount rate times 100 to convert a fraction to a percent.

The Interest Rate

A dollar available today is more valuable than a dollar available one period from now if investment opportunities exist. There are two primary reasons why real investments can generate an interest return.

1. Some types of capital increase in value through time because of changes in physical characteristics, for example, cattle, wine, and trees.
2. There are many work processes where roundabout methods of production are desirable, leading to increased productivity. If you are going to cut down a large tree, it may be worth investing some time to sharpen your axe. A sharp axe may result in less time being spent cutting down trees (including sharpening time) than working with a dull axe. If you are going to dig a hole, you might want to build or buy a shovel, or even spend the time to manufacture a back-hoe if it is a big hole. The investment increases productivity sufficiently compared to the alternative methods of production without capital so that the new asset can earn a return.

These characteristics of capital lead to a situation in which business entities can afford to pay interest for the use of money. If you invest $1 in an industrial firm, the firm may be able to pay you $1 plus interest if your savings enabled the firm to use some roundabout method of production or to delay the sale of a product while it increased in value.

Future Value

Assume that you have $1 now and can invest it to earn r interest. After one period, you will have $1 plus the interest earned on the $1. Let FV be the future value and r be the annual interest rate. Then

$$FV = 1 + r$$

Repeating the process, at time 2 you will have

$$FV = (1 + r) + r(1 + r) = (1 + r)^2$$

and the future value of $1 invested for n periods is

$$FV = (1 + r)^n$$

If $r = .10$ and $n = 2$, we have

$$FV = (1 + r)^n = (\$1.10)^2 = \$1.21$$

If, instead of starting with $1, we start with a present value, PV, of $50, the value at time 2 is

$$FV = PV(1 + r)^n$$

$$FV = 50(\$1.10)^2 = \$60.50 \tag{2.1}$$

The $50 grows to $55 at time 1. The $55 grows to $60.50 at time 2.

Equation (2.1) is the standard compound interest formula for the future value of a present sum. The term $(1 + r)^n$ is called the accumulation factor. Equation (2.1) shows how to calculate future values of a present sum: the dollar amount that you will have n years in the future if a present sum of PV dollars is compounded for n years at an interest r per year.

The power of compounding (earning interest on interest) is dramatic. It can be illustrated by computing how long it takes to double the value of an investment. Table 2.1 shows these periods for different values of r.

A useful rule of thumb in finance is the "double-to-72" rule, where for wide ranges of interest rates r, the approximate doubling time is $.72/r$. Note how closely the rule approximates the values in Table 2.1. With a .10 time value factor, an investment will double in value every 7.3 years. The rule of thumb gives 7.2 years.

Frequently, to make business decisions instead of computing future values, we shall want to work with present values.

TABLE 2.1   Time Until Doubling

Interest Rate (r)	Time Until Initial Value is Doubled
.02	35.0 years
.05	14.2
.10	7.3
.15	5.0
.20	3.8

Time Indifference: Present Value

Today over 90 percent of large firms use some form of discounted cash flow (DCF) techniques in their captial budgeting (investment decision making). To perform a DCF analysis, we must find the present value equivalents of future sums of money. For example, if the firm will receive $100 one year from now as a result of a decision, we want to find the present value equivalent of the $100. Assuming that the money is worth (can be borrowed or lent at) .10 per year, the $100 is worth $90.91 now. The indifference can be shown by noting that $90.91 invested to earn .10 will earn $9.09 interest in one year; thus, the investor starting with $90.91 will have $100 at the end of the year. If the investor can both borrow and lend funds at .10, the investor will be indifferent between receiving $100 at the end of the year or $90.91 at the beginning of the year.

If the .10 interest rate applies for two time periods, the investor will be indifferent about receiving $82.64 today or $100 two years from today. If the $82.64 is invested to earn .10 per year, the investor will have $90.91 after one year and $100 at the end of two years.

The unit of time can be different from a year, but the unit of time for which the interest rate is measured must be the same as the unit of time for measuring the timing of the cash flows. For example, the .10 used in the example is defined as the interest rate per year and is applied to a period of one year.

Starting with equation (2.1) we have

$$FV = PV(1 + r)^n \tag{2.1}$$

Dividing both sides of that equation by $(1 + r)^n$, we obtain

$$PV = \frac{FV}{(1 + r)^n}$$

Using C_n to denote the cash flow at the end of period n and r to denote the time value of money, we find that the present value PV of C_n is

$$PV = \frac{C_n}{(1 + r)^n}$$

or, equivalently,

$$PV = C_n(1 + r)^{-n} \tag{2.2}$$

where $(1 + r)^{-n}$ is the present value of $1 to be received at the end of period n when the time value of money is r. The term $(1 + r)^{-n}$ is called the present value factor.

Computing Present Value Factors

There are three common methods for computing present value factors: tables, hand calculators, and microcomputers.

The present value factor for various combinations of time periods and interest rates is found in Appendix Table A at the back of this book.

Any hand calculator with the capability to compute y^x can be used to compute present value factors directly. If y^x is used, then $y = 1 + r$ and $x = -n$. For example, to find the present value factor for $r = .10$ and $n = 5$ using a typical calculator, we would place 1.1 in the calculator, press the y^x button, insert 5, press the "$+/-$" button to change 5 to minus 5, and press the "=" button to find .62092.

A third method is to use a spreadsheet program on a microcomputer. With a typical spreadsheet program, define three one-cell ranges named FV, n, and R. Enter the values of the future cash flow, the number of periods, and the interest rate in the corresponding cells. Then, in the fourth cell, type the present value formula + FV*(1 + R)$_\wedge$ − n. Enter the formula into the cell by depressing the "return" key. If your spreadsheet is set for automatic recalculation (this is usually the default setting), the contents of the cell should show the present value of the future amount FV. To find a different present value, change the entries in the FV, n, or R cells. The present value cell will be instantly updated. (Beware: If your spreadsheet has a function labeled @PV, it probably gives the present value of an annuity, not the present value of a single payment.)

EXAMPLE 2.1

What is the present value of $1 to be received three time periods from now if the time value of money is .10 per period?

In Appendix Table A the .10 column and the line opposite n equal to 3 give .7513. If you invest $.7513 to earn .10 per year, after three years you will have $1. Also, $(1.10)^{-3} = .7513$.

What is the present value of $100 to be received three time periods from now if the time value of money is .10? Since $(1.10)^{-3} = .7513$, the present value of $100 is

$$PV = \$100 \ (.7513) = \$75.13$$

If $75.13 is invested at time 0, the following growth takes place.

Time	Investment at Beginning of Period	Interest	Investment at End of Period
0	$75.13	$7.513	$82.643
1	82.643	8.264	90.907
2	90.907	9.091	100.000

If investors can earn .10 per period and can borrow at .10, then they are indifferent between $75.13 received at time 0 or $100 at time 3.

With present value factors, we can compute the present value of any single cash flow. But in most applications, we need to be able to compute the present value of a sequence of cash flows. There are a few general rules that can be used to calculate the present value of any sequence of cash flows. The first rule is called the present value addition rule.

Present Value Addition Rule

The present value of any sequence of cash flows is the sum of the present values of each of the cash flows in the sequence.

EXAMPLE 2.2

What is the present value of two cash flows, $100 and $200, to be received at the end of one and two periods from now, respectively, if the time value of money is .10?

Period (n)	Cash flow (C_n)	Present Value Factors Using a .10 Interest Rate	Present Value (PV)
1	$100	.9091	$ 90.91
2	200	.8264	165.28
			Present value using .10 = $256.19

By using the formula for the present value of a future cash flow and the present value addition rule, one could calculate the present value of any possible cash flow.

Present Value Multiplication Rule

The present value factor for n years is equal to the product of the present value factor for t years and the present value factor for $(n - t)$ years.

For example, using an 8 percent discount rate, the present value factor for a dollar to be received in 3 years is .7938, and the present value factor for a dollar in 9 years is .5002. Therefore the present value of a dollar in 12 years is .7938 × .5002 = .3971.

Bond Values

We will illustrate present value computations by calculating the present value of a $1 bond that pays interest once a year at a rate equal to the discount rate. If the bond has a life of one year, the cash flow to be received in one year for $1 of principal is $(1 + r)$ dollars. The present value is $(1 + r)/(1 + r)$, which equals one. Now suppose the bond has a life of two years. The cash flows are

Actual Cash Flows for Two-Period Bond

	Period 1	Period 2
Cash flow	r	$1 + r$

We can replace the cash flow in period 2 by its present value in period 1, which we have already seen is 1.

Equivalent Cash Flows for Two-Period Bond

	Period 1	Period 2
Cash flow	$1 + r$	

We have already seen that these cash flows have a present value of 1. So a two-period bond with a coupon rate equal to the discount rate will sell for its principal value. The results for a three-period bond should come as no surprise.

Actual Cash Flows for Three-Period Bond

	Period 1	Period 2	Period 3
Cash flow	r	r	$1 + r$

As before, we can replace the period 3 cash flow by its present value (1) in period 2. These equivalent cash flows are the same as the actual cash flows for a two-period bond. So we know their present value is 1.

This leads to the following generalization: When the coupon rate on a bond equals the discount rate, and the next cash flow occurs one year from one, the present value of the bond will equal its principal amount, regardless of the life of the bond.

Present Value of an Annuity

An annuity is a sequence of n equal cash flows, one per period. If the first payment occurs one period from now, the annuity is called an ordinary annuity or an annuity in arrears. We will find the present value of an annuity by starting with the relationship we just derived for the present value of a coupon bond. Let $B(n, r)$ represent the present value of an ordinary annuity. The interest rate is r, and there are n annual payments of $1 each. The present value of a $1 coupon bond can be represented as

$$rB(n, r) + (1 + r)^{-n} = 1$$

On the left-hand side, the first term represents the present value of all n interest payments, including the final payment in year n; the second term represents the present value of the principal repayment in year n. We have already seen that the total present value equals 1 for all n. Rearranging the above equation to solve for $B(n, r)$ gives an explicit formula for the present value of an annuity.

$$B(n, r) = \frac{1 - (1 + r)^{-n}}{r} \tag{2.3}$$

Many practical problems require knowing the present value of an annuity, and using this formula is easier than computing the present value of each term.

Appendix Table B at the back of this book gives the present values of ordinary annuities of $1 per period for different values of r and n. Many hand calculators also are equipped for computing the present value of an annuity.

If C dollars are received at the end of each period instead of $1, we can multiply the present value of $1 per period by C to obtain the present value of C dollars per period. That is, for an ordinary annuity for C dollars per period, the present value is

$$PV = C \times B(n, r) \tag{2.4}$$

Many microcomputer spreadsheet programs have a function that will compute the present value of an ordinary annuity, given the quantities labeled C, n, and r in equation (2.4). It is customary in spreadsheets to use the symbol PV for this function, although it is actually an annuity function rather than a present value function.

EXAMPLE 2.3

The ABC Company is to receive $1 a period for three periods, the first payment to be received one period from now. The time value factor is .10. Compute the present value of the annuity.

There are three equivalent solutions.

a. From Appendix Table B,

$$B(3, .10) = 2.4869$$

b. By equation (2.3),

$$B(3, .10) = \frac{1 - (1 + r)^{-n}}{r} = \frac{1 - .7513}{.10} = \frac{.2487}{.10} = 2.487$$

c. By addition of the first three entries in the .10 column in Appendix Table A,

$$(1.10)^{-1} = .9091$$
$$(1.10)^{-2} = .8264$$
$$(1.10)^{-3} = .7513$$
$$\overline{B(3, .10) = 2.4868}$$

If, instead of $1 per period, the amount is $100, then using equation (2.4), we could multiply $2.487 by 100 and obtain $248.70.

An Annuity Due

When the first payment is at time 1, we have an ordinary annuity. When the payment occurs at the beginning of each period, we have an annuity due (also called an annuity in advance). Equation (2.3), repeated here, gives the present value of an ordinary annuity.

$$B(n, r) = \frac{1 - (1 + r)^{-n}}{r}$$

If we have $(n + 1)$ payments, with the first payment taking place immediately, we would merely add $1 to the value of the preceding equation. Thus, if $B(3, .10)$ equals $2.4868, a four-payment annuity with the first payment at time 0 would have a present value of $3.4868. An n-period annuity due is nothing more than an $(n - 1)$ period ordinary annuity plus the initial payment.

Present Value of a Perpetuity

A perpetuity is an annuity that goes an forever (an infinite sequence). If we let n of equation (2.3) go to infinity, so that the annuity becomes a perpetuity, then the $(1 + r)^{-n}$ term goes to zero, and the present value of the perpetuity using the equation becomes

$$B(\infty, r) = \frac{1}{r} \tag{2.5}$$

Thus, if $r = .10$ and the series of cash receipts of $1.00 per period are infinitely long, investors would pay $10.00 for the infinite series. They would not pay $11.00, since they could invest that $11.00 elsewhere and earn $1.10 per period at the going rate of interest, which is better than $1.00 per period. Investors would like to obtain the investment for $9.00, but no rational issuer of the security would commit to pay $1.00 per period in return for $9.00 when $10.00 could be obtained from other lenders for the same commitment.

Although perpetuities are seldom a part of real-life problems, they are useful, since they allow us to determine the value of extreme cases. For example, if $r = .10$, we may not know the present value of $1 per period for 50 time periods, but we do know that it is only a small amount less than $10, since the present value of a perpetuity of $1 per period is $10, and 50 years is close enough to being a perpetuity for us to use 10 as an approximate value:

$$B(\infty, r) = \frac{1}{r} = \frac{1}{.10} = \$10$$

Intuitive Interpretation

By rearranging the ordinary annuity equation, we can put the formula for an ordinary annuity in a slightly different form, which has a very intuitive interpretation.

$$B(n, r) = \frac{1}{r} - \frac{1}{r}(1 + r)^{-n}$$

On the right-hand side, the first term is the present value of a perpetuity. The second term, which is subtracted from the first, is the product of two present values. One is the present value of a perpetuity, and the second is the present value of $1 to be received in n years. Think of the annuity as the difference between two perpetuities. The first is a perpetuity of inflows beginning at the end of period 1. The second is a perpetuity of cash flows that are not to be received, thus that are subtracted from the perpetuity, with the first subtraction occuring at the end of period $(n + 1)$. The cash flows of the two perpetuities and the annuity are as follows.

	Period									
	1	2	3	4	...	n − 1	n	n + 1	n + 2	...
First perpetuity	1	1	1	1		1	1	1	1	1
Second perpetuity	−	−	−	−		−	−	−1	−1	−1
Annuity for n periods	1	1	1	1	...	1	1	0	0	0

A Flexible Tool

We now have the tools to solve a wide range of time value problems that have not been described. While we could introduce other formulas, we prefer to adapt the three basic formulas that have been introduced.

For example, if a $60-per-year annuity for 20 years were to have its first payment at time 10 and if the interest rate is .10, the present value is

$$PV = CB(n, r)(1 + r)^{-t} = 60B\ (20, .10)\ (1.10)^{-9}$$
$$= 60\ (8.5136)\ (.4241) = \$216.64$$

```
         CB(n, r)      60       60
    ├──────────┼────────┼────────┼──────────
    0    ...   9       10       11      ...
```

Note that if the first annuity payment is at time 10, we only have to discount the annuity for 9 years to find the present value, since $B(n, r)$ gives the annuity value as of the end of period 9.

If one were to invest $216.64 at time 0 to earn .10 per year, then at the end of period 10 (time 10) one could withdraw $60 and could withdraw $60 a year for 20 years ($1,200 in total). If we turned the problem around, we could determine how much we would have at time 29 if we saved $60 per year for 20 years, with the first amount saved starting at time 10.

$$FV = \$216.64\ (1.10)^{29} = \$216.64\ (15.8631) = \$3,437$$

Equivalently,

$$FV = \$60B\ (20, .10)\ (1.10)^{20} = \$600\ (8.5136)\ (6.7275) = \$3,437$$

Now let us do the same problem but assume that the annuity starting at time 10 is a perpetuity. The present value at time 9 is $60/.10 = $600. The present value of the $600 at time 0 is

$$PV = \$600\ (1.10)^{-9} = \$600\ (.4241) = \$254.46$$

Another approach to solving for the present value is to compute the present value of a perpetuity and subtract the present value of a nine-period annuity:

$$PV = \$600 - \$60B\ (9, .10) = \$600 - \$60\ (5.7590) = \$254.46$$

It is important that you realize the extreme flexibility of the basic time-discounting tools. These tools are sufficient for solving any time value problem.

Annual Equivalent Amounts

In many situations we will desire to determine the annual equivalent of a given sum. For example, what is the annual equivalent over 20 years of $100,000 received today if the time value of money is 10 percent?

The answer to this question lies in equation (2.4) which, when solved for the annual cash flow, is

$$C = \frac{PV}{B(n, r)} \tag{2.6}$$

That is, to find the annual equivalent C of a present sum PV, that sum is divided by the annuity factor $B(n, r)$, where r is the time value of money and n is the number of years over which the annual equivalent is to be determined.

Calculations of this type are particularly useful in the management of financial institutions such as insurance companies or banks, where customers make periodic payments over an extended time period in return for a lump-sum immediate loan.

EXAMPLE 2.4

The ABC Company wishes to borrow $10,000 from the City Bank, repayable in three annual installments (the first one due one year from now). If the bank charges .10 interest, what will be the annual payments?

From equation (2.6),

$$C = \frac{10,000}{B(3, .10)}$$

$$= \frac{10,000}{2.4869} = \$4,021$$

and the loan amortization schedule is

(1)	(2)	(3)	(4)	(5) = (2) + (3) − (4)
		Interest		
Time	Beginning Balance	.10 of (2)	Payment	Ending Balance
0	$10,000	$1,000	$4,021	$6,979
1	6,979	698	4,021	3,656
2	3,656	366	4,021	0

The loan amortization schedule starts with the initial amount owed. Column 3 shows the interest on the amount owed at the beginning of the period. Column 4 is the debt payment and column 5 shows the ending debt balance. The ending debt balance is equal to the beginning debt balance plus the period's interest less the debt payment.

The process is repeated for the life of the debt. If the present value of the debt payments is equal to the initial beginning balance (as it will be using the effective cost of debt), the ending balance after the last debt payment will be equal to zero.

Nominal and Annual Percentage Rates

In most capital budgeting decisions, the decision makers assume that cash flows occur at the end of the year and interest is compounded annually; in other types of financial analysis, particularly with loan and savings transactions, it is sometimes convenient to use months or some other unit of time. Appendix Tables A and B are for "periods" of time where the periods may be defined to be any unit of time.

It is useful to distinguish between the effective and the nominal rate of interest in cases where the interest rate is stated in terms of one period of time but applied over a different period of time with compounding (reinvestment of the principal plus accrued interest). For example, if the nominal annual rate of interest is .10 per year and the nominal quarterly rate of interest is .025, with interest being compounded quarterly, the annual percentage rate (APR) is 10.38 percent.

Let

$$r\ =\ \text{the annual discount rate (APR)}/100$$

$$j\ =\ \text{the nominal rate for a year}$$

$$\frac{j}{m}\ =\ \text{the effective rate for a fraction of a year}$$

$$m\ =\ \text{the number of compoundings in a year, for example,}$$
$$\text{for quarterly compoundings, } m\ =\ 4$$

The nominal annual rate is equal to j. For the example, $j = .10$ and $m = 4$, and the effective rate for a quarter is .025. The annual discount rate r may be computed using

$$1 + r = \left(1 + \frac{j}{m}\right)^{m}$$

or

$$r = \left(1 + \frac{j}{m}\right)^{m} - 1 \qquad (2.7)$$

For the example, we have

$$r = (1.025)^{4} - 1 = 1.1038 - 1 = .1038$$

Thus, the APR is 10.38 percent.

For example, suppose that a bank pays a nominal 7.75 percent annual interest rate on savings but compounds quarterly. The nominal rate per quarter is $7.75/4 = 1.9375$ percent per quarter. The annual percentage rate is

$$(1.019375)^{4} - 1 = .07978 = 7.98 \text{ percent}$$

or very nearly 8 percent. If a competing bank offers the same nominal rate but compounds daily, the daily effective rate is $7.75/365 = .021233$ percent per day, and the annual percentage rate in this case is

$$(1 + .0775/365)^{365} - 1 = .08057 = 8.06 \text{ percent}$$

In this instance, going from quarterly to daily compounding increases the annual percentage rate by about .08 percent per year. The difference may be negligible to an individual with a savings account of only a few thousand dollars, but it is important to a corporate treasurer responsible for investing temporarily excess funds that may amount to millions of dollars. On $10 million, the interest rate differential amounts to $8,060 per year.

As was indicated, the choice of time period varies from one situation to another. Most short-term instruments have interest compounded on a daily basis. A $1,000 90-day loan at nominal 8.5 percent annual interest, assuming a 365-day year, would require a payment of

$$\$1,000 \left(1 + \frac{.085}{365}\right)^{90} = \$1,021.18$$

Stating the cost of this loan as a annual percentage rate yields

$$\left(1 + \frac{.085}{365}\right)^{365} - 1 = .0887$$

or 8.87 percent per year.

Continuous Cash Flows and Continuous Discounting

While it is generally assumed in this book that cash flows occur instantaneously at the end of a period and that interest is compounded annually, either or both of these assumptions may be varied. Interest may be compounded monthly, weekly, daily, or continuously. Instead of assuming that the cash flows occur at the end of a year, they may also be presumed to occur monthly, weekly, daily, or continuously. We now explain continuous compounding of interest.

Assume that a nominal annual interest rate of .12 is compounded twice during the year. If m is the number of annual compoundings, for $m = 2$ we have

$$\left(1 + \frac{j}{m}\right)^m = \left(1 + \frac{.12}{2}\right)^2 = (1.06)^2 = 1.1236$$

The annual percentage rate is 12.36.

If $m = 12$,

$$\left(1 + \frac{.12}{12}\right)^{12} = (1.01)^{12} = 1.1268$$

APR = 12.68 percent.

If $m = 365$, so that we have daily compounding of interest,

$$\left(1 + \frac{.12}{365}\right)^{365} = (1.000329)^{365} = 1.12747$$

If m is allowed to increase beyond bound (approach infinity), we obtain e^{jn} as the accumulation factor, where e is equal to 2.71828 and is the base of the natural or Naperian system of logarithms. If $j = .12$ and $n = 1$, we have $e^{.12} = 1.12750$. The use of continuous compounding leads to a larger future value than does the use of discrete compounding.

We can use e^{jn} to find the future value and e^{-jn} to find the present value for n years with interest compounded continuously at an annual rate of j:

$$FV = e^{jn} \qquad (2.8)$$

$$PV = e^{-jn} \qquad (2.9)$$

EXAMPLE 2.5

Let

$$j = .02$$
$$n = 1$$

To compute the present value of a dollar to be received at time 1, assuming that interest is compounded continuously,

$$PV = e^{-jn} = e^{-.02}$$

$$PV = e^{-.02} = (2.71828)^{-.02}$$

We can make use of a calculator or table for finding values of e^{-x}.

$$e^{-.02} = .9802$$

The .9802 resulting from continuous compounding can be compared with .9804, which is the present value of a dollar, using 2 percent compounded annually. The difference between annual compounding and continuous compounding increases as the level of interest rates increase.

Examples of the present values using different interest rates (j) and different time periods (n) follow.

EXAMPLE 2.6

j (Continuous Interest Rate)	n (Number of Periods)	jn	Present Values (e^{-jn})
.05	1	.05	.951229
.05	2	.10	.904837
.05	3	.15	.860708
.15	1	.15	.860708
.075	2	.15	.860708

Any calculator that includes the e^x and $\ln x$ functions can be used to make these calculations.

We can convert from interest rates assuming annual compounding to equivalent interest rates assuming continuous compounding, and vice versa. Suppose that r is the rate assuming annual compounding, and j is the equivalent rate assuming continuous compounding. Then the following relation must hold if we are to have the same present or future value independent of discrete or continuous discounting.

$$(1 + r) = e^j$$

or

$$r = e^j - 1$$

or

$$j = \ln (1 + r)$$

To convert from a continuous rate j to the corresponding annual compounding rate, we use $r = e^j - 1$. To convert from annual compounding at the rate r to the equivalent continuous rate j, use $j = \ln (1 + r)$. Table 2.2 shows the continuous equivalents of some representative annual rates. For interest rates below 10 percent, the differences between continuous compounding and annual compounding are not of practical significance for most capital budgeting applications. When r or j becomes large, the divergence between their values becomes large.

TABLE 2.2   Continuous Interest Rates Equivalent to Various Annually Compounded Interest Rates

Annual Rate (r)	Equivalent Continuous Rate $j = \ln (1 + r)$
.01	.00995
.02	.01980
.03	.02956
.04	.03922
.05	.04879
.10	.09531
.15	.13976
.20	.18232
.25	.22314
.30	.26236
.40	.33647
.50	.40547
1.00	.69315
11.00	2.48491
22,025.46	10.00000

EXAMPLE 2.7

Compute the annual percentage rate (APR) to a corporation for a debt with a 12 percent nominal cost if the interest is compounded.

a. Annually

.12

APR = 12 percent.

b. Every six months.

$$\left(1 + \frac{.12}{2}\right)^2 - 1 = .1236$$

APR = 12.36 percent.

c. Every month.

$$(1.01)^{12} - 1 = .1268$$

APR = 12.68 percent.

d. Continuously.

$$r = e^{.12} - 1 = .1275$$

APR = 12.75 percent.

Continuous Payments

Instead of $1 being received at the end of each year, there may be m payments per year, each payment being an amount of $1/m$ dollars. The total received during each year is $1. If m becomes very large (approaches a limit so that we receive $1 per year in a large number of small installments), the present value of a series of such payments extending over n years, with interest compounded continuously at a rate j, will be

$$\text{Present value of a continuous annuity} = \frac{1 - e^{-jn}}{j} \qquad (2.10)$$

EXAMPLE 2.8

A corporation expects to receive $3,650,000 during a year. The corporation wants to use a discount rate equivalent to 5 percent for 6 months. We want to compare the present value of this amount under various assumptions about when it will be received. Keep the APR constant in all the comparisons.

If the funds are received at the beginning of the year, the present value is $3,650,000. Assuming the money is received in one lump sum at the end of the year, the appropriate discount rate is $(1.05)^2 - 1 = 10.25$ percent.

$$PV = 3,650,000/1.1025 = \$3,310,658$$

Assuming the money is received in one lump sum in the middle of the year, the appropriate discount rate is 5 percent per half year period.

$$PV = \$3,650,000/1.05 = \$3,476,190$$

Assume the money is received in 12 equal payments of $304,167 at the end of each month. To find the appropriate discount rate, solve

$$(1 + r)^{12} = 1.1025$$

$$(1.1025)^{1/12} = 1.00816$$

$$r = .00816 = 0.816 \text{ percent per month}$$

$$B(12, .00816) = [1 - (1.00816)^{-12}]/.00816 = 11.38668$$

$$11.38668 \, (3,650,000/12) = 3,463,448$$

Assume the money is received in 365 equal installments of $10,000 each. The appropriate daily discount rate is

$$r = (1.1025)^{1/365} - 1 = .00026738 \text{ per day}$$

$$B(365, .00026738) = 347.7105$$

$$347.7105 \, (10,000) = \$3,477,105$$

Assume the money is received continuously. The appropriate continuously compounded discount rate is

$$e^{j} = 1.1025$$

$$j = \ln (1.1025)$$

$$= .09758$$

The annuity factor for one year is

$$[1 - e^{-.09758}]/.09758 = .95275885$$

The present value of the cash flow is

$$.95275885 \, (\$3,650,000) = \$3,477,570$$

The largest change in the present value comes from assuming the money comes in midyear instead of at the end of the year. The remaining assumptions would have very little effect on a typical capital budgeting decision. They might be important in some financial decisions.

Equation 2.10 applies if there is continuous discounting of a continuous cash flow. However, it is possible to have one without the other. If either the cash flows are discrete or the discounting is discrete, then the discrete annuity formula can be used, as explained below.

If the cash flows are continuous, but interest is compounded on a discrete basis, no accuracy is lost by treating the cash flows as discrete. Suppose interest is compounded m times per year at a nominal rate of j per year. There are m periods in the year. The effective interest rate in each period is j/m. The present value of an annuity of $1 per year lasting n years ($n \times m$ periods) is

$$(1/m) \times B(n \times m, \; j/m)$$

For example, suppose j is .12, m is 12 and the annuity lasts for 10 years, or 120 months.

$$\begin{aligned}
(1/12) \times B(120,.01) &= (1/12) \times [(1/.01) \times (1 - 1.01^{-120})] \\
&= (.08333) \times (100) \times (1 - .30299) \\
&= 5.80838
\end{aligned}$$

If the cash flows are discrete, but interest is compounded continuously, convert the interest rate to the equivalent rate for the period whose length is the time between cash flows. Suppose the nominal interest rate is 12 percent per year compounded continuously. Cash flows are received at the rate of $1 per month for 120 months. The effective monthly interest rate is

$$e^{.01} - 1 = .01005$$

The present value of the annuity is

$$\begin{aligned}
12 \times B(120, .01005) &= 12 \times (1/.01005) \times (1 - 1.01005^{-120}) \\
&= 12 \times 99.50249 \times (1 - .3012) \\
&= 834.3878.
\end{aligned}$$

Conclusions

Most investment analyses performed by a company are made on the basis of annual cash flows. Finer divisions of time are usually unwarranted in light of the roughness of the cash flow estimates. Some firms use present value tables that assume the cash flows are distributed evenly over the year or occur at the midpoint of the year in question rather than at the end of the year, as do the present value tables at the end of this book.

Most financial decision making can be reduced to evaluating incremental or alternative cash flows. There are three steps in the analysis. First, the relevant incremental cash flows must be estimated. Second, there must be some means of dealing with uncertainty if the cash flows are not known with certainty. Third, there must be some way to take into consideration the time value of money. The material in this chapter is essential for dealing with the time value of money to determine the present and future values of certain sums of money to be received or paid at various times. In the next chapter, we shall apply the time value concepts to the valuation of investments.

REVIEW EXAMPLE 2.1

a. If the interest rate per month is .025, compounded monthly, what is the annual equivalent rate?

b. If $100 will grow into $118 in one year, what is the continuous rate of growth?

c. If $100 will grow continuously at .20 for one year, what is the discrete annual rate of growth that will lead to the same future value?

d. What is the continuous equivalent to a .20 discrete rate of discount?

Solution

a. $(1.025)^{12} - 1 = .3449$

b. $100e^{j} = 118$
$e^{j} = 1.18$
$j = \ln 1.18 = .1655144$

c. $1 + r = e^{j} = e^{.20} = 1.2214$
$r = .2214$

d. $e^{j} = 1 + r$
$j = \ln (1 + r) = \ln (1.20) = .18232$

REVIEW EXAMPLE 2.2

Exactly 15 years from now, Jones will start receiving a pension of $20,000 a year. The payments will continue forever. How much is the pension worth now, assuming that money is worth .10 per year?

Solution

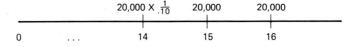

		20,000 × $\frac{1}{.10}$	20,000	20,000
0	. . .	14	15	16

The present value at time 14 is $20,000/.01 = $200,000.
The present value at time 0 is

$$200,000 \ (1.10)^{-14} = 200,000 \ (.26333)$$
$$= \$52,666$$

REVIEW EXAMPLE 2.3

a. Twelve rental payments of $1,000 will be paid monthly at the end of each month. The monthly interest rate is .01. What is the present value of the payments?

b. If the payments are at the beginning of each month, what is the present value?

Solution
  a. $1,000B (12, .01) = $1,000 (11.2551) = $11,255
  b. $1,000 [B(11, .01) + 1] = $1,000 (10,3676 + 1) = $11,368 or
     $11,255 (1.01) = $11,368

PROBLEMS

2.1 Assume a .05-per-year time value of money. Compute the value of $100 (a) received 1 year from now, (b) received immediately, (c) received at the end of 5 years, (d) received at the beginning of the sixth year, (e) received at the end of 50 years, (f) received at the end of 50 years but with an interest rate of .10.

2.2 Assume that the interest rate is .10. Compute the present value of $1 per year for four years (first payment one year from now) using three different methods (Table A, Table B, and an equation).

2.3 Assume a .05 time value of money. Compute the value of the following series of payments of $100 a year received for (a) five years, the first payment received one year from now; (b) four years, the first of five payments received immediately; (c) ten years, the first payment received one year from now; (d) nine years, the first of ten payments received immediately.

2.4 Assume a .05 time value of money. The sum of $100 received immediately is equivalent to what quantity received in 10 equal annual payments, the first to be received one year from now? What would be the annual amount if the first of 10 payments were received immediately?

2.5 Assume a .05 time value of money. We have a debt to pay and are given a choice of paying $1,000 now or some amount X five years from now. What is the maximum amount that X can be for us to be willing to defer payment for five years?

2.6 We can make an immediate payment now of $10,000 or pay equal amounts of R for the next five years (first payment due one year from now). With a time value of money of .05, what is the maximum value of R that we would be willing to accept?

2.7 If the interest rate per month is .05, compounded quarterly, what is the annual equivalent rate?

2.8 If a firm borrowed $100,000 for one year and paid back $9,455.96 per month, what is the cost of the debt?

2.9 A firm can save $10,000 per year for 15 years. If the time value of money is .10, how much better off will the firm be after the 15 years if it accomplishes the saving?

2.10 If the time value of money is .10, how much do you have to save per year for 20 years to have $50,000 per year for perpetuity? Assume that the first deposit is immediate and that the first payment will be at the beginning of the twenty-first year.

2.11 If $100 earns .08 per year, how much will the investor have at the end of 10 years? What is the present value of $100 due in 10 years if money is worth .08?

2.12 What is the present value of $20 per year for perpetuity if money is worth .10?

2.13 Refer to problem 2.12. If the first payment is to be received in 11 years, what is the series of payments worth?

2.14 You are the loan officer of a bank. The ABC Company wants to borrow $100,000 and repay it with four equal annual payments (first payment due one year from now). You decide that the ABC Company should pay .10 per year on the loan.
   a. What is the annual payment?
   b. Complete the following debt amoritization table.

Period	Amount Owed (Beginning of year)	Interest	Principal	Amount Owed (End of Year)
1	$100,000			
2				
3				
4				

   c. What would be the annual payment if the first of four equal payments is due immediately?

2.15 **a.** If the interest rate per month is .02, compounded monthly, what is the annual effective equivalent rate?
   b. How much do you have to save per year for 10 years in order to have $50,000 per year for perpetuity? $r = .08$. The first $50,000 payment will be received at time 21.
   c. If $100 will grow into $120 in one year, what is the continuous rate of growth?

2.16 Assume a .10 interest rate. How much is an ordinary perpetuity of $1,000 per year worth?

2.17 Assume a .10 interest rate (you can borrow and lend at that rate). Specify which you would prefer:
   a. $10,000 in cash or $1,000 per year for perpetuity (first payment received at the end of the first period).
   b. $10,000 in cash or $1,100 per year for perpetuity (first payment received at the end of the first period).

c. $10,000 in cash or $900 per year for perpetuity (first payment received at the beginning of the first period).

2.18 **a.** What would be the annual payments on an 8-percent-per-annum installment loan of $1,000 with repayment over three years?

b. Write out the amortization schedule for the loan.

c. Now suppose that the payments were to be made on a semiannual basis; what would the semiannual payments be? Assume the .08 is a nominal rate.

d. Is the total paid in case (c) less or more than in the former case? Why?

2.19 With a continuous discount rate of .08, what is the present value of $400 per year received continuously for five years?

2.20 Assume that you have just purchased a $75,000 house. One bank will give you a 9 percent mortgage with repayment in equal annual installments over 20 years with $15,000 down payment. Another bank wants a 10 percent rate of interest but will give you a 25-year equal-annual-installment mortgage with a $15,000 down payment. Assuming that you have the $15,000, which of the two deals will minimize the annual payment?

2.21 **a.** How much do you have to save per year (at the end of each year) for 40 years in order to have $10,000 per year for perpetuity, first receipt starting in year 41? Use .10 as the time value factor.

b. If the interest rate being charged is .04 per quarter, compounded quarterly, what is the annual equivalent rate? Use discrete discounting.

2.22 Exactly 20 years from now Jones will start receiving a pension of $10,000 a year. The payments will continue for 30 years. How much is the pension worth now, assuming money is worth .05 per year?

2.23 **a.** If the interest rate per month is .04, compounded monthly, what is the annual equivalent rate?

b. If $100 will grow into $110 in one year, what is the continuous rate of growth?

c. If $100 will grow continuously at .20 for one year, what is the discrete annual rate of growth?

d. What is the continuous equivalent to a .20 discrete rate of discount?

2.24 **a.** We can make an immediate payment now of $10,000 or pay equal amounts of R for the next four years (first payment due one year from now). With a time value of money of .10, what is the maximum value of payment that we would be willing to make?

b. Now assume that the first of the *five* payments is *immediate*. What is the maximum value of payment we would be willing to make?

2.25 **a.** Mr. Jones has 10 years until retirement. He wants to save enough to have $20,000 per year after retirement for perpetuity. Money will earn .10. How much should he save each year? Assume that the first "draw down" in savings takes place at time 11.

    b. Mr. Smith is spending $12,548 more than he earns each year. He is borrowing at the end of each year at a cost of .10. Assume that he does this for 10 years. How much interest will he be paying each year, starting at the end of year 10 (beginning of year 11)?

2.26 The ABC Company can invest $4,000 and earn $5,000 one year later.

    a. What is the annual return that will be earned if discrete discounting is used? used?

    b. Now assume that the return will occur after one week. With discrete discounting, the annual return is _____. With continuous discounting, the annual return is _____.

2.27 The XYZ Company has borrowed $100,000. Payments will be made over a four-year period (first payment at the end of the first year). The bank charges interest of .20 per year.

    a. The annual payment will be _____.

    b. The debt amortization schedule is

Amount Owed (Beginning of Period)	Interest	Principal
1. $100,000		
2.		
3.		
4.		

    c. If there are five payments with the first payment made at the moment of borrowing, the annual payment will be _____.

2.28 The ABC Company can invest $4,000 in a single positive-payment investment and earn .12 per year.

    a. What is the total value of the investment after 15 years if discrete growth is used?

    b. What is the total value of the single positive-payment investment after 15 years of continuous growth (at an annual continuous rate of .12)?

    c. With discrete discounting, the annual interest rate is .20. With continuous discounting, the annual interest rate that will give the same present value as the .20 discrete rate is _____.

2.29 The XYZ Company has borrowed $40,000. Equal payments will be made over a three-year period (first payment at the end of the first year). The bank charges interest of .15 per year.

    a. The annual payment will be _____.

    b. The debt amortization schedule is _____.

Amount Owed (Beginning of Period)	Interest	Principal Payment
1. $40,000		
2.		
3.		
4.		

   c. If there are four equal payments with the first payment made at the moment of borrowing, the annual payment will be _____ .

2.30 **a.** An investor will save $1,000 per year for 10 years (first payment at time 1). At time 10, the investor will have _____ , and starting at time 11, the investor will be able to spend _____ per year. The interest rate is .20.

   b. Mr. Jones has 10 years until retirement. He wants to save enough to have $20,000 per year after retirement for perpetuity. Money will earn .20. How much should he save each year? Assume that the first "draw down" in savings takes place at time 11.

2.31 Assume that a bank charges .01 interest per month. You borrow $50,000, to be paid by equal payments over a 35-month period, first payment to be due one month from now. How much will you have to pay each month? What is the annual effective interest cost?

2.32 The newspaper headline states "Baseball Player Signs for $1.4 Million." A reading of the article revealed that the player will receive $100,000 per year for six years. He will then receive $40,000 per year for 20 years.

$$6 \times 100,000 = \quad 600,000$$
$$20 \times 40,000 = \quad \underline{800,000}$$
$$\text{Total} = 1,400,000$$

Assuming that the player can borrow and lend funds at .10 per year, what is the present value of his contract?

2.33 Assume a bank charges .03 interest per quarter. You borrow $50,000, to be paid by equal quarterly payments over a 36-month period, first payment one quarter from now. How much will you have to pay each quarter? How much would an annual payment have to be?

2.34 Assume the O-I Company has outstanding $10,000,000 of 4 percent bonds, maturing in 20 years (paying $400,000 of interest per year). The current interest rate is .10. What is the present value of the debt?

2.35 Assume the I-O Company has outstanding $10,000,000 of 10 percent bonds maturing in 20 years (paying $1,000,000 of interest per year). The current interest rate is .04.

a. What is the present value of the debt?

b. If the bonds can be called at a price of $10,500,000, how much could the firm pay to accomplish the refunding? Assume zero taxes.

2.36 Compute the present value for a bond that promises to pay interest of $50 a year for thirty years and $1,000 at maturity. The first interest payment is one year from now. Use a rate of discount of .05.

2.37 Estimate the present value of a bond that promises to pay interest of $30 a year for thirty years and $1,000 at maturity. The first interest payment is one year from now. Use a .03 rate of discount. After estimating the present value, compute it using the present value tables.

2.38 A twenty-year $1,000 bond promises to pay .045 interest annually. The current interest rate is .05. How much is the bond worth now? How much would the bond be worth if the current interest rate were .04?

2.39 Exactly twenty years from now Smith will start receiving a pension of $10,000 a year. The payments will continue for perpetuity. How much is the pension worth now, assuming money is worth .10 per year?

2.40 Assume a .05 interest rate. How much is a perpetuity of $1,000 per year worth?

2.41 Assume a .10 interest rate. How much is a perpetuity of $1,000 per year worth if the first payment is at time 21?

REFERENCES

Archer, S. H., G. M. Choate, and G. Racette, *Financial Management* (New York: John Wiley & Sons, 1983).

Brealey, R., and S. Myers, *Principles of Corporate Finance* (New York: McGraw-Hill Book Company, 1984).

Brigham, E. F., *Financial Management: Theory and Practice* (New York: The Dryden Press, Division of CBS College Publishing, 1982).

Glasgo, P. W., W. J. Landes, and A. F. Thompson, "Bank Discount, Coupon Equivalent, and Compound Yields," *Financial Management*, Autumn 1982, pp. 80–84.

Hawawini, G. A., and A. Vora, "Yield Approximations: A Historical Perspective," *The Journal of Finance*, March 1982, pp. 145–155.

Kellison, S. E., *The Theory of Interest* (Homewood, IL: Richard D. Irwin, 1970).

Public Information Department, Federal Reserve Bank of New York, *The Arithmetic of Interest Rates* (New York: Federal Reserve Bank of New York, 1981).

Schall, L. D., and C. W. Haley, *Financial Management* (New York: McGraw-Hill Book Company, 1983).

Van Horne, J. C., *Financial Management and Policy* (Englewood Cliffs, NJ, Prentice-Hall, 1983).

CHAPTER 3

Capital Budgeting: The Meaning of Net Present Value

The theory is one of investment opportunity and human impatience as well as exchange.

Irving Fisher, The Theory of Interest, as Determined by Impatience to Spend Income and Opportunity to Invest It (New York: Kelley & Millman, 1954), p. 149.

A Capital Budgeting Decision

A capital budgeting decision is characterized by costs and benefits that are spread out over several time periods. This leads to a requirement that the time value of money be considered in order to evaluate the alternatives correctly. Although in actual practice we must consider risk as well as time value, in this chapter we restrict the discussion to situations in which the cash outlays, cash inflows, and time value of money are all known with certainty. There are sufficient difficulties in just taking the time value of money into consideration without also incorporating risk factors. Moreover, when the cash flows are finally allowed to be uncertain, we shall suggest the use of a procedure that is based on the initial recommendations made with the certainty assumption, so nothing is lost by making the initial assumption of certainty.

In this chapter we shall attempt to present in a systematic and positive way our reasons for recommending the use of the net present-value measure. We hope to make clear the advantages as well as the limitations of this method. It is by no means a cureall for the problem of the manager harassed by the difficult problems of developing, evaluating, and choosing long-run investments.

We believe that the net present value method can make a definite and important contribution to the solution of the problems of making investment decisions. But it is vitally important that the users understand what it is they are accomplishing by discounting the cash flow of an investment and what they are not accomplishing. Unfortunately, some of those who have advocated use of this procedure have done so for the wrong reasons or have made claims for it that cannot be fulfilled.

Rate of Discount

We shall use the term *time value of money* to describe the discount rate. One possibility is to use the rate of interest associated with default-free securities. This rate does not include an adjustment for the risk of default; thus, risk, if present, would be handled separately from the time discounting. In many situations it is convenient to use the firm's borrowing rate (the marginal cost of borrowing funds). The objective of the discounting process is to take the time value of money into consideration. We want to find the present equivalent of future sums, neglecting risk considerations. Later we shall introduce several techniques to adjust for the risk of the investment.

Although the average cost of capital is an important concept that should be understood by all managers and is useful in deciding on the financing mix, we do not advocate its general use in evaluating all investments.

Classification of Cash Flows

We shall define conventional investments as those having one or more periods of outlays followed by one or more periods of cash proceeds. Borrowing money is a kind of negative investment or loan-type of cash flow in which one or more periods of cash proceeds are followed by one or more periods in which there are cash outlays. Loan-type investments have positive cash flows (cash inflows) followed by periods of negative cash flows (cash outlays). There are also nonconventional investments in which periods of outlays and periods of proceeds alternate more than once. With nonconventional investments, there is more than one sign change in the sequence of the cash flow. With a conventional investment or loan, there is one sign change. The possibilities may be illustrated as follows.

	Sign of Flow for Period			
	0	1	2	3
Conventional investment	−	+	+	+
Loan type of flows	+	−	−	−
Nonconventional investment	−	+	+	−
Nonconventional investment	+	--	−	+

Incremental Cash Flow

Investments should be analyzed using the appropriate after-tax incremental cash flows. Although we shall initially assume zero taxes so that we can concentrate on the technique of analysis, it should be remembered that the only relevant cash flows of a period are after all tax effects have been taken into account.

The definition of incremental cash flows is relatively straightforward: If the item changes the bank account or cash balance, it is a cash flow. These cash flows must be adjusted for opportunity costs (the value of alternative uses). For example, if a warehouse is used for a new product and the alternative is to rent the space, the lost rentals should be counted as an opportunity cost in computing the incremental cash flows.

It is generally advisable to exclude financial types of cash flows from the investment analysis. One common error in cash flow calculations is to include interest payments on debt in the cash flows and then apply the time-discounting formulas. This results in double counting the time value of money, if the receipt of the debt principal and its repayment are excluded. This topic is covered in Chapter 5.

Special Assumptions

The computations of this chapter make several assumptions that are convenient but are not essential. They simplify the analysis. The assumptions are

1. Capital can be borrowed and lent at the same rate of interest.
2. The cash inflows and outflows occur at the beginning or end of each period rather than continuously during the periods.
3. The cash flows are certain, and no risk adjustment is necessary.

In addition, in choosing the methods of analysis and implementation, it is assumed that the objective is to maximize the wellbeing of stockholders, and more wealth is better than less.

The Net Present Value Decision Criterion

The net present value is a direct application of the present value concept. Its computation requires the following steps: (1) Choose an appropriate rate of discount, (2) compute the present value of the cash proceeds expected from the investment, (3) compute the present value of the cash outlays required by the investment, and (4) sum the present values of the proceeds minus the present value of the outlays. This sum is the net present value of the investment.

The recommended accept-or-reject criterion is to accept all independent investments whose net present value is greater than or equal to zero and to reject all investments whose net present value is less than zero.

With zero taxes, the net present value of an investment may be described as the maximum amount a firm could pay for the opportunity of making the investment without being financially worse off. With such a payment, the investor would be indifferent to undertaking or not undertaking the investment. Because usually no such payment must be made, the expected net present value is an unrealized capital gain from the investment, over and above the cost of the investment used in the calculation. The capital gain will be realized if the expected cash proceeds materialize. Assume an investment that costs $10,000 and returns $12,100 a year later. If the rate of discount is 10 percent, a company could make a maximum immediate outlay of $11,000 in the expectation of receiving the $12,100 a year later. If it can receive the $12,100 with an actual outlay of only $10,000, the net present value of the investment will be $1,000. The $1,000 represents the difference between the present value of the proceeds, $11,000, and the actual outlay of $10,000. The company would have been willing to spend a maximum of $11,000 to receive $12,100 a year later.

The following example illustrates the basic computations for discounting cash flows, that is, adjusting future cash flows for the time value of money, using the net present value method.

Assume that there is an investment opportunity with the following cash flows.

	Period		
	0	*1*	*2*
Cash flow	−$12,337	$10,000	$5,000

We want first to compute the net present value of this investment using .10 as the discount rate. Appendix Table A gives the present value of $1 due *n* periods from now. The present value of

$1 due 0 periods from now discounted at·any interest rate is 1.000.

$1 due 1 period from now discounted at .10 is .9091.

$1 due 2 periods from now discounted at .10 is .8264.

The net present value of the investment is the algebraic sum of the three present values of the cash flows.

	1	*2*	*3*
			Present Value
Period	*Cash Flow*	*Present Value Factor*	*(Col. 1 × Col. 2)*
0	−$12,337	1.0000	−$12,337
1	10,000	.9091	9,091
2	5,000	.8264	4,132
		Net present value = $	886

The net present value is positive, indicating that the investment is acceptable. Any investment with a net present value equal to or greater than zero is acceptable using this single criterion. Since the net present value is $886, the firm could pay an amount of $886 in excess of the cost of $12,337 and still break even economically by undertaking the investment. The net present value calculation is a reliable method for evaluating investments.

We next want to consider the underlying reasons why net present value computations are a reasonable approach to the evaluation of investments.

A Bird in the Hand

Most managers will agree that a dollar in the hand today is more valuable to them than a dollar to be received a year from now. There are a variety of reasons for this preference. A survey may reveal the following answers to the inquiry "Why is a dollar in hand today worth more to you than a dollar to be received in one year?"

Risk:
As a manager, I live in an uncertain world. A dollar in the bank is something I can count on. A promise to pay me a dollar in one year is only a promise until I actually get the money. The promise may be made in perfectly good faith, but any number of things may occur between now and next year to prevent the fulfillment of the promise.

Immediacy:
Human nature naturally attaches more weight to present pleasures than to the more distant joys. Offer a young man the choice between a trip to Europe during the coming summer or a trip five summers from now, and he will nearly always choose the earlier trip. We would always prefer to receive a given total amount of after-tax income as soon as possible.

Alternative Investments:
A dollar received now is more valuable than a dollar to be received five years from now because of the investment possibilities that are available for today's dollar. By investing or lending the dollar received today, I can have considerably more than a dollar in five years.

We have suggested three separate reasons for attaching more weight to dollars on hand than to dollars that may be received in the future. Each reason is a correct one in important respects. But the last one of them by itself is sufficient justification for using discounted cash flow procedures in evaluating investment proposals. The other two reasons, insofar as they are appropriate in any situation, need to be taken into account in other ways. Let us consider each of the three reasons in turn.

Uncertainty

Our first hypothetical respondent stressed the fact that one can never be certain about the receipt of future cash. We would not disagree. In fact, we would generalize and say that one can never be certain about the future value of present cash held. It can be lost or stolen, the bank in which it is deposited might fail, or our ability to benefit from it may be impaired by death or injury.

It is not the need to allow for uncertainty that is in question, but the suitability of using the present value approach to make this allowance. The inappropriateness of using high discount rates as a general method of allowing for uncertainty may be illustrated by cases in which there is great uncertainty about the cash flows in the near future but relatively little uncertainty about the more distant cash flows. Suppose that we are considering investing in a building that, once it is built, could be rented on the basis of a long-term lease. The prospective lessee is willing to sign a contract now, and its credit standing is excellent, so that there is minimum uncertainty about the ability to meet the rental payments. There may be considerable uncertainty about how much it will cost to construct the building, however. In a situation such as this, it is difficult to justify using a high rate of discount applied to the relatively certain future cash receipts. There is considerable uncertainty about the magnitude of the cash outlays required to build the building, but varying the discount rate will have little effect on the present value of these outlays, because they will occur in the near future.

Some suggestions for handling data to improve the judgments of the risks involved in investments will be discussed later. No completely satisfactory and universally applicable method is known, however.

Subjective Time Preference

The second reason suggested as a justification for discounting future income is the time preference of the individuals involved. There are individuals who would prefer an additional $100 of consumption immediately to the opportunity of obtaining an additional $110 of disposable income a year from now. Such individuals might be acting rationally if they rejected a riskless opportunity to invest $100 today in such a way that it would return $110 in one year if acceptance of the investment required a corresponding reduction in the investor's immediate consumption.

But acceptance of the investment will not require a reduction in immediate consumption if opportunities to borrow money at less than 10 percent are also available now. Suppose the individuals in question accept the investment and at the same time borrow $100 at 5 percent to maintain their immediate consumption. At the end of a year the proceeds from the investment will enable them to pay off the loan, plus its accrued interest, and still retain an additional $5.

In general, the subjective time preferences of the owners of a corporation do not need to be consulted in making investment decisions for that corporation, provided the corporation can obtain additional funds in the capital market and invest its excess funds, if any, on the capital market. It is only the rates at which the corporation can obtain or lend funds that are relevant. Accordingly, the purpose of a business enterprise in discounting expected future cash proceeds is not to take account of the subjective time preferences of the owners (unless the owners do not, for one reason or another, have access to the capital market).

The manager of a business owned by a small group of individuals may, and sometimes should, adjust the investment policy of the company to take into consideration the cash requirements of the owners. But the shareholders of a large corporation are usually a diverse group. They may pay marginal tax rates on dividends of anywhere from zero (for certain individuals and nonprofit institutions) to over 50 percent. At any given time, some shareholders will be reinvesting a part of their dividend receipts, while others will be reducing their portfolios. The large corporation cannot easily adjust its investment policy to the needs of individual shareholders.

Investment Opportunities and Alternative Uses of Money

The purpose of discounting the cash flows from an investment is to determine whether the investment produces a more valuable flow of cash than the best available alternative. In the case of an independent investment proposal, the consequences of accepting the investment are to borrow more funds or to lend less outside the firm. If the costs of borrowing are the same as the rate that could be earned by lending elsewhere, the borrowing and lending alternatives are equivalent. It should be mentioned that the term *borrowing* is used here in a very broad sense to include raising additional equity as well as the more conventional forms of debt.

Investment Financed by Borrowing

To illustrate the meaning of the present-value computation when the investment must be financed by borrowing, we may use an investment, that requires an initial outlay of $10,000 and offers proceeds of $11,506 at time 1. At a 10 percent rate of interest, the net present value of the investment is $460, and the present value of the proceeds is $10,460. The value of the proceeds expected from the $10,000 investment is sufficent to pay off the principal and accrued interest on a loan of $10,460 at 10 percent payable at time 1. One way of interpreting the meaning of the present value calculation is to realize that a firm could borrow a total of $10,460 at 10 percent. It could then apply $10,000 of the loan proceeds to buying the investment and immediately distribute the remaining $460 as a dividend to the owners. The $11,506 of proceeds from the investment would be sufficient to repay the loan and interest.

We mentioned earlier that making allowances for the subjective time preferences with respect to receipt of income is not the purpose of the discounting process as long as the income recipient has access to the capital market. In the case of the preceding example, we assumed that the owners of the firm chose to receive the profit resulting from the investment in the year it was made. Actually, any pattern of cash receipts, such that their present value was equal to $460, could have been selected. If some or all of the income withdrawals were deferred to time 1, the actual withdrawals that could be made would exceed $460. Suppose the owners elected to borrow $10,000, the amount required to undertake the investment, and to withdraw their proceeds only after the initial loan had been repaid. Under these circumstances, the owners would be enabled to withdraw $506 at the end of the year, because this amount has a present value of $460 with an interest rate of 10 percent.

Investment Financed Internally

So far we have considered the case where the investment within the firm was to be financed by obtaining additional capital from outside the firm. This may seem to be an artificial comparison to a company whose past operations are generating enough cash to undertake all the worthwhile investments that seem to be available within the Company. This situation is not uncommon. It is a mistake to assume that internally generated funds are "free," however, because there is the possibility of lending funds outside the firm. For example, if a riskless possibility of earning 10 percent from loans outside is available, then risk-free internal investments should be compared with these external profit opportunities; other wise, the company may undertake internal investments that are not so profitable as those outside of its funds.

Consider the previous example. In the situation in which the funds to finance the investment were obtained from outside the firm, we said that we could interpret the fact that the investment had a net present value of $460 as meaning that a loan equal to the amount required to finance the investment, plus $460, could be negotiated and the excess over immediate needs ($460) withdrawn; the proceeds from the investment then would be sufficient to repay the entire loan.

Assume that the firm has funds available from internal sources. The owner has estimated that by applying $10,000 of those funds to the internal investment, the company could generate cash proceeds of $11,506 at time 1. We could ask how much money the firm would have to lend outside at 10 percent in order to generate cash proceeds of $11,506. Because the present value of $11,506 at 10 percent is $10,460, it would require an external loan of that amount to generate the same cash proceeds that would be generated internally from an investment of only $10,000.

In the case where funds are available from internal sources and external lending opportunities to earn 10 percent per year are available, the fact that an internal investment with a net present value of $460 is available means that $10,460 would have to be lent externally to generate the same cash proceeds as the internal investment of $10,000.

As in the previous case, the subjective time preferences of the owners should not affect the choice between the internal or external investment loan. If the owner wants to consume now, then up to $10,460 can be borrowed and up to $460 can be consumed now if the owner currently has zero assets. The investment generating $11,506 of proceeds can be used to repay the loan of $10,460 plus $1,046 of interest.

One further interpretation of the net present value of $460 of the investment is possible. The $460 is like an unrealized capital gain. For an expenditure of $10,000 we obtain the right to proceeds whose present value totals $10,460 and whose net present value is $460. Before investing, we have $10,000 in cash; after investing, we have prospects of cash proceeds whose present value is $10,460. Thus, our asset position can be improved in terms of present values (by $460) by making the investment.

Present Value Factors as Prices

To understand the approach to capital budgeting taken in this book, it is helpful to think of dollars that are received or paid at different times (dated dollars) as being different commodities. Present value factors are the prices of these dated dollars.

An investment is essentially a production process in which near dollars are used up to produce distant dollars. To determine whether an investment is profitable, we need to calculate whether the value of the distant dollars to be received is greater than the cost of the near dollars that are used to start the production process. To do this, we multiply the quantity of each different dated dollar by its price. Prices of dated dollars are measured in present dollars, just like the prices of oranges and grapefruits. If the value of the distant dollars produced by an investment is greater than the value of the near dollars used up, then we can say the investment is profitable. The magnitude of these profits is a measure of how desirable the investment is.

Whether two amounts can be treated as identical or must be distinguished depends on whether the market treats them as perfect substitutes. A rational person would give a firm a discount for making a loan payment a year early. That is, the lender would accept less than a dollar paid today to settle a payment of one dollar due in a year. A dollar now and a dollar a year from now are different if the interest rate is positive.

To illustrate these ideas, suppose that a business is considering an investment opportunity that requires an immediate outlay of $100, which would generate proceeds of $60 at the end of each of the next two years. If the decision makers understood that dollars received at different times had different value, they would request more information to make the investment decision. The additional data needed are today's prices (or values) for dollars to be received one and two years from now. Today's price for a dollar to be received today is $1. If the price of a dollar to be received one year from now is $.9091 and the price of a dollar two years from now is $.8264 (reflecting a 10 percent time-value factor), the manager is in a position to evaluate the future cash flows. One can multiply the price of each of the three kinds of dollars involved by their quantities and find the net benefit in terms of today's dollars. Thus,

Value of second period's proceeds	$.8264 × 60 = $ 49.58
Value of first period's proceeds	$.9091 × 60 = 54.55
Total value of proceeds in terms of today's dollars	104.13
Less required outlay in today's dollars	100.00
Equals net value of the investment in terms of today's dollars (NPV)	$ 4.13

The example illustrates, first, that the process of making investment decisions involves using market prices (when possible) to put otherwise noncomparable quantities (dollars of different time periods) on a comparable basis in terms of today's dollars. Second, the net present value of an investment is equivalent to the net benefit from an investment in terms of today's dollars.

Intuitive Explanations of Percent Value

Consider an investment that will generate cash flows of $10,000 one year from today and will cost $8,000. With a discount rate of 5 percent, the investment has a net present value of $1,524 [that is, ($10,000 × .9524) − 8,000]. The $1,524 is the present value of the unrealized profit that the firm will earn if the expectations are realized by operations one period after the expenditure of the $8,000. The present value of the investment will be $9,524, and the cost is only $8,000, so there will be $1,524 of unrealized profit associated with the investment. An accountant would report $2,000 of income in period 1, but if 5 percent of $8,000 is subtracted, we obtain a net earnings after interest of $1,600. The present value of $1,600 is $1,524.

Revenues		$10,000
Less:		
Depreciation	$8,000	
Interest	400	8,400
Net income		$ 1,600

The preceeding income measure is after the capital cost ($400) on all capital and will equal the actual interest paid only if the investment is financed entirely with debt.

The previous example illustrated the fact that the net present value is equal to the present value of future incomes (after an interest cost on capital), but it was a one-period case. Now consider an investment with an outlay of $8,000 followed by benefits one year later of $1,000 and benefits two years later of $11,000. This investment has a net present value of $2,000 using a .10 rate of discount. Using straight-line depreciation, we get the following two income statements.

	Year 1	Year 2
Revenues	1,000	11,000
Depreciation	4,000	4,000
Income (loss) before interest	(3,000)	7,000
Interest (.10)	800	400
Net income	(3,800)	6,600

The present value of the income measures is

$$PV = -3,800\,(1.10)^{-1} + 6,600\,(1.10)^{-2} = \$2,000$$

Again the present value of the incomes is equal to the net present value of the investment. If we changed the method of depreciation, it would not change this relationship.

The relationship between the net present value measure and accounting concepts is considered in detail in Chapter 10.

Another useful interpretation of the net present value of the investment is that the firm could afford to pay $1,524 more than the cost of the investment and still break even (on a present value basis) on the investment. For example, if the firm paid $9,524 for the investment, 5 percent interest on $9,524 would be $476. Since the investment will earn $10,000, there will be enough cash to pay the original investment of $9,524 plus the $476 interest cost on the investment.

Describing the net present value of an investment as the amount that one could afford to pay in excess of the initial cost is helpful in giving management an estimate of the amount of room for error that is in the estimation of the cost of the investment. It is a useful intuitive definition of net present value.

Logical Basis for the Net Present Value Method

In our discussions of the net present value method, we have chosen to present our explanation in terms that have a maximum intuitive appeal. If the desirability of the net present value method depended only on its intuitive appeal, there would be the possibility that somebody might discover or invent another method that had even stronger intuitive appeal. Our confidence in the net present value method is derived from the fact that it is at least as good as any other solution to the problem of measuring the economic worth of an investment under certain well-defined circumstances.

First, we assume that the owners of a firm want investment choices that offer the greatest satisfaction. The entity can be thought of as a single individual, a family unit, a business firm, or some other organizational entity. The satisfaction that the owner of the entity derives from the investment decisions depends upon the amount and timing of the cash flows that can be withdrawn from the business operations. It may be helpful to think of these cash flows as consumption. In a business organization, the analogue to consumption on the part of an individual are dividends and other forms of cash payments made to stockholders.

The decision maker faces two sets of decisions that together determine the pattern of consumption the owner will be able to enjoy. One set of decisions concerns investment choices; the second determines how these investment choices will be financed.

Each possible investment alternative may be described by a series of cash flows representing the amount that would be paid out or received in each period. The size and timing of the cash flows associated with each investment choice are assumed here to be known in advance and with certainty. The number of separate investment choices open to the decision maker may be small or extremely large.

It is assumed that there is a known market rate of interest at which the firm can lend as much as it wants or borrow as much as it wants. The only restriction on borrowing is that loans must be repayable out of future cash flows.

How should the decision maker select from among the available investment options in such a way that it will be possible to achieve the maximum attainable level of satisfaction? All the investment opportunities should be arranged into groups. Only one investment from each group will be accepted. Some of the groups may contain only one option; others may contain a large number of options. From each group, select the investment whose net present value is algebraically the largest when the net present value is computed at the market rate of interest. If this investment has a positive net present value, accept it; otherwise, reject all the investments in that mutually exclusive group.

Now imagine that the decision maker has selected from among all the investment options the ones that have a positive net present value and that do not violate the restriction that no more than one from each group of investments can be accepted. These investments will determine the amount of money the firm will receive or must pay out in each time period as a result of the investments.

Assume that the decision maker has two independent investment opportunities with the following cash flows projected.

| | Period | | |
Investment	0	1	2
A	−$ 900	$1,000	
B	− 1,500		$2,000

The rate of interest (this is both the borrowing and lending rate) is assumed to be .05. All we need know to make the investment decisions is the net present value of these two investments ($52.40 for A and $314 for B). Because the two net present values are positive, the investments should be undertaken, and no further information or computations are required. The investor can borrow the funds at a cost of .05 and repay the debt using the cash flows from the investments. There is no question that the funds should be obtained to finance the investments. The conclusion not only holds for the two investments illustrated, but is valid for any investment with a positive net present value using the .05 borrowing rate. (Remember that there is no uncertainty; thus, the cash flows of the investments are known.)

We can make the decision to undertake the investments without considering the consumption preferences of the owners. If $X are available, these funds can be consumed, and $2,400 can be borrowed to finance the investments. The value of $X does not affect the investment decision. We assume, other things being equal, that the owners prefer more consumption to less. Specifically, if two patterns of consumption are identical in all time periods except one, and if the first pattern of consumption results in more consumption in a given time period than the second pattern of consumption, the owners will prefer the first to the second.

Accepting investments A and B will enable the investors to finance any pattern of consumption they may desire, provided the present value of the amounts consumed does not exceed the sum of the net present values of the investments accepted, in this case $366.40. If the investors are presented with a third independent investment option whose net present value is positive, they should accept it. By doing so, they will be able to increase the amount they consume in one or more periods without having to decrease consumption in any period. On the other hand, if the investors are presented with another investment option whose net present value is negative, they should reject it. Accepting it would require them to reduce, in one or more periods, the amounts consumed.

The details of the investors' consumption preferences do not need to be known in order for one to advise them about which investments to accept. One would need to know something about these consumption preferences in order to advise them about how to finance the investment—that is, what loans they should make and when they should be repaid. But the decision to invest is independent of consumption preferences as long as funds can be borrowed (obtained from external sources) or lent at the specified market interest rate.

Qualifications

The problem we have just described is not exactly the problem faced in practice by managers. There are two important ways in which managers might feel that the problems they face are different from the problem just described.

The managers may feel that the financial alternatives open to them are not considered in the preceding problem. They may feel that they are not able to obtain any additional funds, or, that, if they borrow, the lender may impose undesirable restrictions on their actions; or they may not know for future dates what the cost of borrowing or the return from lending will be. In any of these circumstances the present value method, as we have described it, is not strictly applicable. Second, the managers may not feel they are able to predict with perfect certainty the cash-flow consequences of their investment alternatives. Thus, they cannot describe the outcome of making an investment in terms of a single set of cash flows. Rather, there may be a large number of possible cash flows, any of which could be the outcome of selecting the particular investment, and the managers do not know in advance which one of the possible outcomes will occur.

Later we shall consider what modifications should be made to the net present value method to make it more useful as a method of selecting investments in these more general circumstances. .

Net Terminal Value

The net present value of an investment transmits all the information that is needed from an economic point of view (if the net present value is positive, the alternative is acceptable). If it is desired to make a point, however, it is frequently more impressive to switch to net terminal value. For example, assume a decision will save $10,000 a year for twenty years. The time-value factor is 10 percent. The present value of these saving is $85,136. After twenty years, however, the firm will have, as a result of the savings, $572,750 (assuming reinvestment at 10 percent). This latter number is more impressive than $85,136 and might benefically be inserted into an argument.

Time Zero

We will generally assume the outlay takes place at time zero. When is time zero? The choice of time zero will affect the magnitude of the net present value, but it will not affect the decision. Essentially, when we shift time zero forward or backward, we are merely multiplying by $(1 + r)^x$, where the exponent x may be positive or negative.

For example, assume an investment requires an outlay of $1,000 in 1990 and generates cash flows of $1,210 a year later in 1991. At a ten-percent discount rate, if 1990 is defined to be year zero, the net present value is $100. If 1991 is defined to be year zero, the net present value is $-\$1000\,(1.1) + \$1,210 = \$110$.

The Rollback Method

When using a simple hand calculator (one where there is no present value button), it is sometimes convenient to use a rollback method of calculation to compute the net present value of an investment. One advantage of this procedure is that the present values at different moments in time are obtained. Consider the following investment.

Time	Cash Flow
0	−$7,000
1	5,000
2	2,300
3	1,100

Assume that the discount rate is .10.

The first step is to place the cash flow of period 3 ($1,100) in the calculator and divide by 1.10, to obtain $1,000, the value at time 2. Add $2,300 and divide the sum by 1.10, to obtain $3,000, the value at time 1. Add $5,000 and divide by 1.10, to obtain $7,273, the value of time 0. Subtract $7,000, to obtain the net present value of $273.

Why a Positive NPV?

In a competitive economy one would expect abnormal profit opportunities to be eliminated by the competitive process. If this is so, why might a firm have projects proposed that have positive NPV? For one thing, even competitive economies have situations where there is less-than-perfect competition. Technological breakthroughs generating new products can give rise to positive investment opportunities. Second, there can be opportunities for increased efficiency because of past inefficiencies or because new manufacturing or distribution processes have been developed. New markets or new production locations can develop because of political change; thus, the first firms entering the market can reap positive present values.

Unfortunately, one explanation of why projects have positive NPVs is that too often the persons doing the analysis are excessively optimistic and have failed to consider adequately the full effects of the competitive forces on the future cash flows. In some cases, firms have even failed to consider the effects of their own project on the market prices of the inputs and outputs. The consequences of internal investments as well as the consequences of actions of competitors must be considered in computing the cash flows that are used to evaluate an investment.

Conclusions

The discounting for time is an essential part of any capital budgeting project evaluation process. We want to be able to compute present value equivalents of future sums so that the cash flows of different time periods can be added together, to compute an overall measure of investment worth.

While some measures of value will be as effective as the net present value measure under some circumstances, no alternative method will be as reliable and flexible as the net present value method.

PROBLEMS

3.1   Assume a cost of money of 10 percent. How much could you afford to pay now for $1,000 per year (payable at the end of each year, with the first payment a year from now) for (a) five years; (b) ten years; (c) twenty years; (d) thirty years; (e) perpetuity?

3.2   It costs $20,000 to make a new machine that promises to return cash flows of $10,000 per year for five years. Assume a cost of money of 10 percent. How much could you pay the owner for the patent rights to this machine and still be no worse off than if the new machine were not made?

3.3   If the patent rights for the machine described in problem 3.2 could be purchased for $10,000, what is the largest extra dividend the company could declare immediately on the basis of the net cash flows expected from these transactions?

3.4   Assume the transactions described in problem 3.3 were financed by a "loan" costing 10 percent. How large a loan would be required? Set up a payment schedule for this loan so that the machine is self-financing.

3.5   If the "loan" described in problem 3.4 were to be repaid in a single payment (including "interest") at the end of five years, what financial arrangements would be required?

3.6   There are two investments that have different degrees of risk associated with them. With the first investment, it is thought that a dollar to be received one period from now is worth $.9524 today (implying a 5 percent rate of discount). With the second investment, it is thought that a dollar to be received one period from now is worth $.9091 (implying a 10 percent rate of discount). Use the implied rates of discount to determine the value today of $1 to be received fifty years from now, for each of the two investments.

3.7   Mr. Jones can borrow $1,000 or more at a cost of 6 percent. He has an investment opportunity costing $1,000 that will earn 10 percent. Should his consumption preferences affect the amount he invests or borrows?

3.8   Bank A promises to pay its depositors 8 percent interest, *compounded continuously*, on one-year time deposits.

   Bank B makes the same payments to its depositors on one-year time deposits, but describes itself as paying X percent interest compounded annually. X is _____ percent. (Show the formula you used to derive X.)

3.9   In the United States it is customary for bonds to pay interest semiannually. That is, a $1,000 face-value bond is described as paying 8 percent if interest of $40 is paid every six months. In some countries, it is customary to pay interest annually. In those countries, a $1,000 face-value bond is described as paying 8 percent if interest of $80 is paid every twelve months.

   If you were willing to pay $1,000 for a bond that would pay $1,080 in one year, what would you be willing to pay for an otherwise identical bond that paid $40 in six months and $1,040 in one year?

3.10   An investment has the following cash flows.

0	−11,712
1	10,000
2	5,000
3	1,000

a. Compute the net present value using 10 percent.
b. Using straight-line depreciation, compute the present value of the income after capital costs using a 10 percent discount rate.
c. Should the investment be undertaken?

3.11   Miss Jones has been offered a desirable investment opportunity that will cost $10,000 and will return 15 percent per year. She has $10,000 available, but she has wanted to buy a new automobile that also costs $10,000.

What facts are relevant to the decision as to whether or not she makes the investment?

3.12   A decision will save $10,000 per year for twenty years. The time-value factor is 10 percent.
a. What is the present value of the savings?
b. What will the firm have after twenty years if the savings are reinvested?

3.13   Use continuous discounting to compute the present value of $1,000 for the following situations.

	Annual Discount Rate j	Number of Years Until Receipt of the Cash n
1	.01	100
2	.10	10
3	.20	5
4	.25	4
5	.05	20
6	.05	40
7	.05	100

3.14   *Long-Range Financial Planning*

For this problem, ignore income taxes. Assume money can be borrowed or lent at 12 percent per year.
a. Jacques and Jackie are very good friends. Together they have $100,000 in cash. If they did not work but were willing to use up their $100,000, what level annual rate of consumption could they afford for the next eight years? (At the end of year 8, they would be broke.)

b. What level rate of consumption could they afford if they wished to preserve their capital? (At the end of year 8, they would still have $100,000.)

c. Jacques and Jackie believe that if they both got jobs, they would be able to earn $20,000 a year for the first four years and $25,000 a year for the next four. What annual increase in consumption would be made possible if they work? (Consumption is to remain at the same level every year.)

d. Jacques and Jackie are actually planning to go into the retail sporting goods business. They first plan to open one store, and four years later, when it is established, they expect to open a second. They do not believe that they can handle more than two stores.

They estimate that it requires an outlay of $100,000 (mostly for working capital) to start a store. The estimated cash proceeds and outlay for the first eight years are shown here.

End of Period	Outlays	Operating Proceeds
0	−100,000	0
1		10,000
2		20,000
3		30,000
4	−100,000	30,000
5		40,000
6		50,000
7		60,000
8		60,000
Present values	−163,550	164,494

Assuming that the stores could be sold at the end of year 8 for the value of the working capital at that time ($200,000), what is the NPV of the investment? Use 12 percent as the discount rate.

3.15   What is the maximum possible level rate of consumption if Jacques and Jackie go into business for themselves and preserve their capital? (Their net worth will be $100,000 at the end of year 8. See the pro-forma balance sheets). The discount rate is 12 percent.

Now			
Cash	$100,000	Net worth	$100,000

At End of Year 8, Balance Sheet Before Business Is Liquidated			
Working capital	$200,000	Bank loans	$100,000
		Net worth	100,000

3.16 The town of Itheker has been planning some sewer improvements. The cost of constructing the improvements is $1,000,000. The improvements are to be financed by borrowing money, to be repaid over a thirty-year period. In answering parts (a), (b), and (c) of this question, assume level repayments over the next thirty years.

    a. What annual repayment would be required if interest rates were 6 percent?

    b. What level annual payments would be required if the interest rates were 12 percent?

    c. How much of the first payment referred to in (b) would go toward interest expense and how much toward repayment of principal?

    d. An obscure provision of the New York State Constitution has the effect of requiring that at least $25,000 of principal be repaid during each of the first two years. What would the total payment be in the first year if the principal repayment were exactly $25,000 and if interest rates were

        1. 6 percent.

        2. 12 percent.

3.17 The manager of a pension fund (the fund is not subject to taxation) considered that the appropriate cost of money for his fund was a continuously compounded rate of 12 percent. The manager had excess cash, which he was planning to invest in a bond. He was considering two alternatives. Both bonds were of the very highest quality, and both promised to pay $1,000 at maturity in five years. The domestic bond promised to pay interest at six-month intervals, each payment being $62. The first payment would be received in six months and the last at maturity. The other alternative was a Eurodollar bond, which promised to pay interest at annual intervals, each payment being $128. The first payment in this case would be received in one year and the last at maturity.

    Which bond would you recommend that the pension manager purchase?

REFERENCES

Gitman, J., and J. R. Forrester, Jr., "A Survey of Capital Budgeting Techniques Used by Major U.S. Firms," *Financial Management*, Fall 1977, pp. 66–71.

Hastie, K. Larry, "One Businessman's View of Capital Budgeting," *Financial Management*, Winter 1974, pp. 36–44.

Kim, S. H., and E. J. Farragher, "Current Capital Budgeting Practices," *Management Accounting*, June 1981, pp. 26–30.

Pinches, G. E. "Myopia, Capital Budgeting and Decision Making," *Financial Management*, Autumn 1986, pp. 6–19.

Trippi, Robert R., "Conventional and Unconventional Methods for Evaluating Investments," *Financial Management*, Autumn 1974, pp. 31–35.

CHAPTER 4

Measuring Investment Value: Decisions with Certainty

How far the majority of our agricultural and industrial plants lag behind
the most progressive model establishments in their own fields! And even
the latter, in all probability, fall just as far short of the ideal of truly
perfected equipment.

> —*Eugene von Böhm-Bawerk, Capital and Interest, Vol. II,* Positive
> Theory of Capital *(South Holland, IL: Libertarian Press, 1959; first
> published in 1888), p. 85.*

In this chapter we shall describe four of the more commonly used procedures for
making capital budgeting decisions. We shall not attempt to describe all the
variations that are possible or all the faulty procedures that are used. If you
understand the basic elements of a correct procedure, you will soon be able to
distinguish between correct and incorrect procedures. The two basic correct
capital budgeting techniques presented in this chapter are applicable to a wide
range of decisions found throughout the economy, both in the profit and
not-for-profit sectors.

Methods of Classifying Investments

Any useful scheme of evaluating investments must be based on a classification of
types of investments. Different kinds of investments raise different problems,
are of different relative importance to the firm, and will require different persons
to evaluate their significance. Through the classification of different types of
investments, each investment proposal will receive attention from persons
qualified to analyze it.

Investments may be classified according to the following categories.

1. The kinds of scarce resources used by the investment. For example, does the investment require important amounts of cash, floor space, or the time of key personnel? (Personnel may also be classified: sales, production, research, top management, legal staff, and so on.)
2. The amount of cash investment that is required. For example, with respect to the amount of immediate cash outlays required, we could classify investments as requiring less than $500, between $500 and $50,000, and over $50,000.
3. The way in which benefits from the investment are affected by other possible investments. Some investments stand on their own feet. Others will be improved or will be successful only if supplementary investments are made; still others will be useless if competing investments are accepted. For example, the worth of another forklift truck may depend on whether or not the plan for adding an automatic conveyor system is accepted.
4. The form in which the benefits are received. Investments may generate greater cash flows, reduce the risks associated with poor business conditions, reduce the accident rate, improve employee morale, or eliminate a community nuisance such as excessive smoke or noise.
5. Whether the incremental benefits are the result of lower costs (efficiency) or increased sales or whether the investments merely prevent a decline in sales or market share.
6. The functional activity to which the investments are most closely related. For example, an oil company may classify investments according to the following activities: exploration, production, transportation, refining, or marketing.
7. The industry classification of the investment. For example, the manager of a conglomerate may want to know if the investment being considered has to do with its professional football team, steel production, or space activities.
8. The degree of necessity. Some investments are necessary in the sense that, if they are not undertaken, the entire operation stops (if stoppage is desirable, the *necessity* may not be absolute). Other investments are highly optional and move the firm in a new direction.

Many other methods of classification could be suggested (for example, energy saving, new products, maintaining market share, capacity expansion, pollution control). Clearly, no single scheme of classification will be equally valid for all uses or for all companies. The essential task is to develop a classification system for investments that is appropriate to the activity of the business and the organizational structure of the particular company.

We are primarily concerned with investments for which both the resources used and the benefits to be received can be measured to an important degree in terms of cash flows. Second, the analytical methods developed in this book will be most useful for investments that are important enough to the firm to warrant a relatively careful study of their potential profitability. Next, we shall consider a classification of investments that is based on the way the benefits from a given investment are affected by other possible investments.

Dependent and Independent Investments

In evaluating the investment proposals presented to management, it is important to be aware of the possible interrelationships between pairs of investment proposals. A given investment proposal may be economically independent of, or dependent on, another investment proposal. An investment proposal will be said to be *economically independent* of a second investment if the cash flows (or more generally, the costs and benefits) expected from the first investment would be the same regardless of whether the second investment were accepted or rejected. If the cash flows associated with the first investment are affected by the decision to accept or reject the second investment, the first investment is said to be economically dependent on the second. It should be clear that when one investment is dependent on another, some attention must be given to the question of whether decisions about the first investment can or should be made separately from decisions about the second.

Economically Independent Investments

In order for investment A to be economically independent of investment B, two conditions must be satisfied. First, it must be technically possible to undertake investment A whether or not investment B is accepted. Thus, it is *not* possible to build a school and a shopping center on the same site; therefore, the proposal to build one is not independent of a proposal to build the other. Second, the net benefits to be expected from the first investment must not be affected by the acceptance or rejection of the second. If the estimates of the cash outlays and the cash inflows for investment A are not the same when B is either accepted or rejected, the two investments are not independent. Thus, it is technically possible to build a toll bridge and operate a ferry across adjacent points on a river, but the two investments are not independent because the proceeds from one will be affected by the existence of the other. The two investments would not be economically independent in the sense in which we are using the term, even if the traffic across the river at this point were sufficient to operate profitably both the bridge and the ferry.

Sometimes two investments cannot both be accepted because the firm does not have enough cash to finance both. This situation could occur if the amount of cash available for investments were strictly limited by management rather than by the capital market or if increments of funds obtained from the capital market cost more than previous increments. In such a situation, the acceptance of one investment may cause the rejection of the other. But we will not consider the two investments to be economically dependent. To classify this type of investment as dependent would make all investments for such a firm dependent, and this is not a useful definition for our purposes.

Economically Dependent Investments

The dependency relationship can be classified further. If a decision to undertake the second investment will increase the benefits expected from the first (or decrease the costs of undertaking the first without changing the benefits), the second investment is said to be a *complement* of the first. If the decision to undertake the second investment will decrease the benefits expected from the first (or increase the costs of undertaking the first without changing the benefits), the second is said to be a *substitute* for the first. In the extreme case where the potential benefits to be derived from the first investment will completely disappear if the second investment is accepted, or where it is technically impossible to undertake the first when the second has been accepted, the two investments are said to be *mutually exclusive.*

It may be helpful to think of the possible relationships between investments as being arrayed along a line segment (see Figure 4.1). At the extreme left, investment A is a prerequisite to investment B. In the center of the line, investment A is independent of investment B. At the extreme right-hand end of the line, investment A is mutually exclusive with respect to investment B. As we move to the right from the left-hand side of the line, we have varying degrees of complementariness, decreasing to the right. Similarly, the right-hand side of the line represents varying degrees of substitutability, increasing to the right.

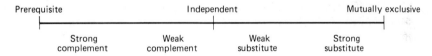

FIGURE 4.1   Investment Relationships

Statistical Dependence

It is possible for two or more investments to be economically independent but statistically dependent. Statistical dependence is said to be present if the cash flows from two or more investments would be affected by some external event or happening whose occurrence is uncertain. For example, a firm could produce high-priced yachts and expensive cars. The investment decisions affecting these two product lines are economically independent. However, the fortunes of both activities are closely associated with high business activity and a large amount of discretionary income for the "rich" people. This statistical dependence may affect the risk of investments in these product lines, because the swings of profitability of a firm with these two product lines will be wider than those of a firm with two product lines having less statistical dependence.

Measures of Investment Worth

Here we introduce some methods of evaluating the worth of investments that are in common use or have been frequently recommended as being desirable. If we take a group of investment proposals and rank them by each of these methods, we shall find that each method will frequently give a different ranking to the same set of investment proposals. In fact, it can be said that the different measures will only accidentally give identical rankings to a set of investment proposals. Although we shall not to be able to rank economically independent investments in a useful manner, we shall normally be able to make decisions without such rankings.

Various executives faced with the same set of investment possibilities, but using different measures of investment worth, will tend to make dissimilar investment decisions. Clearly, all the measures that will be described here cannot be equally valid. We shall attempt to determine which of the measures have some legitimate reason for use and to isolate the circumstances under which they will tend to give satisfactory results.

In current business practice, each of the methods selected has its advocates, and frequently they are used in combination with each other. Because investment proposals are rarely accepted by top management solely on the basis of such analyses, it may be argued that the choice of method is of little significance because the investment decision is likely to be influenced by many different factors. Insofar as the executives making the final decision are aware of the risks involved and are intimately familiar with the proposals, know the possible technical or operating problems that may be encountered, and realize the potential erosion of earnings resulting from competitive action or changing technology, this criticism may very well be valid. In most large organizations, however, it is impossible for the top management officials, who must finally approve or disapprove investment proposals, to be intimately familiar with the details of each and every proposal presented to them. To the extent that this intimate knowledge is impossible or impractical, these executives must rely upon the economic evaluations prepared by their subordinates. To make reasonable choices in weighing alternative investments, it is increasingly necessary that various proposals be evaluated as nearly as possible on some uniform, comparable basis. In such circumstances, although the measure of economic worth of an investment should never be the sole factor considered in making a final decision, it should play an important part in the evaluation of the investments under consideration by the firm.

The fact that various measures give different rankings and indicate different accept-or-reject decisions to identical sets of investment proposals is a matter of concern. Substantial improvements in efficiency and income may result if a more adequate measure can be discovered and widely adopted. Any such progress first requires a more general agreement about the desirable characteristics to be possessed by a good index of the economic worth of an investment. We assume that the objective is to maximize the wellbeing of the common stockholders.

The Elements of a Cash Flow Projection

To arrive at the set of projected incremental cash flows used in evaluating any investment, it is usually necessary to project the impact of the investment on the revenues and expenses of the company. Some investments will affect only the expense components (such as cost-saving investments), whereas others will affect revenues as well as costs. Projecting how various expense and revenue items will be affected if the investment is undertaken is not an easy task, for incremental impacts are often difficult to assess. In some cases, such as the impact of a new product on the sales of an existing product that is considered a substitute, the problem is the uncertain extent of the erosion. In other cases, such as with overhead items (such as accounting services, plant security, a regional warehouse system), the problem arises because there is not a well-defined relationship between the incremental action contemplated and these costs; no exact solution exists to these knotty problems.

An investment in plant or equipment to produce a new product will probably also require an investment in current assets less current liabilities (working capital). There may be an increase in raw material, work-in-process, and finished goods inventories. Also, if there are sales on credit rather than cash, accounts receivable will increase; that is, sales per the income statement will be collected with a lag, and there will be an increase in accounts receivable. Finally, not all payables will be paid immediately, and this lag will manifest itself in an increase in current liabilities (reducing the need for other financing). Thus, a working capital investment (a negative cash flow and a need for capital) usually accompanies the direct investment in plant and equipment.

One can assume that the working capital investment is fully turned into cash at the hypothesized end of the project. That is, it is assumed that inventories are depleted, receivables are collected, and payables are paid. Hence, over the life of the project, the sum of the working capital changes should be zero if this assumption is accepted. However, the commitment of resources to working capital has a cost (the time value of money) even if those resources are ultimately freed.

Two Discounted Cash Flow Methods

We shall first introduce the two primary discounted cash flow investment evaluation procedures, net present value (NPV) and internal rate of return (IRR). After a brief discussion of these two measures of investment worth, we shall describe a series of four hypothetical investments. The four hypothetical investments have been designed so that for two selected pairs, it is possible to decide that one investment is clearly preferable to the other. If a measure of investment worth indicates that one investment is better when the other investment is actually better, then clearly there is a danger in using that measure. We shall find that some measures can easily be eliminated as general decision rules because in some situations they give obviously wrong answers and another measure gives the "right" answer. We shall conclude that the net present value method is better than the other possible methods.

We offer two proposed measures of investment worth that, as a group, could be called the discounted cash flow, or DCF, measures. Before proceeding to analyze them, it is desirable to explain again the concept of the present value of a future sum, because in one way or another this concept is utilized in both these measures.

The Net Present Value Method

The net present value method of evaluating investments is built on the assumption that we can define the appropriate discount rate to be used to find present value equivalents of future sums.

If the net present value of the investment's cash flows is positive, then the investment is acceptable. The output of the net present value method of investment evaluation is an absolute dollar amount.

Internal Rate of Return

Many different terms are used to define the internal rate of return concept. Among these terms are *yield, interest rate of return, rate of return, return on investment, present value return on investment, discounted cash flow, investor's method, time-adjusted rate of return*, and *marginal efficiency of capital*. In this book, *IRR* and *internal rate of return* are used interchangeably.

The internal rate of return method utilizes present value concepts. The procedure is to find a rate of discount that will make the present value of the cash proceeds expected from an investment equal to the present value of the cash outlays required by the investment. Such a rate of discount may be found by trial and error. For example, with a conventional investment, if we know the cash proceeds and the cash outlays in each future year, we can start with any rate of discount and find for that rate the present value of the cash proceeds and the present value of the outlays. If the net present value of the cash flows is positive, then using some higher rate of discount would make them equal. By a process of trial and error, the approximately correct rate of discount can be determined. This rate of discount is referred to as the internal rate of return of the investment, or its IRR.

The IRR method is commonly used in security markets in evaluating bonds and other debt instruments. The yield to maturity of a bond is the rate of discount that makes the present value of the payments promised to the bondholder equal to the market price of the bond. The yield to maturity on a $1,000 bond having a coupon rate of 10 percent will be equal to 10 percent only if the current market value of the bond is $1,000. If the current market value is greater than $1,000, the IRR to maturity will be something less than the coupon rate; if the current market value is less than $1,000, the IRR will be greater than the coupon rate.

The internal rate of return may also be described as the rate of growth of an investment. This is more easily seen for an investment with one present outlay and one future benefit. For example, assume that an investment with an outlay of $1,000 today will return $1,331 three years from now.

This is a .10 internal rate of return, and it is also a .10 growth rate per year.

Time	Beginning-of-Period Investment	Growth of Period	Growth Divided by Beginning-of-Period Investment
0	$1,000	$100	$100/$1,000 = .10
1	1,100	110	$110/$1,100 = .10
2	1,210	121	$121/$1,210 = .10
3	1,331	—	

The internal rate of return of a conventional investment has an interesting interpretation that may be referred to at this point. It represents the highest rate of interest an investor could afford to pay, without losing money, if all the funds to finance the investment were borrowed and the loan (principal and accrued interest) were repaid by application of the cash proceeds from the investment as they were earned.

We shall illustrate the internal rate of return calculation using a basic example where the investment has a net present value of $886 using .10 as the discount rate. (See the following table for the cash flows.) We want to find the rate of discount that causes the sum of the present values of the cash flows to be equal to zero. Assume that our first choice (an arbitrary guess) is .10. We find that the net present value using .10 is a positive $886. We want to change the discount rate so that the present value is zero. Should we increase or decrease the rate of discount for our second estimate? Since the cash flows are conventional (negative followed by positive), to decrease the present value of the future cash flows, we should increase the rate of discount (thus causing the present value of the future cash flows that are positive to be smaller).

Period	Cash Flow	Present Value Factor (10%)	Present Value
0	−$12,337	1.0000	−$12,337
1	10,000	.9091	9,091
2	5,000	.8264	4,132
		Net present value =	$ 886

Let us try .20 as the rate of discount.

Period	Cash Flow	Present Value Factor (20%)	Present Value
0	−$12,337	1.0000	−$12,337
1	10,000	.8333	8,333
2	5,000	.6944	3,472
		Net present value =	−$ 532

The net present value is negative, indicating that the .20 rate of discount is too large. We shall try a value between .10 and .20 for our next estimate. Assume that we try .16.

Period	Cash Flow	Present Value Factor (16%)	Present Value
0	−$12,337	1.0000	−$12,337
1	10,000	.8621	8,621
2	5,000	.7432	3,716
		Net present value =	0

The net present value is zero using .16 as the rate of discount, which by definition means that .16 is the internal rate of return of the investment.

Although tables give only present value factors for select interest rates, calculators and computers can be used for any interest rate.

Net Present Value Profile

The net present value profile is one of the more useful devices for summarizing the profitability characteristics of an investment. On the horizontal axis we measure different discount rates; on the vertical axis we measure the net present value of the investment. The net present value of the investment is plotted for all discount rates from zero to some reasonably large rate. The plot of net present values will cross the horizontal axis (have zero net present value) at the rate of discount that is called the internal rate of return of the investment.

Figure 4.2 shows the net present value profile for the investment discussed in the previous section. If we add the cash flows, assuming a zero rate of discount, we obtain

$$-\$12,337 + \$10,000 + \$5,000 = \$2,663$$

The $2,663 is the intersection of the graph with the Y axis. We know that the graph has a height of $886 at a .10 rate of discount and crosses the X axis at .16, since .16 is the internal rate of return of the investment. For interest rates greater than .16, the net present value is negative.

Note that for a conventional investment (minus cash flows followed by positive cash flows), the net present value profile slopes downward to the right.

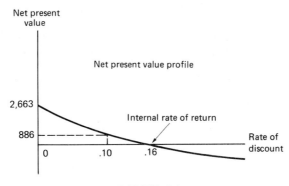

FIGURE 4.2

The net present value profile graph can be used to estimate the internal rate of return by plotting one negative value and one positive value and connecting the two points with a straight line. The intercept with the X axis will give a sensible estimate (not the exact value) of the internal rate of return.

We shall now consider four different investment opportunities and will apply four different investment criteria to these investments.

Four Investments

In Table 4.1 four hypothetical investments are described in terms of the initial cost of each and the net cash flows expected during each year of earning life. Assume the four investments are mutually exclusive (only one investment will be accepted). The salvage value or terminal value of each is assumed to be zero. We shall illustrate the ranking that may be given to these investments by each measure of investment worth under consideration.

To avoid complexities, we will assume that there are zero taxes and no uncertainty. An evaluation of the risk or uncertainty associated with an investment is a crucial part of the investment decision process. Also, all

TABLE 4.1   Cash Flows of Hypothetical Investments

Investment	Initial Cost	Net Cash Flows per Year	
		Year 1	Year 2
A	$10,000	$10,000	
B	10,000	10,000	$1,100
C	10,000	3,762	7,762
D	10,000	5,762	5,762

investments must be placed on an after-tax basis. The concepts of risk or uncertainty and taxation are complex, however, and it has seemed advisable to take these problems up separately later in the book.

Ranking by Inspection

It is possible in certain limited cases to determine by inspection which of two or more investments is more desirable. Two situations in which this is true are the following.

1. Two investments have identical cash flows each year through the final year of the short-lived investment, but one continues to earn cash proceeds in subsequent years. The investment with the longer life would be more desirable. Thus, investment B is better than investment A, because all factors are equal except that B continues to earn proceeds after A has been retired.

2. Two investments have the same initial outlay and the same earning life and earn the same total proceeds. If at the end of every year (during their earning life) the total net proceeds of one investment are at least as great as, and for at least one year are greater than, the total for the other investment, then the first investment will always be more profitable. Thus, investment D is more desirable than investment C, because D earns $2,000 more in year 1 than investment C does; investment C does not earn this $2,000 until year 2. The earning of $2,000 more in the earlier year leads to the conclusion that investment D is more desirable than investment C.

Payback Period

The payback period is one of the simplest and one of the most frequently used methods of measuring the economic value of an investment. The *payback period* is defined as the length of time required for the stream of cash proceeds produced by an investment to equal the original cash outlay required by the investment. If an investment is expected to produce a stream of cash proceeds that is constant from year to year, the payback period can be determined by dividing the total original cash outlay by the amount of the annual cash proceeds expected. Thus, if an investment required an original outlay of $300 and was expected to produce a stream of cash proceeds of $100 a year for five years, the payback period would be $300 divided by $100, or three years. If the stream of expected proceeds is not constant from year to year, the payback period must be determined by adding up the proceeds expected in successive years until the total is equal to the original outlay.

Ordinarily, the administrator would set some maximum payback period and reject all investment proposals for which the payback period is greater than this maximum. Investigators have reported that maximum payback periods of two, three, four, or five years are frequently used by industrial concerns. The relatively short periods mentioned suggest that different maximum payback periods are required for different types of investments, because some kinds of investments (construction, for example) can seldom be expected to have a payback period as short as five years.

Assume that the payback period is also used to rank investment alternatives, with those having the shortest payback periods being given the highest ranking. The investments described in Table 4.1 are ranked by this method in Table 4.2.

Let us check the reasonableness of the ranking given the investments by the cash payback approach. Investments A and B are both ranked as 1 because they both have shorter payback periods than do any of the other investments, namely, one year. But investment A earns total proceeds of $10,000, and this amount merely equals the cost of the investment. Investment B, which has the same rank as A, will not only earn $10,000 in the first year but also $1,100 in the next year. Obviously, investment B is superior to A. Any ranking procedure, such as the payback period, that fails to disclose this fact is deficient.

Consider investments C and D modified so as to cost $11,524. They would be given identical rankings because both would return their original outlay by the end of the second year. The two investments are in fact similar, with the single exception that out of identical total returns, more proceeds are received in the first year and less in the second year from investment D than is the case with C. To the extent that earnings can be increased by having $2,000 available for reinvestment one year earlier, D is superior to investment C, but both would be given the same ranking by the payback period measure.

Thus, the cash payback period measure has two weaknesses: (1) It fails to give any consideration to cash proceeds earned after the payback date, and (2) it fails to take into account the differences in the timing of proceeds earned prior to the payback date. These weaknesses disqualify the cash payback measures as a general method of ranking investments. They are useful as a general measure of risk (all things equal, a two-year payback is less risky than a ten-year payback).

TABLE 4.2 **Payback Period**

Investment	Payback Period (Years)	Ranking	Calculations of Payback
A	1.0	1	
B	1.0	1	
C	1.8	4	$1 + \dfrac{\$6,238}{\$7,762} = 1.803$
D	1.7	3	$1 + \dfrac{\$4,238}{\$5,762} = 1.736$

Return on Investment

The methods described in this section are commonly referred to as rate-of-return analysis or return-on-investment (ROI) analysis. Terminology is a problem because both these terms are also used to describe other procedures. We shall consistently use internal rate of return only when we refer to a discounted cash flow calculation and return on investment to refer to an income divided by investment calculation.

To get a measure of efficiency, analysts frequently use the ratio of the firm's income to the book value of its assets. Some companies also use this measure as a means of choosing among various proposed internal investments. When this measure is used, the average income is computed after depreciation. If the denominator in the ratio is the book value of the investment, the value of both the numerator and the denominator will depend on the depreciation method used. An alternative procedure is to divide the average income by the cost of the investment (the accrued depreciation is not subtracted).

The ratio of income to book value is a common and useful measure of performance, but it is less useful as a device for ranking investments. Table 4.3 shows that the same ranking of 1 is given to investments C and D, although D is preferable to C. This procedure fails to rank these investments correctly because it does not take into consideration the timing of the proceeds.

An alternative procedure (see Table 4.4) is to divide income by the cost of the investment (accumulated depreciation not being subtracted). For purposes of measuring performance and computing return on investment, the use of undepreciated cost will give lower measures than will the use of book value. Both measures illustrated fail to take into consideration the timing of cash proceeds. It is this failing that leads to incorrect decisions from the use of either of the two methods.

TABLE 4.3   Average Income on Book Value

Investment	Average Proceeds	Average Depreciation[a]	Average Income (Proceeds Less Depreciation)	Average Book Value[b]	Income on Book Value (%)	Ranking
A	$10,000	$10,000	$ 0	$5,000	0	4
B	5,550	5,000	550	5,000	11	3
C	5,762	5,000	762	5,000	15	1
D	5,762	5,000	762	5,000	15	1

[a] Assuming straight-line-depreciation.
[b] Investment divided by 2.

TABLE 4.4   *Average Income on Cost*

Investment	Cost	Average Income	Average Income on Cost (%)	Ranking
A	$10,000	$ 0	0	4
B	10,000	550	5.5	3
C	10,000	762	7.6	1
D	10,000	762	7.6	1

Discounted Cash Flow Methods

We have considered payback and return on investment as methods for measuring the value of an investment. Payback indicated that B is as desirable as A. ROI indicated that C is tied with D. But B is clearly better than A, and D is better than C. On the basis of such an example, we have been able to reject payback and ROI as general methods of evaluating investments.

These two measures failed to consider the timing of cash proceeds from the investments. The payback period represents one extreme in this regard because all the proceeds received before the payback period are counted and treated as equals, and all the proceeds received after the payback period are ignored completely. With the return on investment, the proceeds were related by simple averaging techniques to such things as the original cost of the investment or its book value. Neither of these methods succeeded in bringing the timing of cash proceeds into the analysis.

We have seen that the measures of investment worth previously considered may give obviously incorrect results because they fail either to consider the entire life of the investment or to give adequate attention to the timing of future cash proceeds. The discounted cash flow concept provides a method of taking into account the timing of cash proceeds and outlays over the entire life of the investment. We now return to the two measures of investment worth already introduced that incorporate present value concepts.

Internal Rate of Return

In Table 4.5 we show the internal rate of return for each of the investments listed in Table 4.1 and the ranking of investments that would result if this method were used.

It is instructive to examine the rankings given by this method applicable to each of the pairs of investments in this list for which we were earlier able to determine the more desirable investment of each pair.

We previously compared two pairs of investments and decided that investment B was preferable to A and D to C. In each case, if preference had been

TABLE 4.5   Internal Rate of Return of the Investments

Investment	IRR (%)	Ranking
A	0	4
B	10	1
C	9[a]	3
D	10	1

[a] Approximate measure.

determined by using the internal rate of return of an investment method, the pairs would be given the correct ranking. This is the first method that we have used that gives the correct rankings of both pairs.

$$
\begin{array}{llll}
A, & 0\% & C, & 9\% \\
B, & 10\% & D, & 10\%
\end{array}
$$

Net Present Value

It is instructive to note the rankings that will be given to the hypothetical investments of Table 4.1 by the net present value method, using two sample rates of discount. In Table 4.6 we present the results of using the net present value method and a 6 percent rate of discount.

In discussing the measures of investment worth that do not use the discounted cash flow method, we pointed out that the relative ranking of certain pairs of these four investments was obvious. That is, it is obvious from examining the cash flows that investment B is preferable to A, and D is preferable to C. The reader may note that in each case the net present value method using a 6 percent rate of discount ranks these investment pairs in the correct relative order.

In Table 4.7 the same investments are ranked by the net present value method using a 30 percent rate of discount instead of 6 percent. The relative ranking of investments C and D does not change with the changes in the rate of

TABLE 4.6   Net Present Values of the Investments—Rate of Discount is 6 Percent

Investment	Present Value of Cash Flow	Present Value of Outlay	Net Present Value	Ranking
A	$ 9,430	$10,000	−$570	4
B	10,413	10,000	+413	3
C	10,457	10,000	+457	2
D	10,564	10,000	+564	1

TABLE 4.7   Net Present Values of the Investments—Rate of Discount is 30 Percent

Investment	Present Value of Proceeds	Present Value of Outlay	Net Present Value	Ranking
A	$7,692	$10,000	−$2,308	3
B	8,343	10,000	−1,657	1
C	7,487	10,000	−2,513	4
D	7,842	10,000	−2,158	2

discount. Investment C, which was ranked second when a 6 percent rate of discount was used, is ranked fourth when the 30 percent discount rate is used. The ranking of investment D is changed from first to second by the change in the rate of discount. The higher rate of discount results in the proceeds of the later years being worth less relative to the proceeds of the early years; thus, the ranking of B goes from 3 to 1, but D is still ranked ahead of C.

Even with a 30 percent rate of interest, the present value method maintains the correct ordering of each of the two pairs of investments for which an obvious preference can be determined. Thus we still find investment B preferred to A, and D preferred to C. This result is not an accident resulting from the specific choice of hypothetical investments and discount rates used in our examples. Whenever it is possible to determine obvious preferences between pairs of investments by the methods described earlier, the present value method will rank these investments in the correct order, no matter what rate of discount is used to compute the present value, as long as the same rate of discount is used to determine the present value of both the investments.

Summary of Rankings

The rankings given by each measure of investment worth for each of the hypothetical investments described in Table 4.1 are summarized in Table 4.8. The most striking conclusion to be drawn from Table 4.8 is the tendency for each measure of investment worth to give a different ranking to the identical set of investments. This emphasizes the need to give careful consideration to the choice of measures used to evaluate proposed investments. All four methods cannot be equally valid. By considering specific pairs of investments, we have shown that the measures of investment worth that do not involve the use of the discounted cash flow method can give rankings of investments that are obviously incorrect. For this reason, these measures will be excluded from further consideration.

The rankings given the investments by the net present value measures are not identical to that given by the internal rate of return of an investment measure. Neither of these rankings can be eliminated as being obviously incorrect; yet,

TABLE 4.8 Summary of Rankings

Measure of Investment Worth	Investment			
	A	B	C	D
Payback period	1[a]	1[a]	4	3
Average income on book value or cost	4	3	1[a]	1[a]
Internal rate of return	4	1[a]	3	1[a]
Net present value				
At 6%	4	3	2	1
At 30%	3	1	4	2

[a] Indicates a tie between two investments.

because they are different, they could lead to contradictory conclusions in certain situations. In Chapter 5 we shall continue our investigation in an attempt to determine whether the net present value or the internal rate of return measure is more useful to a decision maker.

Limitation of Investment Rankings

In this chapter we discussed the ranking of four mutually exclusive investments and showed that, given a carefully defined set of investments, we can make definite statements about the relative desirability of two or more investments. If the investments are not restricted to mutually exclusive investments, we will find our ability to rank investments very limited. It is difficult to rank independent investments so that the rankings can be used to make decisions.

Generally, we shall not be concerned with the "ranking" of investments; instead, we shall

1. Make accept or reject decisions for investments that are independent (that is, if we undertake one investment, the cash flows of undertaking the other investments are not affected).
2. Choose the best of a set of mutually exclusive investments (that is, if we undertake one, either we would not want to undertake the other or we would not be able to because of the characteristics of the investments).

Although the decision-making objectives are somewhat more modest than the objective of ranking investments, we shall still encounter difficulties. There is nothing in our recommendations, however, that will preclude a manager from applying qualitative criteria to the investments being considered to obtain a ranking. The ranking that is so obtained is likely to be difficult to defend. Fortunately, for a wide range of decision situations, a manager can make decisions without a ranking of investments.

Discounted Payback

Instead of computing the length of time required to recover the original investment, some analysts compute the length of time required until the present value turns from being negative to positive. This computation gives a break-even life of the asset or a discounted payback period. If the life of the asset exceeds this break-even life, the asset will have a positive present value. The discounted payback period can be used to make accept or reject decisions for independent investment decisions, since any investment with a discounted payback period will at least earn the required return.

Assume an investment with the following cash flows.

Time	Cash Flow
0	−$2,487
1	1,000
2	1,000
3	1,000
4	1,000
5	1,000

Figure 4.3 shows the cumulative present values (with a discount rate of 10 percent) for the investment. It has a discounted payback period of three years, and Table 4.9 (p. 80) shows the calculations, assuming a 10 percent rate of discount.

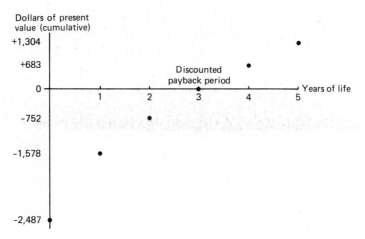

FIGURE 4.3   Discounted Payback Period

Relationship Between Payback Period and Internal Rate of Return

If an investment is expected to earn equal proceeds each year of its life and if the life of the investment is known, it is possible to construct a theoretically correct

TABLE 4.9 Present Values for Different Lives

| Period i | Net Present Value for Life of i | Cash Flows and Present Values for Period | | | | | |
		0 (−$2,487)	1 ($1,000)	2 ($1,000)	3 ($1,000)	4 ($1,000)	5 ($1,000)
0	−$2,487	−$2,487					
1	−1,578	−2,487	$909				
2	−752	−2,487	909	$826			
3	0	−2,487	909	826	$752		
4	+683	−2,487	909	826	752	$683	
5	+1,304	−2,487	909	826	752	683	$621

payback period that will lead to the same accept or reject decisions as the present value rule. Because of the limiting assumptions, especially equal annual proceeds, this formula has limited usefulness in making decisions, but it does illustrate the weakness of certain payback conventions. In particular, it shows that the longest acceptable payback period depends on the life of the investment and the time value of money.

The payback period is defined as the period of time required to recover the initial investment, or as the cost of the investment divided by the proceeds per period. In equation form, with equal proceeds per period,

$$\text{Payback period} = \frac{\text{cost of investment}}{\text{proceeds per period}}$$

The present value rule is that an investment should be accepted if the sum of the present values of the proceeds from the investment is greater than the cost of the investment. The symbol $B(n, r)$ stands for the present value of an annuity of $1 per period for n periods (the life of the investment) discounted at a rate of r per period. We assume that r is known and is the appropriate discount rate for the firm. With equal annual proceeds we would accept the investment, using the present value rule, if the following inequality is satisfied:

$$(\text{Proceeds per period}) \times B(n, r) \geq \text{cost of investment}$$

If the proceeds per period are positive, we can divide both sides of the preceding inequality by the proceeds per period without changing the sense of the inequality sign. When we do this, the right-hand side becomes cost of investment divided by proceeds per period, which is the payback period. This leads to the following formulation of the present value rule:

$$B(n, r) \geq \text{payback period} \quad \text{or} \quad \text{Payback period} \leq B(n, r)$$

This shows that an investment with positive equal annual proceeds over its n-year life will have a positive NPV if and only if its payback period is less than $B(n, r)$. As the life of the investment increases, so does the maximum acceptable payback period. As the life tends to infinity, the maximum acceptable payback period approaches an upper limit of $1/r$.

Sometimes we may not be sure what life we can expect for an investment. In this case the preceding formula can also be used to find the minimum acceptable life of an investment whose payback period is known. To do this, we find the smallest value of n for which $B(n, r)$ is greater than the investment's payback period. The values of $B(n, r)$ are listed in Appendix Table B.

EXAMPLE 4.1

The ABC Company requires a two-year payback period or less before accepting equipment. A piece of equipment is being considered that costs $5,000 and that is expected to earn cash proceeds per year of $1,000 for a life of ten years. The relevant discount rate is 10 percent per year. Should the equipment be purchased?

The equipment has a payback period of five years; thus, it seems to be undesirable in view of the company's two-year payback criterion. Because it has a life of ten years, however, it could have a payback period of up to six years ($B(10, .10) = 6.1446$) and would still be acceptable.

Now assume that the equipment has a perpetual life. The reciprocal of the payback period of five years is .2. This is also the internal rate of return of the investment:

$$\text{Internal rate of return} = \frac{\text{income}}{\text{investment}} = \frac{1,000}{5,000} = .2$$

If, instead of a perpetual life, we had assumed a very long life, the reciprocal of the payback period would have approximated the IRR of the investment.

What Firms Do

Prior to 1960 very few corporations used discounted cash flow methods for evaluating investments. Recent surveys indicate that the situation has changed. Gitman and Forrester showed in a 1976 study that 67.6 percent of the major U.S. firms responding used internal rate of return as either the primary or secondary method and that 35.7 percent used net present value (see Table 4.10).

In an independent study (see Table 4.11), Scholl, Sundem, and Gaijsbeck found that 86 percent of the major firms responding used internal rate of return or present value, thus confirming the magnitude of the Gitman–Forrester study (see Table 4.11).

TABLE 4.10   What Firms Do: A Survey in 1976

Technique	Capital Budgeting Techniques in Use			
	Primary		Secondary	
	Number	Percent	Number	Percent
Internal (or discounted) rate of return	60	53.6%	13	14.0%
Rate of return (average)	28	25.0	13	14.0
Net present value	11	9.8	24	25.8
Payback period	10	8.9	41	44.0
Benefit/cost ratio (profitability index)	3	2.7	2	2.2
Total responses	112	100.0%	93	100.0%

Source: L. J. Gitman and J. R. Forrester, Jr., "A Survey of Capital Budgeting Techniques Used by Major U.S. Firms," *Financial Management*, Fall 1977, pp. 66–71.

TABLE 4.11   Percentage of Firms Using Method

Method	Percentage of Firms
Payback	74%
Accounting return on investment	58
Internal rate of return	65
Net present value	56
Internal rate of return or present value	86
Use only one method (of which 8 percent is a DCF method)	14

Source: L. D. Scholl, G. L. Sundem, W. R. Gaijsbeck, "Survey and Analysis of Capital Budgeting Methods," *Journal of Finance*, March 1978, pp. 281–287. There were 429 firms selected and 189 responses. The firms were large and stable. A major financial officer was sent the survey.

A study by Kim and Guin indicates that by 1985, 70 percent of the firms surveyed used discounting methods as an exclusive or primary method.[1] This is probably due in part to the widespread use of personal computers with spreadsheet programs that significantly reduce the effort required to calculate DCF measures.

Where We Are Going

There are many different ways of evaluating investments. In some situations, several of the methods will lead to identical decisions. We shall consistently

---

[1] S. H. Kim and L. D. Guin, "A Survey of Empirical Studies of Capital Budgeting Practices," *Business and Public Affairs*, Fall 1986, Table 1.

recommend the net present value method as the primary means of evaluating investments.

The net present value method ensures that future cash flows are brought back to a common moment in time. For each future cash flow, a present value equivalent is found. These present value equivalents are summed to obtain a net present value. If the net present value is positive, the investment is acceptable.

In cases of uncertainty, additional complexities must be considered, but the basic framework of analysis will remain the net present value method.

Conclusions

An effective understanding of present value concepts is of great assistance in the understanding of a wide range of areas of business decision making. The concepts are especially important in financial decision making, since many decisions reached today effect the firm's cash flows over future time periods.

It should be stressed that this chapter has only discussed how to take the timing of the cash flows into consideration. This limitation in objective (and achievement) should be kept in mind. Risk and tax considerations must still be explained before the real-world decision maker has a tool that can be effectively applied. In addition, there may be qualitative factors that management wants to consider before accepting or rejecting an investment.

It is sometimes stated that refinements in capital budgeting techniques are a waste of efforts because the basic information being used is so unreliable. It is claimed that the estimates of cash proceeds are only guesses and that to use anything except the simplest capital budget procedures is as futile as using complicated formulas or observations of past market levels to determine which way the stock market is going to move next.

It is true that in many situations reliable estimates of cash proceeds are difficult to make. Fortunately, there are a large number of investment decisions in which was proceeds can be predicted with a fair degree of certainty. But even with an accurate, reliable estimate of cash proceeds, the wrong decision is frequently made because incorrect methods are used in evaluating this information.

When it is not possible to make a single estimate of cash proceeds that is certain to be accurate, it does not follow that incorrect methods of analysis are justified. If the investment is large, the use of a careful and comprehensive analysis is justified, even if this means that the analysis will be more complicated and costly. With small tactical investments, somewhat less involved methods might be used because a more complex analysis would not be necessary, but again there is no need to use inferior methods that decrease the likelihood of making correct investment decisions.

When all the calculations are completed, judgmental insights may be included in the analysis to decide whether to accept or reject a project.

REVIEW EXAMPLE 4.1

Assume that a firm has a cost of money of .15. It is considering an investment with the following cash flows.

Time	Cash Flow
0	−$27,000,000
1	+12,000,000
2	+11,520,000
3	+15,552,000

Should the investment be accepted?

Solution

The net present value using .15 as the discount rate is

Time	Cash Flow	Present Value Factor	Present Value
0	−$27,000,000	1.15^{-0}	−$27,000,000
1	+12,000,000	1.15^{-1}	10,435,000
2	+11,520,000	1.15^{-2}	8,711,000
3	+15,552,000	1.15^{-3}	10,226,000
		Net present value =	$ 2,372,000

The net present value is positive, and the investment is acceptable. The internal rate of return is .20 and larger than the .15 cost of money.

Appendix: Discounted Cash Flow Formulations

Net Present Value and Internal Rate of Return

The basic mathematical relationships for the present value and the internal rate of return of an investment follow.
    Let

$$C_t = \text{cash flow of at the end of period } t;$$

$$i = \text{time value of money of the firm;}$$

$$r = \text{internal rate of return of the investment;}$$

$$\text{NPV} = \text{net present value of the investment;}$$

$$n = \text{life of the investment.}$$

Then the net present value of an investment is

$$\text{NPV} = \sum_{t=0}^{n} C_t(1 + i)^{-t}$$

The internal rate of return of an investment is found by solving the following equation for r:

$$\sum_{t=0}^{n} C_t(1 + r)^{-t} = 0$$

or, equivalently,

$$\sum_{t=1}^{n} C_t(1 + r)^{-t} = -C_0$$

C_0 is the outlay and is negative. The equation is solved by a trial-and-error procedure, as illustrated in the section of this chapter entitled "Internal Rate of Return."

PROBLEMS

4.1 Compute the net present value for each of the following cash flows. Assume a cost of money of 10 percent.

	Period					
Investment	0	1	2	3	4	5
A	$(1,000)	$100	$100	$100	$100	$1,100
B	(1,000)	264	264	264	264	264
C	(1,000)					1,611

4.2 Compute the internal rate of return for each of the cash flows in problem 4.1.

4.3 Compute the payback for each of the cash flows in problem 4.1. If the maximum acceptable payback period is four years, which (if any) of the cash flows would be accepted as a desirable investment?

4.4 Assume a cost of money of 5 percent. Compute the net present values of the cash flows of problem 4.1.

4.5 Assume a cost of money of 15 percent. Compute the net present values of the cash flows of problem 4.1. Compare with the results obtained from problems 4.1 and 4.4.

4.6   The Arrow Company is considering the purchase of equipment that will return cash proceeds as follows.

End of Period	Proceeds
1	$5,000
2	3,000
3	2,000
4	1,000
5	500

Assume a cost of money of 10 percent.

What is the maximum amount the company could pay for the machine and still be financially no worse off than if it did not buy the machine?

4.7   **a.** An investment with an internal rate of return of .25 has the following cash flows.

Time	Cash Flow
0	C_0
1	+$8,000
2	+10,000

The value of C_0 is _____ .

b. If the firm financed the investment in (a) with debt costing .25, the debt amortization table (using the funds generated by the investment to repay the loan) would be

Time	Amount Owed	Interest	Principal Payment
0			
1			
2			

4.8   Compute the net present value (use a cost of money of .15) and the internal rate of return for each of the following investments.

Investment	Period 0	Period 1	Period 2
A	$(1,000)		$1,322
B	(1,000)	$ 615	615
C	(1,000)	1,150	

4.9   Recompute the net present values using (a) a cost of money of .20 and (b) a cost of money of .05 for each of the investments of problem 4.8.

4.10   Prepare a schedule showing that, with a rate of growth of .15 per year, $1,000 will grow to $1,322 in two years.

4.11   Determine the internal rate of return of the following investment.

Period	Cash Flow
0	$(9,120)
1	1,000
2	5,000
3	10,000

4.12   How much could you pay in excess of the indicated cost for the investment in problem 4.11 if the cost of money were .10?

4.13   Assume that you can only invest in one of the three investments of problem 4.8.
   a. Using the internal rates of return of the three investments, which is preferred?
   b. Using the net present value method and a cost of money of .05, which is preferred?

4.14   A company uses a 10 percent discount rate. Assume equal annual cash proceeds.
   What should be the maximum acceptable payback period for equipment whose life is 5 years? What are the maximum acceptable paybacks for lives of 10, 20, and 40 years and infinite life?

4.15   Assume that the discount rate is 5 percent and answer problem 4.14.

4.16   Assume that $r = .06$. A new machine that costs $7,000 has equal annual cash proceeds over its entire life and a payback period of 7.0 years.
   What is the minimum number of full years of life it must have to be acceptable?

4.17   Compute the internal rate of return of the following investments.

		Period		
Investment	*0*	*1*	*2*	*3*
A	−$10,000	$4,747	$4,747	$ 4,747
B	−10,000			17,280

Compare the two investments.
   Which do you prefer? Are you making any assumption about the reinvestment of the cash flows?

4.18 Determine the internal rate of return of the following investment.

Period	Cash Flow
0	−$15,094
1	10,000
2	10,000
3	1,000

4.19 Draw the net present value profile for the investment of problem 4.18.
Using a hand calculator and the rollback method described in the chapter, compute the net present value using a discount rate of .10.

4.20 Assume a discount rate of 3 percent and a machine that generates a constant annual amount of savings.
What is the maximum acceptable payback period if the life of the machine is (a) 5 years, (b) 10 years, (c) 15 years, and (d) 20 years?

4.21 Assume interest rates of 6 percent and 12 percent and answer problem 4.20.

4.22 Find the net present value at a 5 percent discount rate for each of the following three investments.

	Period		
Investment	0	1	2
A	−$18,594	$10,000	$10,000
B	−18,140	0	20,000
C	−19,048	20,000	0

4.23 Assume a discount rate of 5 percent from time 0 to time 1 and of 7 percent from time 1 to time 2.
Find the net present value of each of the three investments in problem 4.22.

4.24 Assume a discount rate of 5 percent from time 0 to time 1 and of 3 percent from time 1 to time 2.
Find the net present value of each of the three investments in problem 4.22.

4.25 An investment costing $31,699 will earn cash flows of $10,000 a year for eight years. The rate of discount is 10 percent.
What is the discounted payback period?

4.26 Assume that two investments have the following sets of cash flows. Based on the analysis, it is decided that A is more desirable.
Evaluate the conclusion.

		Period	
Investment	*0*	*1*	*2*
A	−$19,008	$10,000	$12,000
B	−19,008	12,000	10,000

	A		B	
	1	*2*	*1*	*2*
Revenue	$10,000	$12,100	$12,100	$10,000
Straight-line depreciation	9,504	9,504	9,504	9,504
Income	$ 496	$ 2,496	$ 2,496	$ 496
Average investment	14,256	4,752	14,256	4,752
ROI	.03	.50	.17	.11
Average ROI	.26		.14	

4.27   The Super Company used a ROFE (return on funds employed) method of evaluating investments. The income of each period is divided by the average assets used during the period. This is done for each period, and then an average ROFE is computed of all the ROFEs.

The controller of the Super Company defends the procedure, since it is consistent with the performance evaluation procedures that are used after the investment is acquired.

The company is currently evaluating two investments (A and B).

		Period	
Investment	*0*	*1*	*2*
A	−$20,000	+$11,000	+$12,100
B	−20,000	+12,100	+11,000

	A		B	
	Year 1	*Year 2*	*Year 1*	*Year 2*
Revenue	$11,000	$12,100	$12,100	$11,000
Depreciation	10,000	10,000	10,000	10,000
Income	$ 1,000	$ 2,100	$ 2,100	$ 1,000
Average investment	15,000	5,000	15,000	5,000
ROFE	.067	.420	.140	.200
Average ROFE	.24		.17	

The firm requires a .20 return for an investment to be acceptable. The firm acquired investment A.

Which investment is more desirable?

4.28   Assume the following set of cash flows and a discount rate of 10 percent. What is the investment's net present value?

Period	Cash Flows
0	−$11,000
1	1,000
2	10,000
3	5,000

4.29   (*Problem 4.28 continued*)   If you were to take the cash flows from the investment and use them to repay a 10 percent loan of $11,000 that was used to finance the investment, how much cash would you have at time 3? What is the present value of this cash amount?

4.30   **a.** If the investment of problem 4.28 costs $12,930, what is the investment's internal rate of return?

b. If funds were borrowed at 10 percent to finance the investment and if the cash flows were used to repay the debt, how much cash will the firm have at time 3?

4.31   The ABC Company has determined that its cost of money is .12; however, because of a series of necessary nonproductive (not generating cash flows) investments, it has found that on the average a discretionary investment must earn .15 in order for the firm to break even.

The firm has a chance to undertake an investment that has an internal rate of return of .14 and no risk. This investment also will not affect the amount of nonproductive investments needed.

Should the investment be accepted?

4.32   The ABC Company has signed a contract with the XYZ Company agreeing to share the profits (equally) on a $1 million investment if the profits are in excess of a .24 return. If the investment does not earn in excess of .24, ABC should get all the cash generated.

It is agreed that the investment is risky.

The expected cash flows of the investment agreed to by ABC and XYZ are

Period 0	Period 1	Period 2	Period 3	Period 4
−$1,000,000	+$300,000	+$300,000	+$1,200,000	+$400,000

Devise a procedure in which the profits are split. The ABC Company does not want to have to collect a refund from XYZ in the future, since XYZ's future is uncertain and a refund might not be collectible. The ABC want to recover its investment and the .24 return before splitting with XYZ. Assume that the cash flows shown occur. Illustrate your profit-splitting arrangement.

REFERENCES

See the references for Chapters 1–3.

C H A P T E R   5

Mutually Exclusive Investments

Long-range investing under rapidly changing conditions, especially under
conditions that change or may change at any moment under the impact of
new commodities and technologies, is like shooting at a target that is not
only indistinct but moving and moving jerkily at that.

J. A. Schumpeter, Capitalism, Socialism, and Democracy *(New York:
Harper & Row, 1947), p. 88.*

Net Present Value

In Chapter 4 we compared four commonly used measures of investment worth.
We saw that neither of the two discounted cash flow procedures for evaluating
an investment is obviously incorrect. In many situations the internal rate of
return (IRR) procedure will lead to the same decision as the net present value
(NPV) procedure. There are also times when the internal rate of return may lead
to different decisions from those obtained by using the net present value
procedure. In this chapter we will continue our study of the two discounted
cash-flow procedures. We will conclude that when the two methods lead to
different decisions, the net present value method tends to give better decisions.

It is sometimes possible to use the IRR method in such a way that it gives the
same results as the NPV method. For this to occur, it is necessary that the rate of
discount at which it is appropriate to discount future cash proceeds be the same
for all future years. If the appropriate rate of interest varies from year to year,
even if that pattern of variation is known in advance, then the two procedures
may not give identical answers.

It is easy to use the NPV method correctly. It is much more difficult to use the
IRR method correctly. We recommend the use of the net present value method,

and in this chapter we shall explain why we believe the internal rate of return method is inferior. In the process we shall show how that method could be used more correctly.

Accept or Reject Decisions

Frequently, the investment decision to be made is whether to accept or reject a project where the cash flows of the project do not affect the cash flows of other projects. We speak of this type of investment as being an independent investment. With the internal rate of return procedure, the recommendation with conventional cash flows is to accept an independent investment if its IRR is greater than some minimum acceptable rate of discount. If the cash flow corresponding to the investment consists of one or more periods of cash outlays followed only by periods of cash proceeds, this method will give the same accept or reject decisions as the net present value method, using the same discount rate. Because most independent investments have cash flow patterns that meet the specifications described, it is fair to say that in practice, the internal rate of return and net present value methods tend to give the same recommendations for independent investments.

Consider an investment with an immediate outlay of $100 and benefits of $115 one year from now. Its net present value profile is shown in Figure 5.1. With discount rates of less than 15 percent, the net present value is positive; with rates larger than 15 percent, the net present value is negative. At 15 percent, the net present value is zero; the investment has an internal rate of return of 15 percent.

Figure 5.1 illustrates an investment that has an internal rate of return of 15 percent. If the required rate is less than 15 percent, the investment is acceptable

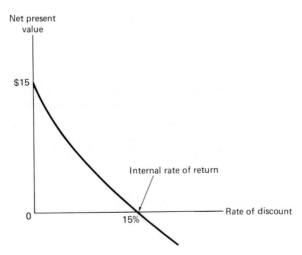

FIGURE 5.1 Net Present Value Profile

using the IRR method, and the figure shows that the net present value will be positive if the discount rate is less than 15 percent. With a conventional investment, the NPV method and the IRR method will lead to consistent accept and reject decisions.

It is sometimes suggested that one of the advantages of the internal rate of return procedure is that it may be utilized without deciding on a minimum acceptable discount rate, whereas the net present value method requires that this rate be incorporated into the computations. The weakness of the position becomes evident when we consider the accept-or-reject type of investment decision. To reach a decision, the internal rate of return of an investment must be compared with the minimum acceptable discount rate. The discount rate is no less important to IRR than to net present value, although it enters at an earlier stage in the computations with the net present value method.

Mutually Exclusive Investments

If undertaking any one of a set of investments will decrease the profitability of the other investments, the investments are substitutes. An extreme case of substitution exists if undertaking one of the investments completely eliminates the expected proceeds of the other investments. Such investments are said to be mutually exclusive.

Frequently, a company will have available two or more investments, any one of which would be acceptable, but because the investments are mutually exclusive, only one can be accepted. For example, assume that a company is trying to decide where to build a new plant. It may be that either of two locations would be profitable. But the company will have to decide which one is likely to be the more profitable because only one new plant is needed. An oil company may need additional transport facilities for its products. Should it build a pipeline or acquire additional tankers and ship by water? Either of these alternatives may result in a net profit to the firm, but the company will wish to choose the one that is more profitable. Suppose that it has decided to build the pipeline. Should a 6- or 10-inch-diameter pipeline be installed? Again, the problem is to choose the more profitable of these alternatives. In all these situations, the choice is between mutually exclusive investments.

Mutually exclusive investment alternatives are common in industry. The situation frequently occurs in connection with the engineering design of a new installation. In the process of designing such an installation, the engineers are typically faced at a great many points with alternatives that are mutually exclusive. Thus, a measure of investment worth that does not lead to correct mutually exclusive choices will be seriously deficient. In this light, the fact that the two discounted cash flow measures of investment worth may give different rankings to the same set of mutually exclusive investment proposals becomes of considerable importance.

Incremental Benefits: The Scale Problem

The IRR method's recommendations for mutually exclusive investments are less reliable than are those that result from the application of the present value method because the former fail to consider the size of the investment. Let us assume that we must choose one of the following investments for a company whose discount rate is 10 percent: Investment A requires an outlay of $10,000 this year and has cash proceeds of $12,000 next year; investment B requires an outlay of $15,000 this year and has cash proceeds of $17,700 next year. The internal rate of return of A is 20 percent, and that of B is 18 percent.

A quick answer would be that A is more desirable, based on the hypothesis that the higher the internal rate of return, the better the investment. To see why this answer may be wrong, consider that an internal rate of return of 1,000 percent on an investment of a dime for one year is likely to be a poor substitute for a rate of 15 percent on $1,000 for one year if only one of the investments can be undertaken and if the time factor is less than 15 percent.

When only the IRR of the investment is considered, something significant is left out—and that is the *size* of the investment. The important difference between investments B and A is that B requires an additional outlay of $5,000 and provides additional cash proceeds of $5,700. Table 5.1 shows that the IRR of the incremental investment is 14 percent, which is clearly worthwhile for a company that can obtain additional funds at 10 percent. The $5,000 saved by investing in A can earn $5,500 (a 10 percent return). This is inferior to the $5,700 earned by investing an additional $5,000 in B.

Figure 5.2 shows both investments. It can be seen that investment B is more desirable (has a higher present value) as long as the discount rate is less than 14 percent.

We can identify the difficulty just described as the scale or size problem that arises when the internal rate of return method is used to evaluate mutually exclusive investments. Because the IRR is a percentage, the process of computation eliminates size; yet, size of the investment is important.

TABLE 5.1   Two Mutually Exclusive Investments

Investment	Cash Flows 0	Cash Flows 1	Internal Rate of Return (%)
A	−$10,000	$12,000	20
B	−15,000	17,700	18
Incremental (B–A)	−$ 5,000	+$ 5,700	14

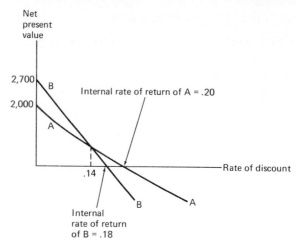

FIGURE 5.2   Two Mutually Exclusive Investments

Timing

The scale problem is sometimes more difficult to identify than in the preceding example. Assume that there are two mutually exclusive investments both requiring the same initial outlay. This case seems to be different from the one we have just discussed because there is no incremental investment. Actually, the difference is superficial. Consider investments Y and Z, described in Table 5.2. Suppose that they are mutually exclusive investments for a company whose cost of money is 5 percent. The internal rate of return of Y is 20 percent, whereas that of Z is 25 percent. If we take the present value of each investment at 5 percent, however, we find that the ranking is in the opposite order. The present value of Z is less than the present value of Y. Neither investment can be said to be obviously superior to the other, and both require the same cash outlays at time 0.

TABLE 5.2

Investment	Cash Flows for Period			Internal Rate of Return (%)	Net Present Value at 5%
	0	*1*	*2*		
Y	−$100.00	$ 20.00	$120.00	20	$27.89
Z	−100.00	100.00	31.25	25	23.58

Suppose that we attempt to make an incremental comparison, as follows.

Period 0	0	Cash flows identical
Period 1	−$80.00	Cash flow of Y is less than that of Z
Period 2	$88.75	Cash flow of Y exceeds that of Z

We see that the cash flow of Y is $80.00 less in year 1 and $88.75 more than Z in year 2. As before, we can compute the IRR on the incremental cash flow. An outlay of $80.00 that returns $88.75 one year later has a rate of 10.9 percent. An investment such as this would be desirable for a company whose cost of money is less than 10.9 percent. Again, we are really dealing with a problem of the scale of the investment, but in this case, the opportunity for the additional investment occurs one year later.

The same result can be reached by a somewhat different route if we ask how much cash the company would have on hand at the end of the second year if it accepted investment Y or if it accepted investment Z. Both investments give some cash proceeds at the end of the first year. The value of the investment at the end of the second year will depend on what is done with the cash proceeds of the first year. Assume that the cash proceeds of the first year could be reinvested to yield 5 percent. Then investment Y would result in a total cash accumulation by the end of the year of $141 (105 percent of $20 plus $120). Investment Z would result in a cash accumulation of only $136.25 (105 percent of $100 plus $31.25).

Figure 5.3 shows that investment Y is to be preferred as long as the appropriate discount rate is less than 10.9 percent. If the rate is in excess of 10.9, then Z is to be preferred.

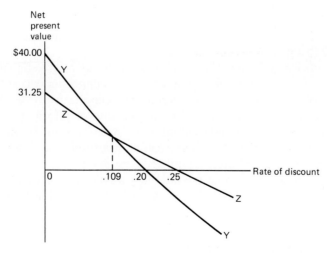

FIGURE 5.3   Two Mutually Exclusive Investments

One disadvantage associated with the use of the internal rate of return method is the necessity of computing the IRR on the incremental cash proceeds in order to determine which of a pair of mutually exclusive investments is preferable. If there are more than two mutually exclusive investments, we shall have to conduct an elimination tournament among the mutually exclusive investments. Taking any pair, we compute the internal rate of return on the incremental cash flow and attempt to decide which of the two investments is preferable. The winner of this round is then compared in the same manner with one of the remaining investments until the grand champion investment is discovered. If there are 151 investments being considered, there will have to be 150 computations, because 150 investments will have to be eliminated.

Reinvestment Assumption

It is frequently claimed that the internal rate of return method assumes reinvestment at the internal rate of return. At best this claim is inexact. The internal rate of return of an investment can be computed without any assumption about the utilization of the funds generated by the investment. For example, an investment generating cash flows that are consumed will have the same internal rate of return as an investment whose cash flows are invested, if the cash flows of the two investments are identical.

In general the cash flows from an investment may be reinvested in some productive investment, or consumed, or saved (which usually mean acquiring a liability issued by another economic unit or reducing outstanding liabilities). It is hoped that they will be allocated to the most valuable of these alternatives. Similarly, the cash inflows required to make the investment may be obtained by foregoing some other investment, by reducing consumption, or by increasing outstanding liabilities. It is hoped that the cash will be obtained from the least costly of these alternatives. It is not even necessary to know the cost of the cash used or the value of the cash produced by an investment to calculate its internal rate of return. But these costs and values are necessary to decide if an investment is acceptable.

If we are comparing two mutually exclusive investments that have the same internal rate of return, then the relevant opportunity cost for cash will affect the choice. We would be indifferent between the two investments if the opportunity cost were equal to the internal rate of return. If the mutually exclusive investments have different internal rates of return the opportunity cost is again relevant to the choice and we cannot assume that funds are reinvested at the internal rate of return of either investment.

The statement that the internal rate of return calculation assumes that funds are reinvested at the internal rate of return is not likely to be harmful, but it is not exactly correct.

We conclude that one does not need to know the reinvestment rates to compute the internal rate of return. However, one does need to know the reinvestment rates to compare alternatives.

Loan-type Flows

So far in this chapter we have discussed the investment type of cash flows. Now let us consider loan-type cash flows (positive flows followed by negative flows or outlays) from the viewpoint of the borrower. Instead of a negative slope, the net present value profile will now have a positive slope. Consider a borrowing of $10,000 where $12,100 is to be repaid at time 2. The net present value using a zero rate of discount is a negative $2,100 and the present value is zero at 10 percent. Figure 5.4 shows the net present value profile of the borrowed funds. The maximum height of the net present value profile is $10,000, the amount borrowed.

The characteristic of loan-type flows is that their net present value increases with higher rates of discount. By constrast, with a pure investment-type cash flow, the net present value decreases with higher rates of discount.

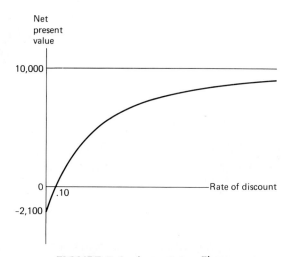

FIGURE 5.4   Loan-type Flows

Multiple Internal Rates of Return

When the internal rate of return method is used, the ability to choose the best of two investments depends on whether a given series of incremental cash flows is like a conventional investment—in which case the higher the rate, the better—or whether it is like a loan—in which case the lower the rate or interest cost, the better. The following illustrates a case in which the choice is not obvious. The cash flows represented by two mutually exclusive investments, R and S, are given in Table 5.3. The last line, labeled I, shows the incremental cash flows (that is, R–S). The cash flows, R and S, are conventional investments because they have outlays *followed by proceeds*. But for investment I, the outlays of

TABLE 5.3

Investment	Cash Flows for Period			Internal Rate of Return
	0	1	2	
R	−$100	+$ 30	+$130	.30
S	0	−280	+350	.25
I	−$100	+$310	−$220	.10 and 1.00

period 0 are followed by proceeds in period 1 and then by further outlays in period 2. With this kind of cash flow, we cannot say "The higher the internal rate of return, the better," or "The lower the internal rate of return, the better."

Suppose that the mutually exclusive investments R and S are available to a company whose cost of money is 15 percent. If the IRR of the incremental cash flows I is 10 percent, should the company accept R or S? If the IRR of the incremental cash flows I is 100 percent, should the company accept R or S? It turns out that the present value of the cash proceeds is equal to the present value of the cash outlays at a 10 percent rate of discount and at a 100 percent rate of discount. The internal rate of return of I is *both* 10 and 100 percent.

Interpretation of Multiple IRRs

To help illustrate the relationship between the internal rate of return of an investment and the present value measure, and to explain why multiple IRRs occur and how they should be interpreted, it is helpful to introduce a graph. In Table 5.3, we described the three series of cash flows, R, S, and I. For R, S, and I in Figure 5.5, the vertical axis represents the net present value of the corresponding cash flow for various possible rates of interest, which are measured along the horizontal axis. By net present value we mean the algebraic sum of the present value of the proceeds and the present value of the outlays.

Because the IRR of a cash flow is defined as the rate of discount that makes the net present value zero, the IRR is the point at which the net present value line crosses the horizontal axis (which measures the rate of discount). For R, the net present value line drops as the rate of discount increases. At discount rates lower than 30 percent, the net present value is positive; at discount rates greater than 30 percent, it is negative. This general configuration typifies those conventional investments in which a series of cash outlays is followed by a series of cash proceeds.

The left-hand part of the graph for I is typical of that of a loan; the right-hand part has the downward slope typical of the ordinary investment. This series of cash flows would be worthwhile at rates of discount between 10 and 100 percent; outside this range it is not advisable.

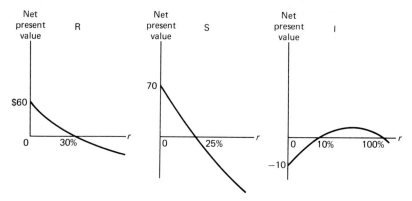

FIGURE 5.5   A Multiple Rate of Return

In this case a simple calculation of the net present value of the investment at the correct rate of discount would have provided the correct answer and would have bypassed the problem of multiple internal rates of return. Figure 5.6 shows that investment R has a higher present value at rates of discount in excess of 10 percent. The two curves cross again at 100 percent, but normally the values at such high interest rates are not relevant.

A "Paradox"

Figure 5.6 shows if that the firm has a .15 required return, the investment I should be accepted; but if the firm's required return were to decrease to .08, the investment would be rejected. This seems to be a paradox, but fortunately, there is a logical explanation.

At relatively low discount rates, investment I is more like a loan than a conventional investment. The firm will accept a .10 "loan" if money costs .15 but will reject a .10 "loan" if money costs .08.

The cash flows of the unconventional investment I can be broken down into two components, a one-period investment and a one-period loan. To do this, we assign part of the cash proceeds of period 1 to the investment and the remainder to the loan. Let us consider the cash flows of investment I and a basic $100 investment earning .15 and a $195 loan costing .15.

	Time 0	Time 1	Time 2
Investment I	−$100	+$310	−$220
Investment	− 100	+ 115	
Loan		+ 195	− 224.25

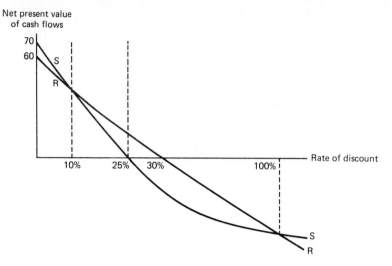

FIGURE 5.6   A Multiple Rate of Return

The $195 loan requires an outlay of $224.25 at time 2, but investment I requires an outlay of only $220, thus, it is more desirable.

If we replaced the .15 investment and loan with a .08 investment and loan, we would have

	Time 0	Time 1	Time 2
Investment	−100	+ 108	
Loan		+ 202	− 218.16

The $218.16 outlay is less than $220; thus, investment I is inferior to lending and borrowing at .08.

Converting Multiple IRRs to a Single IRR

If an upper-level manager is told that an investment has two internal rates of return, one of 0 percent and one of 100 percent, it is apt to be confusing. A 0 percent return is not acceptable, but a 100 percent return is outstandingly good. What decision should be made? We know that the use of net present value can solve the dilemma, but not everyone is willing to abandon the internal rate of return method, even in situations where it cannot be used.

One solution is to adjust the cash flows in such a way to eliminate the possibility of multiple IRRs. Then a new internal rate of return is calculated from the adjusted cash flows. If this new internal rate of return is greater than the minimum acceptable cutoff rate, the investment can be accepted. Otherwise, it can be rejected. The problem is to find a procedure for adjusting the cash flows that will eliminate the possibility of multiple rates of return but will not make undesirable investments seem desirable or vice versa. There are a number of procedures that do this. All of them adjust the cash flows so that the present value of the adjusted cash flows is the same as the present value of the original cash flows using the minimum acceptable cutoff rate as a discount rate. The precise value of the new internal rate of return calculated from the adjusted cash flows will vary, depending on which new adjustment method is used. In each case, however, the value of the new internal rate of return will be greater than the cutoff rate if and only if the original cash flows had a positive present value at the cutoff rate.

Using one of these methods offers a solution to the multiple IRR problem. Based on reasonable assumptions, it offers a workable measure that can be compared to the minimum cutoff rate for accept or reject decisions. Given that the investment really does have two internal rates of return, it would be surprising if we could wave our hands and convert a complex investment into an exactly economically equivalent investment with one internal rate of return. The adjusted investment is similar to the original investment, but not exactly equivalent. We will illustrate two methods for adjusting cash flows to eliminate multiple internal rates of return.

Let us consider the investment just used in which there is outlay of $100, followed at time 1 by benefits of $310 and an outlay at time 2 of $220. This investment has two internal rates of return, 10 percent and 100 percent, and is graphed in Figure 5.5. Either of two procedures (there are other variations) may be used to obtain one IRR. With the first procedure, the negative cash flows that follow positive flows are discounted back using the cutoff rate until they are at least balanced by positive cash flows of a prior period. Begin with the most distant cash outlays and continue until the adjusted cash flows are in the form of a conventional investment.

The second procedure is to proceed as if positive cash flows will be reinvested at the cutoff rate. They are accumulated forward in time until they eliminate all subsequent negative cash flows. Assume initially that the cutoff rate is 8 percent.

Using the first procedure, we discount $220 one period by 8 percent. This is a negative present value of $204, which, when added to the cash flows of time 1 of $310, is $106. The new investment has an outlay of $100 and returns at time 1 of $106. This is a 6 percent internal rate of return. Reject the investment, since 8 percent is required.

Using the second procedure, we would accumulate $310 using 8 percent for one period and obtain $334.80, which is added to the $220 outlay to obtain a net of $115. An investment of $100, leading to benefits of $115 in two periods, is an internal rate of return of approximately 7 percent. Again we should reject.

With an 8 percent cutoff rate, both computational methods lead to a reject decision, since the unique internal rate of return in each case is less than the cutoff rate (even though the two IRRs of the unadjusted investment are both greater than 8 percent). Inspection of Figure 5.5 also indicates that with a time-value factor of 8 percent the investment should be rejected.

If the cutoff rate were raised to 12 percent, we would then have $220 with a present value (discounted for one time period) of $196, which, when subtracted from $310, gives $114. This is a 14 percent IRR on an outlay of $100, and the investment is acceptable, since 14 percent is larger than 12 percent.

If we had accumulated $310 by 12 percent, we would have $347 at time 2, which must be reduced by the time 2 outlay of $220 to $127. This is a two-period 13 percent IRR on $100, and again the investment is acceptable. Inspection of Figure 5.5 indicates that with a 12 percent time-value factor, the investment is acceptable.

If the cutoff rate being used to make the accept or reject decision is also used to convert the basic nonconventional cash flows to a conventional set of cash flows (with one internal rate of return), the accept or reject decision will not be changed. If the present value is positive before the adjustment, the present value will be positive after the adjustment. If one rate of discount is being used as the cutoff rate (the hurdle rate) and another discount rate is used to convert the cash flows to conventional cash flows, however, then the investments can be changed from acceptable to nonacceptable or from nonacceptable to acceptable. Thus, we return to the fact that, in evaluating a nonconventional cash flow stream, one should compute and plot its net present value profile. From these techniques one should be able to make a reasonable accept or reject decision.

Significance of Nonconventional Cash Flows

We define conventional investments (or loans) as those in which there were one or more periods of net cash outlays (or net proceeds) followed by one or more periods of net cash proceeds (or net outlays). It is important to determine whether a series of cash flows is conventional because *a conventional investment will have one and only one positive internal rate of return.*

If an investment is not conventional, we consider it to be a nonconventional investment. With a nonconventional investment, any one of the following situations is possible.

1. The investment has *no* internal rate of return.
2. The investment has *one* internal rate of return.
3. The investment has *more than one* internal rate of return.

An example of a nonconventional investment with two internal rates of return was given in Figure 5.6. An example of a nonconventional investment with no internal rate of return would be an investment having cash proceeds of $100 and

$150 in periods 1 and 3, respectively, and cash outlays of $200 in period 2. This "investment" does not have an internal rate of return, but it has a positive present value for all rates of discount.[1] It is possible for an investment to have more than two internal rates of return. Suppose an investment has cash outlays of $1,000 and $591.25 in periods 0 and 2, and cash proceeds of $430 and $262.5 in periods 1 and 3. This investment has internal rates of return of 5, 25, and 100 percent.

While multiple-rates-of-return situations are not frequently encountered in practice, they occur with enough frequency so that they should be understood. In the oil industry they occur because the rates at which oil and gas are pumped out of a well are mutually exclusive alternatives. When the incremental benefits are computed, the net cash flow stream is likely to have more than one sign change (timing choices frequently give rise to multiple rates of return). Strip mining of coal gives rise to an initial expense of clearing the overburden (a negative cash flow), the mining of the coal (periods of positive cash flows), and then the returning of the land to its original condition (a negative flow).

A nuclear power plant has large negative cash flows because of the decommissioning costs, and this can result in multiple rates of return. But probably the most common situation is real estate, where the analysis is made in terms of the owners' cash flows net of debt. There are the initial outlays followed by rents and tax benefits, but then there are debt repayments and decreased tax benefits, resulting in negative flows. There may be another positive cash flow when the asset is sold. Deciding to replace equipment now or later frequently produces multiple rates of return.

Capital Budgeting Russian Style

Even Russia is not immune to the necessity of making capital budgeting decisions. In December 1980 the Soviets refused to pay 8 percent for debt money from European banks, which was necessary to finance a twin gas pipeline from Siberia to Western Europe. The twin pipeline would have cost $14 billion and would have generated $19 billion of revenue per year for twenty years. They considered 8 percent to be an excessively high cost of money.

In July 1981 the Soviets arranged financing for a single pipeline. The loans cost between 9 and 10 percent. The single pipeline would generate revenues of about $10 billion annually and would cost about $9 billion.

It was planned to build the second pipeline on completion of the first line (in about three years). At that time the second pipeline would cost $6 billion.

---

[1] Mathemaically, finding an internal rate of return for this series of cash flows is equivalent to finding a real number x that would satisfy the equation

$$0 = 100 - 150x^2.$$

But this equation has no solution in the domain of real numbers.

The alternatives were as follows.

	Time 0	Time 3	Time 4	Time 5	Time 6	...	Time 24
Twin pipeline	−14	+19	+19	+19	+19		+19
One pipeline followed by second	−9	+10 −6	+10	+10	+10		+10 +9
Difference	−5	+15	+9	+9			

How much could the Soviets have paid for borrowed funds to finance the second pipeline immediately? It can be argued that the given estimates of costs and revenues are inexact. That is true (for example, the opportunity cost of the gas should be included as outlays), but the magnitudes and the pattern of the cash flows give an indication of the direction in which the decision should be slanted. It would be interesting to know the exact numbers that were used.

Ranking Independent Investments

We can safely use the present value method to choose the best of a set of mutually exclusive investments only when the rate of discount used is an appropriate opportunity cost. As soon as we use the present value method to rank independent investments for the purpose of choosing a cutoff rate above zero present value (some investments with positive present values will be rejected), the rate of discount used in computing the present values becomes inappropriate, because the true opportunity cost is higher than the rate chosen.

EXAMPLE 5.1

The time value of money of the firm has been compounded to be .10. There are two independent investments, C and D, with the following characteristics:

Investment	Cash Flows for Period		Internal Rate of Return	Present Value (using .10)
	0	1		
C	−$ 5,000	$10,000	1.00	$ 9,091 − 5,000 = $4,091
D	− 20,000	30,000	.50	$27,273 − 20,000 = $7,273

Using the net present values, we would choose D over C. Using as the opportunity cost the internal rate of return of the rejected investment C (1.00), we find the present values to be

$$\text{Present value of C} = \$5,000 - 5,000 = 0$$
$$\text{Present value of D} = \$15,000 - 20,000 = -\$5,000$$

If we used the internal rate of return of the last investment accepted, D (.50), we would have as present values

$$\text{Present value of C} = \$6,667 - 5,000 = \$1,667$$

$$\text{Present value of D} = \$20,000 - 20,000 = 0$$

With both of these rates of interest, we find that C is preferred to D but, with an interest rate of .10, D is preferred to C. Figure 5.7 shows that as long as the appropriate time-value factor is less than 33 percent, the investor prefers investment D, but that if the discount factor is greater than 33 percent, investment C is preferred.

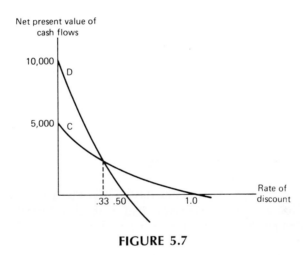

FIGURE 5.7

The problem becomes even more complex when we consider the opportunity costs of money for many time periods and where we have many sets of mutually exclusive investments. The choice of the best of each set will depend on the opportunity cost that is chosen.

Thus, we make no claim that the present value method can be used to rank independent investments where that ranking will be used to eliminate some independent investments with positive present values. This problem will be taken up again when we discuss capital rationing.

Duration: A Sensitivity Measure

Assume that there are two mutually exclusive investments with the same present value. Which is to be preferred?

Let us consider an approach similar to computing payback, for, like payback, it considers the entire life of the asset. Its name is *duration*. The duration of an investment is its weighted average life, where the weights are the present value of the cash flows received in the period (P_t).

$$\text{Duration} = \frac{\sum tP_t}{\sum P_t}$$

An investment with a single cash flow of $330.99 in year 3 would have a present value of of $248.68 (with a discount rate of .10) and a duration of 3. Assume an investment has three equal cash flows of $100, with the first payment to be received one period from now. The discount rate is .10. The duration of this investment is

$$\text{Duration} = \frac{1(100)(1.10)^{-1} + 2(100)(1.10)^{-2} + 3(100)(1.10)^{-3}}{100(1.10)^{-1} + 100(1.10)^{-2} + 100(1.10)^{-3}} = 1.94$$

Both investments have a present value of $248.60, but one has a duration of 1.94 and the other has a duration of 3. If we think that the rate of interest may increase, we might prefer the investment with the shorter duration, since its present value would decline by less as a result of the interest rate increase. This conclusion is valid if the interest rates of all periods change by the same amount.

Present Value and Future Value

The recommendation of this book is that net present value is a very useful calculation. Some managers find it useful to use the value at the end of the planning horizon for the investment being considered. There is no harm in converting from a present value analysis to a terminal value analysis, since the two calculations differ only by a factor of $(1 + r)^n$. Consider the following two mutually exclusive investments.

	Time 0	Time 1	Time 2	NPV (.10)
A	−1,000	1,331		210
B	−1,000		1,452	200

The net present value calculation indicates that A is preferred to B. If we can earn .10 on the $1,331 received at time 1 with A, then at time 2 we will have $1,464.10 with A, as opposed to $1,452 with B. This is an advantage of $12.10. The difference in net present values is $10, which converts to $12.10 in value at time 2.

In the preceding example both A and B cost $1,000. If the initial investments differed, then all the cash flows would have to be converted into values as of time 2.

Why IRR Is Popular

Managers like the IRR, since they consider it important to know the differential between the proposed investment's internal rate of return and the required return. This is a measure of safety that allows an evaluation of the investment's return compared to its risk. If an investment has an IRR of .30 when the required return is .12, this is a large margin, which allows for error. A net present value measure does not give the same type of information to management.

Conclusions

If a corporation knows its cost of money and can either obtain additional funds from the market at the cost of money for desirable internal investments or invest any excess funds externally at that cost of money, then either of the two discounted cash flow procedures can be used to make correct investment decisions.

If the net present value method is used, the rules for making correct investment decisions are quite simple in principle. They are

1. For each investment proposal, compute the net present value of the proposal, using the cost of money as the discount rate.
2. If the choice is between accepting or rejecting the investment, accept it if its net present value is greater than zero and reject it if the net present value is less than zero.
3. If a set of comparable mutually exclusive investment proposals is available and the net present value of each investment is greater than zero, but only one can be accepted, accept the one for which the net present value is the greatest.

The internal rate of return method can also be used to make correct investment choices, provided that the cost of money is the same in all future time periods. If used properly, this method will in fact lead to the same choices as the net present value method. But the rules that must be followed are quite complex if the internal rate of return method is to be used properly. The complexities arise from the following considerations.

1. A single investment may have more than one internal rate of return. The present value of the cash proceeds from an investment may equal the present value of the costs at both x and at y percent. This may mean that the investment is profitable only if the cost of money is between x and y percent, or it may mean that the investment is profitable only if the cost of money is less than x percent or greater than y percent.
2. If a group of two or more mutually exclusive investments is available, a

direct comparison of their internal rates of return will not necessarily lead to the correct choice of the best alternative. If the cost of money is the same in all future periods, it is possible to analyze the investment proposals two at a time, decide which one of each pair is more desirable, and then compare the more desirable investment with one of the others to decide which of those two is more desirable, continuing until, by a process of elimination, the best one can be determined. By contrast, the present value method indicates immediately which one of a group of mutually exclusive proposals is more desirable.

3. In interpreting the internal rate of return of a single investment, it is necessary first to determine whether the cash flows correspond to an ordinary conventional investment or to a loan from the point of view of the borrower.

4. It may not be possible to define the internal rate of return for a cash flow series. In this case, it is easiest to interpret the cash flow series using the net present value method.

5. If the cost of money is not expected to be the same in all future time periods, the internal rate of return method can not be used to give the same decisions as the net present value method.

For most purposes, the net present value method is simpler, easier, and more direct. The remainder of this book will proceed in terms of this approach.

The "conflict" between present value and internal rate of return disappears if the graph of present values is used for comparing investments. The internal rate of return is the intersection of the net present value profile graph and the X axis, and the present value is the vertical height from the X axis to the graph. Using the internal rate of return as the rate of discount, the net present value is zero.

REVIEW EXAMPLE 5.1

There are two mutually exclusive investments. Assume an interest cost of 8 percent. Choose the better of the two investments.

		Period		
Investment	0	1	2	Internal Rate of Return (%)
A	−$10,000	0	$12,100	10
B	−10,000	$5,762	5,762	10

Solution

By inspection, A is more desirable (you can also compute the net present value). The funds are invested longer at the desirable return of .10.

$$NPV(A) = \frac{\$12,100}{(1.08)^2} - \$10,000 = \$374$$

$$NPV(B) = \frac{\$5,762}{(1.08)^2} + \frac{\$5,762}{(1.08)^1} - \$10,000 = \$275$$

PROBLEMS

5.1 Accept or reject the following independent investment proposals using the internal rate of return and net present value procedures and a cutoff rate of 10 percent.

	Period		
Investment	0	1	2
A	$(10,000)	$ 2,000	$12,000
B	(10,000)	10,500	
C	10,000	(12,000)	

5.2 **a.** There are three mutually exclusive investments. Which of the three investments should be chosen? Assume a cutoff rate of 10 percent.

	Period				Internal Rate
Investment	0	1	2	3	of Return (%)
A	$ (1,000)	$ 505	$ 505	$ 505	24
B	(10,000)	2,000	2,000	12,000	20
C	(11,000)	5,304	5,304	5,304	21

b. Compute the incremental cash flow for investments B and C in problem 5(a). Compute the internal rate or rates of return of this incremental cash flow. Is investment B or C more desirable?

5.3 The Apple Company wishes to choose between two different machines that accomplish essentially the same task (the machines are mutually exclusive). A comparison of the cash flows of the two machines shows that if the less expensive of the two machines is chosen, there will be a saving of $1,000 at the time of purchase, but there will be additional outlays of $333 per year over the five-year life of the machines. The cost of money for the Apple Company is 10 percent. Compute the internal rate of return of the incremental cash flows and determine whether the cheaper of the two machines should be purchased. Make the same decision using the net present value procedure.

5.4   There are two mutually exclusive investments. Assume a discount rate of 10 percent. Choose the better of the two investments.

Investment	Period 0	Period 1	Period 2	Internal Rate of Return (%)
A	$ (16,050)	$10,000	$10,000	16
B	(100,000)	60,000	60,000	13

5.5   There are two mutually exclusive investments. Assume an interest cost of 5 percent. Choose the better of the two investments.

Investment	Period 0	Period 1	Period 2	Internal Rate of Return (%)
A	$(10,000)	$5,760	$12,1000	10
B	(10,000)	$5,762	5,762	10

5.6   Assume an interest rate of 15 percent. Choose the better of the two investments of problem 5.5.

5.7   There are two mutually exclusive investments. Assume an interest rate of 5 percent. Choose the better of the two investments.

Investment	Period 0	Period 1	Period 2
A	−$600	$500	$600
B	− 700	800	400

5.8   Compute the relative cash flows of investment (B − A) of problem 5.7. Comment on the computation of the internal rate of return of this investment.

5.9   There is an investment with the following cash flows.

Period 0	Period 1	Period 2
−$50	$150	−$100

Assume an interest rate of .05.

Is the investment acceptable? What are the internal rates of return of the investment?

5.10 **a.** Compute the internal rates of return of the following two investments.

Period	X	Period	Y
0	−$ 9,089	0	−$ 7,118
1	+1,000		
2	+10,000		
3	+1,000	3	+10,000

b. Compute the net present values of the investments if the appropriate rate of discount is .10.

5.11 **a.** Compute the internal rates of return of the following three investments.

	Period 0	Period 1	Period 2
A	−$10,000	$11,500	
B	−10,000	6,151	$ 6,151
C	−10,000		13,226

b. Compute the amount the investor will have at time 2 if the funds received at time 1 can be reinvested to earn .15.
c. For each of the three investments, graph the present value profile.
d. Which investment is to be preferred if the ratte of discount is .10?

5.12 The ABC Company is considering undertaking an investment that promises to have the following cash flows.

Period 0	Period 1
−$50	$90

If the firm waits a year, it can invest in an alternative (that is, mutually exclusive) investment that promises to pay

Period 1	Period 2
−$60	$100

Assume a time value of money of .05.
Which investment should be firm undertake? Use the net present value and the internal rate of return methods.

5.13   The IBC Company is considering undertaking an investment that promises to have the following cash flows.

Period 0	Period 1	Period 2	Period 3
−$100	$150	$50	$50

If it waits a year, it can invest in an alternative (that is, mutually exclusive) investment that promises to pay

Period 1	Period 2	Period 3
−$150	$250	$50

Assume a time value of money of .05.

Which investment should the firm undertake? Use the present value method and the internal rate of return approaches. With the IRR approach, use the incremental cash flows.

5.14   The Arabian Oil Company is considering an investment that can be undertaken this year or postponed one year. The investment cash flows if the investment is undertaken now would be as follows.

Period 0	Period 1
−$100	$200

The cash flows if it is delayed one period would be as follows.

Period 1	Period 2
−$100	$200

Assume a time value of money of .05. Should the company invest now or delay one year? First use the internal rate of return method and then use the net present value method.

5.15   The IBC Company is considering undertaking an investment that promises the following cash flows.

Period 0	Period 1	Period 2
−$100	$80	$80

If the company waits a year, it can make the following investment.

Period 1	Period 2
−$220	$280

Assuming a time value of .10, which investment should the firm undertake? Use both the net present value and IRR approaches. With the IRR method, use incremental cash flows.

5.16   Assume that there are two mutually exclusive investments. Which of the two investments would be chosen using the index of present value? Assume a cost of money of 10 percent. The index of present value equals the present value of benefits divided by the present value of the outlays.

	Period	
Investment	0	1
A	−$ 4,000	$11,000
B	−20,000	33,000

5.17   Assume that there are two mutually exclusive investments.
Which of the two investments would be chosen using the index of present value? The index of present value equals the present value of benefits divided by the present value of the outlays. Assume a cost of money of 10 percent.

	Period	
Investment	0	1
A	−$4,000	$11,000
B	−4,000	−10,000
		21,000

5.18   Assume that an investment has the following cash flows.

Period 0	Period 1	Period 2
−$10,000	$21,600	−$11,600

This investment has IRRs of 0 and .16. Assume that the firm has a time value of money of .10 (it can borrow at .10). Divide the investment into two components, a fictitious investment of $10,000 at time 0, returning $11,000 at time 1, and the borrowing of $10,600 at time 1, requiring an outlay of $11,600 at time 2.
Determine whether the basic investment is desirable.

5.19   Assume that an investment has the following cash flows.

Period 0	Period 1	Period 2
$10,000	−$21,600	$11,600

The investment IRRs of 0 and .16. Assume that the firm has a time value of .10 (it can borrow at .10). Divide the investment into two components, a fictitious borrowing of $10,000 at time 0, paying $11,000 at time 1, and an investment of $10,600 at time 1, earning $11,600 at time 2.

Determine whether the basic investment is desirable.

5.20   Assume that an investment has the following cash flows.

Period 0	Period 1	Period 2	Period 3
$10,000	$10,000	$10,000	−$29,000

The firm uses the internal rate of return method of evaluating investments and has a hurdle rate of .10.

Is the investment desirable?

5.21   There are two mutually exclusive investments with the following cash flows.

	Cash Flows for Period		
Investment	0	1	2
R	−$162,727	$190,909	$ 60,000
S	−90,000	20,000	160,000

Which of the two investments do you prefer if the firm's time value of money is (1) .05, (b) .20, (c) .30?

5.22   The ABC Company can save $200,000 immediately by reducing its finished-goods inventory. Lost sales due to stockouts will be $30,000 per year as a result of the reduction, however. This decision offers a 15 percent internal rate of return.

Should the change be accepted if the cost of money of the firm is 10 percent?

5.23   The controller of the A-Can Company is evaluating the status of a plant. Currently, the plant is losing $1 million per year (cash flow). If the plant is shut down, there will be $5 million of closing costs (out of pocket).

An alternative is to modernize the plant at a cost of $10 million. This will cause the cash flow per year to be $500,000. Assume that this cash flow will continue for perpetuity, as will the $1 million negative cash flow associated with doing nothing.

What should the company do? The company is not sure which discount rate it should use to evaluate this decision.

5.24 In 1978 Cornell University's Teagle Hall management instituted a plan that reduced the inventory of gymwear by eliminating the "dead" inventory stored in the lockers. The new system did result in increased labor cost through time, however, since each customer now had to go through the service line twice, whereas before each customer went through the line once.

Assuming that the cash flows were computed for the decision to implement the system, and assuming that the internal rate of return was unique and equal to 30 percent, should Cornell have adopted the new system?

The cash flows were calculated by assuming that students and professors waiting in line have zero value to their time.

5.25 Is the plant that offers the highest internal rate of return the most desirable plant (in a set of mutually exclusive alternatives)?

5.26 Consider the following three mutually exclusive investments.

	Investment		
Period	A	B	C
0	−$2,000	−$800	−$1,450
1	200	0	500
2	1,000	600	700
3	1,400	600	700

a. If the time value of money is 6 percent, which investment is most desirable?
b. Which investment has the highest internal rate of return?

5.27 Consider the following investment cash flow patterns over time: −$100, 240, −$143, for periods 0 through 2, respectively.

At what rates of discount will the net present value of the investment equal zero? Solve this problem algebraically (remember that if $a^2 X^2 + bX + c = 0$, then $X = \dfrac{-b \pm \sqrt{b^2 - 4ac}}{2a}$

5.28 Consider two mutually exclusive investments.

	Period 0	Period 1	Internal Rate of Return (%)
Investment A	−$ 10,000	$ 12,500	25
Investment B	−110,000	127,500	16

Which investment should the firm accept? Assume that the firm uses .10 as the rate of discount.

5.29 There are two mutually exclusive investments. Assume a cost of money of 10 percent.

Choose the better of the two investments.

| | Period | | | Internal Rate |
Investment	0	1	2	of Return (%)
A	−$ 16,050	$10,000	$10,000	16
B	−100,000	60,000	60,000	13

5.30 A firm has an office building that will earn cash flows of $20 million per year at the end of each year (for perpetuity) if left unchanged. It can tear down the building and put up a new building at a cost of $100 million. The building will have an infinite life.

There are zero taxes. The firm uses a .10 discount rate. The land can be sold for $42 million, and it is expected that this price will stay constant.

The depreciated cost (book value) of the present building is $45 million (exclusive of land), and the replacement cost is $86 million.

a. What annual (constant) cash flows have to be achieved for the firm to replace the old and build the new? Assume a perpetual life and constant cash flow.

b. How (if at all) does the answer to (a) change if the firm can sell now for $250 million (both building and land)?

REFERENCES

Bacon, P. W., "The Evaluation of Mutually Exclusive Investments," *Financial Management*, Summer 1977, pp. 55–58.

Bierwag, G. O., Kaufman, G. G., and Toevs, A., "Duration: Its Development and Use in Bond Portfolio Management," *Financial Analysts Journal*, July/August 1983, pp. 15–35.

Dorfman, R., "The Meaning of Internal Rates of Return," *Journal of Finance*, December 1981, pp. 1011–1021.

Emery, G. W., "Some Guidelines for Evaluating Capital Investment Alternatives with Unequal Lives," *Financial Management*, Spring 1982, pp. 14–19.

Henderson, Glenn V., Jr., "On Capitalization Rates for Riskless Streams," *Journal of Finance*, December 1976, pp. 1491–1493.

Meyer, R. L., "A Note on Capital Budgeting Techniques and the Reinvestment Rate," *Journal of Finance*, December 1979, pp. 1251–1254.

Nicol, D. J., "A Note on Capital Budgeting Techniques and the Reinvestment Rate: Comment," *Journal of Finance*, March 1981, pp. 193–195.

Pratt, J. W., and J. S. Hammond III, "Evaluating and Comparing Projects: Simple Detection of False Alarms," *Journal of Finance*, December 1979, pp. 1231–1241.

Ruback, R. S., "Calculating the Market Value of Riskless Cash Flows," *Journal of Financial Economics*, March 1986, pp. 323–339.

CHAPTER 6

The Determination and Use of Cash Flows

I really don't know one plane from the other.... To me they are all
marginal costs with wings.
   Alfred E. Kahn, C.A.B. chairman. New York Times, April 23, 1978.

Accounting theory suggests three basically different methods of recording a cash outlay for an asset or cost factor; these in turn affect the measurement of income. The outlay may be considered to be an expense of the period in which it is incurred, or to represent the acquisition of a wasting asset that will be charged to expense over a number of future periods, or to represent the acquisition of a nonwasting asset, in which case it is never charged to expense. The first is typified by outlays for a sale executive's salary; the second, by outlays for plant and equipment; and the third, by outlays for land. For some outlays a reasonable case can be made for one or another accounting treatment. Thus, outlays for research, certain types of advertising, and some kinds of maintenance may be treated as current expenses or capitalized and depreciated over a longer period; outlays for land may be treated as wasting assets if the important characteristics of the land are its possession of certain minerals or soil fertility, or as partially nonwasting if its site value is considered.

The accounting treatment accorded a particular outlay will influence the amount and timing of income measurement. But in the absence of income taxes, the choice of investments should not be influenced by the method of accounting for a particular outlay. The amount and timing of the cash outlays and the amount and timing of future cash proceeds are what is relevant to the choice of investments.

In the case of corporations subject to income taxes, the accounting treatment adopted for income tax purposes must be considered in evaluating a potential investment, because the choice will affect the amount and timing of income tax payments. Because income taxes do not affect all investments in the same manner, it is necessary to place cash flows associated with each investment on an after-tax basis before evaluating the investments. In this chapter we shall be concerned with the mechanics of computing the after-tax cash flows associated with investments. We shall consider separately the problems associated with depreciable assets, nondepreciable assets, and outlays chargeable to current expense.

Cash Flows

We can define an investment as a commitment of resources made in the hope of realizing benefits that are expected to occur some time in the future. According to this definition, neither the resources nor the benefits need be in the form of explicit cash flows. A decision to have an executive spend a month studying the capabilities of various types of electronic data processing equipment would be an investment in the sense of this definition. The executive's time is a scarce resource. The month could have been spent in other activities that are valuable to the firm. In the first instance, at least, the expected benefits will be increased knowledge by management of a relatively new technology. Thus, there is no explicit cash outlay or cash inflow, but there is an investment.

In previous chapters, it was argued that investments ought to be evaluated in terms of the present value of the cash flows expected from them, in preference to any other measures of investment worth that have been suggested. We have not given a complete or careful definition of the term *cash flows*, however. In the present chapter we expect to do this as well as to explain some of the difficulties that arise in applying a cash flow analysis to investment proposals.

Cash Flows and Profits

Cash flows are not identical with profits or income. Changes in income can occur without any corresponding changes in cash flows. During a period of investment in plant, receivables, and inventories, a corporation can even experience a decrease in cash at the same time that income is increasing. One main advantage of the cash flow procedure is that it avoids difficult problems underlying the measurement of corporate income that necessarily accompany the accrual method of accounting. These accounting problems include the following.

1. In what time period should revenue be recognized?
2. What expenses should be treated as investments and therefore capitalized and depreciated over several time periods?

3. What method of depreciation should be used in measuring income as reported to management and stockholders (as distinct from income measurement for tax purposes)?
4. Should LIFO (last in, first out), FIFO (first in, first out), or some other method be used to measure inventory flow?
5. What costs are inventoriable? Should fixed, variable, direct, indirect out-of-pocket, unavoidable, administrative, or selling costs be included in evaluating inventory?

There are disagreements as to the answers to each of these questions. Different approaches may lead to different measures of income. If income is used to evaluate investment worth, investments may look good or bad, depending on how income is measured. The utilization of cash flows minimizes many of these complications.

The Use of Cash Flows

In evaluating an investment, we suggest that the cash flows of the investment be used in the analysis. We are not interested in the conventional "cost" of the investment, but rather in the cash outlays required and the timing of these cash flows. We are not using the earnings of period 1, but rather the cash flows of period 1. These distinctions can be important. A builder may tell us that a construction project will cost $1 million, but this is not sufficient information. We want to know when the outlays will be required. For example, if the outlays are made on completion of the building, the cost is truly $1 million. If the payment is required one year prior to completion, the true cost is $1 million plus the interest on the $1 million for one year. The use of expected earnings to measure the benefits of an investment would require a much more sophisticated accounting system than is currently being used by any corporation. The earnings figures resulting from current accounting practices are not usable for investment evaluation without adjustment. Also, even with improved measures of income, there would remain the question of whether the use of cash flows or earnings is more appropriate. If earnings are measured correctly, both measures should give identical net present values. The advantage of the use of the cash flow is that the receipt of cash is an objective, clearly defined event that leads to a significantly different situation than before the receipt of cash.

A sale on account is an economic event recorded by the accountant and affecting accounting income. But the firm has not yet received the cash, it cannot spend the cash, and the ultimate collection of the cash is uncertain. For purposes of investment analysis, we are more interested in the moment when the cash is to be received. At that moment the firm reaches a new decision point. The cash may be returned to the stockholders by the payment of a dividend. It may be used to retire debt, increase the working capital, or acquire new long-lived assets.

It might be suggested that to be correct, the dollar of cash received in period 1 should be followed to its disposition at the end of the firm's life. However, we find it more convenient to take the receipt of cash associated with a specific asset to be a self-contained event, and we do not normally concern ourselves with the final disposition of the dollar. The assumption that cash flow can be borrowed and lent at a given discount rate allows us to make this simplifying assumption.

Thus, for purposes of investment analysis, unlike conventional accounting, we choose the receipt or disbursement of cash to be the crucial event. It should not be thought that a sale on account or other accruals are ignored. A sale on account in period 1 will affect the expected cash collection in period 2; hence, it is brought into the analysis in period 2, the period in which the firm has the cash in hand and has reached a decision point.

Absolute and Relative Cash Flows

When cash flows are being compared with zero cash flows, we shall speak of absolute cash flows. In evaluating the present value of these cash flows, using a 10 percent rate of interest, we are implicitly comparing this investment with an investment that would return 10 percent, thus having a zero net present value.

A second method of analysis would be to compare directly one alternative with the other. In looking at the cash flow estimates, for example, we can subtract the cash flows of one alternative from the cash flows of the second alternative. The incremental cash flows can be called relative cash flows, and we can compute the present value of this series of relative cash flows. It can be shown that the present value of this series of relative cash flows will be the same as the difference between the present values of the absolute cash flows from the two alternatives. Thus, the present value method will lead to the same conclusion as to the relative worth of the two alternatives, whichever of the approaches is used.

There is an important difference between the two series of cash flows, however. With the series of absolute cash flows, if the investment were accepted and actually began to operate, we could compare, period by period, the actual cash flows with our previous forecasts. There is not, however, any similarly indentifiable series of cash flows that could be compared with the relative cash flow estimates.

Importance of Considering All Alternatives

Apart from those difficulties in making estimates of relative cash flows, which are a byproduct of the difficulties of estimating the incremental effects of various actions of the firm, there is an important conceptual danger that must be avoided in estimating relative cash flows. As explained, an estimate of relative cash flows always involves a comparison of two alternatives. The size of the estimated relative cash flows from making a particular investment will depend upon the alternative that is used as a basis of comparison. *This means that almost any investment can be made to seem worthwhile if it is compared with a sufficiently bad alternative.*

In general, an investment should not be accepted unless the present value of the absolute cash flows that it will generate are positive. As long as all feasible alternatives are considered (including doing nothing or abandoning what is currently being done), it makes no difference which acceptable alternative is chosen as the standard of comparison. The choice of a standard of comparison may lead to mistaken conclusions only if some advantageous alternatives (such as ceasing production entirely) are excluded from the analysis, or an unacceptable alternative is used as the basis of comparison.

EXAMPLE 6.1   Absolute and Relative Cash Flows

A new modernized store replacing an old store is expected to earn 25 percent. Should it be accepted if the firm has a 10 percent cost of money? The cash flows (a perpetuity) are

Time 0	Time 1	Time 2	Time 3
−$1,000,000	+$250,000	+250,000	⋯

Conclusion: We have to know what the present store is earning. Are the cash flows shown absolute or relative cash flows?

EXAMPLE 6.2   (*Continuation of Example 6.1*)

Now assume thaat the cash flows of Example 6.1 are absolute flows and that the old store is currently earning $200,000 a year. The relative cash flows for "new minus old" are

Time 0	Time 1	Time 2	Time 3
−$1,000,000	$50,000	$50,000	⋯

This is a 5 percent return, and the new store is clearly not acceptable, even though it earns $250,000 per year, unless we add new information (such as a changing competitive situation) that will adversely affect the $200,000 currently being earned.

EXAMPLE 6.3   (*Continuation of Example 6.1*)

Now assume that the cash flows of Example 6.1 are relative cash flows and that the old store is losing $200,000 per year. The firm still uses a 10 percent cost of money.

	Time 0	Time 1	Time 2	Time 3
Continue old		−$200,000	−$200,000	...
New	−$1,000,000	50,000	50,000	...
New–old	−$1,000,000	$250,000	$250,000	...

The relative cash flow has a 25 percent internal rate of return.

The 25 percent return is not valid, since the new is being compared to an unacceptable alternative. Both alternatives are unacceptable. If there are no better alternatives, the store should be shut down. The undesirability of the new store is illustrated if "new" is compared to "shut down" and if shutdown has zero cash flows. The 5 percent return is not sufficient to justify investment.

	Time 0	Time 1	Time 2	Time 3
New	−$1,000,000	$50,000	$50,000	$50,000
Shut down		0	0	0
New–shut down	−$1,000,000	$50,000	$50,000	$50,000

These examples illustrate the fact that all the alternatives must be considered.

Opportunity Costs

Usually, the cash outlays included in the computation of net cash flows are the outlays incurred because of the investment. Outlays that would be incurred by the firm whether or not the investment is accepted should not be charged to a particular investment project. Thus, the practice of allocating a share of general overhead to a new project on the basis of some arbitrary measure, such as direct labor hours or a fraction of net sales, is not recommended *unless* it is expected that general overhead will actually increase if the project is accepted.

On the other hand, in some instances an investment project may require the use of some scarce resource available to the firm, although the explicit cash outlays associated with using that resource may be nonexistent or may not adequately reflect the value of the resource to the firm. Examples are projects that require a heavy drain on the time of key executive personnel or that use valuable floor space in a plant or store already owned by the business. The cost of using such resources are called opportunity costs, and they are measured by estimating how much the resource (the executives' time or the floor space) would earn for the company if the investments under consideration were rejected.

It may appear that the practice of charging opportunity costs against an investment project when no corresponding cash outlay can be identified is a violation of, or exception to, the procedure of evaluating investments in terms of actual cash flows. Actually, including opportunity costs is not as much an exception to the cash flow procedure as an extension of it. The opportunity cost charged should measure net cash flows that could have been earned if the project under discussion had been rejected. Suppose that one floor of a factory building owned by a business could either be rented out at $1,200 per month or be used to produce a new product. By charging a rental opportunity cost of $1,200 per month against the new product, a more meaningful measure of the cost to the company of producing it is obtained. An alternative procedure would be to estimate the relative cash flow from the new product compared with that produced by renting the extra space and not producing the new product.

In some instances it will be extremely difficult to estimate opportunity costs. The temptation then is to use some other more easily identifiable basis of charging for the use of such things as floor space or executive time. This temptation must be viewed with some skepticism. The pro rata share of the costs of owning a building may be much higher or much lower than the true opportunity costs of using that space. When there is really no basis for estimating the opportunity costs associated with the use of a factor, such as the time of certain key executives, it may be preferable to note merely that the proposed projects is likely to require some amount of attention from such key executives.

The only valid justification for the prorating of the out-of-pocket costs to the proposed project would be if the costs are a reasonable basis for estimating the opportunity cost. For example, if an additional executive can be hired for the same salary as a present executive, the opportunity cost of using some of the present executive's time should not be greater than this current salary (a new executive could be hired). If it is felt that the managers are currently earning their salaries when they are doing their least profitable tasks, the cost should not be less. Thus, we can correctly say that the opportunity cost of an executive's time is equal to the actual salary that would be paid to the next executive who could be hired.

Cash Flow Determination

Acquiring Assets Without Cash Disbursements

The term *cash outlay* is also applied to a transaction in which an asset is acquired by incurring a long-term debt or by issuing stock. Even though there may be no explicit borrowing of cash, receipt of cash, and disbursement of cash, these transactions are assumed to occur when an asset is acquired via a promise to pay in some distant time period and the transaction is treated as if there has been a cash outlay as well as a source of new capital.

Some investments are acquired by the issuance of common stock. In such a situation there is no disbursement of cash, and there is a tendency to evaluate such opportunities as if there are no cash outlays. This tendency is wrong. The cash that could have been obtained by a public offering of the common stock has an opportunity cost, and in an economic sense it is a cash outlay. The method of analysis for an issuance of stock should be identical to the analysis used when there is an explicit cash outlay. The cost of using common stock capital will be taken into consideration when the cash flows are discounted and adjusted for uncertainty.

Working Capital

In focusing attention on outlays for plant and equipment, it is possible to lose sight of the fact that the working capital needed to operate the investment project should also be included in computing the investment outlays. If residual working capital is recoverable at the termination of operations, this causes the investment to have a net terminal value that should be taken into consideration. Increases in current liabilities are subtracted from the increase in current assets to compute the use of cash. It is assumed that the additional current liabilities do not change the proportion of current liabilities to other sources of capital.

An investment in plant assets will usually lead to funds being tied up in working capital. This will include the cash necessary to meet payroll and other bills, funds invested in the raw material, work-in-process and finished-goods inventories, and receivables from customers. The size of these items will depend on the exact nature of the capital investment, but all the previously mentioned fund requirements will usually accompany an investment in long-lived assets. The one possible exception would be an investment that would decrease the need for working capital by increasing efficiency. Examples of this nature are accounting machines that expedite the billing to customers or storage facilities and inventory control devices that reduce the amount of inventory that must be kept on hand.

A working capital need arising because of the investment (required by the investment increase) has the effect of increasing the investment outflow today. If the investment has a limited life the working capital is expected to be recovered at the end of the life of the investment, the recovery of the working capital in the last period should be considered as cash proceeds and treated in the same manner as the other cash flows are treated. It should not be thought that ignoring the working capital investment and the recovery of working capital will balance each other out. The factor that must be considered is the required return on the working capital during the period of use.

When an asset is acquired by the incurrence of a noninterest-bearing current liability, there is no cash outlay. It is the timing of the actual cash disbursement that is important. Thus, if the investment results in an increase in inventories of $100 and the source of capital is an increase in current liabilities of $100, the net cash outlay that is required in the period of inventory acquisition is zero. If the $100 increase in inventories required cash outlays of $20 and current liabilities increased by $80, then the net cash outlays in the period of inventory acquisition is $20. A net increase in working capital (leaving out interest-bearing debt) needed by an investment is a use of capital and thus a negative cash flow. If the use of the investment increases the working capital that is available and the firm can use this working capital in other projects, this is a positive cash flow.

The cash flow caused by working capital is equal to the change of the net working capital, or in more detail:

$$\text{Cash flow used} = \frac{\text{increase in working}}{\text{captial assets}} - \frac{\text{increase in current liabilities}}{\text{that are noninterest-bearing}}$$

An interesting problem arises with accounts receivable. Assume an investment where a credit sale of $100 with the incremental costs of the sale being $40 is projected for time 1. Working capital is expected to increase by $100 at time 1. But the cost of the sale is $40. Is the investment in accounts receivable $100 or $40?

The investment is $40, but the easy and correct solution is to use $100 as the expected use of cash to increase working capital. There will also be $60 of income reported, and the net use of cash flow is $40, which agrees with the conclusion just reached that the investment is $40.

Interest Payments and Other Financial Flows

The treatment of interest expense and other financial cash flows is one of the most frequent sources of confusion and error in defining cash flows. We first state some basic principles and then illustrate them with simple examples. We shall also illustrate some of the most common mistakes that occur.

To avoid confusion on this topic it is important to maintain a clear distinction between project flows and financial flows. Ordinarily, in defining the cash flows to be used for analyzing capital budgeting projects, we prefer to consider only project cash flows and to exclude all financial flows. Interest expense and principal repayments are financial flows, and would be excluded using our preferred approach. However, sometimes it is useful to analyze the equity cash flows associated with a project. In particular, the use of equity cash flows is very common when analyzing real estate projects. When the equity cash flow approach is used, all of the financial cash flows associated with debt must be considered. These include the cash proceeds from borrowing money and the outlays for its repayment and for the interest expense. If income taxes are relevant, each cash-flow stream should be on an after-tax basis. We shall now illustrate these points, first ignoring taxes (assume the investor is tax exempt), and then explicitly considering taxes.

Assume that a capital budgeting project requires an outlay of $1,000 and promises to return $1,080 at the end of one period. Initially we assume there is no uncertainty. The $1,000 outlay will be used to acquire an asset. The proceeds of $1,080 consist of revenues from operating the asset and from disposing of it at the end of the year. No interest expense has been subtracted. In defining project cash flows we do not specify who provided the money for the project or to whom the proceeds will go. To evaluate the project, we do need the cost of money; assume it is 6 percent. The project cash flows and their net present value and the internal rate of return are as follows:

A Correct Analysis

Time	0	1	NPV (6%)	IRR
Project flows	−$1,000	$1,080	$18.87	8%

If the required rate of return is 6 percent, the investment is desirable. It has a positive NPV and an IRR greater than the cost of money.

Some managers may feel uncomfortable about excluding interest expense from the project cash flows. Thus, let us consider the outcome when they are included. Suppose the owners of the project financed it by borrowing $1,000 at time zero and repaid the loan when the project terminated. The interest expense at time 1 would be $60. The project cash flows before and after interest expense are given below, along with the corresponding NPVs and IRRs.

A Common Mistake

Time	0	1	NPV (6%)	IRR
Project flows	−$1,000	$1,080	$18.87	8%
Interest expense		−60	−56.60	
Project flows after interest expense	−$1,000	$1,020	−$37.73	2%

By combining interest expense with the project cash flows, we have made a good project look bad. The NPV is negative and the IRR is less than the cost of money. Including interest expense as a part of the project cash flows would incorrectly lead to a reject decision. Therefore one conclusion is: _Don't include interest expense as a part of project cash flows_. Because discounting takes the time value of money into account, there is no need to subtract the interest expense. To do so amounts to double counting interest expense. Alternatively, the error can be described as including the cost of borrowing money, but not including the benefits received from borrowing. To understand this second interpretation let us include all of the debt cash flows, not just the interest expense. This is done in the following table.

An Alternative Analysis: Correct if the Debt Rate is Used

Time	0	1	NPV (6%)	IRR
Project flows	−$1,000	$1,080	$18.87	8%
Debt flows	+1,000	−1,060	0.00	6%
Equity cash flows	0	$ 20	$18.87	

Notice that when the discount rate used is the cost of borrowing, the equity and project cash flows have the same NPV. This is true even if there is less than 100 percent debt financing as is shown in the next table.

A Second Example

Time	0	1	NPV (6%)	IRR
Project flows	−$1,000	$1,080	$18.87	8%
Debt flows	+500	−530	0.00	6%
Equity cash flows	−$ 500	$ 550	$18.87	10%

A second important generalization from the previous examples is: *When the cost of debt is used as the discount rate, the NPV of the project cash flows and the NPV of the equity cash flows are the same.* One might be tempted to infer from this conclusion that it makes no difference whether project cash flows or equity cash flows are used for capital budgeting. Be careful. Two qualification are necessary. Using equity cash flows instead of project cash flows would make no difference if decisions were always made using NPV with the cost of debt as the discount rate. But decisions are frequently made using other criteria, such as IRR, or using NPV with discount rates higher than the cost of debt. Using a discount rate higher than the cost of money is a common means of allowing for risk. It has other consequences also.

First consider IRR. The project cash flows have an IRR of 8 percent. Because the cash flows are conventional, they will have a positive NPV at any discount rate below 8 percent. When 100-percent debt financing is used, the IRR of the equity cash flows is undefined (there is no outlay). Because the equity cash flows are all positive, we could consider them to have an infinite rate of return. When 50 percent of the initial outlay is debt financed, the project cash flows have an IRR of 10 percent. (See the above table.) This is an example of a third important generalization. *Whenever the NPV of the project cash flows is positive at the cost of debt, the IRR of the equity cash flows can be increased by using more debt.* Being that this distortion takes place if IRR is used, and since IRR is frequently used as an investment measure, we recommend using project cash flows to analyze investments. We are not against using debt to finance projects; it is frequently appropriate. We do recommend caution in using equity cash flows to analyze projects; the use of equity cash flows can make the IRR look better than it would if only investment flows were used.

Next consider NPV. The equity cash flows and the project cash flows have the same NPV if the cost of debt is used as the discount rate. But it is common practice to discount cash flows at a higher discount rate "to allow for risk." *If the discount rate used to calculate the NPVs is higher than the cost of debt, then the NPV of the equity cash flows will be greater than the NPV of the project cash flows.* It is even possible that the equity cash flows will have a positive NPV even though the project cash flows have a negative NPV. This is illustrated in the following table, in which we take the project with 50 percent debt, but calculate the NPV at 9 percent instead of 6 percent "to allow for risk."

Using a Risk-Adjusted Discount Rate

Time	0	1	NPV (9%)	IRR
Project flows	−$1,000	$1,080	−$ 9.17	8%
Debt flows	+500	−530	13.76	6%
Equity cash flows	−$ 500	$ 550	$ 4.59	10%

What is happening here? Let us first note that the NPV of the project flows is negative and the IRR of those flows is less than the discount rate; thus both project measures are signalling project rejection. Second, note that the NPV of the debt flows is positive. This makes sense. If a 9-percent discount rate is used, the opportunity to borrow at 6 percent has a positive value; that is, the meaning of the positive NPV for debt flows in this instance. Finally, look again at the equity cash flows. The NPV of the equity flows is positive, and the IRR of those flows is greater than the discount rate; thus both measures signal project acceptance. The NPV of the equity flows is equal to the algebraic sum of the NPV of the project flows plus the NPV of the debt flows. In this case, the algebraic sum of a small negative project NPV and a larger positive debt NPV gives a positive equity NPV.

Is looking at the NPV of the equity cash flow of a levered project a useful way of analyzing levered projects? Two factors drive the result. One is the use of a discount rate above the cost of debt; the second is the use of equity cash flows instead of project cash flows. Each factor has some intuitive appeal. The combination of the two produces some interactions that are not necessarily understood or desired.

The most common reason for using a discount rate greater than the cost of debt is that the decision maker considers the project to be risky and therefore requires a return greater than the cost of debt to compensate for the risk. This is intuitively appealing and frequently produces the desired results when applied to project cash flows. In this instant the project does not supply enough extra return to meet the decision-maker's standard.

Financing the project with debt makes the equity cash flows more risky than they would be if no debt were used. One strongly suspects that if the unlevered cash flows provide an unsatisfactory return for the risk involved, then the project with leverage should also be rejected (remember there are no taxes). An analysis that leads to the opposite conclusion should be used with considerable caution.

Conclusions

It is important to distinguish between project cash flows and financing cash flows. Including interest expense with the project cash flows is clearly incorrect. Our preference is to use project cash flows wherever possible. If there is a strong reason to consider equity flows, we recommend clearly separating the project cash flows and the financing cash flows and displaying how they combine to produce equity cash flows. Similarly, whatever analytical tool is used—NPV, IRR, or any other—it should be applied to each of the three types of cash flows, not just to the equity flows.

When the debt rate is used to calculate the NPVs, the NPV of the equity cash flows will be the same as the NPV of the project cash flows. When the discount rate used is greater than the debt rate, the NPV of the equity cash flows will be greater than the NPV of the project cash flows. The equity NPV may even be positive when the project NPV is negative.

With projects having conventional cash flows, if the IRR of the project is greater than the cost of debt, the IRR of the equity cash flows will be greater than the IRR of the project cash flows. In this case, the analyst can make the IRR of the equity cash flows as high as desired by applying enough debt.

The Tax Shield of Interest

So far we have not explicitly considered taxes. The operation of the project may generate some tax liabilities and some tax shields; the use of debt may also. Everything that has been said about project flows, financing flows, and equity flows is applicable in the presence of taxes if all flows are put on an after-tax basis, and the after-tax cost of money is used for discounting. The presence of taxes complicates the calculations, but introduces no new principles. Taxes do introduce new opportunities to make mistakes. A common mistake, which we will illustrate, is to treat the tax shield from debt as part of the project cash flows, while ignoring the rest of the debt flows. We first illustrate a correct approach, and then the consequences of including the interest tax shield.

Since the mistake results in making an undesirable project look good, we start the example with a project that would be undesirable if analyzed correctly. We continue the assumption that the before-tax cost of money is .06. The relevant tax rate is .34; assume that the appropriate after-tax cost of money is .0396 $[.06 \times (1 - .34)]$. We first consider the project cash flows. As shown in the following table the project has a 5 percent return before taxes and a 3.3 percent return after taxes. The period 1 proceeds of $1,050 would be subject to taxes of $357, but this is reduced by $340 as a result of the depreciation.

Time	0	1	NPV (3.96%)	IRR
Before-tax project flows	−$1,000	$1,050	$10.00	5%
Gross tax liability		−357	−343.40	
Depreciation tax shield		340	327.05	
After-tax project flows	−$1,000	$1,033	−$ 6.35	3.3%

We next consider the effect of taxes on debt. Suppose the owners are considering 100-percent debt financing. The following table puts the debt flows on an after-tax basis by subtracting the interest tax shield from the before-tax debt flows.

A Correct After-tax Analysis of Debt

Time	0	1	NPV (3.96%)	IRR
Before-tax debt flows	$1,000	−$1,060.00	−$19.62	6%
Interest tax shield		20.40	19.62	
After-tax debt flows	$1,000	−$1,039.60	−$ 0.00	3.96%

With the information from the previous two tables, we construct an after-tax equity analysis by combining the after-tax project cash flows and the after-tax debt flows. This is illustrated in the following table.

An After-tax Equity Analysis: Correct if the Debt Rate is Used

Time	0	1	NPV (3.96%)	IRR
After-tax project flows	−$1,000	$1,033.00	−$6.35	3.30%
After-tax debt flows	$1,000	−$1,039.60	−$0.00	3.96%
After-tax equity flows	$0	−$6.06	−$6.35	

Again, the project should be rejected. We can now illustrate the common mistake, referred to earlier, of attaching the interest tax shield from the debt to the project cash flows, while ignoring the rest of the debt cash flows. When the tax shield from the debt is attached to the project cash flows, the bad project appears to be acceptable; it has a positive NPV and an IRR greater than the cost of money. These are faulty calculations.

An Incorrect After-tax Analysis of a Project with Hidden Debt

Time	0	1	NPV (3.96%)	IRR
Before-tax project flows	−$1,000	$1,050.00	$10.00	5.00%
Gross tax liability		−357.00	−343.40	
Depreciation tax shield		+340.00	327.05	
Interest tax shield		+ 20.40	19.62	
After-tax project flows	−$1,000	$1,053.40	$13.27	5.34%

Salvage and Removal Costs

The salvage and removal costs introduce no real problem if we keep in mind that we are interested in the periods when cash outlays are made or when cash flows into the firm. In the following descriptive material, the term *salvage* refers to net salvage; removal costs have been subtracted.

Let us first consider the salvage value of the new investment. Any funds obtained from selling the new investment when it is retired will increase the flow of cash in the last period. Thus, the salvage of the new investment will increase the cash flow of the last period of use.

When the investment is being made to replace an item of equipment currently being used, there are two additional salvage values to be considered: (1) the salvage value now of the old equipment and (2) the salvage value that the old equipment would have at the end of its physical or useful life (whichever comes first) if it were not replaced now. If the asset is replaced now, the present salvage will have the effect of increasing the cash flow of this period (or decreasing the required cash outlay). However, if the old equipment is being retired now, the salvage that would have been obtained at the end of its life will not be obtained. Thus, there is a decrease in the relative cash flows of that last period because of the salvage that will not be obtained at that time. To summarize, the absolute cash flow effects are

Salvage value of the new equipment. Increase the cash flow of the last year of use for the buy alternative.

Present salvage value of the old equipment. Increase the cash flow for this year (decrease the cash outlay) for the buy alternative.

Salvage value of the old equipment at time of normal retirement. Increase the cash flow of that year (because the salvage value would be obtained if the replacement did not take place). This cash inflow applies to the absolute cash flows of the "continue-the-old" alternative.

The analysis of the cash flows arising from salvage is complicated by the fact that the cash flow analysis may be made in terms of relative or absolute cash flows. If the cash flows are relative, we compute the cash flows from buying the new equipment minus the cash flows that would occur if the old equipment were retained. To analyze the absolute cash flows of the several alternatives, the cash flows of retaining the old would be computed, as would the cash flows of purchasing the new equipment. The present salvage value of the old equipment and the future salvage value of the new equipment would affect the cash flow of the alternative of purchasing the new equipment. The salvage value on retirement of the old would affect the cash flow of retaining the old equipment.

EXAMPLE 6.4

Assume that the present equipment has a salvage value now of $1,000 and an expected salvage value in five years of $400 (at which time the equipment would be physically unusable). The new equipment will have a salvage value at the time of its expected retirement in year 10 of $650. All figures are on an after-tax basis. The cash flows arising from the salvage values would be as follows.

		Year	
	0	5	10
Absolute flows of			
Retaining the old		$400	
Purchasing the new	$1,000	____	$650
Relative flows of			
Replacing now	$1,000	$(400)	$650

Terminal Value

Salvage value is one form of terminal value. Another form is the release of cash necessary to operate the investment. Other examples of items that may result in released cash at the cessation of operations are collections of accounts receivable and reduction in required inventories. All these items gave rise to outlays of cash when they were purchased and then lagged in their generation of cash. When the outlays of cash cease because the production is being phased out, the coming periods will have increases in cash flows resulting from the conversion of these noncash current assets into cash; similarly, reductions of current liabilities reduce cash.

Even when $100 of working capital can be converted into $100 of cash, there is a timing cost. Assume that $100 is invested in working capital at time 0 and that the working capital is converted into $100 of cash at the end of the asset's life at time 10. Use a .15 time value factor.

Present value of outlay at time 0	$100
Present value of benefits at time 10	25
Net cost	$ 75

Cash Flow and Uncertainty

Each computation of cash flows makes specific assumptions about the level of business activity, actions of competitors, future availability of improved models of machines, costs of factors of production, future sales, and the like. Because there is a large amount of uncertainty connected with each of these factors, it should be appreciated that computations using the net present value method are indications of value rather than measures with 100 per cent certainty and accuracy. A more detailed discussion of the consequences of uncertain estimates and some suggestions for making analyses when basic assumptions are subject to uncertainty are presented in later chapters. It should be stressed that any decision about investments must be based on as complete a consideration of all the relevant factors as it is possible to provide and that the probable net present value of an investment proposal is only one factor, although a very significant one, to be considered in arriving at a final decision.

Income Taxes and Cash Flows

All decisions must be made on an after-tax basis. The income taxes are computed by applying the expected tax rate for each period to the taxable income (excluding interest charges) of that period. The taxable income will not be equal to the cash flow of the period, and frequently the taxable income will be different from the income computed in accordance with generally accepted accounting principles. The taxable income is defined by the tax laws established by government. The accounting income is defined by the accounting authorities (the Financial Accounting Standards Board). No matter what method is being used to accept or reject investments, it will be necessary to compute the income for tax purposes so that the tax can be computed.

In the case of corporations subject to income taxes, the timing of revenues and expenses adopted for income tax purposes must be considered in evaluating a potential investment, since the choices will affect the amount and timing of income tax payments. Because income taxes do not affect all investments in the same manner, it is necessary to place cash flows associated with each investment on an after-tax basis before evaluating the investments.

Governments have available many devices for encouraging or discouraging firms to undertake investments. Among the variables are the method of depreciation, the allowed life of assets, the treatment of salvage, and investment tax credits or investment allowances. Instead of investment tax credits, some countries use investment allowances or grants where firms are actually paid a percentage of the cost of the investment. Whatever the terminology, the economic effect to such tax benefits is to reduce the cost of the investment.

Business managers should be knowledgeable as to the nature of the current tax laws and sensitive to changes in the laws. The tax laws are a powerful tool for governments to influence the level of investments. Businesses should make decisions that are consistent with the tax laws under which they will have to operate.

After-Tax Flows

If revenues are $100 and the tax rate is .34, the firm will pay $34 of taxes and will net $66. The calculation is

$$(1 - t)R$$

where t is the tax rate and R is the revenue. A variation would be to write the expression as

$$R - tR$$

where tR is the incremental tax. Note that R is being multiplied by $(1 - t)$ to reduce it to an after-tax cash flow measure.

If out-of-pocket expenses are E, the after-tax cash flow expense is

$$(1 - t)E$$

or, equivalently,

$$E - tE$$

where tE is the tax savings arising from being able to deduct E from the taxable income. If the out-of-pocket expenses are $100, the after-tax cash flow expense is $66.

If the expense is a noncash-utilizing expense, then the calculation is modified. Define depreciation expense deductible for taxes to be Dep_t; then the cash flow effect of deducting Dep_t depreciation for taxes is

$$tDep_t$$

Thus, if there is $100 of depreciation expense taken for taxes, the cash flow effect will be a positive $34 with a .34 tax rate.

Measuring the Effects of Depreciation Expense on Cash Flows

Suppose that we are considering the purchase of a new piece of equipment. If there were no income taxes, the cash proceeds resulting from the use of the equipment could be estimated by subtracting the additional cash outlays required to operate the equipment from the additional revenues that result from acquiring it. The depreciation expense does not affect the cash proceeds. That is,

$$\text{Before-tax cash proceeds} = \text{revenues} - \frac{\text{expenses other than}}{\text{depreciation}}$$

The term *cash proceeds* is used here to refer to the proceeds generated by operating the investment. It assumes that all revenues are accompanied by an immediate generation of cash equal to the revenues. It also assumes that there are no changes in net working capital. For a nonprofit hospital or government bureau, this is the only calculation that would be necessary.

Now assume that there are income taxes. It is necessary to subtract the additional income tax liability that occurs because of the investment.

$$\text{After-tax proceeds} = \text{revenues} - \text{cash outlays} - \text{income tax}$$

or, equivalently,

$$\text{After-tax proceeds} = \text{revenues} - \frac{\text{expenses other than}}{\text{depreciation}} - \text{income tax}$$

The income tax liability is computed by applying the income tax rate to the additional taxable income. It is the amount of tax that actually has to be paid.

One allowable deduction for purposes of computing the tax liability is the tax depreciation of the investment. It is possible to express the determination of the income tax in the following way

$$\text{Income tax} = \text{tax rate} \times \text{taxable income}$$

and

$$\text{Income tax} = \text{tax rate} \times (\text{revenues} - \text{expenses other than} \\ \text{depreciation} - \text{tax depreciation})$$

It can be seen that the higher the depreciation taken for income tax purposes, the lower the income tax will be and the greater the after-tax cash proceeds. Substituting in the equation for after-tax proceeds gives

$$\text{After-tax proceeds} = (1 - \text{tax rate}) \times (\text{revenues} - \text{expenses} \\ \text{other than depreciation} - \text{tax depreciation}) \\ + \text{tax depreciation} \qquad (6.1)$$

or, rearranging terms in the above equation,

$$\text{After-tax proceeds} = (1 - \text{tax rate}) \times (\text{revenues} - \text{expenses} \\ \text{other than depreciation}) + (\text{tax rate} \\ \times \text{tax depreciation}) \qquad (6.2)$$

These two equations are mathematically equivalent and therefore give identical answers, although one or the other formula may be easier to use in a particular instance. The final equation is particularly useful, because it highlights the fact that the cash proceeds of the period are increased by the allowable tax depreciation times the tax rate. Thus, we can compute the present value of the "tax savings" by multiplying the depreciation by the expected tax rate of each period and discounting that amount back to the present. For convenience, we assume that the first depreciation deduction and the resulting tax saving take place exactly one year after the single outlay associated with the investment. This is a simplification, since the exact timing of the savings will depend on the timing difference between the investment outlays and the tax payments.

Let

$$C = \text{the after-tax proceeds}$$

$$t = \text{the tax rate}$$

$$R = \text{the revenues}$$

$$E = \text{the expenses other than depreciation}$$

$$Dep_t = \text{the depreciation expense taken for taxes}$$

Then, rewriting the last two equations, we have

$$C = (1 - t)(R - E - Dep_t) + Dep_t$$

and

$$C = (1 - t)(R - E) + tDep_t \tag{6.3}$$

This equation highlights the fact that the higher the period's tax depreciation expense, the larger the period's cash flow if the tax expense can be used to shelter taxable income.

EXAMPLE 6.5

Assume that the tax rate is .34, revenue is $150, the out-of-pocket expenses are $50, and the depreciation for taxes is $80. We have

$$t = .34$$

$$R = 150, \quad E = 50, \quad Dep_t = 80$$

Using the above preceding equations, we have

$$C = (1 - t)(R - E - Dep_t) + Dep_t$$
$$= .66(\$150 - \$50 - \$80) + \$80$$
$$= \$13.20 + \$80.00 = \$93.20$$

$$C = (1 - t)(R - E) + tDep_t = .66(\$100) + .34(\$80)$$
$$= \$66 + \$27.20 = \$93.20$$

The exact method of computing the cash flows is a matter of taste. A wide range of different methods will be equally correct.

Accelerated Cost Recovery System (ACRS)

In August 1981 the United States Congress passed a law that introduced a new method of tax depreciation expense calculation. Even the words *depreciation expenses* were dropped and the term *recovery allowances* was introduced. The objective of the legislation was to accelerate the tax deductions. Capital assets were divided into five classes, with four of the classes defined in terms of a number of years. The fifth class was real estate (written off over 18 years using an accelerated method).

In May of 1985 the President of the United States proposed that the ACRS be abandoned in favor of a slower rate of writeoff, and in 1986 the tax law was revised so that the depreciation tax shields became less generous than those offered by the ACRS provisions.

The 1986 Tax Reform Act

The basic depreciation methods for nonreal property (tangible personal property) under the 1986 Tax Reform Act are 200 percent declining balance and 150 percent declining balance, both with a switch to straight-line depreciation.

TABLE 6.1   Depreciation Classes: 1986 Tax Reform Act

| ADR Midpoint Life | ACRS with Asset Depreciation Range (ADR) Method | | |
	ACRS	Depreciation Method	Special Explanations
4	3 years	200% declining balance	Excludes automobiles and light-purpose trucks
Between 4 and 10 (4 < x < 10)	5 years	200% declining balance	Includes automobiles, light trucks, some equipment
Between 10 and 16 (10 < x < 16)	7 years	200% declining balance	Railroad track, some agricultural structures
Between 16 and 20 (16 < x < 20)	10 years	200% declining balance	None
Between 20 and 25 (20 > x < 25)	15 years	150% declining balance	Includes some plant and equipment
Longer than 25 (x > 25)	20 years	150% declining balance	Excludes real property with an ADR midpoint life of 27.5 years or more
Not relevant	27 ½ years	Straight line	Residential rental property
Not relevant	31 ½ years	Straight line	Nonresidential real property

The owner of the asset can use straight-line depreciation instead of declining balance. Table 6.1 shows the six declining-balance classes and the two real-property classes. Note that the asset depreciation range (ADR) midpoint lives are used to determine the ACRS asset class.

Except for real property (residential and nonresidential), a half-year convention is to be used. This means that a five-year ACRS asset will be depreciated over a six-year period.

EXAMPLE 6.6

Assume a $100,000 asset that fits the five-year ACRS 200 percent declining balance class. The straight-line depreciation rate is 20 percent, and twice that is 40 percent. We have

Year	Calculation	Amount of Depreciation Expense
1	(.40 × 100,000) 1/2	$ 20,000
2	.40 × 80,000	32,000
3	.40 × 48,000	19,200
4	.40 × 28,800 or $\dfrac{28,800}{2.5} = 11,520$	11,520
5	.40 × 17,280 = 6,912 or 11,520	11,520
6	11,520 × 1/2	5,760
		$100,000

With a three-year ACRS class (a four-year ADR midpoint life), we would have

Year	Calculation	Amount of Depreciation Expense
1	(2/3 × 100,000) 1/2	$ 33,333
2	2/3 × 66,667	44,444
3	2/3 × 22,223 = 14,815 or $\dfrac{22,223}{1.5}$ = 14,815	14,815
4	22,223 − 14,815 =	7,408
		$100,000

Appendix Table D gives the depreciation expense for each year of the assets life for the different ACRS asset classes. Straight-line depreciation may also be used.

EXAMPLE 6.7

A piece of new equipment costs $10,000. It can be depreciated for tax purposes using the three-year ACRS method class, and the ACRS has been decided upon. The equipment is expected to have no salvage value on retirement. The company uses straight-line depreciation in its accounting. The equipment is expected to bring an increase in annual revenues (sales are all for cash) of $8,000 for four years and additional annual costs requiring cash outlays of $4,000 (not including depreciation of the equipment). The income tax rate is 34 percent. The cost of money is 10 percent (after tax).

The first step is to compute the taxable income and income tax of each year. This is accomplished in Table 6.2.

It should be noted that the use of a tax rate of 34 percent for all years carries an assumption that the tax rate will not be changed. If a change is expected, the tax rates of the future years should be used.

The second step is to compute the cash flows to each year (Table 6.3). It is important to note that the accounting depreciation does not enter into this computation at all, but the depreciation for tax purposes influences the income

TABLE 6.2   Computation of Income Tax

Year	Revenues	Other Costs	Depreciation for Tax Purposes	Taxable Income	Tax Rate (%)	Income Tax
1	$8,000	$4,000	$3,333	$ 667	34	$ 227
2	8,000	4,000	4,444	−444	34	−151
3	8,000	4,000	1,482	2,518	34	856
4	8,000	4,000	741	3,259	34	1,168

TABLE 6.3   Computation of Cash Flows

Year	Revenue	Other Costs	Income Tax	Cash Flows
1	$8,000	$4,000	$ 227	$3,773
2	8,000	4,000	−151	4,151
3	8,000	4,000	856	3,144
4	8,000	4,000	1,108	2,892

tax and thus does indirectly affect the proceeds. Using the following equation to compute the cash flows of year 2, we would have

$$\text{After-tax cash flows} = (1 - .34)(\$8,000 - \$4,000 - \$4,444) + \$4,444$$
$$= -\$293 + \$4,444$$
$$= \$4,151$$

Alternatively, we would also have

$$\text{After-tax cash flows} = (1 - .34)(\$8,000 - \$4,000) + (.34 \times \$4,444)$$
$$= \$2,640 + \$1,511$$
$$= \$4,151$$

The next step is to compute the present value of the cash flows, using 10 percent as the rate of discount (see Table 6.4). The present value of the cash flows is $11,198. This is larger than the cash outflows of $10,000; thus, the investment is to be accepted.

TABLE 6.4   Computation of the Present Value of Cash Flows

Year	Cash Flow	Discount Factor (Using 10%)	Present Value of the Cash Flows
1	$3,773	.9091	$ 3,430
2	4,151	.8264	3,431
3	3,144	.7513	2,362
4	2,892	.6830	1,975
			$11,198

The Tax Rate

Let us assume that the statutory tax rate is 34 percent and that we are making a capital budgeting analysis. What rate should be used for decisions if the actual tax expense divided by reported income for the previous period is 30 percent?

The differences arise because of provisions in the tax code such as tax-exempt interest, investment tax credits, accelerated depreciation, and various other tax-avoidance possibilities. A normal taxpaying corporate entity may have any tax rate from 0 to 34 percent. What rate should be used?

We could argue that the rate applicable to the marginal investment should be used. The rate may be zero for the next investment because of a large tax-loss carryover; however, the tax rate might still change to 34 percent on an additional investment that would cause a positive tax payment.

A firm with tax losses that would otherwise not be used would be incorrect if it used 34 percent. If there is expectation that an investment for a zero tax firm will move the firm to a tax status of 34 percent, then there is some tax cost, however. If we would expect the firm to be able to keep itself in a zero tax status at no cost, then the tax rate should be zero. But a zero tax rate tends to be unrealistic, since most companies are only temporarily zero tax, and profitable investments tend to cause taxes, either now or in the future. We advocate the use of a marginal tax rate that would be between 0 and 34 percent. The choice of the rate will depend on the incremental effect on taxes of undertaking the investment. The tax analysis is further complicated in the United States by the 20 percent alternative minimum tax provision passed in 1986.

EXAMPLE 6.8

The ABC Company earned $100 million before tax and $90 million after tax. The effective tax rate was .10 of before-tax income and .11 of after-tax income. The low tax rate was caused by investment tax credits and the treatment of foreign taxes. There are no unused tax credits.

What tax rate should be used on the next investment?

If $100 of income will result in $34 of taxes, then a .34 tax rate should be used.

Depreciation Methods

Using Depreciation Tables

The depreciation tables in the appendix to this book enable us to take a short-cut in the calculations. Instead of computing the actual cash flows of each year, we separate the calculation into several subcomponents. The steps in the calculations are

1. Compute the present value of the after-tax cash proceeds without considering the depreciation expense tax shield. This is an "incorrect" calculation, which will be corrected by step 4.
2. Compute the investment tax credit (this is zero after 1986 in the U.S.).
3. Compute the present value of the depreciation tax savings using the appropriate tables.
4. Combine the cost of investment and the information from steps 1–3 to compute the net present value.

EXAMPLE 6.9

Let us consider the acquisition of equipment that costs $1,000,000. The asset can be depreciated using the five-year property class schedule. The investment has a life of twenty years and will earn cash flows (before tax) of $151,515 per year. The corporate tax rate is .34. The firm has a .10 cost of money.

1. The after-tax cash flow (before considering depreciation) is $151,515 (1− .34), or $100,000. The present value factor for the annuity is 8.5136, and the present value is $851,360.
2. The ITC equals zero.
3. The present value of depreciation per dollar of investment is .77326, or $773,260 for a $1,000,000 investment. The present value of the tax savings is .34(773,260), or $262,908.
4. The net present value of the investment is

$$NPV = -1,000,000 + 262,908 + 773,260 = \$36,168$$

The investment is marginally desirable.

Additional Complications Affecting Choice of Depreciation Methods

The examples presented in the preceding section are intended primarily to illustrate the type of analysis when we know what depreciation method we want to use. In some situations we need to determine the most advantageous method of depreciating a wasting asset. The present value approach can be used to determine the most advantageous method of depreciating an asset. A full treatment of the complications that arise in determining a proper and acceptable method of depreciation under the internal revenue code would require a book in itself and is beyond the scope of this chapter. Some of the more important complications that may arise in practice will be mentioned briefly, however.

In the examples presented, it was assumed that the assets to be depreciated would have no salvage value at the end of their expected useful life. Following present tax laws, expected salvage value does not affect the recovery allowance.

Another complication is that many companies use the group method of depreciation instead of the unit method. Under the group method, the rate of depreciation is based on the average life of many units of like items (for example, telegraph poles). This rate of depreciation is then applied to the balance of unretired units. As the units are retired, no loss or gain is recognized at the time of retirement. The depreciation of successive periods is based on the estimate of average life (which is computed by using mortality experience for this type of asset) and the number of units that are retired in each period. Thus, the use of the group procedure of depreciation requires a forecast of the number of units in use in each period in order to compute the depreciation of each period as well as a rate of depreciation.

A final complication is the timing of tax payments and of tax savings resulting from depreciation. In the past years, tax payments have lagged the earning of corporate income, but at present they have been advanced to such an extent that to assume that the tax payment (or the tax saving) occurs at the end of the period in which income is earned is reasonable.

The Effect of Tax Computation on Investment Analysis

Terminal Value

High costs of money, high tax rates, and long-lived assets, combined with accelerated depreciation for tax purposes, can result in the presence of terminal value adversely affecting the desirability of an investment.

EXAMPLE 6.10

Assume a discount rate of 10 percent, a 34 percent tax rate, a life of the twenty years for the asset, and a tax depreciation method that allows a company to write off the depreciable asset over 5 years, using straight-line depreciation. In this case, $100 of depreciable assets may be worth more than $100 of terminal value.

The present value of $100 of after-tax terminal value due in twenty years, assuming a rate of interest of 10 percent, is

$$\$100 \times .1486 = \$14.86 \quad \text{(present value of salvage)}$$

The $100 of additional depreciable assets (assuming no salvage value) will reduce taxes a total of $34, or $6.80 per year. The present value of an annuity of $1 per period for five periods, with an interest rate of 10 percent, is $3.7908.

$$\$6.80 \times 3.7908 = \$25.78 \quad \text{(present value of the tax deductions)}$$

With these facts, the $100 of tax deduction is worth more than the $100 of terminal value. Note that the facts of this situation are reasonable and close to reality: The corporate tax rate is 34 percent; depreciable assets do frequently have lives of twenty years; 10 percent is not excessively high for a discount rate; and assets are frequently written off for tax purposes over a period of five years.

The ideal situation from the point of view of the investor would be to write off the investment for tax purposes as if it had no salvage and then to wait and see if any salvage develops. The taxpayer is going to be better off with a conservative estimate of salvage.

The preceding analysis leads to several interesting conclusions. First, a depreciable asset that is deductible for tax purposes is more desirable than an asset that is not depreciable for tax purposes. Second, other things being equal, an expenditure that can be expensed immediately for tax purposes is more desirable than an expenditure that must be written off for tax purposes over a period of years. Thus, under the present tax code, increasing net revenues by the same amount through research is more desirable than increasing net revenues by the same amount through increasing plant and equipment, since research may be expensed immediately, but plant and equipment must be depreciated.

Changes in Inventories

The computation of cash flows makes use of the cash expenditures for factors of production in the period of outlay when computing the amount of outlays. Some of the factors of production may be lodged in inventory at the end of the accounting period and thus not charged against the revenues of the period. This would affect the cash flows of the period, because the items would not be expensed for purposes of computing income taxes. The income taxes of this period will be higher than they would be if all cash expenditures were expensed for tax purposes. In some future accounting periods, these items will be expensed and will result in taxes for that period being reduced, thus in effect increasing the cash flows (by decreasing taxes) in a period long after the cash expenditure was made. Thus, buildups of inventory required by an investment will adversely affect the desirability of the investment by requiring an immediate cash outlay, whereas the cash flows, both by reducing income taxes and by generating revenues upon sale of the items, are delayed for one or more periods. The inventories must generate enough cash flows not only to recover the initial outlay of funds, but also to pay the interest costs of the differences in time of outlay and recovery of cash.

Present Value

We have defined the net present value of an investment as the amount a firm could afford to pay for an investment in excess of its cost. This implicitly assumes a zero tax rate. With a corporate tax rate of t_c, the amount that a firm would be willing to pay for a stream of benefits must take into consideration the fact that the benefits will be taxed and that the amount paid for the investment generally will be deductible for tax purposes. If D is the present value of the depreciation deductions per dollar of investment cost, using accelerated depreciation, the cost of an investment (C) net of the tax savings from depreciation is

$$C(1 - t_c D).$$

Setting this equal to the present value of the benefits of the investment, we can then solve for C, the amount we could afford to pay for the investment.

EXAMPLE 6.11

An investment will result in cash proceeds of $10,000 per year before tax and $6,600 after tax ($t_c = .34$) for a period of ten years. The time value of money is

.10 after taxes. If we use a five-year ACRS class, how much could we pay for the investment?

The present value of the benefits is

$$\$6{,}600 \times B(10, .10) = \$6{,}600 \times 6.1446 = \$40{,}554$$

The present value of depreciation deductions (from Appendix Table C) per dollar of investment is .77326.

$$C(1 - t_cD) = 40{,}554 \quad \text{and} \quad (1 - t_cD) = (1 - .34 \times .77326) = .73571$$

$$C = \frac{40{,}554}{.73571} = \$55{,}122$$

We could pay $55,122 for an investment that has cash flows with a present value of $40,554, because the tax depreciation deductions reduce the cost of the investment from $55,122 to $40,554.

Timing of Tax Payments

The timing of income tax payments is relevant to the investment analysis if the payment of the tax occurs in a time period significantly later than the earning of the proceeds. We consider the cash outlay to occur when the actual cash disbursement occurs, not when the obligation to pay is created.

EXAMPLE 6.12

Assume that firm has an opportunity to invest $18,500 today in promoting a sport contest. The promised return to be received one year from today is $24,000. The income tax of $1,870 (assuming a 34 percent tax rate) is to be paid two years from today. The interest rate is 20 percent. The schedule of cash flows would be as follows.

@ 20%

Year	Cash Flows	Present Value Factor	Present Value of Cash Flows
0	$(18,500)	1.0000	($18,500)
1	24,000	.8333	20,000
2	(1,870)	.6944	(1,299)
			$ 201

The net present value is positive and therefore the investment should be undertaken.

If the income taxes were paid during period 1, the cash flows of that period would be $22,130, and the net present value of the cash flows, using a 20 percent rate of discount, would be a negative $58. This would indicate that the investment should not be undertaken.

Conclusions

Investment analysis uses cash flow because it is theoretically correct and because it is easier to define and use than accounting incomes.

The cash flow can be defined to be equal to the change in the company's bank account as long as the debt flows and other financing flows are excluded and the opportunity costs are included. If some debt flows are included, then all debt flows must be included, and the resulting net cash flow will be the change in the stockholders' position.

Changes in working capital affect the cash flow. Cash earning of $100 will increase working capital and will be a positive cash flow. Cash amounting to $100 that is required to be on deposit in a bank because of the investment is also an increase in working capital, but this is a negative cash flow because now capital is required to finance the $100 cash sitting in the bank. Changes in net working capital caused by undertaking an investment change the amount of capital needed.

The most important thing to remember is that the present value of the depreciation deductions times the tax rate is the economic value of the depreciation tax savings, and this amount effectively reduces the cost of acquiring a depreciable asset.

REVIEW EXAMPLE 6.1

The following events are assumed to take place at time 1. Determine the cash flow for investment evaluation purposes. The tax rate is .34.

Credit sales	$ 40,000	
Cash sales	100,000	
Out-of-pocket expenses	75,000	
Income taxes	12,880	(reflects the $7,000 interest expense tax shield and the $30,000 depreciation)
Depreciation (accounting)	20,000	
Depreciation (tax)	30,000	
Change in net working capital (increase)	8,000	(includes $28,000 of accounts receivable that only cost $20,000 incrementally)
Interest expense	7,000	
Principal payment	16,000	

Solution

Cash from operations:		
Sales		$140,000
Less		
Out-of-pocket expenses	75,000	
Income taxes	9,520	65,480
Subtotal		$ 74,520

To eliminate interest tax savings,

$$
\begin{aligned}
\text{Subtotal} &= \$74,520 \\
\$7,000 \times .34 &= \underline{\$\ 2,380} \\
&\ \ \ \$72,140
\end{aligned}
$$

Less the increase in working capital   <u>8,000</u>
Cash flow $64,140

The tax calculation was

	With Interest	*Without Interest*
Revenue	$140,000	$140,000
Expenses	75,000	75,000
Dep_t	30,000	30,000
Interest	7,000	
Total expenses	$112,000	$105,000
Taxable income	28,000	35,000
Tax rate	× .34	× .34
Tax	$ 9,520	$ 11,900

$$\$11,900 - \$9,520 = \$2,380 \text{ tax shield of interest}$$

or

$$\$7,000 \times .34 = \$2,380 \text{ tax shield of interest}$$

Note:

   a. Depreciation (accounting) of $20,000 does not affect any of the calculations.
   b. Interest expense is excluded (or eliminated).
   c. Principal payment is excluded.
   d. The difference between the book amount of receivables and the cost of receivables does not affect the calculations (two items are affected, and they self-balance).

PROBLEMS

6.1   The following facts relate to an investment costing $10,000 that is being considered by the ABC Company.

	Period	
	1	2
Cash revenues	$12,000	$12,000
Depreciation	5,000	5,000
Net income	$ 7,000	$ 7,000

The company intends to declare dividends of $12,000 in period 1 and $12,000 in period 2 as a result of the investment. The company is not subject to income taxes.

What are the cash flows of the two years for purposes of the analysis of the investment?

6.2. For problem 6.1, assume that all the sales were made on account and that collection lagged the sale by one period. The company will distribute dividends equal to the cash generation.

What are the cash flows of each year?

6.3 An investment will require an increase in the following working-capital items.

Cash	$1,000,000
Accounts receivable	3,000,000
Inventories	6,000,000

It is also expected that current liabilities will increase by $4 million.

How will the preceding items affect the cash flows of the investment?

6.4 In computing the cash flows of a period, should interest payments be included or excluded? Explain.

6.5 The ABC Company is considering an investment in a new product. The information for one year is as follows:

Sales	$200,000
Manufacturing costs of sales	80,000
(includes $20,000 of depreciation)	
Selling and administrative expenses	40,000
(directly associated with the product)	
Equipment purchases	10,000
Decrease in contribution of other products	5,000
Increase in accounts receivable	15,000
Increase in inventories	20,000
Increase in current liabilities	30,000
Income taxes associated with product income	12,000
Interest on bonds expected to be used in financing	18,000

Compute the cash flow that can be used in the present value computations of this investment.

6.6 A product is currently being manuafactured on a machine that has a book value of $10,000 (20 years ago it was purchased for $50,000). The costs of the product are as follows.

	Unit Costs
Labor, direct	$ 4.00
Labor, variable indirect	5.00
Other variable overhead	2.50
Fixed overhead	2.50
	$14.00

In the past year 10,000 units were produced and sold for $10 per unit. It is expected that the old machine can be used indefinitely in the future and that the price will continue to be $10 per unit.

An equipment manufacturer has offered to accept the old machine as a tradein for a new version. The new machine would cost $80,000, after allowing $15,000 for the old equipment. The projected costs associated with the new machine are as follows.

Labor, direct	$ 2.00
Labor, variable indirect	3.50
Other variable overhead	4.00
Fixed overhead	3.25
	$12.75

The fixed overhead costs are allocations from other departments plus the depreciation of the old equipment. Repair costs are the same for both machines.

The old machine could be sold on the open market now for $6,000. Ten years from now, it is expected to have a salvage value of $1,000. The new machine has an expected life of 10 years and an expected salvage of $10,000.

There are no corporate income taxes. The appropriate time discount rate for this company is .05. It is expected that future demand for the product will remain at 10,000 units per year.

Evaluate whether the new equipment should be acquired.

6.7 The ABC Company is considering an investment in a new product. The information for one year is as follows.

Sales (all on accounts)	$200,000
Manufacturing costs of sales	90,000
(include $20,000 of depreciation and $6,000 of fixed-cost	
allocations from service departments)	
Selling and administrative expenses	40,000
(directly associated with the product)	
Equipment purchases	10,000
(purchased on account and not yet paid)	
Decrease in contribution of other products	5,000
Increase in accounts receivable	15,000
Increase in inventories	20,000
(includes $4,000 depreciation)	
Increase in current liabilities	30,000
Income taxes associated with product income	12,000
Interest on bonds expected to be used in financing	18,000
Increase in accumulated depreciation	19,000

Compute the cash flow that can be used in the present value computations of this investment.

6.8 Assume that an investment is financed partially by sinking-fund bonds and that there is a requirement to place $50,000 per year into a sinking fund.

Does this information affect the computation of the cash flows for the investment analysis? A sinking-fund requirement mandates that cash or the bonds themselves be set aside for the debt retirement.

6.9 Compute the cash flow effect (change) caused by the following items. The tax rate is .34. Assume the firm is paying taxes.
   a. Revenues increase by $100 _____.
   b. Labor expenses increase by $100 _____.
   c. Tax depreciation expense increases by $100 _____.
   d. Accounting depreciation increases by $100 _____.

6.10 The A Company is currently earning $13,000,000 per year on $100,000,000 of stockholders' equity, or a return of 13 percent. One plant with a cost base of $10,000,000 earns $800,000 of cash per year, or 8 percent.

The chairman of the board has set a target ROI of 15 percent. The company has received an offer of $5,000,000 for the plant. The pro forma return on investment (assuming the $5,000,000 from the sale of the plant is returned to investors) is

$$ROI = \frac{\$12,200,000}{\$90,000,000} = 13.5\%$$

Should the plant be sold?

6.11 The X Company will use a .10 discount rate in evaluating an investment that costs $1,500,000. For each year of its 15-year life, the investment will have the following same revenues and out-of-pocket expenses. The firm uses straight-line depreciation. The first year's income statement is

Revenues	$280,000
Out-of-pocket expenses	30,000
Interest	150,000
Depreciation expense	100,000
Income	$ 0

The company has a zero tax rate.
   Should the company undertake the investment?

6.12 Assume that the cash flows of an investment are

0	−$1,500,000
1–15	250,000

The rate of discount to be used is .10.
   Should the company undertake the investment?

6.13 The National Money Company, in deciding whether to make or buy, considers only direct labor and direct material as being relevant costs. The sum of these two costs factors is compared with the cost of purchasing the items, and a decision is made on this basis.
   Appraise the make-or-buy procedure of the National Money Company.

6.14 The National Money Company has an investment opportunity that offers $1 million of cash flows a year for perpetuity. It requires a cash outlay of $19.6 million for plant and equipment and the necessary inventory. It is estimated that an additional $500,000 of cash will have to be carried as a compensating balance during the period of the investment. The company has a time value of money of .10.
   Is the investment acceptable?

6.15 To make a new product, inventories must be increased by $5 million.
   Should this be considered a cash outlay?

6.16 Would you expect the relevant costs for decision making (such as the make-or-buy decision) to be higher or lower than the accounting costs computed on an absorption costing basis?

6.17 Assume that the Internal Revenue Code allows a tax credit of .10 of the cost of eligible investments to be deducted from the amount of federal income taxes payable. It also allows the use of accelerated depreciation. The tax base is not reduced by the investment tax credit.
   Assume a marginal income tax rate of .34 and an after-tax discount rate of .12.

a. How much is $1 of tax credit worth today?

b. How much is the "right" to deduct $1 of depreciation today worth today?

c. Assume that we pay $1 million for equipment eligible for the tax credit. The equipment will be depreciated for tax purposes in 10 years. What is the cost of the equipment? What is the cash flow of the period of purchase of the equipment? What do we know about the value of the equipment as of the beginning of the period after the taking of tax credit?

6.18 Assume a tax rate of .34, a before-tax rate of discount of .15, and an after-tax rate of .099.

a. If the firm is basically profitable, what is the present value of $1 of tax-deductible expense incurred and paid for at the end of period 1?

b. If the firm is operating at a loss, what is the present value of $1 of tax-deductible expense incurred and paid for at the end of period 1?

6.19 Compute the present value of the right to deduct $1 million in depreciation immediately compared with the right to deduct the $1 million 20 years from now. The tax rate is .34, and the after-tax rate of discount is .10.

6.20 The AB has a borrowing cost of .10 and a tax rate of .4. It uses an after-tax borrowing rate of .06 to evaluate riskless investments (cash flows are certain). It can invest $1,000 to earn $1,080 of net revenues (before tax) one period hence. The cash flows are certain, and the firm has taxable income. The following calculations have been done.

Revenue		$1,080
Depreciation	1,000	
Interest	100	1,100
Tax loss		$ 20
Tax rate		× .4
Tax saving		$ 8

The cash flows used were

Time 0	−$1,000	
Time 1	+1,088	(including $8 tax savings)

The present value, using .06 as the discount rate, is

$$-\$1,000 + \$1,088(1.06)^{-1} = -\$1,000 + \$1,026 = +\$26$$

The investment was accepted.
   Evaluate the decision.

6.21 Manufacturers of heavy electric generating equipment have been arguing for years over the value of buying in advance of need. The following analysis was presented by one manufacturer in order to persuade utilities to order in advance under a buy-and-store plan.

Cost of boiler if purchased a year early and stored	$1,000,000
(90 percent of the purchase price would be paid immediately and 10 percent one year, later, when the boiler is completed)	
Storage costs for one year	10,000
(this amount would be paid two years from now)	

It is expected that there will be an 8.5 percent increase in cost ($85,000) if the purchase is delayed one year.

Assuming a short-term interest rate of .04, the interest cost of buying early is $36,000. With a .52 tax rate, the after-tax interest cost is $17,200. Comparing the $85,000 of cost saving with the storage cost plus the interest indicates that it is desirable to purchase early.

Assume that the boiler is to be placed into use two years from now.

The after-tax cost of money of the company considering the purchase is 7 percent.

Prepare an estimate of the incremental after-tax cash flows resulting from ordering a boiler immediately. The estimated cash flows should be suitable for determining the value of advance ordering, using a discounted cash flow approach. Assume that the boiler would be depreciated on a straight-line basis over a 20-year period from the date it is installed and ready to use. These is no investment tax credit.

6.22 The following projections for an investment apply for the coming year (the forecasted tax rate is .34).

Revenues (credit sales)	$100,000
Accounting depreciation	30,000
Tax depreciation	40,000
Interest expense	5,000
Principal payment	12,000
Receipt of receivables	93,000
Increase in receivables	7,000
Increase in net working capital (where working capital includes receivables)	29,000

a. Assuming that the firm is on an accrual basis for taxes, determine the expected tax expense that will be *paid*.

b. The tax expense to be used for the investment evaluation cash flow calculation is _____ .

c. Determine the cash flow for purposes of evaluating the investment: _____ _____ . The cash flow will be discounted using an after-tax discount rate based on using a composite of all types of capital.

6.23 Assume a tax rate of .34 and a rate of discount of .20 before tax and .132 after tax.

   a. If the firm is basically a profitable operation, what is the present value of $1 of tax-deductible expense incurred and paid for at the end of period 1?

   b. If the firm is a loss operation what is the present value of $1 of tax-deductible expense incurred and paid for at the end of period 1?

6.24 Compute the present value of the right to deduct $1 million in depreciation immediately compared with the right to deduct the $1 million in thirty years. The tax rate is .34, and the after-tax rate of discount is .192.

6.25 The AB has a borrowing cost of .14 and a tax rate of .34. It uses an after-tax borrowing rate of .0924 to evaluate riskless investments (cash flows are certain). It can invest $1,000 to earn $1,100 of net revenues (before tax) one period hence. The cash flows are certain, and the firm has taxable income. The following calculations have been done.

Revenue		$1,100
Depreciation	1,000	
Interest	140	1,140
Tax loss		$ 40
Tax rate		× .34
Tax saving		$13.60

The cash flows used were

Time 0	−1,000.00	
Time 1	+1,113.60	(including $13.60 tax savings)

The present value using .0924 as the discount rate is

$$-1,000 + 1,113.60 \, (1.0924)^{-1} = -1,000 + 1,019 = +19$$

The investment was accepted. Evaluate the decision.

6.26 While discussing the pros and cons of an automated collator with an executive of a large corporation, the dean of a school in a large university said, "You are lucky; with a tax rate of .40, you pay only $6,000 for a $10,000 machine."

Assume that there is a labor saving of $2,500 per year associated with the collator being considered. The expected life is ten years, and the before-tax time value of money is .05 to both the university and the corporation. Assume the present value of tax depreciation is .89786 per dollar of cost for this asset. Who has more incentive to purchase the machine, the university or the corporation?

6.27   Continuing problem 6.26: Assume that a university and a corporation both are considering spending $5 million for an administrative office building. The expected life is fifty years. Take the depreciation into consideration; what is the net saving to each? The tax rate is .40, and the time value of money is .05 before taxes (.03 after taxes to the corporation). The alternative for both is to rent at a before-tax cost of $300,000 per year with a cancelable lease. The present value of tax depreciation for this asset is .634516 per dollar of cost.

6.28   The Old Company is currently producing a product that sells for $7.00 per unit, and the variable costs of manufacturing are $6.00 per unit. The company produces and sells 1,000,000 units per year and expects this level of production and sales in the future. The total market is 2,000,000 units. The fixed costs (including overhead) allocated to the product are $1,200,000 per year. The company has an opportunity to purchase new equipment costing $9,000,000 and having an expected life of twenty years. The IRS will accept the twenty-year life for taxes. The present value of tax depreciation for this asset is $.676799 per dollar of cost.

   The equipment will reduce variable costs to $4.50 per unit. Because of the method of cost allocation, the fixed costs allocated (including the equipment depreciation) will increase to $1,600,000 per year.

   The tax rate is .34. The appropriate rate of interest to be used in this type of investment decision has been determined by the company to be 6 percent. Maintenance expense will be constant throughout the equipment's life.

   The board of directors of the company is very much concerned with an investment's payback, ROI, and its effect on earnings per share. However, it does believe that all decisions should be made in the best interests of the firm's common stockholders.

   Should the equipment be purchased? Explain.

6.29   The XYZ Company has an investment that costs $6,000 and has a life of three years. The tax rate is .48.

   The asset will earn $10,000 the first years, $9,000 the second, and $7,000 the third. There are $5,500 of out-of-pocket expenses per year.

   Working capital will be $1,000, then $1,600, then zero.

   The time discount rate is 10 percent.

   The present value of the depreciation tax savings is $2,464 for this asset.

   Using the following worksheet, evaluate the investment.

Worksheet for Problem 6.29

	Period 1	Period 2	Period 3
Revenues or savings (cash and receivables			
Out-of-pocket expenses	____	____	____
Income before taxes			
Taxes (.48)	$____	$____	____
Income after taxes	$____	$____	____
Plus: Net working capital decrease			
Less: Net working capital increase	____	____	____
Cash flow	$____	$____	____
Present value factors			
Present values	════	════	════

Total present value of savings $____

Cost of investment $____

Less:
PV of dep. times
Tax rate (.48)   ____
Net cost   ____

Net present value   ____

6.30 *The NSV Manufacturing Company*

A product is currently being manufactured on a machine that is fully depreciated for tax purposes and has a book value of $10,000 (it was purchased for $30,000 twenty years ago). The costs of the product are as follows:

	Unit Costs
Labor, direct	$ 4.00
Labor, variable indirect	2.00
Other variable overhead	1.50
Fixed overhead	2.50
	$10.00

In the past year 10,000 units were produced and sold for $18 per unit. It is expected that with suitable repairs the old machine can be used indefinitely. The repairs are expected to average $25,000 per year.

An equipment manufacturer has offered to accept the old machine as a tradein for a new version. The new machine would cost $60,000 after allowing $15,000 for the old equipment. the projected costs associated with the new machine are as follows.

Labor, direct	$2.00
Labor, variable indirect	3.00
Other variable overhead	1.00
Fixed overhead	3.25
	$9.25

The fixed overhead costs are allocations from other departments plus the depreciation of the equipment.

The old machine could not be sold on the open market. The new machine has an expected life of ten years and no expected salvage at that time.

The current corporate income tax rate is .40. For tax purposes, the cost of the new machine may be depreciated in ten years. The appropriate after-tax time discount rate for this company is .10. The present value of the tax depreciation is .701 per dollar of cost for this machine.

It is expected that future demand of the product will stay steady at 10,000 units per year. (a) Should the new equipment be acquired? (b) If the product can be purchased at a cost of $7.80 per unit from a reliable supplier, should it be purchased or made? Explain.

6.31 *The XYZ Manufacturing Company*

A product is currently being manufactured on a machine that is fully depreciated for tax purposes and that has a book value of $10,000 (it was purchased for $30,000 twenty years ago). The costs of the product are as follows.

	Unit Costs
Labor, direct	$ 4.00
Labor, indirect	2.00
Variable overhead	1.50
Fixed overhead	2.50
	$10.00

In the past year 1,000 units were produced and sold for $18 per unit. It is expected that the old machine can be used indefinitely. An equipment manufacturer has offered to accept the old machine as a tradein for a new version. The new machine would cost $60,000 after allowing $15,000 for the old equipment. The projected costs associated with the new machine are as follows.

Labor, direct	$2.00
Labor, indirect	3.00
Variable overhead	1.00
Fixed overhead	3.25
	$9.25

The fixed overhead costs are allocations from other departments plus the depreciation of the equipment.

The old machine could be sold on the open market now for $5,000. Ten years from now it is expected to have a salvage value of $1,000. The new machine has an expected life of ten years and an expected salvage of $10,000.

The current corporate income tax rate is .40, and the capital-gain tax rate is .25. Any salvage from sale will result in a capital gain at the time of retirement. (For tax purposes, the entire cost may be depreciated in ten years). The appropriate after-tax time discount rate for this company is .10. The present value of the tax depreciation is .701 per dollar.

It is expected that future demand of the product will stay steady at 1,000 units per year. (a) Should the equipment be acquired? (b) If the product can be purchased at a cost of $7.80 per unit from a reliable supplier, should it be purchased or made? Explain.

6.32   *Chem Co.*

Assume there is a .10 investment tax credit. The company leaves out the .10 investment tax credit (ITC) in evaluating an investment. It requires a .26 internal rate of return.

a. Assume a life of one year (but still eligible for the ITC). What is the effective required return?

b. Assume a ten-year life and constant benefits. What is the effective required return?

c. Repeat part (b), assuming a perpetual life.

d. Assume the benefits are decaying at a rate of .24 per year. What is the effective required return?

6.33   RST Corporation is considering introducing a new product. The product could be manufactured on a machine costing $15,000. The life of the product and machine is five years. Startup costs (which can be expensed) are $5,000 in year 1 and $2,000 in year 2. Expected unit sales are 3,000 in years 1 and 5 and 5,000 in years 2, 3, and 4. The product would contribute $2.00 per unit before taxes towards fixed overhead and profit. The firm is subject to an income tax rate of 40 percent. Working capital of $5,000 would be required in year 1 and would be returned in year 5. The machine would be depreciated with a five-year life using the SYD methods for taxes. The first year's depreciation is $2,000. The machine has no salvage value and is not eligible for an investment tax credit. Working capital would be financed by a bank loan at a before-tax rate of 8 percent, which would be renewed each year. The firm expects to have taxable income from other operations in each of the next five years. Calculate the total after-tax cash flow per period that you would use in deciding whether to accept or reject this investment opportunity. Enter the totals in the last row of the table on this page. Use the other rows in the table to show the details of your calculations. Label each row if you use it.

RST Corporation Cash Flow Summary

Item	0	1	2	3	4	5
(1) Capital outlay	−15,000					
(2)						
(3)						
(4)						
(5)						
(6)						
(7)						
(8)						
(9)						
(10) Total after-tax cash flow						

Period spans columns 0–5.

6.34 The Seymour Products Co. Inc. is currently bottling furniture polish on a machine that is fully depreciated for tax purposes. The old machine has a market value of $5,000 now, and it is expected that in ten years, because of inflation, it would have a salvage value of $6,000.

The old machine could be traded in on a new machine with an additional cash payment of $28,000. The new machine has an expected life of ten years and is expected to have a salvage value of $2,000 at that time.

The current corporate tax rate is 22 percent, and the capital gain tax rate is 10 percent. The new machine would have a tax base of $34,000 and for tax purposes could be depreciated over a life of ten years. Straight-line depreciation will be used.

It is expected that future demand for the product will stay steady at 10,000 units per year. Unit costs with the old and new machines would be as follows.

	Unit Costs	
	Old	New
Labor, direct	$0.70	$0.40
Labor, indirect	0.15	0.05
Raw materials	.30	.30
Fixed overhead	.15	.25

Fixed overheads are allocations from other departments and do not include depreciation of the equipment.

With either machine, unit revenues would be $1.25 per unit for the entire ten-year period. The appropriate after-tax cost of money for this company is 9 percent.

What action would you recommend to the management of this company? Justify your recommendation by calculating an appropriate measure of the benefits to be derived from each of the alternatives that you consider.

6.35   The XYZ Company has an investment that costs $6,000 and has a life of three years. The tax rate is .46. The asset will earn $10,000 the first year, $9,000 the second, and $7,000 the third. There are $5,500 of out-of-pocket expense per year. Working capital will be $1,000, then $1,600, then zero. The $1,600 of working capital will be worth $400 on termination. The time discount rate is 10 percent. Using the optimum method of depreciation, the present value of the depreciation per dollar of asset is .855427, and, with a depreciable cost of $6,000, the present value of depreciation is $5,133. The format shown in the box on page 163 should be used to evaluate the investment.

6.36   There is a marginal tax rate of .4 and an after-tax time-value factor is .06. Assume there are no other uses for the plant or equipment and that their book value for taxes is $12,000,000. The annual out-of-pocket costs of making the product are $300,000. The annual costs of buying are $400,000.

If retained, the plant and equipment will be depreciated over 20 years, using the straight-line method of depreciation.

Should the product be made or bought?

6.37   The Packaging Company has developed a new product. While the prospects look good, there are considerable production risks and, all things being equal, it would prefer to build a pilot plant to test the production process and then build the production plant. The following cash flows have been projected.

Time 0	Time 1	Time 2	Time 3	Time 4
−$4,000,000	+$100,000	+$1,000,000	−$25,000,000	+$5,000,000

Worksheet for Problem 6.35

	Period 1	Period 2	Period 3
Revenues or savings (cash and receivables)			
Out-of-pocket expenses	——	——	——
Income before taxes			
Taxes (.46)	$——	$——	——
Income after taxes	$——	$——	——
Plus: Net working capital decrease Less: Net working capital increase	——	——	——
Cash flow	$——	$——	——
Present value factors			
Present values	══	══	══

Total present value of savings	$——
Cost of investment	
Less:	——
PV of dep. times	
Tax rate (.46)	——
Net cost	——
Net present value	——

Problem 6.37 (*continued*).

Assume that the $5,000,000 of benefits will continue for perpetuity, the $4,000,000 plant will be abandoned at time 3, and the firm uses a 10 percent discount rate. It has a requirement that investments have a payback period of five years or less.

If the pilot plant is bypassed, the outlay of $25,000,000 and benefits of $5,000,000 per year will take place (starting in year 1).

What do you recommend?

6.38   Assume that the tax law says that you can expense the cost of equipment for tax purposes when the asset is acquired. The tax rate is .34. The ABC Company has the opportunity to invest in a piece of equipment that costs $299,060 and will earn $100,000 per year for five years.

a. Compute the before-tax internal rate of return.

b. Compute the after-tax internal rate of return.

c. Compute the after-tax internal rate of return if the tax rate is .70.

REFERENCES

Ang, James S., Jess H. Chua, and Ronald Sellers, "Generating Cash Flow Estimates: An Actual Study Using the Delphi Technique," *Financial Management*, Spring 1979, pp. 64–67.

Angell, R. J., and T. R. Wingler, "A Note on Expensing Versus Depreciating Under the Accelerated Cost Recovery System," *Financial Management*, Winter 1982, pp. 34–35.

Beardsley, G., and E. Mansfield, "A Note on the Accuracy of Industrial Forecasts of the Profitability of New Products and Processes," *Journal of Business*, 1978, pp. 127–135.

Brealey, R., and S. Myers, *Principals of Corporate Finance* (New York: McGraw-Hill, 1984).

Brown, K. C., "A Note on the Apparent Bias of Net Revenue Estimates for Capital Investment Projects," *Journal of Finance*, September 1974, pp. 1215–1227.

——, "The Rate of Return of Selected Investment Projects," *Journal of Finance*, September 1978, pp. 1250–1253.

Cooper, I., and Julian R. Franks, "The Interaction of Financing and Investment Decisions When the Firm Has Unused Tax Credits," *The Journal of Finance*, May 1983, pp. 571–583.

Doenges, R. Conrad, "The 'Reinvestment Problem' in a Practical Perspective," *Financial Management*, Spring 1972, pp. 85–91.

Finnerty, J. D., *Corporation Financial Analysis* (New York: McGraw-Hill, 1986).

Hobbs, J. B., "How to Select the Optimal Tax Recovery Method for Depreciable Property," *The Journal of Taxation*, July 1983, pp. 48–52.

Maloney, K. J., and T. I. Selling, "Simplifying Tax Simplication: An Analysis of Its Impact on the Profitability of Capital Investment," *Financial Management*, Summer 1985, pp. 33–43.

Marsh, P. R., and R. A. Brealey, "The Use of Imperfect Forecasts in Capital Investment Decisions," *Proceedings of the European Finance Association 1975* (Amsterdam: North Holland Publishing Company, 1975).

McCarty, D. E., and W. R. McDaniel, "A Note on Expensing Versus Depreciating Under the Accelerated Cost Recovery System: Comment," *Financial Management*, Summer 1983, pp. 37–39.

Miller, E. M., "Uncertainty Induced Bias in Capital Budgeting," *Financial Management*, Autumn 1978, pp. 12–18.

Smidt, S., "A Bayesian Analysis of Project Selection and of Post-Audit Evaluations," *Journal of Finance*, June 1979, pp. 675–688.

Statman, M., and T. T. Tyebjee, "Optimistic Capital Budgeting Forecasts: An Experiment," *Financial Management*, Autumn 1985, pp. 27–33.

Tull, D. S., "The Relationship of Actual and Predicted Sales and Profits in New-Product Introductions," *Journal of Business*, July 1967, pp. 233–250.

Zhu, Yu, and Irwin Friend, "The Effects of Different Taxes on Risky and Riskfree Investment and on the Cost of Capital," *The Journal of Finance*, March 1986, pp. 53–66.

PART II

Capital Budgeting Applications and Some Operational Problems

Reporter: "Coach, what are you going to do to raise your winning percentage above 50 percent?"

Coach with record of five wins and five losses in the past year: "Win one or more games more than last year."
Anonymous

This part of the book deals with applications of capital budgeting techniques to break-even analysis, make or buy decisions (Chapter 7), and selected problems in application of discounted cash flow techniques. Also, in this section we apply the more basic capital budgeting tools to types of decisions that are more specialized than those in the first chapters.

One issue that has concerned managers is the situation that occurs when there are projects that require more capital than is available. This capital-rationing problem is discussed in Chapter 8. Chapter 9 discusses the problems of making capital budgeting decisions when there is inflation. Chapter 10 relates the capital budgeting decision and the problem of measuring performance after the investment has begun operations. Chapter 11 deals with buy versus lease, a specialized, but common, decision.

Chapters 12 through 14 stretch one's imagination in the area of investment decisions (investment timing, fluctuating rates of output, and using additional information). Chapter 15 acknowledges that complexities are introduced when a company makes investments in a foreign country. Chapter 16 considers the special problems that arise when a government attempts to evaluate investments. In Chapter 17 we attempt to outline a reasonable approach to applying the theories and techniques of the previous chapters.

CHAPTER 7

Annual Equivalent Costs and Replacement Decisions

What is usually called a reasonable wage, or a reasonable profit, proves on investigation to be not so much "reasonable" as "usual," to be in fact the wage or profit determined by free competition under the prevailing conditions of time and place.

Knut Wicksell, Lecture on Political Economy, Vol. 1 (London: George Routledge and Sons, 1946), p. 51.

Annual Equivalent Cost

Investments tend to involve large expenditures that benefit many time periods and to have lives that are longer or shorter than the time period for which the decision is being made. In these situations we may find it useful to compute the annual equivalent cost of utilizing a long-lived asset. This concept has a large number of potential uses, including computing the cost of making a product and solving the decision problem when different alternatives or components have different lives.

Consider an investment that has an expected life of 20 years and that costs $2 million. It is easy to divide the $2 million by 20 and obtain an annual cost of $100,000 per year. The difficulty is that this cost computation leaves out the capital cost (the interest factor) and is an incomplete calculation.

Assume there is an investment outlay of $2,000,000 and that the investment has a life of 20 years. We would like to replace the $2,000,000 outlay with a series of annual costs that have a present value of $2,000,000 and thus are economically equivalent. Let us assume that the firm has a 10 percent time value of money. Define R to be the annual equivalent cost of the initial outlay. Then,

$$B(20, .10)R = \$2,000,000$$

$$8.5136R = \$2,000,000$$

$$R = \$234,918$$

The firm would be indifferent between the immediate outlay of $2,000,000 and an annual outlay of $234,918 occurring at the end of each time period. We would say that the annual equivalent cost is $234,918, where the cost is measured at the end of each of 20 time periods. Remember that if we had divided the cost by the 20 years of life, we would have obtained an annual cost of $100,000. The equivalent annual cost is about 2.35 times as large as the incorrect calculation that omits the interest cost.

Make or Buy Decisions

As an example of the use of the annual equivalent cost concept, consider a make or buy decision. The CBD Corporation requires 10,000 units per year of a metal part used in several of its major products. Demand for the part will remain at this level for the next 20 years. CBD has been purchasing the part from a reliable outside supplier at a cost of $20 per unit. The purchasing manager has proposed that the company make the product itself at a saving of $5 per unit and has justified the recommendation with the following data.

	Per Unit	Per Year
Cost of making		
Labor and material	$ 5.00	$ 50,000
Depreciation expense	10.00	100,000
Total	$15.00	$150,000
Cost of buying	$20.00	$200,000

The depreciation expense results from the acquisition of a specialized machine at a cost of $2,000,000 that will be needed if CBD is to make the part itself. The machine has no other applications and would have a life of 20 years. CBD Corporation has a long-term credit arrangement with an insurance company under which it could borrow the $2,000,000 needed to acquire the machine at an interest cost of 10 percent per year. If CBD borrows, it can arrange whatever repayment terms it wishes for the loan. Or if CBD has available excess funds, those funds could be applied to a partial repayment of existing loans under this agreement, thereby saving interest of 10 percent per year, or the funds could be used for capital outlays earning 10 percent. The cost of funds is 10 percent.

The purchasing manager's analysis of the cost of making is incomplete, in that it fails to consider the time value of money. We will assume that the labor and material expense will be incurred at the end of each year so that their present value will be less than the eventual outlay. But the payment for the machine is made at the start, so that the cost is $2,000,000. The present value of making 10,000 units per year is $2,425,680, and the present value of the cost of buying is only $1,702,720.

	Outlays	Present Value Factors	Present Values
Cost of making			
Labor and material	$ 50,000	8.5136	$ 425,680
Equipment cost	2,000,000	1.0000	2,000,000
Total			$2,425,680
Cost of buying	$ 200,000	8.5136	$1,702,720

While the foregoing analysis is correct, it may not be meaningful to executives who are not familiar with present value calculations. Additionally, the present value calculation does not provide a convenient means of evaluating the savings from buying on a per-unit basis.

An alternative approach is to present the analysis in terms of annual equivalent costs. With this approach, the annual equivalent cost per unit can be obtained by dividing the total annual equivalent cost by the number of units expected to be produced per year. The resulting annual equivalent cost per unit will be fully comparable to the $20 cost per unit of buying. The analysis might be presented as follows.

	Per Unit	Per Year
Cost of making		
Labor and material	$ 5.00	$ 50,000
Equipment ($2,000,000/8.5136)	23.49	234,918
Total	$28.49	$284,918
Cost of buying	$20.00	$200,000

The annual equivalent cost of the equipment can be explained as the annual payment that would be required to amortize a $2,000,000 loan at 10 percent with 20 equal annual payments. Or the $234,918 can be interpreted as the annual amount by which future debt service payments could have been reduced over the next 20 years if the $2,000,000 had been paid to the equipment supplier at the time of acquistion.

Instead of assuming that the annual expenditure for the parts takes place at the end of the period, we could assume that the expenditure takes place at the beginning of the period. We would then have for the annual equivalent cost.

$$[1 + B(19, .10)]R = \$2,000,000$$

$$9.3649R = \$2,000,000$$

$$R = \$213,563$$

A third possibility is to assume continuous outlays for the parts. For this purpose, we must use continuous discounting. If the discrete interest rate is $r = .10$, compounded annually, the corresponding equivalent continuous interest rate j can be found from the following equality.

$$1 + r = e^j$$

Taking the natural logarithm of both sides (using a computer or calculator), we find for $r = .10$ that $j = .0953$. A continuous interest rate of .0953 gives the same present value as the discrete rate of .10 used with $(1 + r)^{-n}$. With continuous discounting, we then have an annual cost of \$223,893.

$$R\left(\frac{1 - e^{-20j}}{j}\right) = \$2,000,000$$

$$R\left(\frac{1 - .1487}{.0953}\right) = \$2,000,000$$

$$R = \frac{\$2,000,000}{8.9328} = \$223,893$$

One important application of annual equivalent costs occurs in situations where mutually exclusive alternatives have different lives. We shall define this to be a problem of comparability of life.

Comparability

A group of investments will be said to be comparable and mutually exclusive if the profitability of subsequent investment possibilities will be the same, regardless of which investment is accepted or if all are rejected, but only one investment of the group can be accepted. Investment alternatives should be combined into groups that are both mutually exclusive and comparable before a final decision is made.

For example, a new plant could be heated by using forced hot air or steam. These are mutually exclusive alternatives. They are not comparable, however, if an air-conditioning system will be installed at some time in the future. The air-conditioning system would cost less to install in a building already equipped with air vents, and the present value of this difference in expected costs should be taken into account when choosing the heating system. Including the installation costs of the air-conditioning system will make the two alternatives comparable.

The importance of having mutually exclusive investments comparable is a matter of degree. In choosing a heating system for a new plant, the importance of the fact that future installation of air conditioning would be more expensive with steam heating will depend on the likelihood that air conditioning will eventually be required, the lapse of time until it may be required, the extent of the extra installation costs, and so on. In deciding whether a group of mutually exclusive alternatives is sufficiently comparable for practical purposes, one must apply a reasonable approach.

Mutually Exclusive Alternatives with Different Lives

Must mutually exclusive investment alternatives have the same lives in order to be comparable? The answer is no. In some instances, investment alternatives with different lives will be comparable; in other instances, equal future time periods are necessary to achieve comparability.

An example of comparable mutually exclusive alternatives not having the same life occurs in connection with deciding how to exploit a new patented product. One alternative is to sell the patent rights to another firm. This results in a single lump-sum payment. The patent may also be exploited by manufacturing and selling the product.

In this example the two choices are comparable, although the expected cash proceeds from one would extend only one year and from the second, for a longer period of time. The two alternatives should be compared using the net present value of each over its own life. For example, if selling the patent rights would generate immediate cash proceeds of $2 million and manufacturing and selling the product would produce cash flows having a net present value of $1.5 million over a 12-year period, the immediate sale is more desirable. We are assuming that at the expiration of life of each asset, the firm will invest in assets that earn the time value of money.

When mutually exclusive investments have unequal lives and there is a necessity to make the alternatives comparable, we have a choice of assumptions that we can make.

1. We can assume that the firm will reinvest in assets of exactly the same characteristics as those currently being used.
2. We can make specific assumptions about the reinvestment opportunities that will become available in the future.

The present value method will lead to a correct decision with both assumptions as long as the facts of the decision are consistent with the method chosen.

In theory, the second alternative is both the preferred and the easier one to describe. While it is easy in theory, however, it is difficult to implement in practice because it requires a great deal of forecasting about the future.

As an example, suppose that there are two mutually exclusive investments, A and B, with the following characteristics.

		Cash Flows for Period		
Investment	0	1	2	3
A	−$10,000	$12,000		
B	−10,000	5,000	$5,000	$5,000

A and B may be different types of equipment that perform the same task, with A having a life of one year and B, a life of three years. With a cost of money of 10 percent, the net present values of the cash flows of A and B are as follows.

Investment	Net Present Value of Cash Flows
A	$ 909
B	2,434

Investment B would seem to be the more desirable investment; however, this analysis is incomplete if we assume that after one year the equipment of type A (or similar equipment) will again be purchased. Where it is assumed that investment A will be repeated at the beginning of periods 2 and 3 (assumption 1), the following cash flows would occur for investment A.

		Period		
Investment	0	1	2	3
A	−$10,000	−$10,000	−$10,000	
		12,000	12,000	$12,000
Total	−$10,000	$ 2,000	$ 2,000	$12,000

The present value of the cash flows as now presented is $2,488 for investment A; thus, A is marginally more desirable than B. When the mutually exclusive investments have unequal lives, we may want to take into consideration the possibility of reinvesting in a similar type of equipment. If we choose assumption 2, we have to forecast the nature of the equipment available after one period and after two periods for investment A.

In most situations, the lowest common multiple of the lives of the two investments results in a length of time longer than the life of the longest-lived alternative. For example, if there are two types of equipment, one of which has a life of 3 years and the other of 8 years, the lowest common multiple of lives is 24 years. In a situation such as this, the equivalent cost per year, the cost for perpetuity, or the present value of the costs for 24 years can be computed. The equipment with the lowest cost would be the most desirable alternative. The two methods of computation being discussed will lead to the same decision. We are assuming there are no changes in the cost of the equipment through time.

EXAMPLE 7.1

Assume that two pieces of equipment have the following characteristics.

Equipment	Expected Life (Years)	Initial Cost	Operating Cost per Year
X	3	$10,000	$2,000
Y	8	30,000	1,500

This problem can be solved by taking the lowest common multiple of 8 and 3, 24 years, and by computing the costs for a 24-year period.

Annual Equivalent Cost

An alternative procedure for solving Example 7.1 is to compute the annual equivalent cost of an outlay of $10,000 every 3 years, and the annual equivalent cost of an outlay of $30,000 every 8 years.

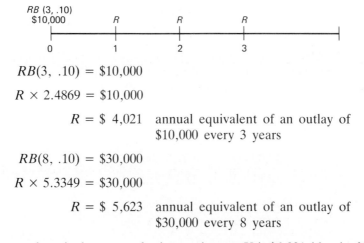

$$RB(3, .10) = \$10,000$$

$$R \times 2.4869 = \$10,000$$

$$R = \$\ 4,021 \quad \text{annual equivalent of an outlay of } \$10,000 \text{ every 3 years}$$

$$RB(8, .10) = \$30,000$$

$$R \times 5.3349 = \$30,000$$

$$R = \$\ 5,623 \quad \text{annual equivalent of an outlay of } \$30,000 \text{ every 8 years}$$

The annual equivalent cost of using equipment X is $6,021 (that is, $2,000 + $4,021), and the annual equivalent cost of using equipment Y is $7,123 (that is, $1,500 + $5,623). On the basis of annual equivalent costs, X is the more desirable equipment.

The comparison between the annual equivalent costs of equipment X and equipment Y will be valid only if both annual equivalents are expressed in the same price level. Adjusting for inflation is the topic of Chapter 9. Briefly, the annual equivalents shown in the example will be at the same price level if the discount rate used to compute the annual equivalents is a real discount rate.

To find the present value of the cost of using each type of equipment for 24 years, we multiply the annual equivalent cost for each type of equipment by the annuity factor for 24 years. Since $B(24, .10) = 8,9847$, the present values are as follows:

$$X: \$6,021 \times 8.9847 = \$54,097$$
$$Y: \$7,123 \times 8.9847 = \$63,998$$

Since both annual equivalent costs are multiplied by the same annuity factor, the relative merits of the two alternatives are not changed if we compare their present values instead of their annual equivalent costs. X remains more desirable than Y.

To find the cost of using the equipment forever, we multiply the equivalent cost per year by the present value of a perpetuity. The general formula for the present value of a perpetuity of $1 a period is

$$\text{Present value of a perpetuity} = \frac{1}{r}$$

where r is the appropriate rate of interest.

Since r is equal to .10, the factor in this example is 10. The present value of using equipment X forever is $10 \times \$6,021$, or $60,210. The present value of using Y is $71,230.

Components of Unequal Lives

An investment alternative (possibly one of several mutually exclusive investments) may be made up of several components of unequal lives. For example, we may have a building with a life of 50 years costing $5 million, a furnace with a life of 25 years costing $4 million (exclusive of lining), and a furnace lining costing $1 million with a life of 4 years. With a time value of money of .05, the annual equivalent cost for each of the first 4 years of operation is

$$\frac{\$5,000,000}{B(50, .05)} = \frac{\$5,000,000}{18.25593} = \$273,884 \quad \text{cost of building}$$

$$\frac{\$4,000,000}{B(25, .05)} = \frac{\$4,000,000}{14.09394} = \$283,810 \quad \text{cost of furnace}$$

$$\frac{\$1,000,000}{B(4, .05)} = \frac{\$1,000,000}{3.54595} = \underline{\$282,012} \quad \text{cost of furnace lining}$$

$$\text{Total annual equivalent cost} = \$839,705$$

The expression $1/B(n, r)$ is called a capital recovery factor. When taxes are not a consideration, a simple rule for converting from the initial cost of an item of capital equipment to the corresponding annual equivalent cost is to multiply the initial cost of the equipment by the corresponding capital recovery factor. When this procedure is used to find the annual equivalent cost of a collection of equipment with varying lives, there is the implicit assumption that each item of equipment will be replaced at the end of its useful life by another item having the same annual equivalent cost. This assumption would be satisfied if each item of equipment were replaced by another having the same cost and the same life. If we are summing the annual equivalent costs of several facilities, as illustrated above, the annual equivalent must be in dollars of the same price level. To accomplish this, the discount rate used to select the capital recovery factor must be a real discount rate. (Refer to Chapter 9, in which we consider inflation, for a more complete discussion.)

Cost of Excess Capacity

Assume that the ABC Chemical Corporation has extra boiler capacity and is considering the addition of a new product that will take one half of the extra capacity. How is the cost of the boiler brought into the analysis? The quick, easy answer is to say there is no relevant boiler cost, since the cost is a sunk cost. Unfortunately, this conclusion may not be correct. Add the information that undertaking the new product and using one half of the excess capacity moves up the expected date of purchase of a new utility system from five to three years in the future. This acceleration of future purchase has costs, and these costs are part of the new product decision.

Assume that the expected cost of the boiler acquisition is $2.595 million, and it has an estimated life of 15 years. With a cost of money of .05, the annual equivalent cost per year of use is

$$\frac{\$2,595,000}{B(15, .05)} = \frac{\$2,595,000}{10.38} = \$250,000$$

Without the new product, years 4 and 5 will not have the cost of a new boiler. With the new product, there is an additional equivalent cost of $250,000 for years 4 and 5.

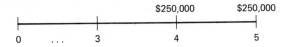

The present value of the additional costs at time 0 is $401,550.

$$.8227 \times \$250,000 = \$205,675$$
$$.7835 \times \$250,000 = \ \ 195,875$$
$$\text{Present value} = \$401,550$$

An advocate for the new product might argue that the cost should be less because the degree of utilization of the new boiler during the first two years of its use will be very low, and there will not be any wear and tear. If we assume no wear and tear (also no obsolescence), there would only be the interest cost of $129,750 (.05 of $2,595,000) occurring four and five years in the future. Just taking interest into account gives a cost of approximately $208,404 present value.

$$.8227 \times \$129,750 = \$106,745$$
$$.7835 \times \$129,750 = \underline{101,659}$$
$$\text{Present value} = \$208,404$$

Generally, some decrease in value (that is, depreciation) should be recognized, however. Thus, the present value of the cost of adding the product is not exactly defined. One estimate is $401,550, but it could be $208,404 if we assume that the life of the new equipment is not shortened or maintenance increased by the early purchase. Including either of these estimates is better than assuming that there is no cost associated with using the excess capacity.

We may want to perform an analysis in which we do not include the capacity cost but rather consider abandoning the product when capacity is reached and it is time to add new facilities. This possibility should be checked out, but generally it is appropriate to assume that once the product is added, it will be produced in the future. This will tend to occur because of the momentum principle (it is difficult for a firm to change directions) and because, after the costs of getting a product under way have been incurred, there is a good chance that if the original forecasts are realized, an economic analysis would indicate the desirability of continuing the sale of the product and taking advantage of the goodwill that was created.

The Replacement Decision

A special classification of investment decisions involves the replacement of currently owned assets. One method is to compute the absolute cash flow of each alternative. A second method is to compute the savings resulting from using the new asset instead of old asset. These savings are then discounted back to the present and equated to the cost of the asset in order to find the internal rate of return, or the net present value of the savings.

One of the problems in this type of analysis is the treatment of depreciation. The book depreciation of the new asset and the old should be excluded. The cost of the new asset is already taken into consideration by treating it as an outlay at the time of purchase. The book depreciation of the old asset is not relevant, because it is a sunk cost and has no real economic significance. The expense of utilizing the old asset would be recognized in the accounts whether the asset is replaced or not. Any decrease in salvage value of the old asset is relevant and should be taken into consideration. Also, any tax basis of the old asset is relevant, as are tax shields from depreciation expense.

EXAMPLE 7.2

The time value of money is 10 percent. If the net present value is positive using 10 percent or if the internal rate of return from replacement is greater than 10 percent, the asset should be replaced.

The following facts are available.

	Old Asset	New Asset
Cost new	$100,000	$ 70,000
Book value	60,000	—
Estimated remaining useful life (with zero salvage now and at the end of 10 years)	10 years	10 years
Costs per year (including labor, power, maintenance, and so on from replacement)	$200,000	$190,000

Should the asset be replaced? Assume zero taxes.

The present value of the cost for ten years of not replacing is

$$\text{PV of cost} = \$200,000B\ (10,\ .10) = \$200,000\ (6.1446) = \$1,229,000$$

The cost of replacing is

$$\text{PV of cost} = \$190,000B\ (10,\ .10) + \$70,000$$
$$= \$1,167,000 + \$70,000$$
$$= \$1,237,000$$

The cost of not replacing is somewhat smaller than the cost of replacing. The cost and the book value of the old asset do not enter the analysis.

Instead of computing the absolute cash flows and their present value, we can compute the present value of the net savings.

$$\text{Advantage of replacing} = \$10,000B\ (10,\ .10) - \$70,000$$
$$= \$61,447 - \$70,000 = -\$8,553$$

Again, replacing is not desirable.

Now assume that the *new asset* will have a salvage value equal to $5,000 at the end of ten years. The salvage of the new asset may be considered to *increase the cash flows* of the last year.

If the *old asset* has an expected *salvage value* today of $20,000 (and no value ten years hence), then the net cost of replacing the old asset will not be $70,000 but $50,000. This amount is obtained by subtracting the value of the salvage of the old asset, $20,000, from the cost of the new asset, $70,000. If the old asset has expected salvage value at the end of the ten years, then we should decrease the savings of the last year (because if the equipment is replaced, there will be no salvage of the old equipment in the tenth year) by the amounts of the salvage expected in the tenth year.

EXAMPLE 7.3

Assume that the savings are $10,000 a year and that the initial cost of the new equipment is $70,000. The following facts also apply.

Salvage now of the old	$20,000
Salvage in ten years of the old	1,000
Salvage in ten years of the new	5,000

The cash flows, assuming we replace now, are as shown.

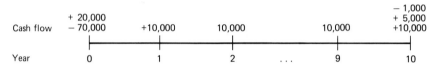

The $1,000 is subtracted in year 10 because the salvage of the old equipment is being taken now and will not be taken in year 10. By retiring the old now, we are increasing the present cash flow by $20,000 and decreasing the flow in year 10 by $1,000.

We now have the following cash flows.

Time	Continue Old Asset	Replace with New Asset	Advantage of New
0		+$20,000 salvage of old − 70,000	+$20,000 − 70,000
1–10	−200,000	−190,000	+ 10,000
10	+ 1,000	+ 5,000 salvage of new	+ 4,000

The relative net present value of replacing is

$$\text{Advantage of new} = -\$50{,}000 + \$10{,}000B\,(10, .10) + \$4{,}000\,(1.10)^{-10}$$
$$= -\$50{,}000 + \$61{,}446 + \$1{,}542$$
$$= \$12{,}988$$

The net present value is positive, and the investment (the replacement) should be undertaken.

The foregoing solution assumes away a very interesting problem. How do we know that the new equipment will have a life of ten years? The life of the new equipment can be determined if we make assumptions relative to the expected salvage of each year, the repair costs of each year, and the type of equipment likely to be encountered in the future. Assuming that these events can be expressed in mathematical formulas, a mathematical solution can be derived.

Replacement Chains

Suppose that a real estate company is considering whether to remodel a motel and continue operating it for an additional ten years or to raze it and build a new motel that would have an economic life of twenty years.

If the alternatives were comparable, we would compare the present value of expected cash outlays and proceeds from the two unequal-lived streams. In this instance, however, the two investments are not comparable. If the company chooses to remodel the existing motel now and scrap it after ten years, the company will then have the options of selling the land, building a new motel, or using the land in some other way. These possibilities must be taken into account in making the present decision.

One possibility is to convert the two investments into annual equivalent cash flows. Suppose that the company has a cost of money of 10 percent and that remodeling the old motel would produce a net present value at 10 percent of $100,000 during the next ten years. To convert this into annual equivalent cash flows, we would find the annual amount for ten years that has a present value of $100,000. Similarly, if the expected net present value from building a new motel is $125,000, we would find the twenty-year annuity that has a present value of $125,000. At 10 percent, the annual equivalent payments are $16,274 and $14,682. With this system, the alternative having the larger annual equivalent cash flow is more favorable. See Table 7.1.

Note that, by using net present value, building a new motel is favored; by using annual equivalent returns, remodeling the present is better. Using net present value, we ignore any profits that could result from using the land during years 11 through 20, when the present motel will be torn down if it is remodeled now. This creates a bias toward the alternative of building a new motel now. On the other hand, by converting to annual equivalent returns, we assume that an investment as profitable as remodeling the current motel will reappear ten years from now. Another possible assumption would be that ten years from now it will be possible to build a new motel that would be as profitable and long-lived as the new motel to be built now. Although it may turn out, upon investigation in a particular case, that this assumption is reasonable, we cannot assume that this will be the case.

TABLE 7.1 Comparison of Present Value and Annual Equivalents for Motel Example

Alternatives	Horizon Life	Present Value Over Horizon	Annual Equivalent Return Over Horizon
Remodel	10	$100,000	$16,274
Build new	20	125,000	14,682

If we considered ourselves sufficiently clairvoyant, we might attempt to estimate the cost of building a new motel ten years from now and also the cash proceeds that would be generated by operating this new motel. Even this would not solve the problem if this new motel is expected to last longer than an additional ten years, because the two alternatives would not then be comparable.

Sometimes a practical solution is found by putting an upper or lower limit on the value of potential future opportunities. For example, in the motel problem one can safely estimate that, if the motel is remodeled now, in ten years there will be a potential cash flow at least equal to the value of the land at that time. It may turn out that even an optimistic estimate of the value of the land will not be sufficient to make the alternative of remodeling the old motel more attractive than the prospect of constructing a new motel. But the values of the land at times ten and twenty must be considered to obtain a correct solution.

Public Utilities and Annual Cost

The annual cost of using long-lived assets is important to a public utility, since it is allowed to recover its costs as well as a return on the investment. Just how the utility is allowed to allocate the cost of assets serving more than one year affects groups of consumers in different ways.

Assume an asset costing $1,000,000 has a life of two years. If the utility assigns $500,000 of depreciation expense to each year (straight-line depreciation) and it is allowed to earn .10 on the investment, we have the situation shown in Table 7.2. Note that the consumers in year 1 pay more than the consumers in year 3.

To equalize the annual cost to the consumers, we will determine an annual equivalent cost (AEC).

$$\text{AEC} = \frac{1,000,000}{B\,(2,\,.10)} = \frac{1,000,000}{1.73554} = \$576,190$$

Table 7.3 shows the new situation with the annual cost to consumers now a constant $576,190.

We split the AEC into a depreciation expense component and an allowed return component, where the allowed return is .10 of the book investment. The

TABLE 7.2 Straight-Line Depreciation

Year	Investment	Depreciation Expense	Allowed Return	Total Allowed Revenue
1	$1,000,000	$500,000	$100,000	$600,000
2	500,000	500,000	50,000	550,000

TABLE 7.3   Annual Equivalent Cost

Year	Investment	Depreciation Expense	Allowed Return	Total Allowed Revenue
1	$1,000,000	$476,191	$100,000	$576,191
2	523,809	523,809	52,381	576,190

depreciation expense is equal to the $576,190 minus the amount of income. Equivalently, the depreciation expense is equal to the change in value of the asset. We have

Time	Value of Investment	Value of Investment	Depreciation: Change in Value
0	$\dfrac{576,190}{1.10} + \dfrac{576,190}{(1.10)^2} =$	$1,000,000	
1	$\dfrac{576,190}{1.10} =$	523,809	$476,191
2	0	0	523,809

But now let us assume there is .06 inflation, and it has been decided that the real cost to consumers should be constant. Let R be the real cost per year. Now we want

$$\frac{R}{1.10} + \frac{1.06R}{(1.10)^2} = 1,000,000$$

$$1.10R + 1.06R = 1,210,000$$

$$R = \$560,185$$

and

$$1.06R = \$593,796$$

Table 7.4 shows the new situation when the amount charged to consumers is constant in real terms but increases in terms of nominal dollars.

TABLE 7.4   Constant Real Costs to Consumers

Year	Investment	Depreciation Expense	Allowed Return	Total Allowed Revenue
1	$1,000,000	$460,185	$100,000	$560,185
2	539,815	539,814	53,982	593,796

The depreciation expense for year 1 is obtained by subtracting the $100,000 of allowed return from the $560,185 of total allowed revenue. A comparable calculation is made for year 2.

Thus, for a public utility where the revenue to be earned by an asset is defined by public policy objectives, the amount of annual cost will be different than with a competitive firm where the revenue earned is only indirectly (if at all) related to the cost of an asset or the portion of the cost assigned to a specific time period.

Conclusions

Although techniques such as those we are recommending force one to make difficult estimates in the face of imperfect and incomplete information, they have the advantage of focusing attention on the important unknowns. Simpler techniques achieve their simplicity by using general assumptions about the nature of future opportunities rather than conjectures that are tailor-made to a particular situation. They save time and effort but result in a less precise analysis of the decision-making situation.

REVIEW EXAMPLE 7.1

The NSV Manufacturing Company currently manufactures a product on a machine that is fully depreciated for tax purposes and has a book value of $10,000 (it was purchased for $30,000 20 years ago). The costs of the product are as follows.

	Unit Costs
Labor, direct	$ 4.00
Labor, variable indirect	2.00
Other variable overhead	1.50
Fixed overhead	2.50
	$10.00

In the past year 10,000 units were produced and sold for $18 per unit. It is expected that, with suitable repairs, the old machine can be used indefinitely. The repairs are expected to average $25,000 per year.

An equipment manufacturer has offered to accept the old machine as a tradein for a new version. The new machine would cost $60,000 after allowing $15,000 for the old equipment. The projected costs associated with the new machine are as follows.

Labor, direct	$2.00
Labor, variable indirect	3.00
Other variable overhead	1.00
Fixed overhead	3.25
	$9.25

The fixed overhead costs are allocations from other departments plus the depreciation of the equipment. The old machine could not be sold on the open market. The new machine has an expected life of 10 years and no expected salvage at that time. The current corporate income tax rate is .40. For tax purposes, the cost of the new machine may be depreciated in 10 years. The appropriate after-tax time discount rate for this company is .10. Assume that the present value of depreciation deductions per dollar of cost is .701. It is expected that future demand of the product will stay steady at 10,000 units per year.

a. Should the new equipment be acquired?

b. If the product can be purchased at a cost of $7.80 per unit from a reliable supplier, should it be purchased or made? Explain.

Solution

Cost of using the old:

$$PV = -.6 \ (\$75,000 + \$25,000 \ B \ (10, .10))$$
$$= -.6 \times \$100,000 \times 6.1446$$
$$= -\$369,000$$

Costs of using the new:

$$PV = -\$60,000 - .60 \ (\$60,000 \times 6.1446)$$
$$= -\$60,000 - \$221,000$$
$$= -\$281,000$$

The tax savings from the depreciation is

$$\text{Tax savings} = \$60,000 \times .4 \times .701 = \$17,000$$

$$\text{Net cost} = \$281,000 - \$17,000 = -\$264,000$$

Replace because $264,000 is less than $369,000.
The annual equivalent after-tax cost of using the new equipment is

$$R = \frac{\$264,000}{6.1446} = \$42,960 \text{ per year}$$

$$\frac{\$42,960}{10,000} = \$4.30 \text{ per unit}$$

Let X be the maximum before-tax cost per unit we would be willing to pay. The after-tax cost is $.6X$, where X is the before-tax cost.

$$\$7.80 \times .6 = \$4.68, \text{ after-tax cost of buying}$$

The after-tax cost of making is $4.30. The before-tax cost of making is

$$.6X = 4.30$$

$$X = \$7.17, \text{ before-tax cost of making}$$

We would not be willing to pay the $7.80 cost per unit to buy the product. Produce the product unless the capacity of the plant can be used on other products, in which case these other products should be considered.

PROBLEMS

7.1 The Roger Company has the choice between two different types of dies. One type costs less, but it also has a shorter life expectancy. The expected cash flows after taxes for the two different dies are as follows.

			Period		
Die	0	1	2	3	4
A	$(10,000)	$8,000	$8,000		
B	(12,000)	5,000	5,000	$5,000	$5,000

The cost of money of the firm is 10 percent.
   Choose the more desirable die. Explain.

7.2 Assume that there are two mutually exclusive investments that have the following cash flows.

	Period		Internal
Investment	0	1	Rate of Return (%)
A	$(10,000)	$12,000	20
B	(5,000)	6,100	22

Assume that either investment will require modification to the basic building structure, which will cost $1,000, and that this amount is not included in the preceding computations. The cost of money is 10 percent.
   a. Compute the actual internal rates of return of the investments.
   b. Does the additional $1,000 change the ranking of the two investments? Explain.

7.3 Consider the following two mutually exclusive investments.

| | Period | | Internal |
Investment	0	1	Rate of Return (%)
A	$ (20,000)	$ 30,000	50
B	(100,000)	130,000	30

Assuming a cost of money of .10, which investment is to be preferred?

7.4 An existing machine must be replaced. Two new models are under consideration. Both cost $15,000. Model X will generate savings of $10,000 per year and
has a life of two years. Model Y will generate savings of $18,000; it has a life of
one year. The machine will be needed for two years.

Which model should be purchased if the cost of money is .05?

7.5 Assume that two pieces of equipment have the following characteristics.

Equipment	Expected Life (Years)	Initial Cost	Operating Cost per Year
A	9	$20,000	$10,000
B	5	25,000	8,000

At a cost of money of .10, which equipment is the more desirable?

7.6 The A Corporation's computer currently has excess capacity. The controller
would like to prepare and distribute a report that would take approximately one
hour a day of the computer's time. The computer could do this task and still have
excess capacity. The annual cost of this type of computer is $1 million a year.
The discount rate is .05. The long-range planning group estimates that without
the report, the corporation would be shifting to a more powerful computer five
years from now. With the report, it estimates the shift to be four years from now.
The new computer will cost $1.5 million per year. Assume that the computer
payments take place at the end of each year.

What is your estimate of the cost of adding the report?

7.7 The New York State Utility Company is considering the construction of a new
utility plant. It has accumulated the following cost information.

	Fossil Plant (Oil and Gas)	Nuclear Plant
Initial outlay	$60,000,000	$100,000,000
Annual operating cost	15,000,000	20,000,000[a]

[a] This is the projected cost for year 1. It is expected that the operating costs of the
nuclear plant will decrease by $2,000,000 per year and level off at $10,000,000. The
expected decrease is a result of decreased fuel costs. Both plants have an expected
useful life of 50 years.

Assume a time value of money of .05 per year.
a. Which plant should be built?
b. Assume that if the nuclear plant is not built, the needed electricity can be purchased at a cost of $16 million per year. Should it be built?

7.8 Assume that the cost of the needed electricity in Problem 7.7 is $17 million.
a. Should the nuclear plant be built?
b. Compute the present value today of building (that is, completing) the nuclear plant six years from now, when the operation costs would be $10 million per year, compared to buying electricity.

7.9 The A Corporation is considering the construction of a new plant to build a component part that it is currently purchasing. It has the following information.

	Cost	Expected Life
Plant	$20,000,000	40 years
Utilities	10,000,000	20 years
Equipment	15,000,000	10 years

The operating costs are estimated at $5 million per year, assuming an output of 1 million units of product per year.

The corporation uses a discount rate of .05. It can purchase the product at a cost of $10 per unit.

Should the new plant be built (on a straight economic basis)?

7.10 A company is considering two alternative marketing strategies for a new product. Introducing the product will require an outlay of $15,000. With a low price, the product will generate cash proceeds of $10,000 per year and will have a life of two years. With a high price, the product will generate cash proceeds of $18,000 but will have a life of only one year. The cost of money for the company is .05.

Which marketing strategy should be accepted?

7.11 Compare your answers to problems 7.4 and 7.10. Are the relevant cash flows the same in both problems? If not, why?

7.12 State Electric wants to decide whether to repair or replace electric meters when they break down. A new meter costs $30 and, on the average, will operate for 12 years without repair. It costs $18 to repair a meter, and a repaired meter will, on the average, operate for 8 years before it again needs a repair. Repairs can be made repeatedly to meters because they are essentially rebuilt each time they are repaired. It costs $6 to take out and reinstall a meter. The time value of money is .05.

Should the company repair old meters or buy new meters?

7.13 Assume that an investment requires an initial outlay of $12,337 and that the revenues from the investment are $10,000 in year 1 and $5,000 in year 2. Assume that an interest rate of .05 should be used.

Using annual equivalent revenues and costs, determine whether the investment is acceptable.

7.14   The following facts apply to an investment that the ABC Company is considering:

> Plant costs $1 million with a life of 50 years.
> Equipment costs are $2 million with a life of 20 years.
> Annual fixed costs are $180,000, of which $100,000 are incremental with the decision (but excluding depreciation) and $80,000 are allocations from other departments and projects. These costs could be avoided if the product is discounted in the future.
> The net revenue contribution per unit sold is $2.
> The cost of money of the firm is .10.
> It is expected that 1 million units of product will be used per year.

How many units have to be produced and sold per year to break even? If 1 million units are produced, what will be the per-unit cost?

7.15   Assume that the plant and equipment described in problem 7.14 have been purchased. One million units of the product are needed in the coming year. These units can be purchased at a cost of $1.20 per unit from a reliable supplier. The variable manufacturing costs per unit are $.20. If the units are purchased, the plant and equipment will be shut down (this can be done with little additional cost). They have no alternative use.

Should the units be made or bought? Assume that the probability of the product being supplied on time and the quality of the product are the same whether made or bought.

7.16   If the plant in problem 7.15 requires working capital of $1.5 million (cash outlay), should the units be made or purchased?

7.17   Assume that the plant and equipment of problem 7.14 have been purchased. There is a marginal tax rate of .4 and an after-tax time value factor is .06.

Should the units be made or bought? Assume that there are no other uses for the plant or equipment and that their book value for taxes is $12 million. The annual out-of-pocket costs of making the product are $300,000. The annual costs of buying are $400,000.

If retained, the plant and equipment will be depreciated over 20 years using the straight-line method.

Should the product be made or bought?

7.18   The Bright Machine Tool Shop is considering replacement of the equipment in a section of its shop. The equipment performs a function that could be completely eliminated. A comparison of the present equipment being used with new equipment indicates that the following relative cash flows would result if the new machine were purchased instead of continuing with the old.

Period 0	Period 1
$(10,000)	$12,000

The internal rate of return of the investment is 20 percent, and the cost of money is 15 percent. The net present value of the investment is $435. Based on the positive net present value, the decision was made to replace the present equipment.

In the period of operation, the machine performed exactly as predicted, and all costs were as predicted. The absolute cash flows were as follows.

Period 0	Period 1
$(10,000)	$11,000

Comment on the investment decision made by the Bright Machine Tool Shop.

7.19 The Dotted Airline Company is considering replacement of its fleet of ten two-engined planes with five new-model jets. One jet can replace two of the present planes. The airplane company has prepared an analysis showing that each new plane will cost $343,000 and will earn cash proceeds of $100,000 per year for five years. Assume that after five years, the salvage value will be zero for both the new and old planes. The analysis was based on the load and operating characteristics of the new plane and the past experience of the airline, as well as on the number of passengers and the routes traveled, adjusted in a reasonable manner for additional passengers who will be attracted by the new planes.

The planes currently being used are considered to be safe workhorses, but they are not as glamorous as the new planes. In competition with jets, they are expected to earn net cash proceeds of only $10,000 per year per plane. There is no discernible trend of earnings. The present planes now have a zero salvage value.

The cost of money of the Dotted Airline is 10 percent. Assume that the company has access to the necessary funds.

Should the Dotted Airline purchase the new jets? Explain. What would be your recommendation if the salvage value is now $40,000 on an old plane?

7.20 A new piece of equipment being considered costs $75,816 and has a useful life of five years. It will cost $10,000 in out-of-pocket expenses per year to operate. The cost of money is .10. An alternative to the equipment is to use a labor-intensive process that would cost $38,000 per year. This $38,000 includes $15,000 of depreciation expense for the currently used machine (the machine has no other use but does have a replacement cost of $25,000). The tax rate is zero.
a. Prepare an analysis of the alternatives. What should the firm do?
b. If the equipment will make 1,000 units of product per year, what will be the cost per unit if the new equipment is purchased?

7.21 The Ithaca Manufacturing Company has excess capacity and is considering manufacturing a component part that is currently being purchased. The estimate of the cost of producing one unit of product is as follows.

Direct labor	$2.00
Material	3.00
Variable overhead	1.00
Fixed overhead (based on generally accepted accounting procedures)	2.50
	$8.50

The average increase in net working capital that will be required if the item is produced internally is $50,000.

The firm uses 100,000 of the parts per year. The unit cost of purchasing the parts is $6.05. Assume a zero tax rate.

Should the company make or buy the parts?

7.22 The XYZ Manufacturing Company is currently manufacturing its product on a machine that is fully depreciated for tax purposes and that has a book value of $10,000 (it was purchased for $30,000 20 years ago). The costs of the product are as follows.

	Unit Costs
Labor, direct	$ 4.00
Labor, indirect	2.00
Variable overhead	1.50
Fixed overhead	2.50
	$10.00

In the past year 1,000 units were produced and sold for $18 per unit. It is expected that the old machine can be used indefinitely. An equipment manufacturer has offered to accept the old machine as a trade-in for a new version. The new machine would cost $60,000 after allowing $15,000 for the old equipment. The projected costs associated with the new machine are as follows.

Labor, direct	$2.00
Labor, indirect	3.00
Variable overhead	1.00
Fixed overhead	3.25
	$9.25

The fixed overhead costs are allocations from other departments plus the depreciation of the equipment.

The old machine could be sold on the open market now for $5,000. Ten years from now it is expected to have a salvage value of $1,000. The new machine has an expected life of ten years and an expected salvage of $10,000.

The current corporate income tax rate is .40, and the capital gain tax rate is .25. Any salvage from sale will result in a capital gain at the time of retirement. (For tax purposes, the entire cost may be depreciated in ten years using straight-line depreciation.) The appropriate after-tax time discount rate for this company is .10.

It is expected that future demand of the product will stay steady at 1,000 units per year.

a. Should the equipment be acquired?

b. If the product can be purchased at a cost of $7.80 per unit from a reliable supplier, should it be purchased or made? Explain.

REFERENCES

See the references for Chapters 1–6 and 12.

CHAPTER 8

Capital Budgeting Under Capital Rationing

In practice we have tacitly agreed, as a rule, to fall back on what is, in truth, a convention. The essence of this convention—though it does not, of course, work out quite so simply—lies in assuming that the existing state of affairs will continue indefinitely, except insofar as we have specific reasons to expect a change.

> J. M. Keynes, The General Theory of Employment, Interest and Money *(New York: Harcourt, Brace & Company, 1936), p. 152.*

In the preceding chapters we concluded that, under conditions of certainty, if a firm could borrow or lend funds at a given market rate of interest, it should accept independent investments when the investments have positive net present values at this market rate of interest. In this chapter we consider situations in which the assumption that a firm can borrow or lend any quantity of funds that it desires at a given market rate of interest is not valid. There are two distinctly different situations in which this assumption may not hold.

One of these situations arises because of a decision by management either to limit arbitrarily the total amount invested or the kind of investments the firm undertakes or to set acceptance criteria that lead it to reject some investments that are advantageous when judged by market criteria. For example, instead of using the market interest rate, it might use some higher rate as a cutoff or hurdle rate.

A second situation that must be considered is when there is a difference between the market rate of interest at which the firm can borrow money and the market rate at which it can lend.

Both situations are frequently labeled *capital rationing*. To distinguish between them, we shall refer to the former situation as *internal capital rationing* and to the latter as *external capital rationing*. External capital rationing is actually the result of market imperfections or transaction costs.

Two observations should be noted. First, capital rationing in both the first and second form is present throughout the economy, but usually to a relatively minor degree, and thus may frequently not be incorporated into the analysis (although it should not be ignored without trying to estimate its impact). Second, when capital rationing is present, there is no simple solution to the internal investment decision. Two possible approaches are offered. The first possibility is to make simplifying assumptions where appropriate and to recognize that the answer obtained is an approximation. The second approach is to use mathematical techniques to develop possible solutions, following different possible investment alternatives (including all possible combinations of investments through the succeeding years). This analytical technique may lead to a sound solution to the capital-budgeting decision under capital rationing, but it is complex and requires detailed knowledge of future investment alternatives that is frequently not available.

External Capital Rationing

In this chapter the term *borrow* is used when a firm obtains capital from the market by issuing any type of security. The term *lend* is used to mean the use of funds to purchase any type of security. We specifically assume that borrowing takes place in such a way that the borrowing firm's capital structure (the relative proportion of the various kinds of securities it has issued) is not changed. Thus, borrowing would normally involve issuing both debt and equity securities. Similarly, we assume that lending means acquiring a portfolio of securities that has approximately the same average risk characteristics as the assets presently owned by the firm.

Under conditions of certainty, the term *lending* could be interpreted literally, because there is no problem of risk. Under uncertainty, we want to define lending so that the process does not change the risk characteristics of the firm's assets compared to expanding the firm's operations by investing internally. A firm is lending if it purchases the securities of other firms whose assets have the same risk characteristics as its own assets.

A firm may purchase its own securities in amounts proportional to their market value. Suppose that a firm has only equity shares outstanding, and it buys some of its own shares. The effect is very nearly the same as if it had used the same amount of cash to pay a cash dividend. It differs from lending in that it is not expected that the funds will be returned to the corporation.

If capital markets were such that a firm could lend or borrow as much money as it desired at the going rate of interest, this rate of interest would be the same for both the borrowing and lending transactions. The goal of profit maximization would then require that the firm accept all independent investments whose present values were positive, using this rate of interest. With such capital markets, the choice of investments would not be dependent on the amount of funds available to the firm, because by an appropriate combination of borrowing and lending, each firm could finance investments that had positive present values.

This theoretical situation is an ideal never encountered in practice. There will almost always be some divergence between the rates of interest at which the firm can lend surplus funds and the rates at which it can borrow funds. The size of the gap may vary for many reasons, including the effect of the underwriting costs of raising new money and the fact that there may be hidden costs or risks connected with one or another of the investments. Another reason is that money lenders may prefer firms having certain characteristics, thus driving up the cost of borrowing by firms that lack these characteristics.

If the borrowing rate and the lending rate are almost equal, little is lost by neglecting the difference and speaking of a market rate of interest. If the difference is large, it cannot be ignored in determining the investment and financial policies of the firm. This gives rise to the situation we describe as external capital rationing.

A partial solution to the capital budgeting process with external capital rationing can be described as follows: Assume that a schedule is prepared showing the total current net outlays required in period 0 for investments having a positive present value at various rates of discount. Such a schedule will show greater current outlays at lower rates of interest, because some investments whose present values are negative at high discount rates will have positive present values at low discount rates. The schedules are shown by curves $I–I$ in Figures 8.1(a), (b), and (c). We let the distance $0Q_1$ represent the quantity of internally generated funds available for investment during the current period. Three situations are possible. In Figure 8.1(a) the vertical line drawn up from point Q_1 intersects curve $I–I$ at a rate of interest higher than r_2, the borrowing rate. This indicates that some investments that would be profitable at a cost equal to the borrowing rate could not be financed from internally generated funds. It would be profitable for the firm to borrow an amount Q_1Q_2 to enable it to accept all investments that would be profitable at the borrowing rate. It would not be profitable to borrow any more than this amount, because all remaining investments have negative present values at the borrowing rate of discount.

In Figure 8.1(b) the internally generated funds currently available are more than sufficient to enable the firm to undertake all the investments that would be profitable when evaluated at the lending rate of interest. Only $0Q_2$ dollars would be invested internally. The remaining funds, Q_1Q_2, would either be invested externally by buying the securities of other organizations or used to reduce the capitalization of the firm by returning the funds to the suppliers.

A third possibility is that the firm has sufficient funds to accept all independent investments whose present values are positive when evaluated at the borrowing rate, but that the firm does not have enough funds to accept all investments whose present values are positive when evaluated at the lending rate. This is illustrated in Figure 8.1(c). Under those circumstances the firm

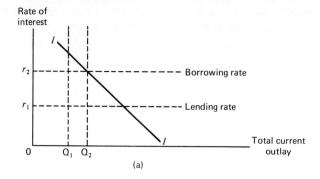

(a)

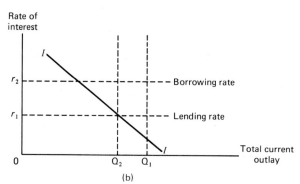

(b)

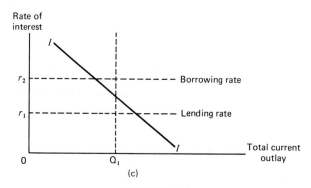

(c)

FIGURE 8.1

would neither borrow any additional funds nor lend any part of its present funds, and the proper rate of discount for investments would be lower than the borrowing rate but higher than the lending rate.

Based on this analysis, an incomplete set of rules for dealing with individual investment projects can be derived. Consider independent projects for which accept or reject decisions are appropriate. Evaluate the present value of the cash flows from the project at the borrowing rate. If the present value is positive, the project should be accepted. Projects that meet this test will be worth accepting even if money must be borrowed to finance them. If the project is not accepted by this rule, evaluate the present value of the cash flows from the project at the lending rate. If the present value is negative, the project should be rejected. A project whose present value is negative at the lending rate should be rejected even if the firm has surplus funds.

These two rules will not lead to definite decisions for all projects. There may be some independent projects whose present values are negative at the borrowing rate and positive at the lending rate. For such projects no strict rules can be given. The final decision will depend partly on the firm's financial position and partly on management's objectives.

A similar set of tests can be applied to pairs of mutually exclusive alternatives, but in this case the cash flows that should be used are the incremental cash flows. If the best of a set of mutually exclusive alternatives can be identified utilizing these two tests, it is still necessary to consider whether this best alternative should be accepted or rejected when considered as an independent investment.

Strictly speaking, these rules are applicable only to conventional cash flows. Modifications to handle cases in which the cash flow sequences alternate between outlays and proceeds are possible but are beyond the scope of this book.[1]

The analysis of this chapter assumes a capital market with a significant difference between the borrowing and lending rates. The solution suggested is only approximate, because we have not indicated what assumption is being made as to the probable lending and borrowing rates in the future and the firm's position relative to them. The appropriate interest rates in future time periods are relevant to decisions made in the present because they affect the profitability of funds reinvested at those times. Cash flows expected in each future time period should be discounted at the rate of interest that will apply in that period. If we predict future lending and borrowing rates, we can assume that the appropriate rate of discount for each future period will lie somewhere between these upper and lower limits. Occasionally, a firm will have some basis for predicting whether in a given future year it is more likely to be operating somewhere near its borrowing rate or near its lending rate. If a firm, even in a growing industry, is faced with a temporary excess of capacity, it may feel safe in predicting that for the next few years it will have more internally generated funds than it needs for the available profitable investment alternatives. This can be reflected by using a rate of discount for these years that is relatively close to the lending rate. In other cases, the firm may anticipate product improvements that are presently in the research and development state but that are expected to be perfected within a few years. If the introduction of these innovations will require large-scale capital investments, the firm may feel confident in predicting that it

---

[1] On this point, see Gordon Pye, "Present Values for Imperfect Capital Markets," *Journal of Business*, January 1966, pp. 45–51.

will be likely to be operating relatively close to its borrowing-rate point during the years these investments are being made. See Figure 8.1(c) and assume that curve *II* has shifted upward to the right (meaning there are more profitable investments) until the situation is described by Figure 8.1(a). In this situation the borrowing rate is applicable.

Although such predictions of future cutoff rates under external capital rationing are inevitably rather crude, they serve a useful purpose if the predicted rates are in the right general direction. By using a high rate of discount for a future year in which there is likely to be a shortage of internally generated funds relative to the available investment opportunities in that year, the firm is recognizing that the opportunity cost of funds may be higher in some periods than in others. Investment proposals that release funds for use in periods when the demand is greatest will thus be preferred, all other things being equal, over investments that utilize funds in the periods of high demand. Similarly, if excess funds are likely to be available, the use of a lower discount rate will tend to lead toward the choice of investments that do not generate funds during these periods. The opportunity cost of funds during periods of excess funds is low; thus, a low rate of discount is appropriate.

If a company is in a situation of external capital rationing, it may be useful for the top management to predict the appropriate cutoff rate that will apply in future years. By this means, the investment planning in various parts of the organization can be coordinated in terms of the best available estimates of future cash needs and requirements for the company as a whole. If fluctuating cutoff rates are expected in the future, the company may wish to prepare and use present value tables that show the appropriate discount factors to be used for each future period.

EXAMPLE 8.1

Suppose a firm expects that its appropriate cutoff rate will be 5 percent for periods 1, 2, and 3 and 10 percent for periods 4 and 5. The firm is considering two mutually exclusive investment alternatives. Both require initial outlays of $100 now. Investment G will return $150 in year 3; investment H will return $200 in year 5. The present value of G's proceeds is $150 (1.05)$^{-3}$ = $150 (.8638) = $130. The present value of H's proceeds is $200 (1.05)$^{-3}(1.10)^{-2}$ = $200 (.8638) (.8264) = $200 (.7138) = $143. Investment H, with a net present value of $43, is preferred to G, with a net present value of only $30.

Internal Capital Rationing

There are two types of internal capital rationing. In the first, the firm sets a cutoff rate for investments that is higher than the firm's cost of money. In the second type, the firm decides to limit the total amount of funds committed to internal investments in a given year to some fixed sum, even though investments having positive present values at the firm's cost of money may be rejected as a result of this decision.

Consider the first kind of internal capital rationing. Suppose a firm requires that investments must have a positive present value at 15 percent, even though the firm has identified its cost of money to be 10 percent. If the same cutoff rate is maintained from year to year, the cutoff rate in future years will be known, and the firm can evaluate all investments *as if* the cost of money were 15 percent.

But, although a definite cutoff rate is available, the logic of using that rate to discount cash flows is no longer completely correct. The rate of discount used should measure the alternative uses of funds available to the firm. In the present instance, however, it indicates only that an investment of $1 now yielding less than 15 percent will not be undertaken. If next year the company has more internally generated funds than it is willing to invest following the 15 percent cutoff rule, then an extra dollar of funds that becomes available will have an opportunity cost that is less than 15 percent. How much less will depend on what use the firm makes of the "excess" cash that it will not invest internally.

Internal Capital Rationing and Dividend Policy

In the second type of internal capital rationing, the cutoff rate is not specified, but the maximum amount that will be invested is determined by top management, because it is unwilling to go to the market to obtain additional funds, even though there are desirable investments. This reluctance to go to the market may result from a wish to prevent outsiders from gaining control of the business or from a feeling that there will be a dilution of earnings if additional equity funds are raised under the given market conditions.

In these circumstances, the correct amount and selection of investments will depend on the firm's dividend policy. One possibility is that the firm will maintain (over the life of the investments) the current level of dividends, regardless of any increases in earnings that may come about because of additional investment. Assume that past investments will support the dividend; then the net cash flows generated in future periods by the investments of the current period will be available for reinvestment in the period in which they are earned. The amounts of cash available for investment will vary from period to period, as will the desirability of investments (the demand schedule for investments may shift). This situation may result in the firm rejecting internal investments with IRRs greater than the borrowing rate. For this reason, it will be very difficult to make predictions of future cutoff rates (the opportunity costs for future cash flows).

Even if the firm has an overabundance of cash, it should not invest the funds in investments with a negative net present value. Such investment would result in the reinvested dollars having less value than the dollars paid as dividends. It is unnecessary for the firm to accept investments whose IRRs are less than the IRRs of alternative opportunities available to the stockholders, because these same investments are generally available to the corporation.

Ranking of Investments

If management views a situation as being one of capital rationing, this is apt to lead to a request to the investment analyst for the ranking of independent investments. The decision for the independent investments is no longer a matter of accept or reject decisions, but management wants to know the ranking of investments so that it can choose the best set of investments.

There are many procedures that seem to give a reliable ranking of investments, but that appearance is an illusion. There is no sure proof procedure for the ranking of independence investments. The problem is that ranking implies the use of a cutoff rate above the cost of money and a rejection of investments that would be acceptable except for the rationing situation. This implies that the use of the conventional cutoff rate as a discount rate is not valid, since the opportunity cost for funds will be higher. Also, the opportunity cost of future time periods may well be different from that of the present as the capital rationing either becomes more tight or less tight.

Let us consider the use of net present value as a ranking technique. First, the net present value does not tell us how much capital had to be committed to the investment. Two small investments may well be better than one large investment, even though the large investment has a larger net present value than either of the two small investments (but not larger than their sum). Second, the net present value is the result of an assumption about the time value of money that with rationing may not be appropriate. Neither of these difficulties is bothersome in the absence of capital rationing, but with capital rationing, they eliminate present value as an effective means of ranking investments.

The internal rate of return method is intuitively appealing, but we already know that an investment with a lower internal rate of return might be more desirable than an investment with a higher internal rate of return. Figure 8.2 shows that investment B is preferred to investment A if the time-value factor being used is less than r, even though the internal rate of return of A is larger than that of B.

A third popular method of ranking investments is the index of present value (present value of benefits divided by benefit of outlays). There are several difficulties in using this technique to rank independent investments. For example, the index depends on whether an outlay decreases the numerator (is deducted from benefits) or increases the denominator (increases the outlays). Since the classification is of necessity somewhat arbitrary, this is a severe weakness. A second problem is that the technique does require the use of a rate of discount in a situation where the ultimate choice of investments and rejection of investments will determine the opportunity cost of funds. A third problem is the fact that investments come in different sizes; thus, we might not be able to undertake the mix of investments indicated by the ranking. The index of present value fails to consider effectively the size of the investment.

Recognizing that certain individuals have the audacity to pick a Miss Universe, we should be able to rank investments. And so we can, as long as the

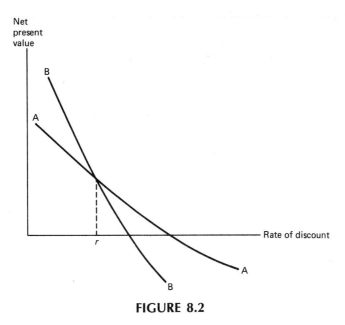

FIGURE 8.2

ranking is placed in somewhat the same perspective as the Miss Universe contest. A reasonable (not exactly correct) ranking can be obtained using either internal rate of return or index of present value. If desired, the present value of different sets of investments can be computed and an attempt made to maximize present value (but remember, the discount rate should represent the opportunity cost of funds).

In addition to these complexities, if risk considerations are also brought into the analysis, then we must conclude that the ranking of independent investments for a capital situation is truly more like choosing Miss Universe than it is an exact scientific technique.

We can safely use the net present value method to choose the best of a set of mutually exclusive investments only when the rate of discount used is an appropriate opportunity cost. As soon as we use the net present value method to rank independent investments for the purpose of choosing a cutoff rate above the cost of money (some investments with positive present values will be rejected), the rate of discount used in computing the net present values becomes the inappropriate rate to use because the true opportunity cost is higher than the rate chosen.

EXAMPLE 8.2

The time value of money of the firm has been computed to be .10. There are two independent investments, C and D, with the following characteristics.

Investment	Cash Flows for Period		Internal Rate of Return	Present Value Using .10
	0	1		
C	−$ 5,000	$10,000	1.00	$9,091 − $5,000 = $4,091
D	− 20,000	30,000	.50	$27,273 − $20,000 = $7,273

Using the internal rate of return C is ranked 1, and D is ranked 2. Using the net present values, we would choose D over C. Using the internal rate of return of the rejected investment C (1.00) as the opportunity cost, we find the present values to be

$$\text{Present value of C} = \$5,000 - \$5,000 = 0$$

$$\text{Present value of D} = \$15,000 - \$20,000 = -\$5,000$$

Now C is better than D.

If we used the internal rate of return of the last investment accepted, D (.50), we would have as present values

$$\text{Present value of C} = \$6,667 - \$5,000 = \$1,667$$

$$\text{Present value of D} = \$20,000 - \$20,000 = 0$$

With rates of interest of .50 and 1.00, we find that C is preferred to D, but with an interest rate of .10, D is preferred to C. Figure 8.3 shows that as long as

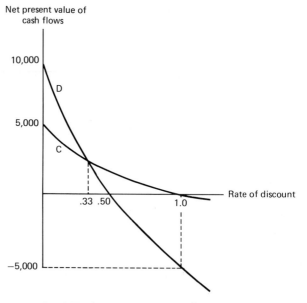

FIGURE 8.3   Two Mutually Exclusive Investments

the appropriate time value factor is less than 33 percent, the investor prefers investment D, but that if the discount factor is greater than 33 percent, investment C is preferred.

The problem becomes even more complex when we consider the opportunity costs of money for many time periods and where we have many sets of mutually exclusive investments. The choice of the best of each set will depend on the opportunity cost that is chosen.

Index of Present Value (or Profitability Index)

Some authors suggest dividing the present value of cash proceeds by the present value of the investment type of outlays to obtain an index of present value (proceeds per dollar of outlay, both expressed in terms of present value). This calculation is also called the profitability index of an investment.

The index of present value method is a variant of the present value method; its appeal lies in the fact that seemingly it can be used to rank investments. We shall attempt to show that the resulting ranking of mutually exclusive investments is frequently spurious. If our objective is limited to accept or reject decisions, the index of present value (accept all investments with an index greater than 1) will give results identical to those of the present value method.

EXAMPLE 8.3

The cost of money is 10 percent. Assume that an investment has the following cash flows.

Period 0	Period 1	Period 2
−$1,500	$1,000	$1,000

The present value of the $1,000-a-period cash proceeds is $1,736. The index is 1.16.

$$\text{Present value index} = \frac{\$1,736}{\$1,500} = 1.16$$

One rule to use with an independent investment is the following: If the index is larger than 1, accept the investment. This rule is sound. If the index is greater than 1, however, the net present value is also positive, and the computation of the present value index is unnecessary.

A second rule is this: Evaluate mutually exclusive investments by their indexes; choose the investment with the highest index. This rule may lead to the correct decision, but it may just as well lead to incorrect decisions because of two factors: scale of the investment and classification of cash flows.

EXAMPLE 8.4   Scale

Assume two mutually exclusive investments with the cash flows indicated. Which is the more desirable for a cutoff rate of 10 percent?

	Period			
Investment	0	1	2	Present Value Index
X	−$1,500	$1,000	$1,000	1.16
Y	−3,100	2,000	2,000	1.12

The index measure indicates that X is preferred to Y. A computation of present values will show that Y is better, however (a net present value of $371 for Y compared to $236 for X). The present value index is a ratio of benefits to outlay. But it fails to consider the scale of the investment in the same manner as do other ratio measures, such as return on investment and internal rate of return. This point can be seen more clearly if we look at the incremental investment consequent on moving from X to Y. We shall label that investment Y–X.

	Period			
Investment	0	1	2	Present Value Index
Y–X	−$1,600	$1,000	$1,000	1.08

The index is greater than 1; thus, the incremental investment is desirable. The problem of scale can be solved by comparing pairs of investments, but this is unnecessary because the problem can be solved more easily by using the net present value method. Also, the problem of the classification of cash flows still exists.

EXAMPLE 8.5   Classification of Cash Flows

The second difficulty with the present value index is that it requires a distinction be made between deductions from cash proceeds and investment-type outlays. Assume the following two mutually exclusive investments and a 10 percent time value factor.

		Period		Present Value Index
Investment	0	1	2	
A Net flows	−$1,500	$1,000	$1,000	1.16
B Proceeds		2,000	2,000	1.07
Outlays	−1,500	−1,000	−1,000	

$$\text{Present value index (A)} = \frac{\$1,000.00\,(1.10)^{-1} + \$1,000.00\,(1.10)^{-2}}{\$1,500.00}$$

$$= \frac{\$1,735.54}{\$1,500.00} = 1.16$$

$$\text{Present value index (B)} = \frac{\$2,000\,(1.7355)}{\$1,500 + \$1,000\,(1.7355)} = \frac{\$3,471.08}{\$3,235.54} = 1.07$$

The index measure chooses A over B. Close inspection of the cash flows of the investments shows that the investment net cash flows are identical for both investments. The cash flow difference is only a matter of classifying the $1,000 outlays of B as investments or as deductions from cash proceeds, as with A. Any procedure that depends on arbitrary classifications rests on quick sand. For example, are advertising expenditures an expense or an investment? A partial solution to this problem is to use net cash flows.

A misconception about the present value index is that it will rank independent investments. This ranking is not reliable. If the company does not intend to accept all independent investments with a positive present value (or an index greater than 1), the cost of money used will not be the appropriate rate of discount, and the index ranking will not be reliable. It is not claimed here that the net present value method may be used to rank independent investments. It is claimed only that the net present method will lead to more easily obtained decisions involving choices between mutually exclusive investments and will give equally correct accept or reject decisions when applied to independent investments.

Programming Solutions

There exists a large number of programming solutions to the capital rationing situation.[2] A typical solution is to maximize an objective function that consists of

[2] For example, see J. D. Forsyth and D. C. Owen, "Capital Rationing Methods," in R. L. Crum and F. G. J. Derkinderen (Eds.), *Capital Budgeting Under Conditions of Uncertainty.* (Boston: Martinus Nijhoff, 1981).

a sum of present values of future dividends. But this assumes away a large percentage of the problem, since it assumes we know what rate of interest to use to discount the future benefits. Also, to solve the problem, we not only need the information concerning currently available investments but also what investments will be available in the future.

The basic structure of the programming solution will be to maximize the present value of the future dividends (or net cash flows) subject to the summations of all of a period's cash flows (positive and negative) minus a period's dividend being equal to or less than the cash available from all the sources. This inequality must hold for all time periods. There would be an additional constraint that would insure that only one of a set of mutually exclusive investments could be accepted.

We will illustrate the general solution approach using a very simplified example. Assume we have only $10,000 to invest at time 0 and cannot obtain external funds at time 1. We have the following investment opportunities.

	Time 0	1	2
X_1	$-10,000$	0	$12,100$
X_2	$-10,000$	$+11,400$	
X_3		$-10,400$	$12,000$

Assume that the investors in this firm use a .08 discount rate. We want to maximize the present value of future dividends. We have

$$\text{Undertake } X_1: \text{PV} = \frac{12,100}{(1.08)^2} = \$10,373$$

or

$$\text{Undertake } X_2 \text{ and then } X_3: \text{PV} = \frac{1,000}{1.08} + \frac{12,000}{(1.08)^2} = \$11,214$$

With X_2, then X_3, there is a $1,000 dividend at time 1 and a $12,000 dividend at time 2. This is better than a dividend of $12,100 at time 2, which we receive with X_1.

While we solved the problem by inspection, the programming formulation would be

$$\text{Maximize} = \Sigma \text{ PV of all future dividends}$$
$$\text{Subject to:} \quad 10,000X_1 + 10,000X_2 + 0X_3 + D_0 \le 10,000$$
$$0X_1 - 11,400X_2 + 10,400X_3 + D_1 \le 0$$
$$-12,100X_1 + 0X_2 - 12,000X_3 + D_2 \le 0$$
$$X_1, X_2, X_3 \ge 0$$

where X_i is the number of units of X_i investment.

If X_1 and X_2 were mutually exclusive investments, then we would also have $X_1 + X_2 \leq 1$. We can also restrict the values of X_i to be either 0 or 1 (but we would then have to use *integer* programming).

Because of the immense information requirements (knowledge of future investments), we are not as enthusiastic regarding programming solutions to capital rationing situations as are some other authors. Also, there is disagreement about whether or not it is correct to maximize the present value of future dividends discounted at the investors' opportunity cost of capital. It is difficult to find corporations that have successfully applied programming techniques to solving capital rationing problems.

Capital Rationing and Risk

Up to this point, we have assumed certainty and that the firm's problem was to ration too little capital among too many projects. In Chapter 18 we introduce uncertainty. With uncertain outcomes, investments might have expected returns larger than the firm's weighted average cost of capital but still be rejected because they are too risky. Thus, with uncertainty, capital rationing considerations become relevant only after the investments have been deemed to be acceptable using some type of time value–risk adjustment calculations.

Conclusions

Capital rationing in one form or another exists to some extent in most corporations. We may distinguish among minor and severe cases of capital rationing. In the minor cases the present value rules suggested in this book may be used with confidence. In the more severe forms of capital rationing, the net present value method may still be used, but it is now less correct to use a constant rate of discount for all future years. The rate of discount used for each future year must reflect the cost of obtaining additional funds, the value of external investments available to the firm, the internal opportunity cost of funds, or the desires of the owners for present versus future proceeds.

We make no claim that the net present value method can be used to rank independent investments where that ranking will be used to eliminate some independent investments with positive present values. Recognizing that certain individuals have the audacity to pick the best movie of the year, we should be able to rank investments. And so we can, as long as the ranking is placed in somewhat the same perspective as the best-movie contest. A reasonable (not exactly correct) ranking can be obtained using either internal rate of return or index of present value. If desired, the present value of different sets of investments can be computed and an attempt made to maximize present value (but remember, the discount rate should represent the opportunity cost of funds).

In addition to the foregoing complexities, if risk considerations are also brought into the analysis, then we must conclude that the ranking of independent investments for a capital rationing situation is truly more like choosing the best movie than it is an exact scientific technique.

PROBLEMS

8.1 The ABC Company is planning its investment budget. Currently, it can raise money at a cost of .06. It assumes that its stockholders are able to invest funds so as to earn .04. There are also opportunities for the company to lend its funds and earn .04.

  a. Assume that the company expected a large amount of investment opportunities. What discount rate should it use in making investment decisions?

  b. Assume that the company expected a large amount of cash compared to internal investment opportunities. What rate of discount should it use in making decisions?

  c. Assume that the company expected a shortage of cash for the coming 24 months but then expected a surplus amount of cash. What does this imply about the rate of discount to be used?

8.2 The ABC Company has a stable dividend policy ($2 per share per year). It also has a policy of not raising new capital from the market. The policy is to invest the available funds after payment of the dividends (excess cash is invested in marketable securities). What does this imply about the use of the present value method of making investment decisions?

8.3 The ABC Company has more investment opportunities than it can use (it is unwilling to borrow or issue more common stock). Management estimated that the investment cutoffs for the next two years will be as follows.

Year	Cutoff
0–1	.20
1–2	.30

It is attempting to choose between two mutually exclusive alternatives, both of which will require an initial outlay now and will pay off at the end of two periods.

What discount rate should be used in evaluating the mutually exclusive investments? What rate would you use if the investments had a life of one year? [*Hint:* $(1 + R_n)^n = (1 + r_1)(1 + r_2) \dots (1 + r_n)$, where r_i is the value of money of period i and R_n is the equivalent interest rate for the n periods.]

8.4 The president of the ABC Company wants a ranking of three investments. The firm considers its cost of money to be .05. The following three independent investments are ranked.

| | Cash Flows of Period | | | Net Present Value, | |
Investment	0	1	2	Using .05	Ranking
A	−$1,000	$1,120		$66.69	3
B	− 1,000		$1,210	97.47	1
C	− 1,000	400	775	83.89	2

The firm has $1,000 of uncommitted funds available (without borrowing) for investments. Based on the preceding ranking, the president decides to accept investment B. It is then revealed that, because investment B has a IRR of .10, this could be considered to be the investment cutoff rate (other investments that have already been approved have higher IRRs).

Evaluate the decision process.

8.5 In answering the following questions, assume that $1 one year from now is worth $0.90 today, and $1 two years from now is worth $0.75 today. Dollars can be bought and sold at these prices. There are no transaction costs.

A firm anticipates that it will have a surplus of dollars one year from now but a shortage two years from now.

a. The present value of the surplus of dollars that is forecast for one year from now is $2,000. What is the amount of the surplus in terms of dollars available in one year?

b. By how much would the net present value of the firm change if all of the surplus-year-1 dollars are sold (now) and the proceeds used to buy more year-2 dollars?

c. How many year-2 dollars can be obtained in the transaction described in question b?

d. What is the present value of an annuity of a dollar per year for two years at these prices?

e. What is the interest rate the firm would have to pay on a one-year loan, negotiated now, with the funds to be received one year from now and paid back two years from now? That is, the cash flow from the point of view of the borrower would be as follows.

	Time 0	Time 1	Time 2
Amount	0	+100	−100 $(1 + r)$
Find r			

8.6 An investor can earn .05 (before taxes) in default-free investments. He is considering purchasing stock in a corporation that will pay a dividend of $10 a year for perpetuity (assume this information is known with certainty). The investor is in a marginal .7 tax bracket.

a. Compute the value of the stock to the investor.

b. Compute the value of the stock, assuming that an investor has a marginal tax rate of .4.

c. Compute the value of the stock for the investors of parts (a) and (b). Assume that there are tax-exempt securities that can be purchased to yield .03.

8.7 Assume a situation where it is known that the dividend of $10 a year of problem 8.6 will not begin for eleven years and that the price at the end of ten years will be $200. The capital gains tax rate is .25, the after-tax opportunity cost to high-tax investors is .03, and the after-tax opportunity cost to low-tax investors is .05.

a. How much would a high-tax investor be willing to pay for the stock now? Assume that he will sell at the end of ten years for $200. Why is this selling assumption reasonable?

b. How much would a low-tax investor (say zero tax) be willing to pay for the stock now? Would he sell at the end of ten years?

8.8 Recompute parts (a) and (b) of problem 8.7. Assume that the expected price at the end of ten years is $100.

8.9 Refer to problem 8.7.

a. How much would the high-tax investor be willing to pay for the stock at the end of year 9? How much would the low-tax investor be willing to pay?

b. How much would the high-tax investor realize in year 9 if she liquidated her investment at a price of $190? Assume that she paid $130 for the investment.

c. Compute the present value of the investment at the end of year 9. Assume that the high-tax investor intends to hold until year 10 and sell at $200.

8.10 The ABC Company prefers to finance investments internally to the extent possible. However, it has adopted the following polices, which are applied unless there are significant qualitative considerations that justify an exception for a particular project.

a. Investments are not accepted unless they can earn at least 11.1 percent after taxes on a discounted cash flow (DCF) basis, even if excess funds are available.

b. Investments are not rejected if they will earn 25 percent or more after taxes on a discounted cash flow (DCF) basis, even if internally generated funds are not available.

The following table shows the cash flows for a series of independent investments. Use the ABC Company's criteria to classify each investment as.

A	Must accept
R	Must reject
U	Uncertain

Investments		Cash Flows			Classification
D	−$100	$50	$50	$ 50	
E	− 100			200	
F	− 100	80	50	30	
G	− 100	30	50	80	
H	− 100	10	40	70	

8.11 The ABC Company has opened 100 new stores. It has incurred a great deal of expenses associated with opening the stores, and the stores have not yet built up enough clientele to be profitable. However, the stores are operating at profit levels exceeding expectations, and there are indications that they will be very profitable in the future. It is obvious that the stock market has not yet digested this latter fact, and the stock of the company is currently depressed compared to management's appraisal of value. The company has the opportunity to acquire an additional fifty stores this year, but to do so will require new stockholder capital acquired from the market (it has borrowed all it feels it is prudent to borrow and cannot obtain more capital from its current stockholders). Without the new capital, the stockholders can expect to earn an equivalent annual yield of .15 on the current market value of their investment (assume that there is $100 million shares of stock outstanding). The stock is currently selling at $100 per share and paying a $6-per-share dividend. The earnings are $7.50 per share ($7.5 million in total).

The new investments would require $10 million to be obtained by issuing 100,000 new shares of common stock. The investment would return $1.2 million per year available for dividends for perpetuity. The stockholders desire a .08 return per year on their incremental investments.

a. Should the corporation issue the new shares and undertake the investment?

b. What would be your recommendation if the corporation had the necessary cash already available?

8.12 Change the statement of problem 8.11 so that the present stockholders can expect to earn dividends of $6 per share or an equivalent annual yield of .06 for perpetuity unless the new investment is undertaken. Should the new investment be undertaken?

8.13 Change the statement of problem 8.11 so that the present stockholders can expect to earn $ 8 million, or an equivalent return of .08 per year on the current market value of their investment, if the new investment is not undertaken. Should the new investment be undertaken?

8.14 The ABC Company currently has outstanding $1 million of .05 debt with a maturity of two years. The only way it can finance a $500,000 investment would be by refinancing the $1 million with $1.5 million of .08 debt, also maturing in two years. The investment would pay $55,000 in year 1 and $555,000 in year 2 (the investment has a yield of .11). The firm has a cost of capital of .10.

Cost of equity	.12 × .5 = .06
Cost of debt	.08 × .5 = .04
	.10

Should the investment be accepted?

8.15 The CDE Company can borrow and lend funds at an interest rate of .08. It can invest $11 million in a risky project that on the average will lead to net cash flows of $1 million per year. A consultant has suggested that the firm use its cost of capital of .10 in computing the present value of the investment. The investment's life is extremely long. Insurance can be purchased that will guarantee the $1 million per year. Should the investment be undertaken? How much could the firm afford to pay for the insurance?

8.16 *Production-Line Problem*

Three new machines are required for a proposed improvement to the production line in the Charles Corporation main plant. Each has a life of five years and no salvage value. The proposed improvement requires all three machines. There are zero taxes.

Machine A costs $400,000 to buy; it could be leased for $115,000 per year of five years. Machine B costs $1,000,000 to buy; it could be leased for $285,000 per year for five years. Machine C costs $500,000 and is not available for lease.

If all three machines are installed, there will be operating savings of $600,000 per year for each of the next five years. (There would be no benefit to installing just two of the machines.)

The cost of money for the Charles Corporation is 8 percent. (Money could be borrowed or lent at that rate.) The president, H. Arvard, seldom accepts investment proposals that have an internal rate of return of less than 20 percent.

a. In your opinion, what decision in this matter is in the best interests of stockholders? (If your decision is to make the improvement, specify whether A and/or B are to be bought or leased.) Why?

b. Of the proposals that might be acceptable to the president, which one is best for stockholders?

8.17 The Big Manufacturing Company (BMC) has a plant that is currently losing $1 million of cash per year. This loss is expected to continue into the future unless either of two actions is taken

The plant can be closed down at a one-time cost of $10 million (there is a large amount of pension obligation). Alternatively, $12 million can be invested to modernize to earn $600,000 of cash flow per year (a perpetuity).

The analysis of the firm have concluded that the $12 million should not be invested, since the investment will earn only 5 percent per year, and that the plant should be closed down. The firm has a weighted average cost of capital of 15 percent and a borrowing cost of 12 percent (it has debt outstanding). Its tax rate is zero.

a. What should BMC do?

b. What should BMC do if the investment opportunity is not available?

DISCUSSION QUESTIONS

8.A A small oil company owns ten different oil-producing properties. It wants to raise capital for more drilling, but the owner does not want to dilute his ownership, and thus the firm cannot sell any common stock. It has borrowed up to its debt capacity.

What do you recommend?

8.B In September 1987 the Commonwealth Utility Company announced it would discontinue its stock dividend policy. The policy of the company had been to issue stock dividends of 1 to 2.4 percent equal to the earnings in excess of the cash dividends. The stated purpose of the stock dividends was to help finance expansion without public offerings of common stock. The dividends were stopped because it was feared that a further increase in the common stock equity ratio would increase the company's overall cost of money. Discuss the company's use of stock dividends.

REFERENCES

Bacon, P. W., "The Evaluation of Mutually Exclusive Investments," *Financial Management*, Summer 1977, pp. 55–58.

Balas, Egon, "An Additive Algorithm for Solving Linear Programs with Zero–One Variables," *Operations Research*, July–August 1965, pp. 517–549.

Baumol, W., and R. Quandt, "Investment and Discount Rates Under Capital Rationing—A Programming Approach," *Economic Journal*, June 1965, pp. 317–329.

Bernhard, Richard H., "Mathematical Programming Models for Capital Budgeting—A Survey, Generalization, and Critique," *Journal of Financial and Quantitative Analysis*, June 1969, pp. 111–158.

Burton, R. M., and W. W. Damon, "On the Existence of a Cost of Capital Under Pure Capital Rationing," *Journal of Finance*, September 1974, pp. 1165–1174.

Carleton, W. T., "Linear Programming and Capital Budgeting Models: A New Interpretation," *Journal of Finance*, December 1969, pp. 825–833.

———, C. L. Dick, Jr., and D. H. Downes, "Financial Policy Models: Theory and Practice," *Journal of Financial and Quantitative Analysis*, December 1973, pp. 691–709.

Crum, R. L., and F. G. J. Derkinderen (Eds.), *Capital Budgeting Under Conditions of Uncertainty* (Boston: Martinus Nijhoff Publishing, 1981).

Elton, E. J., "Capital Rationing and External Discount Rates," *Journal of Finance*, June 1970, pp. 573–584.

Fogler, H. Russell, "Overkill in Capital Budgeting Technique?" *Financial Management*, Spring 1972, pp. 29–62.

Forsyth, J. D., and D. C. Owen, "Capital Rationing Methods," in R. L. Crum and F. G. J. Derkinderen (Eds.), *Capital Budgeting Under Conditions of Uncertainty* (Boston: Martinus Nijhoff, 1981), pp. 213–235.

Hirshleifer, J., "On the Theory of Optimal Investment," *Journal of Political Economy*, August 1958, pp. 329–352.

Lorie, J. H., and L. J. Savage, "Three Problems in Rationing Capital," *Journal of Business*, October 1955, pp. 229–239.

Lusztig, P., and B. Schwab, "A Note on the Application of Linear Programming to Capital Budgeting," *Journal of Financial and Quantitative Analysis*, December 1968, pp. 427–431.

Manne, A. S., "Optimal Dividend and Investment Policies for a Self-Financing Business Enterprise," *Management Science*, November 1968, pp. 119–129.

Merville, L. J., and L. A. Tavis, "A Generalized Model for Capital Investment," *Journal of Finance*, March 1973, pp. 109–118.

Myers, S. C., "A Note on Linear Programming and Capital Budgeting," *Journal of Finance*, March 1972, pp. 89–92.

———, and Gerald A. Pogue "A Programming Approach to Corporate Financial Management," *Journal of Finance*, May 1974, pp. 579–599.

Rychel, D. F., "Capital Budgeting with Mixed Integer Linear Programming: An Application," *Financial Management*, Winter 1977, pp. 11–19.

Thompson, H. E., "Mathematical Programming, The Capital Asset Pricing Model and Capital Budgeting of Interrelated Projects," *Journal of Finance*, March 1976, pp. 125–131.

Weingartner, H. M., *Mathematical Programming and the Analysis of Capital Budgeting Problems* (Englewood Cliffs, NJ: Prentice-Hall, 1963).

———, "Capital Rationing: *n* Authors in Search of a Plot," *Journal of Finance*, December 1977, pp. 1403–1431.

Whitmore, G. A., and L. R. Amey, "Capital Budgeting Under Rationing: Comments on the Lusztig and Schwab Procedure," *Journal of Financial and Quantitative Analysis*, January 1973, pp. 127–135.

C H A P T E R 9

Capital Budgeting and Inflation

Among the many misfortunes which bring ruin to entire states ... four
are the most serious: internal dissension, a high death rate, poor harvests
and the corruption of money....

Nicholas Copernicus, "A Method of Coining Money," 1528.

The basic principles of capital budgeting are applicable when there is a risk of inflation as well as when the risk of inflation is negligible. However, it is not always easy to apply these principles correctly when the risk of inflation is of primary importance. The purpose of the present chapter is to offer some suggestions about how to consider inflation in an effective manner. When inflation is possible, future cash flows may differ not only in their timing but in their puchasing power, and we may want to determine whether money flows or purchasing-power flows are more useful in describing the outcomes of an investment and in making decisions about alternative investments. In addition, selecting an appropriate discount rate in the presence of inflationary risks is more complex. The principal conclusion of this chapter is that investments can be analyzed using either money cash flows or purchasing-power flows, as long as the analysis is done in a consistent manner.

What Is Inflation?

In a dynamically growing economy, price changes take place constantly. In the highly organized markets for securities and for some commodities, it is normal for prices to change from one transaction to the next. In other cases—for example, most real estate leases—prices (rents, in the case of a lease) are fixed by contract for a period of years. Sometimes the price of a particular good or service may exhibit an upward or downward trend that can last for months, years, or even decades.

The price changes that are the result of shifts in the supply or demand for particular goods and services do not imply any change in the general price level. Increases in the price of some goods or services may be offset by decreases in others, so that the average level of prices can remain more or less constant. A change in the average price level takes place if there is a strong tendency for many prices to move up (or down). Inflation is a rise in the average price level; deflation is a decline in the average price level. In the United States, price-level changes have tended to be inflationary during most of the last half-century; during the preceding half-century, the price-level changes tended to be deflationary.

Although the idea of an average price level is a useful tool, it is important to be aware of its limitations. The statisticians who construct price-level indexes must decide what goods to include in the index and what weight to assign to each. A commonly used index, the consumer price index, is designed to measure the average price of the goods consumed by an average-sized middle-income urban family. It is a reasonable measure for this purpose, but the price level it records may not accurately reflect the buying habits of a specific family or of a business enterprise. Many families and almost all business organizations will have important components of their revenues or expenses whose movements are not closely tied to the average price level of consumer goods. In these circumstances, careful consideration of the prices of specific goods and services of particular importance to the decision makers is required. In evaluating capital budgeting decisions, a manager must consider not only the possible effects of inflation, but also the effect of long-run trends in the relative prices of products and of important categories of expenditures.

This point is particularly important because the prices of many of the most important goods and services purchased by firms are not directly included in the commonly used price indexes. Labor is the prime example. Wage and salary payments are a major expense item for almost every business. Yet wage rates are not directly included in price indexes used to measure the rate of inflation or deflation. Labor costs, however, are reflected in the costs of the consumption goods and services that are included in the price indexes.

Real Cash Flows

Up to this point we have described investments in terms of cash flows. If the price level rises, the purchasing power of a dollar will decline. For some purposes, it may be equally useful to measure the costs and benefits of an investment in terms of dollars of constant purchasing power. Suppose that an investment will return $100 this year and $100 next year. If the price level rises 4 percent between now and next year (the price index is 100 for this year and 104 for next year), the $100 to be received next year will have a purchasing power in terms of this year's dollar of $100/1.04 = R\$96.15$.

To distinguish in this chapter between cash flows measured in dollars and cash flows measured in terms of purchasing power, the former will be referred to as nominal cash flows and the latter as real cash flows. The symbol $R\$$ will be used to denote real cash flows. Thus, in the example used in the previous paragraph, $R\$96.15$ is the real cash flow of the investment next year.

Real Cash Flows and Nominal Flows

The process of analyzing a capital investment project involves at least two distinct steps. First, the costs and benefits of the project must be described in some meaningful way. Second, the costs and benefits must be evaluated in terms of the goals and objectives of the decision maker. In each if these steps the decision maker has a choice of whether money cash flows or real cash flows will be used.

It has long been recognized that one of the disadvantages of an unstable price level is that it makes the task of appropriately analyzing the economic advantages and disadvantages of different alternatives more difficult and complex. In the present chapter it is our intention to illustrate with specific examples techniques that may be used to take the possibility of inflation into account.

Although capital budgeting decisions may be made using either nominal or real flows, there may be differences in our ability to estimate the necessary inputs, the costs and benefits of an investment project. If revenues or costs are mainly determined by market forces in the period in which the outlays are made or the revenues received, estimates in terms of real cash flows may be more accurate than estimates of nominal cash flows. But if future costs and revenues are determined by long-term fixed-price contractual relationships, estimates in terms of nominal flows are likely to be more accurate.

Money values are converted into real values by dividing the monetary value by an appropriate price-index relative. For example, suppose than an investment promises to return $100 per year for the next two years and that the cash proceeds measured in money values are certain. At 9 percent, the present value of the monetary value is $175.91. Suppose that the price index for the current period is 140; it is expected to be 145.6 next year and 151.424 the following year. We wish to convert the nominal values in all three years to real values in terms of this year's price level. To do this, the first step is to construct price-index relatives for each of the three years. A price-index relative is a ratio of two price-index values. The value in the numerator is the value of the price index for the year in which the cash flows will occur. The denominator is the price index of the base period (the real values are to be expressed in terms of the purchasing power of that period). The price relatives are $140/140 = 1$ for the current period, $145.6/140 = 1.04$ for next year, and $151.424/140 = 1.0816$ for the following year.

To convert nominal values to real values, the nominal values for a given period are divided by the price-index relative for that period. The real value of the $100 to be received next year is $R\$96.154$ ($100/1.04$), and the real value of the $100 to be received the following year is $R\$92.456$ ($100/1.0816$). If real cash flows are used, it is not appropriate to use the nominal observed market costs of capital as a discount rate. A "real" cost of money must be estimated.

The Use of Specific Prices

Suppose that a firm is considering investing $10,000 in a machine that has a useful life of five years. For simplicity, assume that for tax purposes the original cost of the machine will be depreciated (zero salvage) on a straight-line basis over its life. With the machine, one worker using 2,000 pounds of raw materials per year can produce 1,600 units of product per year. In current prices the machine will cost $10,000; the worker, $8,000 per year; and the raw material, $2 per pound. The firm is subject to a combined federal and state corporate income tax rate of 60 percent. The product can be sold for $10 per unit.

In each of the five years, if there are no changes in any of these prices, the cash flow will be as follows.

Revenues 1,600 × $10	$16,000
Labor expense	8,000
Raw material expense	4,000
Income taxes	1,200
Net cash flow	$ 2,800

These numbers are reproduced in column 1 of Table 9.1.

Even with no change in the general price level, specific prices may still change. For example, assume labor expense will rise by 10 percent if there is no change in the price level. This will increase labor expense by $800, reduce tax payments by $480, and reduce the cash flow by $320 to $2,480. The resulting cash flows are shown in column 2 of Table 9.1.

TABLE 9.1 *Examples of Effects of Price Level and Labor Expense Changes on Nominal and Real Cash Flows*

	Column 1	Column 2	Column 3
Assumptions			
Real wages	No change	+10%	+10%
Price level	No change	No change	+10%
Nominal cash flows			
Revenues	$16,000	$16,000	$17,600
Expenses			
Labor expenses	8,000	8,800	9,680
Raw material	4,000	4,000	4,400
Income taxes	1,200	720	912
Net cash flow	$2,800	$2,480	$2,608
Real cash flows	R$2,800	R$2,480	R$2,371

Now suppose that the general price level increases by 10 percent and that this price-level change is reflected in strictly proportional changes in the product and raw material prices. Suppose also that real labor expense increases by an additional 10 percent in real terms to $9,680. Calculating the cash flow under these assumptions, we have the following.

Revenues: 1,600 × $11	$17,600
Labor expense	9,680
Raw material expense	4,400
Income taxes	912
Net cash flow	$ 2,608

The cash flows under these assumptions are shown in column 3 of Table 9.1.

Comparing the nominal net cash flows of columns 2 and 3, a firm might conclude that, despite a 10 percent increase in real wages, inflation is to its advantage. The nominal net cash flow is $128 higher with a 10 percent increase in the price level than without it ($2,608 compared to $2,480). But with a 10 percent inflation, the money cash flow of $2,608 in year 5 is equivalent, in purchasing power, to $(1/1.10) \times ($2,608) = R$2,371$. It is this amount that should be compared to $2,480, which will be received (real and nominal cash flow) without inflation. With inflation the firm's real cash flow is R$109 less than without inflation.

The three situations just described are summarized in Table 9.1. The table is intended to illustrate the importance of making realistic assumptions about how specific prices are likely to change with or without general price-level inflation.

Real and Nominal Discount Rates

In previous sections we have stated that the cash flows from a project could be described in terms of nominal cash flows or real cash flows. In the present section we discuss the choice of a discount rate. The value of an asset should not depend on whether it is analyzed in nominal terms or in real terms as long as the appropriate discount rate is used in each case. With nominal cash flows, the discount rate used should be the nominal discount rate. With real cash flows, the discount rate used should be a real discount rate. The failure to follow these apparently simple rules is a frequent source of errors in project evaluation.

To illustrate the relationships between the two discount rates, we first ignore tax effects. (Assume the decision maker is in the zero tax bracket.) With annual compounding, if j is the annual rate of inflation and i is the real rate of interest, then the corresponding nominal rate of interest is

$$r = (1 + j)(1 + i) - 1 \qquad (9.1)$$

or, equivalently,

$$r = j + i + ij \qquad (9.2)$$

For example, if we require a real rate of interest of .03 and expect a rate of inflation of .10, then the required nominal rate of interest to give an equivalent real return will be

$$r = .03 + .10 + .003 = .133$$

The same relationship can also be used to solve for the real rate of interest, given the nominal rate and the expected rate of inflation. For example, suppose the expected rate of inflation is .10, and we observe a nominal rate of interest of 13.3 percent. What is the corresponding real interest rate? Solving equation 9.2 for i gives

$$i = (r - j)/(1 + j) \qquad (9.3)$$

and substituting the assumed values gives

$$i = (.133 - .10)/(1.1) = .033/1.1 = .03$$

In valuing an asset, we have two choices. We can use nominal cash flows and the nominal rate of interest or the corresponding real cash flows and real interest rate. Suppose, under the conditions just described, we observe a bond that promises interest payments of $133 per year for three years, with the principal of $1,000 to be repaid at the end of the third year. At the nominal discount rate of 13.3 percent, the present value of the bond should be $1,000. This presumption is verified in the following calculations.

Period	Nominal Cash Flow	Nominal Present Value Factor (.133)	Present Value
1	$ 133	.8826	$ 117.39
2	133	.7790	103.61
3	1,133	.6876	779.00
			$1,000.00

The same present value would result if we first convert the nominal cash flows to real cash flows and discount these at the corresponding real interest rate of .03. This is illustrated in the following calculations.

Period	Nominal Cash Flow	Price Level Relative	Real Cash Flows	Real Present Value Factor	Present Value
n	(1)	(2) = $(1 + j)^n$	(3) = (1)/(2)	(4) = $(1 + i)^{-n}$	(5) = (3)(4)
1	$ 133	1.10	$120.91	.9709	$ 117.39
2	133	1.21	109.92	.9426	103.61
3	1,133	1.331	851.24	.9151	779.00
					$1,000.00

We first used nominal cash flows and nominal discount rates and obtained a present value of $1,000. We then converted the money (nominal) cash flows to real cash flows and used a real discount rate to again obtain a present value of $1,000. If nominal cash flows are used, it is important that a nominal discount rate be used. However, if real cash flows are used, it is necessary to use a real discount factor. The real cash flows cannot sensibly be discounted using the nominal discount rate.

In the preceding examples, we used assets or liabilities that promised nominal cash flows. Now suppose that an asset is available that is expected to provide R$100 per year for three years, for example, a lease with a price-index escalator clause. What is the value of the lease? The easiest approach is to discount the real cash flows using the real interest rate of 3 percent. In this case, we can use the annuity factor $B(3, .03) = 2.8286$. Therefore, the value of the asset is $282.86. An alternative approach is to translate the real cash flows into nominal cash flows at the assumed 10 percent rate of inflation and evaluate the nominal cash flows using the nominal interest rate. The calculations are shown here. The present value is again $282.86.

Period	Real Cash Flow	Price Level Relative	Nominal Cash Flow	Nominal Present Value Factor	Present Value
1	R$100	1.10	$110.00	.8826	$ 97.09
2	100	1.21	121.00	.7790	94.26
3	100	1.331	133.10	.6876	91.51
					$282.86

Inflation Analysis: A Simplified Approach

Let us consider an investment with the following cash flows projected, assuming a zero inflation rate.

Time	Cash Flows
0	−$2,100
1	1,300
2	1,200
3	1,100

Given the zero inflation rate, the firm uses a .10 discount rate, and the investment has a $900 net present value.

If the projected inflation rate is .05, the nominal interest rate can be expected to be

$$.10 + .05 + .05 (.10) = .155$$

and the projected nominal cash flows and their present value are

Time	Cash Flows: Nominal Dollars	Present Value Factors	Present Value
0	−$2,100	1.00	−$2,100.00
1	1,365	1.155^{-1}	1,182
2	1.323	1.155^{-2}	992
3	1,273.3875	1.155^{-3}	826
			NPV =$ 900.00

If all the cash flows and the discount rate are adjusted for the .05 inflation, the net present value is not changed by the inflation assumption. For example, let us assume there is .05 price deflation (the prices are .95 of the prices of the previous period). The nominal interest rate is

$$r = .10 - .05 - .05\,(.10) = .045$$

and the projected cash flows are

Time	Cash Flows: Nominal Dollars	Present Value Factors	Present Value
0	−$2,100	1.000	−$2,100
1	1,235	1.045^{-1}	1,182
2	1,083	1.045^{-2}	992
3	943.1125	1.045^{-3}	826
			NPV =$ 900

With zero taxes, if the analysis is done correctly, and if we assume that all nominal prices change at the assumed rate of inflation (real prices remain constant), and if the relations between the real rate of interest and the nominal rate of interest are as described by equation (9.1), then the projected NPV of the project will not be affected by the assumed rate of inflation. This is illustrated in the two preceding tables, in which the NPV of the project is $900 when the assumed rate of inflation is zero percent, when the assumed rate of inflation is 5 percent, and when there is 5 percent deflation. If the real value of the firm's input or output prices, or the real rate of interest is affected by the inflation rate, then the net present value will change.

Tax Effects

The analysis in the previous section considered inflation, but not income taxes. Without taxes the nominal rate of discount should reflect the expected future rate of inflation, so that changes in expected inflation do not change the expected real interest rate. Previous chapters have considered tax effects, without explicitly considering inflation. In general, investors who are taxed will realize lower after-tax returns than investors who are not. However, there are interactions between the tax effects and the inflation effects. This section considers both taxes and inflation.

Suppose an investor expects that the rate of inflation will be j per year. The investor wishes to analyze a proposed investment by discounting real flows. What is the relevant discount rate? The nominal rate of interest on taxable default-free debt is r. If the investor were exempt from taxes, the answer could be obtained by applying equation 9.3. But the relevant nominal return for a taxable investor is the highest after-tax return available. A taxable investor buying taxable nominal default-free debt will realize an after-tax nominal return of $(1 - t)r$, where t is the investor's marginal tax rate. The relevant after-tax real return to the taxable investor depends on the investor's tax rate. We denote it by $i(t)$, to emphasize that the value of i depends on the marginal tax rate, t. The after-tax real return to the taxable investor can be expressed as

$$i(t) = \frac{1 + r(1 - t)}{1 + j} - 1 \tag{9.4}$$

Note that equation 9.4 is analogous to equation 9.1. By rearranging the terms in equation 9.4, it can be expressed in a form analogous to equation 9.3 as follows:

$$i(t) = \frac{r(1 - t) - j}{(1 + j)} \tag{9.5}$$

If there is no inflation then $j = 0$ and $i(t) = r(1 - t)$, as we would expect. Suppose that the marginal income tax rate is 30 percent, the inflation rate is 6 percent per year, and nominal default-free taxable debt returns 11 percent. Then $i(.30) = .0160$.

$$i(.30) = \frac{.11\,(1 - .3) - .06}{1.06} = .0160.$$

An investor in the zero tax bracket with a nominal return of .11 and the same expected rate of inflation would have an after-tax real return of

$$i(0) = \frac{.11\,(1 - .0) - .06}{1.06} = .0472.$$

A Tax-exempt Alternative

Now assume there is the possibility of investing in insured (risk-free) tax exempt bonds to earn r_e. If r_e is larger than $r(1 - t)$, then r_e is the effective opportunity cost for investing funds and we have

$$i(t) = \frac{1 + r_e}{(1 + j)} - 1 = \frac{r_e - j}{1 + j} \tag{9.6}$$

Continuing the above example, when $j = .06$, $t = .30$, and $r = .11$, now assume $r_e = .09$. Since $r_e > r(1 - t)$, we use equation 9.6 to obtain

$$i(0) = \frac{.09 - .06}{1.06} = .0283.$$

The rate obtained using the tax-exempt investment alternative is larger than the .0160 obtained previously and is the effective real opportunity cost for the investor. However, if there are laws preventing borrowing at .0160 and investing at .0283, the .016 rate is effective if the investment is financed with debt. The tax-exempt real rate may not be feasible in that situation.

The Real Return

With a positive inflation rate, the real after-tax return of the taxable investor can be negative, even though before-tax nominal rates of return are positive. Situations in which real after-tax returns were negative for taxable investors occurred during the high inflation periods of the 1970s.

In the presence of expected inflation, the nominal rate of interest can be thought of as having two components, a real return and an adjustment for inflation. In the absence of taxes, investors who expect inflation and who are considering an investment in nominal debt will demand an expected real return that is at least as great as the real return they could obtain by buying a real asset—such as land—whose price could be expected to increase with inflation. Thus, the nominal return will equal the normal real return and an additional amount to cover the reduction in the purchasing power of the principal. This relationship, called the "Fisher effect" after the economist who first studied it Irving Fisher, is the basis for equations 9.1 and 9.2.

When Fisher did his studies, income taxes were not a major issue for investors, and he formulated the relationship on a before-tax basis. This is still the relevant relationship for tax-exempt investors. The U.S. tax laws do not distinguish between the real return and the inflation adjustment component. Both are taxed. Taxable investors would like a nominal return that is large enough so that their after-tax real return does not decline because of inflation. If a taxable investor in a given tax bracket receives an unchanged real return, investors in lower tax brackets receive a larger real return, and investors in higher tax brackets receive a lower real return. The latter will either have to settle for a lower real return or try to shift into assets that provide better inflation hedges. The tax bracket at which after-tax real returns do not change will be referred to as the "marginal" tax bracket.

A modification of the Fisher effect is called the Darby effect. The Darby effect predicts that in the presence of expected inflation, nominal interest rates will rise by enough so that expected after-tax real return of taxpaying investors in the marginal tax bracket will remain constant, so that security returns can compete with returns on real assets. The Darby effect is the basis for equations 9.5 and 9.6.

How is all of this relevant to capital budgeting? If you want to know how the investments under consideration would be affected if there were changes in the expected rates of inflation, you need to know how nominal interest rates will change in response to changes in the expected rates of inflation.

The Fisher and Darby relations do not provide simple answers to the question of how the after-tax real discount rate will be affected by changes in the expected rate of inflation. However, they do provide a framework for thinking about the answers and they provide upper and lower limits on the possible values. If the Fisher relation holds, we should expect equations 9.1 and 9.2 to be valid. If the Darby effect holds, then nominal interest rates will adjust so that the relationships in equations 9.5 and 9.6 are satisfied. Each of these equations implies a prediction about how the nominal interest rate is affected by changes in the expected rate of inflation. The predicted nominal rate from the Darby-effect equations will be greater or equal to the predicted nominal rate from the Fisher-effect equations. This will be illustrated in the following example.

To simplify assume that $r_e < r - tr$, so tax-exempt debt is not relevant for a taxable investor. Assume also that we know the equilibrium real interest rate $i(t)$, which taxable investors demand in order to hold nominal debt instead of real assets. We can solve equation 9.5 for the Darby effect predicted nominal return, r as follows:

$$r = \frac{j + i(t) + ji(t)}{1 - t} \tag{9.7}$$

If the required minimum real interest rate before taxes is the same for taxable and tax-exempt investors, then $i(t) = i(1 - t)$. In this case, substituting $i(1 - t)$ for $i(t)$ in equation 9.7, we have the following equality, in which i represents the real rate of interest to a tax-exempt investor:

$$r = \frac{j}{1 - t} + i + ij. \tag{9.8}$$

This represents the Darby effect prediction of the nominal interest rate.

If the relevant tax rate equals zero, as predicted by the Fisher effect, then equation 9.8 is reduced to equation 9.2 and we have

$$r = j + i + ij. \tag{9.2}$$

Thus, the predicted nominal rate of interest for a given expected rate of inflation depends on the assumed (or equilibrium) tax rate and will take a value between $j + i + ij$ and $j/(1 - t) + i + ij$. If the required real interest rate before tax is affected by the tax rate of investors, then a wide range of possibilities exists for the equilibrium nominal rate. An analysis of empirical studies of how interest rates have actually responded to changes in expected inflation is beyond the scope of this work.

Table 9.2 shows the wide range of nominal interest rates that might be projected under various assumptions. The minimum rates arise with the zero tax rate assumption and correspond to the nominal rate obtained from equation 9.2.

TABLE 9.2 Nominal Interest Rates Consistent with Various Expected Rates of Inflation and Marginal Tax Brackets, Assuming a 3% Real Return for Tax-exempt Investors

Expected Rate of Inflation	Tax Rate			
	0%	15%	30%	45%
i	Nominal Interest Rates			
3%	6.1%	6.6%	7.4%	8.5%
6%	9.2%	10.2%	11.8%	14.1%
9%	12.3%	13.9%	16.1%	19.6%
12%	15.4%	17.5%	20.5%	25.2%
15%	18.5%	21.1%	24.9%	30.7%

The maximum rates correspond to the nominal rates resulting from a 45-percent tax rate applied to equation 9.7. Values are given in Table 9.2 for various expected rates of inflation and for four different tax rates. All projections assume a 3-percent real rate.

Conclusions

During periods of rapidly changing prices, managers tend to question the use of dollar cash flows. The maintenance of purchasing power becomes an objective. Investments can be analyzed using either money cash flows or real cash flows, but the analysis must be done in a consistent manner. If real purchasing power units are used (dollars adjusted for purchasing-power changes), the nominal (observed) discount rates cannot be used. If nominal dollars unadjusted for purchasing power changes are used the real rate of interest cannot be used.

While the maintenance of real purchasing power may be considered to be desirable, an investment may still be acceptable in the absence of uncertainty if its return is larger than the cost of money (for example, the borrowing rate) without considering the purchasing-power changes.

PROBLEMS

9.1 Assume that the price level is expected to increase by .05 in the coming year. What return do you have to earn on an investment of $100 to earn .06 on your investment in terms of real purchasing power?

9.2   A one-year $100 debt security is issued to yield .10. It is expected that there will be .08 inflation during the next year. What return, in real terms, will the security earn if the prediction of price-level change actually is fulfilled?

9.3   A three-year $100 debt security is issued to yield .10 ($133.10 will be paid after three years). It is expected that there will be .08 inflation per year during the time period. What return, in real terms, will the security earn if the prediction of price-level change actually occurs?

9.4   The ABC Company is building a plant that is expected to cost $10 million to service the capacity needs of the firm for the next three years. For another $2 million it can build excess capacity that is expected to fill the needs for an additional seven years. It is expected that it will cost $3 million to make the identical changes three years from now. The firm's cost of money is .10. Should the excess capacity be purchased?

9.5   The UVW Company is considering an investment costing $1 million. The expected IRR is .04. Debt funds can be obtained to finance this investment at a cost of .05. The justification offered for the investment is that there is expected to be inflation; thus, there will be a gain at the expense of the bondholders (they will be holding fixed dollar claims). The .04 IRR of the investment includes appropriate adjustments in cash flows because of the expected inflation. The lives of the investment and the debt are comparable. Can the investment be justified?

9.6   Assume a firm expects a 9-percent-per-year increase in wage rates and in the price level and a 10 percent time-value factor (costing of borrowing).

A piece of equipment costing $331,210 will save 5,000 hours of labor per year. Initially, each hour is worth $20.

The life of the equipment is four years.

Should the equipment be purchased? There are zero taxes.

9.7   (*Continuation of problem 9.6.*) Assume the 9 percent increase in wage rates still applies to the firm, but there is a 15 percent inflation in the economy. The cost of borrowing is still 10 percent. The firm wants to translate future dollars into current purchasing power and make the following calculations.

100,000	$= 100{,}000 \times 1.10^{-1}$	$= 90{,}909$
$109{,}000 \times 1.15^{-1} =$	$94{,}800 \times 1.10^{-2}$	$= 78{,}347$
$118{,}000 \times 1.15^{-2} =$	$89{,}800 \times 1.10^{-3}$	$= 67{,}468$
$129{,}503 \times 1.15^{-3} =$	$85{,}200 \times 1.10^{-4}$	$= \underline{58{,}193}$
	$\overline{369{,}800}$	$\overline{298{,}917}$

The NPV $= -331{,}210 + 294{,}900 = -36{,}310$. The investment was rejected. Evaluate.

9.8   An asset costs $10,000 now. It will return a perpetuity R$400 per year with no risk. (The dollar amount paid out will grow in proportion to the rate of inflation.) The time value of the money is 10 percent.

Is this a desirable investment if the expected rate of inflation is 8 percent? Explain. Ignore taxes. Illustrate your explanation with a simple numerical example, if possible.

9.9 Dr. M. Upham has $100,000 cash, which she wants to invest. Her marginal tax rates are 60 percent for ordinary income and 20 percent for capital gains. She expects the rate of inflation to be 12 percent. She can buy a high-grade municipal bond costing $100,000 that pays interest of 9 percent ($9,000) per year. This interest is not taxable. There are no capital gains or losses.

a. If a high-grade corporate bond were available that was just as safe as the municipal bond, what interest rate on the corporate bond is required so that Dr. Upham would be indifferent between the two bonds?

b. In fact, the comparable corporate bond available pays an interest rate of 15 percent ($15,000) per year. This interest is taxable as ordinary income. There are no capital gains or losses. What interest rate on the municipal bond is required so that Dr. Upham would be indifferent between the two bonds?

c. Dr. Upham has read that investments should be analyzed in real (purchasing-power) terms. Dr. Upham's alternatives are either a nontaxable municipal bond paying 9 percent or a taxable corporate bond paying 15 percent. What is the best *real* rate of return that she can expect to earn?

(Calculate your answer to the nearest 1/10 of one percent.)

d. In order to increase her real return, Dr. Upham consulted a real estate broker. He suggested a tract of land that was *worth* $113,700, which he said was sure to increase in value by the same percentage amount as the price level. Furthermore, the land could be picked up at a bargain price of $100,000 because the seller needed cash. The broker said the cash flows would be

0	1	2	3
−100,000	0	0	150,000

Dr. Upham realized that these were before-tax cash flows and that the $50,000 profit would be taxable at the capital gains rate. Find the real NPV of this investment, using a real after-tax interest rate of 1 percent.

e. Find the real NPV of the investment described in part (d) if the best alternatives available to the doctor are the bonds previously described.

9.10 *Con-Chem-Co.*

Con-Chem-Co. has specified standard methodology for evaluating investments. They specified in 1990 a 26 percent IRR "regardless of the project or division."

One of the directions given in the manual is "Deflate the current dollar cash flows to obtain the results in today's dollars." Annual deflators were supplied.

The deflators to be used for the five years starting in 1990, are

1990	1.00
91	.90
92	.80
93	.73
94	.68
95	.63

Assume that five-year debt costs Con-Chem-Co. .14 percent. There is a .46 tax rate, and the after-tax cash flows (current dollars) of an investment are

1990	−1,000
91	+ 200
92	+ 200
93	+ 200
94	+ 200
95	+1,200

The cash flows are certain.
a. Prepare the analysis as it would be prepared by Con-Chem-Co.
b. Should the investment be undertaken?

9.11   A company requires a 26 percent "real return." With a 15 percent inflation rate, what nominal (current dollar) return must the firm earn?

9.12   Assume a 9 percent inflation rate (with an equivalent increase in wage rates) and a 10 percent time-value factor (cost of borrowing).
   A piece of equipment costing $250,000 will save 4,000 hours of labor per year. Initially, each hour is worth $20.
   The life of the equipment is three years.
   Should the equipment be purchased? There are zero taxes.

9.13   An investment costs $1,000 and, with no inflation, the expected cash flows are $1,000. With a 20 percent inflation, the cash flows are expected to be $1,180.
   Funds can be borrowed at a cost of 15 percent.
a. Using the borrowing rate, should the investment be undertaken?
b. What real return does the investment earn if inflation occurs?
c. Should the investment be accepted?

9.14   Company A can borrow funds at 15 percent. It is considering an investment that has an outlay of $1,000 and $1,000 of benefits in real purchasing power terms at time 1. A 20 percent inflation rate is forecasted.
   Should the investment be accepted?

9.15   Assume that investors want a real return of .04 percent, and there is an inflation rate of 16 percent. What nominal return must be earned?

9.16   Assume that there is a 16 percent rate of inflation. A $1,000 investment earns a return of 20.64 percent. What real return is earned?

9.17   Assume that a firm has borrowed $1,000 and is paying 20.64 percent interest per year. There is a 16 percent inflation rate. What is the real cost of the borrowed funds?

9.18   Does a firm benefit from using debt instead of common stock during a period of inflation?

9.19   Miss Smith is currently earning $30,000 and is paying an average tax rate of .4 and a marginal rate of 70 percent.

With an inflation rate of 10 percent, what pay increase does Miss Smith require to maintain her standard of living?

9.20   (*Continuation of problem 9.19*). Miss Smith would like to earn a real return of 4 percent before tax and $(1 - .7)(.04) = .012$, or 1.2 percent, after tax.

What nominal interest rate would she have to earn if the marginal tax stays at .7 and if there is an inflation rate of .10?

9.21   What interest rate would you use to find the annual equivalent cost in constant (real) dollars of owning a home that could be purchased for $100,000 now? Assume the homeowner is in the 30 percent income tax bracket, that he expects the rate of inflation to be 6 percent per year, and that the home would be financed with a $80,000 mortgage at an interest rate of 10 percent. The remaining $20,000 would be obtained by selling securities, with an opportunity cost of 15 percent per year before taxes. The homeowner believes that there is no correlation between short-term changes in the rate of inflation and short-term changes in the rate of return on the stock market.

DISCUSSION QUESTION

9.A   Which is more risky, a mortgage bond or common stock of a large oil company? Explain.

REFERENCES

Baldwin, C. Y., and R. S. Ruback, "Inflation, Uncertainty, and Investment," *Journal of Finance*, July 1986, pp. 657–669.

Bodie, Z., "Common Stocks as a Hedge against Inflation," *Journal of Finance*, May 1976, pp. 459–470.

Brenner, M., and I. Venezia, "The Effects of Inflation and Taxes on Growth Investments and Replacement Policies," *Journal of Finance*, December 1983, pp. 1519–1527.

Cooley, Philip L., Rodney L. Roenfeldt, and It-Keong Chew, "Capital Budgeting Procedures Under Inflation," *Financial Management*, Winter 1975, pp. 12–17.

Darby, Michael, "The Financial and Tax Effects of Monetary Policy on Interest Rates," *Economic Inquiry*, June 1975, pp. 266–76.

Day, T. E., "Real Stock Returns and Inflation," *Journal of Finance*, June 1984, pp. 493–502.

Fama, Eugene, "Inflation Uncertainty and Expected Returns on Treasury Bills," *Journal of Political Economy*, June 1976, pp. 427–448.

———, and G. William Schwert, "Asset Returns and Inflation," *Journal of Financial Economics*, 5 November 1977, pp. 115–46.

Ezzell, J. R., and W. Z. Kelly, Jr., "An APV Analysis of Capital Budgeting Under Inflation," *Financial Management*, Autumn 1984, pp. 49–54.

Feldstein, Martin, "Inflation, Income Taxes, and the Rate of Interest: A Theoretical Analysis," *American Economic Review*, December 1976, pp. 809–820.

———, "Inflation and the Stock Market," *American Economic Review*, December 1980, pp. 839–847.

Findley, M. C., and A. W. Frankle, "Capital Budgeting Procedures Under Inflation," *Financial Management*, Autumn 1976, pp. 83–90.

Gandolfi, Arthur, "Inflation, Taxes and Interest Rates," *Journal of Finance*, June 1982, pp. 797–807.

Hong, Hai, "Inflation and the Market Value of the Firm: Theory and Tests," *Journal of Finance*, September 1977, pp. 1031–48.

Jaffe, J. F., "Corporate Taxes, Inflation, the Rate of Interest, and the Return of Equity," *Journal of Financial and Quantitative Analysis*, March 1978, pp. 55–64.

Kim, M. K., "Inflationary Effects in the Capital Investment Process: An Empirical Examination," *Journal of Finance*, September 1979, pp. 941–950.

Mehta, D., M. D. Curley, and Hung-Gay Fung, "Inflation, Cost of Capital, and Capital Budgeting Procedures," *Financial Management*, Winter 1984, pp. 48–53.

Miles, James A., "Taxes and the Fisher Effect: A Clarifying Analysis," *Journal of Finance*, March 1983, pp. 67–77.

Modigliani, Franco, "Debt, Dividend Policy, Taxes, Inflation and Market Valuation," Journal of Finance, May 1982, pp. 255–273.

———, and Richard A. Cohn, "Inflation, Rational Valuation, and the Market," *Financial Analysts Journal*, March–April 1979, pp. 23–44.

Nelson, Charles R., "Inflation and Capital Budgeting," *Journal of Finance*, June 1976, pp. 923–931.

Rappaport, Alfred, and Robert Taggart, Jr., "Evaluation of Capital Expenditure Proposals Under Inflation," *Financial Management*, Spring 1982, pp. 5–13.

Schall, L. D., "Taxes, Inflation and Corporate Financial Policy," *Journal of Finance*, March 1984, pp. 105–126.

Schwert, G. W., "The Adjustment of Stock Prices to Information About Inflation," *Journal of Finance*, March 1981, pp. 15–29.

Stulz, R. M., "Asset Pricing and Expected Inflation," *Journal of Finance*, March 1986, pp. 209–223.

Wilcox, James A., "Why Real Interest Rates Were So Low in the 1970's," *American Economic Review*, March 1983, pp. 44–53.

CHAPTER 10

Accounting Concepts Consistent with Present Value Calculations

What you're saying, then, is that just because all the professionals in the field believe it, it must be right. If this were really true, the world is flat.
Joel Segall, from the Autumn 1969 Newsletter of the Graduate School of Business, *University of Chicago*

Much of the economic analysis of evaluating prospective capital investments relies heavily on concepts such as cash flows and their net present value. This is in contrast to the usual accounting practice where the investment review emphasizes such concepts as revenue, depreciation, income, and return on investment. The purpose of this chapter is to show that the discounted cash flow approach and the main accounting concepts can be reconciled, provided that the accounting concepts are appropriately defined.

We will consider two different methods that give identical net results. The first method includes all cash flows (including investment outlays) in the computation of depreciation and income. The second method excludes investment cash flows after the investment begins operations.

Economic Depreciation: Including All Cash Flows

If we are given the cash flow stream associated with an asset and an appropriate interest rate, we can define the net present value of the cash flows associated with the asset during all succeeding time periods and denote this present value as $V(t)$. $V(0)$ is the present value at time 0 (end of zero period), and $V(1)$ is the present value at time 1. $V(t)$ is after any new investment at time t.

The economic depreciation during period t will be defined as the change in present values during this period. That is, $D(t)$ is the depreciation of period t. $D(t)$ is defined as

$$D(t) = V(t - 1) - V(t)$$

In the usual case, where the present values have declined over the period, depreciation will be a positive quantity. If the present values increase during the period, depreciation will be negative, and we shall refer to the negative value of depreciation as appreciation. If $N(t)$ is the cash flow of the t period (positive for inflows and negative for outflows), the income of the period is defined as the cash flow of the period minus the depreciation of the period. That is, if income is denoted by $Y(t)$, then

$$Y(t) = N(t) - D(t)$$

Return on investment can be defined as the ratio of the income of the period to the present value of the asset at the end of the previous period. If r is the discount rate used in this analysis, each period's return on investment will be equal to r. That is,

$$\frac{Y(t)}{V(t - 1)} = r$$

if $V(t - 1) \neq 0$

The measure of depreciation expense being used in this section is not consistent with the conventional accounting definition, since $V(t)$ is affected by any additional investment. Because the cash flows and depreciation are both affected by the same amount (and in opposite directions), the net income will be consistent with accounting measures of income.[1]

Consider two investments A and B where the cash flows of the one investment supply the cash needed to undertake the second investment. The appropriate rate of discount is 10 percent.

		Time	
	0	*1*	*2*
A	−$17,355	$10,000	$10,000
B		−10,000	11,000
A + B	−$17,355	$ 0	$21,000

Table 10.1 shows the computation of $V(t)$ for the joint investment A plus B. Exhibit 10.1 shows the computation of depreciation, income, and return on investment.

[1] This is not exact but will be close enough for purposes of this chapter. See H. Bierman, Jr., "A Further Study of Depreciation," *The Accounting Review*, April 1966, pp. 271–274.

TABLE 10.1 The Computation of V(t) for A + B (r = .10)

Period	End-of-Period Cash Flow	For V(0) Present Value Factor	For V(0) Present Value	For V(1) Present Value Factor	For V(1) Present Value
1	$ 0	.9091	$ 0		
2	21,000	.8264	17,355	.9091	19,091
			V(0) = $17,355		V(1) = $19,091

EXHIBIT 10.1 Depreciation, Income, and Return on Investment

For period 1, we have

$$D(1) = V(0) - V(1) = 17,355 - 19,091 = -1,736$$
$$Y(1) = N(1) - D(1) = 0 - (-1,736) = 1,736$$

$$r = \frac{Y(1)}{V(0)} = \frac{1,736}{17,355} = .10$$

For period 2, we have

$$D(2) = V(1) - V(2) = 19,091 - 0 = 19,091$$
$$Y(2) = N(2) - D(2) = 21,000 - 19,091 = 1,909$$

$$r = \frac{Y(2)}{V(1)} = \frac{1,909}{19,091} = .10$$

The returns on investment for both years are .10, which is also the internal rate of return of the joint investment.

The procedure described so far can be used without the necessity of distinguishing between cash flows from operations and investment-type cash flows. Investment-type cash flows result from acquiring or disposing of new assets. If this distinction is ignored, then $V(t)$ must be interpreted as the present value of the cash flows from all present assets and all planned additions and deletions in future periods. Similarly, $D(t)$ must be interpreted as the net depreciation of the period, that is, the decrease in value of the existing assets less the increase in asset values resulting from any net additions during the period. Thus, investment A decreased in value by $8,264 in period 1 (this amount is derived in the next section), but there is an additional investment of $10,000; thus, the value of $D(1)$ is a negative $1,736. The asset value increased by $1,736.

Economic Depreciation: Excluding Investment Flows

The preceding procedure is operational. It does work. But the definition of depreciation that is used is not intuitively appealing, since depreciation is affected by the amount of investment made during the period. This "error" is washed out because the cash flows are also reduced by the amount of the investment, and income is not affected.

The procedure to be illustrated aims at using a definition of depreciation that is more consistent with the definition that is used by accountants. Unfortunately, the introduction of this definition of depreciation does lead to some complexity. There is a real gain, however. Frequently, it is desirable to distinguish explicitly between cash flows from operations and investment-type cash flows. The basis for the distinction is that operational cash flows do not directly affect the cash flows of future periods, but investment-type cash flows do. For example, an advertising outlay designed to increase future sales would be an investment; an advertising outlay designed to increase only current sales would be an operational cash flow. Also, the procedure allows the evaluation of discrete investments rather than requiring the evaluation of large sets of investments.

To implement the procedure, let $I(t)$ be defined as an investment type of cash flow occuring in period t. This is a negative cash flow that is incurred because the present value of the positive cash flows associated with the action is sufficiently large to warrant the expenditure. If there are investment-type cash flows encountered in period t, we have

$$I(t) + d(t) = V(t - 1) - V(t)$$

or

$$d(t) = V(t - 1) - V(t) - I(t)$$

where $I(t)$ is a negative quantity if there have been investment outlays, and $d(t)$ is net depreciation. Note that $d(t) = D(t) - I(t)$. The value of $I(t)$ is included, since $V(t)$ reflects the investment, and the objective is to obtain a depreciation measure that is independent of $I(t)$.

EXAMPLE 10.1

To illustrate these concepts, suppose that the discount rate is 10 percent and that interest is compounded annually. The case flows associated with the hypothetical asset A are as follows. The cash flows occur at the end of each period.

Period	End-of-Period Cash Flow
0	−$17,355
1	10,000
2	10,000

The calculations of the net present values of the remaining cash flows at various points in time are presented in Table 10.2. The calculations of depreciation, income, and return on investment are presented in Exhibit 10.2.

The income of period 1 is $1,736, which is exactly the same as with the previous procedure illustrated in Exhibit 10.1. The depreciation expense is now $8,264, whereas it was previously a negative $1,736, but this difference did not affect the income measures.

If we now consider investment B and define B to be essential to A, then the cash flows at time 2 are $21,000, and we have (as previously computed)

$$V_0 = 17,355$$

$$V_1 = 19,091$$

$$V_2 = 0$$

TABLE 10.2   Calculation of Net Present Value of an Asset at Various Points in Time ($r = .10$)

Period	End-of-Period Cash Flow	For V(0) Present Value Factor	For V(0) Present Value	For V(1) Present Value Factor	For V(1) Present Value
1	$10,000	.9091	$ 9,091		
2	10,000	.8264	8,264	.9091	9,091
			V(0) = $17,355		V(1) = $9,091

EXHIBIT 10.2   Depreciation, Income, and Return on Investment for Asset Described in Table 10.2

For period 1

$$d(1) = 17,355 - 9,091 = 8,264$$

$$Y(1) = 10,000 - 8,264 = 1,736$$

$$r = Y(1)/V(0) = 1,736/17,355 = .10$$

For period 2

$$d(2) = 9,091 - 0 = 9,091$$

$$Y(2) = 10,000 - 9,091 = 909$$

$$r = Y(2)/V(1) = 909/9,091 = .10$$

But now, to compute $d(1)$, we have

$$d(1) = V(0) - V(1) - I(1)$$

where $I(1) = -10,000$.

$$d(1) = 17,355 - 19,091 - (-10,000) = \$8,264$$

This depreciation expense measure is equal to that previously obtained (Exhibit 10.2) and is not affected by the new investment. Following the procedure of this section, an investment in the period does not affect the depreciation expense of the period.

Assets with Positive Present Values

In the preceding example, we assumed that, before the first cash flow occurs, the net present value of the cash flows associated with the asset is 0. (The IRR of the investment is equal to the time value of money). We shall now consider investment opportunities whose net present value is positive. How can we measure income and depreciation in such cases?

The example presented earlier will serve to illustrate this case if we assume that the appropriate time-value factor for the firm is .05. As shown in Table 10.3, the net present value of the A investment is $1,239.

One solution is to recognize $1,239 of additional income at time 0, then act as if the asset cost $18,594 and depreciate that amount over its life. The 5 percent rate of interest would be used for discounting, and the return on investment each period after time 0 would be 5 percent. The computations are illustrated (in Table 10.4 and Exhibit 10.3).

This procedure requires the adjustment of the cost of an asset to its value as well as the recording of income and acquisition. Because of the subjective nature of the inputs, many would object to the procedure.

An alternative approach would be to use the internal rate of return of the investment as the discount rate. If this is done for investment A, the computations would be identical to those shown in Table 10.2 and Exhibit 10.2.

TABLE 10.3 *Computation of Net Present Value (r = .05)*

Period	Cash Flow	Present Value Factor (5%)	Present Value
0	−$17,355	1.0000	−$17,355
1	10,000	.9524	9,524
2	10,000	.9070	9,070
			Net present Value $1,239

TABLE 10.4   Calculation of Net Present Value of an Asset (r = .05)

Period	End-of-Period Cash Flow	For V(0)		For V(1)	
		PV Factor	PV	PV Factor	PV
1	$10,000	.9524	$ 9,524		
2	10,000	.9070	9,070	.9524	9,524
			V(0) = $18,594		V(1) = $9,524

EXHIBIT 10.3   Depreciation, Income, and Return on Investment for Asset Described in Table 10.4

For period 1	For period 2
$d(1) = 18,594 - 9,524 = 9,070$	$d(2) = 9,524 - 0 = 9,524$
$Y(1) = 10,000 - 9,070 = 930$	$Y(2) = 10,000 - 9,524 = 476$
$r = 930/18,594 = .05$	$r = 476/9,524 = .05$

The use of an asset's internal rate of return has the advantage of simplicity. But assets with identical cash flows except for the initial outlay would be recorded at values that are not equal to the present values that would be obtained using a common discount factor. For example, two investments with exactly the same benefit stream would be recorded differently if they cost different amounts (their internal rates of return would differ). This is, of course, consistent with generally accepted accounting practice. But it would lead to two identical benefit streams being recorded at different values and leading to different returns on investments. This practice would tend to reduce the usefulness of the return-on-investment calculation as a managerial control device. Suppose that two managers are in charge of the two assets. If both do as well as expected with their assets (that is, achieve the cash flows predicted for their assets), one will have a low return on investment, and the other, a higher return on investment. Thus, the return on investment measures not their operating ability, but the ability (or luck) of whoever originally uncovered the investment opportunities.

We can adjust the first procedure illustrated for those who do not want to recognize the unrealized appreciation as income. Suppose that the asset is carried on the books under two headings: (1) cost of the asset and (2) the difference between the present value and the cost of the asset. The cost would be reduced each period by a depreciation expense computed by taking the change in the present value of the cash flows using the IRR (the interest rate that makes the present value of the investment equal to 0). The difference between the value and the cost would be reduced each year by an additional amount calculated so that the total of the two asset accounts equaled the value of the asset. These calculations are illustrated in Tables 10.5 and 10.6. The incomes and returns on investment for the investment in period 2 are shown in Exhibit 10.4.

The use of the IRR has the advantage of being somewhat more simple to compute and to present.

TABLE 10.5   Computation of Incomes

Period	Revenue	Depreciation (Based on Value)	Income (Based on Value)	Realized Gain	Income (Based on Cost)
1	$10,000	$ 9,070	$ 930	$ 806	$1,736
2	10,000	9,524	476	433	909
	20,000	$18,594	$1,406	$1,239	$2,645

TABLE 10.6   Computation of Realized Capital Gains*

Period	Depreciation (Based on Value)	Depreciation (Based on Cost)	Realized Gain
1	$ 9,070	$ 8,264	$ 806
2	9,524	9,091	433
	$18,594	$17,355	$1,239

* We could also have taken the difference in incomes resulting from the use of the two methods of depreciation. Identical results would have been obtained.

EXHIBIT 10.4   Income and Return on Investment Calculations for Asset with Positive Net Present Value

Period 2	
Revenue	$10,000
Less: Depreciation of original cost	9,091
Income (based on cost of asset)	909
Less: Reduction in unrealized capital gain of asset	433
Income (based on value of asset)	$ 476

$$\frac{\text{Income (based on cost of asset)}}{\text{Depreciated cost of asset}} = \frac{909}{9,091} = 10\%$$

$$\frac{\text{Income (based on value asset)}}{\text{Depreciated value of asset}} = \frac{476}{9,524} = 5\%$$

Tax Effects

The preceding discussion applies if there are no income taxes or if the cash flows and the discount rates used are on an after-tax basis. In general, given the present tax structure, the value of an asset or investment opportunity will depend on the tax status of the investor. Thus it may be profitable for the investor who undertakes an investment to sell the resulting asset to another investor whose tax status is different. This concept is the basis for many tax shelters.

Consider an investment where there is an expenditure of $17,355 and then the investor receives $10,000 a year (before tax) for two years. The present value of the benefits is $18,594, using .05 as the discount rate. This is the value to a zero tax investor at time 0.

Suppose that the original investment has been made by A, that A is subject to a marginal tax rate of 40 percent on his taxable income, and that taxable income is computed using straight-line depreciation on the cost of the asset. Since A is subject to a tax rate of 40 percent, if the before-tax interest rate is .05, A's after-tax interest rate will be .03. Table 10.7 shows the present value of A's after-tax cash flows from the asset at a discount rate of .03, provided the asset is retained.

Since the investment is worth $18,594 to the zero tax investor and only $18,122 to A, a sale by A is likely to occur (the gain to be taxed at the statutory rate for capital gains). If A receives an offer of $18,594, the capital gain would be 18,594 − 17,355 = $1,239. With a .20 capital gains tax ($248), A would net $18,346, which is larger than $18,122.

Valuation Not Affected by Taxes

Opportunities for transactions motivated by differences in tax status would be eliminated if taxable income were determined by using depreciation based on present value. When this convention is adopted, two investors who expect the same before-tax cash flows from an asset will assign it the same value at each point in time, even though each investor values the asset by discounting a dif-

TABLE 10.7   Value of an Asset to an Investor in the 40 Percent Tax Bracket if It Is Held

Before-Tax Cash Flow	Depreciation for Taxes	Taxable Income	Income Tax	After-Tax Cash Flow	Present Value Factor (.03)	Present Value
$10,000	$ 8,677.5	$1,322.5	$ 529	$ 9,471	.9709	$ 9,195
10,000	8,677.5	1,322.5	529	9,471	.9426	8,927
$20,000	$17,355.0	$2,645.0	$1,058	$18,942		$18,122

ferent set of after-tax flows. This is consistent with P. A. Samuelson's definition of income.[2]

We will assume the same investment as just described, but we will now assume a .10 before-tax interest rate. The investor is again subject to an income tax rate of 40 percent.

Taxable income is defined as the change in the present value of the future cash flows from an asset. If interest payments for such a taxpayer are tax deductible and the interest received is included in taxable income, such a taxpayer would use an after-tax rate of .06 if the before-tax interest rate was .10.

We previously computed (Exhibit 10.2) the incomes and depreciation of each year and obtained $V_0 = 17,355$ and $V_1 = 9,091$, $d(1) = 8,264$ and $d(2) = 9,091$ for a zero tax investor.

Using these depreciation expenses for taxes, we obtain the results shown in Table 10.8.

In Table 10.9, the after-tax cash flows and the after-tax discount rate of .06 are used to calculate the value of the asset at various times. At each time, the value of the asset is the same on an after-tax basis as was computed on a before-tax basis for each year.

TABLE 10.8   Income Tax and After-Tax Cash Flows when Taxable Income is Defined in Present Value Terms

Period	End-of-Period Before-Tax Cash Flow	Depreciation	Income	Tax	End-of-Period After-Tax Cash Flow
1	$10,000	$8,264	$1,736	$694	$9,306
2	10,000	9,091	909	364	9,636

TABLE 10.9   Calculation of Net Present Value of an Asset Based on After-Tax Cash Flows (r = .06)

Period	End-of-Period Cash Flow	For V(0) PV Factor	For V(0) PV	V(1) PV Factor	V(1) PV
1	$9,306	.9434	$ 8,779		
2	9,638	.8900	8,576	.9434	9,091
		V(0)	$17,355	V(1)	$9,091

[2] See P. A. Samuelson, "Tax Deductibility of Economic Depreciation to Insure Invariant Valuation," *Journal of Political Economy*, December 1964, pp. 604–606.

Now consider the following investment, shown in Table 10.10, and assume a zero tax investor whose cost of money is .10.

We see in Table 10.11 that the straight-line depreciation expense is equal to the economic depreciation. The net present value of the investment, including the $3,000 outlay, is zero before the outlay is made.

Now assume the investor is taxed at 40 percent and straight-line depreciation is used for taxes (see Table 10.12.)

The present value of the after-tax cash flows using the after-tax borrowing rate of .06 is shown in Table 10.13.

The present values at each moment in time are identical to the values obtained for the zero tax investor.

If the tax rate is changed but the same method of depreciation is used (economic depreciation), the present values of the investment will not be changed.

TABLE 10.10   Zero Tax Investor

Time	Cash Flow	Depreciation	Income	Beginning Investment	Return on Investment
0	−$3,000				
1	1,300	$1,000	$300	$3,000	.10
2	1,200	1,000	200	2,000	.10
3	1,100	1,000	100	1,000	.10

TABLE 10.11   Present Values of Before-Tax Cash Flows

Time	Cash Flow	Time 0 Present Value, Using .10	Time 1 Present Value, Using .10	Time 2 Present Value, Using .10
1	$1,300	$1,181.82		
2	1,200	991.74	$1,090.91	
3	1,100	826.44	909.09	1,000.00
		$3,000.00	$2,000.00	$1,000.00
Change in value:		Period 1 = $1,000	Period 2 = $1,000	Period 3 = $1,000

TABLE 10.12   Calculation of After-Tax Cash FLows

Time	Cash Flow	Depreciation Expense	Income Before Tax	Tax	After-Tax Cash Flow
1	$1,300	$1,000	$300	$120	$1,180
2	1,200	1,000	200	80	1,120
3	1,100	1,000	100	40	1,060

TABLE 10.13   Present Values with t = .40

Time	Cash Flow	Time 0 Present Value, Using .06	Time 1 Present Value, Using .06	Time 2 Present Value, Using .06
1	$1,180	$1,113.20		
2	1,120	996.80	$1,056.60	
3	1,060	890.00	943.40	1,000.00
		$3,000.00	$2,000.00	$1,000.00

The values are invariant to the tax rate if the depreciation expense used in the tax calculations is equal to the before-tax change in value and if the after-tax discount rate used to accomplish the time discounting is equal to the market before-tax rate (the same for all investors) times the amount 1 minus the taxpayer's marginal tax rate.

With the method of depreciation illustrated, transactions will not take place because of differentials in tax rates.

If the cost of the asset is less than $3,000, say $2,000, the procedure will still work if the asset is written up to its present value of $3,000 and if the tax depreciation expense is based on this $3,000 of present value.

Internal Rate of Return and Taxes

Let us assume a situation where an investment type of outlay may be deducted for taxes at the time the outlay is made rather than being depreciated over time.

We want to show that the internal rate of return after tax equals the internal rate of return before tax.

Assume the before-tax cash flows are

$$C_0, C_1, C_2, \ldots C_i \ldots C_N$$

where C_i is the cash flow of period i.

The after-tax present value is

$$\text{NPV} = (1 - t)C_0 + \frac{(1 - t)C_1}{1 + r} + \frac{(1 - t)C_2}{(1 + r)^2} + \cdots + \frac{(1 - t)C_n}{(1 + r)^n} = 0$$

where r is the internal rate of return.

Dividing both sides by $(1 - t)$, we obtain

$$\text{NPV} = C_0 + \frac{C_1}{1 + r} + \frac{C_2}{(1 + r)^2} + \cdots + \frac{C_n}{(1 + r)^n} = 0$$

where r is the before-tax internal rate of return.

The fact that the internal rate of return is not affected by the tax rate requires that C_0 and all subsequent cash flows be treated as taxable expenses or incomes in the years in which they occur.

Consider the following investment with an internal rate of return of .10.

Time	Before-Tax Cash Flow
0	−$3,000
1	1,300
2	1,200
3	1,100

With immediate expensing and a .40 tax rate, the cash flows and their present values would be

Time	After-Tax Cash Flow	Present Value (.10)
0	−1,800	−$1,800.00
1	780	709.09
2	720	595.04
3	660	495.87
		NPV = $ 0

The before- and after-tax internal rate of return are both .10. The internal rate of return is not affected by the tax rate.

The net present value would be reduced by an increase in the tax rate unless the rate of discount being used is the internal rate of return.

This analysis is also applicable to certain types of retirement funds, commonly known as Keogh plans. The basic tax rules applicable to these plans are (1) the cash invested in one of these funds is tax deductible in the year in which it is invested; (2) dividends, interest, and capital gains realized by such a fund are not taxable as long as the money remains in the fund; and (3) cash withdrawn from such a fund is fully taxable in the year it is withdrawn. Suppose that the money invested in an Keogh is used to purchase assets that provide an internal rate of return of 10 percent before taxes. Then the after-tax internal rate of return to the investor is also 10 percent. This is illustrated with the following simple example, for an investor in a 40 percent tax bracket and an asset whose IRR is 10 percent.

Time	Before-Tax Cash Flow	After-Tax Cash Flow
0	−$3,000	−$1,800
5	4,832	2,899

The after-tax cash flows will have a positive present value for any discount rate less than 10 percent. The internal rates of return of both the before- and after-tax cash flows are equal to .10.

Taking the Long-Run Perspective Without Neglecting the Short Run

Critics of the business scene have emphasized the tendency of business firms to focus on the short-run effects rather than the long-run consequences of decisions.[3] Part of the blame has been placed on graduate schools of business and their MBA programs, but this is an invalid accusation, since for the past thirty years just about 100 percent of these schools have taught the use of internal rate of return and net present value in making investment decisions. These are long-run perspectives. It is a very rare member of the academic community who would advocate focusing on the return on investment (ROI) of year 1 or year 2 for an investment with a life of twenty years. Unfortunately, managers do use such measures.

If the excessive focus on the short run was not learned at school, where was it learned? Partially, it was learned on the job by observation of the paycheck (or, more accurately, the bonus payment) and a reading of the job agreement. A concern for short-run changes in the stock price also has motivated an excessive attention to the near-term effects of investments.

When corporations compensate top managers, there is a tendency to reward a manager for:

1. Increases in total earnings.
2. Improvements in ROI.
3. Improvements in earnings per share (EPS).

All things equal, it is both fair and desirable to reward managers who achieve increases in total earnings, improve ROI, and cause EPS to increase. It is only when we look closely at these measures that we see possible difficiencies in their use.

An intelligent operating officer will realize when a decision will benefit one of the preceding measures but will harm the firm. Then why is the bad decision made? Financial incentives geared to the short-run measures will cause the most conscientious managers to give serious consideration to an alternative that will benefit their take-home pay. Equally important is the fact that a decision that

---

[3] See Robert H. Hayes and David A. Garvin, "Managing as if Tomorrow Mattered," *Harvard Business Review*, May–June 1982, pp. 70–79. Also, Robert H. Hayes and William J. Abernathy, "Managing Our Way to Economic Decline," *Harvard Business Review*, July–August 1980, pp. 67–77.

would harm the paycheck is likely to be rejected even if the decision is likely to be beneficial in the long run.

It is unintelligent to offer rewards for a type of action and then think it immoral (or lacking in intelligence) when the managers act in a manner consistent with the incentives.

We will not suggest an abandonment of the short-term income measures but rather an adjustment in their calculation and an expansion to the use of other measures to supplement them. It would be more dramatic (and theoretically correct) to conclude that only measures that considered the entire life of the assets being used should be the basis of the performance measurement. But this approach would neglect the very natural desire of managers to know how both they and their subordinates are doing right now. We are naturally too impatient to wait until the year 2000 to find out how we did in 1990.

The Suggestion

The basic suggestion of this section is to convert the short-run measures of performance into long-run measures. This conversion will be accomplished using present value depreciation. Present value depreciation locks all the years together, so that if an investment is desirable, each year of life will show desirable performance measures.

EXAMPLE 10.2

Assume that a firm has .10 time value factor and uses straight-line depreciation. Consider an investment that has the following cash flows.

0	1	2	3	4
− 200,000	50,000	60,000	100,000	171,875

With a .10 hurdle rate, the investment is desirable on a discounted cash basis (it has an internal rate of return of .25). If the firm borrows the entire investment cost an interest rate of .10 and the forcasts are realized, the following income statements will result if straight-line depreciation is used.

	Year			
	1	*2*	*3*	*4*
Revenue	$50,000	$60,000	$100,000	$171,875
Depreciation	50,000	50,000	50,000	50,000
Interest	24,000	15,000	10,000	5,000
Income	−$20,000	−$5,000	$ 40,000	$116,875

The first two years of operations have losses and, if one focuses on total earnings, ROI, or earnings per share of the two early years, the tendency will be to reject this investment. Only if one considers the entire life does the investment become desirable. This type of conflict situation is apt to arise whenever the benefits start low and increase through time.

We will first consider an accounting solution (there are several possible accounting solutions). Using the internal rate of return to compute present values and defining $V(t)$ to be the present value at time t and $d(t)$ to be the present value depreciation for the tth period, we have

Time: t	V(t)	d(t)
0	$200,000	
1	200,000	0
2	190,000	10,000
3	137,500	52,500
4	0	137,500
		$200,000

$d(t)$ is equal to the change in value of the asset rather than the cost of the asset divided by the life or some other mechanical calculation. The income statements and returns on investment are now

	Year			
	1	2	3	4
Revenue	$ 50,000	$ 60,000	$100,000	$171,875
Depreciation	0	10,000	52,500	137,500
Income before interest	50,000	50,000	47,500	34,375
Investment	$200,000	$200,000	$190,000	$137,500
ROI	.25	.25	.25	.25

The investment now favorably affects total earnings, ROI, and earnings per share of each year. Each year has an ROI equal to the internal rate of return of the investment.

We now reach a very important generalization. If an investment is economically desirable, the method of accounting used to evaluate performance should not indicate that any year's operations is not acceptable if the actual results are the same as the planned results. A method of accounting that shows bad performance measures when the performance is good is not acceptable accounting. Only if the actual results fall short of those forecasted should the measures of performance indicate less-than-acceptable performance.

A second solution to the problem just illustrated is to delay the performance evaluation (and bonus payment) until the end of the entire four-year planning horizon. This procedure would ensure that the short-run considerations would not be the crucial factor in analyzing the investment. The disadvantages are that managers want to track the progress being made to achieve goals and that the wait for a bonus would be excessively long with long-lived investments.

EXAMPLE 10.3

Assume that a firm has a choice between two plants. One plant will be adequate for two years, at which time an expansion, good for another four years, will be built. The other plant will be good for the entire six-year period. The firm requires a return of .10 on its investments.

The expected cash flows are

	Time 0	1	2	3	4	5	6
Plant A	−$10,000	$6,500	$ 6,500 −44,966	18,000	$18,000	$18,000	$18,000
Plant B	−36,566	6,500	6,500	18,000	18,000	18,000	18,000

Using straight-line depreciation and funds borrowed at cost of .10, the income statements for the first two years will be

	Plant A		Plant B	
	Year 1	Year 2	Year 1	Year 2
Revenue	$6,500	$6,500	$6,500	$6,500
Depreciation	5,000	5,000	6,094	6,094
Interest	1,000	500	3,600	3,000
Income	$ 500	$1,000	−$3,194	−$2,594

The income statements indicate a superiority for Plant A. There are positive incomes in both year 1 and year 2, while Plant B has two loss years. The managers with their bonus based on total income or earnings per share have a strong bias for Plant A. If the example is made more dramatic by moving the time of plant expansion for A to year 10, we can easily sense the incentive to exploit the possibility of achieving ten good years and letting the next manager worry about the plant expansion.

Now let us consider the economics of the two alternatives. Plant B costs $26,566 more at time 0 but saves $44,966 at time 2. By building Plant B, the firm earns .301 per year incrementally. Unless uncertainty is introduced, it is clear that Plant B should be built if the company requires a .10 return on its investments.

The earnings-per-share incentives are identical to those of total earnings in this type of situation. Plant A will favorably affect earnings per share, and Plant B will have an adverse effect for the first two years. In addition, the returns on investment for two years also point to Plant A as the preferred choice.

Thus, a short-run incentive approach will result in Plant A, even though the discounted cash flow calculations make clear that in this situation Plant B is to be preferred.

Solutions

One suggestion is to require that all economically feasible alternatives be submitted to top management so that mutually exclusive investment decisions are not made at the operating level. Another possibility is for top management to consider the entire planning horizon rather than the year-by-year performance. This would imply that the size of a bonus would depend on more than the conventional accounting measure of the early years of operation. A comparison of the planned results and the actual results would be more important than the absolute value of accounting measures.

Following this proposal, there would not be an incentive to choose A rather than B, since both alternatives budget $6,500 of cash flows for the first two periods. If the actual results are $6,500, both investments will show identical performance.

The final suggestion is again to modify the method of accounting. Moving from straight-line depreciation to the use of present value depreciation will modify B's results so that the losses of periods 1 and 2 are eliminated. The values at time 0, 1, and 2 and depreciations for periods 1 and 2 for plant B are

| | Plant B | |
Time	Value (Using .25)	Depreciation
0	$36,566	
1	39,207	−$2,641
2	42,509	− 3,302

Plant B's internal rate of return of .25 is used as the discount rate.

The depreciation expenses are negative, indicating the asset is becoming more valuable from time 0 to time 1 and from time 1 to time 2. Income statements for Plant B for the first two years are now

	Year	
	1	2
Revenue	$ 6,500	$ 6,500
Depreciation	−2,641	−3,302
Income before interest	9,141	9,802
Investment	$36,566	$39,207
ROI	.25	.25

Now investment B is more than competitive with investment A.

The Problem Can Disappear

We want to illustrate a situation where the problem of ROI distortion that is being described will not be relevant. Assume that an investment with a life of three years will have cash flows of

Time	Cash Flows	Depreciation Expense	Income	ROI
0	−$3,000			
1	1,100	$1,000	$100	.033
2	1,210	1,000	210	.105
3	1,331	1,000	331	.331

The internal rate of return is .10, but the ROI in year 1 is only .03.

Now assume that identical investments will be made each year, but the dollar size of the investment will grow by .10.

Time	Investment of Year 0	Investment of Year 1	Investment of Year 2
0	−$3,000		
1	1,100	−$3,300	
2	1,210	1,210	−$3,630
3	1,331	1,331	1,331
4		1,464.1	1,464.10
5			1,610.51

Let us consider the ROI of year 3 (subtract the depreciation expense to obtain each year's income).

$$\text{ROI} = \frac{(1{,}331 - 1{,}000) + (1{,}331 - 1{,}100) + (1{,}331 - 1{,}210)}{1{,}000 + 2{,}200 + 3{,}630} = \frac{683}{6830} = .10$$

In each year after year 2, the ROI will be equal to the investment's internal rate of return, independent of the depreciation method.

Unfortunately, the growth in investments is not as uniform in practice as is illustrated in the preceding example. The problem being described will not always be eliminated by identical investments growing at the same rate as the investment's internal rate of return.

Conclusions

It is generally accepted accounting practice to use some method of depreciation accounting that is well defined and is independent of the economic characteristics of the asset being depreciated. For tax purposes, the objective of depreciation accounting is to write the asset off as rapidly as possible (more exactly, to maximize the present value of the writeoffs). For accounting purposes, the objective is to allocate the cost of the asset over its useful life. This chapter has suggested two alternative methods of defining depreciation. One method accomplishes the important objective of equating the return on investment of the asset to its internal rate of return. If we are willing to record an adjustment to the cost of the asset to its present value, the second method leads to the return on investment being equal to the time-value factor (rate of discount defined to be appropriate) for the firm in each year of use. These procedures have the advantage of eliminating the types of distortions in the measurement of return on investment associated with the use of straight-line depreciation or accelerated depreciation when the cash flows do not decrease rapidly through time.

We know that investment decisions should be made using the available information for the entire life of the investment. The measures of performance should do likewise, or distortions will be introduced if there is a focus on the short-run measures.

If the accounting measures are converted from conventional measures to economic measures, significant improvements in the measures of performance result. They become reconciled to the economic measures of investment worth.

The severity of the distortions resulting from the use of conventional accounting were understated in the examples given in this chapter, since straight-line depreciation was used. If any of the accelerated depreciation methods had been used, the distortions would have been even larger. The performance of the early years of use would have appeared even worse than was indicated in the examples.

We have to move to a system of measuring performance where a desirable investment has desirable measures of performance as long as the actual results coincide with the forecasted results.

PROBLEMS

10.1 An asset costs $15,277 and will earn proceeds of $10,000 a year for two years. The cash is received at the end of each period. The time value of money is .20.
  a. Compute the internal rate of return of the investment.
  b. Compute the depreciations in value of the asset, the incomes, and the returns on investment for the two years of life.

10.2 An asset cost $25,620 and will earn proceeds of $10,000 in year 1 and $20,000 in year 2. The time value of money is .10.
  a. Compute the internal rate of return of the investment.
  b. Compute the depreciations in value of the asset, the incomes, and the returns on investment for the two years of life.

10.3 An asset costs $26,446 and will earn proceeds of $20,000 in year 1 and $10,000 in year 2. The time value of money is .10.
  a. Compute the internal rate of return of the investment.

b. Compute the depreciations in value of the asset, the incomes, and the returns on investment for the two years of life.

10.4   An asset costs $20,000 and earns proceeds of $11,000 in year 1 and $10,500 in year 2. The time value of money is .05.

a. Compute the internal rate of return of the investment.

b. Compute the depreciations in value of the asset, the incomes, and the returns on investment for the two years of life.

10.5   An asset costs $20,000 and will earn proceeds of $12,000 in year 1 and $11,000 in year 2. The time value of money is .10.

a. Compute the internal rate of return of the investment.

b. Compute the depreciations in value of the asset, the incomes, and the returns on investment for the two years of life.

10.6   An asset costs $15,778 and will earn cash proceeds of $10,000 a year for two years, the first payment to be received two years from now. The sales will be made at the end of periods 1 and 2, and the collections, at the end of periods 2 and 3. The time value of money is .10.

Compute the depreciations, the incomes, and the returns on investment for the life of the investment.

10.7   An asset costs $8,505 at time 0 and an additional $8,000 at time 1. It will earn proceeds of $10,000 a year for two years, the first payment to be received two years from now. The time value of money is .10.

Compute the depreciations, the incomes, and the returns on investment for the life of the investment.

10.8   (*Continuation of problem* 10.7.) What is the value of the investment at time 1 (after the second investment) if the actual investment outlay was only $5,000 at time 0 and $4,000 at time 1? What is the value at time 2? Assume that the expected benefits are unchanged.

10.9   The XYZ Company wants to know the cost of a new building it has constructed. It paid the builder an advance of $2 million and paid the remainder when the building was completed two years later (total amount paid to the builder was $3 million).

a. Determine the cost, assuming that the building was financed with .05 debentures.

b. Determine the cost, assuming that the building was financed entirely by stock.

10.10   An investment costs $14,059 and has expected cash flows of

Period 0	Period 1	Period 2
−$14,059	$10,000	$5,000

The time value of money of the firm is .05. Management wants a system for reappraising capital budgeting decisions.

a. Assume that the accounting measures of expense (except for depreciation) and revenues would be the same as the preceding. Prepare statements of income and return on investment that would be reasonable tools for reappraisal of the decisions.

b. Assume that the cash flows just indicated apply, but the accounting measure of net revenue in period 1 is $14,762, and the net revenue in period 2 is $0. What is the depreciation of periods 1 and 2?

10.11 **a.** Find the income, depreciation and return on investment during periods 1 and 2 using an interest rate of 25 percent (no taxes are payable).

Period	End-of-Period Before-Tax Cash Flows
0	−$16,000
1	+ 16,000
2	− 7,000
3	+ 15,000

b. Assume a tax rate of 40 percent on income defined in present value terms. What are the after-tax cash flows for periods 1 and 2?

10.12 Consider the following before-tax cash flows.

0	1	2
−100	0	+144

Suppose an investor is in the 60 percent tax bracket. Find the after-tax internal rate of return on this investment for each of the following circumstances.

a. The outlays come from after-tax funds. The taxes are paid using the present value definition of income. (Assume a before-tax discount rate of 20 percent.)

b. The outlays come from after-tax funds. The proceeds are taxed using an income concept based on historical cost and straight-line depreciation.

c. The outlays come from before-tax funds and are tax deductible. All proceeds are taxable when realized. (This is how some pension plans work.)

10.13 Consider the following before-tax cash flows.

Period	0	1	2
End-of-period cash flow	−$8,000	+$15,000	−$5,000

a. Find the income and depreciation during period 1, using present value accounting. Assume no taxes and an interest rate of 6 percent in all periods.

b. Find the income and depreciation during period 2, using present value accounting. Assume no taxes and an interest rate of 6 percent in all periods.

c. Assume a tax rate of 25 percent on income defined in present value terms. What are the after-tax cash flows for periods 1 and 2? (Assume the taxpayer has other taxable income in both periods.)

10.14 Given the following data.

Period	End-of-Period Before-Tax Cash Flows
0	−$12,000
1	+ 12,000
2	− 6,000
3	+ 12,000

a. Find the income, depreciation, and return on investment during period 1, using an interest rate of 12 percent (no taxes are payable).

b. Find the income, depreciation, and return on investment during period 2, using an interest rate of 12 percent (no taxes are payable).

c. Assume a tax rate of one third on income defined in present value terms. What are the after-tax cash flows for periods 1 and 2?

DISCUSSION QUESTIONS

10.A The tax laws allow accelerated depreciation. Assume that an investment has equal cash flows in each year over its entire life.

Without taxes, what timing of depreciation expense would you recommend to measure income appropriately? What does this imply about the tax depreciation deduction?

10.B A power generating plant cost NY Electric Utility $500,000,000. It has an expected life of five years. The firm is allowed a .10 return on capital.

Prepare a schedule showing investment, depreciation expense, allowed return, and total amount paid by consumers if the consumers pay an equal amount each year.

10.C Assume there is .04 inflation and it is desired that in each year consumers will pay the same real total revenue. Prepare a schedule for the situation similar to that done for problem 10.16.

REFERENCES

Bierman, Harold, Jr., "A Reconciliation of Present Value Capital Budgeting and Accounting," *Financial Management*, Summer 1977, pp. 52–54.

Dearden, John, "The Case Against ROI Control," *Harvard Business Review*, May–June 1969, pp. 124–35.

Ijiri, Juji, *Theory of Accounting Measurement*, Studies in Accounting Research, No. 10 (Sarasota, FL: American Accounting Association, 1975).

———, "Cash-Flow Accounting and Its Structure, "*Journal of Accounting, Auditing and Finance*, Summer 1978, pp. 331–48.

———, "Recovery Rate and Cash Flow Accounting," *Financial Executive*, March 1980, pp. 54–60.

Mauriel, John J., and Robert N. Anthony, "Misevaluation of Investment Center Performance," *Harvard Business Review*, March–April 1966, pp. 98–105.

Solomon, Ezra, "Alternative Rate of Return Concepts and Their Implication for Utility Regulation," *Bell Journal of Economics and Management Science*, Spring 1970, pp. 65–81.

Solomons, David, *Divisional Performance Measurement and Control* (Homewood, Il: Irwin, 1965).

Buy or Lease

Practical men, who believe themselves to be quite exempt from any intellectual influences, are usually the slaves of some defunct economist.
J. M. Keynes, The General Theory of Employment, Interest and Money *(New York: Harcourt, Brace & Company, 1936), p. 383.*

When we use the term *lease* in this chapter, we shall be referring to a financial type of lease, that is, a lease where the firm has a legal obligation to continue making payments for a well-defined period of time. We are excluding from consideration the type of lease where an asset is acquired for a short period of time to fill a temporary need and then leasing is stopped. (A familiar example of this latter type of lease is the renting of an automobile at an airport.) We shall first deal with leases where there is a buy-or-lease option and the firm has already made the decision to acquire the asset. In this situation, the buy-or-lease decision becomes a financing decision. We shall then discuss the situation where the firm must decide whether to buy, lease, or do nothing. We shall conclude that many financial leases are very similar to debt and should be treated in essentially the same manner as debt. A legally oriented person would be able to point out the differences between a lease and debt (especially when there is a failure to pay the required payments), but we shall concentrate on the similarities, and the decision maker can bring the differences into the analysis in a qualitative manner.

The basic problem in analyzing a lease is that there is implicit debt financing accompanying the acquisition of the right to use an asset. Since the debt is implicit rather than explicit, conventional methods of analysis can be faulty unless they are carefully used. Normally, we exclude debt-financing flows and their tax effect from the investment analysis. With leasing, the debt flows are interwoven with the investment flows, and the extraction is more complex.

Borrow or Lease: The Financing Decision

We shall first assume a zero tax rate and analyze the financial aspects of the lease-versus-buy decision. Assume that a company is considering the lease or purchase of a piece of equipment. The firm has decided to acquire the equipment. The equipment will incur operating costs and will generate revenues that are unaffected by whether the equipment is leased or purchased. Thus, for any lease-or-buy decision, there will be many cash flows that are common to both decisions. There are, however, differences in the cash flows related to the method of financing the equipment. On the one hand, we have the cash flows associated with buying, and on the other, the cash flows associated with leasing. Assume that the equipment costs $100,000; we can borrow the $100,000 at a cost of .05 per year or we can lease the equipment at a cost of $29,000 per year. Should we lease or buy, assuming that the equipment has an expected life of four years? Because we have decided to acquire the asset, the only decision is the type of financing.

There is an easy method of solving the buy-versus-lease decision with zero taxes. Since the lease payments are $29,000 per year, the decision maker can make a phone call to the firm's bank and ask what payments would be required annually for four years to repay a $100,000 loan. If the amount is less than $29,000 (with .05 debt the payment is $28,201), then buy–borrow is more desirable than leasing (all other things equal and zero taxes).

We can also compute the present value of the two alternatives. The present value of the cash outlays with leasing is $29,000 times the present value of an annuity for four periods using an interest rate of .05.

$$\$29,000 \times 3.5460 = \$102,834$$

The present value of the immediate cash outlay associated with buying is $100,000, and we again prefer buying (and borrowing). The present value of the debt payments of $28,201 per year is also $100,000 if we use the borrowing rate of .05.

If the discount rate used in the analysis is the same as the interest rate that the firm would have to pay if it actually attempted to finance the purchase of the asset by a loan, the particular loan repayment schedule chosen will not affect the present value of the loan. Suppose that an amount C is borrowed, and interest of k percent is paid on the principal plus accrued interest outstanding. Using k as the discount rate, we find that the present value of the payments required to repay the loan will always be C, whatever loan repayment schedule is chosen.

By equating the present value of the four $29,000 lease payments to the $100,000 cost of the asset, we can determine the implicit interest cost of leasing.

$$29,000B\,(4,\,k) = 100,000$$

$$B\,(4,\,k) = 3.4483$$

By trial and error (or by inspecting Appendix Table B), we find that k is approximately equal to .062. The leasing is an expensive method of debt financing compared to borrowing from the bank. With zero taxes, this is a sensible solution.

The purpose of this phase of the analysis is to determine whether the proposed lease is financially attractive. Because the lease is presumed to require a contractually predetermined set of payments, it is reasonable to compare the lease with an alternative type of financing available to the company that also requires a contractually predetermined set of payments, that is, a loan. In this analysis we are only determining whether leasing or borrowing is preferable.

The conclusions to this point can be summarized as follows: We can buy a piece of equipment for $100,000; it has an expected life of four years. The firm could borrow the money to finance the purchase at an interest cost of 5 percent. The equipment could also be acquired through a lease. If the annual lease payments were $29,000 per year for four years, there would be a financial cost disadvantage to leasing, because the present value of the lease payments at 5 percent is larger than the amount that would have to be borrowed to finance the purchase through borrowing. If the lease payments required were less than $28,201, the lease would have a financial cost advantage.

A Lease Is Debt

Now assume the firm normally uses a .10 weighted average cost of capital to evaluate investments, and the asset will earn cash flow benefits of $31,000 per year. The net present value of buying is

$$\text{NPV (buying)} = 31,000B\ (4, .10) - 100,000$$
$$= 31,000\ (3.1699) - 100,000 = -\$1,733$$

The present value of buying is negative, and buying is not acceptable.
A conventional calculation of the present value of leasing would be

$$\text{NPV (leasing)} = (31,000 - 29,000)\ B\ (4, .10)$$
$$= 2,000\ (3.1699) = \$6,340$$

The net present value is positive (using any interest rate), and leasing seems to be acceptable. But this analysis is in error, since the lease is debt and we are discounting the debt at a higher discount rate than the cost of borrowing. We just concluded that if the project is acceptable, buying is better than leasing. We cannot now conclude that leasing is better. Leasing costs $29,000 per year, and buying with debt costs $28,201. Buying costs less than leasing. The net present value of buying if the debt is included in the cash flows is

$$\text{NPV (buying)} = (31,000 - 28,201)\ B\ (4, .10)$$
$$= 2,799\ (3.1699) = \$8,873$$

which is better than the $6,340 of leasing.

The problem with including the debt flows in the buy analysis when the discount rate is larger than the borrowing rate is that the net present value is then affected by the rate at which the debt is repaid.

A reasonable solution is to compute the net present values using the cost of debt.

$$\text{NPV (buying)} = 31{,}000B\ (4,\ .05) - 100{,}000$$
$$= 31{,}000\ (3.5459) - 100{,}000 = \$9{,}923.$$
$$\text{NPV (Leasing)} = (31{,}000 - 29{,}000)\ (3.5459) = \$7{,}092$$

If we include the debt flows in the buy analysis, the net present value of the debt flows will now be zero, since all flows are being discounted using the cost of debt.

The analysis we have presented may be used to decide whether direct borrowing with an explicit debt security is more desirable or less desirable than leasing. We have not attempted to present an analysis here that proves debt is more or less attractive than other types of financing. We have kept the capital structure the same for both alternatives. Since a lease is debt, the buy alternative must also use debt to make the two alternatives comparable.

The analysis we have presented cannot be used to decide whether the asset should be acquired, nor can it be used to decide whether the firm should have more or less financial leverage. If it has been decided that acquiring the use of the equipment is desirable, the analysis can be used to determine whether to buy or lease the equipment. The specific actions that should be taken will depend on whether additional financial leverage is desirable.

The analysis of this section is incomplete in several respects. It cannot tell us whether the equipment should be acquired at all, and it cannot tell us whether additional financial leverage is desirable.

In addition, the preceding analysis assumes a zero tax rate. It is necessary to take income taxes into consideration to make the analysis more realistic, because incomes taxes will tend to influence the choice.

Buy or Lease with Taxes: Using the After-tax Borrowing Rate

With taxes, there are two reasonably correct approaches to analyzing lease versus buy. The easiest solution is to use the after-tax borrowing rate as the discount rate. If the firm wants to use some type of risk-adjusted rate, then arriving at a reasonable solution is much more complex.

Let us now consider the effects of a corporate income tax of 40 percent. With an income tax, we shall want to put all cash flows on an after-tax basis, and because interest expense is deductible for tax purposes, we shall use an after-tax discount rate. If a discount rate of 5 percent was appropriate on a before-tax basis for borrowed funds, the corresponding after-tax rate can be assumed to be $(1 - .4)\ .05 = .03$.

Because lease payments are a deductible expense in computing income subject to taxes, annual lease payments of $28,201 per year will become after-tax cash flows of $(1 - .4)$ $28,201, or $16,921 per year. The present value of the after-tax lease payments, using a 3 percent discount rate, will be $16,921 × 3.7171, or $62,897. This calculation can only be justified if the after-tax borrowing rate is being used.

The cost of the equipment is $100,000, and we shall consider borrowing that amount in order to finance purchase of the machine. The exact pattern of after-tax cash flows will depend on the debt repayment schedule. If the lender charges 5 percent per year, equal payments of $28,201 per year for four years would be one repayment schedule sufficient to repay the interest and principal on the loan. To put these cash flows on an after-tax basis for the borrower, we need to determine for each year how much of this amount will be considered a payment of interest and how much a repayment of principal. Only the interest expense portion is allowed as an expense for tax purposes. A different repayment schedule would lead to a different pattern of after-tax cash flows; but provided interest were computed on the remaining debt balance, the present value of the after-tax cash flows required to repay the principal and interest of the loan will always be $100,000. For example, suppose that the firm pays interest at $5,000 per year for four years and repays the principal in a lump sum at the end of the fourth year. The after-tax interest payments are $3,000 for each year. The present value of the debt using .03 as the discount rate is

$$\$3,000 \times 3.7171 = \$ \ 11,151$$

$$\$100,000 \times .88849 = \underline{88,849}$$

$$\$100,000$$

We want to compute the cash flows of borrowing the funds to buy the equipment. If we subtract the present value of the positive cash flows associated with borrowing (plus $100,000) from the present value of the after-tax cash payments (a negative $100,000), we find that borrowing has a zero present value.

If we compare the $100,000 immediate cost of the asset with the $62,897 present value of the lease payments, there appears to be an advantage in favor of the lease when taxes are taken into account. However, depreciation tax deductions have not yet been considered. If the equipment is leased, the lessee cannot deduct depreciation. If the equipment is purchased, the right to deduct depreciation expense for tax purposes is obtained. With a tax rate of 40 percent, each dollar of depreciation expense will save $.40 of taxes. The present value of the tax savings resulting from depreciation will depend on the timing of the depreciation expense. If depreciation is charged on a straight-line basis over a four-year period, the value of the tax savings each year will be $10,000 ($.4 \times \$25,000$), and the present value of the tax savings will be $10,000 × 3.7171 = $37,171. Subtracting this from the cost of the investment gives a net present value of after-tax cash flows of $62,829 for the borrow-and-buy decision. This is slightly less than the present value of the lease payments ($62,897).

If a more rapid method of depreciation were used, there would be a more clearly defined advantage in favor of buying. For example, if the twice-straight-line, declining-balance method of depreciation were used, the present value of the tax savings could be computed using Appendix Table D. With an interest rate of 3 percent and a life of four years, the present value of the tax deduction privilege is as follows: $100,000 \times .4 \times .946539 = \$37,862$. Subtracting this amount from $100,000 gives a net present value of $62,138 for buying and borrowing, which is $759 less than the present value for leasing.

The tax savings that result from charging depreciation if the asset is owned are not contractual, as are the other cash flows we are considering. Frequently, however, there is little uncertainty associated with the amount and timing of these tax savings. Regardless of whether the particular piece of equipment performs as anticipated, the right to charge depreciation expense will generate tax savings as long as the firm as a whole has taxable income. Even if the firm does not have taxable income in any particular year, the tax-loss carry-forward and carry-back provisions of the law provide a high degree of assurance that tax savings will result, although their timing might change slightly. It should be remembered that there is also no guarantee that there will be enough revenues so that the full lease payments can be used to reduce taxes. The preceding analysis used the after-tax borrowing rate. If any other discount rate is used, the analysis is more complex.

One important difference in buying, compared to leasing, is that the firm that buys an asset owns the asset at the end of the time period of the lease. To the extent that the asset has net value at that time, this is also a net cash flow for the buy analysis. This difference will be illustrated when we discuss the buy–lease analysis for acquisition of land.

Is the Equipment Worth Acquiring?

In the previous sections, we have shown that the present value of the cost (using twice-straight-line depreciation) of acquiring the equipment is $62,138 if it is bought and $62,897 if leased. To decide whether it is worth buying the equipment, we need to compare the present value of the benefits with the net cost of $62,138.

Suppose that the equipment has a life of four years and would lead to before-tax cash savings of $31,000 per year. The after-tax cash savings are $(1 - .4) \times \$31,000$, or $18,600 per year. The present value of the tax savings that would result from the right to charge depreciation expense on the equipment has already been calculated and subtracted from the purchase price of the equipment, so these tax savings should not be considered again.

Using the after-tax interest rate of 3 percent, we find that the present value of the savings from operating the machine is

$$\$18,600 \times 3.7171 = \$69,138$$

Subtracting the present value of the costs of equipment from the present value of the savings, we have a net present value of $7,000 (that is, $69,138 − $62,138), indicating that we can accept the machine on a borrow-and-buy basis if we are willing to accept a return equal to the after-tax borrowing rate. We can expect that the firm will want to make an adjustment for risk.

In situations such as this, we may be able to estimate the cost of acquiring the asset with a high degree of confidence, whereas the savings that would result from having the use of the asset are subject to considerable uncertainty. If the firm has not had experience with similar equipment, there may be some question as to whether the savings in cost per unit of product (or other measure of the rate of usage) will be as high as anticipated. In addition, there may be some uncertainty about the number of units of product that will be needed and about the equipment's anticipated life. For these and other reasons, a decision about whether the machine should be acquired will to a great extent depend upon management's judgments and risk preferences.

Using a Risk-Adjusted Discount Rate

If some rate other than the after-tax borrowing rate is used, then we cannot merely find the after-tax present value of leasing by computing the present value of the after-tax leasing flows. Doing this creates a bias for leasing by including lease debt flows and their tax effects in the present value calculation.

The first step using a risk-adjusted rate (say .10) is to compute the debt equivalent of the lease payments.

$$29,000B \ (4, \ .05) = \$102,834$$

The second step is to compute a debt amortization schedule for the debt equivalent.

Time	Amount Owed	Interest	Principal = 29,000 − Interest
0	$102,834	$5,142	$23,858
1	78,976	3,949	25,051
2	53,925	2,696	26,304
3	27,621	1,381	27,619
4			

The "Principal" column gives us the base tax deduction that is the equivalent to the depreciation tax deduction of buying. The present value of these tax deductions converted into tax savings is

$$\text{Present value} = .4\left[\frac{23,858}{1.10} + \frac{25,051}{(1.10)^2} + \frac{26,304}{(1.10)^3} + \frac{27,619}{(1.10)^4}\right]$$

$$= .4 \ (81,019) = 32,408$$

The net cost of leasing is

$$\text{NPV (leasing)} = 102{,}834 - 32{,}408 = \$70{,}426$$

The net cost of buying using straight-line depreciation for taxes is

$$\text{NPV (buy)} = 100{,}000 - 25{,}000 \ (.4) \ B \ (4, \ .10)$$
$$= 100{,}000 - 10{,}000 \ (3.1699) = 100{,}000 - 31{,}699 + \$68{,}301$$

Buying costs less than leasing.

Risk Considerations in Lease-Versus-Borrow Decisions

We begin this chapter by suggesting that many leases are essentially financing instruments, comparable to debt contracts. It is desirable to consider the risks associated with the financial decisions (borrow or lease) that we have been considering.

For practical purposes, it may be reasonable, in some circumstances, to treat the financial cash flows as being free of any uncertainty. This assumption will not always be valid, as we shall see. If the likelihood of any substantial deviation from our predictions is very small, the time and cost involved in any detailed analysis of the uncertainties may not be worth the effort. The main justification for treating these financial cash flows as essentially certain for practical purposes is that their amounts and timing are largely determined by legal contracts that the firm acquiring the asset will have to fulfill. The lease contract determines the amounts and timing of the lease payments; the debt contract determines the amounts and timing of the debt repayments by the firm acquiring the asset. The depreciation expense charges allowed for tax purposes are not contractual, but they are fixed by law and, in the presence of a large amount of other income and stable tax rates, are reasonably certain.

Given a specific set of contracts, it might be possible to analyze the cash flows under various foreseeable alternatives. What would happen if the firm could not meet the legal requirements? Would it be declared bankrupt? Could the lease be terminated earlier? Could the loan be extended or renewed, or is it callable?

Possible changes in the corporate income tax rates are worth considering. If a decrease in the corporate income tax is anticipated, it will tend to raise the after-tax cash flows (benefits, net of costs) for any of the alternatives considered. The effect of this increase on the net present value of any alternative, however, will be somewhat offset by the fact that a decrease in tax rates will also tend to increase the appropriate after-tax discount rate and to decrease the value of the expense deductions, thus changing the relative desirability of buying or leasing. Some leases specify a minimum term and contain an option allowing the lessee to extend the lease for a longer time period. In these circumstances, uncertainty about how long the capital asset will be needed may influence the choice between leasing or buying.

The effects of these sources of uncertainty could be analyzed in detail if such an analysis were considered worthwhile. The following section illustrates such an analysis when there is uncertainty about how long the asset will be needed.

Leases with Uncertain Lives

Suppose that a piece of equipment is needed. The initial cost of the equipment, if it is bought, is $100,000. The equipment can be used for up to four years. After that time, a physical replacement will be necessary. The asset will be depreciated on a straight-line basis. If at any time the asset is no longer needed, it can be sold for its book value. The before-tax cost of borrowing is 5 percent, and a corporate income tax rate of 40 percent is applicable.

If the equipment is purchased, the cost will depend on how long it is used. Table 11.1 shows how the present value of the costs of owning the equipment will vary with the length of time that it is needed, assuming the salvage value of the equipment equals its book value. Table 11.2 shows the assumed costs of leasing.

Suppose that the equipment is also available on a lease basis. The lease requires rental payments of $28,333 per year [equal to (.6)($28,333) = $17,000 after taxes]. The lease is for a period of four years. It can be canceled by the lessee at the end of any annual period. There is a penalty of $5,000 if the lease is canceled at the end of the first year, but no penalty if it is canceled in later years. The lessor cannot cancel the lease.

Table 11.2 compares the present value of the costs of owning versus leasing for periods from one to four years.

If the equipment is used one year, the after-tax cost will be $17,000 plus 60 percent of the $5,000, or $20,000, with a present value of $19,417.

TABLE 11.1   Present Values of Costs of Owning Equipment for t Years

Item	Length of Time Equipment Is Owned (t)			
	1	2	3	4
Present value of purchase outlays	$100,000	$100,000	$100,000	$100,000
Present value of tax shield from depreciation	9,709	19,135	28,286	37,171
Present value of salvage*	72,816	47,130	22,879	0
Net present value of costs	$ 17,475	$ 33,735	$ 48,835	$ 62,829

* Salvage for four successive years is as follows.

Year	Amount
1	$75,000
2	50,000
3	25,000
4	0

TABLE 11.2   Present Values of Costs of Owning and Leasing

	Number of Years Equipment Is Used			
	1	2	3	4
Owning	$17,475	$33,735	$48,835	$62,829
Leasing	19,417	32,529	48,086	63,191

If it were certain how long the equipment would be needed, Table 11.2 could be used to decide whether to lease or buy. For example, if the equipment were needed for either one or four years, it would be less expensive to buy it. Suppose that four years is the most probable length of time the equipment will be needed. Although buying is less expensive if the equipment is needed for four years, it does not follow that buying is the best decision, since there is some probability that the life will be different from four years.

Another approach is to calculate the expected present value of the two alternatives of buying or leasing. This requires assigning a probability to each year to reflect the likelihood that the equipment will be needed for that length of time but not longer. Table 11.3 illustrates the necessary calculations for a hypothetical set of probabilities. On an expected present value basis, the costs of leasing are less than the costs of buying. A change in probabilities might change the conclusion.

TABLE 11.3   Expected Present Values of Leasing Versus Buying

Number of Years Equipment Will Be Used	Probabilities	Buying		Leasing	
		Present Value of Costs	Probability × Present Value	Present Value of Costs	Probability × Present Value
1	.1	$17,475	$ 1,747	$19,417	$ 1,942
2	.2	33,735	6,747	32,529	6,506
3	.3	48,835	14,651	48,086	14,426
4	.4	62,829	25,132	63,191	25,276
	1.0		Expected PV = $48,277		Expected PV = $48,150

The Rate of Discount

Some analysts of the buy-versus-lease decision do not want to use the after-tax borrowing rate as the rate of discount. They argue that the residual value of the asset and the tax savings from depreciation deductions are not different from other cash flows associated with buy decisions, and it is appropriate to test the sensitivity of the buy–lease decision to changing the rate of discount.

Leasing combines the elements of investment and financing. If we use a discount rate other than the after-tax cost of borrowing, the buy-versus-lease analysis becomes much more complex. The complexity arises because the debt flows are excluded from the buy analysis and included with the lease analysis. We want the two analyses to be comparable relative to the treatment of the debt flows and the tax deductions arising from the nondebt flows. The following analysis illustrates an approach to comparability by isolating debt effects in the lease and excluding them from the cash flows to be discounted. The remaining cash flows are then compared to the buy cash flows at various interest rates.

Since depreciation is deductible if we buy, we want to isolate a deduction with leasing that is comparable to depreciation. With leasing, the noninterest component of the lease payment is deductible (whereas with buying, the principal payment associated with the debt is not deductible), and we shall treat this "principal" payment with leasing as being comparable to depreciation generated with the buy alternative.

Let us consider the following cash flows of buying.

> Investment flows
>> Cost of investment
>> Depreciation tax savings
>> Positive after-tax cash flows (benefits) and residual value
> Debt flows
>> Principal payments
>> Interest flows
>> Interest tax-shield savings

We have listed six different cash streams, but the list can be reduced by combining the two debt flows (principal and interest) and the two tax shields (depreciation and interest). The debt flows are contractual, thus relatively risk-free. The riskiness of the tax deductions (savings) depends on the firm's total taxable income and possible changes in tax laws. The after-tax benefits and residual value are likely to be high-risk (but the benefits are common to both the buy and lease alternative; thus, their effect is neutral). Time discounting is not likely to affect significantly the present value of the investment cost, since the outlays are close to time 0. We can define a different discount rate for each cash flow with a different riskiness.

The cash flows of the lease alternative divided into its components for purposes of this analysis are

> Lease outlay–interest equivalent
> Lease outlay–principal equivalent
> Lease tax deduction–interest equivalent
> Lease tax deduction–principal (depreciation) equivalent

It is important that each of the lease cash flow components be discounted at the same magnitude of interest rate as the buy alternative.

One Recommendation

For lease: Discount the interest and principal components at a before-tax discount rate to determine the debt equivalent of leasing. Subtract the present value of the lease tax deduction–principal (depreciation) equivalent.

For buy-borrow: Only use the investment flows: Subtract the present value of the depreciation tax savings from the cost of investment.

A Second Recommendation

If all the lease flows just listed are discounted, this is equivalent to including the debt flows in the buy analysis. Now many alternatives is possible. One important consideration is to have the debt included in the buy analysis be comparable to the debt included in the lease analysis. This is a second best solution.

The recommended solution is to use the after-tax borrowing rate to evaluate the alternatives.

Leasing of Land

In making investment decisions, we generally separate the cash outlay (the investment) from the financing (the source of the cash). The two are tied together by the use of a given rate of discount that measures the time value of money for the firm.

In leasing decisions involving land, it may not always be possible to separate an investment from its financing, as they frequently become interwoven. In fact, in some situations it is not clear whether the land is being purchased or leased. Assume a situation where land is being leased, but the company leasing the land can acquire the land for a nominal price at the end of twenty years. Are the lease payments for the use of the land, or are they for the use of money during the twenty-year period plus payments for the land?

We shall assume the following situation: Company A owns land and has offered to lease it to Company B at a cost of $80,242.65 per year for twenty years. After the twenty years, A retains ownership of the land.

B is a very large, stable company, and A considers a lease with B to be the equivalent of a certain cash flow. Using the current long-term debt rate of .05, B finds the before-tax present value of the $80,242.65 per year to be $1 million.

A has offered to sell the land to B for $1 million. (A would not be taxed on this transaction.) Should B buy? B can obtain long-term funds at a cost of .05. These funds would have to be repaid at the end of twenty years. B's tax rate is .40, and B has taxable income.

B's analysis is as follows.

Cost of Leasing

The after-tax cost of leasing is obtained by multiplying the lease by the tax and present value factors. The present value of an annuity for twenty periods using .03 is 14.8775.

$$\text{After-tax cost of leasing} = (\$80,242.65) \times .60 \times 14.8755$$
$$= \$716,000$$

Cost of Buying Land

The cost of buying is the immediate outlay of $1 million. The after-tax cost of leasing is less than the cost of buying. In considering the buy decision, however we ignored the value of land at the end of the twenty years. The cash flow of the twentieth year may affect the decision.

We will compare the $716,000 after-tax cost of leasing with the $1 million after-tax cost of buying and compute the break-even value of land (at the end of twenty years). Let X be the value of the land after twenty years.

$$\$716,000 = \$1,000,000 - X(1 + .03)^{-20}$$
$$\$284,000 = .5537X$$
$$X = \$513,000$$

Based on the after-tax computation, if the land is expected to have a value of less than $513,000, we should lease; otherwise, we should buy. A change in the rate of discount would change the necessary residual value.

We can compare the two alternatives year by year. Assume that the land will be worth its present purchase price at the end of twenty years. The lease plan does not have a buy option.

With a balloon payment debt (constant interest payments), the after-tax cash flows (in dollars) are as follows.

	Year			
	1	2	3–19	20
Lease	−$48,146	−$48,146	−$48,146	−$ 48,146
Buy	− 30,000	− 30,000	− 30,000	− 30,000 interest
				− 1,000,000 repayment of debt
				+ 1,000,000 value of land
Difference (lease–buy)	−$18,146	−$18,146	−$18,146	−$ 18,146

The $18,146 is the extra cost (per year) of leasing compared to buying. Assuming that the land does not depreciate in value through time, the advantage is clearly with buying. If the lease payments were $50,000 per year before tax, there would be indifference between buying and leasing.

Changing the timing of the debt repayment would not change the basic conclusion as long as the interest rate of the loan and the discount rate were equal.

Lease and Buy

There is an additional complication. Suppose that Company B can lease and then buy the land for $300,000 at the end of twenty years. A lease decision is preferable, based on the after-tax economic analysis. The Internal Revenue Service will probably object to the deduction of the lease payment for tax computations, however, and will consider a large part of the cash outlay as being a payment for the land (which it is).

Leasing of land is a possible method of financing the use of land. If we remove the mystery from the decision process, we find that leasing may be more desirable than purchasing if there exists a difference of opinion relative to the value of land upon termination of the lease. If Company A thinks the value of land will be increasing, it may lease to B at a price that seems low to B, if B thinks the value of the land will decrease. To the extent that the Internal Revenue Service allows lease payments for land to be deductible when there is an option to buy at a reduced price (that is, a price less than the expected market price) at the termination of the lease, there may be a tax advantage to leasing land. But this tax advantage cannot be automatically assumed, as it is likely that the lease payments will be interpreted to be a purchase payment and thus not deductible for tax purposes.

Leveraged Leases

There are three major financial parties to a leveraged lease: the lessee; the long-term creditor, who furnishes the major portion of the financing; and the lessor, who is the equity participant. The lessor furnishes a relatively small percentage of the capital but is considered by the tax authorities to be the owner and thus is able to take the tax deductions associated with the asset (the investment tax credit and accelerated depreciation deductions). Congress periodically defines the conditions necessary for the lessor to be considered the owner for tax purposes. These conditions include

1. Lessor's equity as a percentage of cost.
2. The value of the asset at the end of lease.
3. The remaining life at the end of lease.

4. The option price to buy at the end of the lease.

5. Lessor must expect to make a profit apart from taxes.

A leveraged lease is characterized by the lessor using a large amount of debt to finance the asset. Frequently, there will be a party organizing the lease financing, and one of the groups will be the equity participants (the lessor).

Leveraged leases may give rise to multiple-rate-of-return equity investments. The lessor will supply equity capital and will make an initial investment outlay to acquire the asset that will be leased (this is a negative cash flow). There will then be periods of positive cash flows caused by the investment tax credit (if any) and tax-reducing depreciation deductions. These positive cash periods will be followed by periods of negative cash flows associated with cash outlays (debt repayments) as well as increased tax payments arising from the reduced tax shield (the reduced depreciation deductions resulting from the use of accelerated depreciation). Finally, there is a positive cash flow if the asset has residual value.

It is important to remember that these are cash flows to the equity investors, not basic investments flows.

An investment may have more than one internal rate of return if there is more than one sign change in the cash flow sequence. A conventional investment has one or more periods of outlays followed by one or more periods of benefits (the cash flows have one sign change). A multiple-yield investment has additional outlays after the benefits have started, so that there is more than one sign change in cash flows.

EXAMPLE 11.1

Assume that a piece of equipment having a life of six years and costing $210,000 can be financed with $150,000 debt, costing 10 percent (the debt payments are $34,441 per year). The equipment can be leased to a firm at $40,000 per year. The tax rate is .4, and there is no investment tax credit. We assume zero salvage value to simplify the example. The tax depreciation method used is the sum of the years' digits.

The cash flows are shown in Table 11.4. Table 11.5 shows the debt amortization.

The $19,559 cash flow of time 1 is computed as follows.

Revenue		$ 40,000
Tax depreciation	$60,000	
Interest	15,000	−75,000
Loss		−$35,000
Tax rate		× .40
Tax saving		−$14,000

TABLE 11.4   Computation of Cash Flows

Time	Outlay	Revenue	Depreciation	Interest	Tax	Cash Flow
0	−$60,000					−$60,000
1		$40,000	$60,000	$15,000	−$14,000	19,559*
2		40,000	50,000	13,056	− 9,222	14,781
3		40,000	40,000	10,917	− 4,367	9,926
4		40,000	30,000	8,565	574	4,985
5		40,000	20,000	5,977	5,609	− 50
6		40,000	10,000	3,131	10,748	− 5,189

* $40,000 − $34,441 − tax = $5,559 − tax = $19,559, where the $34,441 is the annual debt payment.

TABLE 11.5   Debt Amortization Table

Time	Amount Owed	Interest	Debt Amortization Principal Payment
1	$150,000	$15,000	$19,441
2	130,559	13,056	21,385
3	109,174	10,917	23,524
4	85,650	8,565	25,876
5	59,774	5,977	28,464
6	31,310	3,131	31,310

$$\underset{\text{Revenue}}{40,000} + \underset{\text{Tax saving}}{14,000} - \underset{\text{Debt outlay}}{34,441} = 19,559$$

The sum of the years is $6(1 + 6)/2 = 21$, and the first year's depreciation is $6/21 \times \$210,000 = \$60,000$. The depreciation of each year is $10,000 less than that of the previous year.

The cash flows shown in Table 11.4 have an interesting pattern. There is an immediate outlay, followed by four periods of benefits, followed by two periods of outlays. This is potentially a multiple-yield investment (this investment can have as many as two internal rates of return).

The positive cash flow of periods 1 to 4 reflects the rental payments received that are tax shielded by the accelerated depreciation taken for tax purposes. The cash flows go negative as the tax-depreciation expense shield becomes small and the debt payments continue. The owner would like to abandon the asset at the end of period 4 (the last year of positive cash flows) but would have to be careful of depreciation expense recapture provisions as well as the loan provisions, since the obligation to pay continues. If the loan is a nonrecourse loan, there would be an incentive to abandon (or donate) the equipment if there is no depreciation recapture.

Conclusions

Leasing is an important financial device. For smaller firms without access to debt money, it may be the only way of acquiring equipment. But for many potential lessees the option to buy is available, and, with ready access to the debt-capital market, the relevant decision is to compare buy–borrow and lease, since firm lease commitments are, in effect, debt-type obligations. Furthermore, in focusing on the incremental cash flows of buy–borrow and lease, the use of the after-tax borrowing rate enables us to choose the form of the debt. The use of a conventional investment hurdle rate or WACC to discount the lease flows is in error.

Many firms have made the wrong financing decision by not following these principles. Comparing buy (without including debt flows) with lease flows using a high discount rate creates an inherent bias toward the leasing alternative, and we suspect that the phenomenal growth rate in leasing witnessed in the past few years is, in part, the result of faulty analysis.

There are no easy rules of thumb to help decide which alternative is preferable, even when the intangibles are ignored. Calculating and comparing the net present after-tax cash flows of the two alternatives will provide a guideline with respect to these factors if the correct discount rate and correct cash flows are employed.

REVIEW EXAMPLE 11.1

Assume that the A Corporation can obtain a ten year noncancellable lease of $12,500 per year for an asset that it wants. The lease payment is due at the end of each year. The asset will have zero value at the end of ten years.

The asset would cost $70,000 if purchased. It will earn gross cash flows of $13,500 per year.

Corporate taxes are .46. The asset fits in the five-year accelerated cost recovery system (ACRS) class life. Assume there is a .10 investment tax credit (ITC) and if it is taken, the depreciation base for taxes is .95 of the cost.

The corporation can borrow money repayable in equal installments at a before-tax cost of .13. It has a weighted average cost of capital of .15 and a cost of equity capital of .20. Round the discount rate to three decimals.

Assume that the firm has decided to acquire the asset. Assume that the firm is willing to use the borrowing rate (before or after tax, as is appropriate). If the asset is leased, the lessor will take the ITC.

The net of tax cost of buying is _____.

The net of tax cost of leasing is _____.

Present Value of Depreciation of $1,000,000 of Assets Under ACRS

Discount Rate	Class Life			
	3 Years	5 Years	10 Years	15 Years
01	979156	969618	949194	928486
02	959001	940615	902132	864282
03	939507	912912	858479	806496
04	920645	886436	817933	754358
05	902386	861118	780223	707203
06	884707	836893	745105	664453
07	867582	813701	712360	625607
08	850988	791487	681788	590226
09	834904	770198	653211	557930
10	819309	749784	626466	528385
11	804183	730201	601407	501299
12	789507	711404	577900	476415
13	775263	693353	555825	453508
14	761435	676010	535071	432377
15	748007	659340	515539	412848
16	734962	643309	497136	394764
18	709968	613040	463395	362398
20	686343	584973	433263	334347

Solution

Net cost of buying = $70,000 − .46 ($70,000) (.813701) .95 − $7,000

= $38,109

Net cost of leasing = $12,500 (1 − .46) B (10, .07) = $47,409

REVIEW EXAMPLE 11.2

The A Corporation wants to use its WACC of .15 to evaluate all investment types of alternatives. Prepare an analysis using .15 to evaluate investment flows. Use the facts of Example 11.1.

a. What is the net of tax cost of buying?
b. What is the net after-tax cost of leasing (round off to nearest dollar in calculating?
c. What is the present value of the "depreciation equivalents" with leasing if .07 is used as the discount rate?

Solution

a. $70,000 − .46 ($70,000) (.95) (.65934) − $7,000 = $42,831 = net cost of buying

b. $12,500 (5.42624) − .46 ($29,630) = $54,198 = net cost of leasing

c. $44,532 and the tax savings are $44,532 × .46 = $20,485

The $44,532 is obtained by discounting the "principal payments" using .07.

Beginning of Year	Amount Owed	Interest (.13)	Principal
1	$67,828	$8,818	$ 3,682
2	64,146	8,339	4,161
3	59,985	7,798	4,702
4	55,283	7,187	5,313
5	49,970	6,496	6,004
6	43,966	5,716	6,784
7	37,182	4,834	7,666
8	29,516	3,837	8,663
9	20,853	2,711	9.789
10	11,064	1,438	11,062

Present value (.15) = $29,630
Present value (0.7) = $44,532

PROBLEMS

11.1 Assume zero taxes. Equipment can be leased at $10,000 per year (first payment one year hence) for ten years or purchased at a cost of $64,177. The company has a weighted average cost of capital of 15 percent. A bank has indicated that it would be willing to make the loan of $64,177 at a cost of 10 percent.

Should the company buy or lease? There are not uncertainties. The equipment will be used for ten years. There is zero salvage value.

11.2 If the bank in problem 11.1 was willing to lend funds at 9 percent, should the company buy or lease?

11.3 If the company in problem 11.2 pays $64,177 for the equipment, it will save $10,000 a year lease payments for ten years.

What internal rate of return will it earn on its "investment?"

11.4 Continuation of problem 11.1. Now assume a marginal tax rate of .4. Assume that the funds can be obtained for .10 at a bank. The company uses sum-of-the-years' digits depreciation for taxes.

Should the firm buy or lease? (Assume that the present value of the depreciation deductions is .79997 per dollar of depreciable assets using .06 as the discount rate.)

11.5   Continuation of problem 11.1. Now assume a marginal tax rate of .4 and that a loan can be obtained from the bank at a cost of 9 percent.

Should the firm buy or lease? Using .054, the percent value of depreciation is .811. Use .054 as the discount rate.

11.6   Continuation of problem 11.5. Assume that the lease payments of $10,000 start immediately and that they are paid at the end of each year. There are ten payments.

Compute the present value of leasing; compare the present value with that obtained for problem 5.

11.7   Assume that there is a .4 marginal tax rate. An asset with a life of three years can be bought for $25,313 or leased for $10,000 per year. Funds can be borrowed at a cost of .09 (payments of $10,000 per year).
   a. What is the present value of the debt (the liability) if the funds are borrowed at a cost of 9 percent? Assume that the payments to the bank are $10,000 per year.
   b. What is the present value of the lease payments of $10,000 (the liability).

11.8   Continuation of problem 11.5.
   a. Include the borrowing cash flows in the buy analysis. Assume equal payments of debt. How does this change the net cost?
   b. Assume that the net cost of buying was computed using the cost of capital of 15 percent. Now include the borrowing cash flows. How will this change the net cost of buying (you do not have to compute the present value)?

11.9   What factors might make a lessor's expected cost of acquired and disposing of equipment less than the lessee's expected cost?

11.10   Why are leasing companies (lessors) so highly levered?

11.11   Consider the following investment.

Cash Flows at Time			
0	1	2	Internal Rate of Return
−$1,000	$576	$576	10%

If debt can be obtained at a cost of 5 percent, determine the net present value of the equity cash flows discounted at 15 percent if

a. No debt is used to finance the investment.

b. $500 of debt is used to finance the investment.

c. $900 of debt is used to finance the investment.

Repeat the calculations using 5 percent at the discount rate.

11.12 Suppose that $100,000 is borrowed at 8 percent and is to be repaid in three equal annual installments. Prepare a debt amortization table and show that the net present value of the after-tax cash flows of the debt is zero using the after-tax cost of debt as the discount rate. The tax rate is 40 percent.

11.13 Suppose that a firm has substantial taxable income and a small amount of depreciable assets.

a. What are the after-tax equity cash flows if it buys a machine for $800,000, takes a 10 percent investment tax credit, and leases the machine to a user for $120,000 per year for eight years payable at the beginning of each year? Further, suppose that the firm borrows $700,000 at 10 percent to help finance the purchase of the machine and that the bank is to be repaid in three equal installments. Assume a 40 percent tax rate. It is expected that the machine will be worth $160,000 (after tax) at the end of eight years. The entire $800,000 of cost can be depreciated using straight-line depreciation for tax purposes over a five-year life.

b. If the next best alternative is to earn 15 percent after tax, is this a good investment?

11.14 **a.** MBI has offered to sell or lease computing equipment that has an expected life of three years to Cornell University. If the equipment purchased, the initial cost would be $2 million. If it is leased, the annual lease payments would be $800,000 per year. Cornell can borrow money at about 7 percent on its endownment and pays no taxes. Ignoring salvage value, what should Cornell do?

b. MBI has offered the same deal to EXNOX Corporation. If EXNOX can borrow money at 10 percent, has a weighted average cost of capital of 11 percent, and has a 40 percent marginal tax rate, what should EXNOX do? Assume straight-line depreciation with a life of six years, a 7 percent investment tax credit, and no salvage value.

11.15 The ABC Company can purchase a new data processing machine for $35,460 or rent it for four years at a cost of $10,000 per year. The estimated life is four years. The machine will result in a saving in clerical help of $11,000, compared with the present manual procedure. The corporation has a cost of capital of .10 and a cost of available short-term debt of .05. The incremental tax rate is .52. Assume that the investment tax credit does not apply. The following analysis was prepared for the two alternatives.

Buy Analysis

	0	1	2	3	4
Outlay	−$35,460				
Savings before tax		$11,000	$11,000	$11,000	$11,000
Depreciation[a]	—	17,730	8,865	4,432	4,432
Taxable income		$(6,730)	$ 2,135	$ 6,568	$ 6,568
Tax on savings (.52 of income)		(3,500)	1,110	3,415	3,415
Net cash flow		$14,500	$ 9,890	$ 7,585	$ 7,585
Present value factor (using .10)		.9091	.8264	.7513	.6830
Present values	−$35,460	$13,182	$ 8,173	$ 5,699	$ 5,181

[a] Assume that the depreciation of each year for tax purposes is computed using the twice-straight-line method of depreciation with a life of four years.

The net present value is −$3,255, using .10 as the discount rate.

Lease Analysis

Gross savings	$11,000	$11,000	$11,000	$11,000
Lease payments	−10,000	−10,000	−10,000	−10,000
Savings before taxes	$ 1,000	$ 1,000	$ 1,000	$ 1,000
Income tax	520	520	520	520
Net savings	$ 480	$ 480	$ 480	$ 480

The buy alternative was rejected, since the net present value was −$3,225. The lease alternative was accepted, since the present value of the savings is positive for any positive rate of discount.

Comment on the decision to lease

11.16 The assistant treasurer of the ABC Company has argued that the firm should use the after-tax borrowing rate to compare the lease alternative to the buy–borrow alternative for an asset when the firm has already decided to proceed with the asset.

The treasurer is unimpressed with the position, stating that "Just this past summer we issued preferred stock, common stock, and long-term debt. Why should we use the after-tax debt rate to discount for time when we know that capital has a higher cost than that to the firm? We will have to enter the market again this winter. The debt rate does not measure the average cost of obtaining capital."

Evaluate the position of the treasurer.

11.17 The tables on pages 276–277 were prepared for a real estate partnership. Assuming the data were reasonable forecasts based on the information available to the analysts at the time, can this be a feasible equity investment?

Projected Partnership Taxable Income (Loss)

Years	Gross Rentals	Interest Income	Gross Income	Interest Expense	Depreciation and Amortization	Expenses	Partnership Taxable Income (Loss)
1983	$ 447,058	$ 206,635	$ 653,693	$ 750,865	$ 345,245	$ 147,268	$ (589,685)
1984	2,261,260	613,140	2,874,400	3,478,054	1,839,491	261,849	(2,704,994)
1985	2,285,436	490,545	2,775,981	3,440,696	1,912,641	237,418	(2,814,774)
1986	2,309,205	357,555	2,666,760	3,378,662	1,900,814	213,517	(2,826,233)
1987	2,429,946	220,770	2,650,716	3,302,112	1,900,814	192,366	(2,744,576)
1988	2,638,939	95,755	2,734,694	3,185,491	1,782,722	173,208	(2,406,727)
1989	3,029,211	7,095	3,036,306	3,049,753	1,450,000	142,802	(1,606,249)
1990	3,055,081	0	3,055,081	3,067,441	1,450,000	140,780	(1,603,140)
1991	3,081,109	0	3,081,109	3,105,142	1,450,000	141,131	(1,615,164)
1992	3,106,979	0	3,106,979	3,143,842	1,450,000	141,480	(1,628,343)
1993	3,371,338	0	3,371,338	2,531,152	1,450,000	76,313	(686,127)
1994	3,397,208	0	3,397,208	2,531,152	1,450,000	77,494	(661,438)
1995	3,422,107	0	3,422,107	2,531,152	1,450,000	78,695	(637,740)
1996	3,449,107	0	3,449,107	2,531,152	1,450,000	79,960	(612,005)
1997	3,474,005	0	3,474,005	2,531,152	1,450,000	81,232	(588,379)
1998	4,414,516	0	3,414,516	2,531,152	1,164,997	94,902	623,465

Projected Partnership Cash Flow

	A	B	C	D	E	F	G	H
		Source of Funds				Use of Funds		Partnership Net Cash Flow
Year	Gross Income	Total Investor Contributions	Loan	Cash Flow	Interest Paid	Principal Paid	Disbursements	Net Cash Flow
1983	$ 447,058	$ 349,511	$2,762,258	$	$ 533,408	$ 0	$3,025,414	$ 5
1984	2,261,260	1,479,005	648,500	0	3,052,152	0	1,334,395	2,218
1985	2,285,436	1,529,495	0	0	3,139,837	577,442	95,434	2,218
1986	2,309,205	1,473,230	0	0	3,070,412	618,342	91,463	2,218
1987	2,429,946	1,364,000	0	0	2,986,575	715,419	89,905	2,047
1988	2,638,939	1,125,520	0	0	2,861,803	808,234	92,715	1,707
1989	3,029,211	719,345	0	0	2,714,236	691,321	101,187	241,812
1980	3,055,081	0	0	0	2,711,475	0	101,794	241,812
1991	3,081,109	0	0	0	2,736,891	0	102,406	241,812
1992	3,106,979	0	0	977,661	2,762,153	0	103,014	241,812
1993	3,371,338	0	0	0	2,542,879	977,661	110,026	718,433
1994	3,397,208	0	0	0	2,531,152	0	111,466	754,590
1995	3,422,107	0	0	0	2,531,152	0	112,916	778,039
1996	3,449,107	0	0	0	2,531,152	0	114,451	803,504
1997	3,474,005	0	0	0	2,531,152	0	115,972	826,881
1998	4,414,516	0	0	0	2,531,152	0	139,047	1,744,317

REFERENCES

Ang, J., and Pamela P. Peterson, "The Leasing Puzzle," *Journal of Finance*, September 1984, pp. 1055–1065.

Beechy, T. H., "Quasi-Debt Analysis of Financial Leases," *Accounting Review*, April 1969, pp. 375–381.

Bierman, H., Jr., "Analysis of the Buy-Lease Decision: Comment," *Journal of Finance*, September 1973, pp. 1019–1021.

Bower, R. S., "Issues in Lease Financing," *Financial Management*, Winter 1973, pp. 25–34.

———, R. C. Herringer, and J. P. Williamson, "Lease Evaluation," *Accounting Review*, April 1966, pp. 257–262.

Brealey, R. A., and C. M. Young, "Debt, Taxes, and Leasing—A Note," *Journal of Finance*, December 1980, pp. 1245–1250.

Childs, C. R., and W. G. Gridley, "Leveraged Leasing and the Reinvestment Rate Fallacy," *The Bankers Magazine*, Winter 1973, pp. 53–61.

Copeland, T. E., and J. Fred Weston, "A Note on the Evaluation of Cancellable Operating Leases," *Financial Management*, Summer 1982, pp. 60–66.

Crawford, P. J., C. P. Harper, and J. J. McConnell, "Further Evidence on the Terms of Financial Leases," *Financial Management*, Autumn 1981, pp. 7–14.

Financial Accounting Standards Board (FASB), FASB No. 13 (Stamford, CO: 1976).

Franks, J. R., and S. D. Hodges, "Valuation of Financial Lease Contracts: A Note," *Journal of Finance*, May 1978, pp. 657–69.

Lewellen, W. G., M. S. Long, and J. J. McConnell, "Asset Leasing in Competitive Capital Markets," *Journal of Finance*, June 1976, pp. 737–798.

McConnell, J., and J. S. Schallheim, "Valuation of Asset Leasing Contracts," *Journal of Financial Economics*, August 1983, pp. 237–262.

Miller, M., and C. Upton, "Leasing, Buying and the Cost of Capital Services," *Journal of Finance*, June 1976, pp. 761–786.

Myers, S. C., D. A. Dill, and A. J. Bautista, "Valuation of Financial Lease Contracts," *Journal of Finance*, June 1976, pp. 799–820.

O'Brien, J. J., and B. H. Nunnally, Jr., "A 1982 Survey of Corporate Leasing Analysis," *Financial Management*, Summer 1983, pp. 30–35.

Offer, A. R. "The Evaluation of the Lease Versus Purchase Alternatives," *Financial Management*, Summer 1976, pp. 67–74.

Roenfeldt, R. L., and J. S. Osteryoung, "Analysis of Financial Leases," *Financial Management*, Spring 1973, pp. 74–87.

Schall, L. D., "The Lease-or-Buy and Asset Acquisition Decisions," *Journal of Finance*, September 1974, pp. 1203–1214.

Sorensen, Ivan W., and Ramon E. Johnson, "Equipment Financial Leasing Practices and Costs: An Empirical Study," *Financial Management*, Spring 1977, pp. 33–44.

Vanderwickin, P., "The Powerful Logic of the Leasing Boom," *Fortune*, November 1973, pp. 132–194.

CHAPTER 12

Investment Timing

Bill Shankly, manager of Liverpool's defending champions in the English Soccer League, comments: "The way some people talk about modern football [soccer], anyone would think the results of just one game [were] a matter of life and death. They don't understand. It's much more serious than that."

New York Times, *January 13, 1974, p. 7.*

In this chapter the term *timing* will be used to refer to decisions about when a new investment should be undertaken and when an investment should be terminated. For certain categories of investment decisions, the question of when to start is critical. An investment may seem desirable if the only alternatives considered are to accept or reject the investment now. If the alternative of undertaking the investment at a later time is possible, however, that may be preferable to accepting the investment now. In principle, the timing problem could be handled by considering a mutually exclusive set of alternatives: undertaking the investment now or undertaking it one period from now, or two periods from now, and so on. But more efficient techniques for approaching this problem are available. We shall consider some of these in this chapter.

Frequently, in making investment decisions, the useful life of the investment must be determined. This can be accomplished in at least two ways. First, the desirability of an investment may be affected by the estimate of its useful life. Thus, the estimated profits from growing trees are critically affected by assumptions about when they will be harvested. Second, the decision to undertake an investment may require terminating an existing investment. Planting a new crop of trees may require harvesting the existing stand of trees; buying a new car may require selling the old one. In these cases, the salvage value of the existing investment, the costs incurred, and the revenues that might be received if it were not scrapped now will influence the decision of when to undertake the new investment.

279

In timing problems, the relationships among the cost and revenue streams of the various alternatives are frequently complex. But the basic principles at work are not difficult to understand. To help focus on the basic principles, we begin with a simple example of a class of situations in which timing problems are important, but no investment decision is involved.

Basic Principles of When to Start and Stop a Process

In Figure 12.1, the curve R represents the contribution to overhead (revenues minus variable costs) that will be generated at time t of a day if the business is operating. The line F represents the fixed costs that could be avoided if the business were not operating at time t. On the X axis, time is measured from 0 to 24 hours.

Let us first make the assumption that the business must operate around the clock if it operates at all. For example, a private water works company may be obliged to operate 24 hours a day if it operates at all, even though the contribution to overhead produced during certain nighttime hours does not even cover the avoidable fixed costs of the time period. In these circumstances there is no timing problem, and it will be economically desirable to operate only if the total area under the R curve exceeds the total area under the F curve over the entire cycle of operations.

In some situations the manager is free to decide when to operate and when to shut down. For example, the owner of a supermarket may not be obliged to operate on a 24-hour basis. In this situation, considering only explicit revenues and costs, the enterprise should operate only during the interval in which the contribution to overhead from operations exceeds the avoidable fixed costs of operating. In Figure 12.1 this interval extends from t_1 to t_2. The operations should start at t_1 and cease at t_2, since between these points $R \geq F$; in other words, the contribution exactly equals or is larger than the avoidable fixed costs.

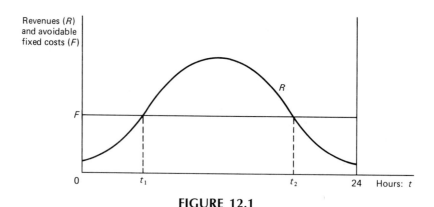

FIGURE 12.1

The conclusion from these illustrations is that if there is a choice about when to start and stop an operation, it should be started when revenues equal costs and are rising; it should be stopped when revenues equal costs and are falling.

As we shall see, this simple rule is really applicable to all the situations considered in this chapter. In applying the rule, the conceptual difficulties center on identifying the relevant revenues and costs.

Growth-type Investments[1]

Suppose that a firm owns a tract of land and is considering planting a crop of trees. It wishes to determine the net present value of that investment. Since the net present value will depend on when the trees are harvested, an estimate of that date is required. If the firm makes the investment, it is prepared to harvest the trees when the net present value of the investment is maximized.

Let

$f(t)$ = net revenue (net of all finishing expenses) obtainable if the trees are harvested in year t

$f'(t)$ = slope of $f(t)$, that is, the rate at which the obtainable net revenue is changing with time

i = market rate of interest

C = cost of planting trees

e^{-it} = present value factor for time t

P = net present value of the investment

The net present value of the investment if the trees are harvested at time t is

$$P(t) = -C + f(t)e^{-it} \qquad (12.1)$$

The determination of the optimum time to harvest the trees can be seen in Figure 12.2. The curve $f(t)$ begins at 0 and increases, rapidly at first, and then more gradually. The paths $a_0 a_1$ and $b_0 b_1$ are time-transformation curves that enable us to convert future values into present values at the assumed interest rate i. The present value of a_1 is a_0, and the present value of b_1 is b_0. The time transformations have a slope equal to i times their height. (Their heights are $a_0 e^{it}$ and $b_0 e^{it}$.) The present value of the investment is maximized if the trees are harvested at t_2, when the value of the trees is b_1 and the net present value of the investment equals $(-C + b_0)$. At t_2 the $f(t)$ curve is tangent to the time-transformation curve. It follows that the slope of the $f(t)$ curve is $if(t_2)$ at t_2.

---

[1] This section is based in part on Harold Bierman. Jr., "The Growth Period Decision," *Management Science*, February 1968, pp. B-302–B-309.

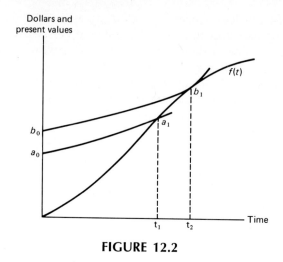

FIGURE 12.2

Thus, the value of t at which the present value of the investment is maximized must satisfy the condition that

$$f'(t) = if(t) \qquad (12.2)$$

Recall that $f'(t)$ is the increase in the value of the trees per year. Thus, the condition for an optimum is that the increase in the value of the trees must equal the interest rate times the value of the trees.

In terms of the criteria for stopping referred to in the previous section, the increase in the value of the trees if they are not harvested corresponds to the revenues, and the interest on the value of the trees corresponds to the fixed cost that can be avoided by harvesting.

The rule previously described for deciding when to harvest ignores the value of the land on which the trees are planted. If additional land of comparable quality is available in any desired amount at no cost, the economic value of the land is zero, and it need not be considered in deciding when to harvest trees growing on it.

Ordinarily, the value of the land must be considered. Suppose that if the trees were harvested, the cleared land would be worth an amount $V(t)$ at time t. In that case, the avoidable fixed costs incurred if the trees are allowed to grow include both the interest on the value of the standing trees and the interest on the value of the land. In these circumstances, a necessary condition that should be met when the trees are harvested is

$$f'(t) = i[f(t) + V(t)] \qquad (12.3)$$

Of course, the value of the land depends on its best available use. For example, if the best use of the cleared land is for farming, then $V(t)$ should reflect the value of the land in that use.

Suppose, however, that the best use of the land is growing trees. Then, although equation 12.3 is still formally correct, it is not very helpful. When the trees are harvested depends on the value of the land, but the value of the land will depend on how often the trees growing on it can be harvested. In this case, the value of the land must be determined on the assumption that the trees growing on it are harvested and replanted at intervals that maximize the value of the land.

We have already shown that the present value of one crop of trees, if they are harvested at the end of t years, is

$$P(t) = -C + f(t)e^{-it} \tag{12.1}$$

Assume that the trees are replanted every T years and that we want to determine the optimum value of T. Let $V(T)$ be the present value of the land under these circumstances. Then $V(T)$ is determined as follows.

$$V(T) = P(T) + P(T)e^{-iT} + P(T)e^{-i2T} + P(T)e^{-i3T} + \cdots$$

Summing this infinite series,

$$V(T) = \frac{P(T)}{1 - e^{-iT}} = \frac{-C + f(T)e^{-iT}}{1 - e^{-iT}} \tag{12.4}$$

We want to select the value of T that maximizes $V(T)$. It can be shown that the value of T that maximizes $V(T)$ satisfies the following relationship:

$$f'(T) = i[f(T) + V(T)]. \tag{12.5}$$

In practice, the best way to determine the optimum value of T is by trial and error, using equation 12.4. Equation 12.5 is basically the same as equation 12.3, but in deriving equation 12.5 we have given an explicit method of determining the value of the land in its use for growing trees. Equation 12.5 can be interpreted as follows: A crop of trees should be allowed to grow until the annual increase in its value declines to the point where it is equal to the market interest rate times the sum of the value of the current stand of trees plus the present value of the future crops of trees that could be grown on the land if the present crop were harvested now.

EXAMPLE 12.1

Trees growing at .15 per year are currently worth $1,000,000. The land on which the trees are growing has alternative uses that are worth $5,000,000 (this value is not expected to change).

Money is worth .10.
Should the trees be harvested now?
If harvested now,

Value of harvesting now = $1,000,000 + $5,000,000 = $6,000,000

If harvested one year from now,

$$\text{Value of harvesting in one year} = \frac{\$1,000,000 \ (1.15) + \$5,000,000}{1.10}$$

$$= \$5,590,00$$

Harvesting now is better.

Change the alternative use value of the land to zero. Does this change the decision?

$$\text{Value of harvesting now} = \$1,000,000$$

$$\text{Value of harvesting in one year} = \frac{\$1,000,000 \ (1.15)}{1.10} = \$1,045,000$$

Delaying a year is now better than harvesting immediately.

The fact that the land had an alternative use worth $5,000,000 caused the harvest to be accelerated. This alternative use can be thought of as being future generations of trees waiting to be planted. The sooner they are planted, the sooner they will have value.

A more complex and more accurate solution would have the alternative use value of the land be a function of the length of time the trees are allowed to grow. This is illustrated next.

Tree Farm Example

Suppose that the net realizable value of a crop of trees on a particular parcel of land as a function of their age is given by the following equation.

$$F(t) = -350 + 60t - .5t^2, \quad \text{for } 10 \leq t \leq 30 \tag{12.6}$$

Assuming a continuously compounded rate of interest of 5 percent per year, Table 12.1 shows the net realizable value of the trees from one growth cycle at various ages, their percentage rates of growth, and their present value. If the value of the land is ignored, the trees would be allowed to grow until the rate of increase in their value declines below 5 percent (in year 23). This is the age at which the present value of the realizable value of the trees is maximized.

Suppose, however, that after the trees were harvested the land could be sold for $500 or converted to some other use whose value was $500. In that case, the amount realized when the trees were harvested would be $500 + f(t)$.

Table 12.2 shows the appropriate calculations in this case. Under these circumstances, it would pay to harvest the trees when they are between the fourteenth and fifteenth year. After that time, the rate of increase in the value of the trees is less than 5 percent of the amount that could be realized by cutting the trees and putting the land to some other use. This is also the age at which the present value of the land and trees is maximized.

TABLE 12.1   One Cycle

Age of Trees t	Realizable Value $f(t)$	Annual Increment in Value $f'(t)$	Rate of Increase in Value $f'(t)/f(t)$	Present Value Factor e^{-it}	Present Value $f(t)e^{-it}$
10	$200	$50	.2500	.6065	$121.30
11	250	49	.1960	.5770	144.25
12	298	48	.1611	.5448	162.35
13	346	47	.1358	.5220	180.61
14	392	46	.1173	.4966	194.67
15	438	45	.1027	.4724	206.91
16	482	44	.0913	.4493	216.56
17	526	43	.0817	.4274	224.81
18	568	42	.0739	.4066	230.95
19	610	41	.0672	.3867	235.89
20	650	40	.0615	.3679	239.14
21	690	39	.0565	.3499	241.43
22	728	38	.0522	.3329	242.35
23	766	37	.0483	.3166	242.52*
24	802	36	.0449	.3012	241.56
25	837	35	.0418	.2865	239.80
26	872	34	.0390	.2725	237.62

* Maximum present value.

TABLE 12.2   Land Value is $500

Age of Trees t	Realizable Value of Land and Trees $500 + f(t)$	Annual Increment in Value $f'(t)$	Rate of Increase in Value $\dfrac{f'(t)}{500 + f(t)}$	Present Value Factor e^{-it}	Present Value $e^{-it}[500 + f(t)]$
10	$ 700	$50	.0714	.6065	$424.55
11	750	49	.0653	.5770	432.75
12	798	48	.0602	.5448	434.75
13	846	47	.0556.	.5220	441.61
14	892	46	.0516	.4966	442.97
15	938	45	.0480	.4724	443.11*
16	982	44	.0448	.4493	441.21
17	1,026	43	.0419	.4274	438.51
18	1,068	42	.0393	.4066	434.25
19	1,110	41	.0369	.3867	429.24
20	1,150	40	.0348	.3679	423.09
21	1,190	39	.0328	.3499	416.38

*Maximum present value.

If the most economical use of the land is to grow trees, the value of the land in this use must be determined. But the value of the land depends on the frequency at which crops are harvested and the costs of planting a new crop. Table 12.3 shows the value of the land when crops are harvested at various ages, if the cost of planting is $50. This is an application of equation 12.4. Harvesting in year 17 maximizes the present value of the land.

Table 12.4 applies equation 12.5 to this situation. Both equations 12.4 and 12.5 result in an optimum life of seventeen years per crop (or slightly more if fractional years are allowed).

TABLE 12.3   Value of Land

Ages of Trees t	Net Present Value of One Crop of Trees Growing for t years $P(t) = -50 + e^{-it}f(t)$	Annunity Factor $\dfrac{1}{1 - e^{-it}}$	Value of Land $\dfrac{P(t)}{1 - e^{-it}} = V(t)$
10	$ 71.30	2.54	$181.10
11	94.25	2.36	222.82
12	112.35	2.20	246.81
13	130.61	2.09	273.25
14	144.67	1.99	287.39
15	156.91	1.90	297.41
16	166.56	1.82	302.46
17	174.81	1.75	305.29*
18	180.95	1.69	304.94
19	185.89	1.63	303.09
20	189.14	1.58	299.22

* Maximum present value.

TABLE 12.4   Return Earned

t	$V(t)$	$f(t)$	$f'(t)$	$\dfrac{f'(t)}{V(t) + f(t)}$
10	$181.10	$200	50	.1312
11	222.82	250	49	.1036
12	246.81	298	48	.0881
13	273.25	346	47	.0759
14	287.39	392	46	.0677
15	297.39	438	45	.0612
16	302.46	482	44	.0561
17	305.29	526	43	.0517*
18	304.94	568	42	.0481
19	303.09	610	41	.0449
20	299.22	650	40	.0421

*Closest to .05.

Equipment Replacement

The question of when to replace an existing piece of equipment with another machine that will perform the same function is very similar to the question of when to harvest a crop of trees. In the case of trees, we are seeking to maximize the net present value of the revenues that we can receive from the land, whereas in the equipment-replacement problem, we are seeking to minimize the net present value of the costs that will be incurred from owning and operating a sequence of machines.

In the machine problem, the costs incurred by retaining the existing machine are the costs of operating it for the current period (including any necessary repairs and maintenance), the decline in its salvage value during the current period, and the interest on the current salvage value of the existing machine. If the machine is retained for one additional period, we benefit by delaying for that length of time the costs of acquiring and operating all subsequent replacement machines. The magnitude of the latter cost is measured by the market interest rate times the present value of the costs of acquiring and operating all subsequent replacements. This present value will depend critically on how long each subsequent replacement equipment is retained. Thus, the decision about when to replace the current machine requires an estimate of the economic value of its anticipated replacements, just as the decision about when to harvest a crop of trees depends on the future use that will be made of the land occupied by the trees.

The Strategy of Capacity Decisions

One of the most important decisions a corporation can make is the capacity decision. How large a plant should be built and when it should be built are two crucial decisions. An intelligent capacity strategy will greatly enhance a firm's profitability. Excess capacity and the resulting large capital costs lead to severe drops in profit. On the other hand, a shortage of capacity gives competition an opportunity to increase its share of the market and to come more rapidly down its learning curves.

We shall consider capacity strategy from several points of view, first assuming a firm in isolation and then considering a firm in a competitive environment. Elements of game theory will be used to illustrate the complexity of the decision.

The Basic Decision

The basic decision presents the problem of choosing the best of a set of mutually exclusive investments. Each of the alternatives provides a different timing for building capacity.

Consider the following two alternatives.

	Time 0	Time 1	Time 2
A	−10,000		−14,400
B	−18,000		

With alternative A, a small addition is made at time 0; then a second addition is made at time 2. With alternative B, we build the same capacity at time 0 as we obtain over the two periods with alternative A.

Which alternative is better? Assume the firm has a time value factor of .20. The present value of A's outlays is $20,000, while B costs only $18,000. B is thus better than A, for in addition to costing less, B also supplies a cushion of capacity over the two-year planning period.

With a time-value factor sufficiently higher than .20, the preference could shift to A. For example, if the time-value factor is .40, the present value of A is $17,347. This causes A to be more desirable than B.

Performance Measurement and the Timing Decision

The timing decision for alternatives A and B was made on a straight economic basis (the maximization of the present value of the stockholder's position). It is well known that actual decisions are multidimensional, with other factors being considered beside the net present value.

Assume the firm's time-value factor is .20, so that B is more desirable than A. We now add the positive cash flows to the analysis.

	Time 0	Time 1	Time 2	Time 3	Time 4
A	−$10,000		−$14,400		
		+$6,000	+$ 7,200	+$8,800	+$10,080
B	− 18,000	+$6,000	+$ 7,200	+$8,800	+ 10,080

Assume a four-year life for the product being made and the use of straight-line depreciation. We have the following data for years 1 and 2 for the two investments (assuming a two-year life for the first unit of A and a four-year life for B).

	Year 1		Year 2	
	A	B	A	B
Revenues	$6,000	$6,000	$7,200	$7,200
Depreciation	5,000	4,500	5,000	4,500
Income	$1,000	$1,500	$2,200	$2,700
Investment	10,000	18,000	5,000	13,500
ROI	.10	.083	.44	.20

A is superior to B in both year 1 and year 2 based on income and return on investment. But with a 20 percent time-value factor, we know that B is better than A. The measure of performance being used is deficient. The cost of B includes the cost of excess capacity that will be used in periods after period 2. The first two periods should not be penalized for the acquisition of the excess capacity.

A shift to prevent value depreciation solves the problem. It is inappropriate that the entire initial investment of B be considered an investment of the first two time periods. It should not be depreciated using straight-line depreciation. One way or another, the performance measurement procedure must take these factors into consideration if the capacity decision is not to be distorted. Assume the following values and depreciation expenses are computed using B's internal rate of return of .252.

	Investment B	
Time	Value (.252)	Depreciation
0	$18,010*	
1	16,550	$1,460
2	13,520	3,030
3	8,050	5,470
4	0	8,050

* There is a rounding-off error.

The incomes and returns on investment of B are

Year	Revenues	Present Value Depreciation	Income	Investment	ROI
1	$ 6,000	$1,460	$4,540	$18,010	.252
2	7,200	3,030	4,170	16,550	.252
3	8,880	5,470	3,410	13,520	.252
4	10,080	8,051	2,029	8,051	.252

A comparable method of income measurement for A would lead to an ROI of .20 for each year. Now B is not only to be preferred on an economic basis (a higher net present value), but is also preferred using ROI for each year.

Competitors: Preempting the Market

The strategy of preempting the market is very attractive. In an expanding market a company builds before its competitors, thus making it unprofitable for others to build.

For example, assume there are 1,000,000 units of demand not being satisfied. It is expected that the cost of building capacity for 1,000,000 units per year is

$10,000,000 and that the contribution margin per unit is $2. The life cycle of the product is expected to be ten years (for simplicity, we will assume) constant revenues over that period.

If 1,000,000 units per year can be sold, the net present value of the investment with a .10 time value factor (6.1466 is the annuity factor) is

$$2,000,000 \ (6.1446) = \begin{array}{r} \$12,289,000 \\ -10,000,000 \\ \hline \$\ 2,289,000 \end{array}$$
$$\text{Net present value}$$

Assume the market is not expected to exceed 1,000,000 units per year. Therefore, if the firm builds, a competitor building additional capacity would face the expectation of selling less than 1,000,000 units. Also, the possibility of a smaller contribution margin than $2 exists if competitors force the price down. From a strictly present value analysis basis, the investment is not likely to be desirable given that a competitor is already building a plant with a capacity of 1,000,000.

The plans of competitors can thus affect the desirability of capacity expansion.

It is very likely that a firm and its competitors can lapse into a form of "prisoner's dilemma." Consider a situation where the net present value of firm A will be as follows.

Firm A's Net Present Value Conditional on B's Actions

	A Does Not Build	A Builds	Maximum Profits
B does not build	$1,000,000	$2,289,000	$2,289,000
B builds	0	500,000	500,000

An analysis of the preceding table indicates that if B does not build, A is better off building, and if B builds, A is better off building. A has a strong incentive to build.

Now consider Firm B's profits.

Firm B's Net Present Value Conditional on A's Actions

	A Does Not Build	A Builds
B does not build	$1,000,000	$ 0
B builds	2,289,000	500,000
Maximum Profits	$2,289,000	$500,000

The maximum profits for B occur when B builds if A builds, or if A does not build. B thus has a strong incentive to build.

Let us assume that both A and B build. If both firms build, each firm will make profits of $500,000. This sum is less than the $1,000,000 of profits that both firms will earn if both firms do not build.

While both firms acting in their own interest should build, when they do so, they will find that they have reached an inferior profit position.

A possible solution (but likely to be illegal in some countries) is for the firms to talk with each other to decide that not to build is preferable to both firms building. Still another possibility might be for the firms to merge, if that is legal.

If the firms cannot talk, then it is likely that they will learn through time that certain actions will not be profitable.

For example, A may decide to build in the hope that B will not think that building is profitable. B will see, however, that $0 of net present value without building is less than $500,000 with building and will decide to build. Firm A will regret the construction.

Now assume that A and B's profits are negative if both firms build. On a straight profit basis, B should not build if A builds first. However, B might choose to teach A a lesson by building the capacity even though it is not needed. If A suffers losses from building excess capacity, it might be satisfied with a more modest expansion in the next building cycle. An improved solution might be for both firms to build 500,000 units of capacity (the economics of this alternative are not given) and to share the market growth.

In some situations, the capacity expansion will also result in changes in efficiency. The firm that does not expand and improve efficiency will be at a competitive disadvantage. This will also act as an incentive for B to expand when A expands.

The strategy of constructing preemptive capacity can backfire if the competitor feels that conceding the market can have adverse long-run effects and thus reacts by building capacity, even though the market will not absorb all the capacity of the industry.

Conclusions

The economic analysis of capacity expansion without competitors is a straight forward, mutually exclusive investment decision until one considers the accounting measures of performance. These measures require adjustment so that there is not a conflict between the accounting measures and the economic measures of investment desirability.

With shifts to considering strategy in a competitive situation, the possibility of a prisoner's dilemma appears. The strategy of constructing preemptive capacity is balanced off by a strategy that attempts to teach the competitor that such a strategy is not profitable. Exact correct answers are lacking in a competitive situation, but we gain instead an appreciation of the degree of complexity that exists when there are competitors.

It is important to realize that the prices (and possibly costs) that exist before the capacity expansion might not be in effect after the capacity expansion. Observed prices and costs are not likely to be reliable indicators of price and costs when capacity and efficiencies are changed.

PROBLEMS

12.1   Trees growing in value at .15 per year are currently worth $1,000,000. The land itself (without the trees) is worth $5,000,000 now and one year from now. Money is worth .10. Should the trees be harvested now?

12.2   What is your answer to problem 12.1 if the trees are growing at .20 per year and money is worth .05?

12.3   High Voltage Electric Company has $10 million of debt outstanding, which pays 7 percent interest annually. The maturity date of the securities is fifteen years from the present. There are $100,000 of bond issue costs and $200,000 of bond discount currently on the books.

Assume that a fifteen-year security could be issued, which would yield 6 percent annually. The issue costs on the new issue would be $300,000, and the call premium on the old issue would be $500,000.
a. The company has a 10 percent cost of capital. Assume a zero tax rate. Should the old bonds be replaced with new securities?
b. Assume a discount rate of 7 percent. What would be your answer?

12.4   Referring to problem 12.3, how would your answer be affected by the possibility of interest rates decreasing in the future and the new bonds being issued for a thirty-year period?

12.5   Max A., the general manager of a mining company, is in need of advice. In answering, ignore uncertainty and assume the cost of money is 10 percent. All data (including the cost of money) are in real after-tax dollars.

Dry Gulch is an operating mine. Ore can be produced and sold this year for a contribution of $200 per ton. However, if production is delayed a year, a contribution of $210 per ton could be realized. Would you recommend waiting? Explain.

12.6   (*Continuation of problem 12.5.*). Wet Rock contains mineral deposits. Max plans to develop the property so that it can be mined, and then he will sell it to someone else to be mined. It will cost $1,000,000 and take about a year to get the property ready to sell. If development is started now, the property could be sold for $1,200,000 in one year. Max estimates the selling price will increase by 5 percent per year, but he anticipates no increase in development costs. Thus, the possible cash flows include the following.

Decision	Time 0	Time 1	Time 2	Time 3
Develop now	−$1,000,000	$1,200,000	$ 0	$ 0
Develop in one year		−1,000,000	1,260,000	0
Develop in two years			−1,000,000	1,323,000

If Max must develop the property now or next year, what should he do? Explain.

12.7 (*Continuation of problem 12.6.*) Max decides not to develop the property referred to in problem 6. However, at the beginning of year 2, he suffers a heart attack and takes a one-year's leave of absence. On returning at the end of year 2, he discovers that, in his absence, the property has been developed but not yet sold. An offer to buy the property for $1,323,000 is in hand. Max is convinced that he can get 5 percent more by waiting another year. He feels the $1,000,000 expenditure was a sunk cost that would not affect his decision. He is inclined to wait at least another year. He wants your advice about when to sell before making up his mind.

12.8 Woodrow owns a plot of land in the South. The land, with no timber on it, is worth $500. The $500 value of the land is based on its potential as residential land. At present, the land is forested. The timber on the land is now ten years old and could be sold for $2,000 now. However, Woodrow estimates that the value of the timber will increase by $500 per year for the foreseeable future. If Woodrow's objective is to earn a 10 percent return on his money, how many more years should he wait to harvest his timber? (For this question, assume $500 is the correct value of the land.)

12.9 (*Continuation of problem 12.8.*) After the timber is harvested, it would cost $500 to plant another crop of timber. Ten years after planting, the crop would be worth $2,000 and would increase in value by $500 per year.

Should Woodrow sell the land for residential purposes (value $500) after the present crop is harvested, or should he plant another crop?

12.10 The ABC Company has $10 million of debt outstanding, which pays .05 (that is, $500,000) interest annually. The maturity date of the securities is twenty years from the present.

Assume that a new twenty-year security could be issued that would yield .04 per year. The issue costs would be $800,000, and the call premium on redemption of the old bonds is $100,000.

Assume a zero tax rate for this company. The hurdle rate of the firm is .10. Should the present bonds be refunded?

12.11 (*Continuation of problem 12.10.*) How would your answer be modified if the maturity date of the new issue were thirty years instead of twenty years?

12.12 The BCD Company has $10 million of debt outstanding, which pays .06 annually. The maturity date of the securities is twenty years from the present.

Assume that new securities could be issued that would have the same maturity date. The issue of the new securities would be $2.7 million; there is no call premium on the present debt. Assume a zero tax rate. Determine the rate of interest or yield rate of new securities at which the firm would just break even if they refunded. Determine to the nearest percent.

12.13   The York State Electric Corporation has $100 million of debentures outstanding, which are currently paying interest of 5.5 percent ($5.5 million) per year. The bonds mature in 24 years.

It would be possible currently to issue 30-year debentures of like characteristics that would yield 5 percent. The firm considers its cost of capital to be 8 percent. The marginal tax rate is .4.

The analysis in Table 12.5 has been prepared (see page 295). Should the firm refund? Explain briefly.

12.14   The Bi-State Electric and Gas Corporation has $25 million of debentures outstanding, which are currently paying interest of 4.5 percent ($1.125 million) per year. The bonds mature in 24 years.

It would be possible to currently issue 30-year debentures of like characteristics that would yield 4 percent. The firm considers its hurdle rate to be 8 percent. The marginal tax rate is .50.

The following analysis has been prepared.

Cash Outlays	Before Taxes	After Taxes
Premium at $52 per $1,000	$1,300,000	$650,000
Duplicate interest for 30-day call period less interest received on principal at 2% due to temporary investment	54,000	27,000
Refunding expense (80% of $220,000 total expense of new issue based on remaining life of old issue of 24 years)	176,000	88,000
Call expense	25,000	12,500
Less tax saving resulting from immediate write off of unamortized debt discount and expense		−18,000
		$759,500

Should the firm refund? Explain.

TABLE 12.5 *York State Electric Refunding Calculations*

	Before Taxes	After Taxes
Cash Outlays		
Premium at $50 per $1,000	$5,000,000	$3,000,000
Duplicate interest for 30-day call period less interest received on principal at 1.4% due to temporary investment	300,000	180,000
Refunding expense (80% of $250,000, total expense of new issue based on remaining life of old issue of 24 years)	200,000	120,000
Call expense	50,000	30,000
Less tax saving due to immediate write off of unamortized debt discount and expense		(20,000)
Total cash outlay of refunding		$3,310,000
Interest Calculations		
Annual interest—old issue at 5.5%	$5,500,000	$3,300,000
Annual interest—new issue at 5%	5,000,000	3,000,000
		300,000
Total after-tax interest—old issue—discounted at 8% for 24 years* (present value factor = 10.5288)		34,700,000
Total after-tax interest—new issue—discounted at 8% for 24 years (present value factor = 10.5288)		31,600,000
Total after-tax discounted interest savings resulting from refunding		$3,100,000
Total after-tax cash outlay of refunding		3,310,000
Net savings due to refunding at effective interest rate of 5%		$ (210,000)

* The remaining life of the old issue.

DISCUSSION QUESTIONS

12.A   Why may a supermarket stay open during certain hours even though fixed operating costs are not recovered in these hours?

12.B   The formulation

$$f'(t) = rf(t) \quad \text{or} \quad r = \frac{f'(t)}{f(t)}$$

where r is the internal rate of return is sometimes suggested (let growth continue until r is maximized). Using the example of the chapter, with land free, what does this imply about the growth period? What is the deficiency of the solution?

REFERENCES

Alchain, A., *Economic Replacement Policy*, RAND Report No. R-224 (Santa Monica, CA: The RAND Corporation, 1952).

Baldwin, C. Y., "Optimal Sequential Investment When Capital Is Not Readily Reversible," *Journal of Finance*, June 1982, pp. 763–782.

Bellman, R., "Notes in the Theory of Dynamic Programming—III: Equipment Replacement Policy," RAND Report No. P-632, *Journal of Society for Industrial and Applied Mathematics*, September 1955.

Bowman, E. H., and R. B. Fetter, *Analysis for Production Management*, rev. ed. (Homewood, Il: Richard D. Irwin, Inc., 1961).

Durand, D., "Comprehensiveness in Capital Budgeting," *Financial Management*, Winter 1981, pp. 7–13.

Howe, Keith M., "Does Inflationary Change Affect Capital Asset Life?" *Financial Management*, Summer 1987, pp. 63–67.

Preinreich, G. A. D., "The Economic Life of Industrial Equipment," *Econometrica*, January 1940, pp. 12–44.

Terborgh, G., *Business Investment Policy* (Washington, D.C.: Machinery and Allied Products Institute, 1958).

Venezia, I., and M. Brenner, "The Optimal Duration of Growth Investments and Search," *Journal of Business*, July 1979, pp. 393–407.

See also the references for Chapter 1.

CHAPTER 13

Fluctuating Rates
of Output

There is less in this than meets the eye.
Attributed to Tallulah Bankhead, J. Bartlett, Familiar Quotations
(Boston: Little, Brown, 1955), p. 941.

Special investment decision-making problems occur if a firm is faced with a choice of two or more types of equipment to produce a product and if there will be fluctuations in the rate of output at which the equipment will be operated. The fluctuations in output may be the result of seasonal fluctuations in demand (which cannot be offset by storage), or the fluctuations may result because the rate of output needed is increasing or decreasing through time. We shall illustrate the case in which the fluctuations are due to seasonal factors. A similar, but more complicated, analysis would apply if demand were growing or falling. This analysis will assume the product cannot be inventoried. The opportunity to have inventory carried over to satisfy peak demand would make the analysis more complex. The decision is to determine the type or amount of equipment that should be purchased.

When there are fluctuations in the rate of output, the amount of productive capacity needed will be determined by the peak rate of output required. The seasonal pattern will determine whether the average amount produced during the year is a high or low percentage of the available capacity.

Assume there are several types of equipment available, some types having higher fixed costs, but lower variable costs, than others. If only one type of equipment can be used, the average percentage of capacity used will influence the choice. For plants that operate at a high average percentage of capacity, equipment with high fixed costs and low variable costs is likely to have lower total costs. If the seasonal fluctuations are such that the plant operates at a low average percentage of capacity during the year, the equipment with lower fixed costs and higher variable costs is more likely to have lower total costs.

We will first determine which one of several types of equipment a firm should use if all the types of equipment can do the same task but have different costs for different levels of operations. Each type of equipment will have a fixed and variable cost component. The second problem to be solved is a situation where the production needs vary, and it is possible to buy one or more different types of equipment to service different levels of demand. Demand through time will be looked at as a pyramid where different horizontal slices of the pyramid can be serviced with different types of equipment. The objective will be to minimize the total cost for the year.

A Plant with One Type of Equipment

Suppose there is a choice between manual and semiautomatic equipment and that a plant is to be built in which only one type of equipment can be used. The product cannot be stored. (The basic cost data on the equipment are shown in Table 13.1.) We wish to compare the total costs of a plant containing either all manual equipment or all semiautomatic equipment. The total costs consist of the fixed costs and variable costs. In comparing fixed costs for the two types of machines, we need to compare equal capacities. One way to do this is to restate the data in terms of fixed costs per unit of capacity by dividing the annual equivalent fixed costs per year per machine by the annual capacity of the machine. This gives the fixed cost per year for a capacity of one unit of output per year. On this basis, the fixed cost per unit for the manual equipment is $3,200/40,000 = \$.08$, and the fixed cost per unit for the semiautomatic is $33,000/100,000 = \$.33$. The semiautomatic equipment has higher fixed costs than the manual, but this is offset by the fact that this type of equipment has lower variable costs.

If the equipment were to be operated at full capacity, the total costs of the semiautomatic equipment would be $\$0.33 + 0.50 = \$0.83$ per unit of output, while at full capacity the total costs of the manual equipment would be $\$.08 + 1.00 = \$1.08$ per unit of output. Thus, at full capacity, the semiautomatic equipment is less costly. But if, because of seasonal factors or because of

TABLE 13.1   Basic Data on Equipment Types

Type	Capacity Per Machine (Units Per Year)	Annual Equivalent Fixed Costs Per Machine (Dollars Per Year)	Variable Costs Per Unit (Dollars Per Unit)	Annual Equivalent Fixed Costs Per Unit (Dollars Per Unit)
Manual	40,000	$ 3,200	$1.00	$.08
Semiautomatic	100,000	$33,000	$0.50	$.33

design characteristics, the equipment is not going to be operated at full capacity all year, the conclusion might be different. We can determine a break-even average fraction of capacity (p) such that the total cost of the two types of machines will be the same. If the actual rate at which the plant will be operated is greater than p, semiautomatic equipment will be preferred; if it is less, manual equipment will be preferred. We assume the plant capacity is equal to a common multiple of the equipment capacities (say 4,000,000 units).

$$.08 + 1p = .33 + .5p$$

$$p = \frac{.25}{.5} = .5$$

Figure 13.1 shows this analysis graphically. If the average fraction of capacity utilized exceeds the break-even fraction of .5, then semiautomatic equipment is preferred. If it is less than .5, then manual equipment is less costly.

We could also solve for p using total costs, as follows: If manual equipment is used, 100 machines will be required to meet the capacity needs of 4,000,000 units: $(4,000,000/40,000) = 100$. The total annual fixed costs for 100 machines will be $100 \times \$3,200 = \$320,000$. If semiautomatic equipment is used, then 40 machines will be required: $(4,000,000/100,000) = 40$. The total annual fixed costs will be $40 \times \$33,000 = \$1,320,000$. The break-even quantity, Q, can be determined from the following equation.

$$320,000 + 1Q = 1,320,000 + .5Q$$

$$Q = 1,000,000/.5$$

$$= 2,000,000$$

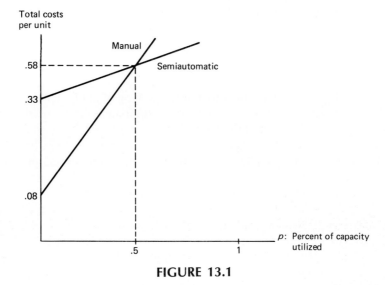

FIGURE 13.1

Previously we solved for $p = .5$. With a capacity of four million units, a utilization factor of .5 implies a break-even production level of 2,000,000 units per year.

To determine the capacity needed and the average percentage of capacity at which the plant will be operated, the seasonal pattern of production must be known. This information is contained in Table 13.2 for a hypothetical example.

TABLE 13.2   Seasonal Production Pattern

Period	Required Production (Units Per Quarter)
January–March	$ 200,000
April–June	600,000
July–September	1,000,000
October–December	600,000
Total annual production	$2,400,000

Since the actual fraction of capacity to be utilized is .60, the semiautomatic plant would be preferred. At that level of utilization, since the indifference amount of utilization is .5, it has a lower total cost.

Assume the product cannot be inventoried. To determine the equipment capacity required, we observe the highest rate of production that is required. In the third quarter, 1,000,000 units must be produced. A plant that could produce 1,000,000 units in one quarter could produce 4,000,000 units in one year if it operated at a level rate. So the required capacity for the plant is 4,000,000 units per year. Because of seasonal fluctuations in demand, the actual output will be only 2,400,000 units per year. Therefore, the average fraction of capacity utilized will be .60, or 60 percent.

Optimum Equipment Mix

So far we have assumed that only one type of equipment will be utilized. But in some circumstances several types of equipment can be used in the same plant or productive system. For example, a power-generating system may contain atomic energy generating capacity, fossil fuel capacity, and gas turbine capacity.

In designing a plant that contains several types of equipment, the objective is to have the correct amount of each type of equipment in order to minimize costs. Once a plant has been constructed, it must be operated in the most economical way possible. This requires utilizing the equipment with the lowest variable costs per unit to the maximum extent possible (that is, to its capacity) before resorting to equipment with higher variable costs per unit.

Suppose that we consider the problem of designing an optimum plant to meet the required rates of production specified in the previous example, where the required capacity of 4,000,000 units per year can be divided between the two types of equipment—manual and semiautomatic—in whatever amounts are considered desirable.

Note that three rates of production occur. In order of size, they are 200,000, 600,000, and 1,000,000 of units per quarter. Based on these required rates of production, the required capacity of the plant can be divided into three components. The first component represents the base demand of 200,000 per quarter (equivalent to 800,000 per year). The second component represents the increment in capacity necessary to increase production from 200,000 per quarter to the next level of 600,000 per quarter. So this component requires a capacity of 400,000 per quarter (equivalent to 1.6 million per year). The final component represents the increment in capacity necessary to increase production from 600,000 per quarter to 1,000,000 per quarter. This component, therefore, also requires a capacity of 400,000 per quarter.

We now know that the plant will consist of three equipment components, one with a capacity of 800,000 units per year and two (not necessarily of the same type) with a capacity of 1.6 million units per year. To select the appropriate type of equipment for each of these components, we need to know for what part of the year each will be used. To determine this, we must develop a production schedule for the plant. Table 13.3 represents a form that could be used for this purpose. Each row represents one quarter of the year. The first column shows the level of production required during each quarter. To determine a production schedule, the available capacity must be assigned to meet the required production.

At this stage we do not yet know what type of equipment will be used. The eligible types are those that are best for some value of p. The first component is determined by the need to meet the base demand, and this component will have

TABLE 13.3 Seasonal Production Schedule Form for Multiple Component Plant (Units in Thousands)

Quarter	Required Production	Equipment Component 1	2	3	Plant Total
		Quarterly Capacity Per Component			
		200	400	400	
		Production Per Component			
January–March	200				
April–June	600				
July–September	1,000				
October–December	600				
Total annual production	2,400				
Total annual capacity	4,000	800	1,600	1,600	4,000
Average fraction of capacity used	6				

variable costs at least as low as any other component. (If another component had lower variable costs, it would be used before component 1.) Table 13.4 shows the status of the production plan when component 1 is used any time production is needed. Using only component 1, we can satisfy all of the required production in the first quarter and part of the requirements of the other quarters. Since 200,000 units of component 1 can be used every quarter, it will operate at 100 percent of capacity. This is larger than p; thus, the optimal type of equipment for this component is two units of semiautomatic equipment. This equipment is less expensive when operated at or above 50 percent of capacity (p).

Table 13.5 shows the status of the production plan when equipment component 2 is assigned. It will have variable costs that are at least as low as the

TABLE 13.4   Step 1: Seasonal Production Schedule for Multiple Component Plant

Quarter	Required Production	Equipment Component 1	2	3	Plant Total
		Capacity Per Component 200	400	400	
		Production Per Component			
January–March	200	200			200
April–June	600	200			200
July–September	1,000	200			200
October–December	600	200			200
Total annual production	2,400	800			800
Total annual capacity	4,000	800	1,600	1,600	4,000
Average fraction of capacity used	.6	1.0	0	0	.20

TABLE 13.5   Step 2: Seasonal Production Schedule for Multiple Component Plant

Quarter	Required Production	Equipment Component 1	2	3	Plant Total
		Capacity Per Component 200	400	400	
		Production of Components			
January–March	200	200			200
April–June	600	200	400		600
July–September	1,000	200	400		600
October–December	600	200	400		600
Total annual production	2,400	800	1,200		2,000
Total annual capacity	4,000	800	1,600	1,600	4,000
Average fraction of capacity used	.6	1.0	.75	0	.50

remaining equipment. It is not needed in the first quarter, but it is needed in the remaining three quarters. Since it will operate at 75 percent of capacity, semiautomatic equipment is also optimal for this component.

In Table 13.5 we note that additional output beyond component 2 is required only in the third quarter. This output will be supplied by equipment component 3. This component will be used on the average at only 25 percent of its capacity. Therefore, manual equipment will be less expensive for this component. The final production plan is summarized in Table 13.6.

TABLE 13.6   Final Version Seasonal Production Schedule for Multiple Component Plant

Quarter	Required Production	Equipment Component			Plant Total
		1	2	3	
		Capacity Per Component			
		200	400	400	
		Production Per Component			
January–March	200	200			200
April–June	600	200	400		600
July–September	1,000	200	400	400	1,000
October–December	600	200	400		600
Total annual production	2,400	800	1,200	400	2,400
Total annual capacity	4,000	800	1,600	1,600	4,000
Average fraction of capacity used	.6	1.0	.75	.25	.60

More Periods or More Equipment Types

The procedure illustrated can be used to handle problems with any number of periods or any number of equipment types if certain conditions are satisfied.

Two conditions are important with respect to the choice of periods. First, the periods must all be of equal length. Second, although the rate of production may vary from period to period, within any given period it must be constant.

These conditions can usually be satisfied by taking the shortest period of time during which production is constant as the period length. If day-to-day variations in production are relevant, then pick a day as the period length and divide the year into 365 one-day periods. Production in some periods can be zero.

If the number of periods is large, it might be convenient to modify the production planning tables such as is exhibited in Table 13.3. As illustrated, they contain one line per period. With daily periods, this would make a very long table. A modification of Table 13.3 that is useful in this case is to design the table so that each line represents a different level of production. For example, in Table 13.6 there are two periods, the second and fourth quarters, in which the

TABLE 13.7   Final Version Combining Quarters with Equal Production: Seasonal Production Schedule for Multiple Component Plant

Number of Periods	Required Production	Equipment Component 1	2	3	Plant Total
		Capacity Per Componenet 200	400	400	
		Production Per Component			
One	200	200			200
Two	600 × 2 = 1,200	400	800		1,200
One	1,000	200	400	400	1,000
Total annual production	2,400	800	1,200	400	2,400
Total annual capacity	4,000	800	1,600	1,600	4,000
Average fraction of capacity used	.6	1.0	.75	.25	.60

level of production is the same. Table 13.7 is an example of a production plan in which these two quarters have been combined into one line. The line for which required production is 600 per period represents two periods, and for each component used, the production per component is equal to the capacity of the component times two (the number of periods). If you plan to use this modification, carefully compare Tables 13.6 and 13.7.

Procedure for Screening Equipment Types

As illustrated in the previous example, in deciding what equipment to use, we first determine how intensively the equipment will be used. Intensity of usage can be measured as the average actual output during a period divided by the capacity of the machine during the same period. We refer to this as the average percent of capacity utilized or, more briefly, as the average rate of use. For a given average rate of use, there may be one machine that has lower (average total) costs than any other machine, or there may be several machines that have equally low costs. If we look at a particular machine, we can determine at what rates of use its average costs are at least as low as those of any other machine. The collection of rates of use at which the costs of a machine are at least as low as the costs of any other available machine are called the optimum utilization range of the machine, abbreviated as OUR.

The OUR for a particular machine will depend on what other machines are available. Thus, if we add a new machine to the set under consideration, or if we remove a machine, the OURs of the remaining machines may change. For one or more machines, the OUR may be the null set, indicating that the machine should never be used. Especially when there are more than two machines available, it is often convenient to determine the OURs for each machine in advance of making any decisions. The process can be illustrated by an example.

The first step is to convert the fixed costs for each machine into the form of an annual equivalent per unit of capacity. Then list the machines in a table, ranking them in order of fixed costs, with the machine with the highest fixed costs on the first line, and so on. For each machine, show its name, its fixed costs per unit of capacity, and its variable costs per unit. This information is provided for a group of five machines in Table 13.8.

The first step is to see if any machines can be eliminated from consideration Look at the "Variable Costs" column. As we proceed from the top row to the bottom row, the variable costs should increase. This is true except for the Dewore, which has lower variable costs than the Candew. Of course, the Dewore also has lower fixed costs than the Candew. Therefore, the Candew machine is dominated by the Dewore and should not be considered. If you were doing this by hand, you would draw a line through the Candew row and eliminate it from all further consideration. Table 13.9 is similar to Table 13.8, except that the line for Candew has been eliminated. The arrows in the first row of each column indicate the direction in which the numbers should be decreasing.

The next step is to calculate the break-even points between each adjacent pair of machines. In column 4, we show the break-even point between each machine and the machine in the row above. Since there is no row above the Atlas, we put

TABLE 13.8   Basic Data

Equipment Type	Fixed Costs per Unit of Capacity Dollars/Year/Per Unit Capacity	Variable Costs: Dollars/Unit
Atlas	$500	$ 75
Benson	400	200
Candew	375	350
Dewore	350	325
Ensign	175	575

TABLE 13.9   First Estimate of Break-Even Point

Equipment Type (1)	Fixed Costs (2)	Variable Costs (3)	Break-Even Points (4)
Atlas	$500 ↓	$ 75 ↑	1.00 ↓
Benson	400	200	0.80
Dewore	350	325	0.40
Ensign	175	575	0.70

a 1.0 in column 4 on the Atlas line. The break-even points are the difference in fixed costs divided by the difference in variable costs. For line 2

$$F(A) + p\,V(A) = F(B) + p\,V(B)$$
$$p = [F(A) - F(B)]/[V(B) - V(A)]$$
$$p = [500 - 400]/[200 - 75] = .8$$

The optimal utilization range for Atlas equipment is from 1.00 to 0.80. That is, for rates of use from 80 percent to 100 percent of capacity, Atlas is less expensive than any other type of machine.

The break-even points should decline as we proceed down column 4. If they do not, this indicates that at least one of the machines being considered is not efficient. In Table 13.9, the Ensign machine has a break-even with the Dewore of .70, which is greater than Dewore's break-even with Benson. This indicates that the Ensign machine dominates the Dewore machine in this collection. Therefore, we eliminate the Dewore from consideration and repeat the break-even point calculations. While Dewore is better than Ensign, if activity is larger than .70, Benson is better than Dewore for this range. The revised results are shown in Table 13.10.

TABLE 13.10   Second Estimate of Break-Even Points

Equipment Type (1)	Fixed Costs (2)	Variable Costs (3)	Break-Even Points (4)	OURs (5)
Atlas	500↓	75↑	1.00↓	0.80 to 1.00
Benson	400	200	0.80	0.60 to 0.80
Ensign	175	575	0.60	0.00 to 0.600

The break-even point between the Atlas and Benson is not affected by eliminating the Dewore, but the break-even point between the Benson and Ensign is $(400 - 175)/(575 - 200) = 225/375 = .60$. In this case, the break-even points are uniformly decreasing as we go down column 4, so no additional machine types need to be dropped. The optimal utilization ranges for each of the remaining types of equipment are shown in column 5.

Determination of Fixed Costs

Assume that the manual equipment cost $18,081 per machine and is expected to last for ten years. The interest rate is 12 percent per year. We can determine the annual equivalent cost, F, to be

$$FB(10, .12) = 18.081$$
$$5.650223F = 18.081$$
$$F = 3,200$$

This is consistent with the fixed cost used for the manual equipment. For simplicity, taxes have been ignored in this example. When income taxes are relevant, the fixed and variable costs of the equipment should be put on an after-tax basis.

Conclusions

This chapter has illustrated a method of choosing the optimal mix of equipment types when output fluctuates. If desired, algebraic solutions can be prepared that arrive at the same solutions. If products can be stored, the solutions become complex, and complex mathematical solutions are necessary.

PROBLEMS

13.1 A new plant is to be built to produce widgets. Three types of facilities are available: fully automated, semiautomated, and manual. All three facilities have the same expected life and produce widgets that are identical in every respect. Only the cost characteristics of the three types of facilities vary. The fixed and variable costs for each type of facility are shown in Table 13.11. All costs are on an after-tax basis, and fixed costs are expressed in terms of equivalent monthly after-tax flows, after allowing for tax savings from depreciation.

To prevent thefts, each widget is produced with the customer's name engraved on it. The name must be engraved before the widget is assembled. This makes it impractical to maintain an inventory of completed widgets. Instead, production must take place after orders are received. Since demand follows a seasonal pattern, widget production is seasonal as well. The anticipated seasonal pattern of demand (and production) is described in Table 13.11. The peak demand is 600 units per month, and a capacity sufficient to meet this peak demand is needed.

TABLE 13.11   Cost Characteristics of Alternative Types of Widget Production Facilities

Facility Type	Fixed Cost Per Month for Enough Capacity to Produce One Widget Per Month	Variable Cost Per Widget
Fully automated	$20	$25
Semiautomated	14	35
Manual	6	69

Suppose that the plant to be built can contain only one type of facility:

a. Using the demand forecast in Table 13.12, which type of facility should be chosen?

b. If Table 13.12 were modified by raising estimated demand in all months from March through August to 600 units per month, which type of facility should be chosen?

c. If peak demand (and therefore the required capacity) remained at 600 units per month (Q_{max}), how low would average monthly demand ($\bar{Q}$) have to fall before the manual facility would be chosen?

d. Let the total monthly cost of using the ith type of facility be

$$T_i = F_i + \bar{Q} V_i$$

where

T_i = total monthly cost of the ith facility

F_i = fixed cost per month for enough capacity to produce one widget per month using the ith facility

V_i = variable cost per unit for the ith facility

Q_{max} = maximum level of demand per month (equals required capacity)

$\bar{Q}$ = average level of demand (widgets per month)

Make a rough graph with T_i on the vertical axis and $\bar{Q}$ on the horizontal axis.

TABLE 13.12   Estimated Demand

Month	Estimated Demand
January	100
February	100
March	300
April	400
May	600
June	500
July	400
August	400
September	300
October	200
November	200
December	100
Estimated annual demand	3,600 widgets/year

Average monthly demand $(\bar{Q}) = \dfrac{3,600}{12} = 300$ widgets per month

Sketch in the first equation for each of the three facilities on this graph, using $Q_{max} = 600$ and the vlaies of F_i and V_i from Table 13.11.

e. What generalizations can you make about the levels of Q at which each type of facility would be preferred?

f. The following equation was obtained from the first equation by dividing both sides by Q_{max} and letting $p = \bar{Q}/Q_{max}$.

$$\frac{T_i}{Q_{max}} = F_i + pV_i$$

Make a rough graph with T_i/Q_{max} as the vertical axis and p as the horizontal axis. Sketch in the second equation on this graph for each of the three facilities, using the values of F_i and V_i from Table 13.11.

g. Does this graph suggest any further generalizations about the type of facility that would be preferred in problems of this type?

13.2   (*Continuation of problem 13.1.*) Suppose that a widget plant can be constructed that contains more than one type of facility.

a. A widget plant has been constructed that contains six types of facilities. There are 100 units of capacity of each type. In terms of variable costs per widget, facility 1 has the lowest cost, facility 2 the next lowest cost, and so on. You are in charge of scheduling production in this plant and responsible for meeting each month's required production while minimizing variable costs. Plan your production schedule by completing the following table to show for each month the number of units to be produced in each type of facility.

Month	Required Production	Amount to be Produced in Facility Number					
		1	2	3	4	5	6
January	100						
February	100						
March	300						
April	400						
May	600						
June	500						
July	400						
August	400						
September	300						
October	200						
November	200						
December	100						
	3,600						

b. For each of the six types of facilities, compute the fraction of that facility's annual capacity that you plan to utilize.

c. If you were designing this plant and had available only the three types of facilities described in problem 13.1, how many units of capacity of each of the three types would you choose in order to minimize total costs? Of the year's production of 3,600 widgets, how many would be produced in each type of facility?

d. Compute the average total cost per month (averaged over a whole year) for the plant design you chose. Compare these costs with the best plant you could devise using only one type of facility.

13.3   The DEF Company uses a batch-process method to produce product S. The product is very perishable, so inventories are small, and production is geared closely to current sales. There are two seasons for product S, each season lasting six months. The DEF company has been producing and selling product S at the rate of 30 million units per month during the busy season—which lasts for six months. During the six-month slow season, production and sales are only 10 million units per month.

The company is convinced it could sell an additional 5 million units per month during the six-month busy season if additional capacity were available. There is no question that these additional sales would be profitable. There is a question of what type of production equipment should be installed.

The company has a choice between two types of equipment. The batch process equipment is the same as the equipment currently in use. The continuous process equipment was developed a few years ago. Both types are known to be reliable and to produce equally high-quality products. Cost data are given here.

Cost Item	Batch	Continuous

Equivalent annual fixed costs:
  Dollars per year per unit of
  capacity capable of producing
  one unit of product per month.
	$2.20	$5.00

Variable costs of producing one unit of product	0.90	0.50

a. What action would you recommend to the DEF Company if there were no costs savings or salvage values associated with scrapping existing batch capacity?

b. What action would you recommend if fixed costs of $1 per year per unit of capacity could be avoided by scrapping existing batch capacity?

13.4 The Giant Motor Car Company is considering the size that would be most desirable for its next assembly plant. We shall assume that there are the following two alternatives:

	Large Plant	Small Plant
Initial costs	$20,000,000	$4,000,000
Out-of-pocket cost savings per year, assuming the assembly of different numbers of cars per year		
100,000 cars		1,000,000
200,000 cars	0	
300,000 cars	2,000,000	
400,000 cars	4,000,000	

A forecast of car sales indicates the following demand for automobiles assembled in this plant:

First year after completion of the plant	100,000 cars
Second year after completion of the plant	200,000
Third year after completion of the plant	200,000
Fourth year after completion of the plant	300,000
Fifth year and thereafter for the expected life of the plant of twenty years	400,000

The Company has a cost of money of 10 percent. For purposes of this problem, assume an income tax rate of zero. Which one of the two plants is the more desirable?

13.5 Power plant design: A power system is to be constructed. Three types of generating equipment are available. Their costs are given in the following table. There are 8,760 hours in a year.

Type	Fixed Costs: Dollars Per year Per KW of Capacity	Operating Costs: Dollars Per KW Hour of Electricity Produced
Nuclear	$200.00	$0.01
Coal	100.00	0.04
Gas	40.00	0.07

(A kilowatt hour of electricity is produced by operating a kilowatt hour of capacity for one hour.)

Suppose only one type of generating equipment could be used to supply an electrical need with the following characteristics:

Maximum demand, 1,000s of kilowatts	500
Total output per year, 1,000s KW hours	2,630,000

How much capacity should the plant have and which type of plant should be selected?

13.6 (*Continuation of problem 13.5.*) Suppose more than one type of generating unit could be used to supply electrical needs with the following characteristics.

(1) Rate of Output 1,000s of KWs	*(2)* Hours Plant Operates at that Rate	*(3) = (1) × (2)* Total Output 1,000s of KW Hours
500	260	130,000
400	1,200	480,000
350	2,000	700,000
300	2,300	690,000
200	3,000	600,000
Totals	8,760	2,630,000

An economic design for this system will include the following:

Type of Equipment	*Required Capacity* 1,000s of KWs
Nuclear	_____
Coal	_____
Gas	_____

DISCUSSION QUESTIONS

13.A Distinguish between determining the optimum-sized plant and the optimum-sized firm.

13.B Is it better to build a small plant and work it intensively (with overtime and double time) or build a large plant and sometimes have idle capacity?

REFERENCES

Bland, Robert R., "The Cogeneration Project at Cornell University," *Facilities Manager*, Spring 1987 pp. 19–24.

Coleman, J. R. Jr., S. Smidt, and R. York, "Optimum Plant Design for Seasonal Production," *Management Science*, July 1964, pp. 778–785.

Coleman, J. R. Jr., and R. York, "Optimum Plant Design for a Growing Market," *Industrial and Engineering Chemistry*, January 1964, pp. 28–34.

Masse, P., and R. Gibrat, "Applications of Linear Programming to Investments in the Electric Power Industry," in J. R. Nelson, ed., *Marginal Cost Pricing in Practice*, Engelwood Cliffs, NJ: Prentice-Hall, 1964, pp. 215–234.

Nguyen, D. T., "The Problem of Peak Loads and Inventories," *Bell Journal of Economics*, Spring 1976, pp. 242–250.

Seshinski, Eytan, and Jacques H. Dreze, "Demand Fluctuations, Capacity Utilization, and Costs," *American Economic Review*, December 1976, pp. 731–742.

CHAPTER 14

Investment Decisions with Additional Information*

> The chances of success of a given investment (whether of capital or
> labour) depend on the efficiency with which all those who work in the
> same firm cooperate with the factor in question.
>
> J. R. Hicks, "The Theory of Uncertainty and Profit," Economica, May
> 1931, p. 185.

Up to this point it has been assumed that the alternatives available to a decision
maker are to accept or reject investment proposals. In this chapter we consider
the possibility of obtaining more information before making a decision. When
this possibility exists, the decision maker needs to compare the costs and benefits
of additional information in order to decide if obtaining it is worthwhile. If
additional information is collected, the decision maker must combine the new
information and the previously existing information to arrive at a decision. After
a decision to accept a project has been made, the possibility of doing a post audit
arises. Post audits may be done by the decision maker or by a higher level of
management. The purpose of the post audit is to improve and possibly to control
the decision-making process. The danger exists that the results of a post audit
may be misinterpreted, so that it fails to achieve its objective or, in extreme
cases, could lead to affecting adversely the decision-making process.

The three main topics considered in this chapter are (1) deciding if additional
information is worthwhile, (2) using additional and prior information in decision
making, and (3) interpreting the results of post audits.

---

* Parts of this chapter are based on an article by H. Bierman, Jr. and Vithala R. Rao,
"Investment Decisions with Sampling," which appeared in the Autumn 1978 issue of *Financial
Management*.

The analytical techniques illustrated in this chapter are based on formal statistical models. They are strictly applicable only to decision-making situations that conform to the assumptions underlying those models.

A substantial part of the chapter considers situations in which a single type of equipment can be installed in many different locations, and the possibility exists of obtaining additional information by trying the equipment in one location before deciding what to do about the other locations. Any procedure for screening investment proposals, however, can be thought of as a procedure for deciding whether to obtain additional information.

Let us consider a procedure that is typical of the decision-making process in many companies. At each decision-making level before the final one, three alternatives are possible: accept, reject, or send to a higher level. Sometimes rules are specified for the various levels. For example, at level 1 the accept alternative may not be available on proposals involving outlays of more than $10,000. At level 2 the accept alternative may not be available on proposals of more than $50,000. Rules such as this require that larger investments must be submitted to higher levels before an accept decision is possible. Since additional information and analysis are presumably available at each higher level, a decision (or requirement) to submit a proposal to a higher level may be interpreted as a decision to obtain additional information. Usually, a proposal can be rejected at any level. Thus, a decision at one level to submit a proposal to the next higher level implies there is not enough information to lead to a rejection decision. In some organizations that are structured in this way, the final decision makers accept nearly all the proposals that come to them. For example, if an investment survives five possible reject decisions, it is assumed that the investment is a reasonable alternative.

The formal statistical models considered in this chapter may provide some insights into organizational situations like the one just described. Even if the assumptions of the particular statistical models used for illustration do not apply, some helpful generalizations are possible.

The Opportunity to Replicate

Multiplant firms have an opportunity to innovate sequentially that is frequently not available to firms with single plants (unless the single plant has multiple production lines). Consider the development of a new type of equipment in a multiplant company. The analysis for a single unit of equipment indicates a negative net present value. But there is some probability that the equipment would be successful and would have a positive present value in any subsequent use. In other words, there is uncertainty about the outcome, but there is some probability that it would be a desirable investment. In such a situation, the possibility that the firm may miss out on a technological breakthrough may be sufficient motivation for trying the equipment as a sample investment.

If one unit of the equipment has a positive expected net present value, then some may argue that all the units should be acquired for the entire firm. On an expected-value basis, this is true. Under conditions of uncertainty and risk aversion, however, trying the investment on a small scale may help to determine if the forecasted good result will actually occur. If the result is good, then the remainder of the units can be purchased. The cost of this policy is delay of the investments, however, which may be a disadvantage.

An objective of this chapter is to emphasize that an apparently poor individual investment might be good when considered in the broader context of subsequent investments. We also want to show explicitly why the greater the uncertainty, the better it is to obtain additional information, perhaps by trying an investment if the investment can be replicated (although we are not sure the investment should be undertaken until the calculations are made). Some managers will prefer to apply intuition, making the decision without the type of calculations that will be illustrated. The model, however, does incorporate the expert judgment of the decision maker into the decision process.[1] The decision will depend on the decision maker's evaluation of the probabilities of events rather than the intuitive judgment of the effect of the combination of probabilities and outcomes. Most important, the model allows the decision maker to focus on the relevant variables.

The Basic Model

The examples show the investment sampling process where the investment, although initially not desirable, may appear acceptable after considering the consequent opportunity of obtaining additional information and the possibility of sequential decisions. The chance of an improvement of the initially undesirable investment follows logically.

We shall assume initially that undertaking one investment would allow perfect information about what could happen if all the identical investments were undertaken. In a subsequent section, the analysis includes imperfect information. This complicates the analysis but does not change the basic logic of undertaking an investment with a negative expected net present value because of the information that can be obtained.

Figure 14.1 shows the basic model with the net present value of the profits lost by *not* undertaking the investment. V_0 is the random variable "net present value" with mean $\bar{V}_0$ for one unit of equipment, and V_b is the break-even present value. V_b is the value when V_0 is equal to zero; therefore, V_b is defined to be zero. C is the slope of the net present value curve for all units of investment.

[1] The methodology of decision calculus is useful in quantifying the experience and judgment of managers. See John D. C. Little, "Models and Managers: The Concept of Decision Calculus," *Management Science*, April 1970, pp. B466–85.

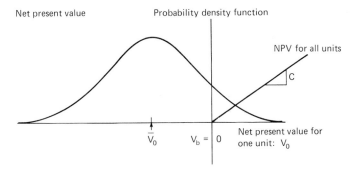

FIGURE 14.1

Since the expected value of V_0, $\bar{V}_0$, is to the left of V_b, the correct decision seems to be to reject the investment. If the investment is rejected, the present value is zero. But V_0 is a random variable with a probability density function. This is a "prior betting distribution." If we are certain that the net present value of the investment is $\bar{V}_0$ (the variance of the distribution is zero), then the investment should be rejected. If there is some probability that $V_0 > V_b$, then further analysis is required.

The value of C is crucially important because it defines the relationship of the net present value potential of all the equipment for different values of the random variable. C depends on the number of units of equipment in which the firm can feasibly invest. The more units of equipment, the steeper the slope.

The profit potential for multiple investments, given an undesirable single investment, is a function of the slope of the net present value line (which in turn depends on the number of units of equipment), the variance of the probability density function, and the distance between $\bar{V}_0$ and V_b.

If $\bar{V}_0$ is less than 0 and if the value of V_0 is positive, the expected profits are

$$C \int_0^\infty V_0 f(V_0) \, dV_0$$

where $f(V_0)$ is the probability density function of V_0. The expected loss of undertaking one unit of investment if V_0 is less than V_b is

$$\int_{-\infty}^0 (-V_0) f(V_0) \, dV_0$$

If the expected present value is positive, the investment ought to be tried. Figure 14.2 shows the net present value if one investment is undertaken and then all investments are undertaken if the actual value of V_0 is greater than V_b. If the actual value of V_0 is less than V_b, then no additional investments are undertaken.

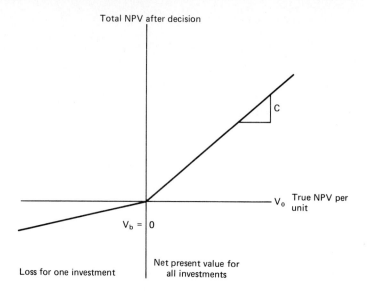

FIGURE 14.2

Numerical Example

Consider an investment that costs $1,000,000. The outcome can either be e_1 or e_2 in all future years.

Event	Probability of Event	Outcome (a Perpetuity)	Present Value	Net Present Value	Expected Present Value
e_1	.4	$150,000	$1,500,000	$500,000	$200,000
e_2	.6	40,000	400,000	−600,000	−360,000
					−160,000

The time-value factor (required return) is 10 percent. The expected present value of the benefits is $840,000 ($1,500,000 × .4 + $400,000 × .6). Since the investment costs $1,000,000 and the expected benefits are only $840,000, the investment has a negative net present value of $160,000. It should be rejected on an expected present value basis.

The firm may have the opportunity to undertake 11 of these investments, however. There is a .4 probability that each unit of equipment will perform to produce a net present value of $500,000, or $5,500,000 in total. There is a .6 probability of 11 units losing $600,000 per unit, or $6,600,000 in total. The expected value is negative ($5,500,000 × 4 − $6,600,000 × .6 = −$1,760,000), and it would seem that the investment is not desirable. But we can modify the uncertainty by buying one item of equipment for a cost of $1,000,000 and a negative expected value. Figure 14.3 shows the decision tree that evolves.

The firm invests in the ten additional units of equipment only if event e_1 occurs and the process proves to be feasible. If the process is feasible, each investment adds $500,000 of net present value. Multiplying the $500,000 by the 11 machines, we find the upper path leading to $5,500,000 of present value. The expected value of path e_1 for eleven units is .4 ($5,500,000) = $2,200,000.

There is .6 probability that the first machine will lose $600,000. This will occur if the event is e_2. This is an expected cost of $360,000. Because the expected value of the e_1 path is $2,200,000 and the expected value of the e_2 path is −$360,000, we would advocate undertaking the single investment in the hope that we will find out that e_1 is the true state of the world. The expected net present value of trying an investment is $1,840,000.

If we changed the probabilities so that e_1 had a probability of .7 and e_2 a probability of .3 then $\bar{V}_0$, the expected NPV per unit of equipment, would be $170,000 (that is, .7 × 500,000 − .3 × 600,000) per unit or $1,870,000 if all 11 units were accepted. Even though the investment is desirable, trying one unit first is still advisable if there is not a long time delay between investments. If all 11 units are undertaken, there is a .4 probability that all the investments will turn out to be bad. The expected loss is 11 times as large as the loss from trying one unit. The expected loss from trying one unit is .3 × 600,000, or $180,000. If all 11 of the investments are undertaken, the loss can be $6,600,000. The advantage of trying one unit is that the loss is limited to $600,000. It increases the expected net present value from $1,870,000 to $2,670,000 (that is, .7 × 5,500,000 − .3 × 600,000). If there is no cost of delay, the sampling of investments is desirable.

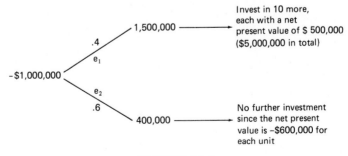

FIGURE 14.3

Sample Investment: Normal Prior Probability and Perfect Information

Assume now that the prior betting distribution of outcomes is normally distributed. (This assumption is not essential and is made only to simplify the arithmetic as we shift from the discrete to the continuous model.) Assume also that once the trial investment is undertaken, we will know how the machine being considered will operate in the other environments of the company.

The prior distribution of outcomes (V_0) for the piece of equipment being considered has a normal distribution of net present values with a mean of ($\bar{V}_0 = -\$2,000$) and a standard deviation of ($\sigma_0 = \$8,000$). Since the distribution is for net present values, the break-even value (V_b) is equal to zero.

The expected net present value is a negative $2,000. If purchase of only one piece of equipment can be undertaken, the project would be rejected. However, assume that the firm uses 500 of these machines. For every dollar increase in net present value of one machine, the total net present value increases by $500. This is C.

Figure 14.4 shows the "betting distribution" on the net present value. If σ_0 equaled zero, and if management were sure that a net present value of $-\$2,000$ would occur, then the project would be rejected. There is some probability, however, that the net present value will be positive. Define EVPI to be the expected value of perfect information. Then

$$\text{EVPI} = C\sigma_0 L(D)$$

where

$$L(D) = \int_{+D}^{\infty} (Z - D)n(Z)\, dZ$$

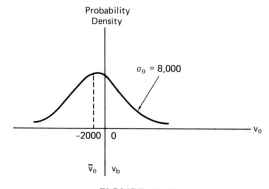

FIGURE 14.4

$n(Z)$ is the unit normal density function for the standardized random variable

$$Z = \frac{V_0 - \bar{V}}{\sigma_0} \quad \text{and} \quad D = \left| \frac{\bar{V}_0}{\sigma_0} \right|$$

For example, we have

$$D = \left| \frac{-\$2,000}{\$8,000} \right| = .25$$

and from a table of normal loss integrals $L(D) = .2863.$[2] The expected value of perfect information for 500 pieces of equipment is EVPI = 500 ($8,000) × (.2863) = $1,145,000.

Define $L(D^*) = D + L(D)$, where D^* results from integrating more than half the density function. The expected cost of undertaking the investment to find out the true value of V_0 is

$$E(L_0) = \int_{-\infty}^{0} (-V_0) f(V_0) \, dV_0 = \sigma_0 L(D^*)$$

For the example, we have

$$L(D^*) = .25 + .2863 = .5363 \quad \text{and} \quad E(L_0) = \$8,000 \, (.5363) = \$4,290$$

Since the expected value of the perfect information is $1,145,000 and the expected cost is only $4,290, the single investment with a negative expected value of $2,000 (considering only one machine) is acceptable.

If the firm could only undertake one unit of equipment:

$$C = \$1 \quad \text{and} \quad \text{EVPI} = \$8,000 \, (.2863) = \$2,290$$

Now the expected cost is $4,290, and the expected value is $2,290. Thus, the expected net present value is a negative $2,000 (equal to the present value of one unit of investment), and the investment would be rejected. There must be

$$\frac{\$4,290}{\$2,290} = 1.87$$

units of investment for the firm to want to sample the investment of this example.

Delaying Other Investments

The sampling procedure (trying one investment before proceeding with the remainder) will result in the delay of other investments, adversely affecting their present values since this is a cost.

[2] A table of loss integrals can be found in H. Bierman, C. Bonini, and W. Hausman, *Quantitative Analysis for Business Decisions*, 7th ed. (Homewood, IL: Richard D. Irwin, 1986), p. 659.

Should this cost be considered? Consider first investments that would otherwise be rejected. If the alternative were to make all the investments now or do nothing, the firm would do nothing. The firm wants to obtain information as cheaply as possible, which is accomplished by undertaking a minimum-sized investment. While the expected value of this investment, taken by itself, is negative, the information that can be gathered justifies undertaking the investment. The fact that the other investments will be delayed is unfortunate, but it does not affect the basic sampling strategy. Delaying the investments decreases their net present value, but it also enables the firm to avoid investing funds in undesirable investments. On balance, the sampling of one investment is a desirable strategy if the investment would otherwise be rejected and if the expected present value of all investments is positive.

Next consider a situation in which $\overline{V}_0$ is greater than zero. If the alternatives were to accept all the investments now or do nothing, the firm would accept all the investments now. In this case, sampling may still be desirable. However, in deciding whether to accept the investments now or wait and collect additional information by sampling (or some other method), the expected decline in present value due to waiting should be considered as an additional cost.

In summary, delaying the startup of other investments should be considered as a cost of acquiring additional information if the investments would otherwise be accepted now. Delay is not a relevant cost if, on the basis of the present information, the investments would be rejected if they all had to be accepted now.

So far we have considered situations in which it may be desirable to obtain additional information. One way of collecting additional information is to sample. This is possible when there are many similar investments, and trying one may provide information about the value of the others. If additional information were costless and could be obtained instantly, it would always be desirable whenever there was uncertainty about the investment's outcome. But in most situations, obtaining information by sampling or further study takes time and money. The decision maker needs to compare the expected value of the additional information with its expected cost to determine whether it is better to decide now or to wait while additional information is collected.

In the examples considered so far, if additional information is obtained, it is decisive: There is no question about what decision should be made. Additional information is sometimes ambiguous. In the next section of the chapter, we focus on the problem of combining prior information and additional information to make decisions.

Imperfect Information

Suppose it has been decided to obtain additional information before making a decision. The additional information can be in the form of a sample, as in the examples in the previous section, or a forecast prepared in some other way.

Suppose that the additional information, after being combined with the prior information, does not eliminate all uncertainty. In this section we consider how the additional imperfect information should be used to make a decision.

Now assume that, after the one investment is made and the results are observed, we still cannot be sure of the desirability of the investment; that is, the information obtained is imperfect. We will now assign a set of probabilities reflecting the reliability of the information. The conditional probabilities exist as shown in Table 14.1. Other probabilities are computed in the appendix to the chapter.

If the investment actually is good, there is still a .1 probability that it may not appear profitable. If the investment actually is not good, there is a .2 probability that it may appear profitable. Extending the example to reflect an initial profitable probability of .4 and .6 not-profitable probability, we will observe either profitable or not-profitable operations. The problem that has to be solved is whether it is desirable to go ahead and make the initial investment. The computations of the relevant revised probabilities are shown in the appendix to this chapter. Figure 14.5 shows the probabilities and the outcomes if purchase of one unit is undertaken to obtain information, and then the decision is whether or not to undertake the additional units.

In Figure 14.5 we have crossed out two inferior paths to simplify the presentation. The expectation of the G path and investing in ten more units is

$$\text{Value of G path} = .75\ (\$5,500,000) - .25\ (\$6,600,00) = \$2,475,000$$

The value of the B path and investing in only one unit is

$$\text{Value of B path} = .077\ (\$500,000) - .923\ (\$600,000) = -\$515,300$$

There is .48 probability of G and .52 probability of B; thus, the expected value of the process if $(.48 \times \$2,475,000 - .52 \times 515,300)$, or \$920,044.

Where we once found that undertaking purchase of one or eleven units with negative expected values was undesirable, now that we can sample, we find that, even with imperfect information, it is desirable to try one unit. The expected present value is \$920,044.

TABLE 14.1   Conditional Probabilities

	Actual State	
Observed Event	Event e_1 (High Present Value)	Event e_2 (Low Present Value)
Investment seems to profitable: G	.9	.2
Investment seems not to be profitable: B	.1	.8

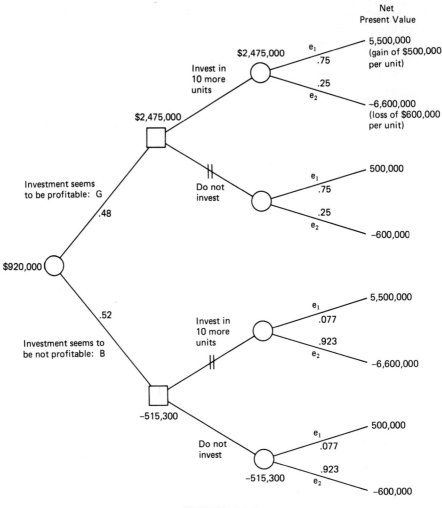

FIGURE 14.5

Imperfect Information: The Normal Distribution

It is convenient to illustrate imperfect information using the normal probability distribution, since the revision of the normal distribution is relatively easy to illustrate.

Assume that, before obtaining additional information, it is estimated that the investment proposal under consideration has an expected net present value of $-\$540,000$. The prior distribution has a standard deviation of $300,000$ and is assumed to be normally distributed. Without additional information, the decision would be to reject the proposal. Rather than rejecting the investment, it has been decided to collect additional information. The new information will provide V_e, an estimate of the true net present value of the project, and will be normally distributed with a standard deviation σ_e, of $250,000. How favorable will the new information have to be in order to justify accepting the project?

It will be helpful to summarize the prior estimates before the new information becomes available in symbols. The expected value, based on prior information, is

$$\bar{V}_0 = E(V_0) = \int_{-\infty}^{\infty} V_0 f(V_0)\, dV_0 = -\$540{,}000$$

$\sigma_0 = \$300{,}000$ [$f(V_0)$ is a normal probability density function].

Define V_e to be the value of the project as estimated only from the new information and V_r to be the revised value of the project as estimated from a combination of the prior information and the new information. It can be shown that, under the assumptions made (normal prior, normal sample),

$$V_r = \frac{\sigma_e^2 V_0 + \sigma^2 V_e}{\sigma_e^2 + \sigma_0^2}$$

$$= \frac{(250{,}000)^2(-540{,}000) + (300{,}000)^2 V_e}{250{,}000^2 + 300{,}000^2}$$

$$= -221{,}311 + .5902 V_e$$

Since V_r incorporates all of the available information, the correct approach is to accept the investment if V_r is greater than or equal to zero. In this example, the revised estimate will be greater than zero if V_e is greater than $375,000.

The critical value of V_e occurs when $V_r = 0$. Defining V_e^* to be the critical value of V_e and solving for it,

$$V_e^* = -\left(\frac{\sigma_e}{\sigma_0}\right)^2 \bar{V}_0$$

In the example just described where $\bar{V}_0 = -540{,}000$, $\sigma_0 = 300{,}000$, and $\sigma_e = 250{,}000$, the above formula yields

$$V_e^* = -(250{,}000/300{,}000)^2(-540{,}000) = \$375{,}000$$

If V_e turns out to be greater than $375,000, we should accept the investment. If V_e turns out to be less than $375,000, we should reject the investment.

The difficult aspect of the approach is obtaining the expected values and the standard deviations of the prior distribution and the sample distribution. In many situations, only subjective estimates are available. The advantage of the model is that it incorporates the available information in a systematic manner into the decision process.

Post-Audit Bias

It is generally agreed that, after an investment is accepted, the results of operations should be compared to the forecasted operations used as the basis of making the accept decision. Management would like to determine whether the forecasts on which decisions are based are biased. A forecast is said to be statistically biased if the average value of the forecast differs from the true value. A common fear of management is that the project sponsors responsible for a project may tend to be too optimistic, resulting in an upward bias in the forcasted net present value. We will describe post-audit bias as existing when the average of the present value forecasts of the accepted investments exceeds the actual value of the investments' present value.[3]

The example used in the previous section will be helpful in considering the post-audit bias problem. There were two forecasts that could be used to make the decision, denoted V_e and V_r. We will refer to them as the sample forecast and the revised or posterior forecast, respectively. When the post audit is done by comparing the actual results with V_e, a post-audit bias problem is likely to be observed. When the post audit is done by comparing the actual results with V_r, there will be no post-audit bias problem. Using V_r, if a difference is observed, the possibility that the forecasts are biased should be investigated.

The post-audit bias as defined here results from the use of V_e, since the prior information is omitted from consideration. The actual results should be compared to the best information that was available for making the decision, the revised estimate of the net present value.

Determining the Extent of the Post-Audit Bias

Suppose a forecast has been made. If the forecast exceeds the critical value V_e^*, the investment proposal will be accepted, and this is a correct decision process. Only after the investment has been implemented, however, will the true net present value, V_0, be known. The observed difference from the forecast can be defined as $(V_r - V_0)$ or, if V_e is used, as $(V_e - V_0)$. Since we assume $V_r = E(V_0)$ the expected bias resulting from the use of V_e is $(V_e - V_r)$. For the preceding example, if we have $V_e = \$1,000,000$, then

$$V_r = -221{,}311 + .5902 V_e$$

$$V_r = -221{,}311 + .5902\,(1{,}000{,}000) = 368{,}908$$

The expected bias from the post-audit use of V_e is

$$V_e - V_r = 1{,}000{,}000 - 368{,}908 = \$631{,}092$$

---

[3] For a more complete discussion of post-audit bias, see Seymour Smidt, "A Bayesian Analysis of Project Selection and of Post-Audit Evaluations," *Journal of Finance*, June 1979, pp. 675–688.

Since the forecast was greater than the prior mean, we should expect a systematic tendency for the forecast of $1,000,000 to be greater than the subsequently observed actual values (positive bias).

The Winner's Curse

A very interesting investment evaluation problem arises because investment decisions are normally made based on uncertain information. The problem is most easily explained in the context of an auction, but it is more general than an auction and can occur with any investment proposal.[4]

Assume a situation where the true (but unknown) net present value of an investment is a negative $10,000,000, and the investment should be rejected. Management has to make its decision based on observations and forecasts that are not reliable. There is uncertainty. Assume that there are three unbiased forecasts that can occur.

Forecast of NPV	Probability of Forecast
−$25,000,000	.25
− 10,000,000	.50
+ 5,000,000	.25

If the forecast is −$25,000,000 or −$10,000,000, the project will be rejected. However, if the forecast is $5,000,000, the project will be accepted because of the faulty information.

One solution is to recognize that some bad projects will be accepted if marginally desirable investments are accepted; therefore, marginal investments should be rejected. However, consider a second investment with a true (but unknown) net present value of $10,000,000, where the decision has to be based on an unbiased forecast in which there are three possible forecast values.

Forecast	Probability of Forecast
+$ 5,000,000	.25
+ 10,000,000	.50
+ 15,000,000	.25

If we were to adjust the NPV of the first investment by subtracting $6,000,000 of net present value for the problem being described, we would reject the first

---

[4] For a theoretical discussion, see J. H. Kagel and D. Levin, "The Winner's Curse and Public Information in Common Value Auctions," *The American Economic Review*, December 1986, pp. 894–920.

investment (which should be rejected), but we would also reject the second investment (which should be accepted). Thus, we have to live with the fact that some unbiased forecasts will lead to incorrect decisions. No adjustment is necessary.

But now we will again consider the first investment. Assume an analyst comes up with the negative $25,000,000 forecast, and the management decides to reject. Later, a second analyst prepares another forecast and this time comes up with a negative $10,000,000, and again there is a reject decision. Finally, after several more analysts also conclude that the investment is not desirable, an analyst forecasts a positive $5,000,000 NPV. If top management is not informed of the first set of analyses, all recommending rejection, but is only given the final analysis recommending acceptance, there is an unacceptable bias introduced. Top management has to be told the results of all the studies, or it will be misled into making a wrong decision.

While the preceding situation is not an auction, it has consequences that are similar to an auction situation. Assume that a situation similar to the first investment is put out to bid. Most of the firms invited to bid will reject the investment based on their forecasts, but if there is a large number of bidders, some of the bidders will forecast a $5,000,000 NPV. They will bid somewhere between $1 and $5,000,000, and one of them will win a bad investment.

Even with the second investment, which is a good investment, some of the bidders will bid as high as $15,000,000 and will pay an excessive amount for the investment, thus turning a good investment into a bad investment.

With a large number of bidders and an opportunity to have different opinions on the future, based on public information, it is possible that excessively optimistic firms tend to win the bid. If so, these firms will suffer a "winner's curse." After suffering losses from bidding too high, we can expect firms to scale down their bids because of a realization that this curse exists.

If a firm has special information regarding the probable outcome, the high bidder may be able to justify the magnitude of its bid. But this is a different situation than was just described.

There are two solutions to the curse associated with auctions. One is to scale down the amount you are willing to bid. This will result in your losing some good investments, but it will also result in losing some bad investments. Auctions require a scaled-down bid. The second solution is to avoid auctions. A major corporation, heavily engaged in acquiring firms, will not engage in an unfriendly acquisition because of the possibility of becoming engaged in an auction (a bidding war). This "arbitrary" rule has a sound theoretical foundation.

In some situations, the amount by which the bid should be reduced can be computed using a Bayesian revision technique, and in other situations, it can only be estimated subjectively. It is reasonable that the amount deducted should increase as the number of bidders increases.

A decision maker has to be aware that the winner's-curse problem can be found in situations that are not formal auctions. It occurs whenever a project has been considered several times within a firm or when one or more external parties have considered and rejected the project or similar projects.

Assume that a firm is considering buying an office building in New York City. If this is the first time the building has been considered by the firm, if the NPV is positive, and if no other firm has been offered the opportunity to buy, a different analysis is appropriate than if many other prospective buyers have rejected the opportunity to buy or, alternatively, if it is the tenth time this firm has evaluated the building (previously the analysis indicated that rejection was the correct decision).

Conclusions

The existence of uncertainty not only raises the possibility that an investment that is acceptable may turn out to be undesirable, but also that an investment that seems to be unacceptable may turn out to be desirable if additional information is obtained. The value of the additional information must be balanced against the cost of the information.

After an investment has been accepted, there is a need to evaluate the results of operating the investment compared to the forecasts used to make the investment decision. The possibility of post-audit bias arises in this situation if the forecast being used in the post audit does not incorporate all the relevant information—in particular, if it leaves out prior information.

If post audits are done using forecasts that incorporate all of the information, there should be no post-audit bias. When such forecasts are used and a bias is detected, it would indeed be a signal that corrective action to improve the forecasts may be appropriate.

Appendix: Calculations to Revise Probabilities

From Table 14.1 we obtain

$$P(G|e_1) = .9 \qquad P(G|e_2) = .2$$
$$P(B|e_1) = .1 \qquad P(B|e_2) = .8$$

The joint probabilities are

$$P(G, e_1) = P(G|e_1) P(e_1) = .9 \times .4 = .36$$
$$P(G, e_2) = P(G|e_2) P(e_2) = .2 \times .6 = \underline{.12}$$
$$P(G) \qquad = \qquad\qquad\qquad\qquad\qquad .48$$
$$P(B, e_1) = P(B|e_1) P(e_1) = .1 \times .4 = .04$$
$$P(B, e_2) = P(B|e_2) P(e_2) = .8 \times .6 = \underline{.48}$$
$$P(B) \qquad = \qquad\qquad\qquad\qquad\qquad .52$$

$$P(e_1|G) = \frac{.36}{.48} = .75 \qquad P(e_2|G) = .25$$

$$P(e_1|B) = \frac{.04}{.52} = .077 \qquad P(e_2|B) = .923$$

PROBLEMS

14.1 You are asked to provide statistical advice about capital budgeting decisions to the president of a corporation. For each project, the president receives an estimate of its expected NPV from the division V. P. (denoted by V_0). He receives as well the standard deviation of the estimate (denoted σ_0). He also has or can obtain a separate estimate of the expected NPV from his corporate finance staff (denoted by V_e). The standard deviation of that estimate is denoted σ_e. The president wants to accept investments whose true NPV is positive and is willing to assume for decision-making purposes that V_0 and V_e are both *unbiased* normally distributed estimates of the true net present value.

The president has the following information already (in millions of dollars).

$$V_0 = .1 \qquad \sigma_e = .06 \qquad \sigma_0 = .08$$

He has instructed his corporate finance staff to obtain V_e. Since a prompt decision is needed, and he will be in Paris for three weeks, he has instructed his secretary to tell the division vice president to go ahead with the investment if V_e is greater than K or to cancel it if V_e is less than K. The correct value of K is _____ (show your calculations).

14.2 For a third project, the president of the corporation already has the following information.

$$V_0 = \$75,000 \qquad \sigma_e = \$1,000,000 \qquad \sigma_0 = \$150,000$$

The uncertainty about this project is all technological. The corporate research laboratory has assured the president that a $100,000 lab experiment could provide perfect information about the value of this project. What is the expected value of perfect information in this case? (Show your calculations.)

14.3 For the project referred to in problem 14.2, the president could contract with an outside consultant to obtain an opinion about the value of the project. The consultant's estimate will be unbiased, will have a standard deviation of $100,000, and will cost $10,000. Which of the following alternatives is best?
a. Obtain perfect information from the lab.
b. Obtain imperfect information from the consultant.
c. Obtain information from both sources.
d. Accept the investment now.
e. Reject the investment now.
Show your calculations.

14.4 The Phil T. Rich Oil Company has a lease on the mineral deposits of a parcel of land. Geologists have provided the following opinions of what might be found if an exploratory well is drilled on this property.

Outcomes	Probability	PV of Resources Discovered (Millions of Dollars)
Only gas deposit	.18	5.0
Only oil deposit	.08	10.0
Both oil and gas	.02	15.0
Neither oil nor gas	.72	0
Total	1.00	

The possible gas deposits are in a geological formation approximately one mile below the surface. A well that stopped at this level could be drilled for $1.2 million ($0.8 million to set up the drill rig plus $0.4 million to drill the first mile). The possible oil deposits are in a formation two miles below the surface. (The extra costs of drilling the second mile are $0.6 million if the drilling contractor is told before drilling begins and $1.1 million if a decision is made after the well has already been drilled for the first mile.)

If Rich Oil does not spend at least $0.5 million exploring for oil on its property, its lease will expire at the end of the year.

Mr. Rich is considering the following alternatives.

a. Do nothing. Let the lease expire.
b. Drill for gas only.
c. Drill for gas; then decide whether to continue to drill for oil.
d. Drill a two-mile-deep well (this would find whatever gas or oil is on the property).

The incremental costs (in millions of dollars) associated with each alternative are

a. 0.
b. 1.2.
c. 1.2 (minimum) or 2.3 (maximum).
d. 1.8.

In answering the following questions, assume that Rich Oil's objective is to maximize the expected net present value of its decision. For alternatives (a), (b), and (d), find the cost of the alternatives, the expected present value of the resources discovered, and the expected net present value of the alternatives. Show all calculations. Which of the three actions is preferred?

14.5 (*Continuation of problem 14.4.*) Mr. Rich has chosen alternative (c). The drill is down to the three-quarter-mile level, and he is beginning to think carefully about the decision that will face him soon. He has rearranged the probability estimate provided by his geologists in the following form.

	Gas Present	Gas Not Present	Raw Totals
Oil present	.02	.08	.10
Oil not present	.18	.72	.90
Column totals	.20	.80	1.00

a. What is the best action for Mr. Rich if gas is found at the one-mile level? Why?

b. What is the best action for Mr. Rich if gas is not found at the one-mile level? Why?

14.6 (*Continuation of problem 14.4.*). Explaining why he chose alternative (c), Mr. Rich replied.

"There were two advantages to that alternative. First, I might find some gas. Second, I would find some information about the possibility of oil. Information is valuable in this business. I know I paid for the information. But it was worth it!"

Do you agree that *in this case*, the information is valuable? Explain. (It is acceptable, but not necessary, to calculate the value of the information to answer this question.)

DISCUSSION QUESTION

14.A George Beardsley and Edwin Mansfield studied the experience of a giant multinational corporation in forecasting the profitability of new products (*Journal of Business*, January 1978). Specifically, the corporation recorded a forecast of the profitability of each new product at the time it was decided to produce the product. Each new product was post-audited nine years later, when its actual profitability was known. Beardsley and Mansfield found that "... the initial forecasts tend to be relatively optimistic in cases where actual profits were small and relatively pessimistic in cases where actual profits were large. Specifically, the forecasts underestimated the profitability of ... new products where they exceeded about $1 million, and overestimated the profitability of less profitable new products. . . " (pp. 130–131).

Two interpretations of these results are listed here. For each interpretation, indicate whether you believe the interpretation given is necessarily wrong or is not necessarily wrong (that is, it could be correct). Give a brief explanation of your reasons.

a. The initial forecasts of new products whose true profitability was less than $1 million may be unbiased estimates of the true profitability of those new products.

b. The initial forecasts correspond to Bayesian revised forecasts that correctly incorporate relevant prior information.

REFERENCES

Bierman, H., Jr., and V. R. Rao, "Investment Decisions with Sampling," *Financial Management*, Autumn 1978, pp. 19–24.

Brown, K. C., "A Note on the Apparent Bias of Net Revenue Estimates for Capital Investment Projects," *Journal of Finance*, September 1974, pp. 1215–1227.

———, "The Rate of Return of Selected Investment Projects," *Journal of Finance*, September 1978, pp. 1250–1253.

Little, John D. C., "Models and Managers: The Concept of Decision Calculus," *Management Science*, April 1970, pp. B466–B485.

Marsh, P. R., and R. A. Brealey, "The Use of Imperfect Forecasts in Capital Investment Decisions," *Proceedings of the European Finance Association 1975* (Amsterdam: North Holland Publishing Company, 1975).

Merrett, A. J., and A. Sykes, *The Finance and Analysis of Capital Projects* (New York, John Wiley & Sons, 1963).

Miller, Edward M., "Uncertainty Induced Bias in Capital Budgeting," *Financial Management*, Autumn 1978, pp. 12–18.

Pruit, Stephen W., and Lawrence Gitman, "Capital Budgeting Forecast Biases: Evidence from the Fortune 500," *Financial Management*, Spring 1987, pp. 46–51.

Schlaifer, R., *Analysis of Decisions Under Uncertainty* (New York, McGraw-Hill Book Co., 1969).

Statman, M., and T. T. Tyebjee, "Optimistic Capital Budgeting Forecasts: An Experiment," *Financial Management*, Autumn 1985, pp. 27–33.

Yawitz, J. B., "Externalities and Risky Investments," *Journal of Finance*, September 1977, pp. 1143–1149.

CHAPTER 15

Foreign Investments

"F.A.S.B 8 is the worst set of rules for foreign exchange accounting I have ever heard of—except for all the others anyone has ever shown me," a senior vice president of the Exxon Corporation once said.[1]
Deborah Rankin, New York Times, May 8, 1978, p. D1.

We will define foreign investments as existing when the benefits to be derived through time are in a different currency than the currency of the initial investment. There is an implication that there will be at least two translations of currencies, one at the time of the initial investment and the second at the time that cash flows are returned to the country of the investing company.

In this chapter we will consider several complexities. The first is the necessity to consider the currency translation. The second is the necessity of considering the nature of the investment. This second problem is not unique to international investments, but it is apt to occur more frequently in this setting. We then briefly discuss taxes, the remission of funds, and risk.

Currency Translation

Assume that two divisions are competing for funds. In one division an investment of $1,000,000 will return a 15 percent return, and in the second division a 35 percent return and a higher net present value can be earned. If these returns have been defined in terms of local currencies, then further adjustments are necessary.

---

[1] One of "the others," F.A.S.B 52, has replaced F.A.S.B 8.

Define

r   to be the required rate of return of the parent company (say in dollars)

j   to be the rate of devaluation of the currency of the investment

k   to be the rate of return that should be required in terms of the currency of the investment

We want

$$1 + r = \frac{1 + k}{1 + j}$$

or

$$k = r + j + rj$$

EXAMPLE 15.1

Assume the C Can Company requires an internal rate of return of .10. It is considering investing \$1,000 in a country with a currency called yen, which is devaluating its currency relative to the dollar at a rate of .20 per year. $r = .10$, $j = .20$, and

$$k = r + j + rj$$
$$= .10 + .20 + .02 = .32$$

Assume that the current exchange rate is \$1 for 1.20 yen and that one year from today the rate is expected to be \$1 per 1.44 yen. If \$1,000 is invested today, the firm wants back \$1,100 one year from today. That is, it must earn .32 on the investment of 1,200 yen, or 1,584 yen.

$$1,200 \ (1.32) = 1,584 \text{ yen}$$

The 1,584 yen will be worth \$1,100,

$$\frac{1,584}{1.44} = \$1,100$$

and the firm will earn 10 percent on its initial investment of \$1,000. In order to earn 10 percent in dollars, the foreign subsidiary had to earn 32 percent in yen. Now let us assume that the exchange rate next period will be .8 (1.20) = .96 yen to a dollar and $j = -.20$. We now have

$$1 + k = (1 + r) \ (1 + j)$$

or

$$k = r + j + rj$$

but

$$j = -.20$$

and

$$k = .10 - .20 - .02 = -.12$$

The investment of $1,000 and 1,200 yen now only has to return 1,200 $(1 - .12) = 1,056$ yen one year from now. The 1,056 yen will convert to $1,100 using the .96 conversion rate.

A Different Approach

The formulation

$$k = r + j + rj$$

is most useful as a device that reminds us that both the corporation's domestic required return and the change in the exchange rate must be considered in evaluating the investments of a foreign subsidiary. Also, the interaction term (rj) is not obvious, and the formulation reminds us of the necessity of including it.

Now we will switch to a more intuitive approach to the problem. Rather than computing an average percentage change in exchange rates or predicting one rate for all periods, the analyst will predict the exchange rate each period. The foreign currency will be converted to dollars to determine the net present value or internal rate of return of the investment. Assume that the following cash flows and forecasted exchange rates exist.

Time	Yen	Conversion Rate	Dollars
0	−1,000,000	100 yen for $1	−$10,000
1	+ 100,000	80 yen for $1	+ 1,250
2	+1,100,000	50 yen for $1	+ 22,000

Using a 10 percent rate of discount, the present value of the yen cash flow is zero. The present value of the dollar cash flow is $9,317.

$$
\begin{aligned}
- 10,000 \times 1.0000 &= - 10,000 \\
+ 1,250 \times .9091 &= 1,136 \\
+ 22,000 \times .8264 &= \underline{18,181} \\
&= \$9,317
\end{aligned}
$$

The internal rate of return moves from 10 percent in yen to 54 percent computed using dollars.

The Irrelevance of Future Plans

It is sometimes argued that only the analysis for the foreign currency should be done, since we are probably going to reinvest the yen in the same country when the yen are earned. Only the exchange rates when the cash flows are returned are alleged to be relevant.

The fact is that if the funds were returned to dollars, they would have an internal rate of return of 54 percent (in the most recent example). If it is more desirable to leave the funds invested in the foreign land, that is a second decision.

There is one exception to the preceding conclusion. This exception occurs if the sequential foreign investments are economically linked. If one investment is made, the second investment follows, and the second investment can only be made if the first investment is made. In these situations, the two sequential investments should be treated as one alternative, and the cash flows converted into dollars only after the second investment is financed.

But if this limited situation does not exist, the analysis should be as if the exchange into dollars takes place for the first investment.

The Leverage Consideration

Frequently, investments in foreign countries are made by forming subsidiary corporations. These subsidiaries often will have one or more partners and are financed heavily with debt. We argue that the additional leverage changes the required return. This conclusion assumes the existence of uncertainty.

Assume a situation where a firm is considering a $10,000 investment in a piece of equipment. The firm uses 10 percent as the rate of discount. There is uncertainty and possibility of two equally likely outcomes:

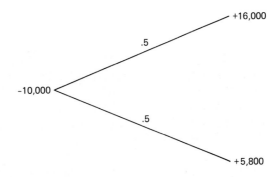

The expected outcome is $10,900, and the expected net present value is $ − 91. Using 10 percent, the investment is not acceptable based on expected net present value.

Let us assume that the firm is financed with .4 debt and .6 common stock and that the following costs apply.

	Capital Structure	Costs	Weighted Costs
Debt	.4	.06	.024
Common stock	.6	.127	.076
Weighted average cost			.100

Right or wrong, assume the firm uses the average capital cost of 10 percent to evaluate investments.

While the equipment has been rejected in the United States, there is an opportunity to buy it for a foreign subsidiary. Since the foreign subsidiary is financed with .5 debt, $5,000 is required as an investment by the parent.

The following stock equity cash flows will occur if the debt costs .07. We assume a one-yen-for-one-dollar exchange rate with no forecasted changes.

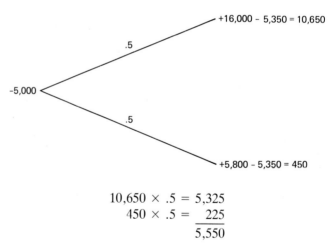

$$10,650 \times .5 = 5,325$$
$$450 \times .5 = \underline{225}$$
$$5,550$$

The $5,550 is an 11 percent return on the $5,000 investment, and the investment is desirable, using the parent's discount rate of 10 percent. The expected net present value is $45. The switch in decisions is caused by the inclusion of more debt and by the switch to the use of stock equity cash flows in the analysis of the foreign investment. Despite the increase in the cost of debt to .07, the investment is now deemed to be acceptable.

The investment of the $5,000 by the parent firm is being evaluated differently overseas than it is being evaluated domestically. Assume that we describe the problem so that the entire investment is domestic, but the subsidiary and its debt still exist. Most business analysts would reject the second analysis, which says that the otherwise unacceptable investment is now acceptable. The investment is made to seem acceptable by the implicit inclusion of debt flows in the analysis and the switch to stock equity cash flows. It is far from obvious that 10 percent is the appropriate discount rate to evaluate the cash flows consisting of the $5,000 outlay followed by $5,550 of expected benefits one period later. We know that with .4 debt the stockholders required a .127 return. The subsidiary has .5 debt, and if the analysis is to be done in terms of the cash flows to the stockholders, then a return larger than .127 must be used.

In the preceding analysis, the inclusion of the additional debt of the subsidiary was made obvious. Frequently, in evaluating investments in foreign subsidiaries, the inclusion of the debt is less obvious. Assume a firm targets 10 percent on funds invested domestically or 15 percent on funds invested overseas. It may not be made clear that the 15 percent return is on funds invested in the stock equity of a subsidiary and only results because of the additional debt that is incorporated in the analysis.

Taxes

The tax laws applicable to international trade are apt to change through time. Thus, only general principles will be discussed in this section.

A primary tax issue is whether a tax paid in a foreign country will be treated as an expense (thus worth t_c per dollar as a deduction where t_c is the domestic corporate tax rate) or as a tax credit (thus worth $1 per dollar as a credit against taxes paid).

A second tax issue arises as to the extent of tax deferral that is feasible by not bringing back the earnings of the subsidiary to the home country. Tax deferral is a powerful incentive, and its possibility will greatly affect decision making. Bringing back earnings and having them taxed compared to keeping them invested without being taxed are forms of mutually exclusive investments.

In some situations government rules will prevent the free flow of funds across national boundaries and thus further complicate decisions on whether to reinvest or commit additional funds.

Remission of Funds

Given legislation limiting the flow of funds, companies tend to develop strategies to facilitate the transfer of funds. Among these strategies are for the parent to supply capital in the form of debt so that payments of interest and principal accomplish the transfer or inflate the intracompany transfer prices for materials or services. These manipulations also affect the taxes of the several jurisdictions under which the companies operate.

One of the simpler techniques for transferring funds is for the subsidiary to declare a cash dividend. Unfortunately, institutional complexities may cause the firm to benefit from more roundabout strategies.

Foreign Investment and Risk

Foreign investment is a form of risk diversification. A foreign investment may be riskier than a domestic investment, but at the same time its overall effect on the risk of the corporation might be to reduce it.

For purposes of illustration, assume that the variance of a domestic investment is 100, while the variance of a foreign investment is 250 (say there is a political risk).

The domestic investment is perfectly correlated with the current investments, however, while the foreign investment is independent of the current investments of the firm.

If the current variance of the firm's investments is 1,600, the variance of the firm with the domestic investment is

$$\text{Var (firm)} + \text{Var (investment)} + 2\sigma_{\text{firm}}\sigma_{\text{investment}}$$

$$1,600 + 100 + 2 (40) (10) = 2,500$$

With the foreign investment we have for the firm's variance,

$$1,600 + 250 = 1,850$$

Even though the variance of the foreign investment is 2.5 times as large as the variance of the domestic investment, it has a significantly more desirable effect on the firms's risk.

The company's stockholders are also likely to benefit from the foreign diversification, since it is a form of diversification that is not likely to be implemented by the average stockholder of the firm.

Conclusions

Assume that we start with two identical risk and return situations relative to the real investments in plant and equipment. One opportunity is domestic, and the second is a foreign subsidiary. If the domestic investment is treated as a conventional investment and the basic investment cash flows are used but the foreign investment's cash flows are those of a residual investor (stockholder), a strong bias is introduced in the analysis for the foreign investment. There should be an upward switch in the required return if the stock equity cash flows are used instead of the investment cash flows.

Second, it should be remembered that the foreign currency must be translated back into the domestic currency in computing the present value or internal rate of return of the investment.

For foreign investments, the primary distinctions compared to domestic investments, aside from the currency exchange problem, are the tax and other institutional factors that affect an investment's cash flows. The tax laws of the country in which the plant is located, the tax laws of the countries in which the plant will do business, and the tax laws of the corporation's domicile are all relevant. But aside from these factors, the investment analysis of foreign opportunities is very similar to that of domestic capital budgeting.

PROBLEMS

15.1 Company A requires a .20 return on its domestic investments. It is considering investing in a foreign subsidiary. The foreign currency is being devalued at a rate of .15 per year. What rate of return should be required?

15.2 Company B requires a .15 return on its domestic investments. It is considering investing in a foreign subsidiary. The foreign currency is appreciating against the dollar. The dollar is depreciating at the rate of .10 per year. What rate of return should be required for an investment in the foreign country?

15.3 Assume that an investment of $1,000 yen will pay $1,380 after one year. If 1 yen will buy $1 at the beginning of the year, and 1.15 yen will buy $1 at the end of the year, what return has been earned on the initial investment of $1?

15.4 Assume that an investment of $1,000 yen will pay $1,035 after one year. If 1 yen will buy $1 at the beginning of the year, and .90 yen will buy $1 at the end of the year, what return has been earned on the initial investment of $1?

15.5 The following cash flows and exchange rates apply to an investment being considered by the C Company.

Time	Exchange Rate	Cash Flow
0	1.20 yen to $1	−12,000 yen
1	1.50 yen to $1	+ 1,200 yen
2	2.00 yen to $1	+13,200 yen

If the parent firm requires a return of 20 percent, is the investment desirable?

15.6 The following cash flows and exchange rates apply to an investment being considered by the D Company.

Time	Exchange Rate	Cash Flow
0	1.20 yen to $1	−12,000 yen
1	.80 yen to $1	+ 1,200 yen
2	.50 yen to $1	+13,200 yen

If the parent company requires a return of 20 percent, is the investment desirable?

15.7   The E Company is thinking of investing $10,000,000 in a foreign subsidiary (no exchange rate changes are expected). The investment is expected to earn 11 percent. The subsidiary is financed .6 with debt and .4 with common stock. The parent has a weighted average cost of capital of .10.

	Cost	Capital Structure	Weighted Cost
Debt	.08	.5	.04
Common stock	.12	.5	.06
			.10

A return of .10 is required on investments. Assume that the capital of the parent is $100,000,000 and the capital of the subsidiary is $50,000,000. Should the $10,000,000 be invested? Explain.

15.8   Assume that the F Company makes decisions using expected monetary value and has a 10 percent time-value factor.

It is considering the following investment.

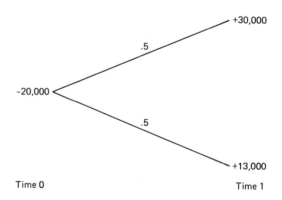

The expected monetary value at time 1 is $\frac{1}{2}(43,000) = \$21,500$. This is a 7.5 percent return on the investment of $20,000.

a. Should the investment be accepted?

b. Now assume that the same investment is being considered by a subsidiary that is financed .7 by debt and .3 by common stock. The debt of the subsidiary costs .05. What expected return will the parent make on an investment of $6,000 in the subsidiary to purchase the equipment? Is the investment acceptable?

15.9   LDC is a poor but progressive country on the northern coast of a large continent in the Southern Hemisphere. The prime minister of LDC has to choose between two tax policies for foreign multinational corporations doing business in LDC. The estimated tax yields over the next four years are as follows.

	Year				
Policy	1	2	3	4	5
A	40	40	0	0	0
B	35	25	25	10	0

Both policies result in shifting the tax burden to foreigners. Whichever policy is adopted, the foreign multinational corporations will eventually learn how to avoid bearing the tax. Some new tax strategy will be required within five years. The prime minister has friends at major international banks who can invest excess funds (if any) at 10 percent or who will lend money at that rate if it can be repaid.

The prime minister wants your advice as to which tax policy she should choose. Explain your recommendation.

REFERENCES

Agmon, T., and Donald R. Lessard, "Investor Recognition of Corporate International Diversification," *Journal of Finance*, September 1977, pp. 1049–1056.

Baker, J. C., and L. Beardsley, "Multinational Companies' Use of Risk Evaluation and Profit Measurement for Capital Budgeting Decisions," *Journal of Business Finance*, Spring 1973, pp. 38–43.

Dufey, Gunter, "Institutional Constraints and Incentives on International Portfolio Investment," *International Portfolio Investment* (U. S. Department of the Treasury OASIA: 1975).

Giddy, Ian H., "An Integrated Theory of Exchange Rate Equilibrium," *Journal of Financial and Quantitative Analysis*, December 1976, pp. 883–892.

Lessard, Donald R., "Evaluating Foreign Projects: An Adjusted Present Value Approach," in Donald R. Lessard (Ed.), *International Financial Management* (Boston: Warren, Gorham, and Lamont, 1979).

Oblak, D. J., and Roy J. Helm, Jr., "Survey and Analysis of Capital Budgeting Methods Used by Multinationals," *Financial Management*, Winter 1980, pp. 37–41.

Rugman, Alan, "Risk Reduction by International Diversification," *Journal of International Business Studies*, Fall 1976, pp. 75–80.

Shapiro, A. C., "International Capital Budgeting," *Midland Corporate Finance Journal*, Spring 1983, pp. 26–45.

———, "Capital Budgeting for the Multinational Corporation," *Financial Management*, Spring 1978, pp. 7–16.

Solnik, Bruno H., "Why Not Diversify Internationally?" *Financial Analysts Journal*, July–August 1974, pp. 48–54.

CHAPTER 16

Economic Evaluation of Investment Proposals: The Government's Point of View

Without development there is no profit, without profit no development.
Joseph A. Schumpeter, Theory of Economic Development *(Cambridge, MA: Harvard University Press, 1934), p. 154.*

In Chapters 1–15 we have been concerned with methods of evaluating the economic worth of proposed investment projects from the point of view of the managers or owners of a business. An investment proposal that appears desirable to the business that proposes it may be considered to be unattractive from the point of view of a government. Similarly, a proposal that is unattractive to a business may be considered to be attractive to the government. The purpose of the present chapter is to introduce the reader to some of the differences between evaluating the economic impact of investment projects from a business point of view and from the point of view of a government agency.

Many executives in private business corporations will encounter situations in which, in order to do their jobs effectively, they must understand how investments are evaluated from a public economic point of view. In most countries today, it is necessary to obtain approvals from one or more government agencies before an important business investment can be undertaken. A proposed investment must be justified not only to a board of directors but to officials from a finance ministry or a government planning office. These officials will be more interested in the cost and benefits from a public point of view than in the profitability to the corporation. Many principles of economic analysis relevant to evaluating investments from the point of view of the owners are also relevant to evaluating investments from a public economic viewpoint, however.

Businesses frequently have to give some attention to the effects an investment has on groups other than the owners of the business proposing it. For example, American businesses have been called upon to cooperate in helping to solve the balance-of-payments problems of the United States. It is not difficult to cite examples in which business investments that were economic from the point of view of the business organization proposing them were opposed by other because of water pollution, air pollution, or detrimental effects on scenic values.

The primary considerations to be incorporated in an evaluation of investments from a public economic point of view are

1. How large are the net benefits that would be derived from the proposed investment?
2. Who would receive the benefits?
3. By what means would the benefits become available to the recipients?

The first question refers to matters of economic efficiency. The second refers to matters of income distribution. The relevance of these two questions should be fairly clear. The relevance of the third question may be less apparent. The means by which benefits are distributed to a group may influence the satisfaction they derive from the benefits. It seems likely, for example, that both American farmers and countries that derive foreign exchange from exports of basic commodities would prefer an increase in income resulting from a higher price for the commodities they sell to an equal increase in income in the form of a grant that has the characteristics of an unearned gift.

Although in principle the answers to all three questions are relevant to deciding on the value of a proposed investment, we shall concentrate in this chapter on the computations that must be made in order to measure the size of the net benefits.

In the following discussion, we shall assume that we begin with an investment proposal that has already been analyzed from the point of view of its profitability to the owners of the business, using the procedures suggested earlier. The process of adjusting this analysis to a public economic point of view can be thought of as consisting of three basic steps.

In evaluating investments, a business uses market prices to estimate the relevant cash flows. However, for a variety of reasons, market prices may not truly reflect opportunity costs of resources used or the opportunity value of the production. Whenever there is a systematic and material difference between the market price and these opportunity prices, the latter should be substituted for corresponding market prices.

A second type of adjustment is necessary when an investment is so large, relative to the markets in which its factors of production will be purchased or in which its products will be sold, that acceptance of the investment will appreciably change the relevant market price or opportunity price of one or more of the resources used or produced. When this is the case, neither the market prices, nor the opportunity costs that would have prevailed without the project, nor the prices with the project will exactly measure the benefits or costs of accepting the project. In these circumstances, we should use a price in between the price that would have prevailed without the project and the price that will prevail with it.

Some investment projects will lead to changes in the efficiency of other economic activities in the society. Such changes in efficiency may be beneficial or detrimental. In either case, it is desirable to take them into account when evaluating the economic worth of investments from a public point of view.

The following sections discuss each of the preceding adjustments in some detail.

Discrepancies Between Market Prices and Opportunity Prices

The opportunity price or cost of a resource is the value of the resource used in its most valuable manner. In a competitive market there is a strong tendency for market prices to represent opportunity prices. Customers will tend to purchase additional units of a product whenever the value of the product to them is more than the price. Similarly, producers will tend to produce an additional unit whenever the price of an additional unit is greater than the extra cost of producing it (where cost is the opportunity cost of the factors of production). In equilibrium, under these conditions, the price of a commodity will measure both the value of an additional unit to customers and the incremental cost of producing it.

Monopoly Pricing

When a commodity is being produced under monopolistic (or oligopolistic) conditions, market prices are likely to differ from opportunity prices. A firm in a monopolistic position will find that it can increase its profits by pricing its products at something more than the extra cost of producing an additional unit. The market price will represent the marginal value of the commodity to the user, but not generally the cost of producing an additional unit.

If an investment proposal involves using factors of production purchased from a monopolistic firm operating within the government's boundaries, a better measure of the cost of the project, from a public economic point of view, can be obtained by substituting an estimate of the marginal cost of the products for the actual market prices.

Unemployed Resources

If, in the absence of the project, a resource would be unemployed, and if the resource cannot be stored, the appropriate opportunity price for using that resource in the project may be less than its market price. In some countries there is considerable unemployment and underemployment of resources, particularly unskilled labor. If a person who would otherwise be unemployed is put to work as a result of a new investment project, the wages paid may considerably overstate the true opportunity cost of using the person in this particular project. In fact, the opportunity to work may have a positive value, taking into consideration the morale of the unemployed workers. With some particularly unpleasant or dangerous work, the opportunity price may be greater than zero. More importantly, if labor must be induced to move from one location to another or be retrained, there may be some significant opportunity costs in employing the labor, even if the alternative would be to leave it unemployed. In addition to the direct cost of moving the workers, there may be costs associated with providing housing, schools, and various government facilities for the additional population at the new location. These are costs that might be avoided if the workers remained in their old location. Even allowing for such costs, the market wage rates are likely to overestimate the opportunity cost of labor when there is chronic unemployment.

Foreign Exchange Shortages

So far we have considered cases in which the market price for using a resource was higher than its opportunity price. There are also important cases in which the market price of a resource is less than its opportunity cost. An important example involves the use of imported goods or services when there are fixed official exchange rates. The official exchange rate may not properly measure the opportunity price of foreign exchange. If a business imports a commodity, the price paid is likely to be the world market price converted to domestic prices at the official exchange rate. The opportunity cost for foreign exchange is a better estimate of the cost to the country of using foreign exchange in this way. Some projects may produce goods for export. The value of a foreign exchange earned by the exports may be underestimated when the official exchange rate is used. The investment project may produce goods that are not exported but are substitutes for imported goods. Such goods may save foreign exchange by reducing the amount that would have otherwise been imported. Again the value of the foreign exchange saving should be estimated by using an opportunity price for an exchange rate to compute the value of the imports rather than the official exchange rate. These discrepancies are reduced or eliminated when exchange rates are allowed to fluctuate freely.

Savings Versus Consumption

Ordinarily, in attempting to evaluate an investment project, we measure the extra income (the benefits less the costs) that would be generated by the project, but we do not concern ourselves with how this income would be used. A justification for stopping with a measure of income is that if the recipients are free to allocate income in any manner they desire, the opportunity value of an additional dollar used for savings will have the same value as an additional dollar used for consumption. In some less developed countries, this assumption may not be valid at the national level. If the country's economic development is inhibited by low levels of savings and investment, the government may consider an increment of income saved and invested to be of greater value in promoting the economic interests of the country than an increment of income used for current consumption. In these circumstances, the government may wish to measure how the income generated by a project is likely to be used. The proportion of income that goes into savings may be given more weight than the proportion that goes into current consumption. The additional value attached to income that is saved and reinvested can be thought of as an opportunity price for savings.

Taxes

A major difference between the way investments would be evaluated from the point of view of the business and from the public point of view is related to the treatment of taxes. The business will be concerned with the after-tax cash flows associated with the investment. This is correct from the public point of view if the taxes are really prices charged for services rendered to the business by government bodies. Examples are tax assessments covering services such as water, sewage, police, and fire protection. Such taxes need to be deducted, but they may require adjustment, as it is unlikely that they reflect the additional cost of providing the additional services used as a result of the investment. Expenditures reflecting the costs of providing such services are a proper deduction from the benefits of an investment from the public economic point of view.

Most tax payments, however, cannot usefully be thought of as payments for identifiable quantities of services rendered a particular business. A large fraction of taxes collected in a government's boundaries may be used for such things as health, education, and national defense (or paying for past wars). A business may benefit from such services in a general way, but there is not likely to be an identifiable relationship between the amount of taxes paid by the business and the amount of benefit received. Because this is the case, the costs and benefits of an investment should be analyzed on an individual basis with an attempt to measure the cost of the government services to be used and the contribution of the investment to the financing of these services.

We have previously mentioned that, if a country's ability to achieve its economic goals is inhibited because savings are too low to finance the desired level of investment, it may be reasonable to attach a high opportunity price to that portion of the project's income that is channeled into savings. Government savings might be used to finance either its own investment projects or those of the private sector. If a government devoted a proportion of its tax revenues to savings and if political or administrative complications did not prevent the effective use of these savings, the extra revenues generated by a new investment project might have more value in contributing to the country's economic goals than the same amount of funds retained in the hands of consumers. This analysis suggests that an opportunity price may in some situations be assigned to government tax revenues. This will increase the measure of benefits associated with investments that generate tax revenues.

Indivisibilities

If a project is so large that the operation of the project would change the market prices of one or more of the inputs purchased or of the products being produced, the net public benefits of the project may not be properly measured using market prices. This may be true even when the market prices represent the opportunity costs of using the resources consumed in the project and the opportunity values of the resources produced. This special evaluation problem arises if for some technological reason the investment must be undertaken on at least a certain minimum scale, large enough so that some of the relevant prices would change as a result of building the project. There are many situations where a series of small incremental investments is not feasible technologically. A jet airport runway must be of a certain minimum size; a dam cannot stop halfway across a river; and a railroad must have at least one set of tracks, preferably with reasonable starting and ending locations.

Suppose that a hydroelectric project results in a 25 percent increase in electric output and that a 50 percent reduction in the price of electricity results in a sufficient expansion of the use of electricity to absorb this extra power. Even if the new price of electricity appropriately measures both the marginal cost of producing an extra unit of electricity and the marginal value of the extra unit in its various uses, the benefits of the investment cannot be measured in terms of revenues collected. Under the assumptions given, accepting the project would lead to a 37.5 percent reduction in total revenues collected by the electric power generating system. If revenues were used as a measure of the benefits, one might conclude that the 25 percent increase in output would lead to a reduction in total benefits.

One difficulty in this case arises because all the electricity is sold at a price that tells how much one small increment of electricity is worth when added to the existing supply. However, the project would add not one small increment to the supply but a very large increment. Consumers as a group should be willing to pay more for the output of the project. The value of this additional increment, expressed as a price per unit, will be an amount somewhere between the market price that would have prevailed without the project and the market price that prevails with it.

The appropriate measure of benefits in such cases is illustrated in Figure 16.1. The vertical axis measures the price per unit, and the horizontal axis measures the rate of consumption in kilowatts per year. The curve ee is a market demand curve for electricity. Each point on the curve shows the quantity that would be sold at the corresponding price. Suppose that without the project a quantity $0A$ would be produced (the marginal cost is AB) and sold at a price of AB. The total revenue collected under these circumstances is measured by the rectangle $0ABS$.

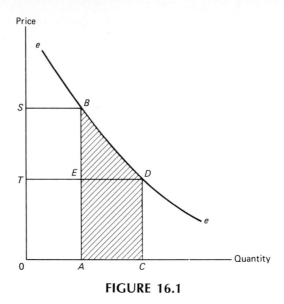

FIGURE 16.1

With the project, an additional quantity AC would be produced (with a marginal cost of CD). The market price will now be CD per unit. If all units are sold at that price, the total revenue collected with the new project would be measured by the rectangle $0CDT$. The additional amount that consumers are willing to pay for an increment of AC units of additional electricity, if the alternative were to do without this increment, is measured by the shaded area $ACDB$. It is this shaded area rather than the change in total revenues that properly measures the extra benefits from having this increment of electricity.

It is still necessary to subtract from these benefits an appropriate measure of the extra costs of providing this electricity. A problem similar to the revenue calculation occurs if a new investment project would materially change the prices of some of the resource inputs used in the project. Figure 16.2 represents an example of this sort. Suppose that, in a country with only one steel mill, it is proposed to build a second steel mill. Both the old and the new steel mills will require metallurgists. With just one steel mill, OG metallurgists would be employed in the old mill at a salary of GH. The curve ss represents the potential supply of metallurgists at various salary levels. With the new mill, let us suppose that the total number who will be required in both the old and new mill increased by an amount GI. (The exact amount of the increase will depend on the demand curve of the product.) To increase the supply by this amount, it will be necessary to pay a wage equal to IJ. The total wage bill for metallurgists with one steel mill is given by the area $0GHL$. The total wage bill for metallurgists with two steel mills is given by the area $0IJK$. The excess of the large area over the small area does not properly measure the extra cost to the country of obtaining the metallurgists required for the new will, however. These extra costs are

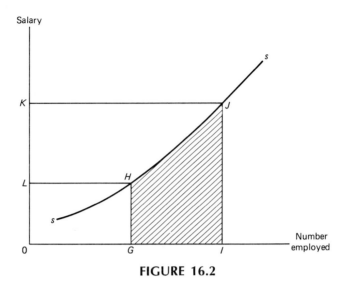

FIGURE 16.2

measured by the shaded area *GIJH*. The additional monetary payments that would in fact be paid to metallurgists if the new mill were built are transfers of income (in this case from the owners of the old steel mill to the metallurgists) in excess of the minimum needed to increase the supply of metallurgists. (For the minimum amount to take place, a discriminatory wage system would have to be used.) The actual wages would be used by a private owner of the mill, including the excess incentive to the workers; they should not be included in evaluating the new mill from the national economic point of view.

External Effects

An investment project may adversely affect the productivity of resources employed in other economic activities or the welfare of the population. To the extent that such changes are compensated for through market or legal institutional arrangement, their effect will tend to be included in the private benefit–cost evaluation of the investment. If the institutional arrangements do not provide for appropriate monetary compensation, these effects should be taken into account by incorporating implicit costs or benefits in evaluating the investment.

Suppose that a factory will produce a large amount of dirt and smoke. Consumers living where the dirt settles will spend more time dusting their furniture and more time and money cleaning clothes. Breathing the polluted air may even shorten their lives. In the absence of an appropriate tax on the factory that reduces its profit and compensates consumers for the additional expense and trouble, the smoke would be an uncompensated external diseconomy that should be taken into account in evaluating a project from the national point of view.

In other cases, an investment may directly affect the productivity of resources employed in other enterprises. If a farmer installs drainage tiles on one field, the productivity of some of the neighbor's fields receiving the runoff may also be increased. An oil company drilling a wildcat well on its own land may provide valuable information about the possibility of oil on adjacent land that it does not control. Sometimes a drilling company is able to obtain compensation from its neighbors for the value of this information in the form of a payment toward the cost of the well, but generally there is no compensation for this type of information. A private utility may build a dam to generate electricity. An uncompensated effect of the dam might be to reduce the danger of flooding on downstream land. Unless it owned the land, the utility would not count this as a benefit derived from its investment. From a public point of view, decreased flood damage is a benefit attributable to the dam.

Investments by Governments

Governments facing investment decisions have exactly the same basic problem as business managers, that is, measuring the costs and benefits of each period and transforming them all back to the present so that one measure of value may be obtained.

Public servants do have a somewhat more difficult problem of measuring benefits because they know they should include the social benefits (and costs) of the project. The business manager may choose to take refuge in profit maximization of the firm and not include the social costs and benefits. (We are not saying that this position is desirable.)

Government projects are not without risk, so the government official is also faced with the necessity of making a risk analysis. The position of a national government is analogous to that of a well-diversified investor when it comes to evaluating project risk. Primary attention must be focused on the systematic risk of the project.

The choice of interest rate is an interesting problem.[1] The government has two basic choices:

1. Its borrowing rate.
2. The opportunity cost to the economy as measured by the cost of funds to business or the required return the firms are using.

The borrowing rate of the government is attractive because it is objectively measured and easily determined. Unfortunately, the rate itself is frequently a

---

[1] For a comprehensive analysis of this problem, see Robert C. Lind et al., *Discounting for Time and Risk in Energy Policy* (Washington, D.C.: Resources for the Future, Inc., 1982).

result of decisions of government (or near-government) officials and may not reflect the opportunity cost of investments to the economy.

The second measure considered is the cost of funds to firms (or their required return); this measure is attractive, but again the information is difficult to obtain. Firms use a wide range of hurdle rates and frequently include risk adjustments. The rate used to take time value of money into account should not include a risk factor.

An added complication is the fact that business firms are taxed and government entities are not. Thus, the investments of government should be placed on the same tax basis as the investments of corporations. This also means that the discount rate used by the government body should be on the same tax basis as the business firm.

For example, if we assume that investors require a return of .06 for both debt and stock, and if there is a .48 corporate tax rate, the following represents the cost of capital calculation if the firm uses 40 percent debt.

	Before-Tax Required Return	Tax Rate	After-Tax Return to Corporation	Return to Investor	Tax Saving from Interest	After-Tax Cost to Corporation
Debt	.0600	.48	.0600	.0600	.0288	.0312
Stock	.1154	.48	.0600	.0600	—	.0600

	After-Tax Cost	Capital Structure	Weighted Average
Debt	.0312	.4	.0125
Stock	.0600	.6	.0360
			.0485

To make its discount rate equivalent, the government body would compute a before-tax required return. Thus, its time value of money would be as follows.

	Before-Tax Required Return	Capital Structure	Weighted Average
Debt	.0600	.4	.024
Stock	.1154	.6	.069
			.093

Although the .093 required return is higher than the .0485 after-tax return of the business firms, it must be remembered that we are placing the government required return on a before-tax basis that is equal to the before-tax required return of the business firm. There is also a difference in the way benefits are measured. The private firm will apply its after-tax required return to the after-tax cash flows from the investment. If the government uses an equivalent before-tax discount rate, it should be applied to the before-tax benefits of the project.

The argument may be made that the required return of government should be lowered because the benefits of a business firm are incorrectly measured (omitting social costs) and the benefits of government enterprises are understated (omitting social benefits). These facts may require an adjustment, but the adjustment should not be in the form of changing the required time-value factor. Also, if either of the .06 required returns included a risk factor, this factor should be excluded by the government in discounting for time.

Cost–Benefit Analysis

The use of the term *cost–benefit analysis* to describe the valuation of government projects is widespread. Although the term might well refer to several different procedures, the usual interpretation is a ratio of the present value of benefits to the present value of costs. This is, of course, the same calculation that we described as the index of present value.

We were critical of the present value index as a method of ranking investments, and all the criticisms carry over to the cost–benefit calculation. Its use may be beneficial, however, if one or more of the following apply.

1. All investments are accepted whose benefit–cost ratio is greater than 1.
2. The best investment is "continuous" and we invest all the funds in it.
3. Only investments with benefit–cost ratios greater than 1 are accepted; then at least the government has chosen acceptable investments. (They may not be the best.)
4. The computation of the benefit–cost ratio initiated a calculation of the benefits and costs of the investment that would otherwise not be made.

How a Federal Government Manager Should Analyze Buy-Versus-Lease Decisions

The navy supply ship was flying its colors, and it was manned by conventional navy enlisted men and officers. But there was something different about this ship. The ship was owned by a major U.S. corporation engaged in a war against taxes. One of the firms's corporate objectives was to reduce its income taxes to zero. The U.S. navy leased the ship.

How should a manager in the federal government make a lease-versus-buy decision? The U.S. government leases many billions of dollars of assets. No one knows how much the federal government spends on leases each year, but from scattered evidence, it would seem to be many billions of dollars.[2] It ranges from the navy leasing supply ships and NASA leasing communications satellites to the TVA leasing nuclear fuel. We want to investigate how a federal government manager should analyze the buy and lease alternatives if the objective is to minimize the present value of the cost to the federal government.

In the interest of achieving economic efficiency (lowest cost), we will subordinate the objective of meeting annual budgetary requirements. The likelihood of managers using the recommendations of this section will depend to some extent on the willingness of Congress to change its budgetary procedures or to enforce economic efficiency.

We will consider the leasing decision in two different ways. First, we will analyze the leasing decision by a unit of the U.S. government (the U.S. navy). Secondly, we will consider all units of the federal government as a single entity and will model the decision from that perspective.

Assume that a federal government department (the U.S. navy) is attempting to minimize the present value of its costs. The timing of the expenditures as well as the amount of expenditure is important to the calculations. An alternative strategy would be for the unit to minimize the cost budgeted for the present or the next year but not use the present value of the cost. While there are practical budgetary reasons for this alternative strategy, we will reject the short-run budgetary considerations in favor of minimizing the present value of the costs over the life of the asset.[3]

We first want to determine the minimum annual lease payment that a lessor with a given time-value factor will need to break even economically. The payment received by the lessor must be equal to or larger than

$$\text{Annual lease payment} = \frac{\text{cost of buying minus present value of tax shelters}}{\text{after tax present value of an annuity for term of lease}}$$

The tax shelters in the numerator would include the value of depreciation tax shields and any investment tax credits. The discount rate used by the lessor will reflect the lessor's after-tax cost of obtaining capital as well as a subjective risk adjustment (possibly equal to zero) for the specific asset being analyzed.

The denominator is equal to 1 minus the lessor's marginal tax rate times the present value of a dollar per period for the term of the lease.

We will next determine the maximum lease payment the federal government manager will be willing to pay if the decision is made on an economic basis from the narrow perspective of the department.

---

[2] See "Navy Cites Some Costs of Leasing," *The New York Times*, March 1, 1983, p. D16. The article says the navy is spending over $2.5 billion on leases per year.

[3] For two different perspectives on time discounting, see R. H. Clark (1978) and R. Thaler (1979).

For the unit of the government, it is necessary that the lease payment be no larger than the maximum payment where

$$\text{Maximum payment} = \frac{\text{cost of buying}}{\text{present value of the annuity for the term of the lease}}$$

If the lease payment required by the lessor is larger than the maximum value just determined, the government manager should not find the lease to be an attractive alternative. Assume that the government uses its borrowing rate as the discount rate. Then the maximum payment just computed is equal to the debt payment the government would make if it bought the asset and made equal annual debt payments. If the prospective lease payment is larger than the debt payment if the asset is purchased, the government should buy.

It should be remembered the government unit and the lessor do not necessarily use the same discount rate. The discount rate can differ because of taxes, risk, or merely different perceived costs. The calculation for the maximum payment by the government unit defines the maximum lease payment to be paid to the lessor. The payment required by the lessor will depend on the discount rate used by the lessor.

If the minimum value required by the lessor is less than the maximum value computed by the government manager, than a leasing contract can feasibly be arranged. Whether or not it can be arranged will depend on the depreciable life of the asset, the rates of discount used by the lessor and the government, the lessor's tax rate, and the value of the investment tax credit. These variables are the inputs into the calculation of the lessor's minimum lease payment and the maximum amount the government should be willing to pay. Although it is likely for leasing not to be desirable, it is necessary for the manager to do the calculations and not jump to conclusions.

In practice the lessor determines the necessary lease payments, and the government manager then only has to determine if the present value of the lease payments is less than the cost of the asset assuming zero residual value.

An equivalent solution for the manager would be to determine if the equal annual debt payment if the asset is purchased is less than the annual lease payment. If it is, then buying is more desirable.

We will do an example where the life is five years. We will see that analysis for the government manager is relatively easy but that it is difficult to draw general conclusions. The calculations of the costs of the two alternatives must be made to reach a sensible decision.

An Example: The Same Discount Rate

Initially assume that the lessor with a tax rate of .34 can borrow funds at .1515 and has an after-tax borrowing rate of .10. The government can borrow at a cost of .10. The government is considering leasing word processors for five years that can be purchased at a cost of $1,000,000. The lessor is not eligible for an investment tax credit. We assume that the lessor and the government use .10 as a discount rate (it is the government's borrowing rate). Using .10, the present value of an annuity for five years is 3.7908.

Assume that the present value of a dollar of depreciation (a five-year class) is .77325 and the present value of the depreciation tax savings is

$$1,000,000 \times .77325 \times .34 = \$263,000$$

For the lessor to break even, it is necessary that the lessor receive

$$\text{Annual lease payment} = \frac{1,000,000 - 263,000}{(1 - .34)\ 3.7908} = \frac{737,000}{2.5019} = \$295,000$$

If the government unit borrowed \$1,000,000 at a cost of .10 per year, it would pay $\frac{1,000,000}{3.7908} = \$263.797$ per year to retire the debt. The debt payment is significantly less than the lease payment, thus, buying is more desirable than leasing.

Leasing can be enhanced by reducing the discount rate used by the lessor below the borrowing rate used by the government. On the other hand, if we assumed the government would have a positive residual value associated with owning, this would enhance buying. If the lessor used a higher discount rate, that would also decrease the desirability of leasing if the lease payment requirements were also increased.

Whether or not leasing is desirable will depend on the lease revenue required by the lessor (\$295,000) in the preceding example. This measure is heavily influenced by the ability of the lessor to use tax deductions, but the single most important factor is the lessor's required rate of return (the discount rate). In the preceding example, the government department and the lessor used the same rate, and buying was clearly preferable.

A Broader Perspective

Instead of having the manager make the decision from the viewpoint of the government subunit, we will now have the manager analyze the decision from the broader perspective of the federal government. This requires that the consequences of the leasing decision to the federal tax collector be considered. There are three tax consequences to be considered: the interest tax shield, the depreciation tax shield, and tax revenues from the lease payments.

If the government debt is purchased by zero tax investors, the present value of the cost of buying will remain at \$1,000,000, and the cost of the government debt will be .10 for the government. The interest received by investors is not taxed; thus, there is no reduction in the borrowing cost of the government.

In the real world, something less than 100 percent of the bonds will be bought by zero tax investors; thus, with a tax rate of .34, the after-tax cost of debt capital for the government is somewhere between .066 and .10. However, we will use the actual borrowing cost of the government without adjusting for taxes (the borrowing cost is correct if the investors are not taxed).

The second tax item to be considered is the depreciation deduction. Every dollar of taxes saved by the lessor is a cost to the government. This factor has to be considered as a cost of leasing to the government.

The lease payments made by the government are income to the lessor; thus, they give use to tax revenues for the government.

An Example

Assume that the lessor with a .34 tax rate requires a .20 return, and the government borrows at a cost of .10 (the after-tax cost is also .10). A $1,000,000 investment will be depreciated by the lessor, and we assume

$$\text{Present value of depreciation using } .20 = \$621,000 \text{ and}$$
$$621,000 \times .34 = \$211,000$$

$$\text{Present value of depreciation using } .10 = \$773,000 \text{ and}$$
$$773,000 \times .34 = \$263,000$$

The lessor wanting to earn a .20 return will charge $400,000:

$$\text{Lease rental} = \frac{1,000,000 - 621,000 \times .34}{(1 - .34)2.9906} = \frac{789,000}{1.9738} = \$400,000$$

where 2.9906 is the present value of an annuity for five years using .20.

From the department's viewpoint, using .10 as the discount rate, the present value of the cost of leasing is $1,516,000.

$$\text{Cost of leasing} = (\$400,000)(3.7908) = \$1,516,000$$

The government's debt payments per year with a borrowing cost of .10 and with a purchase cost of $1,000,000 are $264,000, compared to $400,000 with leasing.

$$\frac{1,000,000}{3.7908} = \$264,000$$

Buying is more desirable than leasing.

We will now compute the cost of leasing from the total government perspective.

If all the government debt was purchased by zero tax investors, so that the government's discount rate was .10, the cost of leasing would be

$$\text{Cost of leasing} = (1 - .34)\,400,000\,(3.7908) + 263,000 = \$1,264,000$$

The leasing cost is reduced from $1,516,000 to $1,264,000, but it is still larger than the buying cost. The $263,000 includes the depreciation tax savings of the lessor. The lease costs are reduced by the tax on the revenues.

In this example, considering the tax effects to the government actually enhances leasing, but not sufficiently to make leasing more desirable than buying. For leasing to be better, the lessor's interest rate would have to be lowered so that the lessor could charge a lower amount, or the borrowing rate of the government would have to be lower so that the present value of leasing and the tax deductions taken by the lessor increased.

If the lessor uses a higher discount rate than the government, it is difficult to show that leasing is more desirable than buying unless the lessor uses a longer estimate of asset life (thus a lower lease rental) than the government projects.

If the lessor's discount rate is larger than the government's borrowing rate, the amount of revenue needed by the lessor to break even will increase. Leasing will become less attractive for the government. By varying the lessor's discount rate and the government's borrowing rate, we can move the preference toward leasing or toward buying. The government's borrowing rate will depend on the tax status of investors in government securities. The lessor's rate will depend on its after-tax borrowing costs as well as on the subjective evaluation of its stock equity capital costs and risk adjustments.

The desirability of leasing may be affected by whether the analysis is done from the perspective of a subunit of the federal government or whether it is done taking into consideration the effects on the federal government's tax collections. Whether including the effect on the tax collecting agency will enhance leasing depends on the taxes on the lease revenues, the value of the depreciation tax deductions, and the value of the taxes on the interest paid by the government.

We can conclude that a government financial manager must evaluate leasing alternatives from the two perspectives. Most importantly, the economic consequences of leasing compared to buying must be computed and understood. Just relying on the annual budgetary consequences as the basis of making the decision is almost certainly going to cost the federal government and the citizens of the country a significantly large amount of money.

Conclusions

It is apparent that different analyses of the desirability of investments may be appropriate for managerial decision making and for decision making where the objective is to take the public economic point of view into consideration. We have suggested several adjustments that might be made to the analysis prepared by the business manager. These adjustments generally require subjective judgments by the analyst.

The business manager might wish for a laissez-faire attitude on the part of government and for the government planners to allow any investment deemed desirable by persons willing to bet their fame or fortune, but the institutional fact remains that in most countries the considerations described in this chapter are relevant.

It is obvious that the manager should be aware of factors taken into consideration by the government planning organization when it attempts to decide whether or not a private investment project should be approved. In like manner, the planning organization that is not aware of the factors considered by the business manager (or owner) in making investment decisions is at a severe disadvantage.

The discussion in this chapter of adjustments that can be made to investment project proposals to make them reflect the projects' effects on the economy should not be interpreted as a recommendation by the authors that governments should institute controls over private investment activity. A full discussion of this issue is beyond the scope of this book, although some points might be mentioned. Market prices may imperfectly measure the national economic benefits of a project, but it does not follow that a system of investment controls would be preferable. Market prices have the advantage of being relatively objective; their use facilitates decentralized decision making and prompt adjustment to changed circumstances. At best, direct government controls have the disadvantage of adding to the time and expense needed to implement investment decisions. There is no guarantee that an attempt to estimate the public economic benefits of a project, requiring as it does a high level of analytical ability and a detailed knowledge of many sectors of the economy, possibly influenced by political considerations, will in practice produce an estimate that is consistently closer to the true measure than the unadjusted private estimate based on market prices.

PROBLEMS

16.1   There are three purchasers of a product; each is willing to pay the following amounts for one unit per period.

Purchaser	Price Purchaser Is Willing to Pay
A	$10 for first unit
A	8 for second unit
B	7
C	5

There are four suppliers; each is willing to supply one unit per period at the following prices or higher.

Supplier	Price
W	$12
X	10
Y	9
Z	8 for second unit
Z	7 for first unit

Assume that the preceding prices for the suppliers also represent their marginal costs.

a. At what price would you expect the product to sell, and how many units would you expect to be sold per period?

b. What total (maximum) revenue would the purchasers of the product be willing to pay? At what total cost would the suppliers be willing to sell?

16.2 A major investment project will employ 100,000 workers. Presently 40,000 of these workers are employed, but the remainder are unemployed. Those who are employed are currently earning $20 million per year; it is expected that they will earn $60 million per year when the new project begins operation. The other workers will earn $30 million.

It will cost $2 million to retrain the workers for their new jobs and $1 million to move them to new living locations. The cost of new governmental and service facilities at their new location will be $10 million.

Describe how the preceding information would be incorporated into the investment analysis from the point of view of the economy.

16.3 The exchange rate for a country is 2 yen for $1. A piece of equipment for an investment project will cost $100,000, or 200,000 yen. The country is short of dollars and wants to conserve its present supply. The planning board wants to choose between two alternative plans: (1) One suggestion is to use an effective exchange rate of 4 yen to $1. (2) Another suggestion is to use a higher discount rate for investments requiring the use of dollars than for investments using only domestic resources. For example, .08 could be used for the former and .04 for the latter. It is felt that there are current uses for dollars that will return, on a present value basis, $2 for every $1 invested.

How would you evaluate the desirability of the equipment?

16.4 The Airplane Company has a cost-plus-fixed-fee contract with the air force to build superjet transports. The government will buy any additional equipment that is needed and that is justified on a cost-saving basis.

The incremental tax rate for the company is .4.

The company has computed the following labor saving for a new piece of equipment that costs $18,334.

Time 1	Time 2
$10,000	$10,000 before tax
6,000	6,000 after tax

The company has an after-tax time value of money of .06, and the federal government has a before-tax time value of money of .05.

Should the equipment be purchased?

16.5 Assume that the appropriate time discount for money is 5 percent on a before-tax basis and that the income tax rate is 40 percent. An investment opportunity is available requiring an outlay of $10,000 in year 0 and producing proceeds of $10,500 in year 1.

Compute the present value on a before-tax and after-tax basis.

16.6 The before-tax cash flows are the same as in problem 16.5, but the outlay of $10,000 in period 0 is chargeable to expense for tax purposes in period 0.

Compute the before-tax and after-tax cash flows.

16.7 The Eastern University has been offered a foundation grant of $2 million to establish a program in the administration of the arts. Although the program has been judged to be acceptable from an academic point of view, the president of the university does not want to accept the grant if it will drain resources from ongoing programs.

The following analysis of the program costs has been prepared.

	Annual Costs
Two professors of specialized interests	$ 60,000
Support of research personnel	40,000
Fringe benefits	9,000
Office space and other overhead	10,000
Student support	30,000
Administration	11,000
Overhead	20,000
Total	$180,000

Should the president accept the grant?

16.8 The time value of money is 6 percent in country R and 8 percent in country P. Country P will not allow foreigners (from country R) to invest directly in country P. Country R is a rich country. Country P is poor. R has a foreign aid program, and it is considering two mutually exclusive proposals for helping country P. These are (1) make a gift of $5 million to country P; (2) make a $20 million loan to country P. Interest on the loan will be 5 percent, paid annually, with the principal to be repaid in a lump sum after twenty years.

You are a legislator in country R, and you will have to vote for one or the other of these two proposals. Assume no uncertainty. Justify your answer, using the net present value method.

a. Which alternative should you favor if you want to minimize the cost to country R of the aid it is providing to country P?

b. Which alternative should you favor if you want to maximize the benefit received by country P from R's foreign aid program?

16.9 A state housing authority will lend funds at a cost of .05 to universities in the state to build student dormitories. The Private University has a proven need for dormitories, expected to cost $50,000,000, which would qualify it for the state loans. The board of trustees of Private has consistently followed a policy of borrowing no more than .4 of the cost of any facility and using the university's own resources for the remainder of the cost. There is $50,000,000 of endowment available (legally) for this type of construction, and members of the board have argued that it should be used. Some argue that while $20,000,000 could be borrowed, they fear the degree of risk that would be associated with having a facility financed with 100 percent debt.

The current interest rate on long-term industrial bonds is .08, and long-term U. S. government bonds are earning .07.

If you were advising the president of the university and the board of trustees, what would you recommend? What would you recommend if the university did not have the $20,000,000 of cash available for construction?

16.10 The U. S. Government has offered to assist a foreign government. For the construction of roads, it will lend $20,000,000, to be repaid 40 years from now. For the first 20 years, no interest will be paid, and then .03 interest will be paid per year (first payment 21 years from today).

The long-term borrowing rate for the U.S. government is .07.

A Senate committee is investigating the cost of foreign aid. Prepare a statement for the committee.

16.11 The present road between Town A and Town B was built 50 years ago and is poorly designed for modern autos. At present the traffic rate is 100,000 trips per year at an average cost (valuing time, fuel, and so on) of $100 per trip. If the road were rebuilt to modern standards, it is estimated the traffic would increase to 1,000,000 trips per year, and the cost per trip would decline to $50.

Estimate the annual equivalent benefits of the rebuilt road. Assume that the demand for road service is linear. (Hint: The "cost" per trip is analogous to the "price" on an ordinary demand curve.)

16.12 In evaluating the Alaskan Gas Pipeline, two separate types of cost and benefit calculations are required. First, it is necessary to calculate the costs and benefits from the point of view of the corporation building the pipeline. Call these *private* costs and benefits. Second, it is necessary to calculate the costs and benefits from the point of view of the entire U.S. economy. Call these the *national* costs and benefits. For each of the following situations, estimate what you consider to be the appropriate dollar measures of the private costs and of national costs. Explain the logic of your calculations. Assume all corporations are subject to a 40 percent tax rate, and all employed persons are subject to a 25 percent income tax rate.

During the intensive construction phase, 20,000 persons will be employed as welders on the pipeline project. Assume that all welders are paid the same wages, whether they are working on the project or elsewhere. Without the project, total employment of welders in the U.S. economy would be 100,000 persons, earning an average of $16,000 per year. With the project, total employment of welders will be 110,000 persons, and their average earnings will be $20,000 per year. Estimate the annual costs of employing welders during the intensive pipeline phase.

16.13 (*Continuation of problem 16.12.*) During the intensive construction phase, 100,000 persons will be employed on the pipeline project in Alaska. Unemployment in the United States will decline by an equal amount. Some persons who are now unemployed will be hired directly to work on the pipeline. Other persons who are now employed will leave their present jobs to work on the pipeline, and presently unemployed persons will fill the positions they vacate.

All of the umemployed persons who will find jobs on the pipeline are now in the 48 states south of the Canadian border. (There is no cyclical unemployment in Alaska.)

The average annual earnings of persons employed on the pipeline is $15,000 per year. The average income and expenditure of persons who are unemployed is $4,000 per year. The cost of living is higher in Alaska, mainly because of higher transportation and fuel costs. An unemployed person would need to spend $6,000 per year in Alaska to obtain the same standard of living that could have been obtained by spending $4,000 per year in the 48 states south of the Canadian border.

Estimate the annual employment costs per person employed on the project.

16.14 (*Continuation of problem 16.12.*) For each of the following items, indicate whether it should be included as a cost. Give a brief explanation.

Corporate income taxes that will be paid to the U.S. government.

Corporate income taxes that will be paid to the Canadian government.

Sales taxes that will be paid to the city of Fairbanks, Alaska.

Salaries for extra policemen who will be hired by the City of Fairbanks, Alaska, to cope with traffic congestion that will be caused by the population increase resulting from the pipeline project.

16.15 The country of Rajah has hired a firm of American consultants to decide on the desirability of a private corporation building a steel mill. The net annual benefits are computed to be $200 million before taxes and $90 million on an after-tax basis. (The taxes are excise and income taxes.) The consultants computed the present value using the $90-million-a-year benefits.

Comment on the computation of the annual benefits.

REFERENCES

Blandin, J. S., and P. C. Frederiksen, "The Role of Discounting," *Defense Management Journal*, November 1978, pp. 12–15.

Clark, R. H., "Should Defense Managers Discount Future Costs?" *Defense Management Journal*, March 1978, pp. 12–17.

Thaler, R., "Why Discounting Is Always Right," *Defense Management Journal*, September–October 1979, pp. 3–5.

The New York Times, "Navy Cites Some Costs of Leasing," March 1, 1983, p. D16.

White, G., "Valuation of Tax Subsidies in Lease-Versus-Buy Comparative Cost Analysis," working paper of the Office of the Secretary of Defense.

CHAPTER 17

A Manual

> But no one has ever won contemporary acclaim as a hero for wise economy and rationality, nor is his name celebrated in history books or attached to magnificent dams—our modern equivalent of pyramids.
>
> *J. Hirschleifer, J. C. DeHaven, J. W. Milliman*, Water Supply, Economics, Technology, and Policy *(The Rand Corporation, The University of Chicago Press, 1960), pp. v-vi.*

Each chapter adds additional complexities to the basic capital budgeting framework. Unfortunately, there is a very real danger of becoming immersed in excessive complexity and losing sight of some basic computations that can be very helpful in evaluating alternative investments. The objective of this chapter is to focus on the utilization of these basic calculations and to suggest that more complex calculations may be appropriate but that one should not ignore the basic calculations that are understandable and intuitively appealing.

We have attempted to make this chapter useful as the foundation for a capital budgeting manual. Its objective is to explain in detail some of the computations necessary to analyze investment proposals when the present value method is used. No attempt is made to explain the theory behind the computations at this point. An attempt is made to give flexible procedures applicable to a wide range of situations.

The chapter is aimed at developing skill in the preparation of forms to be prepared or used by three different groups within the organization. In the first group are the sponsors of the project, the persons who are most familiar with what makes the project desirable and how it will operate. In the second group are the staff persons who must summarize the information obtained from the sponsors. The third group is top management, who must appraise and make the final investment decisions, using the information prepared for them as well as their experience and intuitive judgment.

This chapter focuses attention on the quantitative aspects of the investment decision, but it also allows for the presentation of descriptive material, which tells in detail the pros and cons of different investment opportunities. It should be recognized that each computation requires assumptions about such things as the future level of general business activity, actions of competitors, costs of factors of production, and sales forecasts. Because there is a large amount of uncertainty connected with each of these factors, the resulting computations are, at best, only indications of future operating results.

The authors recognize that it is not possible to devise one set of forms that will be fully satisfactory to every company. The forms presented here are designed to illustrate the main calculations that would be desirable for an analysis of the cash flows that may result from an investment proposal. It is hoped that they will be useful in clarifying the application of the material discussed in earlier chapters and that they will provide a starting point from which a firm unfamiliar with the cash flow method of analyzing investments may proceed in devising administrative practices suitable for its special needs and its particular organizational structure.

The forms presented here can be used directly to compute absolute cash flows or to summarize the results of a relative cash flow comparison. When the figures recorded are relative cash flows, it will ordinarily be necessary to use supplementary work sheets to perform the calculations. Some companies may prefer to have forms that allow space for at least two alternatives. The suggested forms can easily be revised to permit this procedure if it seems desirable.

The Capital Appropriations Request (Form A)

Suggestions from operating personnel on such problems as how to improve processes, replacement of equipment, and possible new products are, of course, desirable. The procedure described here attempts to ensure that all desirable suggestions are properly reviewed by higher levels of management and are given appropriate consideration. (Form A is on pages 367–368.)

The sponsor of an investment project (outlays of over a given amount for plant, equipment, or other out-of-the-ordinary items may be classified as investment projects) should prepare Form A and the necessary supporting material. Because these forms are the basis of the quantitative analysis, they must be carefully prepared. It is recognized that many of the items on the forms are estimates, but they should be reasonable estimates. If the project is accepted, the estimates made on the forms will be reappraised after several periods of operations to determine whether they set forth objectives possible of attainment.

Technical assistance for filling out the forms should be available for the sponsor of the project. Because a staff person will have to process the data, it is desirable that contact be made with the capital budget department early in the

Form A
Capital Appropriations Request Form

Plant or division: Date:
Proposal: Code No.: _____

A. Description and Justification Summary:

B. Risk Analysis Summary:

C. Cash Flow Summary:
    Outlays are bracketed.   Estimated   Internal Rate
                                 Life: _____   of Return: _____

| | Most Probable Outcome | | |
| | Dollars | Present Values Using | |
Period	Cash Flows	After-tax Borrowing Rate ___ %	Cost of Capital ___ %
Total life			
Year 1			
Year 2			
Year 3			
Year 4			
Year 5			
Assuming life is 5 years			
Assuming life is 10 years			
Assuming life is 15 years			
Years 1–			

D. Summary of Economic Measures:
    1. Most probable present values using
        a. The after-tax borrowing rate (say 8%).
        b. The average cost of capital (say 15%).
    2. Internal rate of return _____.
    3. Cash payback period _____.
    4. The effect on accounting income in years:
        1
        2
        3

Form A (Continued)

E. Net Present Value Profile

F. Net Present Value as Function of Life (Discounted Payback)

G. Approvals

Sponsor: _____ Prepared by _____
  (Name)   (Title)   (Name)   (Title)

Routing	Initials	Date	Routing	Initials	Date
Engineering			R & D		
Production			Accounting		
Sales			Div. manager		
Market research					

planning. A staff person should be assigned to assist in the preparation of the forms, to ensure that the data are ready for processing and that all alternatives have been considered. At the time the staff person is assigned to the project, a code number should be selected for the investment project so that references and files of information for the numerous investment projects can be easily identified and coordinated.

Explanations

A. Description and Justification Summary

The description and justification summary should give a brief statement of the nature of the project and of the type of benefits expected. For example: "The purpose of this project is to replace a milling machine with a newer version in order to reduce labor costs per unit processed and to reduce the percentage of defective pieces. An incidental benefit is that there will be a 10 percent increase in capacity for this operation, but this benefit has not been quantified in the cash flow analysis." Is the project to expand capacity, save labor, save energy, etc.?

B. Risk-Analysis Summary

The purpose of the risk-analysis summary is to provide a basis for making a qualitative judgment of the risks to which the project is exposed. This may be done by describing under four main headings uncertain events that, if they occurred, would affect the value of the project to the company. The following classification of uncertain events might be used: (1) unncertain events whose occurrence would affect the cash flows of the project but not the cash flows of other parts of the business; (2) uncertain events whose occurrence would affect the cash flows of the project and of other parts of the business in the same way; (3) uncertain events whose occurrence would have a favorable effect on the project but an unfavorable effect on the rest of the business (or an unfavorable effect on the project but a favorable effect on the rest of the business); (4) the correlation of the project with the overall economy.

C. Cash Flow Summary

The table heading for the cash flow summary assumes that the cash flow forecast will be based on the most probable outcome. If the forecast is actually made on this basis, the main assumptions about various uncertain contingencies should be explicitly described.

Frequently, it will be desirable to prepare more than one cash flow estimate or to prepare the estimate on a different basis than the most probable outcome. In some respects, the expected cash flow would be preferable. The expected cash flow is calculated by taking the sum of each possible outcome weighted by its probability. The calculation is likely to be worthwhile when the most probable outcome is also the best (or the worst) outcome. When net present values of better and worse outcomes are approximately symmetrically distributed around the most probable outcome, the latter can serve as a reasonable approximation to the expected outcome.

D. Summary of Economic Measures

1. *Most probable present values.* The first interest rate used represents the after-tax borrowing rate of the firm. The second rate represents an estimate of the average cost of capital. A graphical presentation of present values for all relevant interest rates should also be prepared.

2. *Internal rate of return.* The computation of the internal rate of return using the estimated cash flows gives the rate of interest for which the present value of the cash flows is equal to zero. The differences between the minimum acceptable return and the IRR gives one measure of the margin for error.

3. *Cash payback period.* The payback period of an investment may be an indication of the amount of risk and is useful information. As a supplemental tool, it is constructive. Used as the primary means of making accept or reject decisions, it is misleading. The payback period is the period of time required for the investors to recover their original investment.

4. *The effect on accounting income.* This is a measure that is computed by many companies. Management frequently wants to know the effect on income in the short run as well as the effect in the long run. The measure requires the preparation of pro-forma income statements.

    Depreciation accounting becomes a crucial computation and component of the income computation. Unfortunately, conventional methods of depreciation accounting (straight-line or accelerated depreciation) can make a slow-starting, long-lived investment seem less desirable than it actually is by loading the early years with excessive depreciation and startup expenses. It should be remembered that these methods are merely accounting conventions and may not be correct measures. However, the fact remains that the income statement will be affected by the accounting procedures, and management is interested in these effects.

E. Net Present Value Profile

This graph gives the present value of the investment for different discount rates. It allows a delay in the choice of the rate of discount in the sense that management can inspect the figure and evaluate whether or not the investment is acceptable for a range of discount rates. For example, if the internal rate of return of the investment is 42 percent, we do not need to know the exact discount rate if the required rate of return is about 15 percent.

F. Net Present Value as Function of Life

The intersection of this graph with the horizontal axis gives a discounted payback break-even point. If the investment has a life equal to or greater than the intersection, the firm at least breaks even on an economic basis.

The residual value of a project is the cash flows that will occur as a result of ending the project. Usually the size of the residual values will vary with the life of the project. Most projects have positive residual values resulting from liquidating working capital and selling unneeded fixed assets. Some projects may have negative residual values because of environmental factors (what will it cost to decommission a nuclear power plant?) or the necessity to pay unemployment compensation, to pay separation allowances, or to fund previously unfunded but vested pension benefits.

The chart showing net present values as a function of life should be clearly labeled to show whether it includes or excludes residual values. An analysis that excludes residual values is easier to prepare, since the cash flow data previously estimated can be used. But such an analysis is incomplete. As a substitute for a complete analysis of residual values, the sponsor might indicate whether they are likely to be large and whether they will be positive or negative. Of particular interest is the residual value associated with assuming a project life of zero years.

Residual values should always be calculated on an after-tax basis. The presence of corporate income taxes usually tends to increase the magnitude of the residual values.

G. Approvals

Space is provided in Form A to indicate the routing of the investment proposal from the original sponsor. The particular routing will, of course, vary from one organization to another. One of the main advantages of a systematic capital budgeting procedure, however, is that it provides a framework for the coordination of planning in this area. For example, consider a proposal sponsored by the production manager for acquiring a new machine that will result in cost saving and also in product improvements. An orderly routing of this proposal to the sales manager concerned will provide a routine mechanism for circulating information about the proposed product improvement. To take full advantage of the possibilities provided by systematic capital budgeting, the sales manager should be encouraged to attach a memorandum indicating whether or not the estimate of increased sales presented by the sponsor is reasonable and including any other pertinent comments. The opportunities for consultation provided by this mechanism will frequently result in further improvements in the character of the investments actually submitted to the final authority. In any case, it will provide valuable information for top management in weighting the important intangible factors almost invariably associated with an investment proposal. Later on, it can be used in comparing actual experience and costs with those predicted. This discipline will induce the sponsors to be more honest and precise in their estimates, and there will be less likelihood of overoptimism.

Estimating Cash Flows from Operations (Form A–1)

Section A

The sales figure should be the dollar value of sales expected to be recognized during the period under consideration. An adjustment for the timing of the actual collection of the cash receipts resulting from such sales is included by incorporating the change in "Increase in accounts receivable" under section C.

Form A–1 **Cash Flows from Operations**

Proposal: _____

Code No. _____

	Year 1 19__	Year 2 19__	Year 3 19__	Year 4 19__	Year 5 19__	Year 6 19__	Year 7 19__	Year 8 19__
	—	—	—	—	—	—	—	—

A. Sales:

B. Expenses (except depreciation):
Direct labor
Materials
Indirect labor
Other manufacturing overhead
Sales and promotion
Administrative
Other (include any investment-type outlays that are expensed for tax purposes in the period of outlay)

C. Increases (decreases) in current liabilities and nondepreciable assets (except finished inventory or work in process):
Increase in accounts receivable
Increase in inventory (supplies and raw material)
Increase in working cash balances
Decrease in current payables (subtract an increase)

D. Adjustments for cash flows in other parts
   of the business resulting from project:
   Decrease in cash proceeds of other
      products
   Cost of space utilized (cost of foregoing
      other uses)
   Use of executive time
   Other

E. Tax adjustments:
   Increase in income taxes before allowing
   for depreciation (see Schedule E)
   Tax savings from depreciation (subtract):
      Outlays of cash (B + C + D + E)

F. After-tax cash flows from operations:
   [A − (B + C + D + E)]

374

Form A–1   Schedule E: Computation of Income Tax (Without Allowing for Depreciation):

	Year 1 19__	Year 2 19__	Year 3 19__	Year 4 19__	Year 5 19__	Year 6 19__	Year 7 19__	Year 8 19__
Sales	—	—	—	—	—	—	—	—
Deductions:								
Beginning inventory*	—	—	—	—	—	—	—	—
Plus: Cost of production incurred†	—	—	—	—	—	—	—	—
Total manufacturing costs	—	—	—	—	—	—	—	—
Less: Ending inventory*	—	—	—	—	—	—	—	—
Cost of goods sold	—	—	—	—	—	—	—	—
Selling and promotion expenses	—	—	—	—	—	—	—	—
Administrative expenses (directly associated with the project)	—	—	—	—	—	—	—	—
Other	—	—	—	—	—	—	—	—
Total deductions	—	—	—	—	—	—	—	—
Amount subject to tax (sales less the total deductions)	=	=	=	=	=	=	=	=
Increase in income taxes before allowing for depreciation (amount subject to tax times tax rate)	—	—	—	—	—	—	—	—

* Includes work in process and finished goods.
† Excludes depreciation of the investment.

If the product or products are partly substitutes for other products already produced by the company, an adjustment for the decline in cash proceeds resulting from the new product should be included under section D. The physical volume and price per unit underlying these calculations should also be included in a schedule.

Section B

In section B, the production cost estimates for each period should be those incurred for the *actual* rate of production expected during that period and *not* an estimated rate for the sales of the period. The actual rate of production during a period may be greater or less than the rate of sales, depending on whether inventories are increasing or decreasing. An adjustment for the cash flows resulting from the tax effect of inventory change is included in section E of Form A–1.

Section B should include all costs incurred because of the investment that would have been avoided if the investment had not been undertaken. Any cost that will be incurred whether or not the investment is undertaken should be excluded from this section. The value of the alternatives uses of any resource for which the cost is unavoidable is discussed in section D.

Section C

In section C, adjustments are made for changes in cash tied up in working capital (other than partly or completely processed inventories). The procedures used in estimating these items are the same as procedures used in preparing cash budgets.

The increase in working cash balances should be the amount estimated as necessary to support the operations resulting from the investment. Excess cash reserves should not be included.

Ordinarily, the items in this section will total to a positive amount (indicating a use of cash) during periods in which the rate of operations is increasing. They will also show negative amounts (indicating a release of cash) during periods when the rate of operations is declining. Similarly, in a period of steady operations, this total will approach zero.

Section D

Most investment proposals will have some effect on the sales, costs, and use of resources in other parts of the organization. Section D is an attempt to allow for such influences. All estimates of cash flows should be on an after-tax basis. Frequently, it will be extremely difficult to arrive at a satisfactory basis for estimating the items in this section because they are often difficult to measure, and wide differences of opinion may exist as to the importance of individual items. An example would be a new product that could partly substitute for an existing product of the firm. If no agreement can be reached as to the degree of substitution, the item may be listed as an intangible. There may be general agreement that sales of the old product will decrease, however, although the amount of the decrease may be in doubt. When some agreement can be reached as to the direction of the effect, if not its size, it is usually wise to include an estimate of the minimal effect and to indicate in the intangible section of Form A that only a minimal estimate has been made and that there is disagreement as to the actual amount. In this case, the estimate of the minimal decline in after-tax cash proceeds resulting from sales of the old product would be included under "Sales of other products."

Section E

Under section E, the item "Increase in income taxes before allowing for depreciation" is computed and obtained from Schedule E. The tax rate used in that schedule should be the tax rate that is expected to apply in that year. The tax rate is applied to the taxable income (excluding the depreciation deduction) expected from the revenues and revenue deductions (associated with the investment) allowable for tax purposes. The tax section of the controller's department should be consulted in computing the taxable income to ensure that the assumptions made in preparing Schedule E are consistent with the method that will actually be used in preparing the tax returns.

Section F

Section F gives the after-tax cash flows from operations that result because of the investment. It should be inserted in column 1 of Form A-3 for further processing.

Computing the Annual Depreciation Charges (Form A–2)

Form A–2 is designed to compute the present value of the tax savings of the depreciation deductions.

Twice-Straight-Line Declining-Balance Method: No Salvage

When the twice-straight-line declining-balance method is used, the Internal Revenue Code allows the taxpayer to switch from this method to the straight-line method applied to the remaining book value and the remaining depreciable life. The switch should be made when the later method is advantageous. Appendix Table D gives the depreciation expense for each year of life using the ACRS method of depreciation. Table C gives the present value of depreciation for the ACRS method.

Summarizing the Cash Flow Information and Computing Present Values (Form A–3)

Form A–3 is provided for the purpose of summarizing all the information on cash flows and also to allow space for computing the present value of these cash flows by years.

If the sum of the present values of the net cash flows (total of column 5 of

Form A–2   ***Computation of Annual Tax Savings from Depreciation***

Proposal:

Code No.: _____

Original Cost of Assets* _____   Expected Salvage Value _____

Expected Life of Assets _____   Depreciation Method _____

Year	(1) Depreciation Expense	(2) Tax Rate	(3) Tax Saving (1) × (2)	(4) Present Value Factor	(5) Present Value of Saving (3) × (4)

*If the outlays are to be made over several periods, attach a schedule showing the timing of the outlays.

Form A–3   Summary of Cash Flows and Computation of Present Values

Proposal:

Code No.: _____

Year	(1) Cash Flows from Operations	(2) Outlays for Assets	(3) Net Cash Flows (1) + (2)	(4) Present Value Factors	(5) Present Value of Cash Flows (3) × (4)

Form A–3) is positive, this means that the investment has passed the test of the present value of cash flows. It promises an internal rate of return greater than the company's rate of discount, thus warranting further consideration, and therefore would ordinarily be recommended to top management. Important exceptions to this rule may arise in the case of mutually exclusive investments (is there another way of accomplishing the same objective that will be even more profitable?) or in cases where the investment has important intangible disadvantages. Similarly, investments with negative present values would not ordinarily be recommended to top management, but exceptions may occur in cases where the investment has important intangible advantages.

Instructions for Using Form A–3

General: Indicate outflows of cash (cash outlays) by bracketing the corresponding figures.

Column 1: This column is filled in from line F of Form A-1.

Column 2: Information for this column is obtained from Form A-2. Check to be sure that outlays charged to expense have been included in the appropriate line of Form A-1. Also include outlays for assets that are nondepreciable.

Column 3: This is the algebraic sum of columns 1 and 2. Enter this column in the appropriate column of Form A.

Column 4: Copy present value factors from the appropriate column of Table A. The present value factor for immediate outlays is always 1.000.

Column 5: This column is computed as the product of columns 3 and 4. If the entry in column 3 is bracketed, the entry on the same row in column 5 should also be bracketed to indicate net cash outlays. This column should also be entered into the appropriate column of Form A.

A Rough Cut for Uncertainty

One of the easiest procedures for introducing the consideration of uncertainty is to prepare two additional sets of forms A, A–1, A–2, A–3. The basic set uses the most probable outcome. The two additional sets would use a pessimistic set of assumptions (say with a 5 percent probability that the actual results will be worse) and an optimistic set of assumptions (say with only a 10 percent probability that the actual results will be better than those contained in the calculations). If these two additional sets of forms are prepared, there will be a 85 percent probability of the actual results being captured within the bounds that were established and a 95 percent probability of exceeding the pessimistic estimate.

Avoiding Errors Resulting from Improper Comparisons

Frequently, the gains from making investments will be so large than no formal analysis is required to justify them. For example, a railroad must either replace a broken rail or abandon the line in which the broken rail occurs. The main danger to be avoided in analyzing such investments is the too-ready assumption that if only the present *necessary* investment is made, future cash flows will proceed indefinitely. If the investment is at all a borderline case, then what is required is a projection, not only of the present investment but also of the necessary additional investments that will be required in the future, thus making it possible to decide whether the whole series of these investments will be profitable.

Otherwise, one may find oneself rebuilding an unprofitable road, rail by rail and tie by tie, with each small expenditure defended as absolutely necessary.

The sales and expenses estimates must always be on a comparative basis. That is, the estimates should attempt to measure the difference between what would occur if the investment under question were undertaken and if it were not undertaken. If the investment will reduce operating costs but not increase sales, then the appropriate entry for sale is 0. Similarly, if the investment will increase both sales and expenses, the amounts of increase of each should be estimated.

Because every estimate of cash flows involves an implied comparison, it is extremely important that a realistic situation be projected as the one likely to occur if the investment is not undertaken. The weakest professional football team would look good in a contest with an Ivy League college team, but no one would use the score of such a contest to judge the professional team's chances of winning the title in its own league. In the same way, an investment may look good if the cash flow analysis is made by comparing its performance against an absurd and unprofitable alternative. Thus, in deciding whether to replace a five-year-old truck now with a new truck, we should not make the comparison as though a decision against replacement meant that the old truck would be operated for another ten years. Similarly, if operating the old truck is unprofitable from the viewpoint that using a common carrier would be less expensive, a decision to replace the old truck with a new model should probably be supplemented by comparing the costs of the new model with the costs of using a common carrier as well as with the costs of continuing to operate the old truck.

Because it is frequently difficult to decide in advance what alternative to the present investment is "realistic," it is important in such situations to try to analyze simultaneously all the significant available alternatives. If all available alternatives are considered, the choice of an unrealistic alternative as the common standard will not bias the results. Thus, if both replacing the old truck with a new model and using a common carrier are compared with the alternative of continuing to operate the old truck, it may become clear that, although buying a new truck may be preferable to continuing to operate the old one (that is, the present value of the cash outlays of the new truck will be less than those of the old truck), using a common carrier is better than buying the new truck (the present value of the cash outlays from using a common carrier is less than from buying a new truck).

Mutually exclusive investments are investments directly and adversely affecting the earning possibilities of each other (for example, ten different models of furnaces being considered when only one furnace is needed). With investments of this type, the appropriate forms should be prepared for each investment. The net cash flow for each investment should be obtained and listed. Form A-3 can be used for this purpose. The investment with the highest present value is the most desirable investment from the point of view of this one criterion. The best investment should be listed on Form A, but the fact that it is one of a set of mutually exclusive investments should be indicated. If top management wants to review the other possibilities, then the entire file of schedules should be presented with this form as a cover sheet.

Bringing in Inflation

There is a very simple and theoretically correct way of bringing inflation considerations into the calculations. If the cash flow forecasts reflect accurately the firm's forecast of inflation, and if the discount rate is the nominal rate (the observed cost of money), the net present value is a theoretically correct measure of value. Thus, if nominal dollars and a nominal discount rate are used, we have taken inflation into consideration correctly.

But some managers will prefer to use real dollars and a real discount rate. They can then vary the assumed rate of inflation and test the sensitivity of the decision to the inflation-rate assumption. This is not to imply that one could not accomplish the same type of analysis using nominal dollars and a nominal discount rate.

A procedure for implementing the use of real dollars and a real discount rate is described in Chapter 9.

Company Manuals We Have Seen

Many corporations have developed their own capital budgeting manuals and forms for presenting the information pertaining to an investment.

There are several minor deficiencies that tend to reappear. One is the calculation of a net present value for a given rate of interest (say the weighted average cost of capital) without calculation of the present value profile. Thus, one might be told that the net present value is negative but not know what would happen if the discount rate were lowered 200 basis points (say from .12 to .10).

Frequently, the calculation is done for a given time horizon (ten years is popular), and the effect of a longer life or a larger residual value is neglected. Also, there are assumptions about cost and revenue trends, but no alternatives are given.

The analysis should be after taxes, but too commonly, some element of tax consequences (such as the investment tax credit) is neglected.

Some companies attempt to combine the information for pro-forma accounting reports and the cash flow information on one form. The result is that it is difficult to see at a glance how the cash flow information for a time period was obtained.

A company should be careful about not including too much current detail in a printed manual. For example, since interest rates will continuously change, the printed manual should not specify the required return. The required return should be updated periodically to be consistent with the most recent economic events.

Conclusions

This chapter has focused on the presentation of basic capital budgeting information. Two important reservations should be noted. First, we have avoided defining one discount rate as *the* hurdle rate. It is essential that management get to see a wide range of investments without good investments being cut off by lower levels of management because they did not meet an artificially high hurdle rate.

Second, the manual presented in this chapter does very little with risk analysis. Throughout the book, suggestions will be made as to how to go about risk analysis. We have preferred not to offer a cookbook approach to risk analysis because we do not think the appropriate recipe currently exists. We would rather stick with the more detailed explanations scattered throughout the book than one recommendation. We do not recommend that risk be taken into account by adjusting upward the rate of discount for all investments.

REFERENCES

Brigham, E. F., "Hurdle Rates for Screening Capital Expenditure Proposals," *Financial Management*, Autumn 1975, pp. 17–26.

Christy, G. A., *Capital Budgeting—Current Practices and Their Efficiency* (Eugene, OR: Bureau of Business and Economic Research, University of Oregon, 1966).

Fremgen J. A., "Capital Budgeting Practices: A Survey," *Management Accounting*, May 1973, pp. 19–25.

Gitman, L. J., and Vincent A. Mercurio, "Cost of Capital Techniques Used by Major U.S. Firms: Survey and Analysis of Fortune's 1000," *Financial Management*, Winter 1982, pp. 21–29.

————, and John R. Forrester, Jr., "A Survey of Capital Budgeting Techniques Used by Major U.S. Firms," *Financial Management*, Fall 1977, pp. 66–71.

Klammer, T. P., "The Association of Capital Budgeting Techniques with Firm Performance," *The Accounting Review*, April 1973, pp. 353–364.

————, "Empirical Evidence of the Adoption of Sophisticated Capital Budgeting Techniques," *Journal of Business*, July 1972, pp. 337–357.

Petty, W. J., David F. Scott, Jr., and Monroe M. Bird. "The Capital Expenditure Decision-Making Process of Large Corporations," *The Engineering Economist*, Spring 1975, pp. 159–172.

————, and Oswald D. Bowlin, "The Financial Manager and Quantitative Decision Models," *Financial Management*, Winter 1976, pp. 32–41.

Schall, L. D., G. L. Sundem, and W. R. Geijsbeek, Jr., "Survey and Analysis of Capital Budgeting Methods," *Journal of Finance*, March 1978, pp. 281–292.

———, and G. L. Sundem, "Capital Budgeting Methods and Risk: A Further Analysis," *Financial Management*, Spring 1980, pp. 7–11.

Soldofsky, R. M., "Capital Budgeting Practices in Small Manufacturing Companies," *Studies in the Factor Markets for Small Business Firms* (Ames, IA: Iowa State University, 1963).

Sundem, G. L., "Evaluating Capital Budgeting Models in Simulated Environments," *Journal of Finance*, September 1975, pp. 977–992.

Capital Budgeting with Uncertainty

Business men play a mixed game of skill and chance, the average results of which to the players are not known by those who take a hand. If human nature felt no temptation to take a chance, no satisfaction (profit apart) in constructing a factory, a railway, a mine or a farm, there might not be much investment merely as result of cold calculation.

J. M. Keynes, The General Theory of Employment, Interest and Money *(New York: Harcourt, Brace & Company, 1936), p. 150.*

In Part III we explore the subject of uncertainty. We suggest solutions that involve market measures of risk and also suggest solutions involving subjective evaluations of risk. From a theoretical point of view, market measures of risk are a much more appealing approach to a solution. However, a practical manager whose goals are more complex than maximizing the market price of the firm's stock may want to modify the theoretical solutions suggested in Chapters 19 and 20.

The two primary market models are the state preference approach of Chapter 19 and the capital asset pricing model of Chapter 20. Chapter 21 introduces strategic net present value and the use of option valuation approaches to expand the application of net present value to considerations that are not normally included in the calculations.

CHAPTER 18

Capital Budgeting with Uncertainty

Ten percent of what I teach is wrong and should be ignored. The problem is that I do not know which ten percent.
  Cornell University Professor

Up to this point we have assumed, explicitly or implicitly, that an investment can be described as a unique sequence of cash flows. The goal of the analysis has been to determine the net present value of the investment, which we have assumed will equal the change in the market value of the firm if the investment is accepted and the decision communicated to the market. With certainty, the market value of an investment can be described in terms of the present value of its future cash flows using a default-free discount rate. This approach is both theoretically correct and practically feasible, since there is only one possible cash flow, and the appropriate discount rate is well defined.

This chapter presents brief discussions of techniques for dealing with capital budgeting under uncertainty. With uncertainty, many alternative sequences of cash flows could occur if an investment were accepted. The decision maker does not know in advance which sequence will actually occur. The goals are still the same; we would like to know the amount by which the market value of the firm would change if the investment were accepted. However, the estimation process is much more complex than with certainty.

With uncertainty, there is somewhat of a conflict between the theoretically correct and the practically feasible approaches. A theoretically correct approach would take into account all possible cash flows. In most cases, this is difficult or impossible, because there may be too many alternatives to be considered, even with the aid of computers.

The techniques for dealing with uncertainty can be classified into three groups. One group of techniques attempts to consider explicitly all alternative sequences of cash flows. The "state preference" approach fits in this group. These techniques are attractive theoretically but are difficult to implement.

Understanding these techniques is useful, even if it may not be practical to use them directly in many real-world situations. The commonly used practical techniques are often methods of approximating the results that would be obtained if a theoretically correct approach were used.

A second group of techniques requires the decision maker to provide a concise summary description of the asset that can be used to make an estimate of its value. For example, the decision maker may estimate the expected cash flows of each period and discount these by an appropriate risk-adjusted discount rate to estimate the value of the asset. In estimating values for bonds, the promised (most likely) cash flows are used in place of the expected cash flows. In the capital asset pricing model (CAPM), it is assumed that the decision maker knows the asset's beta coefficient, which describes the relationship between the value of the asset and the value of the market portfolio. In option pricing models, the decision maker must assume that changes in the value of the asset (or of some closely related asset) follow a particular probability distribution and must specify parameters of the distribution, such as its variance. With the certainty equivalent approach, the uncertain cash flows of each period are collapsed into a single measure that reflects both probabilities and risk preferences. All of these techniques aim to produce an estimated market valuation for the investment proposal.

A third group of techniques is designed to provide a better understanding of the characteristics of an investment, especially its risk. This can be helpful to the decision maker even if the techniques do not produce specific estimates of the market value of the investment. Payback analysis, sensitivity analysis, and strategic planning are examples of this approach.

While it might appear that the three approaches are conflicting, they can be used in a complementary manner. With uncertainty, any investment decision involves a great deal of judgment. In order to make good decisions, the decision maker must (a) understand how the characteristics of the alternative possible cash flow sequences that can result from an investment affect its market value, (b) understand the relevant risk characteristics of the specific investment under consideration (this understanding is facilitated by the third approach), and (c) must combine these understandings into an estimate of the value of the investment (using one of the second approaches) so that the project can be compared to other alternatives.

In the remainder of this chapter, we will give an overview of various approaches to uncertainty. In later chapters, some of the more important techniques will be considered in detail.

The State Preference Approach

The state preference approach to capital budgeting under uncertainty is theoretically correct in the same sense that net present value is a theoretically correct approach under certainty. The net present value and state preference approaches are closely related. It is useful to think of state preference as a generalization of the net present value approach to conditions of uncertainty. To emphasize the similarities, we give brief parallel descriptions of the net present value and state preference approaches.

Certainty

Under certainty, an asset can be fully described by specifying the cash flows it will produce at each future moment in time. Given the asset and the time specified, there can be only one possible cash flow and one possible value. For example, suppose two default-free zero coupon bonds are available. One bond promises to pay $100 one year from now and sells for $95.24. The second promises to pay $100 two years from now and sells for $86.58. We can summarize this by saying that the present value of $1 in one year is

$$\$95.24/\$100 = .9524$$

and the present value of $1 in two years is

$$\$86.58/\$100 = .8658$$

These present value factors are consistent with a 5 percent rate of discount from time 0 to time 1 and a 10 percent forward rate of discount from time 1 to time 2. For example,

$$1/(1.05)(1.10) = .8658$$

is the present value factor for time 2 cash flows.

Present values are "prices" for future dollars. We need one present value factor for each future point in time at which cash flows will occur. These present value factors can be used to estimate values for assets that are being considered. Suppose an asset will produce certain cash flows of $80 in one year and $60 in two years. To estimate the market value of the asset, we multiply its cash flows by the corresponding present value factors, as follows.

$$
\begin{aligned}
\$80 \times .9524 &= \$\ 76.19 \\
\$60 \times .8658 &= \underline{\$\ 51.95} \\
&\ \$128.14
\end{aligned}
$$

To decide whether to accept or reject this investment, the decision maker merely calculates the present value of the future cash flows from the asset and compares them with the cost of the asset. Assets that are worth more than they cost should be purchased or produced.

If an asset is worth more than it costs, the decision maker does not need to consider whether the firm has enough funds to pay for it. The model implicitly assumes that rights to the future cash flows from the asset can be sold for their present value and that the funds can be used to finance the construction of the asset and still leave something for the decision maker. Equivalently, an amount equal to the present value of the asset can be borrowed. With these alternatives, the decision maker does not need to give up present consumption to acquire the asset. The decision maker can always trade present consumption for future consumption on the terms set by the market. Given these market prices, the decision maker's consumption plan is limited only by the present value of the assets' and liabilities' net worth.

Present values reflect the relative scarcity of future output. In this example, the high price of period 1 dollars relative to period 2 dollars reflects a relative scarcity of period 1 output. These present values provide incentives to produce additional output at times when it is in particularly short supply. In addition, they provide incentives to move consumption away from periods of short supply and toward periods of relative prosperity.

We will compare this approach with the state preference approach under uncertainty.

Uncertainty

With uncertainty, there may be more than one possible cash flow that can be produced by a given asset at a given future time. The difficulty of specifying unique cash flows derives from the fact that there is more than one future state of nature that can occur, and the cash flow that will occur on a future date will depend on which state occurs at that time.

For example, suppose only two states of nature are possible at time 1, state A and state B. The two states are mutually exclusive; if one state occurs, the other cannot and vice versa. They are also exhaustive; at time 1, either state A or state B must occur; there are no other possibilities.

Two assets are available. One will produce $100 one year from now if state A occurs but nothing if state B occurs. This asset sells for $45.00. The second asset will produce $100 one year from now if state B occurs but nothing if state A occurs. This asset sells for $50.24 now. We can summarize this by saying that the *state-conditional* present value of a dollar in one year is .4500 (= $45.00/$100 for state A and .5024 (= $50.24/$100) for state B. The .4500 and .5024 are state-conditional present value factors for states A and B, respectively, at time 1.

The state-conditional present values are "prices" for dollars that may become available in different states at different future times. The state-conditional present values can be used to estimate market values for investments that are being considered. Suppose, for example, that someone is considering investing in an asset that will produce cash flows of $80 in year 1 if state A occurs and $60 in year 1 if state B occurs. To estimate the market value of the new asset, we multiply its state-conditional cash flows by the corresponding state-conditional present value factors, as follows.

$$\$80 \times .4500 = \$36.00$$
$$\$60 \times .5024 = \underline{\$30.14}$$
$$\$66.14$$

The same approach can be applied to assets whose cash flows are the same in both states of nature. For example, suppose an asset will produce cash flows of $100 at time 1 in both states A and B. Its market value will be

$$\$100 \times .4500 = \$45.00$$
$$\$100 \times .5024 = \underline{\$50.24}$$
$$\$95.24$$

Notice that this result is consistent with the certainty approach using a present value factor of .9524. The present value approach for certainty can be thought of as a special case of the state-preference approach. With certainty, an asset produces the same cash flows in every state that can occur at a given point in time.

For simplicity, the state-preference approach has been illustrated for an asset with cash flows in only one future period and only two possible outcomes. But the state preference model is not restricted to one period and two states. In later chapters, multiperiod examples will be given. The number of distinct states that are possible usually increases rapidly as the number of periods increases. Moreover, the appropriate cash flows are not merely functions of the states. They may also depend on future decisions of management, such as expanding a plant or abandoning it. The appropriate cash flows at any future state should be projected assuming management has made the appropriate decisions in the previous periods, based on the information available at the time the decision is made. (This is easier to say than to do. Chapter 21 will consider this problem in more detail.)

Comparison of the State Preference and Present Value Approaches

The parallelism between the two approaches should be clear. Under conditions of certainty, cash flows are distinguished only by the time at which they occur. We need a price (present value factor) for each distinct time at which a cash flow will occur. To derive these prices, we need to know the prices of as many different assets as there are different points in time at which cash flows occur. Given these present value factors, we can estimate the value of any other asset if we know the pattern of certain cash flows associated with it.

Under conditions of uncertainty, cash flows are distinguished both by the time and the state at which they occur. We need a price (state-conditional present value factor) for each distinct time–state combination at which a cash flow can occur. To derive these prices, we need to know the prices of as many different assets as there are different time–state combinations at which cash flows occur. Given these present value factors, we can estimate the value of any other asset if we know the pattern of cash flows it will produce under each state at each point in time. It may be impossible, or very difficult, in practice to obtain these state-conditional present value factors for all states relevant to a particular asset.

In the state preference model, the interpretation of uncertainty is more complex. In the example given, state B dollars are more expensive at time 0 than state A dollars. The higher price may reflect the fact that a marginal dollar is more valuable to consumers in state B than in state A (because the marginal utility of what it can purchase is greater). Another possibility is that the average investor assigns a low probability to state A and therefore is not willing to pay a high price for the dollars that would occur only in that state. (Think of a lottery ticket that will pay one hundred dollars, if it is the winning ticket. You might not be willing to buy it for $1 if the chance of winning is one in three hundred.) Both the scarcity of dollars in a state and the probability of the state will influence the state-conditional present values.

Role of Probabilities

In evaluating an asset using the state preference approach, the existence of market-determined state-conditional present value factors would make it unnecessary for the firm to assign probabilities to the states. This would be helpful, since investors may not agree about the state probabilities. The state-preference approach does not require agreement about probabilities. It does require agreement about what states are possible, about the values of state-conditional present value factors, and about the cash flows that will occur from an asset in each state.

Investors may assign their own subjective probabilities to states. Investors who make different probability assignments may disagree about an investment's expected rate of return, but they will not disagree about its market value. Suppose that, in the previous example, one investor, Mr. Jones, believes that the probability of state A is .75 and the probability of state B is .25. Then Mr. Jones' expected period 1 cash flow from the risky investment paying $80 in state A is $80 × .75 = $60. The cost of buying a $80 payoff in state A is $80 × .4500 = $36. For an investor with a .99 probability that state A would occur, this has an expected payoff of $80 × .99 = $79.20.

If Mr. Jones buys the asset paying $80 in state A or $60 in state B, his subjective expected cash flow is $75(= .75 × $80 + .25 × $60). The market value of the investment, as explained on page 390, is $66.14(= .45 × $80 + .5024 × $60). Jones' subjective expected rate of return from the investment is 13.4 percent.

$$\frac{75 - 66.14}{66.14} = .134$$

For another investor, Mr. Smith, who thought the probability of state A was only .6, the expected cash flows would by only $72 (= .6 × $80 + .4 × $60), and his expected rate of return would be only 8.86 percent (= {72 − 66.14}/ 66.14). An investor such as Ms. Gould, who thought there was a probability of

.99 that state B would occur, would expect cash flows of only \$60.20 (= .01 × \$80 + .99 × \$60) and would expect a loss from holding the investment that cost \$66.14. (Investors with beliefs like Ms. Gould's would not find this investment desirable, but would be more attracted to investments only paying off in state B. They might hold portfolios containing some investments that paid off in state A, "just in case" that state happened to occur.)

Although investors may disagree about the probabilities of the two states and about the expected rate of return from the investment, the market value has been established by the investment's state-conditional cash flows and the market's state-conditional present value factors. No investor would have to pay more than \$66.14 for the investment, because the cash flows from the investment can be duplicated by buying a portfolio consisting of the two assets, each of which pays off in only one state. Investors who believe that state B is likely will hold portfolios that are heavily weighted to paying off if state B occurs. Note that the market value of \$66.14 assume payoffs of \$80 if state A occurs and \$60 if state B occurs.

Valuation Models

The second group of approaches for dealing with uncertainty is based on describing the investment project in terms of some summary characteristics that are sufficient to determine its value. The relationship between the assumed characteristics of the project and its economic environment can be referred to as a valuation model.

For example, in the capital asset pricing model (CAPM), if the future cash flow (and the end-of-period terminal value) of an asset is assumed to follow a normal distribution with known parameters (including its covariance with the rate of return on the "market portfolio"), then a value of the asset can be determined. In this example, the parameters of the normal distribution provide an implicit description of the asset's cash flows without requiring as much detail as an explicit use of the state preference approach.

Another example of a class of models that is widely used in security valuation and is beginning to be used in project evaluation are option-pricing models. In these models, the crucial assumption is that the cash flows from the asset whose value we are trying to determine (be it an investment project or a security) can be duplicated by a portfolio of existing assets and securities whose market values are known. In the original application, Professors Black and Scholes demonstrated that the payoff of a call option could be duplicated by a portfolio consisting of short-term debt and common stock, the proportions of which continuously change as the value of the stock changes.

Another example is a class of models that assumes that the asset can be adequately described in terms of forecasts of its expected cash flows. Most techniques popular with practitioners fall into this category, including the use of the weighted average cost of capital (WACC). The two major tasks required by these techniques are estimating the expected cash flows of the asset and adjusting for risk. There is a huge literature dealing with the second task but relatively little discussion about how to estimate expected cash flows. The analyst or decision maker will frequently forecast the expected cash flows without explicitly considering the specific probability distribution of the cash flows. Apparently, many practitioners feel comfortable about their own ability to produce unbiased estimates of expected cash flows in this manner, although they may be skeptical about the ability of their colleagues and coworkers in this regard.[1]

We will illustrate three approaches that could be used to adjust for risk when using expected cash flows to estimate the value of an asset. For this illustration, suppose a firm has the opportunity of acquiring an asset that is expected to generate $100 per year for the next three years. The default-free rate of interest is 5 percent. The present value of the expected cash flows at 5 percent is $272.32. This would be an appropriate estimate of the asset's value if the cash flows were certain. But investors are usually reluctant to pay that much for an asset with uncertain cash flows.

The approach most frequently used by practitioners to adjust for risk is to raise the discount rate. This is the risk-adjusted discount method. The amount added to the default-free rate to allow for risk is called a risk premium. Suppose it is determined (somehow) that the appropriate risk premium in this case is 6 percent, and therefore the appropriate rate of discount for this asset is 11 percent. Discounting the cash flows at 11 percent produces a risk-adjusted present value of $244.37. This is a decrease of $27.95 compared to the present value at the default-free rate.

The difference between the present value at the default-free rate and the present value at the correct risk-adjusted rate is called the risk adjustment of the asset. In this example, the risk-adjusted present value of the asset ($244.37) is about 90 percent of its present value at the default-free rate ($272.32).

A second way of adjusting for risk would be to estimate the appropriate risk adjustment directly and subtract it from the default-free present value. Assume that the risk adjustment is estimated to be $27.95. The risk-adjusted present value of the investment is

$$V_0 = [100/1.05^1 + 100/1.05^2 + 100/1.05^3] - 27.95 = 244.37$$

Just as using a risk-adjusted discount rate implies a risk adjustment, so

---

[1] See Edward M. Miller, "Uncertainty Induced Bias in Capital Budgeting," *Financial Management*, Autumn 1978, pp. 12–18; Meir Statman and Tyzoon T. Tyebjee, "Optimistic Capital Budgeting Forecasts: An Experiment," *Financial Management*, Autumn 1985, pp. 27–33; and Meir Statman and James F. Sepe, "The Disposition to Throw Good Money After Bad: Evidence from Stock Market Reaction to Project Termination Decisions," working paper, Leavey School of Business and Administration, Santa Clara University, April 1986.

estimating a risk adjustment implies a risk premium. However, if the risk adjustment were estimated directly, it is possible that the estimate would turn out to be different than $27.95. Suppose instead that the risk adjustment were estimated as $40.00. The estimated risk-adjusted present value of the asset would then be

$$V_0 = 272.32 - 40 = 232.32$$

If desired, this result could be stated in terms of an equivalent risk-adjusted discount rate by solving the following equation for the internal rate of return, r.

$$232.32 = 100/(1 + r)^1 + 100/(1 + r)^2 + 100/(1 + r)^3$$

In the preceding example, the internal rate of return is equal to 14 percent.

Using a risk-adjusted discount rate to estimate an asset's current value might imply something to the user about its expected future value. If an asset whose risk-adjusted present value is $244.37 is expected to earn a rate of return of 11 percent in period 1 and to pay a cash return of $100 at time 1, its value at the end of period 1 after the $100 cash payment must be expected to be $171.25 ($= 1.11 \times \$244.37 - \$100$). Using this type of interpretation for future time periods, the risk-adjusted discount rate can be thought of as implying something about the expected future values of the asset.

A third possible approach would be to replace the expected cash flow at each point in time by a certainty equivalent and discount these certainty equivalents at the default-free rate. For example, suppose the expected cash flows of $100 per period were replaced by certainty equivalents of $74.36, $98.00, and $98.00 for years 1, 2, and 3, respectively. The present value of the asset estimated by discounting these certainty equivalents at the default-free rate would again be

$$V_0 = 74.36/1.05 + 98/1.05^2 + 98/1.05^3$$
$$70.82 \quad + \quad 88.89 + \quad 84.66 = 244.36$$

With different certainty equivalents, the present value would be different. In the preceding example, the certainty equivalent is less than 75 percent of period 1's expected cash flow, while it is 98 percent of the expected cash flow of the next two periods. This indicates that the asset is expected to be very risky in period 1 but much less risky after that. In other words, much of the uncertainty about the value of the asset that exists at time 0 will be resolved (favorably or unfavorably) by time 1.

Understanding the Project

All of the theoretical frameworks that might be used for the final valuation of a project require that the persons making the valuation have a thorough understanding of the project being proposed. This is true whether one attempts to describe the cash flows in detail, as in the state preference approach, or in some summary manner, as in the use of a risk-adjusted discount rate. In their study of how capital budgeting was actually carried out in a sample of companies, Bower and Lessard found that

> Effort and expenditure are not concentrated in evaluating the summary measures, however, but in gathering the data for the cash flow projections. . . . For a new product proposal capital expenditures will be built up from detailed estimates of equipment requirements, involved probing for prices, and careful analysis of replacement patterns. Manpower requirements, wage rate projections, market size and market share are also subjects of substantial study. Estimates in all these areas and others will be made in terms of outcomes associated with various conditions, so that even when only a single best estimate is called for it will be based on considerations of a series of alternative estimates. . . . The capital budgeting process as we observed it in these seven firms is extremely rich in basic data.[2]

As described in the preceding passage, the cash flow framework is convenient for studying a project and for assembling and summarizing a lot of project-related information. Project analysts who have done their job properly know much more about a project than is indicated by the single set of cash flow estimates usually presented. In fact, one of the most important results of a capital budgeting study is the knowledge gained by the analyst studying the project.

One difficult problem is communicating the essential points that the analyst has learned to higher levels of management, without overwhelming busy executives with more detail than they can reasonably handle. In addressing this communication issue, it must be recognized that frequently the decision maker is not an expert in finance.

There are a number of techniques that can be used in practice to help the analyst understand the project and especially to communicate that understanding in a concise way to management. Among the most important is sensitivity analysis. This is a way of showing how key factors could influence the value of a project. Basically, it involves varying the level of such things as the cost of a key raw material or the demand for the final product and showing how it affects the cash flows and net present value estimates. Other important considerations are the project's flexibility (the extent to which it allows management to adjust to unanticipated conditions rather than committing management to a predetermined course of action) and the relationship of the project to the firm's strategic objectives.

---

[2] Richard S. Bower and Donald R. Lessard, "An Operational Approach to Risk Screening," *Journal of Finance*, May 1973, p. 323. For a critical analysis of capital budgeting techniques from the point of view of an operating manager, see K. Larry Hastie, "One Businessman's View of Capital Budgeting," *Financial Management*, Winter 1974, pp. 36–43.

PROBLEMS

18.1 The present value factor for a dollar at time 2 is .85741. The one-period interest rate at time 0 is .07.

What is the one-period forward rate of interest from time 1 to time 2?

18.2 The present value factor for a dollar at time 3 is .77947. The one-period rate at time 0 is .07, and at time 1, it is .09.

What is the one-period forward rate of interest from time 2 to time 3?

18.3 Assume that only two states of nature, A and B, are possible at time 1. The one-period default-free rate of interest is .07. The present value of a dollar if state A occurs has been determined to be .500000.

What is the present value of a dollar if state B occurs?

18.4 (*Continuation of problem 18.3.*)
a. What is the present value of $1 to be received for certain at time 1?
b. What is the present value of an investment that will pay $1 if either event A or B occurs?

18.5 Assume that the following three investments exist. The default-free one-period interest rate is .07. The investment pays off at time 1.

Investment	Outlay	Event	Payoffs
A	$90	A or B	$107
B	90	A	200
C	90	B	230.11

The market value of a dollar received at time 1 if event A occurs is .50000, and if event B occurs, it is .43458.
a. Which investment is to be preferred?
b. If you think there is .99 probability of event A and .01 probability of event B, which investment do you prefer?

18.6 A $1,000 face-value, two-period .10 bond is now selling at $918.71 because of increased risk.
a. What is the risk premium of the yield to maturity if the two-period default-free rate is .07?
b. What is the present value of the bond using the risk-free rate?
c. What is the risk adjustment of the bond?
d. What is the risk-adjusted present value of the bond?

18.7 (*Continuation of problem 18.6.*) If the certainty equivalent of the $100 at time 1 is $87.14 and that of the $1,100 at time 2 is $958.59, what is the present value of the bond?

REFERENCES

Baron, D. P., "Investment Policy, Optimality, and the Mean-Variance Model," *Journal of Finance*, March 1979, pp. 207–232.

Bogue, M., and R. Roll, "Capital Budgeting for Risky Projects with 'Imperfect' Markets for Physical Capital," *Journal of Finance*, May 1974, pp. 601–613.

Brennan, M. J., "An Approach to the Valuation of Uncertain Income Streams," *Journal of Finance*, June 1973, pp. 661–674.

Brown, D. P., and M. R. Gibbons, "A Simple Econometric Approach for Utility-Based Asset Pricing Models," *Journal of Finance*, June 1985, pp. 359–381.

Epstein, L. G., and S. M. Turnbull, "Capital Asset Prices and the Temporal Resolution of Uncertainty," *Journal of Finance*, June 1980, pp. 627–643.

Fama, E. F., "Risk Adjusted Discount Rates and Capital Budgeting Under Uncertainty," *Journal of Financial Economics*, June 1977, pp. 3–24.

Greer, W., Jr., "Capital Budgeting Analysis with the Timing of Events Uncertain," *Accounting Review*, January 1970, pp. 103–114.

Grinols, E. L., "Production and Risk Leveling in the Intertemporal Capital Asset Pricing Model," *Journal of Finance*, December 1984, pp. 1571–1594.

Hakansson, N., "Optimal Investment and Consumption Under Risk for a Class of Utility Functions," *Econometrica*, September 1970, pp. 587–607.

Hamada, R. S., "Portfolio Analysis, Market Equilibrium and Corporation Finance," *Journal of Finance*, March 1969, pp. 13–31.

Hillier, F., "The Derivation of Probabilistic Information for the Evaluation of Risky Investments," *Management Science*, April 1963, pp. 443–457.

Kroll, Y., H. Levy, and H. M. Markowitz, "Mean-Variance Versus Direct Utility Maximization," *Journal of Finance*, March 1984, pp. 47–61.

Lanstein, R., and W. F. Sharpe, "Duration and Security Risk," *Journal of Financial and Quantitative Analysis*, November 1978, pp. 653–668.

Lintner, J., "The Valuation of Risky Assets and the Selection of Risky Investments in Stock Portfolios and Capital Budgets," *Review of Economics and Statistics*, February 1965, pp. 13–37.

Markowitz, H. M., *Portfolio Selection: Efficient Diversification of Investment*, (New York: John Wiley and Sons, 1959).

Myers, S. C., and S. M. Turnbull, "Capital Budgeting and the Capital Asset Pricing Model: Good News and Bad News," *Journal of Finance*, May 1977, pp. 321–333.

———, "Interactions of Corporate Financing and Investment Decisions—Implications for Capital Budgeting," *Journal of Finance*, March 1974, pp. 1–25.

Perrakis, S., "Capital Budgeting and Timing Uncertainty Within the Capital Asset Pricing Model," *Financial Management*, Autumn 1979, pp. 32–38.

———, and I. Sahin, "On Risky Investments with Random Timing of Cash Returns and Fixed Planning Horizon," *Management Science*, March 1976, pp. 799–809.

Pratt, J., "Risk Aversion in the Small and in the Large," *Econometrica*, January 1964, pp. 122–136.

Rendleman, R. J., Jr., "Ranking Errors in CAPM Capital Budgeting Applications," *Financial Management*, Winter 1978, pp. 40–44.

Rosenberg, Barr, "The Capital Asset Pricing Model and the Market Model," *Journal of Portfolio Management*, Winter 1981, pp. 5–16.

————, and J. Guy, "Prediction of a Beta from Investment Fundamentals," *Financial Analysts Journal*, Part I, May/June 1976, pp. 3–15.

————, and A. Rudd, "The Corporate Uses of Beta," *Chase Financial Quarterly*, Summer 1982, pp. 75–96.

Ruback, R. S., "Calculating the Market Value of Riskless Cash Flows," *Journal of Financial Economics*, March 1986, pp. 323–339.

Rubinstein, M., "An Aggregation Theorem for Securities Markets," *Journal of Financial Economics 1*, September 1974, pp. 225–244.

————, "The Valuation of Uncertain Income Streams and the Pricing of Options," *Bell Journal of Economics 7*, Autumn 1976, pp. 407–425.

————, "The Strong Case for the Generalized Logarithmic Utility Model as the Premier Model of Financial Markets," in H. Levy and M. Sarnat (Eds.), *Financial Decision-Making Under Uncertainty* (New York: Academic Press, 1977).

————, "A Mean-Variance Synthesis of Corporate Financial Theory," *The Journal of Finance*, March 1973, pp. 167–181.

Rudd, A., and Barr Rosenberg, "The 'Market Model' in Investment Management," *Journal of Finance*, May 1980, pp. 597–607.

Schwab, B., and P. Lusztig, "A Note on Investment Evaluations in Light of Uncertain Future Opportunities," *Journal of Finance*, December 1972, pp. 1093–1100.

Senbet, L. W., and H. E. Thompson, "The Equivalence of Alternative Mean-Variance Capital Budgeting Models," *Journal of Finance*, May 1978, pp. 395–401.

Sharpe, W., "Capital Asset Prices: A Theory of Market Equilibrium Under Conditions of Risk," *Journal of Finance*, September 1964, pp. 425–442..

Stapleton, R. C., "Portfolio Analysis, Stock Valuation and Capital Budgeting Decision Rules for Risky Projects," *Journal of Finance*, March 1971, pp. 95–117.

Stiglitz, J., "On the Optimality of the Stock Market Allocations of Investment," *Quarterly Journal of Economics*, February 1972, pp. 25–60.

Thompson, H. E., "Mathematical Programming, The Capital Asset Pricing Model and Capital Budgeting of Interrelated Projects," *Journal of Finance*, March 1976, pp. 125–131.

Van Horne, J. C., "An Application of the Capital Asset Pricing Model to Divisional Required Returns," *Financial Management*, Spring 1980, pp. 14–19.

Weston, J. F., "Investment Decisions Using the Capital Asset Pricing Model," *Financial Management*, Spring 1973, pp. 25–33.

Weston, J. F., and Nai-fu Chen, "A Note on Capital Budgeting and the Three Rs," *Financial Management*, Spring 1980, pp. 12–13.

CHAPTER 19

The State Preference Approach*

Theories that are right only 50 percent of the time are less economical than coin-flipping.

George J. Stigler, The Theory of Price (New York: Macmillan Publishing Co., Inc., 1966), p. 6. (Professor Stigler implicitly assumes decisions with two outcomes.)

This chapter considers the state-preference approach, which was introduced in Chapter 18. The state preference approach is a natural generalization to conditions of uncertainty of the present value approach under certainty.

If the state preference approach is interpreted literally, it would require treating separately each possible sequence of cash flows that could result from an investment. In any complex situation, this would be impossible, even with the help of computers. Nevertheless, there are several reasons for considering this approach. First, there are situations in which actual cash flows can be evaluated using this approach, either because the investments are not complex or because approximations can be used so that each possible cash flow does not need to be considered individually. Second, the state preference approach provides a great deal of intuition about how the characteristics of the cash flow sequence affect the value of an investment. For example, the required rate of return can be derived for an investment, and the required return can be a function of the time and the state of the economy. Third, commonly used asset valuation approaches, such as option-pricing theory and CAPM, can be expressed in state preference terms, which provides valuable intuition.

* This chapter is adapted from a paper written by the authors titled "Capital Budgeting: A Review and a Forecast" published in *Bedrigfskunde*, January 1976.

Prices with Certainty

Consider an investment that will pay $100 for certain after one time period and $200 after two time periods. If the appropriate time-value factor is .05, then we know that a dollar due in one time period is worth $\frac{1}{1.05}$ = .9524 now. We can say that the "price" now of $1 due in one time period is .9524. In like manner, the price now of $1 due in two time periods is .9070. Thus, the present value of the proceeds from the investment is

$$\$100 \times .9524 = \$\ 95$$
$$\$200 \times .9070 = \underline{\$181}$$
$$\$276$$

In a situation of certainty, we would be willing to pay as much as $276 for the right to receive these proceeds.

If, instead of earning $100 at time 1, the investment earned $146, we would merely substitute $146 for $100 in the previous calculations. The .9524 would be unchanged, unless the time-value factor of 0.05 changed.

Prices with Uncertainty

We want to establish analogous "prices" for future dollars when uncertainty exists as for certainty. We will consider first a one-period horizon, where the only form of uncertainty that concerns us is uncertainty about the next period's cash flows. Suppose an investment has two possible cash flows next period. A tree diagram is a convenient way of illustrating the sequence of different possible outcomes that can occur. In this case, there are two branches with two different cash flows, as illustrated. Each branch in the tree diagram represents a different possible state of the world.

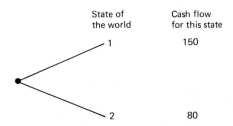

The previous section described an investment that could be evaluated by multiplying the cash flow that would occur at time 1, $100, by a present value factor, .9524, which represents the price of $1 in one period.

EXAMPLE 19.1

To evaluate investments under uncertainty, we suggest multiplying each of the possible cash flows that can occur by prices that represent the value now of a dollar to be received in a future period if a particular state of the world occurs. For example, suppose it was determined that $0.3204 was the right price for a dollar to be received next period if state 1 occurred, while if state 2 occurred, the price is $.6320. The investment evaluation process would be as follows.

(1) State	(2) Value of a Dollar Given the State	(3) Investment Cash Flow for the State	(4) Risk-Adjusted Present Values
1	.3204	$150	$48.06
2	.6320	80	50.56
Totals	.9524		$98.62

Using this approach, the total of the products in the last column—$98.62— would be the value of the cash proceeds.

To emphasize that this approach is a generalization of the use of present value factors under conditions of uncertainty, we recommend calling the prices in column 2 risk-adjusted present value factors, or RAPVFs. The total of the products of columns 2 and 3 in the last column is the risk-adjusted present value of the investment.

Suppose an investment generates cash flows of $100 for certain at time 1. Remember that a certain dollar received at time 1 should be discounted using .05 and is worth $(1.05)^{-1}$, or .9524.

State	RAPVF	Cash Flow	RAPV
1	.3204	$100	$32.04
2	.6320	100	63.20
Totals	.9524		$95.24

When the same flow is received in every state, the cash flows can be evaluated by summing up the RAPVFs over all states and multiplying the total by the certain cash flow. The sum of the RAPVFs over all states is equal to the discount factor that would be applied to a certain cash flow. This approach can be generalized to cover multiperiod investments. As will be shown next, the RAPVFs must be estimated in a systematic fashion to obtain meaningful results.

As mentioned in Chapter 18, the state preference model assumes that everyone agrees about

1. The states that are possible.
2. The value today of $1 to be received in each state.

If everyone also agrees on the cash flows that will be generated in each state, there will be agreement about the value of an asset. Insurance policies are examples of assets that produce specified cash flows if some event occurs but nothing if the event does not occur. Everyone can agree on the cash flows of an insurance policy.

Investors will agree about the values of the RAPVFs for each state if there are markets in which the state conditional cash flows can be purchased or sold separately. Also, if these markets exist, investors and consumers in the economy will be able to allocate their wealth to a portfolio of assets that produces the optimal number of dollars in each state, subject to the decision maker's overall budget constraint. If markets exist and investors assign probabilities to each state, then for each investor, the objective RAPVF for each state can be decomposed into a product of three terms, as described in the next section.

The Three Factors

A risk-adjusted present value factor can be considered to be the product of three terms: the probability that the state will occur, the present value of $1 for certain and a risk-adjustment factor appropriate for that state. The probabilities must sum to 1 over all the states. Suppose, in example 19.1, that the probability of the first state occuring is believed to be .7, and therefore the probability of the second state is .3. Using these values, we can calculate an "expected" cash flow for the risky investment considered previously.

State	Cash Flow	Probability	Expected Cash Flow
1	$150	.7	$105
2	80	.3	24
Totals		1.0	$129

The second term in the product is the present value factor, the meaning of which has already been explained. Under the assumptions of example 19.1, the present value factor would be .9524, which corresponds to a one-period interest rate of 5 percent.

State	Expected Cash Flow	Present Value Factor	Expected Present Value
1	$105	.9524	$100.00
2	24	.9524	22.86
	Total expected	present value	$122.86

The third term in the product leading to the RAPVFs is the risk-adjustment factor. For a given state it represents the value of a dollar in the state. Each state has its own risk-adjustment factor. Just as present value factors represent the price of certain dollars at different points in time, risk-adjustment factors represent the price of dollars in different states at the same point in time. These risk-adjustment factors do not consider either the time value of money or the probability of the event occuring. Ordinarily, we would expect that an additional dollar would be less valuable in states in which we have larger incomes and wealth positions than in states which we have smaller incomes and wealth positions. Therefore, we would expect that the risk-adjustment factor would be below average in states in which most investors have above-average income and wealth and above average in states in which they have below-average income and wealth. (Since the factors depend on income and wealth positions, the magnitudes of the outcomes may affect the values of the risk-adjustment factors if the outcomes are large relative to the decision maker's income or wealth.)

Assume that state 1 in example 19.1 represents prosperity, and state 2 represents a severe depression. Assume a dollar in state 1 is worth $.4806 at time 1 (the investor already has a cash surplus), and a dollar in state 2 is worth $2.212 (the investor is in desperate need of cash). These risk-adjustment factors are applied to the expected present value of the cash flows of each period. Continuing the calculations, we again have an RAPV of $98.62.

State	Expected Present Value	Risk-Adjustment Factor	RAPV
1	$100.00	.4806	$48.06
2	22.86	2.2120	50.56
		RAPV =	$98.62

Multiplying the three components, we obtain for the risk-adjusted present value factors for each state:

$$.7 \times .9524 \times .4806 = .3204$$

$$.3 \times .9524 \times 2.212 = .6320$$

which are the two "prices" we used previously.

We could also multiply each cash flow by the corresponding risk-adjustment factor and probability and sum the resulting products. The sum is called a certainty equivalent. The present value of the certainty equivalents is equal to the risk-adjusted present value. In this example, the certainty equivalent of the

State	Cash Flow	Risk-Adjustment Factor	Probability	Certainty Equivalent
1	$150	.4806	.7	$50.46
2	80	2.2120	.3	53.09
Totals			1.0	$103.55

cash flows is $103.55. Multiplying by the present value factor, .9524 gives the RAPV of the cash flows, $98.62.

The Expected Risk Adjustment

To insure that the certainty equivalent of a certain dollar is equal to unity, the expected value of the risk-adjustment factor over all states must be equal to unity. This requirement is satisfied in this example, as .7 × .4806 + .3 × 2.212 = 1.00.

It is important to recognize that the risk-adjustment factor associated with a state depends on the income and wealth position of the typical investor in that state relative to other states at the same time. For relatively small outcomes, it does not depend on the amount of cash generated by the asset during that state (where the cash flows generated by any one asset are a very small part of the income or wealth of a typical investor).

Countercyclical Assets

While most assets generate more cash flows during prosperity (state 1) than during depressions (state 2), some countercyclinal assets may be available. Suppose there was a countercyclical asset available whose cash flow pattern was as follows.

State of the world	Cash flow for this state	Probability of state
1	80	.7
2	150	.3

The expected cash flows from this asset are $101. Using the RAPVF approach and the factors derived previously, the value of this investment would be as follows.

State	RAPVF	Cash Flow	RAPV
1	.3204	$ 80	$ 25.63
2	.6320	150	94.80
Totals	.9524		$120.43

Although the cash flows associated with ths investment are uncertain and have a lower expected value than those of the first risky investment that we considered, the risk-adjusted present value of the investment is greater. This is because the investment generates more of its flows during the states of nature in which they are most needed. Assets like this have some of the characteristics of insurance and are relatively attractive.

Required Rates of Return

The required rate of return for an asset is defined as the risk-adjusted required return for the uncertain cash flows and is equal to the discount rate that makes the present value of the expected cash flows of an asset equal to its risk-adjusted present value. In the state preference model, the state-conditional cash flows and RAPVFs determine the RAPV of an asset. If we also know the state probabilities, we can calculate the expected cash flow and determine the required rate of return.

For the first asset considered, the expected cash flows are $129, and the RAPV of the asset is $98.62. Therefore, the required rate of return for this asset using $98.62 as the investment basis is

$$\frac{129}{98.62} - 1 = .3081$$

This is a "normal" asset whose uncertain cash flows are larger in good times than in bad times (that is, larger in prosperous states than in depression states).

For the contercyclical asset, the expected cash flows are only $101, but the RAPV of the asset is $120.43. In this case, the asset is worth more than its expected cash flows. The required rate of return for this asset is very low; in fact, it is negative. The required rate of return using $120.43 as the investment basis is

$$\frac{101}{120.43} - 1 = -.1613$$

The low rate of return reflects the fact that the cash flows of the asset are larger in bad times (when cash is in short supply and therefore especially valuable) than in good times (when cash is relatively plentiful, since other assets have large cash payouts).

Application of the RAPV Approach

The risk-adjusted present value approach described in the previous paragraphs is a generalization of the net present value approach covered in the first section of this book. The RAPV approach can be applied in at least two different ways. A direct application would involve defining states of nature, determining the cash flows that would be generated by projects in each state, and estimating the RAPVFs for each state. With these data, the value of a proposed project could be determined. Sometimes this could be an extremely tedious method. The RAPV approach, however, even if not used to make the actual calculations, also offers some very useful insights into such vexing questions as how to compare the relative riskiness of two or more projects. The project that offers downside protection (thus has more valuable cash flows) is relatively more valuable.

Multiperiod Investments

Figure 19.1 shows the probabilities for a two-period investment. The tree diagram provides a useful framework for analysis. For simplicity, only two outcomes are allowed for each node.

We will assume that the default-free one-period rates of interest are

.08 for the first time period

.08 for the second time period if starting from node (1,1)

.03 for the second time period if starting from node (2,1)

Each node is numbered with two numbers separated by a comma. The first number is the node number (starting from the top) and the second number is the time period. Thus, node (3,2) is node 3 in time period 2. There is only one path through the tree diagram from the origin to a particular node.

We define $s(n)$, the (RAPVF) for the nth node at time t, to be $s(n, t)$, where n is the node number and t the time period. We assume that

$$s(1, 1) = .3707 \qquad s(2, 2) = .5552$$
$$s(2, 1) = .5552 \qquad s(3, 2) = .1459$$
$$s(1, 2) = .3707 \qquad s(4, 2) = .8253$$

While we could use the $s(n, t)$ factors for single periods, it is somewhat easier to compute RAPVFs that transform the cash flows to values at time 0. Define

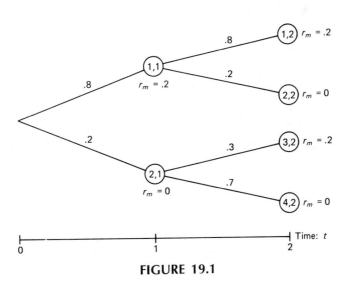

FIGURE 19.1

$S(n, t)$ to be the risk-adjusted present value at time 0 of $1 received at node n and time t. For the example, we have

$$S(1, 1) = s(1, 1) = .37037$$

$$S(2, 1) = s(2, 1) = .55556$$

$$S(1, 2) = s(1, 1) \times s(1, 2) = .37037 \times .37037 = .13717$$

$$S(2, 2) = s(1, 1) \times s(2, 2) = .37037 \times .55556 = .20576$$

$$S(3, 2) = s(2, 1) \times s(3, 2) = .55556 \times .14563 = .08091$$

$$S(4, 2) = s(2, 1) \times s(4, 2) = .55556 \times .82524 = .45847$$

The logic of multiplying $s(2, 1)$ times $s(3, 2)$ to obtain $S(3, 2)$ is the same logic whereby we multiply .9091 times .9091 (where .9091 is the present value of $1 due in one time period) to obtain the present value of $1 due in two time periods. If $1 at node $(3, 2)$ is worth .1459 at time 1, then it is worth .5552 times .1459, or .810, at time 0; thus, $S(3, 2) = .0810$.

Applying the RAPVFs

Now that we have determined the $S(n, t)$'s, the evaluation of an investment is exactly analogous to the net present value calculation. Figure 19.2 shows the cash flows of an investment that costs $300. The facts of Figure 19.1 also apply to Figure 19.2.

The risk-adjusted present value is

Node (n, t)	S(n, t)	Cash Flow	RAPV
(1, 1)	.37037	$432	$160
(2, 1)	.55556	108	60
(1, 2)	.13717	432	59
(2, 2)	.20576	108	22
(3, 2)	.08091	206	17
(4, 2)	.45847	103	47
			RAPV = $365

Since the risk-adjusted present value is $365 and the cost is only $300, the investment is acceptable.

In a world of uncertainty, the same term structure of interest rates could be used to evaluate different assets. Similarly, in a world of uncertainty, the same RAPVFs could be used to evaluate many different assets. In example 19.2 we use the RAPVFs previously derived to evaluate a new asset.

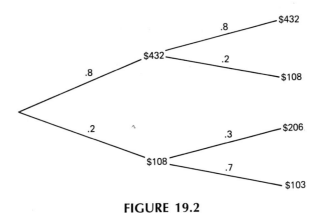

FIGURE 19.2

EXAMPLE 19.2

Assume that an investment will generate $108 at nodes 1 and 2 of period 2 and $103 at nodes 3 and 4. These cash flows are represented in Figure 19.3. If node 1 occurs during period 1, the firm will know that it is to receive $108 for certain in period 2. It will also know the period 2 default-free interest rate, which will be 8 percent in that case. So the future cash flows will be worth $100 at the end of period 1, at node 1.

If node 2 occurs during period 1, the firm will know that it is to receive only $103 for certain in period 2. It will also know the period 2 default-free interest rate, which will be 3 percent in that case. So the future cash flows will be worth $100 at the end of period 1, at node 2.

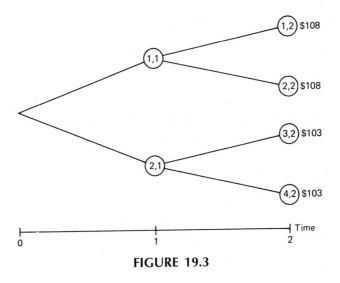

FIGURE 19.3

The value of the asset one period from now looks like this:

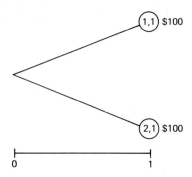

Since the interest rate in period 1 is 8 percent, we would expect the asset to be worth $100/1.08 = 92.59$.

The same answer could be reached using risk-adjusted present value factors on the period 2 cash flows.

Node (n, t)	S(n, t)	Cash Flow	RAPV
(1, 1)	.37037	$ 0	$ 0.00
(2, 1)	.55556	0	0.00
(1, 2)	.13717	108	14.81
(2, 2)	.20576	108	22.22
(3, 2)	.08091	103	8.33
(4, 2)	.45847	103	47.22
			$92.59

Alternatively, we could apply RAPVFs to the end-of-period one-asset values.

Node	S(n, t)	v(n, t)	RAPV
(1, 1)	.37037	100	$37.037
(2, 1)	.55556	100	55.556
			$92.593

Conclusions

In principle, the application of the state preference model illustrated enables us to compute risk-adjusted present value factors for different nodes through time. While the presence of risk precludes the conventional compound interest calculations directly, indirectly we are taking into account the time value of money as well as the risk of the investment.

Once the RAPVFs have been computed, the calculations of the net value of an investment are analogous to the calculations that are made under the assumption of certainty. If the RAPV is greater than the cost of the investment, the risk-adjusted net-present value will be positive and the investment is acceptable. The major obstacle is obtaining RAPVFs in the absence of complete markets.

PROBLEMS

19.1   Evaluate the following investment, assuming an interest rate of .10.

Time	Cash Flow
0	−$8,000
1	10,000

19.2   (*Continuation of problem 19.1.*) Instead of certain cash flows, assume the following time-1 outcomes exist.

State	Probability	Outcome
1	.6	$ 5,000
2	.4	17,500

Evaluate the investment assuming zero risk-adjustment factors.

19.3   (*Continuation of problems 19.1 and 19.2.*) Assume that a risk-adjustment factor of .8 applies to dollars received if state 1 occurs. The discount rate for the certain cash flows is still .10.
   a. Determine the risk-adjustment factor for state 2.
   b. Determine the RAPVFs for states 1 and 2.

19.4   (*Continuation of previous problems.*) Given all the previous facts, evaluate the investment whose cash flows are described in 19.2.

19.5   Evaluate the following investment, assuming an interest rate of .10 per period and certain cash flows.

Time	Cash Flow
0	−$11,000
1	+10,000
2	+5,000

19.6 (*Continuation of problem 19.5.*) Instead of certain cash flows, assume the following outcomes are possible.

	Period 1			Period 2	
State	Probability	Outcome	State	Probability	Outcome
(1, 1)	.5	$ 4,000	(1, 2) and (3, 2)	.4	$6,500
(2, 1)	.5	16,000	(2, 2) and (4, 2)	6	$4,000

The outcomes of period 2 are independent of the outcomes of period 1. Evaluate the investment, assuming a zero risk adjustment.

19.7 (*Continuation of problems 19.5 and 19.6.*) Assume that the following risk-adjustment factors apply.

$$(1, 1) \quad .8 \qquad (1, 2) \text{ and } (3, 2) \quad .9$$

a. Determine the risk-adjustment factors for states (2, 1), (2, 2), and (4, 2).
b. Determine the RAPVFs for all four of the states.

19.8 (*Continuation of previous three problems.*) Given all the previous facts, evaluate the investment.

19.9 Consider the investment described in Figure 19.4.

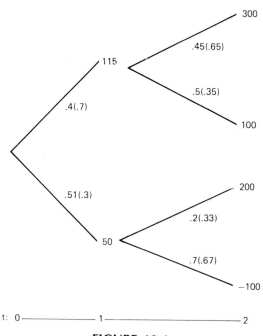

FIGURE 19.4

In Figure 19.4 there are two numbers near the middle of each branch. The first is a one-period RAPVF for that branch. The second (in parentheses) is the conditional probability of the branch, given the previous node. Numbers at the end of each branch are cash flows that will occur if the state corresponding to the branch occurs.

Data in Figure 19.4 apply to questions 19.9 through 19.11.

Find the RAPV at time 0 of an asset that will generate the cash flows described in the tree diagram for this problem.

19.10 (*Continuation of problem 19.9.*) Find the required rate of return on the asset during period 1.

19.11 (*Continuation of problem 19.10.*) Express the value of the asset at $t = 0$ in terms of the present discounted value of its expected future cash flows. (Hint: Use required rates of return as discount rates.)

19.12 The following tree diagram gives values of s (n, t) single-period RAPVFs.

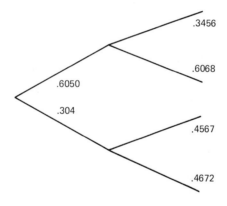

a. Complete the following table.

t	n	$S(n, t)$
1	1	.6050
1	2	.3040
2	1	
2	2	
2	3	
2	4	

b. Find the RAPV of $1 at time 2 if "good times" occur. (Odd-numbered nodes are "good times.")

19.13 The figure provides all the information needed for a complete analysis and evaluation of a simple project with uncertain cash flows for the next two periods: the cash flows (*a*), their probabilities (*b*), and the relevant risk-adjusted present value facts (*c*). Answer the following questions about the project and the economy.

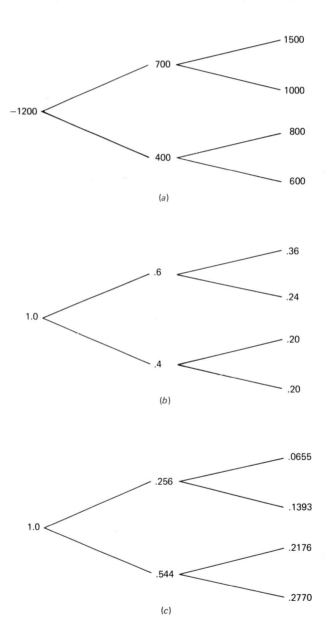

a. What are the expected cash flows from the project at time 0, time 1, time 2?

b. What is the default-free one-period interest rate at time 0? What can you say about the default-free one-period interest rate at time 1?

c. A T-bill paying $1,000 is due at time 1. What is it worth at time 0? A T-bill paying $1,000 is due at time 2. What is it worth at time 0?

d. Find the RANPV of the project.

e. At what discount rate is the present value of the expected cash flows of the project equal to its cost? (This discount rate is the project IRR.)

f. At what discount rate is the present value of the expected cash flows of the project equal to the RAPV of these cash flows? (This discount rate is the required rate of return of the project.)

19.14 (*Continuation of problem 19.13.*) You may have an urgent need for cash at time 1. In addition to the cash generated by the project, there is the possibility of selling the project. (The buyer would obtain whatever cash was generated by the project at time 2.) There are two alternatives.

a. Wait until time 1. Sell then if you need cash. The price would be set at time 1. Both you and the potential buyer would know what the period 1 cash flow is before agreeing on a price. What is the most you could obtain by selling the project at time 1? What is the least you could obtain? What is a reasonable "expected" selling price for the project under these conditions?

b. The other alternative is to make a forward sale. You find a buyer and agree on a price now before either of you knows what the period 1 cash flow from the project is. At time 1, the buyer gives you the cash. You give him the project. (You keep the period 1 cash flow from the project. The buyer gets the period 2 cash flow.) What is a reasonable forward price for the project?

19.15 (*Continuation of problem 19.13.*) There is a possibility of leasing the project. The prospective lessee has an excellent credit rating. The lessee will give you $X at time 1, and again at time 2. In return, the lessee gets to keep any cash generated by the project. What is a fair value for X?

REFERENCES

Arrow, K., "The Role of Securities in the Optimal Allocation of Risk Bearing," *Review of Economic Studies*, April 1964, pp. 91–96.

Banz, R. W., and M. H. Miller, "Prices for State-Contingent Claims: Some Estimates and Applications," *Journal of Business*, October 1978, pp. 653–672.

Black, F., and M. Scholes, "The Pricing of Options and Corporate Liabilities," *Journal of Political Economy*, May–June 1975, pp. 637–654.

Breeden, D. T., and R. Litzenberger, "Prices of State-Contingent Claims Implicit in Option Prices," *Journal of Business*, October 1978, pp. 621–651.

Breeden, D. T., "An Intertemporal Asset Pricing Model with Stochastic Consumption and Investment Opportunities," *Journal of Financial Economics*, September 1979, pp. 265–296.

Debreu, G., *The Theory of Value*, New York: Wiley, 1959.

Fama, E. F., "Risk-Adjusted Discount Rates and Capital Budgeting Under Uncertainty," *Journal of Financial Economics*, August 1977, pp. 3–24.

Gehr, A. K., Jr., "Risk-Adjusted Capital Budgeting Using Arbitrage," *Financial Management*, Winter 1981, pp. 14–18.

Hirshleifer, J., "Investment Decisions Under Uncertainty: Choice Theoretic Approaches," *Quarterly Journal of Economics*, November 1965, pp. 509–536.

——, "Investment Decisions Under Uncertainty: Application of the State Preference Approach," *Quarterly Journal of Economics*, May 1966, pp. 252–277.

Kraus, A., and R. Litzenberger, "Market Equilibrium in a Multiperiod State Preference Model with Logarithmic Utility," *Journal of Finance*, December 1975, pp. 1213–1227.

Rubinstein, M., "The Valuation of Uncertain Income Streams and the Pricing of Options," *Bell Journal of Economics*, Autumn 1976, pp. 407–425.

——, "An Aggregation Theorem for Securities Markets," *Journal of Financial Economics*, September 1974, pp. 225–244.

——, "The Strong Case for the Generalized Logarithmic Utility Model as the Premier Model of Financial Markets," *Journal of Finance*, May 1976, pp. 551–571.

The Capital Asset Pricing Model

One would hope . . . that some day satisfactory solutions will be found to the pervasive and fundamental problem. At present, however, the problem of uncertainty is clouded by uncertainty.

> *Robert Dorfman, A. Maass, et al.,* Design of Water Resource Systems
> *(Cambridge, MA: Harvard University Press, 1962) p. 158.*

In principle, there is a clear criterion for determining whether the financial community considers an investment worthwhile. Worthwhile investments increase the wealth of the owners of the firm's securities.

For example, suppose that the stock of a particular company is currently quoted at $50 per share. During the next year, management will have to make a decision about a major investment opportunity, and the outcome of this decision will become known to the financial community shortly after the decision is made. Management believes that if it rejects this investment opportunity, the company will be able to pay a dividend of $5 per share, its stock will sell for $53 per share one year from now, and a stockholder will have a total value of $58 per share. If the investment opportunity is accepted, however, the company will be able to pay a dividend of only $3 per share (because a larger quantity of cash and retained earnings will be required to help finance the investment), but the price per share at the end of the year will be $57, reflecting the market's recognition of the earnings potential from the new investment. This is a total of $60. Ignoring the important complication of personal taxes, stockholders' wealth will be $2 per share greater if the company accepts the investment than if it rejects it.

In practice, it is not easy to implement this criterion. The major difficulty is predicting how an investment decision will affect the price of a company's stock. Given the present state of knowledge, a totally satisfactory procedure for making such predictions cannot be given. However, we believe that procedures can be suggested that will be helpful in practice to managers.

The necessary tasks can be broken down into two parts: (1) determine the main factors that influence stock prices and (2) determine the relationship between investment projects and these factors.

The present chapter is concerned with a theory of stock prices that is commonly known as the capital asset pricing model, or CAPM. Many of the basic ideas underlying the theory are intuitively appealing and have been known for a long time. It is possible to quantify some of the factors that affect stock prices and the value of real investments.

The basic ideas are as follows: Most investors dislike risk. Other things being equal, most investors would prefer higher returns to lower returns. Whenever it is possible to reduce risk without reducing expected returns, it follows that investors will attempt to do this. It will be assumed that the standard deviation of the rate of return from a portfolio of securities is a reasonable measure of risk. Thus, there is an incentive to use diversification to reduce the standard deviation of a portfolio. For example, if the rates of return from two securities have the same expected value and are independent, it can be shown that a portfolio consisting of both securities in appropriate proportions will have a lower risk than any portfolio that consists of only one of the securities.

To the extent that the rates of return from different securities are not highly correlated, risk-averse investors who diversify their holdings can reduce their total risk. However, to the extent that rates of return from different securities are correlated with one another and thus tend to fluctuate more or less in unison, diversification does not lead to complete risk elimination.

We find it useful to break down risk into two components: (1) risk that can be eliminated by diversification, which is termed *unsystematic* risk, and (2) risk that is still present with an efficient portfolio (all unsystematic risk has been eliminated), which is termed *systematic* risk. The latter reflects how the investments in the portfolio are correlated with the market.

If the costs of diversification are relatively low, investors will not be willing to pay more for a security because it carries a relatively low burden of unsystematic risk (which can be diversified away). Similarly, securities that carry a large amount of unsystematic risk will not suffer a serious price disadvantage.

According to this theory, to the extent that security prices are determined by the activities of the investors who can diversify their portfolios at low cost, the prices of securities will be set in such a way that differentials in expected rates of return will reflect primarily differences in the amount of systematic risk to which the securities are exposed.

Relation to the State Preference Model

The CAPM can be thought of as a special case of the state preference model that is derived by making additional assumptions. When these assumptions hold, assets can be described and evaluated more simply. For example, in the unrestricted state preference model, an asset must be described by specifying the cash flows that it will produce in every possible state. To evaluate the asset, we also need to know the risk-adjusted present value factors for each state. If we assume that the CAPM is true (or true enough for practical application), then all we need to know about an asset can be summarized by two parameters—the expected end of next-period wealth that will result from owning the asset and its beta coefficient. The end-of-period wealth consists of the cash flows generated by the asset during the period and the end-of-period value of the asset. The beta coefficient, which will be discussed later in the chapter, measures the extent to which the end-of-period wealth of the asset is correlated with the end-of-period wealth of a typical asset in the economy.

Most of the chapter will discuss the CAPM using summary concepts such as these. A section near the end of the chapter shows the relation between these summary measures and the state preference model.

The Assumptions

To understand the CAPM and its limitations, it is necessary to understand the assumptions on which the model is based. It is a single-period model with no assumptions being made about the interaction of return and risk through time. It is assumed that the investor is only interested in the expected return and standard deviation (or variance) of the portfolio's outcomes. This is a theoretical deficiency because for most probability distributions, this ignores other information that an investor might consider to be relevant. However, the expected value and variance does define exactly a normal probability distribution.

It is assumed that all investors must be persuaded to take more risk by the prospect of a higher expected return (they are risk-averse). The actions of an investor do not affect price. The investors are "price takers." The investors can invest at the default-free rate (r_f), and generally we assume that they can borrow at the same rate; this assumption is easily dropped. Investors can sell securities they do not own; that is, they can borrow securities to sell them (this is called a short sale). All investors think the same about the expected return and variance of all securities (they have homogeneous expectations), and they are all perfectly diversified.

The quantity of securities to be purchased is fixed and divisible (securities of any dollar amount can be purchased). There are no transaction costs and taxes.

Many of these assumptions could be dropped, and a model very much like the conventional CAPM would be derived. One important function served by this set of assumptions is a simplification of the model so that we are not distracted by elements that are not crucial to our understanding.

Introduction to Portfolio Analysis*

The capital asset pricing model assumes that investors make decisions regarding portfolios of securities. The characteristics of an individual security affect an investor only through the effect on the investor's portfolio. Before proceeding with an explanation of CAPM, we present a brief explanation of the principles of portfolio theory.

Let $r_i(s)$ represent the rate of return that will be realized from security i if state of nature s occurs, and let $p(s)$ represent the probability of state s. To measure the consequences of adding security i to a portfolio (or of changing the proportion of security i if it is already in a portfolio), we need to know the expected rate of return of security i, the variance of the rate of return, and its covariance with the rates of return of other securities.

The expected rate of return of security i, denoted by $E(r_i)$ is defined as a probability-weighted average of the rates of return in each possible state of nature. In symbols

$$E(r_i) = \sum_{\text{all } s} r_i(s)p(s)$$

The variance of the rate of return, denoted by Var (r_i) or σ_i^2, is the expected value of the squared deviations of r_i from $\bar{r}_i$. In symbols

$$\text{Var } (r_i) = E[(r_i - \bar{r}_i)^2]$$
$$= \sum_{\text{all } s} [(r_i(s) - \bar{r}_i)^2 p(s)]$$

The standard deviation, denoted by σ_i, is the square root of the variance.

Suppose that $r_i(s)$ and $r_j(s)$ are the rates of return of securities i and j in state s. The covariance of the rates of return of securities i and j, denoted by Cov (r_i, r_j) or σ_{ij}, is defined as the expected value of the product of the deviations of security i's rate of return from its expected value times the deviation of j's rate of return from its expected value. In symbols,

$$\text{Cov } (r_i, r_j) = E[(r_i - \bar{r}_i) (r_j - \bar{r}_j)]$$
$$= \sum_{\text{all } s} [(r_i(s) - \bar{r}_i) (r_j(s) - \bar{r}_j)p(s)]$$

---

* Much of the analysis performed here is based on articles by Markowitz and Sharpe. See Harry Markowitz, "Portfolio Selection," *Journal of Finance*, March 1952, pp 77–911; and W.F. Sharpe, "Capital Asset Prices: A Theory of Market Equilibrium Under Conditions of Risk," *Journal of Finance*, September 1964, pp. 425–442.

The covariance measures the extent to which the rates of return of the two securities vary across the possible states of nature. For a given state s, if both i and j have above-average rates of return, or if both have below-average returns, the product of the deviations will be positive. Alternatively, if in a given state one security has an above-average rate of return and the other has a below-average rate, then the product of the deviations will be negative. The covariance can be positive, negative, or zero, depending on the relative frequency of these possibilities and the size of the deviations. Among pairs of securities, positive covariances are much more common than negative ones.

The correlation coefficient, ρ, is defined as

$$\rho_{ij} = \frac{\sigma_{ij}}{\sigma_i \sigma_j}$$

The possible values of the correlation coefficient range from -1 to $+1$.

Forming Portfolios

Portfolios are made up of individual securities or groups of securities that are correlated in some manner. Suppose r_1 and r_2 are the rates of return of two securities whose correlation coefficient is ρ. If $\rho = -1$, r_2 and r_1 are perfectly negatively dependent; that is, an increase in r_1 results in a perfectly predictable decrease in r_2. If $\rho > 0$, there is positive correlation, but knowing r_1 does not allow us to predict the exact value of r_2. If $\rho = 0$, r_1 and r_2 are uncorrelated.

In Figure 20.1, the vertical axis measures the expected rate of return of a security or of a portfolio, and the horizontal axis measures the standard deviation of the rate of return. Point A represents security 1, and point B represents security 2. We want to study what will happen if we form a portfolio containing both securities, with a proportion x_1 in security 1 and a proportion x_2 in security 2. We require that $x_1 + x_2 = 1$.

For any portfolio of two securities with x_1 proportion of the investment in security 1 and x_2 in security 2, with $x_1 + x_2 = 1$,

$$\bar{r}_p = x_1 \bar{r}_1 + x_2 \bar{r}_2$$

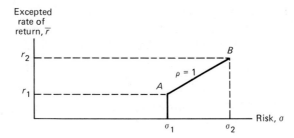

FIGURE 20.1   Perfect Linear Dependence

and

$$\sigma_p^2 = x_1^2\sigma_1^2 + x_2^2\sigma_2^2 + 2x_1x_2\rho\sigma_1\sigma_2$$

where $\bar{r}_p$ is the expected rate of return of the portfolio and σ_p^2 is the variance of the return of the portfolio.

Figure 20.1 shows a situation in which the rates of return of the two assets A and B are perfectly correlated ($\rho = 1$).

If we start at point A, we have 100 percent invested in asset A. As we substitute asset B for asset A, we move up the line to point B. All combinations of asset A and asset B lie on the line connecting points A and B.

The expected return of the portfolio will be a weighted average of $\bar{r}_1$ and $\bar{r}_2$:

$$\bar{r}_p = x_1\bar{r}_1 + x_2\bar{r}_2$$

where x_1 is the proportion invested in asset 1 and x_2 is the proportion invested in asset 2. The standard deviation of the portfolio's return is also a weighted average of the standard deviations of the assets:

$$\sigma_p = x_1\sigma_1 + x_2\sigma_2$$

This simplified expression for the standard deviation of a portfolio can only be used if $\rho = 1$.

If the correlation coefficient is equal to -1, the assets are perfectly negatively correlated. Figure 20.2 shows that when $\rho = -1$, it is possible to attain a zero-risk portfolio. If we start with 100 percent of an investment in asset B, we are at point B. As we substitute some asset A, both the risk and the expected return decrease until point C is reached and the portfolio has zero risk. If still more asset A is introduced, then the investor slides down line CA. There is increasing risk and decreasing expected return.

Any point on line CA is dominated by one or more points on line CB. No investor would want to have an amount of asset A that causes a portfolio to lie on line CA.

The correlation coefficient can take on any value between -1 and $+1$. Figure 20.3 shows the feasible portfolios resulting from different values of ρ. Note that if $\rho = 0$, the locus of feasible portfolios is a curve inside the triangle of ABC. If one starts with investment B, substituting any amount of investment A will reduce risk. If $\rho < 0$, the risk-reduction potential is even larger. This is not surprising, since A has lower risk than B.

However, suppose we start with security A and add some of security B, which is riskier than A and has a higher expected return than A. Provided that $\rho < 1$, there will be portfolios combining A and B that have both higher expected returns and lower standard deviations than A. Therefore, these portfolios will be preferred to A by any investor whose utility for portfolios depends only on their expected rates of return and their standard deviations. This is a remarkable result. Although the expected return of a portfolio is always just a weighted average of the expected rates of return of its component securities, the standard

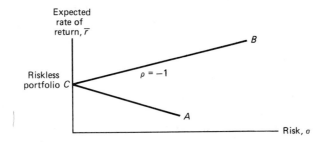

FIGURE 20.2   Perfect Negative Correlation

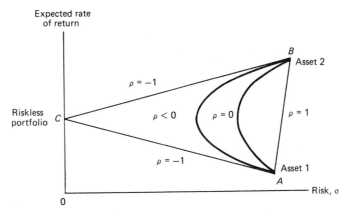

FIGURE 20.3   Two Securities and Different Values of p

deviation of a portfolios return may be less than the average standard deviation of its components. It is for this reason that diversification is beneficial.

In forming portfolios, the feasible region consists of all possible portfolios that can be constructed from the available securities. If all of the available securities are risky (have nonzero standard deviations), the feasible region will lie to the right of the vertical axis or be on the axis (if the correlation coefficient is minus one, there is a combination that lies on the vertical axis). If short positions in securities are not allowed, correlations of exactly minus one will not ordinarily be possible with conventional securities.

The Investors

A risk-averse investor wants a larger expected return as risk (defined as the standard deviation of outcomes) is increased.

The CAPM assumes utility-maximizing investors who (1) are risk-averse, (2)

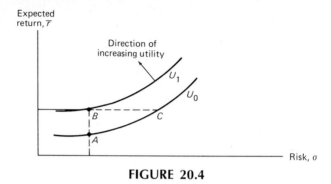

FIGURE 20.4

measure the risk of an investment portfolio by the standard deviation of the rate of return on that investment portfolio, and (3) have indifference curves (different combination of expected return and standard deviation for which the investors are indifferent) that have the shape shown in Figure 20.4.[1] By definition, any point on the indifference curve U_1 is equally desirable for the investor in question; furthermore, since point B has a higher expected return with no change in risk compared to A, a risk-averting investor would find B preferable to A. Finally, point B lies on the indifference curve U_1, and all points on U_1 are preferable to those lying on U_0. Point B is preferred to point C, since it has the same expected return and a smaller amount of risk.

Portfolio Analysis with a Riskless Security

Up to this point we have indicated that an investor, with a set of expectations, should determine the set of efficient portfolios and proceed to find which portfolio of that set lies on the highest indifference utility curve. All we observe are individual portfolios. We have no information about how the market trades expected return for risk with risky portfolios.

The Efficient Frontier

Figure 20.5 shows three portfolios. The expected return is measured on the Y axis, and the standard deviation of the return is measured on the X axis. Using Figure 20.5, we conclude that

1. Portfolio 2 is better than portfolio 1 (the same risk and higher mean return).

[1] See James Tobin, "Liquidity Preference as a Behavior Towards Risk," *Review of Economic Studies*, February 1958, pp. 65-86, for a discussion of the states of nature and modes of investor behavior that imply this assumption.

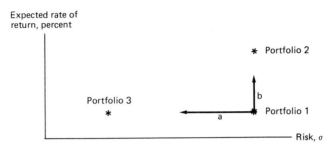

FIGURE 20.5   Choosing Portfolios

2. Portfolio 3 is better than portfolio 1 (same expected return and smaller risk).

Any portfolio that lands within the area bounded by vectors **a** and **b** is better than portfolio 1. It is desirable to move up, to the left, or up and to the left.

If we compare portfolios 2 and 3, we cannot make a definite choice between them. Portfolio 2 has a larger expected return, but it also has more risk. The choice will depend on the investor's preferences.

Taking all portfolios that are not dominated by other portfolios, we can form an efficient frontier of portfolios. All the portfolios on the efficient frontier are eligible for consideration. So far, portfolios 2 and 3 would be on the frontier, but portfolio 1 would not. The choice of a specific portfolio will depend on the investor's preferences.

Fortunately, if we assume the existence of a riskless security and extend portfolio analysis theory to cover that situation, we obtain some useful insights. Government bonds held to maturity are essentially a riskless asset. Therefore, every investor has a riskless security available. "Riskless" as used here refers only to the risk of default and not to other types of risk.

Consider a riskless security earning a pure time value of money rate r_f (such as the rate of return of a one-period U.S. Treasury bill). If a portfolio of the riskless security and a risky portfolio of marketable securities ($\bar{r}_m$, σ_m) were purchased, the expected mean and standard deviation of the different portfolios would lie on the straight line connecting the two points r_f and M. This is shown in Figure 20.6. The reason for the straight line is that the rate of return of a riskless security has a zero correlation with the rate of return of any other risky or riskless security. Point M is the tangent of the line originating at r_f and the efficient frontier determined without considering the risk-free asset. Although there are other possible portfolios made up of the risk-free asset and efficient portfolios (other points on the efficient frontier EE), none of them is as desirable as the portfolios represented by the line $r_f M$. The line $r_f M$ is called the capital market line.

If 100 percent of the portfolio is invested in portfolio M, the investor will earn

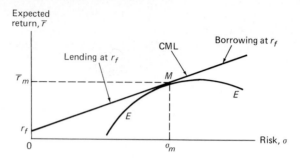

FIGURE 20.6   The Capital Market Line

r_m with risk σ_m. If some risk-free asset is substituted for M, the line $r_f M$ defines the feasible combinations of expected return and risk that are possible.

If the investor supplements the investable resources by borrowing at a rate of r_f and investing in portfolio M, the right-hand extension of $r_f M$ defines the expected return-risk possibilities. Since funds are being borrowed at r_f and invested to earn r_m, where r_m is larger than r_f, the borrowing increases the expected profit, but it also increases the portfolio's risk.

Choose any point on curve EE other than M. Note that for the same risk, a higher expected return can be earned by investing in a mix of M and the risk-free asset and being on the line $r_f M$. The line $r_f M$ offers a set of investment opportunities that is at least as desirable as all points on the efficient frontier (the set of investment opportunities that excludes the risk-free asset).

Different investors (with differing degrees of risk aversion) will have optimal portfolios that lie on different points on the capital market line, but all optimal portfolios will consist of the riskless asset and the portfolio M, which is called the market portfolio.

There are two steps in the determination of the investor's optimum portfolio. Step 1 determines point M, the market portfolio. Assuming that all investors have the same expectations, all investors hold a portion of the same market portfolio. The second step is to determine the optimum point on line $r_f M$. This is the optimum mix of the market portfolio M and the risk-free asset. The theory (originated by Tobin) supporting this two-step process is called the separation theorem.

The market portfolio consists of all risky assets held in the same proportions as their relative total market value. Investors whose common objective is to achieve the maximum amount of diversification would include in their portfolio every security available. Securities are defined here to include common stock and any other security for which there is a market. Thus warrants, convertible bonds, and preferred stock issues would be included in this portfolio.

In deciding how to allocate their assets, the investors do not attempt to anticipate future changes in the value of each security, but use the existing market valuations. Thus, if the outstanding common stock of company X represented .035 percent of the value of the equity of all companies, the stock would represent .035 percent of the equity portion of the portfolio. The investor would literally be buying a share in the capital market; we shall call the resulting investment the market portfolio.

CAPM assumes that because of the diversification characteristics of the market portfolio and the risk aversion of most investors, the prices of the securities in the market portfolio have adjusted so that an investor could not earn a higher rate of return for the same or a lower level of risk in some other form of investment. The level of risk associated with the market portfolio may be too high or too low for a particular investor, however. Investors can lower the level of risk to which they are exposed and still invest in the market portfolio by buying some of the risk-free asset.

Regardless of the location of the optimal portfolio for each investor along the line, each investor (except those at the two extreme points) is trading off risk for return at a rate equal to the slope of the straight line; that is, the slope of each investor's indifference curve at the point of tangency with the efficient portfolio line is equal to the slope of the line. This marginal tradeoff rate between expected return and risk is $(\bar{r}_m - r_f)/\sigma_m$. This tradeoff is available to each investor.

If the investor can borrow at r_f and is willing to accept more risk than σ_m, then the right-hand extension of the line $r_f M$ applies. Whether the investor borrows (moves to the right of M) or invests in a riskless security (moves to the left of M) depends on the investor's risk preferences. But all investors will have the market portfolio, except for those investors who only want the risk-free security.

Note that the optimum portfolio is being chosen, using the expected return and the standard deviation of the portfolio. When we consider the risk of individual securities, we shall consider the covariance of the security with the market portfolio to be a relevant risk measure.

Capital Market Line

Suppose that r_f represents the rate that could be earned on a government security maturing one period from now. For an investor with a one-period planning horizon, there would be no default risk associated with owning a one-period government security. We shall call such a government security a default-free asset, since we are considering only the risk of default. Now consider the possible portfolios that could be constructed by taking combinations of the market portfolio and these government securities. Suppose that our hypothetical investors devoted a proportion α of their assets to the market portfolio and a proportion $1 - \alpha$ to this government security. Assume that the fraction α is between 0 and 1. Denote by $\bar{r}_m$ the expected rate of return from \$1 invested in the market portfolio. Similarly, let σ_m denote the standard deviation of the rate of return r_m from the market portfolio. The expected rate of return on the investors' portfolio, $\bar{r}_p$, is given by

$$\bar{r}_p = (1 - \alpha)r_f + \alpha\bar{r}_m$$
$$= r_f + \alpha[\bar{r}_m - r_f] \qquad (20.1)$$

and the standard deviation of the rate of return on their portfolio is given by

$$\sigma_p = \alpha\sigma_m \qquad (20.2)$$

If the second equation is solved for α and that quantity is substituted into equation 1, the resulting relationship between the expected rate of return of a portfolio and its standard deviation (when the portfolio is a mixture of the market portfolio and a default-free asset) can be rewritten as

$$\bar{r}_p = r_f + \left[\frac{\bar{r}_m - r_f}{\sigma_m}\right]\sigma_p \qquad (20.3)$$

A graphical representation of the relationship in 20.3 is shown in Figure 20.7. Line AD is the capital market line.

If an investor chose an α of 0, all the funds would be held in government securities, and the expected return would be r_f and σ_p would be 0. This corresponds to point A in Figure 20.7. If an investor chose an α of 1, all the funds would be held in the market portfolio, and the expected return would be $\bar{r}_m$ and σ_p and equal σ_m. This corresponds to point C in Figure 20.7. An investor could also reach any point on the straight line from A to C by picking an appropriate value of α between 0 and 1. The points to the right of point C on the market line correspond to value of α that are greater than 1. To reach such points, an investor must be able to borrow at the rate r_f. Suppose that this were the case and that an investor was willing to absorb a level of risk corresponding to a value of $\sigma_p = 2\sigma_m$. The investor could buy \$2 worth of the market portfolio for every dollar of equity owned. The necessary funds would be obtained by borrowing. In effect, the investor would be buying the market portfolio on a 50 percent margin at an interest rate of r_f. The investor's expected return is given by equation 1

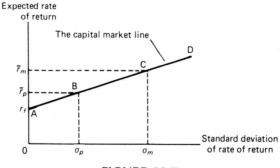

FIGURE 20.7

with α equal to 2. Similarly, the standard deviation of return of the portfolio is given by inserting $\alpha = 2$ into equation 20.2. Since both equations apply, it follows that equation 20.3 is also applicable.

The capital market line applies only to a very special category of portfolios, those consisting of mixtures of the market portfolio and of riskless assets.

The Expected Return of a Security

Assume that an investor owns the market portfolio. In equilibrium, if we add a very small amount of a new security i, the expected return-risk tradeoff that results from the inclusion of i must equal the market's current tradeoff rate. For this to happen, it can be shown that it is necessary that security i's expected return be equal to

$$\bar{r}_i = r_f + (\bar{r}_m - r_f)\beta_i \qquad (20.4)$$

where

$\bar{r}_i$ = the equilibrium expected return of security i

r_f = the return from the risk-free asset

$\bar{r}_m$ = the expected return from investing in the market

β_i = the beta of security i, where $\beta_i = \text{cov}(r_i, r_m)/\sigma_m^2 = \dfrac{\rho_{i,m}\,\sigma_i}{\sigma_m}$

The term $(\bar{r}_m - r_f)\beta_i$ is the adjustment to the risk-free r_f for the risk of security i.

The beta measures the amount of systematic risk, that is, the risk arising because of fluctuations in the market return. There is no adjustment for risk specific to the firm (unsystematic risk) in the CAPM, since it is assumed that the unsystematic risk goes to zero given the very large number of investments (the unsystematic components are independent).

The beta of a security measures how the security's return is correlated with the market's return; thus, it is a measure of the security's systematic risk.

The Security Characteristic Line

The excess return from investing in the market portfolio compared to investing in the risk-free security is $r_m - r_f$. The excess return from investing in security i is $r_i - r_f$. If the excess return for security i is plotted against the excess market return and line is drawn through these points, we obtain the security characteristic line. (See Figure 20.8.) This line can be drawn for any security or portfolio of securities. The slope of this line is the beta (β_i) of the security i, and the intercept is the alpha (α_i).

The alpha of a security is a security's rate of return in excess of the risk-free return when the market earns only the risk-free return (a zero excess return).

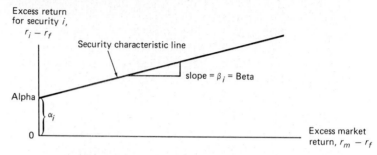

FIGURE 20.8 The Security Characteristic Line

When the market earns a zero excess return, we would expect any security in equilibrium also to earn a zero excess return (an alpha equal to zero). While the weighted average of the alphas of all securities is equal to zero, some securities will have positive alphas and some will have negative alphas based on the observed returns.

If the market thinks that the empirical data leading to a positive alpha will continue in the future, the security is attractive. It will be purchased, and the price will be driven up and the expected return down, so that the expected alpha is equal to zero. Because of market imperfections (including imperfect forecasts), it is not surprising that when time passes and the actual returns are plotted, the alpha of the security will not be exactly equal to zero. The best guess of the alpha of a security, if we think the market is in equilibrium, is zero, but it would be surprising if the actual alpha resulting from the plot of excess returns were zero.

If the CAPM neglects relevant factors that are actually considered by investors, the alpha of a security (or a class of securities) may be expected to be positive or negative because of these neglected factors. For example, the common stock of electric utilities building nuclear generating plants could have negative alphas because the CAPM does not take into consideration specific risk of building nuclear generating plants, but the market does consider this risk.

The following betas were taken from the September 1984 and October 1986 Merrill Lynch publication *Quantitative Analysis* (remember, betas change through time).

	Beta (1984)	*Beta (1986)*
Anchor Hocking	1.0	1.0
Asarco	1.5	1.2
Atlantic City Electric	.7	.7
Chrysler Corp.	1.4	1.3
Eastman Kodak	.6	.8
Five-firm average beta	1.04	1.00

Note that both the high 1984 betas came down and one of the low betas came up.

EXAMPLE 20.1

Assume that the correlation between a security i and the market is .82. The security has a monthly standard deviation of .045, and the market has a monthly standard deviation of .034. The beta of the security is

$$\beta = \frac{\rho_{i,m}\, \sigma_i}{\sigma_m} = \frac{.82\,(.045)}{.034} = 1.085$$

The beta coefficient of a stock (β_i) is widely advocated as the appropriate measure of a stock's risk. It includes the stock's correlation with the market ($\rho_{i,m}$) and the standard deviation of the stock (σ_i) compared to the standard deviation of the market (σ_m).

The beta of a portfolio is the weighted average of the betas of the components.

$$\beta_p = \sum_i x_i \beta_i \qquad (20.5)$$

For example if .6 of the portfolio is invested in a security with a beta of 1.3 and .4 is invested in a security with a beta of .9, we have

$$\beta_p = .6\,(1.3) + .4\,(.9) = .78 + .36 = 1.14$$

Systematic and Unsystematic Risk

It is conventional theory to separate risk into two components. One component is systematic risk, or market risk that represents the change in value resulting from market value changes. Systematic risk can be somewhat reduced by the choice of securities (low-beta securities). Also, reducing systematic risk in this way may increase total risk, since the investor's portfolio will not be perfectly diversified. The second type of risk is residual, or unsystematic risk. This risk is specific to the company (or asset) and is independent of what happens to the other securities. If the investor's portfolio consists of a very large number of securities with no security being a large percentage of the portfolio, then this unsystematic risk can be made to approach zero by a strategy of perfect diversification.

If the costs of diversification are relatively low, investors will not be willing to pay more for a security simply because it carries a relatively low burden of unsystematic risk (which can be diversified away). Similarly, securities that carry a large amount of unsystematic risk will not suffer a serious price disadvantage.

A beta coefficient of unity indicates that a security has the same amount of systematic risk as the market portfolio. A beta coefficient greater (less) than unity indicates the security is riskier (safer) than the market portfolio. Betas based on actual data are prepared by Merrill Lynch, Wells Fargo Bank, and the Value Line investor service, as well as others. These are called historical betas. Fundamental betas would be ex ante estimates based on the capital structure and operating characteristics of the firm.

The Security Market Line

Consider what happens to expected return as we move from a security with a low level of systematic risk to a security with a higher level. We find that, for any security i, the expected return $(\bar{r}_i)$ is

$$\bar{r}_i = r_f + (\bar{r}_m - \bar{r}_f)\beta_i$$

The relationship between expected return and beta is the security market line; it is the major mathematical relationship of the capital asset pricing model. Figure 20.9 shows the security market line. Note that β is measured on the X axis and expected return on the Y axis. M is the market portfolio with a beta of 1. The slope of the line is $(\bar{r}_m - r_f)$. The risk premium is $\beta_i(\bar{r}_m - r_f)$ for a security with beta β_i.

If the risk is $\beta = 1$, then the expected return is $\bar{r}_m$, and the investment has the same expected return as the market portfolio. The security market line leads to a conclusion that if a security has more systematic risk, the market will require a higher return.

Earlier we wrote that

$$\bar{r}_i = r_f + (\bar{r}_m - r_f)\beta_i$$

but since

$$\beta_i = \frac{\text{cov}\ (r_i,\ r_m)}{\text{var}\ (r_m)} = \frac{\rho_{i,m}\sigma_i}{\sigma_m}$$

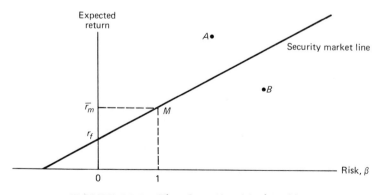

FIGURE 20.9   The Security Market Line

we can write the formulation for $\bar{r}_i$ in a variety of ways by substituting for β. If we define

$$\lambda = \frac{\bar{r}_m - r_f}{\text{var}\,(r_m)}$$

then

$$\bar{r}_i = r_f + \lambda \,\text{cov}\,(r_i, r_m) \qquad (20.6)$$

The equation for $\bar{r}_i$ can be presented in a large number of different forms. All have r_i as a function or r_f, $(\bar{r}_m - r_f)$ and β or the components of β.

Security A of Figure 20.9 is above the security market line. It has a higher expected return than the market requires for its given risk. We can expect the price of A to increase so that its expected return decreases and A returns to the security market line. Investors will buy A, driving its price up and its return down.

Security B is below the security market line. We can expect the price of B to decrease as investors sell it so that its expected return increases, and B will then sit on the security market line. In equilibrium, all securities will be on the security market line.

In understanding the several graphs that have been presented, it is useful to keep the following facts in mind.

	X Axis	Y Axis
Capital market line $\left(\text{the slope is } \dfrac{\bar{r} - r_f}{\sigma_m}\right)$	Standard deviation	Expected return
Security characteristic line (the slope is the beta)	Excess market return	Excess return for security
Security market line (the slope is $\bar{r}_m - r_f$)	Beta	Expected return for a security

All three of the equations describe relationships that should exist in equilibrium if the capital-asset pricing model is correct. The capital market line applies only to portfolios that are a mixture of the market portfolio and the riskless asset. The security market line applies to any security (or portfolio of securities) whose price is in equilibrium. The security characteristic line shows how deviations of the return on the market portfolio from its expected level affects the returns of individual securities or portfolios.

One important factor should be kept in mind. We are interested in return the market expects to earn for a given amount of risk. To determ we need to know the return that is expected to be earned in the ma well as how the risk of a specific security compares to the risk of th model needs expectations in order to be used correctly. All w data based on past events that we may use to estimate th need. For example, one problem is that the beta will change through time. Also, the value of r_f will depend on the maturity of the government security that is used. It is not easy to use the CAPM in an exact manner. One important use of CAPM is in estimating the required rate of return for an asset.

Required Rate of Return Versus Cost of Capital[2]

Suppose that a one-period investment is available whose cost is c. The end-of-period-1 cash flow from the investment is x. Therefore, the rate of return on cost for the investment is

$$r^* = \frac{x}{c} - 1$$

and the expected rate of return on cost is

$$\bar{r}^* = \frac{\bar{x}}{c} - 1$$

where $\bar{x}$ is the expected end-of-period-1 cash flow.

In capital budgeting practice, a commonly used criterion for making accept or reject decisions is to compare the expected rate of return on cost for an investment with the firm's weighted average cost of capital (WACC). The WACC represents the required rate of return for the firm as a whole and, as its name suggests, is an average. Those who advocate this procedure recommend accepting the investment if its expected rate of return on cost exceeds or is equal to the firm's cost of capital. That is, accept if $r \geq$ WACC.

Figure 20.10 shows both the WACC and the security market lines. The two lines imply different investment criteria; in each case the line is the boundary between the accept region (above the line) and the reject region (below the line).

For investments D and G both criteria lead to the same decisions. For F, contradictory recommendations would result. Invest- be rejected by the WACC criterion—but they would be pital asset pricing model approach, even though E yields ree return. Investment C would be accepted using the be rejected using the CAPM approach.

ites one important limitation of the WACC approach: the take into account variations in the riskiness of different approach tends to reject some low-risk projects like F that because their rates of return are more than enough to risk. The WACC approach tends to lead to the acceptance

his section is adapted from Mark E. Rubinstein, "A Mean-Variance Financial Theory," *Journal of Finance*, March 1973, pp. 167–181.

what
ine this,
ket ($\bar{r}_m$) as
e market. The
e shall have are
variables that we

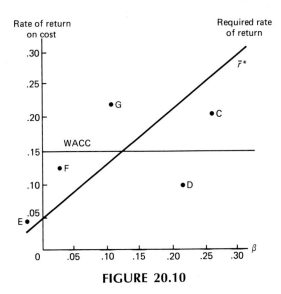

FIGURE 20.10

of high-risk projects, like C, whose expected rates of return are greater than the WACC, but not enough greater to compensate for the beta risk of the project.

Figure 20.10 illustrates a firm with a WACC of .15 and a beta of 1.1.

Making Investment Decisions

The theory of stock prices presented in this chapter can be applied to investment decisions. We illustrate these applications here for an asset with a one-period life. At the same time, we show the connection between the state preference model and CAPM.

If the investment opportunities are economically independent, an accept or reject decision must be made for each investment. In this instance, the criterion that should be used to make the decision is to compare the risk-adjusted present value of the cash flows from the investment with its cost c. Let v be the risk-adjusted present value. If $v - c$ is greater than or equal to zero, the investment should be accepted. If it is negative, it should be rejected. The quantity $(v - c)$ is the risk-adjusted counterpart, under conditions of uncertainty, of the net present value of the investment. Thus, $v - c$ will be called the risk-adjusted net present value, RANPV.

To find the risk-adjusted present value of the cash proceeds, we use the relationship

$$v = \bar{y} - \lambda \operatorname{Cov}(y, r_m), \qquad (20.7)$$

where $y = x/(1 + r_f)$.

The appendix to this chapter shows how equation 20.7 is derived from equation 20.6.

EXAMPLE 20.2

Suppose that r_f is .08 and that the following facts apply to a one-period investment where two states of nature are possible.

State n	Probability of State p	Value of r_m	Cash Flow x
1	.8	.20	$432
2	.2	.00	108

From this we can compute $\bar{r}_m$ and σ_m^2.

n	p	r_m	pr_m	$r_m - \bar{r}_m$	$(r_m - \bar{r}_m)^2$	$p(r_m - \bar{r})^2$
1	.8	.20	.16	.04	.0016	.00128
2	.2	.00	0	−.16	.0256	.00512
			$\bar{r}_m = 16$			$\sigma_m^2 = .00640$

The value of λ is

$$\lambda = \frac{\bar{r}_m - r_f}{\sigma_m^2} = \frac{.16 - .08}{.0064} = 12.5$$

If state 1 occurs, the cash flows are $432, and if state 2 occurs, the cash flows are $108. The covariance between r_m and y, which is, by definition,

$$\sum p(y - \bar{y})(r_m - \bar{r}_m)$$

is shown in the footnote[3] to equal

$$\sum py(r_m - \bar{r}_m)$$

The latter expression is computationally simpler and is used in the examples.

---

[3] $\sum p(y - \bar{y})(r_m - \bar{r}_m) = \sum py(r_m - \bar{r}_m) - \sum p\bar{y}(r_m - \bar{r}_m)$

and

$\sum p\bar{y}(r_m - \bar{r}_m) = \bar{y}(r_m - \bar{r}_m) = 0$

therefore

$\sum p(y - \bar{y})(r_m - \bar{r}_m) = \sum py(r_m - \bar{r}_m)$

The computations of $\bar{y}$ and Cov (y, r_m) follow:

n	x	y	p	py	$(r_m - \bar{r}_m)$	$py(r_m - \bar{r}_m)$
1	432	400	.8	320	.04	12.8
2	108	100	.2	20	−.16	−3.2
				$\bar{y} = 340$		Cov $(y, r_m) = 9.6$

We can now compute v using equation (20.7):

$$v = \bar{y} - \lambda \, \text{Cov}\, (y, r_m)$$
$$= 340 - (12.5)\,(9.60) = 340 - 120 = \$220$$

If the alternatives were to accept or reject, this investment would be acceptable if its cost were less than \$220.

A Simplified Calculation: A State Preference Approach

The preceeding calculation can be simplified by explicitly using a state preference approach to valuation. Let us define $s(n)$ to be the value today of an investment that will pay \$1 at time 1 if node n occurs. For $n = 1$, the value of $s(1)$ can be computed using equation (20.7) as follows.

n	x	y	p	py	$(r_m - \bar{r}_m)$	$py(r_m - \bar{r}_m)$
1	1	.92593	.8	.74074	.04	.02963
2	0	0	.2	0	−.16	0
				$\bar{y} = .74074$		Cov $(y, r_m) = .02963$

$$s(1) = \bar{y} - \lambda \, \text{Cov}\, (y, r_m)$$
$$= .74074 - (12.5)\,(.02963) = .74074 - .37037 = .37037.$$

A similar calculation for $n = 2$ will show that

$$s(2) = .55556$$

To generalize these results, let $p(n)$ be the probability of node n and $r_m(n)$ the value of r_m at that node. Suppose an investment pays \$1 at time 1 if node n occurs and nothing otherwise. The present value of the expected cash flows from such an investment will be

$$\bar{y} = \frac{p(n)}{1 + r_f}$$

The covariance between y and r_m for such an investment will be[4]

$$\text{Cov } (y, r_m) = \frac{p(n)}{1 + r_f} [r_m(n) - \bar{r}_m]$$

Substituting the values for $\bar{y}$ and Cov (y, r_m) in equation 20.7, the value of such an investment will be

$$s(n) = \frac{p(n)}{1 + r_f} [1 - \lambda(r_m(n) - \bar{r}_m)] \qquad (20.8)$$

For example, $s(1)$ could be calculated directly using equation 20.8.

$$s(1) = \frac{.8}{1.08} [1 - (12.5)(.20 - .16)] = (.74074)(1 - .5) = .37037.$$

Equation 20.8 is extremely important, since it simplifies the computation of RAPV. The value $s(n)$ is a time-risk information factor that enables us to compute the risk-adjusted present value of $1 at node n one time period later. It is not dependent on there only being two outcomes. While v gives the risk-adjusted present value of all outcomes stemming from one node, $s(n)$ gives the risk-adjusted present value of one path stemming from a node.

To find the risk-adjusted present value of the investment, we can multiply the values of $s(n)$ by the cash flows and sum:

State	s(n)	x	xs(n)
1	.3704	432	160
2	.5556	108	60
	.9260		$v = \$220$

This value of v agrees with the number obtained previously by using equation 20.7. Equations 20.8 and 20.7 lead to the same solution, but 20.8 has the advantage of being easier to compute. A price is being placed on the value of a dollar in each state (event) that can take place.

EXAMPLE 20.3

We will now consider an investment in which, two possible states may occur (labeled states 3 and 4). The value of r_f is now .03. The following facts apply:

State: n	p	r_m	x
3	.3	.20	206
4	.7	.00	103

---

[4] Remember that Cov $= \sum py(r_m - \bar{r}_m)$ and $y = 1/(1 + r_f)$ at node n and zero elsewhere.

From this we can compute $\bar{r}_m$ and σ_m^2.

n	p	r_m	pr_m	$r_m - \bar{r}_m$	$(r_m - \bar{r}_m)^2$	$p(r_m - \bar{r}_m)^2$
3	.3	.20	.06	.14	.0196	.00588
4	.7	.00	.00	−.06	.0036	.00252
			$\bar{r}_m = .06$			$\sigma_m^2 = .00840$

The value of lambda is

$$\lambda = \frac{\bar{r}_m - r_f}{\sigma_m^2} = \frac{.06 - .03}{.0084} = 3.5714$$

Using equation (20.8),

$$s(3) = \frac{p(n)}{1 + r_f}[1 - \lambda(r_m(n) - \bar{r}_m)] = \frac{.3}{1.03}[1 - 3.5714\,(.14)]$$

$$= .14563$$

$$s(4) = \frac{.7}{1.03}[1 - 3.5714\,(-.06)] = .82524$$

The risk-adjusted present value of the investment is

State	$s(n)$	x	$xs(n)$
3	.1456	206	30
4	.8252	103	85
	.9708		$v = \$115$

The following calculations using the covariance and equation (20.7) also give $115.

n	p	x	y	py	$r_m - \bar{r}_m$	$py(r_m - \bar{r}_m)$
3	.3	206	200	60	.14	8.4
4	.7	103	100	70	−.06	−4.2
				$\bar{y} = 130$		Cov $(y, r_m) = $ 4.2

The value of v is again $115.

$$v = y\,\lambda\,\text{Cov}\,(y, r_m) = 130 - 3.5714\,(4.20)$$
$$= 130 - 15 = \$115$$

Instead of using equation 20.8 the values of $s(n)$ can be computed using equation 20.7 if we make the assumption that x is $1 with node n and zero otherwise. For example, for $n = 3$ we would have

n	p	x	y	py	$(r_m - \bar{r}_m)$	$py(r_m - \bar{r}_m)$
3	.3	1	.9709	.2913	.14	.0408
4	.7	0	0	0	−.06	0
				$\bar{y} = .2913$		$\text{Cov}(y, r_m) = .0408$

$$v = s(3) = \bar{y} - \lambda \, \text{Cov}(y, r_m)$$
$$= .2913 - 3.5714\,(.0408) = .1456$$

Comparable calculations for $s(4)$ again give a value of .8252.

If the investment earns cash flows of $1 with state 3 *and* state 4, we would expect the risk-adjusted present value to be $1/1.03 = \$.97087$, since there is zero risk ($1 will be received no matter what state occurs). Using the values of $s(3)$ and $s(4)$, we obtain $.97087 for the RAPV.

State	$s(n)$	x	$xs(n)$
3	.14563	$1	.14563
4	.82524	1	.82524
		RAPV =	$.97087

The .97087 is equal to $(1 + r_f)^{-1} = (1.03)^{-1}$.

With risky cash flows, we have to take both the time value and the risk of the cash flows into consideration. We find that the values obtained from the use of equation 20.8 can be used as "prices" or transformation factors to find the risk-adjusted present value of cash flows to be received one period from now.

Conclusions

The capital-asset pricing model says that investors have available a market basket of risky securities and the opportunity to invest in securities with no risk of default. Risk preferences of investors dictate a combination of the market basket of the risky securities and the riskless securities. In equilibrium, the return of any security must be such that the investor expects to earn a basic return equal to the return on a default-free security plus an adjustment that is heavily influenced by the "correlation" of the security's return and the market's return. If the return from the investment is positively correlated with the market return, the equilibrium return will be larger than the default-free return. If the correlation is negative, the equilibrium return will be smaller than the default-free return.

It is easy to get lost in a complexity of mathematical symbols and mathematical manipulations. To many readers, the suggested technique will be an example of that situation. However, it is extremely important that you not fail to see the purpose of the calculations.

Today, industry tends to use a "cost of capital" or a "hurdle rate" to implement the discounted cash flow capital budgeting techniques. Both of these measures are "averages" reflecting average risks and average time-value conditions and cannot be sensibly applied to unique "marginal" situations. There is no reason to think that the weighted average cost of capital can be inserted in a compound interest formula and then be applied to any series of future cash flows to obtain a useful measure of net present value that takes both the time value and risk of the investment into consideration.

Now the capital-asset pricing model offers hope for accomplishing a systematic calculation of risk-adjusted present value. The measure reflects the investor's alternative investment return-risk tradeoff opportunities in the same way as the rate of interest on a government bond reflects investment opportunities when there is no default risk.

Even where there is a reluctance to accept immediately the specific calculations of the type illustrated in this chapter, there will be a change in the way that management will look at alternatives.

One important limitation of the capital-asset pricing model for corporate decision making should be kept in mind. The model assumes that the investors are widely diversified and, equally important, it assumes that the managers of the firm are willing to make investment decisions with the objective of maximizing the wellbeing of this type of investor. This means that unsystematic risk (for which the investor is well diversified) may be ignored in the evaluation of investments.

It is well known that objectives of firms and managers are multidimensional and that there will be a reluctance to ignore risk because it does not affect the well-diversified investor. The so-called "unsystematic" risk is not something that is likely to be ignored by a management that includes among its objectives the continuity of existence of the firm.

The models we have used here are simplified. Investors are much more complex in their behavior, and markets are less than perfect. Nevertheless, we feel the conclusions reached are relevant and will be the foundation for a great deal of the financial investment models of the future. Investment decision making under uncertainty is not an easy task, but uncertainty is a characteristic of the world in which managers must operate.

REVIEW EXAMPLE 20.1

The market portfolio has a historically based expected return of .095 and a standard deviation of .035 during a period when risk-free assets yielded .025. The .06 risk premium is thought to be constant through time. Riskless investments may now be purchased to yield .08.

A security has a standard deviation of .07 and a .75 correlation with the market portfolio. The market portfolio is now expected to have a standard deviation of .035.

a. What is the market's return-risk tradeoff?
b. What is the security's beta?
c. What is the equilibrium required expected return of the security?

Solution

a. Market's return-risk trade-off $= \dfrac{\bar{r}_m - r_f}{\sigma_m}$

$$= \frac{.095 - .025}{.035} = 2$$

b. $\beta_i = \dfrac{\text{cov}(r_i, r_m)}{\sigma_m^2} = \dfrac{\rho\sigma_i\sigma_m}{\sigma_m^2} = \dfrac{.75 \times .07 \times .035}{.035^2}$

$$= 1.5$$

c. $\bar{r}_i = r_f + (\bar{r}_m - r_f)\beta_i = .08 + (.06)1.5$

$$= .17$$

There is difficulty in deciding which estimates of market return, risk premium, and market standard deviation to use.

Appendix: Derivation of the RAPV Relationship

We want to show that equation 20.7 follows from equation 20.6.

$$v = \bar{y} - \lambda \, \text{Cov}\,(y, r_m) \tag{20.7}$$

Starting with 20.6 we have

$$\bar{r}_f = r_f + \lambda \, \text{Cov}\,(r_i, r_m) \tag{20.6}$$

we can substitute $\bar{x}/v - 1$ for $\bar{r}$, $x/v - 1$ for r, and then solve the equation for v. In doing this, we take advantage of the fact that for any constant v,

$$\text{Cov}\left(\frac{x}{v} - 1, \, r_m\right) = \frac{1}{v} \, \text{Cov}\,(x, r_m)$$

Making these substitutions, we have

$$\frac{\bar{x}}{v} - 1 = r_f + \lambda\left(\frac{1}{v}\right) \text{Cov}\,(x, r_m)$$

Adding one to both sides and multiplying by v gives

$$\bar{x} = (1 + r_f)v + \lambda \, \text{Cov}\,(x, r_m)$$

Therefore, solving for v,

$$v = \frac{\bar{x} - \lambda \, \text{Cov}\,(x,\, r_m)}{1 + r_f}$$

Note that by definition

$$\bar{y} = \frac{\bar{x}}{1 + r_f}$$

Also, since $y = x/(1 + r_f)$, it follows that

$$\text{Cov}\,(x,\, r_m) = (1 + r_f)\,\text{Cov}\left(\frac{x}{1 + r_f},\, r_m\right)$$

$$= (1 + r_f)\,\text{Cov}\,(y,\, r_m)$$

Substituting these expressions into the equation for v gives

$$v = \frac{\bar{x}}{1 + r_f} - \lambda \frac{\text{Cov}\,(x,\, r_m)}{1 + r_f}$$

$$= \bar{y} - \lambda \frac{(1 + r_f)\,\text{Cov}\,(y,\, r_m)}{1 + r_f}$$

$$= \bar{y} - \lambda\,\text{Cov}\,(y,\, r_m),$$

which is the desired result.

PROBLEMS

For problems 20.1 through 20.9, assume that $\bar{r}_m = .14$, $r_f = .08$, and $\sigma_m = .12$.

20.1 If an investor put half her funds in the market portfolio and half in treasury bills,
   a. What rate of return would you expect her to earn?
   b. What is the standard deviation of returns from her portfolio?
   c. Draw a rough graph with expected return on the vertical axis and standard deviation of return on the horizontal axis. Plot the market portfolio at point C and the investor's portfolio at point B on this graph.
   d. Find the slope of the capital market line.

20.2 If an investor wished to hold a portfolio consisting only of treasury bills and shares in the market portfolio and he wanted an expected return of .12 per year, what proportion of his funds should be invested in the market portfolio? What is the standard deviation of returns from this portfolio?

20.3 On January 1, M.B. University had an endowment worth $100 million. Of this amount, $25 million was invested in treasury bills, and $75 million was invested in the market portfolio. By the following December 31, MBU had earned $2 million in interest and had received dividends of $3 million. These amounts were considered as income and used to pay the current expenses of the university. Except for rolling over treasury bills, no portfolio transactions were undertaken. Although on December 31, MBU's portfolio still held the same number of shares in the market portfolio, the market value of these shares had declined to $60 million because of a general decline in stock prices.

    a. What was the expected annual rate of return on MBU's portfolio on January 1 and its standard deviation?

    b. What was the actual rate of return earned?

20.4   (*Continuation of problem 20.3.*) If no shift has occurred in the capital market line, what rate of return would be expected from the portfolio held by MBU on December 31?

    If MBU wished to modify the composition of its December 31 portfolio so that the expected rate of return was the same as that of its January 1 portfolio, what transactions would be necessary?

20.5   (*Continuation of problem 20.3.*)

    a. By how many standard deviations did the realized return on MBU's portfolio fall short of its expected return?

    b. If the distribution of rates of return can be approximated by a normal distribution, what is the probability of earnings as little as this or less?

20.6   Suppose that it were possible for an investor to borrow, at 8 percent per year, as much as $.75 for every dollar of stock he owned free and clear. Could an investor having $100,000 in cash devise a portfolio consisting only of shares in the market portfolio and treasury bills for which the expected rate of return was 17 percent?

    If it is possible, describe the transactions that would be necessary; if not, explain why it is impossible.

20.7   A retired doctor wants to hold a portfolio consisting only of debt and stock in the market portfolio. She also wants the assurance that, even if the return on the market portfolio were two standard deviations below normal, the rate of return on her portfolio would be no less than −5 percent. What portfolio would you recommend for her?

20.8   The covariance between the rate of return of a stock and the rate of return of the market index is .0192. What is the required rate of return of this stock?

20.9   What is the beta coefficient of the common stock described in problem 20.8?

20.10   If an investment is expected to depress temporarily both accounting income and the current market price of the stock, should the investment be undertaken if it is expected to have a beneficial long-run effect on stock prices?

20.11 Assume the following facts.

	Default-Free Investment	Market Investment
Expected return	.07	.10
Standard deviation	0	.02

Compute the portfolio expected return and risk (standard deviation) if the investment is split .6 in the market portfolio and .4 in the default-free investment.

20.12 (*Continuation of problem 20.11.*) For the information given, determine the equations for the capital market line and the security market line for the investment. What are the slopes of the two lines?

20.13 (*Continuation of problem 20.11.*) Assume that there is an investment j with a covariance of .00064 with the market. Determine the expected return required by the market.

20.14 (*Continuation of problem 20.13.*) If the investment currently has an expected return of .15, what would you expect to happen?

20.15 (*Continuation of problem 20.13.*) If the covariance of the investment with the market were $-.00064$, what would be the expected return required by the market?

20.16 For the information given in problem 20.13, compute the β of the investment. Using the β, compute the expected return required by the market.

20.17 If the β of a security is large, what does this imply about the expected change in value of the stock for small changes in the value of the market portfolio?

20.18 A risky one-period investment requires an immediate outlay of $1,000. The possible proceeds, which will be received in one period, are listed here, along with their probabilities and the corresponding RAPVFs.

Outcome Number n	RAPVF $s(n)$	Probability of Outcome p	Cash Proceeds x
1	.15	.2	$2,000
2	.40	.5	1,500
3	.35	.3	500

a. Find the expected cash flow from the investment.
b. Find the expected rate of return (on the cost) of the investment.
c. Find the required rate of return of the investment.
d. Find r_f.

20.19 The following data apply to the next two questions.

$$r_f = .085$$

State	Probability of State	Rate of Return on Market, Given State
1	.2	.36
2	.4	.21
3	.3	.16
4	.1	−.04

a. Find $\lambda = \dfrac{\overline{r}_m - r_f}{\sigma_m^2}$

b. Find the RAPVFs for states 2 and 3, using the CAPM.

20.20 A security analyst believes that the rate of return that can be earned on default-free securities during the next year is .08 and that the possible one-period rates of return that can be realized from holding the market portfolio and their probabilities are as follows.

Rate of Return	Probability
.30	.30
.20	.40
.10	.25
−.10	.05

a. What is the expected rate of return on the market portfolio?

b. What is the variance of the rate of return on the market portfolio? (You can round to the nearest percent.)

The portfolio manager is responsible for a $100 million pension fund that must be divided between the market portfolio and default-free securities.

c. How much of each should be held to achieve an expected rate of return of 15 percent on the pension portfolio?

d. What would be the standard deviation of the rate of return on the pension portfolio if its expected rate of return were 15 percent?

20.21 Assume the default-free rate, r_f, is .11 and the following additional data.

Outcome Number n	Probability of Outcome p	Rate of Return on Market Portfolio r_m
1	.6	.25
2	.4	.05

a. Find $\lambda = \dfrac{\bar{r}_m - r_f}{\sigma_m^2}$.

b. Find the risk-adjusted present value factors (RAPVFs) for each of the outcomes.

20.22 A risky one-period investment requires an immediate outlay of $150. The possible proceeds, which will be received in one period, are listed here along with their probabilities and the corresponding RAPVFs.

Outcome Number *n*	RAPVF *s(n)*	Probability of Outcome *p*	Cash Proceeds *x*
1	.2175	.6	$300
2	.4014	.3	200
3	.3070	.1	100
	.9259		

a. Find the RANPV of the investment.
b. Find the expected rate of return (on the cost) of the investment.
c. Find the required rate of return of the investment.
d. Find r_f.

REFERENCES

See the references for Chapters 18 and 19.

CHAPTER 21

Valuing Flexibility: An Application of Option Valuation Techniques

There is no good answer to a stupid question.
Russian proverb

Strategic net present value (S-NPV) expands the set of alternatives that the analyst must consider. It recognizes when flexibility exists and places a value on that flexibility.

The value of flexibility can be estimated using the theory of pricing options and the related contingent claims analysis.[1] However, frequently this valuation will be extremely complex, and it will be necessary to substitute a qualitative input.

We will describe types of situations where these tools can be used to evaluate the alternatives. We will stop short of offering a general complex mathematical solution to the types of problems being considered.[2]

There is no question that the application of option theory to capital budgeting decisions is a major capital budgeting development of the 1980s, and managers involved in a firm's capital budgeting process should understand when these concepts can usefully be applied.

---

[1] The initial discovery of the option-pricing approach on which this chapter is based is presented in Fischer Black and Myron Scholes, "The Pricing of Options and Corporate Liabilities," *Journal of Political Economy*, May 1973, pp. 637–659.

[2] A good introduction to option valuation techniques is contained in Robert A. Jarrow and Andrew Rudd, *Option Pricing* (Homewood, IL.: Richard D. Irwin, Inc., 1983).

Before proceeding, we will discuss the basic valuation of options. Each of the situations we will later describe is an option valuation problem. You should distinguish two types of situations. One is where there are enough marketable securities or assets available so that the payoffs of the alternative (the option) being evaluated can be exactly duplicated by a portfolio of one or more alternative securities and assets. This situation will be discussed first. In the second situation, the alternative being evaluated cannot be exactly duplicated by a portfolio of securities and assets. Even in this case, option theory makes an important contribution by calling attention to the existence of the alternatives and the need to value the resulting flexibility.

Options

A person with an option has a choice. In American football, the quarterback calls an option play if he wants to decide whether to pass or run after the play is in progress. In the stock market, an investor might decide to buy a call option, which gives the right to buy the stock later at a price that is determined now. An investment project may incorporate options if, after the project is accepted, there are important decisions that can be made that affect the value of the project. Examples include the option to expand the scale of the project if it is successful, to sell the project if it is unsuccessful, and to develop related businesses because of the knowledge gained by doing the first project.

Our main interest is in evaluating the options that are associated with investment projects, but we will begin by considering procedures for valuing a call option for common stock. This will introduce the basic concepts that we need.

Definition of a Call Option

We begin by defining a call option for common stock.

> A call option is a contract giving its owner the right to buy a fixed number of shares of a specified common stock at a fixed price any time on or before a given date.[3]

In order to fully describe a particular call-option contract, we need to specify the key provisions:

1. The type of common stock that can be purchased.
2. The number of shares that can be purchased.
3. The purchase price at which the shares can be purchased.
4. The last date on which they can be purchased.

---

[3] John C. Cox and Mark Rubinstein, *Options Markets* (Englewood Cliffs, NJ: Prentice-Hall, 1985), p. 1.

5. Whether or not the call option can only be exercised on that last date or on any date up to and including the last date.

6. Who is on the other side of the contract.

There are a number of specialized terms used in connection with options. It helps to learn the language. An owner who takes advantage of the right to buy the common stock is said to be exercising the option. The common stock that can be purchased, such as General Motors, Consolidated Edison, and so on, is called the underlying asset. The purchase price is also called the striking price or the exercise price. The last date on which the stock can be purchased is the maturity date of the contract. Contracts that can be exercised only on the maturity date are said to be European options; contracts that can be exercised at any time up to and including the maturity date are said to be American options. The party on the other side of the contract is said to be the writer. The owner has the right to buy, and the writer has an obligation to sell at the owner's request.

Valuing a Call Option

An option cannot have a negative value. It will have a positive value so long as there is a positive probability that the price of the common stock will be higher than the exercise price sometime during the exercise period. Other factors, such as the dividends forgone by purchasing options rather than purchasing stock, play an important role in the valuation process. To examine the process systematically, we shall first examine the minimum value of an option (called, somewhat misleadingly, its theoretical value). We shall then determine its maximum value. Finally, we shall examine its behavior between these ranges as a function of the uncertain future stock prices and other factors.

Throughout this chapter we shall assume that an option gives the owner a right to acquire *one* share of common stock. Although options may be for more or less than one share, the assumption enables us to simplify notation somewhat.

Minimum and Maximum Values of an Option

The theoretical value of an option is the gain that could be realized if the option were exercised immediately. If the price of the common stock is greater than the exercise price of the option, the gain is the difference between the price of the stock and the exercise price. (We ignore transaction costs.) If the price of the stock is below the exercise price, then the theoretical value is defined to be zero (it would not be rational to exercise the option). Let

$$C_{min} = \text{the minimum (theoretical) value of an option}$$

$$S = \text{the market value of a share of common stock}$$

$$K = \text{the exercise price}$$

Then the theoretical value of an option is

$$(S - K) \text{ if } S > K \text{ and zero if } S \leq K$$

The "theoretical" value is by no means the theoretically correct value of an option. It does, however, set a minimum value for an option if the option could be exercised immediately and the gain realized. The market value of the option will either be equal to or larger than the theoretical value. This is easy to see in the case of an American option, which can be exercised at any time. If the common stock price is $20 and the exercise price is $15, the option cannot sell at less than $5. If the option sold for $3, one could buy the option, exercise it, and sell the stock for $20 and make $2 profit. $(S - K)$ defines the minimum value of the option. $C_{\min}$, depicted in Figure 21.1, is the "theoretical" value.

At the other extreme, the absolute maximum value of an option at any time is the market value of the stock at that time. The option will allow the holder to purchase at the exercise price, but the stock itself can always be purchased on the open market. This price, labeled $C_{\max}$, is also shown in Figure 21.1. If the common stock can be purchased for $20 per share, an investor will not pay as much as $20 for an option to buy a share if the exercise price is some positive amount.

For any current price, the actual value of the option, C, will fall between these two boundaries. C depends on the exercise price, the maturity date of the option, and the distribution of the future prices of the common stock. A longer maturity will increase the option value (move it closer to $C_{\max}$).

In the next section we shall develop a method of valuing an option that is based on arbitrage. Although it is a simplified model, it does illustrate the basic logic behind modern option pricing theory.

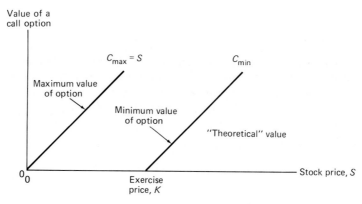

FIGURE 21.1

Option Pricing: A Binomial Model[4]

We shall develop a single-period option pricing model where the stock price can take on only two values in the next period. In the next period, a stock currently selling for a price S will sell for either uS or dS; uS is larger than dS.

An amount B can be borrowed or lent at a rate of r_f, and r is defined as

$$r = 1 + r_f$$

There is zero risk on the debt. The value of r is larger than d, but it is less than u. This is necessary so that there are not riskless profit opportunities involving only the stocks and debt. For example, if both u and d were larger than r, an investment in the stock financed by debt would lead to a certain profit (no risk). No one would want to buy the debt.

Also, if r were larger than both u and d, an investor who invested in bonds would be certain to make more than investors holding stock. No one would want to buy stock.

To prevent these extreme situations, we assume $u > r > d$.

Consider a call option with an exercise price of K that will expire in one period. Let C be the value of the option at time 0. Ultimately, we want to calculate a reasonable value for C. We start by writing down the values of the option at time 1. The value of the option at expiration will depend on the price of the stock at that time.

Let C_u be the value of the call at expiration if the stock price goes to uS at that time.

$$C_u = \text{Max } (uS - K, \ 0)$$

Similarly, let C_d be the value of the call at expiration if the stock price goes down to dS at that time.

$$C_d = \text{Max } (dS - K, \ 0)$$

To value the call at time 1, one period before expiration we will show that the payoffs from the call can be exactly replicated by the payoffs from a properly selected portfolio of stocks and bonds, which is known as the hedge portfolio. Since the call is a perfect substitute for the hedge portfolio, it should have the same value. The value of the hedge portfolio can be determined from the market prices of the stocks and bonds of which it is composed. This provides a value for the call.

---

[4] This section is based heavily on J. C. Cox, S. A. Ross, and M. Rubinstein, "Option Pricing: A Simplified Approach," *Journal of Financial Economics*, September 1979, pp. 229–263, for the multiperiod case.

Constructing a Hedge Portfolio

Suppose the investor wishes to construct a hedge portfolio at time 0 that will have the same payoffs at time 1 as owning a call option. The investor will

1. Buy Δ shares of common stock at a price per share of S.
2. Buy B dollars worth of debt. The value of the debt after one period is rB. The interest rate is $r - 1$.

We want to determine values of B and Δ such that the portfolio will have the same payoff as a call option (see Figure 21.2). The payoff of the option depends on the price of the stock. If the payoff from the hedge portfolio and the option are the same in the event the price of the stock increases, then the following equation will be satisfied.

$$\Delta uS + rB = C_u \tag{21.1}$$

If the payoff from the hedge portfolio and the option are the same in the event the price of the stock decreases, then the following equation will be satisfied.

$$\Delta dS + rB = C_d \tag{21.2}$$

The values of C_u and C_d at time 1 when the option contract matures are known from the characteristics of the option contract and the value of the common stock. Thus, we have two equations and two unknowns. Solving for Δ by subtracting equation 21.2 from 21.1 gives

$$\Delta S(u - d) = C_u - C_d$$

Rearranging, we have

$$\Delta = \frac{C_u - C_d}{S(u - d)} \tag{21.3}$$

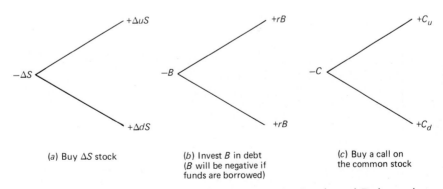

(a) Buy ΔS stock   (b) Invest B in debt (B will be negative if funds are borrowed)   (c) Buy a call on the common stock

FIGURE 21.2 Cash Flows from Investing in Stock and Debt and Buying a Call

The value of Δ is called the hedge ratio because it defines the number of shares of common stock that need to be purchased to balance the cash flows from one call option.

Solving equations 21.1 and 21.2 for B,

$$B = \frac{uC_d - dC_u}{(u - d)r} \qquad (21.4)$$

The portfolio consisting of one call has the same payoffs in each state of a portfolio of B debt and Δ shares of stock. Therefore, in equilibrium, the initial value of the two portfolios must be equal. This requires that the following equation be satisfied.

$$C = \Delta S + B \qquad (21.5)$$

The value of the call, C, must be equal to $\Delta S + B$, or there is an opportunity for profits to be made.

Another point to be noted is that the probabilities of the outcomes u and d were not needed to calculate the value of the call option. These probabilities may affect the value of the call option, but they do so indirectly. If the probability of u were to increase, the stock price S would undoubtedly increase, and from equation 21.5 we can see that an increase in S would increase the value of the call option, C. The model does not tell us how to value the stock. It does tell us how to value the call option, given the price of the stock. In other words, the price of the call is contingent on the price of the stock.

Also, the model does not require that investors agree about the probability of outcome u. Investors who are optimistic that outcome u will occur may be willing to own large quantities of the stock (or of the call). But given the price of the stock, they will agree about the price of call.

We now illustrate the use of the model to determine the composition of the hedge portfolio and the value of a call option for a given set of facts.

EXAMPLE 21.1

$$S = \$100, \qquad u = 1.5, \qquad d = 1.0, \qquad K = \$120$$

$$r_f = .10, \qquad r = 1.10$$

$$C_u = \text{Max}\,(uS - K, 0) = \text{Max}\,(150 - 120, 0) = 30$$

$$C_d = \text{Max}\,(dS - K, 0) = \text{Max}\,(100 - 120, 0) = 0$$

The call option expires in one time period.

The stock price is currently \$100, and after one period, the price will be either \$150 or \$100.

$$uS = 1.5\,(\$100) = \$150$$
$$dS = 1.0\,(\$100) = \$100$$

With the call having an exercise price of $120, the value of the call at the end of the period will be either $30 (with a stock price of $150) or $0 (with a stock price of $100).

To solve for Δ and B we utilize equations (21.3) and (21.4). Since $(u - d) = .5$ and $(C_u - C_d) = 30$,

$$\Delta = \frac{C_u - C_d}{(u - d)S} = \frac{\$30}{.5\,(\$100)} = \frac{\$30}{\$50} = .60 \text{ shares}$$

$$B = \frac{uC_d - dC_u}{(u - d)r} = \frac{-1(\$30)}{.5\,(1.1)} = \frac{-60}{1.1} = -\$54,55$$

The negative value for B indicates that funds should be borrowed.

For each call, .6 of a share or .6 ($100) = $60 of common stock should be purchased and $60/1.1 = $54.55 should be borrowed (the payment of the debt at time 1 will be $60). If u occurs, the value of the portfolio will be

Common Stock	Debt: rB	Total
$150 (.6) = $90	−$60	$30

If d occurs, the value of the portfolio will be

Common Stock	Debt: rB	Total
$100 (.6) = $60	−$60	$0

The $30 and the $0 are the two payoffs given by the call. The initial value of the call is

$$C = \Delta S + B = \$60.00 - \$54.55 = \$5.45$$

The .6 of a share of stock costs $60, of which $54.45 is borrowed at an interest cost of .10. No matter which of the two outcomes occurs, the investor receives the same amount in period 1 as if a call had been purchased.

If a call is selling at a market price different from $5.45, then an arbitrager who knows how to construct a hedge portfolio can make a riskless profit. For example, suppose the call is selling for $10. Since the call is overpriced, the arbitrager will sell (write) calls. A person who sells a call becomes obligated to buy or own stock if the call is exercised, since the stock must be supplied. To guarantee a profit, the arbitrager buys .6 shares of stock and borrows $54.55 at the same time that the call is sold. The period 0 cash flows are then

$$-\$60 + \$54.55 + \$10 = \$4.55$$

In period 1, the arbitrager sells the stock, repays the debt and, if the call is exercised, buys a share of stock in the market and delivers it to the owner of the call in exchange for the exercise price. If the stock goes up, the call will be exercised and the period 1 cash flows will be

$$(1.5)\ 60\ -\ (1.1)\ 54.55\ -\ (1.5)\ 100\ +\ 120$$

$$90\ -\ 60\ -\ 150\ +\ 120\ =\ 0$$

If the stock price remains at \$100, the call will not be exercised, and the arbitrager will sell the stock and use the proceeds to pay off the debt. In this case, period 1 cash flows will be

$$60\ -\ 60\ =\ 0$$

Thus, when the call is overpriced, the arbitrager can sell calls and make a riskless profit equal to the difference between the market price and the net cost of the hedge portfolio. If the call is selling for less than the cost of the hedge portfolio, the arbitrager will reverse all the perceding transactions, selling .6 shares of stock short for \$60, lending \$54.55 at 10 percent, and buying a call. The period 0 cash flows will equal the difference between the correct value of the call and its market price, and the period 1 cash flows will net out to zero. In summary, arbitragers have opportunities for a riskless profit whenever the call price differs from the net cost of the replicating hedge portfolio. Arbitragers who sell calls when they are overpriced and buy them when they are underpriced will prevent the market price of a call from deviating from the market value of the equivalent hedge portfolio. This approach to call valuation is known as valuation by arbitrage.

If we were studying a multiperiod case, the portfolio (stock, debt, and calls) would have to be adjusted so that the appropriate amounts of each were held so that the portfolio was always hedged. If the time periods become very small and trading is continuous, we are then led to the Black–Scholes model of option valuation. The Black–Scholes model is consistent with the binomial model of this section, if we let the time periods become very short and allow continuous trading.

Black–Scholes

In 1973 F. Black and M. Scholes published a paper titled "The Pricing of Options and Corporate Liabilities" in the *Journal of Political Economy*. The model presented in that paper has drastically changed the approach to studying options as well as other securities. They derive a valuation formulation for an option where all the inputs may be observed except one, and for that one input, reasonable estimates can be computed.

Black and Scholes make many assumptions in their derivation. The effect of the assumptions is being tested by many researchers. Among these assumptions are

1. The volatility (standard deviation) of the stock's return may be estimated.
2. There is a risk-free rate that is constant through time.
3. There are no transaction costs, and the seller receives the proceeds from short sales.
4. Taxes are not relevant.
5. There are no dividends.
6. The stock price follows a random walk, and the price at time t is log normally distributed.

The basic logic used by Black and Scholes in deriving their formula is similar to the logic used in the previous single-period binomial example. Their formula is derived by assuming an economic environment in which arbitragers can replicate the payoffs from the call option during the next instant with a hedge portfolio of stocks and bonds. They calculate a value for the call option that is priced so that profitable riskless arbitrage is impossible. Assuming that the stock price follows what is called a lognormal distribution (the natural log of the stock price is normally distribution), then Black and Scholes find the value of an option to be equal to

$$C = SN(h_1) - (r^{-T})KN(h_1 - \sigma\sqrt{T}) \tag{21.6}$$

where

$$h_1 = \frac{\ln \dfrac{S}{K} + \left[\ln r + \dfrac{\sigma^2}{2}\right]T}{\sigma\sqrt{T}} \tag{21.7}$$

$N(h_1)$ = the cumulative normal probability distribution (left tail) for h_1 standard deviations

K = the exercise price

S = the stock price now

$\ln$ = the natural logarithm

$r = 1 + r_f$ = the risk-free interest rate plus 1

T = the time till maturity

σ = the standard deviation of the rate of return of the common stock (this is the only input that cannot be observed)

The Black–Scholes model assumes that the future stock prices will be log normally distributed with a fixed standard deviation, but that is the extent of the assumption about the expected return on the common stock. The expected return of the common stock affects the value of the option in this model only through its effect on the price of the stock.

EXAMPLE 21.2

$$S = \$41.50 \text{ stock price now}$$

$$K = \$40.00 \text{ exercise price}$$

$$T = .4 \text{ time till maturity is } .4 \text{ of a year}$$

$$r = 1 + r_f = 1.05 = \text{interest rate plus } 1$$

$$\sigma = .1124 = \text{standard deviation of the annual meter return of the stock}$$

$$\sigma = .1124$$

$$\frac{S}{K} = \frac{41.50}{10} = 1.0375$$

$$\frac{\sigma^2}{2} = 0.0063$$

$$\ln r = \ln 1.05 = .0488$$

$$\ln \frac{S}{K} = \ln 1.0375 = .0368$$

$$T = 0.4 \text{ years}$$

$$\sigma \sqrt{T} = .0711$$

$$r^{-T} = .9807$$

We need to determine the value of h_1:

$$h_1 = \frac{\ln \dfrac{S}{K} + [\ln (r) + (\sigma^2/2)]T}{\sigma \sqrt{T}} = \frac{.0368 + (.0488 + .0063)\,.4}{.0711}$$

$$= .8277$$

$$h_1 - \sigma \sqrt{T} = .8277 - .0711 = .7566$$

$$C = SN(h_1) - r^{-T} KN(h_1 - \sigma \sqrt{T})$$
$$= \$41.50\, N(.8277) - .9807(\$40.00)N(.7566)$$
$$= \$41.50(.7973) - .9807(\$40.00)(.7838)$$
$$= \$33.00 - \$30.74 = \$2.26.$$

Definition of a Put Option

A *call* option gives the owner the right to buy an asset. A *put* option gives its owner the right to sell an asset. Specifically,

A put option is a contract giving its owner the right to sell a specified asset at a fixed price on or before a specified date.

Just as there are American and European call options, there are American and European put options, which give the owner the right to sell at any time before the specified date (American put) or only on the specified date (European put). Models of the type used to value call options can also be extended to value put options. The basic approach is similar. A hedge portfolio is created that has the same payoff as the put option. The value of the put option is equal to the value of the hedge portfolio. It is beyond the scope of this book to consider the details of valuing put options, but the concept is very useful in capital budgeting situations, as we will see in the remainder of this chapter.

Option Valuation When There Is No Hedge Portfolio

There are many situations in which the decision maker has an option but in which it is not easy to devise a hedge portfolio. Without a hedge portfolio, the value of the option cannot be determined using arbitrage. Nevertheless, the concept of an option may still be valuable.

Option theory contains two important lessons for capital budgeting. The first and most important lesson is that flexibility may be valuable. This lesson is applicable whether or not the option that provides the flexibility can be valued using arbitrage arguments. While ordinary capital budgeting techniques can be used to value options, it is important to remember that the asset being valued is an option. The magnitude of the cash flows that will be generated by an option are usually very sensitive to the state of nature that obtains. The same applies when there is an option component to a complex asset.

The second lesson is that sometimes, with enough ingenuity, it may be possible to devise an appropriate hedge portfolio that can be used to value the option using arbitrage.

Vacant Land

The following example will illustrate the points made in the previous section.[5] We want to value a piece of vacant land in a developed section of a city. It is known that the "highest and best" use of the land is for a condominium apartment building. It is possible to build either a six- or nine-unit building on the land.

A common approach is to determine the best type of building to build on the land and estimate the net present value of the cash flows (excluding the cost of

[5] This example is based on Sheridan Titman, "Urban Land Prices Under Uncertainty," *American Economic Review*, June 1985, pp. 505–514.

the land) that would be generated if such a building were constructed. This provides an estimate of the value of the land for immediate development. But the vacant land has some of the characteristics of an option. If construction is delayed one period, the owner has the option of choosing between a six-unit building or a nine-unit building. The option may be valuable if the most profitable alternative next period could be different from the most profitable current alternative because economic conditions have changed. Consider a specific example.

1. Current interest rate, $k = .12$
2. Current value of a condominium: $100,000 (six units are worth $600,000)
3. Future value of a condominium
   a. Under favorable conditions: $120,000
   b. Under unfavorable conditions: $90,000
4. Construction costs (this year and next)
   a. For six-condominium building: $480,000
   b. For nine-condominium building: $810,000

We also assume that the condominiums can be rented and that the rent would cover the cash outlays (taxes, heat, maintenance, and so on) other than the cost of money that are associated with owning the condominiums. (The model could be adjusted to cover cases in which the rent covered more or less than this amount, but this assumption simplifies the example without eliminating any essential element.[6] There are two alternatives: Develop the land now or develop it next year.

We would like to know which alternative is better and how much the land is worth.

First consider the value of the land if it is developed immediately. With a six-condominium building, the net value is $600,000 − $480,000 = $120,000. With a nine-condominium building, the net value is $900,000 − $810,000 = $90,000. Since the six-condominium building adds more value than the nine-unit building, the land is worth $120,000 if construction is started this year.

Next consider the possibilities if construction is delayed for one period. We do not yet know what condominiums will be worth next period. However, calculations of the sort made in the previous paragraph will indicate that

1. If condominiums are worth $120,000 next year, the best decision will be to construct a nine-unit building yielding a net value of 9 ($120,000) − $810,000 = $270,000.
2. If condominiums are worth $90,000 next year, the best decision will be to construct a six-unit building yielding a net value of 6 ($90,000) − $480,000 = $60,000.

---

[6] Titman assumes the rent exceeds expenses by $8,000. This leads to a difference in the numerical value of his solution and ours.

The conventional capital budgeting approach would be to discount the expected cash flows by an appropriate discount rate to determine the risk-adjusted present value of the land if construction is delayed until next period. Suppose there is a .9 probability of an increase in condominium prices next year. Then the expected value of a condominium next period is $117,000 [.9 (120,000) + .1 (90,000)]. If condominiums are correctly priced, this suggests that the appropriate discount rate is 17 percent [$117,000/1.17 = $100,000]. The expected value of the proceeds from developing the land next period would be .9 ($270,000) + .1 ($90,000) = $252,000. The present value of this amount at 17 percent would be $215,385. This suggests that development should be delayed until next year (which is correct) and that the land is worth $252,000 (which is wrong).

We will now use an option-pricing approach to value the land. The vacant land has the characteristics of a call option. If development is delayed and condominium prices go up, the option will pay off C_u = $270,000 next year (the value with nine units). If development is delayed and condominium prices go down, the option will pay off C_d = $60,000 next year (the value with six units).

It is possible to devise a reasonable hedge portfolio that has the same payoffs as the land and therefore can be used to price the land. In the hedge portfolio for land, condominiums will take the place of stock in the hedge portfolio for a traded call option.

Let S equal the present market value of a condominium. Existing condominiums can be bought or sold for $100,000. Then, in the notation previously used for stock options and measuring all dollar amounts in thousands of dollars, we have the following facts:

$$u = 1.2, \quad d = .9, \quad r = 1.12, \quad S = 100$$
$$C_u = 270 \quad C_d = 60$$

To construct a hedge portfolio, we need to solve for Δ and B, which we can do using equations (21.3) and (21.4).

$$\Delta = \frac{C_u - C_d}{S(u - d)} = \frac{270 - 60}{100\,(.3)} = \frac{210}{30} = 7$$

$$B = \frac{uC_d - dC_u}{(u - d)r} = \frac{72 - 243}{(.3)\,1.12} = \frac{-171}{.336} = -508.93$$

The value of this hedge portfolio is found by using equation (21.5):

$$C = \Delta S + B = 7\,(100) - 508.92 = 191.08$$

Using an option-pricing approach, the value of the land is $191,080. When an option-pricing approach is possible, it is usually more accurate than an estimate computed using discounted expected cash flows.

Option Situations Involving Real Assets

We now consider a series of situations in which the decision maker has an option. There may or may not be securities or other assets that will enable us to form an exact hedge portfolio. Our purpose is to provide examples in which the existence of an option provides flexibility that would affect the value of an investment.

Most situations involving options can be considered to be call options or put options, but they occur in many guises and frequently in combinations.

Call options provide the owner with the option to make an investment or to acquire an asset.

Suppose a firm has decided to build a new factory and is searching for a site. The new factory will contain 100,000 square feet on one floor. To provide parking and fire lanes around the building, a minimum of four acres (about 180,000 square feet) is required. The firm is considering two sites that are equally desirable in terms of location, availability of public facilities, real estate tax rates, and so on. One site, a four-acre lot surrounded by other factories, is available for $160,000. A second site, a six-acre lot, is available for $200,000. Management does not expect to need more than 100,000 square feet of manufacturing space for the foreseeable future.

In this case, the second site provides the option of expanding the factory without relocating. This has some value. We cannot tell whether it is worth $40,000 without further analysis. How certain is management that additional space will not be needed? The more uncertainty about space requirement, the more valuable the option. If the firm buys the first site and then finds that more space is needed, it will have to relocate. This might be easy to do if there are many suitable sites available, or it might be difficult. If relocating is costly or difficult in some other way, the option provided by the extra land is more valuable. The firm may find that even 100,000 square feet is more than it needs, in which case it may wish to sell the site at some future date. The resale value of the factory will depend on how much vacant land is available with it.

One way to analyze this problem is to consider the choice as involving two independent investments. The first investment is the acquisition of four acres of land for a new factory at $160,000. The second investment is the acquisition of two additional acres of vacant land for an additional $40,000. Since the firm is prepared to build a 100,000-square-foot factory now, we can presume that the net present value of accepting the first investment is positive. Since the firm is not prepared to build more than 100,000 square feet of factory space now, we can assume that the second investment has a negative NPV. If the alternatives were to build the factory addition now or never, the decision might be to reject the second investment (buy only four acres).

However, the second site has the characteristics of a call option. The underlying asset is an expanded factory. (If the firm buys the site, it has the option to expand its factory without moving the entire operation to a new site.)

The striking price of the option is the cost of the expansion. At the present time, the value of the underlying asset is less than the striking price. (The value of the expanded factory space is less than its costs of construction.) Therefore, it does not pay to exercise the option by building the new factory now. However, the option has no fixed expiration date, since if it is not exercised now, it can be exercised at any time in the future. Therefore, the value of the option may be greater than zero. If the value of the option is greater than $40,000, the firm should accept the second investment (buy the larger site).

Unexploited investment opportunities typically have the characteristics of an option. The NPV of the investment, as conventionally computed, describes the expected net present value of immediately accepting the investment. This conventionally computed expected NPV is comparable to the theoretical (or minimum) value of a call.

If the investment opportunity will not be available in the future, or if the investment opportunity is certain to be worth less if it is undertaken at a later date, then the NPV is the appropriate decision criterion. However, if it is feasible to delay accepting the investment and there is a chance that the investment may become more valuable in the future because of changing conditions, then the decision about whether or not the investment should be undertaken immediately is comparable to the decision to exercise a call option.

It is not generally optimal to exercise a call option as soon as the underlying asset is greater than the exercise price. The issues of timing discussed in Chapter 12 are relevant here. One important consideration is whether the same investment opportunity is available to competitors. In general, if competitors have access to the same investment, and acceptance by one competitor reduces the value of the investment to the others, then a firm will want to accept investments as soon as their net present values become positive. However, if the firm has a monopoly of the right to accept investments, then it may not be optimal to accept an investment just as soon as immediate acceptance produces a positive expected net present value.

Put Options on Real Assets

Put options provide the owner of an asset with the right to dispose of it on favorable terms.

In some circumstances, the owner of an asset may possess a put option that adds value to the asset over and above its use value to the owner. The necessary circumstances are that a secondary market exist for the asset and that the price at which the asset can be sold in the secondary market may be different than the value of the asset to the present owner. When these circumstances exist, then the minimum value of the put option is the largest of the use value of the asset to the present owner and the resale value of the asset.

The existence of a put option guarantees that the value of an asset will never be less than its resale value. If there is uncertainty about the future use value of the asset, it may not be optimal to sell the asset as soon as its use value falls below the market value. The existence of transaction costs can contribute to a situation in which it is optimal to retain an asset that could be sold for more than its expected use value.

Let us define a specialized asset to be an asset with only one specific use and a generic asset to be an asset for which there are many possible uses. A steel mill is an example of a specialized asset. It is good for making steel and not much else. It is hard to dispose of except by selling the whole steel mill. Except for differences in management (which could be a big exception), there is no reason for the mill to be more valuable to one owner than to another. Even if steel mills were easy to buy and sell, their market price would be reasonably close to their use value.

The value of an option derives from the fact that the exercise price may, under some conditions, differ from the value of the underlying asset. With specialized assets such as steel mills, this is not likely to be the case, and the option of selling the asset is not likely to be of great value.

By contrast, personal computers and airplanes are generic assets, with many possible uses. A firm may buy such an asset for one use. If it turns out not to be valuable in that use, it can be switched to another use within the firm or sold to someone else who has a more valuable use for it.

EXAMPLE 21.3

A firm buys a personal computer for its accounting function and then decides to contract out its bookkeeping. The personal computer can be used for word processing with little change in its hardware.

EXAMPLE 21.4

An airline buys a plane for use on its New York-to-Dallas route. If demand declines, the plane can be shifted to the Chicago-to-San Francisco route. Such an airplane has many uses. On the other hand, if an airplane is especially designed to fly nonstop from San Francisco to Tokyo, it may not be as appropriate for shorter routes.

Conclusions

Strategic net present value (S-NPV) expands the set of alternatives that the capital budgeting analyst must consider. It recognizes when flexibility exists and places a value on that flexibility. The value of flexibility can be estimated using the theory of pricing options; but frequently a quantitative valuation will be extremely complex, and it will be necessary to substitute a qualitative input.

We normally assume that a firm has an infinite life, and an investment in real depreciable assets has a finite life. This latter assumption can be faulty if, at the end of the finite life, the firm's future cash flows will be affected by whether or not the investment is undertaken. The firm will have an option to do the second investment, and that option has a value today.

Admittedly, an intelligent, knowledgeable analyst might place a probability on the positive net present value of a second investment and add this expected value to the net present value of the basic investment. This is economically equivalent to computing the value of the option to undertake the second investment. Option theory causes us to be more sensitive to the opportunities that might exist in the future if we take action today, even where option theory cannot be used to obtain exact quantitative measures, because we cannot find the securities or assets to form zero-value portfolios. This new perspective can be valuable.

There is no question that the application of option theory to capital budgeting decisions will be a major capital budgeting development of the next decade, and managers involved in a firm's capital budgeting process should understand when these concepts can usefully be applied. Even where exact quantitative results cannot be obtained, option theory makes an important contribution by calling attention to the existence of the alternatives and the need to value flexibility that results from a given investment alternative.

REVIEW EXAMPLE 21.1

Determine the equilibrium value of a call if the stock is now selling at $80 and after one period it will sell at either $100 (with .8 probability) or $56 (with .2 probability). The exercise price is $95. Funds can be borrowed or lent at zero risk at .10. The call option expires in one time period.

Solution

$$S = \$80, \qquad u = 1.25, \qquad d = .70, \qquad K = \$95$$

$$C_u = \quad 5, \qquad C_d = \quad 0, \qquad r = 1.10$$

$$\Delta = \frac{C_u - C_d}{(u - d)S} = \frac{5}{(1.25 - .70)\,80} = \frac{5}{\$44}$$

$$= .113636 \text{ and } \Delta S = \$9.09$$

$$B = \frac{uC_d - dC_u}{(u - d)_r} = \frac{-.70\,(5)}{(.55)\,1.10} = -5.785$$

$$C = \Delta S + B = \$9.09 - \$5.79 = \$3.30$$

If a stock price of $100 occurs, we have

$$\$100\,(.113636) = \$11.36 \text{ common stock value}$$
$$5.785\,(1.10) = -6.36 \text{ debt value}$$
$$\text{Sum} = \$5.00 \text{ value of call}$$

If a stock price of $56 occurs, we have

$$\$56 \,(.113636) = \$6.36 \text{ common stock}$$
$$5.785 \,(1.10) = -6.36 \text{ debt}$$
$$\text{Sum} = 0 \text{ value of call}$$

REVIEW EXAMPLE 21.2

The Flexible Company has a great opportunity to invest $40,000,000 for a year. While there is a large probability of earning .54 for the year if there is no tax-law change, there is some probability that only .04 will be earned with a tax-law change. The cost of debt is .10. The RANPV of the investment is zero.

A venture capitalist has offered to invest $10,000,000 in the project if it will be paid $15,000,000 at the end of the year if no tax-law changes take place and will be paid nothing if there is a tax law change.

Should the Flexible Company go ahead with the project?

Solution

$$C_u = \$15,000,000, \qquad C_d = \$0, \qquad u = 1.54, \qquad d = 1.04$$
$$r = 1.10, \qquad\qquad\qquad u - d = .50 \qquad S = \$40,000,000$$

$$\Delta = \frac{C_u - C_d}{(u - d)S} = \frac{15,000,000 - 0}{.5\,(40,000,000)} = .75$$

$$B = \frac{uC_d - dC_u}{(u - d)r} = \frac{1.54\,(0) - 1.04\,(15,000,000)}{.50\,(1.10)} = \frac{20,800,000}{.5\,(1.10)} = -\$28,364,000$$

The debt payment will be (1.10) 37,818,00 = $41,600,000.
Solving for C:

$$C = \Delta S - B = 30,000,000 - 28,364,000 = \$1,636,000$$

The time 0 payment received from the venture capitalist will be $10,000,000. The Flexible Company only needs $1,636,000 to break even. It is ahead by $8,364,000 no matter what happens.

PROBLEMS

21.1 A warrant gives the holder the right to purchase a share of common stock any time in the next five years at a price of $20 per share. The current market price of the stock is $15 per share. No dividends are anticipated, and the stock price is expected to grow to $30. The time value of money is 12 percent.
  a. What is the minimum value of the warrant?
  b. What is the maximum value of the warrant?
  c. What is the present value of the warrant based on a common stock price of $30 at time 5?

21.2 Assume the same facts as in problem 21.1 except that an investor believes that the stock price will increase to $40 per share five years from now.
  What effect will this have on the three warrant values calculated in problem 21.1?

21.3 Assume the same facts as problem 21.1, where an investor believes the stock price will rise to $30 five years from now. The stock pays zero dividends.
  a. Would an expected present value-maximizing investor buy the warrant at a price of $5 or the stock at a price of $15 per share?
  b. Would you prefer to buy one share of common stock or three warrants?

21.4 Assume the same facts as in problem 21.3 except that a $1 dividend per share is anticipated each year.
  What effect will this have on the buy-stock-versus-buy-warrant decision?

21.5 Suppose that the warrant in problem 21.4 could be purchased for $5 and that a common stock price rise to $45 was expected to occur within days.
  What effect will this have on the intrinsic present value and maximum price of the warrant?

21.6 A stock is now selling at $80 per share. You buy a put to sell the stock at $75. The cost of the put is $4. The stock goes down to $72 just before the put expires.
  What was the profitability of buying the put?

21.7 Assume that an investor has $10,000 to invest. Stock can be purchased at $20 per share (500 shares can be purchased). Call options to purchase 100 shares at a price of $25 can be purchased for $500 (options to purchase 2,000 shares can be purchased).
  Compare the change in the investor's wealth from buying the stock and buying the options if the stock price at the expiration of the option is
  a. $35.
  b. $24.

21.8 Determine the equilibrium value of a call if the stock is now selling at $100, and after one period it will sell at either $160 (with .5 probability) or $80 (with .5 probability). The exercise price is $120. Funds can be borrowed or lent at zero risk at .20. The call option expires in one time period.

21.9 (*Continuation of problem 21.8.*) Determine the value of the portfolio after one period for an investor who sold (wrote) a fully hedged call option at the equilibrium price at time zero
  a. If the stock price is $160.
  b. If the stock price is $80.

21.10 If the probability of the stock price going to $160 is .9 instead of .5 and .1 probability of $80 instead of .5, how does this affect the answers to problems 21.8 and 21.9?

21.11   Assume that an investor has computed

$$\Delta S = \$50.00$$

$$B = -\$33.33$$

for a perfectly hedged portfolio. The call option is selling at a price of $20.00.
a. What should the investor do?
b. What risk does the investor have?

21.12   Using the Black–Scholes formulation, compute the value of a option that expires in one year ($T = 1$) if the following facts apply.

$$S = \$45 \text{ stock price now}$$

$$K = \$40 \text{ exercise price}$$

$$r = 1.20 \ (r_f = .20)$$

$$\sigma^2 = .0225$$

$$\sigma = .15$$

21.13   The XYZ Company has the opportunity to invest $32,000,000. At time 1 it will earn either a .30 return ($41,600,000) or a .05 return ($33,600,000). Debt costs .11. The company needs to avoid the possibility of earning only .05. For an expenditure of $3,000,000, it can obtain the right to sell the asset for $41,600,000.

Is the investment desirable without the $3,000,000 expenditure?

Is the investment desirable with the $3,000,000 expenditure?

21.14   The ABC Company has a great opportunity to invest $32,000,000 for a year. While there is a large probability of earning .30 for the year if there are no trade restrictions, there is some probability that only .05 will be earned (with trade restrictions). Since debt costs .11, the earning of .05 could be a very bad event. The firm could not survive with a .05 return.

An investor has offered to advance $4,000,000 for the project. The investor will be paid $8,000,000 at the end of the year if there are no trade restrictions; otherwise the investor receives nothing.

Should the ABC Company go ahead with the project?

REFERENCES

Abel, Andrew B., "Optimal Investment Under Uncertainty," *American Economic Review*, March 1983, pp. 228–33.

Baldwin, C. Y., S. P. Mason, and R. S. Ruback, "Evaluation of Government Subsidies to Large Scale Energy Projects: A Contingent Claims Approach," Harvard Business School working paper, 1983.

Bernanke, Ben S., "Irreversibility, Uncertainty, and Cyclical Investment," *Quarterly Journal of Economics*, February 1983, pp. 85–106.

Black, F., and M. Scholes, "The Pricing of Options and Corporate Liabilities," *Journal of Political Economy*, May 1973, pp. 637–659.

Brennan, M. J., and E. S. Schwartz, "Evaluating Natural Resource Investments," *Journal of Business*, January 1985, pp. 135–157.

————, and ————, "A New Approach to Evaluating Natural Resource Investments," *Midland Corporate Finance Journal*, Spring 1985, pp. 37–47.

Cox, J. C., S. A. Ross, and M. Rubinstein, "Option Pricing: A Simplified Approach," *Journal of Financial Economics*, September 1979 pp. 229–263.

————, and M. Rubinstein, *Option Markets* (Englewood Cliffs, NJ: Prentice-Hall, 1985).

Dukierman, Alex, "The Effects of Uncertainty on Investment Under Risk Neutrality with Endogenous Information," *Journal of Political Economy*, June 1980, pp. 462–475.

Hartman, Richard, "The Effects of Price and Cost Uncertainty on Investment," *Journal of Economic Theory*, October 1972, pp. 258–266.

Jarrow, R., and A. Rudd, *Option Pricing* (Homewood, IL: R. D. Irwin, 1983).

Kensinger, John W., "Adding the Value of Active Management into the Capital Budgeting Equation," *Midland Corporate Finance Journal*, Spring 1987, pp. 31–42.

Majd, S., and R. S. Pindyck, "Time to Build, Option Value, and Investment Decisions," *Journal of Financial Economics*, March 1987, pp. 7–27.

Margrabe, W., "The Value of an Option to Exchange One Asset for Another," *Journal of Finance*, March 1978, pp. 177–186.

Mason, S. P., and R. C. Merton, "The Role of Contingent Claims Analysis in Corporate Finance," in E. I. Altman and M. G. Subrahmanyam, *Recent Advances in Corporate Finance* (*Homewood*, IL: Irwin, 1985), pp. 7–54.

McDonald, Robert, and Daniel R. Siegel, "Investment and the Valuation of Firms When There is an Option to Shut Down," *International Economic Review*, October 1985, pp. 331–349.

Merton, R. C. "The Relationship Between Put and Call Option Prices: Comment," *Journal of Finance*, March 1973, pp. 183–184.

————, "Theory of Rational Option Pricing," *Bell Journal of Economics and Management Science*, Spring 1973, pp. 141–183.

Pindyck, R., "Irreversible Investment, Capacity Choice, and the Value of the Firm," Massachusetts Institute of Technology, Working Paper 1802–86, June 1986.

————, "Uncertainty and Exhaustible Resource Markets," *Journal of Political Economy*, December 1980, pp. 1203–1225.

Robichek, A., and J. Van Horn, "Abandonment Value and Capital Budgeting," *Journal of Finance*, December 1967, pp. 577–590.

Schwab, B., and P. Lusztig, "A Note on Investment Evaluations in Light of Uncertain Future Opportunities," *Journal of Finance*, December 1972, pp. 1093–1100.

Siegel, D. R., J. L. Smith, and J. L. Paddock, "Valuing Offshore Oil Properties with Option Pricing Models," *Midland Corporate Finance Journal*, Spring 1987, pp. 22–30.

Smith, C. W., "Applications of Option Pricing Analysis," in *Handbook of Financial Economics*, J. L. Bicksler. (Ed.) (Amsterdam: North Holland Publishing Company, 1979), pp. 80–121.

———, "Option Pricing: A Review," *Journal of Financial Economics*, March 1976, pp. 3–51.

Stultz, R., "Options on the Minimum or Maximum of Two Risky Assets: Analysis and Applications," *Journal of Financial Economics*, January 1982, pp. 161–185.

Titman, S., "Urban Land Prices Under Uncertainty," *American Economic Review*, June 1985, pp. 505–514.

Trigeorgis, L., "A Conceptual Options Framework for Capital Budgeting," Harvard Business School, Working Paper, October 1985.

———, "Valuation of Shared-Simple-Deferrable Real Options: The Impact of Competitive Interaction on the Value of Real Investment Opportunities," Harvard Business School, Working Paper, revised November 1985.

Trigeorgis, L., and S. P. Mason, "Valuing Managerial Flexibility," *Midland Corporate Finance Journal*, Spring 1987, pp. 14–21.

P A R T   I V

Cases

If we have a correct theory but merely prate about it, pigeonhole it and do not put it into practice, then that theory, however good, is of no significance.

Mao Tse-Tung, "On Practice" (July 1937), in Quotations from Chairman Mao Tse-Tung *(New York: Bantam Books, 1967), p. 176.*

Part IV contains a set of cases for use throughout the course. Most of the cases are based on actual situations, but we have generally changed the names to insure confidentiality.

In addition to the included cases, we have also used in class the following Harvard Business School cases:

The Super Project (9-112-034 Rev.5/80)
The Molecular Compounds Corporation (9-210-088-FM 395)

"Super" deals with the definition of cost and basic DCF versus ROI calculations. "Mocom" deals with evaluation of projects with different risk and performance evaluations.

The Oneida Tomato Company*

The following letter was received by one of the authors from Mr. Walter Payne, the chief executive officer of Oneida Tomato, a food-processing firm, in response to a request to make a case presentation to a capital budgeting class.

I think I am probably the wrong person to speak before your Capital Budgeting class as we are totally unscientific when it comes to this subject. When making capital investment decisions we generally do not give serious consideration to the payback analysis and then compare this payback with alternative uses of capital. Our long-term marketing objectives tend to be the overriding consideration when we decide where to invest capital dollars. In many cases we know that the payback is going to be extremely poor for a number of years, but we make the investment anyway if it is necessary to reach our long-term market penetration goals.

In summary, capital budgeting plays second fiddle to the strategic business policy decisions that are overriding importance in a company such as ours devoted to marketing branded consumer products. I would probably end up contradicting much of your course material and adding little that would be of value in terms of capital budgeting. In many industries, I am sure that a more scientific approach than we use is a valuable management tool. For better or worse, we have never considered it to be particularly significant in our decision-making process.

Oneida is primarily engaged in processing and distributing tomatoes. After some persuasion, the chief executive, Mr. Walter Payne, who is also the founder of the company, agreed to describe a capital budgeting decision recently faced by his firm.

The Oneida Tomato Company obtained most of its raw material from the section of the country in which the company had started and where most of its

---

* Names of persons, places, and things in this case have been changed to preserve confidentiality.

processing plants were located. Sales were also concentrated in that region. Mr. Payne was convinced that the success of the company depended on developing national distribution; he believed that substantial economies in advertising costs could be obtained if the company became a national advertiser. Weather conditions caused substantial variation from year to year in the supply of tomatoes available in any single region of the country. Accordingly, he felt it imperative to develop sources of supply in several regions of the country.

The investment decision that Mr. Payne discussed with the class was the construction of a new tomato processing plant in the Southeast, a region of the country in which Oneida had no previous processing facilities.

Suppose that you are in charge of a study to evaluate this investment. The results of the study will be presented to Mr. Payne before he makes the final decision on this project. Outline the topics that you think should be included in the study. What information would need to be collected to do the study? To what extent would the results of the study depend on judgment? To what extent would they depend on quantitative data? Do you think the results could be expressed in terms of expected cash flows? Explain.

Wellesley Woolen Company

The Wellesley Woolen Company was an old, established Massachusetts textile company. It specialized in woolens used in high-style garments.

The controller stated that the company had not made a major investment decision in recent years. Machines were modernized but were not frequently replaced. In fact, almost all the machines had been purchased over fifteen years ago.

Another member of top management stated, "The woolen industry is intensely competitive. This is illustrated by the fact that mills must work three shifts in order to make a profit. The Wellesley Woolen Company has been able to exist by limiting capital expenditures to modifications of equipment. A large number of the machines now owned were purchased second-hand. The advantages of more modern equipment are that it is somewhat faster, has larger cards, and requires less maintenance. These savings do not justify the purchase of new equipment. Firms that have bought new equipment have run ino difficulties. For example, a new Southern mill was recently closed because the owners couldn't pay for the capital equipment they had purchased."

A seller of textile machinery justified the policy of the Wellesley Woolen Company. The larger number of textile firms going out of business created an extensive market in second-hand textile equipment. This machinery was only slightly less efficient than more recent equipment. In fact, much of the used equipment was built after World War II. Prior to 1950 much of the second-hand equipment had been shipped to foreign markets. but in recent years this market had greatly disappeared. For example, the South American textile manufacturers would rather buy new German textile machinery than second-hand American machinery. They considered the German machinery more efficient and less likely to break down.

One problem encountered by textile machinery salesmen was the reluctance of textile manufacturers to accept radical changes in machinery. They preferred small changes because this did not create new problems of maintenance and repair. They also preferred to have all machines of one type to simplify the spare-parts problem.

Does Wellesley Woolen have an investment decision?

C A S E   3

Norwalk Screw Company

The Norwalk Screw Company was located in Norwalk, Connecticut. It was a privately held corporation, and capital expenditures were financed entirely out of funds generated by operations.

In choosing among different investment possibilities, management relied heavily on its experience. Because management generally had between fifteen and forty years' experience, the capital budgeting computations frequently were not made for specific decisions, although a capital budget was prepared.

An example of an investment decision that was decided affirmatively was the purchase of a zinc plater. The plater was purchased for $20,000. It increased capacity, eliminated expensive subcontracting, and reduced direct labor on this particular plating process from two workers to one. Management was very satisfied with the purchase. Equipment used in the manufacture of screws generally had a long life. It rarely became obsolete, although it was modified and improved.

A decision to be made was whether or not to operate a truck instead of using common carriers in the states of Connecticut and Rhode Island. The traffic manager prepared an analysis of costs and pounds of product transported during December (see Exhibits 1 and 2). The product transported included raw material, finished goods, and products requiring outside work.

EXHIBIT 1   Norwalk Screw Company. Inter-Works Communication

To: Controller
Subject: Truck Operation in Rhode Island and Connecticut

The New England Motor Rate Bureau is increasing the trucking rates 6 percent effective March 10. In an effort to avoid this increase and other future increases, we are planning to operate our own truck on a limited scale in the states of Rhode Island and Connecticut.

At the present time we are planning to use our two-and-one-half-ton truck to start this operation. Connecticut has been selected as the major point due to the fact that

EXHIBIT 2
Norwalk Screw Company: Analysis of Shipments in Rhode Island and Connecticut (Pounds of Freight)

Month of December	Shelton Out	Shelton In	New Britain Out	Hartford Out	Hartford In	Pawtucket Out	New Haven Out	Bridgeport In	Middleton In	Torrington In	Waterville In	Providence In
1	3,000	5,000					1,628					
2	2,662	5,475	2,552	783								
5	5,000	4,494			2,935							
6	3,791	4,412	459						306			600
7	624	940	519				57					
8	5,673	2,977						2,954	1,010			
9	1,530	1,075	3,701		831				128			2,000
12	4,123	5,297					522					
13	704	3,288	430	319	1,360	443			22			
14	2,279	2,206			1,057			2,730				
15	1,928	2,180	2,870	47	374				608			2,000
16	2,773	2,935		1,035	365					3,500		1,700
19	5,000	1,090			217				145	3,000		
20	4,052	1,900		1,022	210							
21	5,000	815			50				247		4,000	
27	4,953	4,825			48							
28	3,400	5,000				1,584						
29	2,112	1,532	2,015								3,500	
30		1,161	4,951		384						3,500	

we have a round-trip movement to Shelton, Connecticut. Each day we have considerable tonnage going to Shelton and coming back to our plant from there. In addition, we have good accounts at New Haven, New Britain, and Hartford, which would enable us to load approximately 5,000 pounds each day. Coming to our plant we also have freight from Bridgeport, Hartford, Torington, and Providence. The freight from Providence is ideal, in that it consists of set-up boxes and a class 1 commodity, which would ride perfectly over a load of screws or coils of brass.

Figures based on actual shipping and receiving during the month of December show that we paid $1,761.81 for both shipping and receiving charges covering nineteen shipping and receiving days, and average of $92.72 per day, or $463.60 per week.

Based on an average round trip of 280 miles per day at $.06 a mile for gas, oil, depreciation, etc., it would cost us $16.80 per day, or $84 a week. The drivers' wages would be approximately $100 per week based on forty hours at $1.82 per hour and ten hours overtime at $2.73 per hour. Our weekly cost would be $184 against $463.60 via common carrier, or a saving of $279.60 per week and $14,259.60 per year.

The service would by no means be limited to the points mentioned above and would be a very flexible operation to satisfy our customers' and our needs. Eventually it could develop into our using our own larger trucks over a greater area. This operation is scheduled to start March 1.

Your comments will be appreciated.

Very truly yours,
R. Smith
Traffic Manager

The analysis of the traffic manager indicated large savings, but the controller rejected the plan.

The cost of a new two-and-one-half-ton truck was $5,000. The company already owned one truck of this type and a pickup truck. Both of these vehicles were driven by one man.

The controller stated: "We generally reject if payback is more than two years." This is the usual approach to investments when the decision can be based on payback or return. Obviously, many investment decisions are made on other bases.

What action should the controller take, based on Mr. Smith's letter?

The Calculating Energy Saver

Joe Sharp, a famous history professor, heated his home with fuel oil. In an average winter he used 800 gallons of oil. Joe read somewhere that it was his patriotic duty to reduce his fuel consumption by adding additional insulation to his house. Also, he thought it might save him some money. Two alternatives were available. Method 1 cost $1,000 and would reduce fuel consumption by 12 percent. Method 2 would cost $1,500 and would reduce his fuel consumption by 15 percent. Fuel oil costs $1.20 a gallon now. Assume a real discount rate of 3 percent and an increase of 1 percent per year in the real price of fuel oil. Joe expects to sell his house in 20 years and move to a warm climate.

1. Measure and compare the investment worth of both methods, using the following:
   payback, IRR, NPV, equivalent annual return, and cost benefit ratio.
2. Which method of insulation do you think is better for Joe? Why?
3. Which measure would you use to explain your preference to Joe? Why? (Assume that he is not familiar with any of the measures.)

The A Company's Manual

The following is an extract from the A Company's manual. Read it and find those sections that you think should be revised.

Appendix: Time-Adjusting Return on Investment

This *Appropriation Request Handbook* uses and discusses an improved method for calculating the rate of return on an investment. This new method, called time-adjusted return on investment, or discounted cash flow, recognizes the principle that time has an economic value. You may also hear this new method referred to as the present value method.

This appendix will explain the theory behind using cash flows and discounting for the timing involved.

A. Why Discount Future Earning Power?

There are two basic reasons for weighing current earnings or cash flows more heavily than those expected in the future.

1. *Uncertainty*. Promise of future potential is based on many things. If any one of a series of things happens, this potential will not be fulfilled. This could consist of labor trouble, unforeseen national disaster, and so on, any one of which could adversely affect earnings.

2. *Alternative uses*. This is the only argument that applies to all capital investment decisions. Cash received in the business today can be reinvested in the operations to earn a profit. Cash expected to be received in the future should be discounted because it is not earning until received. This discount factor should be the required earnings rate, or the rate at which all new capital is expected to generate profit.

B. Required Earning Rate

One method of selecting a required rate is to take the average earning rate expected on funds now invested in the company's operations. This average rate can be adjusted to account for any special considerations that make an individual proposal different from historical averages.

The company has an average cash flow rate of return of approximately 17 percent. This rate is calculated as net profit after taxes from manufacturing operations plus depreciation, divided by net plant and equipment plus inventories.

Because there will always be investments that tend to reduce this historical return, a 20 percent rate of return should be considered a minimum for most future capital requirements. Any capital investment yielding substantially less than a 20 percent return may have merit to the company, but it will require a detailed justification.

C. The Cash Flow Concept

The stream of liquid funds that flow into or out of the business will determine the return on investment. Only cash can be used to purchase personnel, earn interest, or pay dividends.

Net income figures understate actual cash flows from operations because of the depreciation factor. By including this item, we tend to retain funds in the company that would otherwise be distributed in taxes or dividends.

The amount of funds derived from operation of the business, therefore, would be the figure of net income after taxes but before depreciation. The short-cut method of calculating this figure is merely to add back the depreciation charge to net profit after taxes. The result is a very close approximation to the true cash flow.

The stream of liquid funds may now be calculated over the life of a project. The main component parts of this stream are

1. *The project investment.* This, in turn, consists of the original capital investment, any subsequent capital outlay expected, any working capital required, any precious metals to be employed, and so on.
2. *Net profit after tax.*
3. *Depreciation charges.*
4. *Asset recovery.* In some cases, recovery of working capital, precious metals, or equipment can be predicted. When the timing of this recovery is known, the cash generated through tradein or sale should be treated as a cash inflow. In most cases, this timing will be unknown and the cash cannot be so treated.

The sum of all the foregoing components will be the net cash inflow or outflow from the operation.

D. Timing

As discussed, cash in hand at the present is worth more than is the promise of an equivalent amount in the future, since these present funds may be reemployed in some other phase of company operation. To compensate for this discrepancy, a series of present value tables has been drawn up.

These tables given the present value of $1 promised at any time in the future, given the expected earning rate of that money. In other words, the value of a promise to pay $1 to the company four years from now (in year 5) is the same as having $.44 in the treasury right now, if we assume we can earn 20 percent on our money. We therefore discount the promise of future earnings at the rates shown in the present value tables.

The cash inflows and outflows calculated should be tabulated for each year of any project's economic life. The net cash inflow (outflow) figure for each year should then be discounted at the appropriate rate of return to determine its total economic worth to the company.

E. Rate-of-Return Calculation

Projects that are obviously undesirable or those on which rates of return are so low or so high as to require detailed examination may be weeded out through a one-shot procedure: Discount the total annual net cash inflows (outflows) at 20 percent—the company's desired rate for new project investments. The sum of these discounted flows should total at least zero. If the resultant figure is negative, the earning rate on the new project is less than 20 percent. If the discounted sum is positive, the earning rate is greater than 20 percent. Any investment that shows a very large positive or negative discounted figure should be examined in detail.

Fall River Lumber Company

In considering the purchase of equipment for debarking logs, the financial analysis department of the Fall River Lumber Company prepared the following report.

Proposed Debarking Installation for Flakeboard Plant

Introduction

The flakeboard plant is using peeled aspen so that our finished board will have a light-colored appearance. This lighter appearance is felt to be necessary by the sales department if we wish to continue to point our product toward a higher-quality market.

Moreover, as the plant's operating efficiency is a direct function of the life of its flaker knives, the peeled wood will contribute somewhat to increasing this life by eliminating the abrasive action caused by the sand and dirt that are often found within the bark.

However, the primary consideration in maintaining an adequate knife life is that the moisture content in the aspen be sufficient (above 35 percent air dry) to act as a cooling agent on the flaker knives.

If the aspen supplied to the plant is too dry, the flaker knives heat up, thereby becoming dull, and the plant's operations are impaired. Past experience has demonstrated to us that the difference in flaker knife life is almost insignificant between using *freshly peeled aspen* and *freshly unpeeled aspen*, but quite significant between using *dry peeled aspen* and *freshly peeled aspen*.

In the initial stages of operations, the plant used fresh hand-peeled aspen direct from the wood dealers. However, because the hand peeling (commonly known as sap peeling) season lasts only during the trees' annual growth period (a six-week period from spring to early summer), it is only during this time that a sufficient volume (2 cords per person per day) can be maintained. Out of season, this type of production drops to $\frac{1}{2}$ cord per person per day, thus becoming uneconomical. Although a sufficient year's supply of aspen could possibly be bought during the six-week sap-peeling season, the wood would dry out in storage, and the problem of flaker knife life again would become the critical factor.

Chemical debarking must be ruled out as a possibility because the wood becomes too dry in the one-year period that is required for the tree to die and the bark to fall off.

Thus, the use of some kind of mechanical debarking equipment that would ensure a year-round supply of peeled wood with the correct moisture characteristics becomes necessary if we wish to continue producing our lighter-colored flakeboard.

Alternative Solutions

The following proposals exist as a possible means of supplying peeled aspen to the flakeboard plant:

1. Installing permanent debarking facilities at Fall River, employing King or Elmo equipment.
2. Utilizing portable debarkers at Fall River, such as the Leswork.

Recommendations

This study recommends installing a King debarker out in the woodyard. In addition, it recommends the use of mechanical feeding accessories and a bark burner. The estimated savings would be $40,000 per year, compared to our present portable Leswork installation. The total estimated investment would be $70,000. The return on this investment would be at the rate of 57 percent, or payback in one and three quarters years.

Summary of Findings

The problem as outlined in the introduction of this study of determining the most economical and sound engineering method of debarking aspen for the flakeboard plant is complicated.

Basically, it boils down to balancing our rate of production required to supply the flakeboard operations against a capital investment and estimated debarking cost per cord that we are willing to pay for.

Certain assumptions were made. The main ones, subject to the most variability, are

1. The estimated useful life of the debarkers.

2. The estimated repair and maintenance costs.

3. The machine production per hour.

The alternative of *buying peeled wood* is not recommended, and such rejection is based mainly on the following considerations.

1. The wide diversity in the location of the aspen stands, creating a difficult peeling setup in the field.

2. The uncertain supply in the winter season.

3. The higher operating costs for the wood dealer necessitated by his increased handling and depreciation expenses.

4. The possible legal problems arising from buying and renting debarkers to the wood dealers.

5. The reluctance of the wood dealers to debark in the field.

6. The uncertainty of getting clean wood.

Rejection of *portable debarkers at Fall River* is primarily based on a pure cost consideration. Maintaining our estimated production requirements of 1 million square feet per month in the flakeboard plant would necessitate reinvesting in portable debarkers at a rate that would more than offset the initial low investment cost. The low production inherent in these debarkers means running them at their capacity practically around the clock and thereby quickly reaching their estimated life of 5,000 cords.

The choice lies between buying a King debarker, either new or used, or an Elmo. A used King is rejected because its return on investment is less than that of a new King. Both the Elmo and King are substantially the same machine as far as the efficiency in debarking the wood goes. However, the rugged design of the Elmo has kept its repair and maintenance charges well under that of the King. While there are over one hundred King installations in operation, certain companies, such as the United States Paper Company of Flint, Michigan, are replacing their Kings with Elmos, as the latter seemed to hold up better. Nevertheless, the economic advantage evidenced by the higher rate of return of the new King as compared to the Elmo, 57 percent versus 49 percent (see Table 3), takes into consideration this more rugged design of the Elmo; yet this report still concludes that the King investment is the more advantageous for our requirements.

It is well to mention that the inherent savings of using an Elmo or a King debarker lie not only with the increased production (both over twice the hourly capacity of a Leswork), which lowers the total unit cost per cord of wood debarked, but also with the longer estimated life of the machines. The savings are not a result of an overall reduction in manpower.

Although the debarkers themselves do not require operating labor, the machine's higher productive capacities require that such men be utilized as spotters on the infeed and outfeed conveying equipment.

The economics of the study are summarized in Tables 1 to 4. The first three compare the operating costs and investments of a King, an Elmo, and a Leswork

TABLE 1   Cost Estimates for Flakeboard Plant Debarkers

	King (New)	King (Used)	Elmo	Leswork*
Debarker cost (with power)	$23,200	$16,000	$44,000	$4,000
Accessories (conveyors and deck, etc.)	37,425	27,700	52,000	—
Installation	9,650	14,600	9,800	300
Total investment	$70,275	$58,300	$105,800	$4,300
Fixed costs per cord	$0.82	$1.08	$0.74	$0.95
Variable costs per cord	1.16	1.32	0.72	2.87
Total estimated cost per cord	$1.98	$2.40	$1.46	$3.82

* Present Fall River operations (estimated three Lesworks required to meet production demands).

debarking installation. Table 4 summarizes the return-on-investment data of the King and Elmo installations as compared to our present Leswork operations.

Location

The location of a debarker installation is an important factor in determining the efficiency of its operation. The installation could be placed in one of two places:

1. Adjacent to the flakeboard plant.
2. Out in the woodyard.

Wood handling is a major consideration to this location decision, in particular supplying the infeed side of the debarker. On the outfeed side, stacking the slick debarked logs is also a job. If the sticks are maintained with a minimum end-to-end spacing on the infeed conveyor, full utilization of the debarker is obtained. This requires production equipment. With the debarker in the woodyard, the crane could be utilized in unloading the trucks directly onto the infeed-line deck conveyors leading into the debarker, thereby producing at rated capacity. If the volume of trucks is too high at any one period, the crane could stack the wood in ranks adjacent to the infeed table and, in a slack period, feed the debarker from these ranks. Whereas if the crane were brought into the plant site, this would cut down on the yard efficiency for stacking wood when the debarker is not in use. The only other solution would be to use a Cary Lift in place of the crane. However, this means an increased investment of $22,000.

Other advantages of locating the debarker installation in the woodyard are the following.

1. More space, thereby allowing for flexibility of operations.
2. Possible future infeed application utilizing a "hot" pond. This type of wood handling appears to be the most practical way of solving loading into King-type debarkers. The wood is simply dumped into the pond, which

TABLE 2 *Analysis of Total Investment Estimate for Flakeboard Plant Debarkers*

Type of Debarker	King (New)	King (Used)	Elmo	Leswork
Debarker (with power)	$23,200	$16,000*	$ 44,000	$4,000
Building	$(7,000)†	$(4,500)†	$(no exact breakdown given, similar to new King equipment.)	
Infeed and outfeed conveyors	9,000	6,000		
Cross-chain conveyor	10,000	10,000		
Bark conveyor	5,000	3,500		
Starting equipment	1,425	1,200		
Cary lift	(21,400)†			
Bark burner	10,000	3,000		
Special roll conveyor and flipper		2,000		
Spare parts	2,000	2,000		
Total accessories	$37,425	$27,700	$ 52,000	$ —
Dismantling old King equipment and accessories	$ —	$ 5,000	$ —	$ —
Freight—in	250	200	400	50
Power line to woodyard				
2,100-foot wire at $2/foot — $4,200	6,400	6,400	6,400	—
22 poles on 100-foot intervals at $100/pole — 2,200	3,000	3,000	3,000	
Labor and materials to install equipment (3 men, 3 days)				250
Total installation	$ 9,650	$14,600	$ 9,800	$ 300
Total investment	$70,725	$58,300	$105,800	$4,300

* Estimated.
† Not included in totals for accessories.

TABLE 3 Analysis of Cost Estimates per Cord for Fall River Flakeboard Plant Debarkers

Type of Machine	Elmo	King (New)	King (Used)	Leswork (Fall River)
Estimated life*	20,000 hours / 5 years	14,000 hours / 3¾ years	10,000 hours / 2¼ years	2,000 hours / ¼ year
Rated capacity—rough cords per hour Fixed costs per cord	9	7	6	2¼
		Cost estimate per cord		
Depreciation charges: $\dfrac{\text{total equipment cost}}{\text{total estimated life} \times \text{rated capital}}$	$0.59	$0.71	$0.96	$0.90
$\dfrac{\$106{,}000}{20{,}000 \text{ hr} \times 9 \text{ cords/hour}}$ (sample calculation)				
Interest, taxes, insurance: average annual investment × 10%	0.15	0.11	0.12	0.05
$\dfrac{\$106{,}000 \times .1}{2 \times 4{,}000 \text{ hr/yr} \times 9 \text{ cords/hour}}$				
Total fixed costs	$0.74	$0.82	$1.08	$0.90
Variable costs per cord Repairs and upkeep Maintenance (½ hr/8-hr shift)	$0.05+	$0.32+	$0.37+	$0.05
(routine lubrication and adjustment) $\dfrac{\$.125/\text{hour}}{\text{rated capacity}}$	0.01	0.02	0.02	0.05
Operating labor: $\dfrac{2 \text{ men} \times \text{hourly wage} \times 113\%‡}{\text{rated capacity}}$	0.05	0.65	0.75	1.67
$\dfrac{2 \text{ men} \times \$2/\text{hour} \times 113\%}{9 \text{ cords/hour}}$				
Operating supplies and power: 50% hour/rated capacity	0.06	0.07	0.08	0.10
Bark hauling: $\dfrac{\$4/\text{truck/hour} \times 1 \text{ hour/load}}{4 \text{ cords/truckload}}$	—	—	—	1.00
Bark burning	0.10	0.10	0.10	—
Total variable costs	$0.72	$1.16	$1.32	$2.87
Total estimated cost per rough cord	$1.46	$1.98	$2.40	$3.82

* Estimated life based on 16 hr/day × 5 days/wk × 50 wk/yr = 4,000 hr/yr × 5 yr = 20,000 hr.
+ Estimated from actual operations at Great Falls Paper Company (Elmo) and Paper Products (King installation).
‡ Thirteen percent increased for Social Security, workmen's compensation, retirement benefits.

TABLE 4   *Estimated Return on Investment Comparing Proposed Debarkers with Present Leswork Debarker*

	With Bark Burner*		
	Elmo	King (New)	King (Used)
Estimated savings per rough cord	$ 2.63	$ 1.84	$ 1.42
Estimated required rough cords/year†			
(59 cords/day × 360 days)	22,000	22,000	22,000.
Estimated total savings per year	$ 52,000	$40,000	$31,000
Estimated total investment	$106,000	$70,000	$58,000
Estimated return on investment	49%	57%	54%
Payback period	2 years	$1\frac{3}{4}$ years	$1\frac{4}{5}$ years

	Without Bark Burner		
	Elmo	King (New)	King (Used)
Estimated savings per rough cord	$ 1.55	$ 1.05	$ 0.68
Estimated required rough cords/year†			
(59 cords/day × 360 days)	22,000	22,000	22,000
Estimated total savings per year	$34,000	$23,000	$15,000
Estimated total investment	$96,000	$60,000	$48,000
Estimated return on investment	35%	38%	31%
Payback period	3 years	$2\frac{1}{2}$ years	$3\frac{1}{4}$ years

* Cost of burner including installation is $10,000.
† Based on production requirements of fifty finished cords per day, which provides for 1 million square feet of board per month and a 15 percent bark loss.

has impellers submerged in the water. If the sticks are not in contact with the water for more than half an hour, the moisture content of the wood is not affected.

3. Ease of installation, because there would be no interference with the existing supply of wood to the plant.

The principal advantage to locating near the flakeboard plant site is the reduced material handling on the outfeed end. Instead of stacking the wood on trailers for hauling to the plant or in ranks for inventory, it could be fed directly to the flakers. However, this means that the debarking operation is dependent *directly* on the flakeboard plant's operations, for if the plant shuts down, so must the debarker. Otherwise, if the debarker would run when the plant was down, the material handling would increase, since the peeled wood would have to be set off. Out in the woodyard, this would not be the case. Wood racks mounted on rails or the present trailers could be placed under the outfeed-end conveyor and easily removed sideways away from the flow of materials when each rack has been filled.

Bark Disposal

1. Burned in a regular bark burner
2. Utilized as fuel at our boiler house, provided the necessary adapting equipment was installed.
3. Possibly pressed into logs and sold as fireplace wood.
4. Hauled away and dumped as refuse.

This study compares returns with and without a bark burner. (See Table 4.)

If the efficiency of burning is high enough to prevent excessive smoke, the investment in such a piece of equipment would pay for itself by the savings ($1 per rough cord × 22,000 cords per year = $22,000) resulting from eliminating hauling to the dump.

Discussion of Alternative Solutions

1. Portable debarkers at Fall River. It is possible to utilize *a series* of Leswork portable debarkers for the flakeboard plant's wood requirements. At the present time we are barking approximately 45 rough cords per day ($2\frac{1}{2}$ rough cords per hour × 20 hours per day). This appears to be maximum capacity for these debarkers. Assuming a 15 percent bark loss and a 2 percent wood loss, this results in a production of 37 finished cords per day (45 × .83). This is enough capacity for 750,000 square feet of board per month (assuming 1.5 finished cords per 1,000 square feet). Basing our wood requirements at a minimum of 1 million square feet per month, we would need a production of about 50 finished cords per day. Thus, it would be necessary to invest in a minimum of two more debarkers (one for reserve) to fulfill our minimum production requirements. This would be an investment of $12,000 (3 × $4,000), excluding the necessary conveying accessories. However, based on an estimated life of 2,000 hours or 5,000 cords, two thirds of this investment would theoretically be replaced approximately every four months or one third year.

$$\left(\frac{5,000 \text{ cords}}{45 \text{ cords/day} \times 30 \text{ days/month}} = 3.7 \text{ month} \right)$$

Thus, a $12,000 initial investment becomes a $28,000 yearly investment.

Expanding this investment to a comparable figure with the King and Elmo debarkers, the following result is seen.

Type	Elmo	King (New)	Portable Leswork
Estimated life	5 years	$3\frac{1}{2}$ years	4 years
Total investment	$106,000	$70,000	$112,000

2. Permanent debarking facilities. In considering permanent debarking facilities for the Fall River flakeboard operations, the first question that must be answered is what type of bark-removal operation is feasible. Some principal methods of bark removal, apart from manual labor with a spud or draw knife, are the following.

a. By means of friction by tumbling or rotating action, such as the rotating cylindrical drum at Williamsburg.
b. By hydraulic pressure.
c. By shear principle.
d. By the rosser head, or cutter head, principle, such as the present Leswork debarker.

An attempt to debark some aspen in the Williamsburg drum was not successful because the wood was not dry enough to experience sufficient friction for effective bark removal. Since the flakeboard operations demand this higher moisture content in the wood, this generally recognized quick, cheap bark-removal system cannot be utilized.

A hydraulic pressure debarker is ruled out chiefly on the grounds of the water-pollution problem it would create.

The basic feature of a King-type debarker consists of a blunt-edge pressure elastically against the log, which then penetrates the bark down into the cell-forming cambium layer between the bark and wood. Tangential pressure against the bark produces shear stresses between bark and wood sufficient to overcome the strength of the cambium layer. The principal feature of such a machine is the removal of bark at a substantially low wood loss. The trade names of debarkers of this type are the King and the Elmo. Both of these debarkers could be used for our flakeboard operations.

The rosser, or cutter head, principle is employed on the Leswork machine we are now using. While these machines remove the bark sufficiently, the wood loss appears to be higher than with the King type. In addition, as these machines are portable, production is not as great as on the King machines. As an example, the Leswork debarks between 2 and $2\frac{1}{2}$ rough cords per hour, as compared to 5 to 10 rough cords per hour on the King. Nevertheless, the Leswork is a proven debarker that could be utilized in our operations.

Both the King and the Elmo have been utilized in flakeboard operations. It is generally felt that the King does an excellent job in debarking, but the maintenance requirements are high. Moreover, there seems to be more of a problem debarking wood with varying diameters with the King than with the Elmo. (Our operations use wood ranging from 4 to 15 inches in diameter.)

Because the Elmo has been designed for more rugged operations, its weight is approximately $2\frac{1}{2}$ times the King (22,000 pounds versus 9,000 pounds). Its cost is also $20,000 more ($44,000 versus $24,000).

The rating of a debarker is dependent on the number of sticks per cord, the percentage of bark removal required, and the infeed system to the debarker. In addition, under wintertime conditions, it is necessary to slow down the debarker in order to maintain the same percentage of bark removal. For this study, the average rated capacity of the King and Elmo debarkers was based on automatic conveying accessories. It should be kept in mind that manual feeding to either of these debarkers would tend to reduce their rated capacity.

Assume a zero tax rate and a time value of money of .05. What decision should the firm make?

Jacobs Division[*]

Mr. Richard Soderberg, Financial Analyst for the Jacobs Division of MacFadden Chemical Company, was reviewing several complex issues relating to a new product introduction being considered for investment purposes in the ensuing year, 1974. The project, involving a specialty coating material, qualified for investment according to company guidelines. The Jacobs Division Manager, Mr. Reynolds, was fearful, however, that the project might be too "risky." Moreover, Mr. Soderberg believed the only practical way to sell what he regarded as an attractive opportunity would place the product in a weak competitive position over the long run. Finally, he was concerned that the estimates empolyed in the probabilistic analysis were little better than educated guesses.

MacFadden Chemical Company was one of the ten largest in the world with sales in excess of $1 billion. Its volume had grown steadily at the rate of 10% per year throughout the post-war period until 1957. Sales and earnings had grown more rapidly. Beginning in 1957, the chemical industry began to experience overcapacity particularly in basic materials. Price cutting ensued. Also, more funds had to be spend in marketing and research to remain competitive. As a consequence, sales and profits were adversely affected. The company achieved only modest growth in sales of 4% in the 1960's and an overall decline in profits. Certain shortages began developing in the economy in 1972; by 1973, sales had risen 60% and profits over 100% as the result of price increases and near-capacity operations. Most observers believed that the "shortage boom" would be only a short respite from the intensively competitive conditions of the last decade.

* Copyright © 1984 by The Colgate Darden Graduate School of Business Administration of the University of Virginia and by Robert F. Vandell, The Charles C. Abbott Professor of Business Administration. This case was prepared by Professor Vandell and is used with his permission.

There were eleven operating divisions of MacFadden, organized into three groups. Each division had a multiplicity of products centered around one chemical, such as fluoride, sulphur, or petroleum. The Jacobs Division was an exception. It was the newest and smallest division with sales of $30 million. Secondly, its products were all specialty industrial products, such as dyes, adhesives, and finishes, purchased in relatively small lots by a great diversity of industrial customers. No single product had sales in excess of $5 million and many had only $100,000 or so in volume. There were 150 basic products in the division, each with several minor variations. Finally, it was one of the more rapidly growing divisions—12% per year prior to 1973—with a high return on total assets net of depreciation of 13%.

In capital budgeting analysis, there were some corporate-wide guidelines for new investment opportunities: 8% for cost reduction projects, 12% for expansion of facilities, and 16% for new products or processes. Returns were measured in terms of discounted cash flows (internal rate). All calculations were estimated after taxes. Mr. Soderberg believed that these rates and methods were typical of the chemical industry.

Mr. Reynolds, however, tended to demand higher rates for projects in his division, even though its earning's growth-stability in the past marked it as one of the more reliable sectors of MacFadden's operations. Mr. Reynolds had three reasons for wanting to see better returns. First, one of the key variables used in appraising management performance of MacFadden was the growth of residual income (market share, profit margins, etc. were also considered). Residual income was the division's profits after allocated taxes minus a 10% capital charge on total net assets (assets after depreciation). Mr. Reynolds did not like the idea of investing in projects that were too close to the target rate of earnings imbedded in the residual income calculation. Next, many new projects had high start-up costs. Even though they made attractive returns over the long run, these projects hurt overall earnings performance in the short run. "Don't tell me what its (a project's) discounted rate of return is, tell me whether we're going to improve our return on total net assets within three years," Mr. Reynolds was known to say. Finally, Mr. Reynolds was skeptical of estimates. "I don't know what's going to happen here on this project, but I'll bet we overstate returns by 2 to 5% on average," was a typical comment by him. As a result, Mr. Reynolds tended to look for at least 4% in return more than the company standards before he became enthusiastic about the project. "You've got to be hardnosed about taking risk," he said, "By demanding a decent return for riskier opportunities, we've a better chance to grow and prosper."

Mr. Soderberg knew that Mr. Reynolds' views were reflected in actions at decision-making levels throughout the division. Projects that did not have fairly promising return prospects relative to Mr. Reynolds' standards tended to be dropped from analysis or shelved fairly early in the decision process. While this was hard to estimate, Mr. Soderberg guessed that almost as many projects with returns meeting the company hurdle rates were abandoned in this division as were ultimately approved. In fact, the projects submitted were usually so promising Mr. Reynolds rarely said no to a proposal. His capital budgets, in turn, were accepted virtually unchanged at higher management levels, unless top management happened to be unusually pessimistic about business and money prospects.

A new production-process project was often under study for several years after research had developed a "test tube" idea. The properties of the product had to be evaluated in relation to market needs, competition, and the like. A diversity of possible applications tended to complicate this analysis. At the same time, technological studies were under way examining material sources, plant location, manufacturing process alternatives, scale economics, and so on. A myriad of feasible alternatives existed, only some of which could be actively explored. These activities often involved outlays in excess of several hundred thousand dollars before any real feel for the potential of the project could be ascertained realistically. A project manager was assigned to any major project to coordinate this work. "For every dollar of new capital approved, I bet we spent $.30 on business analysis of opportunities," observed Mr. Soderberg, "and that doesn't count the money we spent on research."

The project that concerned Mr. Soderberg at the moment had been dubbed Silicone-X. The product was a special-purpose coating that added slipperiness to a surface. The coating would be used on a variety of products to reduce friction by increasing slide. The uniqueness lay in its hardness, adhesiveness (to the applied surface), and durability. It could be used in almost any application where lubricants might be imperfect in eliminating friction between moving parts. There was a great diversity of situations where Silicone-X might be useful. In terms of market, the product was likely to have a large number of buyers, each ordering small quantities. Only a few firms were likely to buy in yearly amounts larger than 5,000 pounds.

"Test tube batches" of Silicone-X had been tested in a variety of applications inside and outside Jacobs. Comments were universally favorable, although an upper price limit of $2 per pound seemed likely to be the maximum possible. Lower prices were, of course, considered attractive, but this was unlikely to produce large volume. For planning purposes a price of $1.90 per pound was used.

Demand was harder to estimate because of the variety of possible applications. Market-research people had estimated a first-year demand of 1,000,000 to 2,000,000 pounds with 1,200,000 sited as the most likely. Mr. Soderberg empathized with the problem of the market researchers. They had tried to do a systematic job of looking at the segments of most probable application, but the data were not good. "They could spend another year studying it, and state their opinions more confidently. But we wouldn't find them more believable. The estimates are educated guesses by smart people. However, they are also pretty wild stabs in the dark. They won't rule out the possibility of demand as low as 500,000 lbs, and 2,000,000 lbs is not a ceiling to possibility." Once the product was established, however, growth was considered to be pretty good.

Once the product became established, however, demand was likely to grow at a healthy rate—perhaps 10% per year. However, the industries served were likely to be cyclical with swings in volume requirements of plus or minus 20% depending on market conditions.

There was no patent protection in Silicone-X, and the technological know-how involved in the manufacturing process could be duplicated by others in time (perhaps twelve months). "Someone is certainly going to get interested in this product when sales volume reaches $3,000,000 and it's essentially a commodity," observed Mr. Soderberg.

"The product life is likely to be pretty good. We think demand should level off after 8 to 10 years, but the odds are very much against someone developing a cheaper or markedly superior substitute," claimed Mr. Vorst, the Project Manager. As most equipment required for the project was likely to wear out and need replacement after 15 years, give or take a few, this seemed like a natural point to terminate an analysis.

"Fortunately the cost estimates look pretty solid. Basic chemicals, of course, do fluctuate in purchase price, but we have a captive source with stable manufacturing costs. We can probably negotiate a long-term transfer price with Wilson (another MacFadden Division) although this is not the time (sharply higher prices for an apparently temporary period) to do so," added Mr. Vorst.

In his preliminary analysis, Mr. Soderberg tended to use net present value calculations and in this case the discount rate would be 20%. "We can always convert the data to a discounted cash flow rate when we have to do so," said he. "We also work with most likely estimates. Until we get down to the bitter end, there are too many alternatives to consider, and we can't afford probabilistic measures or fancy simulations. A conservative definition of most likely values is probably good enough for most of the subsidiary analyses. We've probably made over 200 present value calculations using our computer programs just to get to this decision point, and heaven knows how many quick and dirty paybacks," observed Mr. Soderberg.

Mr. Soderberg went on to say, "We've made a raft of pretty important decisions that affect the attractiveness of this project. Lord knows, some of them are bound to be wrong—I hope not critically so. In any case, these decisions are behind us. They're buried so deep in the assumptions, no one can find them, and top management wouldn't have time to look at them anyway."

Mr. Soderberg was down to two alternatives: a labor-intensive limited-capacity solution and a capital-intensive solution. "The analysis all points in one direction," he said, "but I have the feeling it's going to be the worst one for the long run."

The labor-intensive method involved an initial plant and equipment outlay of $900,000. This alternative only had a capacity to service 1.5 million pounds. "Even if the project bombs out, we won't lose much. The equipment is very adaptable. We could find uses for about half of it. We could probably sell the balance for $200,000, and let our tax write-offs cover most of the rest. We should salvage the working capital part without trouble. It's the start-up costs and losses that we'll encounter until we decide that the project is no good that are our real risks," summarized Mr. Soderberg. "We can at least get this project on stream in one year's time. In the first year we'll be lucky to satisfy half the possible demand, and spend $50,000 debugging the process." Exhibit 1 shows Mr. Soderberg's analysis of the labor-intensive alternative. The calculations showed a small net present value when discounted at 20%. Mr. Soderberg noted, however, that there was a sizeable net present value if an 8% discount rate was used. The positive present values when related to the negative present values looked particularly attractive.

The capital-intensive method involved a much more sizeable outlay— $3,300,000—for plant and equipment. Manufacturing costs would, however, be reduced by $.35 per unit and fixed costs by $100,000, excluding depreciation, which would increase (depreciation would be over a longer period). The captial-intensive plant was designed to handle 2.0 million pounds, the lowest volume for which appropriate equipment could be acquired. The equipment was more specialized. Only $400,000 of this machinery might be redeployed to other company activities. The balance probably had a salvage value of $800,000. It would take two years to get the plant on stream, and the first operating year volume was likely going to be low—perhaps 700,000 pounds at the most. Debugging costs were likely to be $100,000.

Exhibit 2 presents Mr. Soderberg's analysis of the capital-intensive method. At 20% discount rate, the capital-intensive project had a sizeable negative present value, and appeared much worse than the labor-intensive alternative. However, at an 8% discount rate it looked significantly better.

To gain some perspective, Mr. Soderberg estimated the internal rate on the incremental investment under the labor-intensive method in Exhibit 3. The internal rate was slightly above 14%. As a cost-reduction opportunity, this rate was attractive, but partly because of the expanded capacity. As a part of a new product opportunity, it was unattractive. Mr. Soderberg was not sure how he should look at the project.

Several things concerned Mr. Soderberg about this analysis. Mr. Reynolds would only look at the total return. Thus, the capital-intensive project would not qualify. Yet it seemed the safest way to start the program based on a breakeven analysis (see Exhibit 4). The capital-intensive alternative only needed a demand of 325,900 pounds to break even, whereas the labor-intensive method required 540,000 pounds of sales volume.

Mr. Soderberg was also concerned that competition might develop in the future, and that price cutting would ensue. If the price per pound fell by 20¢, the labor-intensive method would not break even unless 900,000 pounds was sold, and, of course, Jacobs would be sharing the market with a competitor. A competitor, of course, would—once the market was established—build a capital intensive plant, and be in a good position to cut prices by even more than 20¢. In short, there was a risk, given the labor-intensive solution, that Jacobs could not remain competitive with Silicone-X. The better the demand proved to be, the more serious this risk would become.

Once the market was established, Jacobs could build a capital-intensive

EXHIBIT 1   Jacobs Division: Analysis of Labor-Intensive Alternative Silicone-X

				Year			Terminal Year
	0	1	2	3	4	5–15	15
Investments							
Plant and equipment	$ 900,000						
Working capital		$ 140,000	$ 14,000	$ 15,000	$ 17,000	$ 20,000	$381,000
Demand in pounds		1,200,000	1,320,000	1,452,000	1,597,000	n.a.	
Capacity in pounds		600,000	1,500,000	1,500,000	1,500,000	1,500,000	
Units sold		600,000	1,320,000	1,452,000	1,500,000	1,500,000	
Sales price limit		1.90	1.90	1.90	1.90	1.90	
Variable costs per unit							
Manufacture		1.30	1.30	1.30	1.30	1.30	
Marketing		.10	.10	.10	.10	.10	
Marketing total		1.40	1.40	1.40	1.40	1.40	
Contribution per unit		.50	.50	.50	.50	.50	
Contribution in dollars		300,000	660,000	726,000	750,000	750,000	
Fixed costs		210,000	210,000	210,000	210,000	210,000	
Depreciation		60,000	60,000	60,000	60,000	60,000	
Start-up costs		50,000	0	0	0	0	
Total fixed costs		320,000	270,000	270,000	270,000	270,000	
Profit before tax		(20,000)	390,000	456,000	480,000	480,000	
Profit after tax at 50%		(10,000)	195,000	228,000	240,000	240,000	
Cash flow operations		50,000	255,000	288,000	300,000	300,000	
Total cash flow	$(900,000)	$ (90,000)	$ 241,000	$ 273,000	$ 283,000	$ 280,000	$381,000
Net PV at 20%	(900,000)	(75,000)	167,400	158,000	136,500	584,300	24,700
				Net Present Value $95,900 at 20%			
Net PV at 8%	(900,000)	(83,300)	206,600	216,700	208,000	1,469,300	120,000
				Net Present Value $1,237,400 at 8%			

EXHIBIT 2 Jacobs Division: Analysis of Capital-Intensive Alternative Silicone-X

					Year				Terminal Year
	0	1	2	3	4	5	6	7–15	15
Investments									
Plant and equipment	$1,900,000								$(962,000)
Working capital		$1,400,000	$ 160,000	$ 11,000	$ 17,000	$ 20,000	$ 24,000	$ 30,000	(422,000)
Demand in pounds			1,320,000	1,452,000	1,597,000	1,757,000	1,933,000	2,125,000	
Capacity in pounds			700,000	2,000,000	2,000,000	2,000,000	2,000,000	2,000,000	
Units sold			700,000	1,452,000	1,597,000	1,757,000	1,933,000	2,000,000	
Sales price unit			1.90	1.90	1.90	1.90	1.90		
Variable costs per unit									
Manufacture			.95	.95	.95	.95	.95		
Selling			.10	.10	.10	.10	.10		
			1.05	1.05	1.05	1.05	1.05		
Contribution per unit			.85	.85	.85	.85	.85		
Contribution in dollars			595,000	1,234,200	1,357,500	1,493,500	1,643,000	1,700,000	
Fixed costs			110,000	110,000	110,000	110,000	110,000	110,000	
Depreciation			167,000	167,000	167,000	167,000	167,000	167,000	
Start-up costs			100,000	0	0	0	0	0	
Total fixed cost			377,000	277,000	277,000	277,000	277,000	277,000	
Profit before tax			218,000	957,200	1,080,500	1,216,500	1,366,100	1,423,000	
Profit after tax at 50%			109,000	478,600	540,200	608,200	683,000	711,500	
Cash flow operations			276,000	645,600	707,200	775,200	850,000	878,500	
Total cash flow	($1,900,000)		$ 116,000	$ 634,600	$ 690,000	$ 755,200	$ 826,000	$ 848,500	$1,384,000
Present value at 20%	($1,900,000)	($1,166,700)	80,600	366,900	332,900	303,500	276,600	1,144,800	89,800
				Net Present Value at 20% = ($471,600)					
Present value at 8%	($1,900,000)	($1,296,300)	99,500	503,300	507,300	514,000	520,500	3,338,200	436,300
				Net Present Value at 8% = $2,722,800					

499

EXHIBIT 3   Jacobs Division: Incremental Return on Investment Capital-Intensive Alternative

Year	Labor-Intensive Cash Flow	Capital-Intensive Cash Flow	Difference	PV at 14%
0	$(900,000)	$(1,900,000)	$(1,000,000)	$(1,000,000)
1	(90,000)	(1,400,000)	(1,310,000)	(1,149,100)
2	241,000	66,000	(175,000)	(134,700)
3	273,000	644,600	371,600	220,000
4	283,000	690,200	407,200	241,500
5	280,000	755,200	475,200	246,500
6	280,000	871,000	551,000	251,000
7–15	280,000	883,500	573,500	1,212,000
15	381,000	1,284,000	903,000	126,500
			Net present value	$ 14,700

EXHIBIT 4   Breakeven Analysis Silicone-X

	Normal	Labor-Intensive	Capital-Intensive
Fixed costs			
Operations		210,000	110,000
Depreciation		60,000	167,000
Total		270,000	277,000
Contribution per unit		.50	.85
Units to break even		540,000	325,900
Price competitive			
Contribution per unit		.30	.65
Units to break even		900,000	426,200

facility. Almost none of the labor-intensive equipment would be useful in the new plant. The new plant would still cost $3,300,000, and Jacobs would have to write off losses on the labor-intensive facility.

The labor-intensive facility would be difficult to expand economically. It would cost $50,000 for each $100,000 pounds of additional capacity (only practical in 250,000-pound increments). An additional 100,000 pounds of capacity in the capital-intensive unit could be added for $25,000, in contrast.

Pricing strategy was also an element. At $1.90 a pound, Jacobs would invite competition. Competitors would be satisfied with a lower rate of return— perhaps 12%—in an established market. At somewhat lower prices, Jacobs might discourage competition. The project could not be "sold" at lower prices (that is, even the labor-intensive alternative would not provide a rate of return of 20%).

In short, it began to appear to Mr. Soderberg as if the use of a high discount rate forced the company to make riskier decisions and enhanced the prospect of realizing lower rates of return than forecast.

He was also concerned by the fact that the proposals did not consider expansion opportunities. The labor-intensive alternative would look better if 500,000 pounds of capacity were added as soon as demand warranted this action. In two years' time, expansion and, for that matter, cost reduction, could be justified using lower rates of return.

The Modem Corporation

The Modem Corporation (MC) is considering opportunities to modernize (automate) its plant and equipment. Rachele Brown, the president of the firm, is enthusiastic about an automation strategy and sees it as essential if the firm is to stay competitive.

As a first step in the economic analysis of automated equipment, a cash flow net present value calculation was done for one of the more desirable pieces of equipment. The firm conventionally uses .20 to evaluate investment opportunities (debt currently costs .131 before tax). The statutory corporate tax rate is .46.

Exhibit 1 shows the capital budgeting analysis for the $10,000,000 investment. The entire amount of investment is eligible for the .10 investment tax credit. The tax basis of the investment is 9,500,000 ($10,000,000 minus half of the ITC).

EXHIBIT 1

Year	Depreciation Tax Savings	Present Value Factors	PV
1	.15 ($9,500,000) .46 = $655,500	1.2^{-1}	$ 546,250
2	.22 ($9,500,000) .46 = $961,400	1.2^{-2}	667,639
3	.21 ($9,500,000) .46 = $917,700	1.2^{-3}	531,076
4	.21 ($9,500,000) .46 = $917,700	1.2^{-4}	442,564
5	.21 ($9,500,000) .46 = $917,700	1.2^{-5}	366,803

Total present value = $2,554,332

$$\text{net PV} = -\$10,000,000 + \$1,000,000 + \$3,000,000(1 - .46)B(5,\ 20)$$
$$+ \$2,554,332$$
$$= -\$10,000,000 + \$1,000,000 + \$1,620,000(2.9906)$$
$$+ \$2,554,332$$
$$= -\$9,000,000 + \$4,844,772 + \$2,554,332$$
$$= -\$1,600,896$$

The estimated life of the equipment is five years with zero salvage value at the end of that period of time. The firm uses an ACRS method of equipment writeoff for taxes.

The equipment will save $3,000,000 of labor costs per year. It will have a capacity of 2,500,000 units per year. These cost and capacity figures are based on solid information and can be relied on to be correct.

Rachelle accepts the cash flow assumptions that result in the $1,600,896 negative net present value, as shown in Exhibit 1. But she is bothered by the long-run consequences of rejecting the investment. She knows that the firm must modernize if it is to stay competitive. Rachelle also thinks it essential that any investment enhance the financial position of the stockholders. The negative net present value is disconcerting.

There are several other factors not directly incorporated into the cash flow analysis as well. The investment will increase the quality of the output. The product will be more consistent in its characteristics and thus more attractive to the purchasers. The economic value of this characteristic was thought to be too difficult to measure and was not included (its inclusion would have decreased the reliability of the cash flow measures used).

Moreover, the investment would increase the firm's productive capacity by 50 percent. With this increased capacity, the firm could react more rapidly to new orders and deliver goods straight from production rather than from inventory. It is estimated that the average inventory carried during a year could be reduced by $10,000,000. The annual after-tax cost of carrying inventory is estimated to be .25 of the investment.

A third advantage of the new equipment is that it is more reliable and has less down time than the present equipment. This would improve the ability to service customers as well as reduce inventories (this factor did affect the estimated inventory cost reduction).

The product line that the equipment would produce is currently earning $7,000,000 of cash flow per year.

The equipment being considered is a great departure from the equipment used in the past. While it is felt that the five-year life estimate is reasonable, it is also felt that a new generation of this type of equipment will be forthcoming after five years. It is estimated that, even if the current investment is made, $15,000,000 of future cost savings per year are feasible with improved versions of the equipment.

What is your recommendation regarding the investment?

CASE 9

Arkansas Petroleum Company[*]

In May 1974, Mr. Warren Edwards, Financial Vice President of the Arkansas Petroleum Company, was concerned with a number of issues that had been raised recently about the company's capital budgeting policies and precedures. His task was to develop new methods of capital budgeting more appropriate to emerging circumstances.

Arkansas Petroleum Company was a significant domestic oil company with sales of approximately $2.0 billion. The Arkansas Company brand was well known in the midwest, where 90% of its sales were concentrated. Arkansas was diversified outside oil (mostly petrochemicals and coal) and fully integrated. However, crude production represented only 15% of refinery needs, and refined products (about 10%) were purchased. Its strength lay at the marketing end of the process, where it enjoyed a strong 12% market share in its limited regional markets.

Up until 1974, top management determined an overall corporate hurdle rate, based upon the firm's estimated historic average cost of capital, and applied this rate as a minimum return on investment criterion for all operating divisions.

In evaluating an investment opportunity, an operating unit would discount cash flows and outflows at the hurdle rate. Projects with present value ratios greater than 1 (present value of inflows divided by present value of outflows) were given further consideration. A number of projects could not be evaluated exclusively on economic grounds (e.g., office buildings, antipollution devices, security systems), and some projects with inadequate net present value ratios

* Copyright © 1984 by the Colgate Darden Graduate School of Business Administration of the University of Virginia and by Robert F. Vandell, the Charles C. Abbott Professor of Business Adminstration. This case was prepared by Professor Vandell and is used with his permission.

were submitted and approved. Most projects were, however, justified on economic grounds. Riskier projects might not be approved even if their present value ratio, based on expected value calculations, was above 1. While there were no firm guidelines, management tended to use a net present value ratio of 1 only for very low-risk projects. Moderate-risk projects tended to be evaluated against a standard of a 1.2 present value ratio, and high-risk projects usually required a ratio of 1.5. These guidelines were rather fuzzily applied, because of different views about risk. In any case, project economics was only one factor considered in any evaluation.

Capital availability had never been a problem prior to 1974. Arkansas benefited from high cash flows, as the result of depletion allowances. Dividend payouts were low relative to earnings so that retained earnings were favorable. Additional needs had been financed by long-term borrowings. No new equity financings were necessary. However, the debt proportion in the capital structure had risen steadily from 18.2% in 1960 to 46.8% at the end of 1973. Lenders had begun signaling management that the present debt ratio was about as high as the firm could go without seriously jeopardizing bond ratings, or their equivalent, for new issues. Indeed, with the increase in interest costs, coverage ratios were considered very low already, and the debt proportions might have to be further reduced. Mr. Edwards had decided to have a moratorium on new debt issues for at least one year to allow the equity proportion of the capital structure to grow.

In the period 1960 to 1973, financings had been achieved as follows (dollar figures in millions).

Sources		Applications	
Depletion/depreciation	$ 489	New plant	$1359
Retained earnings	307	Working Capital	210
Net debt financing	773		$1569
Total	$1569		

The major sources of capital had all come under pressure recently. As the result of changes in the law with regard to depletion, the percentage of noncash charges divided by gross plant had been declining. Congress was considering even more restrictive depletion allowances, and Mr. Edwards was fearful some adverse decisions might lie ahead. Profits after taxes but before interest as a percentage of capital structure had until recently been declining, whereas interest and dividends had been rising. As a result, retained earnings were squeezed (relative to the dollar value of the capital structure). While price increases, relating to the oil crisis, had reversed this trend, Mr. Edwards was fearful this situation might be temporary. The moratorium on borrowing removed an important source of capital.

At the same time demand for capital was rising as a percentage of gross plant. Some needs related to environment requirements. Inflation had increased the cost of new investments. And the present energy shortage was expected to increase pressures for new investment. Arkansas thus expected to need to raise sizeable amounts of new capital externally to finance its growth. Equity funds would have to be raised for the first time. However, equity markets for Arkansas' stock, as measured by the ratio of market price to estimated twelve-months' future earnings were at their lowest post-war levels. Capital from this source was certainly not attractive.

The funds forecast for the next three years (1975–1977) was (in millions of dollars).

Sources		Applications	
Depletion/depreciation	$ 216	Capital expenditures	$1620
Retained earnings	163	Working capital	214
Total	$ 379		$1834
Short fall	$1455		

The shortage of funds was large compared with Arkansas' net worth at the end of 1973 of $1,019 million.

During the period, Arkansas' cost of capital had declined until 1970. In part this reflected the increased use of debt financing, and in part a rise in the price earnings ratio helped. By 1973, however, a precipitous decline in the price earnings ratio, coupled with a higher average of cost of interest, had increased the capital charge, as shown in Exhibit 1.

Management believed that these costs understated the real cost of money to the firm, because historically Arkansas' growth rate was about 3% above the average for all firms. Management added 3% to the capital cost to recognize the performance superior expected by creditors and stockholders. Some individuals believed that the 3% should apply only to equity capital.

Management did not adjust its hurdle rates, year by year, to recognize changes in the cost of capital. However, the hurdle rate had declined from 11% in 1960 to 9% in 1970. Under 1973 conditions, a 12% hurdle rate seemed more appropriate to Mr. Edwards, although the effective rate was still 9%.

Mr. Edwards was not, however, satisfied with this conclusion. The price earnings ratio for Arkansas stock had since fallen to 6.9 × earnings per share, suggesting an equity cost of 14.4%. Moreover, equity funds would be the main source of capital in the next year or so. He wondered perhaps if this implied that a 17% to 18% hurdle rate might be more appropriate. Clearly the choice of the hurdle rate would affect the amount of expenditures considered attractive, and perhaps their mix as well.

Mr. Edwards was further troubled by the comment made by Arkansas' primary investment banker to the effect, new equity issues would be very difficult to place in the depressed market conditions and prevailing mood, and might be impossible. It seemed to Mr. Edwards that cost of capital measures

**EXHIBIT 1   Arkansas Petroleum Company: Cost of Capital
Calculations, Representative Years**

	Weight	Cost After Tax	Weighted Cost
1960			
Debt	.182	4.3%	.78
Common stock	.818	8.5%	6.95
		Weighted average	7.73%
1965			
Debt	.325	4.8%	1.56
Common stock	.675	7.1%	4.79
		Weighted average	6.35%
1970			
Debt	.436	5.7%	2.49
Common stock	.564	5.5%	3.10
		Weighted average	5.59%
1973			
Debt	.468	6.0%	2.81%
Common stock	.532	11.1%	5.91%
		Weighted average	8.72%

NOTE: The after-tax cost of debt funds represented the average interest of out-standing long-term debt, stated on an after-tax basis. Tax rates averaged about 30 percent of reported income over the period.

Equity cost was determined by dividing a trendline measure of earnings per share for the year by the average of monthly closing prices for the common stock.

were pretty meaningless if capital was unavailable or restricted in quantity. In any case, his measure did not consider the underpricing and issuing costs of raising equity funds, a figure that might be 6–7% of the issue in today's market.

The weighted average cost calculation in Mr. Edwards' mind was backward looking. He wondered whether he should be projecting future capital mixes and their related costs in determining an appropriate hurdle rate. For instance, new debt funds might cost 9.5% to 10.0% at the moment, and if any refinancing were required the marginal cost of the incremental funds would be higher. Weighted average debt costs still reflected some financings in the early 1950's when interest rates were 4%.

Related to this question was how far in the future to project. Forecasting market prices for common equities for six months was problematic enough, let alone trying to anticipate what these prices might become in several years' time. The present moratorium on debt would drastically affect capital costs this year, but over time the impact would diminish. He was uncertain what sort of planning horizon was appropriate, especially given the firm's current unique circumstances.

In recent years Mr. Edwards was concerned by the growth in importance of "nonproductive investments," that is, the necessary investments that did not add to earning power or avoid erosion of earning power directly. In the early 1960's these nonproductive investments amounted to about 10% of the total new fund commitments. Today, largely as a result of environmental laws and pressures, they had increased to 20%. Mr. Edwards believed that in order to earn 12% on all new capital investments, Arkansas now had to earn at least 15% (12% ÷ .8) on its productive investments. This issue needed resolution.

At the time the present value ratio had been adopted for evaluating projects, management was completely satisfied with the intellectual relevance of a hurdle rate, as an expression of the opportunity cost of money. While the notion that the average cost of capital represented this opportunity cost had been debated and its measurement was never considered wholly scientific, it had been accepted. Circumstances had now changed, however. It looked to be difficult, if not impossible, to fund all desirable expenditures in the future because of the prevailing capital scarcity. Mr. Edwards wondered what the relevant notion of hurdle rate should be during periods of capital scarcity and internal fund rationing.

Recently, one of his assistants, Robert Drew, had raised a question about how the hurdle rate should be used. Two years ago, in recognition of inflation, Arkansas had adjusted its methods of present value calculations. In effect, future cash flows were adjusted to reflect the effects of inflation. Estimates of the rates of inflation for various items (e.g., labor costs, prices, construction costs) were supplied by the firm's economic department and plugged into future cash flows. The net cash flows in future years were then deflated by an estimate of the cost of living index to put them in current (common dollar) terms. The common dollar cash flows were then discounted at the hurdle rate to determine the net present value ratio for the project. Mr. Drew argued that the last step was wrong. Cost of capital had risen to reflect investors, views of inflation. (That is, the investor was seeking the same common dollar rate of return as in the past, and to do so had to add to this basic rate, roughly the rate of inflation to determine satisfactory return on investment opportunities.) If this was so the double step of deflating the value of future cash flows and discounting at a hurdle rate, reflecting inflation expectations, overcompensated for inflation. Mr. Edwards believed that Mr. Drew was right in part, but doubted if money-costs yet fully considered inflation expectations. In one sense, this was troublesome, for considering inflationary effects was certainly appropriate in evaluating investment opportunities, yet a procedure that dealt with them incorrectly would only increase confusion and misinformation. To extent inflation did in fact influence money-costs, it also meant that capital would remain expensive, or could become more costly.

Even if the appropriate hurdle rate was clear cut, how the rate should be used within the company in evaluating projects was not. As noted, Arkansas historically had used one rate to discount all projects in all phases of its operations. This practice had come under increasing attack.

Perhaps, Robert Charles, President of the pipeline company presented these views most vigorously:

> Each phase of our business is different, must compete differently, and must draw on capital differently. Pipelines are a regulated industry, and the return on our total capital is limited to about 7%. In most cases, this return is highly certain. The throughput and the profit margins are contracted for on a long-term basis to assure a satisfactory rate of return (by major oil companies who depend on the suppliers). We are not as deeply into pipelines as our competitors, primarily because it is almost impossible to justify an investment with our present single hurdle rate system. This unique constraint adds to our production costs, and in the end weakens our profit margins on sales, and our long-run competitive position.
>
> Given the recognized safety of the investment, many independent pipeline companies can raise most of the capital needed from the debt markets. In projects comparable to the ones we would consider, 85% to 90% of the necessary capital is raised through the debt markets at interest rates reflecting at least A quality. If we could do the same, notice what this would do to our capital costs (using 1973 data):

	Weight	Cost	Weighted Cost
Debt	.85	6.0%	5.10
Equity	.15	11.1%	1.67
		Total	6.77%

> Even at today's high capital costs, pipeline projects develop favorable value ratios. I constrast this with the exploratory drilling division where risks are high and where independents are financed primarily by equity funds (i.e., 11.1%). In my book, their hurdle rate should reflect the cost of equity funds.
>
> There is another subtlety. Our corporate tax rate is 30% on average because of heavy write-offs on exploratory drilling. However, the tax savings are heavily concentrated in one or two operating divisions. The rest of us pay about 50% of our income in taxes. The firm's interest cost before taxes are 8.7%. This should mean that the after-tax cost of interest is only 4.35% for pipelines. Considering taxes properly materially reduces our division's weighted cost of capital (to 5.37%).
>
> In short, I believe that we are really rationing equity funds. We should be seeking a constant rate of return on equity. Those of us who benefit from lower risk, and hence can trade on our equity more extensively, should be penalized because our ability to earn on our assets is restricted in ways not detrimental to very favorable capacity to achieve high returns on our equity, when stated comparably to our competition.

Implicit in Mr. Charles' arguments, as Mr. Edwards understood it, each division in the company would have a different hurdle rate. The costs of the various forms of capital would remain the same (except perhaps for the tax element). However, the mix of capital used would change in the calculation. Low-risk operations would use leverage more extensively while the high-risk divisions would have little or no debt funds. Thus, lower risk divisions would have lower hurdle rates.

Mr. Charles' views were supported by several other division managers. Opposition was just as strong, however, particularly from the divisions whose hurdle rate might be increased. George Pritchett, Division Manager of the Exploratory Drilling Division, expressed his opinion as follows:

Money is all green. We should be putting our money where the returns are best. A single hurdle rate may deprive the underprofitable divisions of investments in order to channel more funds into profitable divisions. But isn't this the aim of the process?

We don't finance each division separately. The corporation raises capital based on its overall prospects and record. The diversification of the company probably helps keep our capital costs down and enables us to borrow more in total than the sum of the capabilities of each division separately. As a result, developing separate hurdle rates is both unrealistic and misleading. All our stockholders want from us is to invest our funds wisely in order to increase the value of their stock. This happens when we pick the most promising projects, irrespective of their source.

Several years ago we installed calculations in our project evaluations in order to determine the expected value of projects. I thought the purpose of this calculation was to take risk and uncertainties fully into account. Multiple hurdle rates will only confuse things by adding a second dimension to our risk appraisals in a way that will obscure the meaning of the basic calculation.

Mr. Charles countered these arguments as follows:

In considering how much to loan us, lenders will consider the composition of risks. If money flows into safer investments over time, their willingness to lend us funds will tend to increase. While multiple hurdle rates may not reflect capital structure changes on a day-to-day basis, over time they will reflect prospects more realistically.

Our stockholders are just as much concerned with risk. If they perceive our business as being more risky than other companies, they will not pay as high a price for our earnings. Perhaps this is why our price earnings ratio is below the industry average most of the time.

Probability calculations leading to expected value measures of the return potential of projects measure average prospects. They do not consider the dispersion around the expected value. Projects with high dispersion should be less attractive.

It is not a question of whether we adjust for risk—we already do. We look for higher present value ratios before we fund riskier projects. The only question in my mind is whether we make these adjustments systematically or not. If we attribute a capital structure to a division or, for that matter, to a project so that the rate of return on equity represents equivalent risks, then we are in a position to pick the projects with the best returns on imputed equity.

At the moment, as I understand it, our real problem is an inadequate and very costly supply of equity funds. If we are really rationing equity capital, then we should be striving for the best returns on equity for the risk. Multiple hurdle rates achieve this objective.

As he listened to these and several similar arguments over the course of several months, Mr. Edwards became increasingly concerned with several other considerations. First, the corporate strategy directed the company towards increasing its integration, particularly towards developing strong crude oil production. One effect of using multiple hurdle rates would be making it more difficult to justify exploratory drilling proposals, since the required rate of return would be increased. In contrast, pipeline investments had a relatively low priority, since they were more in the nature of cost reduction. Drilling and marketing investments tended to build the overall strength of the firm more. Perhaps multiple hurdle rates were the right idea, but the notion that they should be based on capital costs rather than strategic considerations was wrong. On the other hand, perhaps multiple rates based on capital costs should be used, but, in allocating funds, higher net present value ratios should be used for screening projects in divisions that were less strategically important. (Theory was certainly not clear on how to achieve strategic objectives when allocating capital, in Mr. Edwards' mind.)

When the present value ratio replaced the discounted rate of return as the primary economic screening tool, it had been adopted because it was considered an ideal tool for the economic rationing of capital. Capital rationing was now a more material problem for Arkansas. Using a single measure of the cost of money (hurdle rate or discount factor) made the present value ratio results consistent at least in economic terms. If Arkansas adopted multiple rates for discounting cash flows, Mr. Edwards was afraid the calculation would lose its meaning. A present value ratio of 1.2 to 1 would not mean the same thing from division to division. To him, a screening criterion had to be consistent and understandable, or its usefulness would decrease.

Finally, Mr. Edwards was concerned with the problems of attributing capital structures to divisions. In the marketing divisions, for example, a new gas station might be 100% financed either by lease or debt arrangement. This was feasible only because the corporation guaranteed the debt. New gas stations, in Mr. Edwards' mind, were fairly risky, perhaps warranting only a 20% debt structure on average. The financing conventions in this division would make this point difficult to sell. And, in any case, Mr. Edwards considered debt-capacity decisions very difficult to make for the corporation as a whole, let alone for each of its divisions. At best, judgments would be very crude.

Mr. Edwards had two bright young MBA's working for him, and he had discussed the problem of multiple hurdle rates at length with them. Their views differed.

William Lombard stressed that he had learned at his school that the investment decision should never be mixed with the financing decision. A firm should decide what its investments should be, and then how to finance them most efficiently. If leverage were added to a present value calculation it would distort the results. Use of multiple hurdle rates was simply a way of mixing financings with investment analysis. He also believed that a single rate left the risk-decision clean cut. Management could simply adjust its standard (demand present value ratio) as risks increased.

Thomas Gamble, in contrast, noted that the weighted average cost of capital calculation tended to represent an average market reaction to a mixture of risks.

Lower than average risks projects should probably be accepted even though they did not meet a weighted average criterion. Higher than normal risk projects should provide a return premium. While the multiple hurdle rate system was a crude way of achieving this end, it at least was a step in the right direction. Moreover, he believed that the objective of a firm should be to maximize return on equity funds. Since equity funds were and would remain the chief scarce resource being allocated in the foreseeable future, a multiple rate system would tend to maximize returns to stockholders better than a single rate system. The company in effect was still using a single rate and that was its desired rate of return (e.g., 11.1%) on equity funds allocated to divisions and projects.

Mr. Edwards had one further factor to consider. A recently concluded study, reviewing the actual results against forecasts for new investments made 5 to 10 years ago, produced disturbing results. Although the methodology might be debatable, the results nevertheless seemed consistent with his impressions. The real returns on projects, according to the study, were running about three percentage points less than originally forecast on average. In certain divisions and for certain types of projects, results were much worse.

In particular, prices, either for purchased items like foreign crude (30% of Arkansas' total) or for finished products like gasoline, had been difficult to estimate, with serious repercussions on the accuracy of forecasts. The recent Arab oil embargo, related price increases, etc., would only make these forecasts more uncertain in the future.

Mr. Edwards wondered whether this evidence should be used to penalize projects from certain divisions with persisting estimating problems, and if so, how penalties might be put into force, without distorting the usefulness of economic evaluating activities.

Mr. Edwards had no hope that all the issues before him could be resolved systematically. He did want, however, to institute a pragmatic system of appropriate hurdle rates (or one rate) which would tend to facilitate better judgments under the new circumstances faced by Arkansas. He knew that his final resolutions of these issues would not only have to be convincing to himself but understandable and convincing to top management, the division managers, and the individual analysts in the operating divisions.

There were sufficient funds on hand to fund the 1974 capital budget. The capital budgeting process for 1975 would begin with the submission of plans and expenditure proposals in September 1974, by division managers. Some divisions had already begun the planning process. If any changes were to be made in the budgeting analysis, the screening criteria, etc., the announcements would have to be made very shortly.

Community Edison Company

Background

Community Edison (ComEd) is a regulated public utility that produces and sells electricity. ComEd's management has been told by its engineers that some additional equipment must be installed to meet the growth in demand from its customers. The required equipment will cost $100,000. To raise the capital necessary to purchase the equipment, ComEd needs to assure its capital suppliers that the present value of the incremental after-tax cash flows that will result from using this new equipment will at least equal the cost of the equipment, when discounted at 15 percent. In order to get the required after-tax cash flows, ComEd will need to devise an appropriate price schedule, which must be approved by a government agency known as the Public Service Commission (PSC). The PSC will not approve a price schedule if the return on investment (ROI) in any year is more than 15 percent. In calculating the ROI, the PSC uses after-tax accounting earnings divided by the beginning-of-the-year accounting value of the assets.

Additional Facts

A unit of electricity is called a megawatt hour (MWH). The essential facts are

Demand:	Year 1	60 MWH
	Year 2	120 MWH
Cost of equipment		$100,000
Life of equipment		2 years
Operating costs		zero
Salvage value		zero
Income tax rate		40 percent

513

The same financial statements are used by ComEd for income taxes and for financial reporting, and by the PSC for computing ROIs.

General Problem

ComEd's general problem is to find a price schedule that will satsify the requirements of its capital suppliers and of the PSC. The capital suppliers will be satisfied if the present value of the after-tax cash flows discounted at 15 percent is at least $100,000. The PSC will be satisfied if the return on investment is less than or equal to 15 percent each year. There is more than one price schedule that satisfies both of these conditions.

The problem of choosing an appropriate price schedule was discussed at a recent meeting of the board of directors of ComEd. Some directors felt that since the equipment needed would last two years, it should be depreciated by an equal amount in each year. Another group of directors felt that investor confidence would be enhanced if the before-tax revenues of the company were constant from year to year. They favored a financial plan that would achieve this objective. A third group of directors felt that public relations would be improved if ComEd could stabilize the price per unit charged for electricity. The financial vice president, Mr. Moneypenny, stated that any one of these objectives was feasible, but not all three. The board agreed that at the next meeting they would review the financial implications of meeting each set of objectives.

Prepare three versions of the following table for Mr. Moneypenny. Each version should satisfy the objectives of one set of directors.

| | Year | | |
	1	2	Totals
1. Units sales (MWH)	60	120	
2. Price per unit ($/MWH)			
3. Revenues ($)			
4. Depreciation ($)			100,000
5. Before-tax income ($)			
6. Income tax ($)			
7. After-tax income ($)			
8. After-tax cash flow ($)			
9. Beginning of period investment ($)	100,000		
10. ROI	.15	.15	
11. PV of ATCF ($)			100,000

The Algone Case

Memorandum

To: Y.P. Student
Economic Evaluation Manager
Wedoodit Chemical Corporation

From: I. M. Selfmade, President

As you know, the research and development department of our company has developed a new product that we are considering marketing under the brand name of Algone. Algone is an unstable liquid that must be kept under pressure at an extremely low temperature, of approximately $-200°F$. Above this temperature it decomposes within a few minutes. Algone has only one important known commercial application. When a quarter pound of Algone is sprayed through a specially designed applicator onto the feathers of a freshly killed chicken, the feathers completely disappear within seconds. There are no harmful side effects and the product has been approved for use by the Food and Drug Administration.

Wedoodit Chemical is considering two alternative means of exploiting this new product. One possibility is to sell the exclusive rights to the patent to the Chiselem Corporation, which would produce and market Algone. The alternative is for Wedoodit to build a plant to produce the product itself. Chiselem has offered us a straight cash payment of $1 million for the patent rights.

The attached memoranda from the market research manager and the engineering manager provide a basis for evaluating the profit potential of Algone if Wedoodit undertakes to manufacture and market the product itself. As economic evaluation manager, you are expected to specify the type of equipment that would be needed for the most profitable manufacturing facility to produce Algone, to present cash flow estimates for the operation of the facility, and to make a recommendation as to whether or not Wedoodit should sell its patent rights to Algone.

As you know, we have estimated our cost of capital to be 8 percent, and it is company policy to exploit all available investment opportunities that can earn us at least that much.

We are subject to income taxes of 54 percent on incremental income, consisting of 52 percent federal and 2 percent state corporate income tax rates.

Memorandum

To: I. M. Selfmade
      President
      Wedoodit Chemical Corporation

From: V. Gotfigures
        Market Research Manager

Subject: Market Potential for Algone

Total Market

The only significant potential commercial use for Algone is to remove feathers from chickens (broilers) being processed for market. This requires $\frac{1}{4}$ pound of Algone per bird. Approximately 2 billion chickens are consumed in the United States each year. Poultry consumption has been growing rapidly in the last decade as a result of improved technology and lower costs. However, no further growth in this market is expected. The effects of increased population will be offset by growing in this market is expected. The effects of increased population will be offset by growing competition from turkeys and increased consumption of beef as a result of higher consumer incomes.

About half of the poultry is processed in plants in very low-cost labor areas where Algone would be more expensive than other means of removing feathers, or in plants whose layout is not easily converted to this process. Therefore, we expect the total market potential for this process to amount to 1 billion birds per year for the foreseeable future. This would require 250 million pounds of Algone annually, or about 1 million pounds per working day (based on a five-day week and fifty working weeks in the year).

Market Share

Although Algone is patented, news of our discovery has already leaked out to competitors, who are developing similar products not covered by our patents. We are certain to have competitors soon after we begin production. The high capital costs of producing this product and the large potential market will prevent any one firm from dominating the market. We expect to be able to gain and hold 10 percent of the total U.S. market, equivalent to 25 million pounds annually.

Price

Because alternative means of removing chicken feathers are easily available, a market demand for Algone would be very elastic at prices above 12 cents per pound. It is difficult to know how low the price might go, as this would depend on the costs of our competitors and the danger the industry might overexpand, making the business unprofitable for all concerned. Prices below 8 cents per pound would almost certainly be unprofitable. We estimate the price level will fluctuate around 10 cents and recommend using that figure for planning purposes. All price quotations are F.O.B. our plant; customers to absorb freight.

Fluctuations in Demand

Fluctuations in demand are particularly important because Algone is an unstable compound. It cannot be stored except at prohibitive costs. The product must be shipped the same day it is produced. The effective market area for our plant will be limited to those customers who can receive product no more than twenty-four hours after it leaves the plant. The plant will have to operate Saturday through Thursday, because product shipped on Friday would be received on Saturday and would partly decompose by Monday. Poultry-processing plants do not operate Saturdays or Sundays.

Poultry consumption does not fluctuate very much seasonally. But poultry-processing *plant* normally operate only a half-day on Friday. Our production of Algone would be correspondingly lower on Thursday.

Thus, a plant that expects to have an average daily output of 100,000 lb should expect a product fluctuation as follows.

Day of Week	Daily Production (lb)
Sunday through Wednesday	111,000
Thursday	55,000
Average daily production	100,000

Memorandum

To: I. M. Selfmade

From: W. E. Triedit
Manager of Engineering
Design of Pilot Operations Department
Wedoodit Chemical Corporation

A plant location has been selected for the Algone project in consultation with market research and traffic departments. Land and associated development costs (nondepreciable) would be $100,000. We hold a 90-day option on the site.

Two methods of producing Algone have been devised and pilot plant tested. Summary cost figures follow.

Method	Equipment and installation per 1,000 Lb of Daily Capacity	Variable Material and Operating Expense per 1,000 Lb of Algone Produced
A	$80,000	$ 5
B	34,000	45

Either type of equipment would last for ten years, and the costs of equipment and installation would be entirely depreciable. No salvage is expected. Variable costs do not include any depreciation and are on a before-tax basis.

In addition to the equipment listed, capital costs of office, shipping, and miscellaneous utilities would amount to $20,000 per 1,000 pounds of maximum daily output. The various costs of operating these facilities are included in the variable costs of methods A and B.

It would be possible to design a plant that would include a provision for producing Algone by both methods A and B in whatever proportions seem desirable. For example, a 50,000-pound daily maximum production could be achieved in a facility having a capacity of 30,000 pounds using method A and 20,000 pounds using method B. There are no significant shutdown or start-up costs for either method of production.

A plant with a daily output capacity up to 125,000 pounds per day could expect fixed costs (for property taxes, insurance, plant guards, etc.) of about $10,000 per year (excluding depreciation). These costs would all require cash outlays and could be charged to expense for income tax purposes. A plant this size would also require working capital (inventories, accounts receivable, and cash) of about $50,000.

Bokaro Steel Plant

In 1963 the United States Steel Corporation completed for the U.S. government "A Techno-Economic Survey of a Proposed Intergrated Steel Plant at Bokaro, Bihar State, India."

The following quotations are taken from the study:

Profitability—Operations of the plant at Step I levels alone would be unprofitable even though operations are projected at full capacity following completion of start-up. . . . Each year of the projected period produces a cash deficit which reaches $270 million in 10 years or an average annual deficit of $27 million.

Presumably, government of India loans will cover these deficits.

Upon examination of the profitability of Bokaro it is evident that the heavy burden of excise duties and large interest payments on loans are the greatest influences on the results. Production costs on the other hand indicate that Bokaro could be a relatively low-cost steel producer based upon the facilities proposed and the assumptions made with respect to raw materials, manpower and managerial control.

The projected Bokaro expansion in Step II to 2.5 million ingot tons, with operations beginning four years after start of Step I production, will result in profitable operations, when close to 100 percent of capacity is reached, and will remain profitable thereafter.

Since the government of India is assumed to own the mill, it is relevant to mention that during the twenty-year period an estimated $1.0 billion of revenue would accrue to the government of India from the Bokaro operation, through excise duties on ingots, finished steel products, and coal chemical by-products. Income taxes paid by Bokaro would give the government an estimated $0.5 billion. In addition, the "surcharge" of difference between the retention price and selling price would amount to about $1.2 billion during the same period and would accrue to the government.

The selling price is the price paid by a plant's customers; the retention price, the amount it is permitted to keep. Both are set by the government.

Discuss how the items described should affect the analysis of the Bokaro steel plant.

The Eatwell Company

The Eatwell Company is considering the purchase of a new machine to replace one currently in use. The new machine would cost $100,000 and be depreciated over a four-year period on a straight-line basis. It would have no salvage value. Assume a zero investment tax credit in making your analysis.

Let us suppose that the new equipment whose purchase is proposed is to be used to replace an older machine that is fully depreciated and has no salvage value. The older machine could continue in use for another four years, if this were economically desirable. Either machine could be used to produce a part that is a component of one of the company's products. The company's engineering department estimates that the use of the proposed new machine would most likely result in a reduction of $.25 per unit in the manufacturing cost of the component. This cost-reduction calculation takes into consideration savings in direct labor, material, and variable overhead, on a before-tax basis; the cost attributed to depreciation in the new machine is not included in this calculation.

There is some chance that the savings may not be a great as anticipated. The engineering department considers that there is .1 probability the machine produces savings of $.15 per unit, and it further believes that there is .9 probability that savings of $.25 per unit will actually be realized.

Because the total savings that will be realized will depend on the number of units produced, the sales department of the company was asked to estimate total sales for the next four years for the product. The product has an established and stable market. The sales department expected that demand would continue at the present rate for the next four years, in which case total sales would amount to 600,000 units, but added an important qualification. It was known that a competitor was about to introduce a product that might be more satisfactory than the company's product to some customers. If the competitive product was successful, unit sales for the four-year period might be only 400,000. The sales department, however, believed the probability was only .3 that the competitor's product would be successful.

Considering both the engineering and technical uncertainties connected with the proposed new equipment, four possible outcomes (events) need to be considered. These outcomes and their probabilities are given in Table 1. The joint probabilities were calculated on the assumption that the unit cost reduction achieved by the machine would be statistically independent of the unit sales of the product. The assumption seems reasonable in this instance.

The financial consequences of these four outcomes are described in Table 2, assuming a .4 tax rate.

Although the cash flows that might result from using the new equipment are uncertain, the cash outflows associated with a decision to acquire the new equipment, and the tax savings from depreciation, are not certain (see Table 2).

The Eatwell Company produces about one hundred different food products, which are distributed through retail food stores. The machine in question would be used to help manufacture one of these products. The product in question accounts for about 3 percent of sales and of net profits.

TABLE 1   Joint Probabilities of Possible Outcomes Associated with Use of New Equipment

Unit Cost Reduction	Unit Sales		Marginal Probability
	400,000	600,000	
$.25	.27	.63	.90
.15	.03	.07	.10
Marginal Probability	.30	.70	1.00

TABLE 2   Annual After-Tax Savings Before Depreciation

Event	Unit Cost Reduction	Unit Sales for Four Years	(1) Prob-ability	(2) Total Before Taxes	(3) Savings After Taxes: Col. 2 × .6	(4) Annual After-Tax Savings: Col. 3 × $\frac{1}{4}$	(5) Expec-tation: Col. 1 × Col. 4
e_1	$.25	600.000	.63	$150,000	$90,000	$22,500	$14,175
e_2	.25	400.000	.27	100,000	60,000	15,000	4,050
e_3	.15	600.000	.07	90,000	54,000	13,500	945
e_4	.15	400.000	.03	60,000	36,000	9,000	270
			1.00				19,440

Eatwell has a capital structure consisting of 80 percent equity and 20 percent debt. It is able to borrow money on a long-term basis at 5 percent (before taxes). The financial committee estimates that the company's average cost of capital is 10 percent.

The company has no established policy as to the minimum acceptable level of return. It feels that both profitability and risk need to be considered in deciding whether or not an investment is desirable.

Should Eatwell purchase this new machine? What data would you use to defend your judgment?

C A S E   1 4

Rokal Company

The Rokal Company is a small regional hardware wholesaler. In recent years the company has been earning approximately $500,000 per year after taxes. Approximately half the earnings have been paid out as dividends. The stock is closely held by descendants of the founder, many of whom rely on their dividends for a substantial part of their personal income. The board of directors of the company consists of the principal stockholders or their representatives, including the president. Day-to-day management of the company is concentrated in the hands of the president, Mr. John Chalishan, who, it is generally agreed, is the only family member capable of effectively running the business. The board is consulted on important policy matters. Their main objective is to have the company maintain a stable dividend, with some growth if possible.

Recently, several of the board members have become concerned about the possible dangers to dividend stability arising from the fact that management is so heavily concentrated in the hands of the president. In case of a serious sickness or unexpected death, there would be no one else capable of quickly and effectively taking over the management. The board recognized that, in time, an effective professional manager could be found to replace Mr. Chalishan. It also recognized that the company would suffer some financial impairment if it operated without an experienced and energetic head for the six to twenty-four months that would be required to find a new president. The ability of the company to pay its regular dividend during such an interim period was questionable.

The possibility of hiring a potential replacement now was considered but rejected. A person of the necessary experience and ability would be expensive and would have no real future with the company if Mr. Chalishan, who was only forty-seven years old, remained in good health; thus, a new addition might become a source of friction and factionalism.

The board members finally concluded that the purchase of an insurance policy on Mr. Chalishan's life in the amount of $500,000 would be the best way of handling this risk. Inquiries with an insurance broker indicated that a single

TABLE 1   Analysis of Life Insurance Policy As an Investment

Present Value Analysis

Year	Cash Flow	Probability*	Expected Cash Flow	Present Value Factor†	Present Value
0	−$ 15,000	1,000		1,0000	−$15,000
1	500,000	.005	$2,500	.9524	2,381
2	500,000	.005	2,500	.9070	2,268
3	500,000	.005	2,500	.8638	2,160
4	500,000	.005	2,500	.8227	2,057
5	500,000	.005	2,500	.7835	1,959

Net present value $−4,177

Internal Rate of Return Analysis

The discounted cash flow IRR on the expected cash flows
associated with this policy is approximately minus 6 percent.

* Probability based on mortality experience for males of like age and occupation.
† Using a 5 percent discount rate.

payment of $15,000 would provide a five-year term policy on Mr. Chalishan's life, assuming he passed the usual medical examination. The policy provided for renewal if desired with no subsequent medical examination.

When the subject was raised at a board meeting, Mr. Chalishan reacted rather coolly and asked to have the subject tabled until the next meeting. This was done. At the subsequent meeting Mr. Chalishan present an analysis of the was done. At the subsequent meeting Mr. Chalishan presented an analysis of the proposed life insurance policy as an investment, which he felt it was. He recommended that the proposal should be rejected on the grounds that it was an obviously unprofitable investment. He presented Table 1 to justify his opinion.

Can the purchase of a life insurance policy be treated as an investment? Why or why not? Is it reasonable for the Rokal Company to purchase this policy?

CASE 15

The A Chemical Company

The A Chemical Company makes a wide range of products. About 10 percent of its sales and profits are generated by one product, which we will call Basic.

At the current price of $200 per ton, the total world market of Basic is 2 million tons. Currently, A Chemical and a foreign competitor, Nisson Chemical, share the world market.

The following price and cost information applies.

Price per ton	$200
Variable costs	150
Incremental profit	$ 50

Both firms use essentially the same production processes and have the same cost structures. Both firms sell 1 million tons per year.

A major consulting firm has recently studied the market for A Chemical Company and has concluded that the product is in a mature phase of its life cycle and that the demand curve is not apt to shift to the right, allowing additonal price increases.

A university professor has recently published a journal article that could lead to a new manufacturing process for Basic. The A Chemical Company has tested the new process, and the management is convinced that the variable costs could be reduced from $150 per ton to $50 per ton.

The minimum capacity for the new process is 3 million tons per year, and the process would cost $600 million.

The A Chemical Company has a large tax-loss carryover and is not likely to be paying income taxes in the foreseeable future.

The A Chemical Company and Nisson have been competing for a number of years, and given similar cost structures, they have avoided any extreme forms of price competition. The $50 incremental profit per ton is deemed to be a fair return on the capital currently being employed.

The A Chemical Company has been borrowing long-term funds at a cost of .14 and has computed its weighted average cost of capital to be .20. It knows that Nisson uses .10. The A Chemical Company has been using .20 as a hurdle rate to evaluate efficiency-increasing investments in any mature activities with little chance of growth.

There is reason to think that there will be no new significant cost-saving developments in the future and that the demand for the product will stay constant at 2 million tons per year if the price of $200 per ton is not changed. The physical life of the investment is extremely long. It is reasonable to assume that the equipment will have an infinite life.

What do you recommend that the A Chemical Company do?

CASE 16

The Detroit Tool Company

The Detriot Tool Company has 30 divisions. One of its best operating divisions is the auto parts division. This division has capital of $45,000,000 and is earning $15,000,000. This earning measure is equal to the free cash flow generated by the division and can be expected to be constant through time. The division is currently earning a return on investment (ROI) of .33.

The time has come for the president of the tool company to consider a major modernization program for the auto parts division. This automation will need $55,000,000 of additional capital (which is available) and will cause earnings to be $26,000,000. The new ROI will be

$$\text{ROI} = \frac{\$26,000,000}{\$100,000,000} = .26$$

The ROI of the division will decrease from .33 to .26. ROI is an extremely important measure to divisional management, being the basis for the annual bonus (approximately 30 percent management's wages is in the form of a bonus; the higher the ROI, the higher the bonus.)

The tool company has computed its weighted average cost of capital to be .15. It uses the internal rate of return method to evaluate investments combined with the requirement that investment have no more than a four-year payback.

There are no special risks associated with the modernization program. In fact, the risks have been determined to be less than the normal corporate risk.

Should the tool company proceed with the modernization program for the auto parts divisions? There is no thought of selling the division.

C A S E   1 7

The Lansing Lift

The Lansing Lift Company has the opportunity to invest in a new piece of equipment costing $10,000,000. The statutory corporate tax rate is .46.

Exhibit 1 shows the capital budgeting analysis for the $10,000,000 investment. The entire amount of investment is eligible for the .10 investment tax credit (ITC). The tax basis of the investment is $9,500,000 ($10,000,000 minus half of the ITC). The estimated life of the equipment is five years, with zero salvage value at the end of that period of time. The firm uses an accelerated cost-recovery system (ACRS) method of equipment writeoff for taxes.

The equipment will save $3,000,000 of labor costs per year. It will have a capacity of 2,500,000 units per year. These cost and capacity figures are based on solid information and can be relied on to be correct.

$$\text{Net PVC} = -\$10,000,000 + \$1,000,000 + \$3,000,000(1 - .46)B(5, .15)$$
$$+ \$2,881,317$$
$$= -\$10,000,000 + \$1,000,000 + \$1,620,000(3.3522)$$
$$+ \$2,881,317$$
$$= -\$9,000,000 + \$5,430,564 + \$2,881,317$$
$$= -\$688,119$$

EXHIBIT 1

Year	Depreciation Tax Savings	Present Value Factors	PV
1	.15 ($9,500,000) .46 = $655,500	1.15^{-1}	$ 570,000
2	.22 ($9,500,000) .46 = $961,400	1.15^{-2}	726,957
3	.21 ($9,500,000) .46 = $917,700	1.15^{-3}	603,403
4	.21 ($9,500,000) .46 = $917,700	1.15^{-4}	524,698
5	.21 ($9,500,000) .46 = $917,700	1.15^{-5}	456,259
		Total present value =	$2,881,317

Management accepts the cash flow assumptions that result in the $688,119 negative net present value, as shown in Exhibit 1. But it is bothered by the long-run consequences of rejecting the investment. It knows that the firm must modernize if it is to stay competitive.

The analysis considers only the first five years after the investment. Now assume that a new generation of equipment will be available at time 5. This new equipment will build on to the old equipment, automate it, and extend its life. It will cost $10,000,000, have a life of five years, and save an additional $5,000,000 per year (the total annual savings will be $8,000,000).

If the management accepts the fact that this sequence of investments is available, should it invest in the first set of equipment?

C A S E 1 8

The Toledo Glass Company

The Toledo Glass Company uses a basic type of equipment in 5 of its 30 divisions. In total, there are 40 units of this equipment in operation. There has been a technological breakthrough that might result in this equipment becoming obsolete.

The new equipment costs $10,000,000 per unit. There is .3 probability that the equipment will save $6,000,000 per year and .7 probability that it will perform no better than the present equipment. However, if one machine works (saves $6,000,000), all the machines will perform in an identical manner.

Exhibit 1 shows the computation of expected net present value of the depreciation tax shield for the machine being considered. The entire amount of investment is eligible for the .10 investment tax credit. The tax basis of the investment is $9,500,000 ($10,000,000 minus one half of the ITC). The estimated life of the equipment is five years, with zero salvage value at the end of that period of time. The firm uses an ACRS method of equipment writeoff for taxes and a .20 discount rate.

What actions are appropriate?

EXHIBIT 1

Year	Depreciation Tax Savings	Present Value Factors	PV
1	.15 ($9,500,000) .46 = $655,500	1.2^{-1}	$ 546,250
2	.22 ($9,500,000) .46 = $961.400	$1.2^{=1}$	667,639
3	.21 ($9,500,000) .46 = $917,700	$1.2^{=3}$	531,076
4	.21 ($9,500,000) .46 = $917,700	$1.2^{=4}$	442,564
5	.21 ($9,500,000) .46 = $917,700	$1.2^{\div 5}$	366,803
		Total present value =	$2,554,332

530

The Continental Company

Mr. Jeffrey Jones, the president and CEO of the Continental Company, felt a very strong obligation toward the firm's stockholders. In January 1984 he felt that, given the opportunity to earn high returns in fixed-income securities, he had to earn .20 on stockholders' equity capital (long-term debt cost .12). Given a .6 stock/.4 debt capital structure and a .46 tax rate, this was a .146 weighted average cost of capital (WACC).

	Cost	Proportion	Weighted Cost
Debt	(1 − .46).12	.4	.026
Stock	.20	.6	.120
			WACC = .146

The Continental Company had six operating autonomous divisions. These divisions made their own decisions, and the division presidents were compensated using a residual income approach (a .146 capital charge was deducted in computing each unit's income).

Jeffrey had a definite policy of cutting the firm's loses. If a division was not earning a .146 return and there was no specific plan for turning the situation around, the division was sold to the highest bidder. The two most recent sales were to leveraged buyout groups where the management of the divisions became the majority shareholders.

The Ultra Division was currently the worst performing division of the firm. The division used a large amount of plant and equipment, and inspection of the division's most recent balance sheet indicated that the total capital employed was $200,000,000, of which $180,000,000 was invested in plant and equipment.

For the past three years the division's reported accounting earnings were $10,000,000. The ROI was .05

$$\frac{\$10,000,000}{\$200,000,000} = .05$$

and the residual income was

Accounting income	$10,000,000
Capital charge, .146 ($200,000,000)	29,200,000
Operating loss	$19,200,000

While Jeffrey placed a great deal of faith in the accounting reports, he was a convert to price-level–adjusted accounting information. He realized that conventional accounting failed to consider price-level changes, and he considered this omission to be the major deficiency of generally accepted accounting principles. To rectify this failure, he had his controller prepare a price-level–adjusted income statement. The $18,000,000 of book depreciation expense was adjusted to $36,000,000 using an average of GNP price deflators, the consumer price index, and the wholesale price index. Capital was adjusted to $400,000,000 using the same price-level adjustors. And the $10,000,000 of accounting income reported now became an operating loss of $8,000,000.

Jeffrey was not willing to forecast an upward surge in sales and profits; on the other hand, he accepted an assumption that the present profit situation would continue into the future.

Ultra's industry is technologically mature, and there is excess capacity both in the industry and in the division. No significant capital expenditures are planned for the next ten years, but normal maintenance types of capital expenditures would be $2,000,000 per year.

Given the inadequate accounting ROI and, more important, the loss resulting from the use of price-level–adjusted accounting figures, Jeffrey is inclined to sell the Ultra Division to the highest bidder. Feelers have been sent out to likely buyers, and the best cash purchase offer has been $50,000,000. If the division is sold, there will be a $150,000,000 tax loss on divestment, and this loss is worth $150,000,000 × .46 = $69,000,000 in immediate tax deductions; thus, the Continental Company would net out $119,000,000 of cash flow.

Selling out appears to be much more desirable than continuing to operate at a loss (using the residual income or the price-level–adjusted measure).

You have been hired as a consultant. What do you recommend?

The Midwest Company

Karen Smith, the president and CEO of the Midwest Company, decided that it was desirable to review all six of its divisions as potential candidates for divesture. The following summary was prepared.

Division	Capital	Operating Income	ROI	Best Offer Price
A	$200,000,000	$10,000,000	.05	$ 50,000,000
B	300,000,000	30,000,000	.10	200,000,000
C	100,000,000	15,000,000	.15	90,000,000
D	250,000,000	50,000,000	.20	300,000,000
E	80,000,000	20,000,000	.25	130,000,000
F	50,000,000	15,000,000	.30	120,000,000

To simplify an otherwise more complex problem, we shall assume that the operating income is equal to the net cash flow and that we can expect this cash flow to be constant (a perpetuity). The company considers .15 to be an appropriate discount rate for the decision.

If a division is to be divested, which division should it be? Assume that the corporation is not currently paying income taxes and does not expect to in the future.

Appendix Tables

TABLE A Present Value of $1.00* $(1 + r)^{-n}$

n/r	1.0%	2.0%	3.0%	4.0%	5.0%	6%	7%	8%	9%	10%	11%	12%	13%	14%	15%
1	.9901	.9804	.9709	.9615	.9524	.9434	.9346	.9259	.9174	.9091	.9009	.8929	.8850	.8772	.8696
2	.9803	.9612	.9426	.9246	.9070	.8900	.8734	.8573	.8417	.8264	.8116	.7972	.7831	.7695	.7561
3	.9706	.9423	.9151	.8890	.8638	.8396	.8163	.7938	.7722	.7513	.7312	.7118	.6931	.6750	.6575
4	.9610	.9238	.8885	.8548	.8227	.7921	.7639	.7350	.7084	.6830	.6587	.6355	.6133	.5921	.5718
5	.9515	.9057	.8626	.8219	.7835	.7473	.7130	.6806	.6499	.6209	.5935	.5674	.5428	.5194	.4972
6	.9420	.8880	.8375	.7903	.7462	.7050	.6663	.6302	.5963	.5645	.5346	.5066	.4803	.4556	.4323
7	.9327	.8706	.8131	.7599	.7107	.6651	.6227	.5835	.5470	.5132	.4817	.4523	.4251	.3996	.3759
8	.9235	.8535	.7894	.7307	.6768	.6274	.5820	.5403	.5019	.4665	.4339	.4039	.3762	.3506	.3269
9	.9143	.8368	.7664	.7026	.6446	.5919	.5439	.5002	.4604	.4241	.3909	.3606	.3329	.3075	.2843
10	.9053	.8203	.7441	.6756	.6139	.5584	.5083	.4632	.4224	.3855	.3522	.3220	.2946	.2697	.2472
11	.8963	.8043	.7224	.6496	.5847	.5268	.4751	.4289	.3875	.3505	.3173	.2875	.2607	.2366	.2149
12	.8874	.7885	.7014	.6246	.5568	.4970	.4440	.3971	.3555	.3186	.2858	.2567	.2307	.2076	.1869
13	.8787	.7730	.6810	.6006	.5303	.4688	.4150	.3677	.3262	.2897	.2575	.2292	.2042	.1821	.1625
14	.8700	.7579	.6611	.5775	.5051	.4423	.3878	.3405	.2992	.2633	.2320	.2046	.1807	.1597	.1413
15	.8613	.7430	.6419	.5553	.4810	.4173	.3624	.3152	.2745	.2394	.2090	.1827	.1599	.1401	.1229
16	.8528	.7284	.6232	.5339	.4581	.3936	.3387	.2919	.2519	.2176	.1883	.1631	.1415	.1229	.1069
17	.8444	.7142	.6050	.5134	.4363	.3714	.3166	.2703	.2311	.1978	.1696	.1456	.1252	.1078	.0929
18	.8360	.7002	.5874	.4936	.4155	.3503	.2959	.2502	.2120	.1799	.1528	.1300	.1108	.0946	.0808
19	.8277	.6864	.5703	.4746	.3957	.3305	.2765	.2317	.1945	.1635	.1377	.1161	.0981	.0829	.0703
20	.8195	.6730	.5537	.4564	.3769	.3118	.2584	.2145	.1784	.1486	.1240	.1037	.0868	.0728	.0611
21	.8114	.6598	.5375	.4383	.3589	.2942	.2415	.1987	.1637	.1351	.1117	.0926	.0768	.0638	.0531
22	.8034	.6468	.5219	.4220	.3418	.2775	.2257	.1839	.1502	.1228	.1007	.0826	.0680	.0560	.0462
23	.7954	.6342	.5067	.4057	.3256	.2618	.2109	.1703	.1378	.1117	.0907	.0738	.0601	.0491	.0402
24	.7876	.6217	.4919	.3901	.3101	.2470	.1971	.1577	.1264	.1015	.0817	.0659	.0532	.0431	.0349
25	.7798	.6095	.4776	.3751	.2953	.2330	.1842	.1460	.1160	.0923	.0736	.0588	.0471	.0378	.0304
26	.7720	.5976	.4637	.3607	.2812	.2198	.1722	.1352	.1064	.0839	.0663	.0525	.0417	.0331	.0264
27	.7644	.5859	.4502	.3468	.2678	.2074	.1609	.1252	.0976	.0763	.0597	.0469	.0369	.0291	.0230
28	.7568	.5744	.4371	.3335	.2551	.1956	.1504	.1159	.0895	.0693	.0538	.0419	.0326	.0255	.0200
29	.7493	.5631	.4243	.3207	.2429	.1846	.1406	.1073	.0822	.0630	.0485	.0374	.0289	.0224	.0174
30	.7419	.5521	.4120	.3083	.2314	.1741	.1314	.0994	.0754	.0573	.0437	.0334	.0256	.0196	.0151
35	.7059	.5000	.3554	.2534	.1813	.1301	.0937	.0676	.0490	.0356	.0259	.0189	.0139	.0102	.0075
40	.6717	.4529	.3066	.2083	.1420	.0972	.0668	.0460	.0318	.0221	.0154	.0107	.0075	.0053	.0037
45	.6391	.4102	.2644	.1713	.1112	.0727	.0476	.0313	.0207	.0137	.0091	.0061	.0041	.0027	.0019
50	.6080	.3715	.2281	.1407	.0872	.0543	.0339	.0213	.0134	.0085	.0054	.0035	.0022	.0014	.0009

n/r	16%	18%	20%	22%	24%	26%	28%	30%	32%	34%	36%	38%	40%	45%	50%
1	.8621	.8475	.8333	.8197	.8065	.7937	.7813	.7692	.7576	.7463	.7353	.7246	.7143	.6897	.6667
2	.7432	.7182	.6944	.6719	.6504	.6299	.6104	.5917	.5739	.5569	.5407	.5251	.5102	.4756	.4444
3	.6407	.6086	.5787	.5507	.5245	.4999	.4768	.4552	.4348	.4156	.3975	.3805	.3644	.3280	.2963
4	.5523	.5158	.4823	.4514	.4230	.3968	.3725	.3501	.3294	.3102	.2923	.2757	.2603	.2262	.1975
5	.4761	.4371	.4019	.3700	.3411	.3149	.2910	.2693	.2495	.2315	.2149	.1998	.1859	.1560	.1317
6	.4104	.3704	.3349	.3033	.2751	.2499	.2274	.2072	.1890	.1727	.1580	.1448	.1328	.1076	.0878
7	.3538	.3139	.2791	.2486	.2218	.1983	.1776	.1594	.1432	.1289	.1162	.1049	.0949	.0742	.0585
8	.3050	.2660	.2326	.2038	.1789	.1574	.1388	.1226	.1085	.0962	.0854	.0760	.0678	.0512	.0390
9	.2630	.2255	.1938	.1670	.1443	.1249	.1084	.0943	.0822	.0718	.0628	.0551	.0484	.0353	.0260
10	.2267	.1911	.1615	.1369	.1164	.0992	.0847	.0725	.0623	.0536	.0462	.0399	.0346	.0243	.0173
11	.1954	.1619	.1346	.1122	.0938	.0787	.0662	.0558	.0472	.0400	.0340	.0289	.0247	.0168	.0116
12	.1685	.1372	.1122	.0920	.0757	.0625	.0517	.0429	.0357	.0298	.0250	.0210	.0176	.0116	.0077
13	.1452	.1163	.0935	.0754	.0610	.0496	.0404	.0330	.0271	.0223	.0184	.0152	.0126	.0080	.0051
14	.1252	.0985	.0779	.0618	.0492	.0393	.0316	.0253	.0205	.0166	.0135	.0110	.0090	.0055	.0034
15	.1079	.0835	.0649	.0507	.0397	.0312	.0247	.0195	.0155	.0124	.0099	.0080	.0064	.0038	.0023
16	.0930	.0708	.0541	.0415	.0320	.0248	.0193	.0150	.0118	.0093	.0073	.0058	.0046	.0026	.0015
17	.0802	.0600	.0451	.0340	.0258	.0197	.0150	.0116	.0089	.0069	.0054	.0042	.0033	.0018	.0010
18	.0691	.0508	.0376	.0279	.0208	.0156	.0118	.0089	.0068	.0052	.0039	.0030	.0023	.0012	.0007
19	.0596	.0431	.0313	.0229	.0168	.0124	.0092	.0068	.0051	.0038	.0029	.0022	.0017	.0009	.0005
20	.0514	.0365	.0261	.0187	.0135	.0098	.0072	.0053	.0039	.0029	.0021	.0016	.0012	.0006	.0003
21	.0443	.0309	.0217	.0154	.0109	.0078	.0056	.0040	.0029	.0021	.0016	.0012	.0009	.0004	.0002
22	.0382	.0262	.0181	.0126	.0088	.0062	.0044	.0031	.0022	.0016	.0012	.0008	.0006	.0003	.0001
23	.0329	.0222	.0151	.0103	.0071	.0049	.0034	.0024	.0017	.0012	.0008	.0006	.0004	.0002	.0001
24	.0284	.0188	.0126	.0085	.0057	.0039	.0027	.0018	.0013	.0009	.0006	.0004	.0003	.0001	.0001
25	.0245	.0160	.0105	.0069	.0046	.0031	.0021	.0014	.0010	.0007	.0005	.0003	.0002	.0001	.0000
26	.0211	.0135	.0087	.0057	.0037	.0025	.0016	.0011	.0007	.0005	.0003	.0002	.0002	.0001	
27	.0182	.0115	.0073	.0047	.0030	.0019	.0013	.0008	.0006	.0004	.0002	.0002	.0001	.0000	
28	.0157	.0097	.0061	.0038	.0024	.0015	.0010	.0006	.0004	.0003	.0002	.0001	.0001		
29	.0135	.0082	.0051	.0031	.0020	.0012	.0008	.0005	.0003	.0002	.0001	.0001	.0001		
30	.0116	.0070	.0042	.0026	.0016	.0010	.0006	.0004	.0002	.0002	.0001	.0001	.0000		
35	.0055	.0030	.0017	.0009	.0005	.0003	.0002	.0001	.0001	.0000	.0000	.0000			
40	.0026	.0013	.0007	.0004	.0002	.0001	.0001	.0000	.0000						
45	.0013	.0006	.0003	.0001	.0001	.0000									
50	.0006	.0003	.0001	.0000											

* r is the rate of discount and n is the number of time periods.

TABLE B Present Value of $1.00 Received per Period $\dfrac{1-(1+r)^{-n}}{r}$

n/r	1.0%	2.0%	3.0%	4.0%	5.0%	6%	7%	8%	9%	10%	11%	12%	13%	14%	15%
1	.9901	.9804	.9709	.9615	.9524	.9434	.9346	.9259	.9174	.9091	.9009	.8929	.8850	.8772	.8696
2	1.9704	1.9416	1.9135	1.8861	1.8594	1.8334	1.8080	1.7833	1.7591	1.7355	1.7125	1.6901	1.6681	1.6467	1.6257
3	2.9410	2.8839	2.8286	2.7751	2.7232	2.6730	2.6243	2.5771	2.5313	2.4869	2.4437	2.4018	2.3612	2.3216	2.2832
4	3.9020	3.8077	3.7171	3.6299	3.5459	3.4651	3.3872	3.3121	3.2397	3.1699	3.1024	3.0373	2.9745	2.9137	2.8550
5	4.8534	4.7135	4.5797	4.4518	4.3295	4.2124	4.1002	3.9927	3.8897	3.7908	3.6959	3.6048	3.5172	3.4331	3.3522
6	5.7955	5.6014	5.4172	5.2421	5.0757	4.9173	4.7665	4.6229	4.4859	4.3553	4.2305	4.1114	3.9975	3.8887	3.7845
7	6.7282	6.4720	6.2303	6.0020	5.7864	5.5824	5.3893	5.2064	5.0330	4.8684	4.7122	4.5638	4.4226	4.2883	4.1604
8	7.6517	7.3255	7.0197	6.7327	6.4632	6.2098	5.9713	5.7466	5.5348	5.3349	5.1461	4.9676	4.7988	4.6389	4.4873
9	8.5660	8.1622	7.7861	7.4353	7.1078	6.8017	6.5152	6.2469	5.9952	5.7590	5.5370	5.3282	5.1317	4.9464	4.7716
10	9.4713	8.9826	8.5302	8.1109	7.7217	7.3601	7.0236	6.7101	6.4177	6.1446	5.8892	5.6502	5.4262	5.2161	5.0188
11	10.3676	9.7868	9.2526	8.7605	8.3064	7.8869	7.4987	7.1390	6.8051	6.4951	6.2065	5.9377	5.6869	5.4527	5.2337
12	11.2551	10.5753	9.9540	9.3851	8.8632	8.3838	7.9427	7.5361	7.1607	6.8137	6.4924	6.1944	5.9176	5.6603	5.4206
13	12.1337	11.3484	10.6350	9.9856	9.3936	8.8527	8.3577	7.9038	7.4869	7.1034	6.7499	6.4235	6.1218	5.8424	5.5831
14	13.0037	12.1062	11.2961	10.5631	9.8986	9.2950	8.7455	8.2442	7.7862	7.3667	6.9819	6.6282	6.3025	6.0021	5.7245
15	13.8650	12.8493	11.9379	11.1184	10.3797	9.7122	9.1079	8.5595	8.0607	7.6061	7.1909	6.8109	6.4624	6.1422	5.8474
16	14.7179	13.5777	12.5611	11.6523	10.8378	10.1059	9.4466	8.8514	8.3126	7.8237	7.3792	6.9740	6.6039	6.2651	5.9542
17	15.5622	14.2919	13.1661	12.1657	11.2741	10.4773	9.7632	9.1216	8.5436	8.0216	7.5488	7.1196	6.7291	6.3729	6.0472
18	16.3983	14.9920	13.7535	12.6593	11.6896	10.8276	10.0591	9.3719	8.7556	8.2014	7.7016	7.2497	6.8399	6.4674	6.1280
19	17.2260	15.6785	14.3238	13.1339	12.0853	11.1581	10.3356	9.6036	8.9501	8.3649	7.8393	7.3658	6.9380	6.5504	6.1982
20	18.0455	16.3514	14.8775	13.5903	12.4622	11.4699	10.5940	9.8181	9.1285	8.5136	7.9633	7.4694	7.0248	6.6231	6.2593
21	18.8570	17.0112	15.4150	14.0292	12.8211	11.7641	10.8355	10.0168	9.2922	8.6487	8.0751	7.5620	7.1015	6.6870	6.3125
22	19.6604	17.6580	15.9369	14.4511	13.1630	12.0416	11.0612	10.2007	9.4424	8.7715	8.1757	7.6446	7.1695	6.7429	6.3587
23	20.4558	18.2922	16.4436	14.8568	13.4886	12.3034	11.2722	10.3711	9.5802	8.8832	8.2664	7.7184	7.2297	6.7921	6.3988
24	21.2434	18.9139	16.9355	15.2470	13.7986	12.5504	11.4693	10.5288	9.7066	8.9847	8.3481	7.7843	7.2829	6.8351	6.4338
25	22.0232	19.5235	17.4131	15.6221	14.0939	12.7834	11.6536	10.6748	9.8226	9.0770	8.4217	7.8431	7.3300	6.8729	6.4641
26	22.7952	20.1210	17.8768	15.9828	14.3752	13.0032	11.8258	10.8100	9.9290	9.1609	8.4881	7.8957	7.3717	6.9061	6.4906
27	23.5596	20.7069	18.3270	16.3296	14.6430	13.2105	11.9867	10.9352	10.0266	9.2372	8.5478	7.9426	7.4086	6.9352	6.5135
28	24.3164	21.2813	18.7641	16.6631	14.8981	13.4062	12.1371	11.0511	10.1161	9.3066	8.6016	7.9844	7.4412	6.9607	6.5335
29	25.0658	21.8444	19.1884	16.9837	15.1411	13.5907	12.2777	11.1584	10.1983	9.3696	8.6501	8.0218	7.4701	6.9830	6.5509
30	25.8077	22.3965	19.6004	17.2920	15.3724	13.7648	12.4090	11.2578	10.2737	9.4269	8.6938	8.0552	7.4957	7.0027	6.5660
31	26.5423	22.9377	20.0004	17.5885	15.5928	13.9291	12.5318	11.3948	10.3428	9.4790	8.7331	8.0850	7.5183	7.0199	6.5791
32	27.2696	23.4683	20.3888	17.8735	15.8027	14.0840	12.6466	11.4350	10.4062	9.5264	8.7686	8.1116	7.5383	7.0350	6.5805
33	27.9897	23.9886	20.7658	18.1476	16.0025	14.2302	12.7538	11.5139	10.4644	9.5694	8.8005	8.1354	7.5560	7.0482	6.6005
34	28.7027	24.4986	21.1318	18.4112	16.1929	14.3681	12.8540	11.5869	10.5178	9.6086	8.8293	8.1566	7.5717	7.0599	6.6091
35	29.4086	24.9986	21.4872	18.6645	16.3742	14.4982	12.9477	11.6546	10.5668	9.6442	8.8552	8.1755	7.5856	7.0700	6.6166
40	32.8347	27.3555	23.1148	19.7923	17.1591	15.0463	13.3317	11.9246	10.7574	9.7791	8.9511	8.2438	7.6344	7.1050	6.6418
45	36.0945	29.4902	24.5187	20.7200	17.7741	15.4558	13.6055	12.1084	10.8812	9.8628	9.0079	8.2825	7.6609	7.1232	6.6543
50	39.1961	31.4236	25.7298	21.4822	18.2559	15.7619	13.8007	12.2335	10.9617	9.9148	9.0417	8.3045	7.6752	7.1327	6.6605

n/r	16%	18%	20%	22%	24%	26%	28%	30%	32%	34%	36%	38%	40%	45%	50%
1	.8621	.8475	.8333	.8197	.8065	.7937	.7813	.7692	.7576	.7463	.7353	.7246	.7143	.6897	.6667
2	1.6052	1.5656	1.5278	1.4915	1.4568	1.4235	1.3916	1.3609	1.3315	1.3032	1.2760	1.2497	1.2245	1.1653	1.1111
3	2.2459	2.1743	2.1065	2.0422	1.9813	1.9234	1.8684	1.8161	1.7663	1.7188	1.6735	1.6302	1.5889	1.4933	1.4074
4	2.7982	2.6901	2.5887	2.4936	2.4043	2.3202	2.2410	2.1662	2.0957	2.0290	1.9658	1.9060	1.8492	1.7195	1.6049
5	3.2743	3.1272	2.9906	2.8636	2.7454	2.6351	2.5320	2.4356	2.3452	2.2604	2.1807	2.1058	2.0352	1.8755	1.7366
6	3.6847	3.4976	3.3255	3.1669	3.0205	2.8850	2.7594	2.6427	2.5342	2.4331	2.3388	2.2506	2.1680	1.9831	1.8244
7	4.0386	3.8115	3.6046	3.4155	3.2423	3.0833	2.9370	2.8021	2.6775	2.5620	2.4550	2.3555	2.2628	2.0573	1.8829
8	4.3436	4.0776	3.8372	3.6193	3.4212	3.2407	3.0758	2.9247	2.7860	2.6582	2.5404	2.4315	2.3306	2.1085	1.9220
9	4.6065	4.3030	4.0310	3.7863	3.5655	3.3657	3.1842	3.0190	2.8681	2.7300	2.6033	2.4866	2.3790	2.1438	1.9480
10	4.8332	4.4941	4.1925	3.9232	3.6819	3.4648	3.2689	3.0915	2.9304	2.7836	2.6495	2.5265	2.4136	2.1681	1.9653
11	5.0286	4.6560	4.3271	4.0354	3.7757	3.5435	3.3351	3.1473	2.9776	2.8236	2.6834	2.5555	2.4383	2.1849	1.9769
12	5.1971	4.7932	4.4392	4.1274	3.8514	3.6059	3.3868	3.1903	3.0133	2.8534	2.7084	2.5764	2.4559	2.1965	1.9845
13	5.3423	4.9095	4.5327	4.2028	3.9124	3.6555	3.4272	3.2233	3.0404	2.8757	2.7268	2.5916	2.4685	2.2045	1.9897
14	5.4675	5.0081	4.6106	4.2646	3.9616	3.6949	3.4587	3.2487	3.0609	2.8923	2.7403	2.6026	2.4775	2.2100	1.9931
15	5.5755	5.0916	4.6755	4.3152	4.0013	3.7261	3.4834	3.2682	3.0764	2.9047	2.7502	2.6106	2.4839	2.2138	1.9954
16	5.6685	5.1624	4.7296	4.3567	4.0333	3.7509	3.5026	3.2832	3.0882	2.9140	2.7575	2.6164	2.4885	2.2164	1.9970
17	5.7487	5.2223	4.7746	4.3908	4.0591	3.7705	3.5177	3.2948	3.0971	2.9209	2.7629	2.6206	2.4918	2.2182	1.9980
18	5.8178	5.2732	4.8122	4.4187	4.0799	3.7861	3.5294	3.3037	3.1039	2.9260	2.7668	2.6236	2.4941	2.2195	1.9986
19	5.8775	5.3162	4.8435	4.4415	4.0967	3.7985	3.5386	3.3105	3.1090	2.9299	2.7697	2.6258	2.4958	2.2203	1.9991
20	5.9288	5.3527	4.8696	4.4603	4.1103	3.8083	3.5458	3.3158	3.1129	2.9327	2.7718	2.6274	2.4970	2.2209	1.9994
21	5.9731	5.3837	4.8913	4.4756	4.1212	3.8161	3.5514	3.3198	3.1158	2.9349	2.7734	2.6285	2.4979	2.2213	1.9996
22	6.0113	5.4099	4.9094	4.4882	4.1300	3.8223	3.5558	3.3230	3.1180	2.9365	2.7746	2.6294	2.4985	2.2216	1.9997
23	6.0442	5.4321	4.9245	4.4985	4.1371	3.8273	3.5592	3.3253	3.1197	2.9377	2.7754	2.6300	2.4989	2.2218	1.9998
24	6.0726	5.4509	4.9371	4.5070	4.1428	3.8312	3.5619	3.3272	3.1210	2.9386	2.7760	2.6304	2.4992	2.2219	1.9999
25	6.0971	5.4669	4.9476	4.5139	4.1474	3.8342	3.5640	3.3286	3.1220	2.9392	2.7765	2.6307	2.4994	2.2220	1.9999
26	6.1182	5.4804	4.9563	4.5196	4.1511	3.8367	3.5656	3.3297	3.1227	2.9397	2.7768	2.6310	2.4996	2.2221	1.9999
27	6.1364	5.4919	4.9636	4.5243	4.1542	3.8387	3.5669	3.3305	3.1233	2.9401	2.7771	2.6311	2.4997	2.2221	2.0000
28	6.1520	5.5016	4.9697	4.5281	4.1566	3.8402	3.5679	3.3312	3.1237	2.9404	2.7773	2.6313	2.4998	2.2222	2.0000
29	6.1656	5.5098	4.9747	4.5312	4.1585	3.8414	3.5687	3.3316	3.1240	2.9406	2.7774	2.6313	2.4999	2.2222	2.0000
30	6.1772	5.5168	4.9789	4.5338	4.1601	3.8424	3.5693	3.3321	3.1242	2.9407	2.7775	2.6314	2.4999	2.2222	2.0000
31	6.1872	5.5227	4.9824	4.5359	4.1614	3.8432	3.5697	3.3324	3.1244	2.9408	2.7776	2.6315	2.4999	2.2222	2.0000
32	6.1959	5.5277	4.9854	4.5376	4.1624	3.8438	3.5701	3.3326	3.1246	2.9409	2.7776	2.6315	2.4999	2.2222	2.0000
33	6.2034	5.5320	4.9878	4.5390	4.1632	3.8443	3.5704	3.3328	3.1247	2.9410	2.7777	2.6315	2.5000	2.2222	2.0000
34	6.2098	5.5356	4.9898	4.5402	4.1639	3.8447	3.5706	3.3329	3.1248	2.9410	2.7777	2.6315	2.5000	2.2222	2.0000
35	6.2153	5.5386	4.9915	4.5411	4.1644	3.8450	3.5708	3.3330	3.1248	2.9411	2.7777	2.6315	2.5000	2.2222	2.0000
40	6.2335	5.5482	4.9966	4.5439	4.1659	3.8458	3.5712	3.3332	3.1250	2.9412	2.7778	2.6316	2.5000	2.2222	2.0000
45	6.2421	5.5523	4.9986	4.5449	4.1664	3.8460	3.5714	3.3333	3.1250	2.9412	2.7778	2.6316	2.5000	2.2222	2.0000
50	6.2463	5.5541	4.9995	4.5452	4.1666	3.8461	3.5714	3.3333	3.1250	2.9412	2.7778	2.6316	2.5000	2.2222	2.0000

TABLE C Present Value of Declining Balance Depreciation Amounts

Maturity	Discount Rate											
	1%	2%	3%	4%	5%	6%	7%	8%	9%	10%	12%	14%
ACRS Asset Class												
200 Percent Declining Balance												
3	0.98069	0.96202	0.94395	0.92645	0.90950	0.89308	0.87717	0.86173	0.84676	0.83224	0.80445	0.77824
5	0.97264	0.94649	0.92148	0.89753	0.87460	0.85262	0.83155	0.81133	0.79191	0.77326	0.73810	0.70554
7	0.96482	0.93158	0.90016	0.87042	0.84225	0.81553	0.79018	0.76611	0.74322	0.72144	0.68095	0.64413
10	0.95335	0.91005	0.86982	0.83237	0.79747	0.76489	0.73443	0.70593	0.67921	0.65413	0.60840	0.56783
150 Percent Declining Balance												
15	0.92586	0.85955	0.80009	0.74663	0.69845	0.65491	0.61547	0.57966	0.54707	0.51733	0.46523	0.42129
20	0.90538	0.82337	0.75199	0.68961	0.63489	0.58669	0.54407	0.50624	0.47255	0.44242	0.39106	0.34917

Maturity	Discount Rate											
	16%	18%	20%	22%	24%	26%	28%	30%	35%	40%	45%	50%
ACRS Asset Class												
200 Percent Declining Balance												
3	0.75347	0.73005	0.70788	0.68685	0.66690	0.64795	0.62992	0.61276	0.57329	0.53812	0.50663	0.47828
5	0.67535	0.64728	0.62114	0.59676	0.57398	0.55265	0.53265	0.51388	0.47166	0.43515	0.40334	0.37543
7	0.61054	0.57982	0.55165	0.52574	0.50185	0.47979	0.45935	0.44039	0.39852	0.36320	0.33308	0.30715
10	0.53167	0.49929	0.47018	0.44390	0.42010	0.39846	0.37872	0.36065	0.32161	0.28956	0.26286	0.24031
150 Percent Declining Balance												
15	0.38393	0.35190	0.32424	0.30019	0.27913	0.26057	0.24413	0.22948	0.19906	0.17532	0.15633	0.14082
20	0.31456	0.28563	0.26117	0.24029	0.22228	0.20663	0.19290	0.18079	0.15595	0.13682	0.12164	0.10932

TABLE D Depreciation Expense per Year Taking into Account Half-Year Convention and Optimal Switch to Straight Line

	Maturity (ACRS Asset Class)					
Year	20	15	10	7	5	3
1	0.03750	0.05000	0.10000	0.14286	0.20000	0.33333
2	0.07219	0.09500	0.18000	0.24490	0.32000	0.44444
3	0.06677	0.08550	0.14400	0.17493	0.19200	0.14815
4	0.06177	0.07695	0.11520	0.12495	0.11520	0.07407
5	0.05713	0.06926	0.09216	0.08925	0.11520	
6	0.05285	0.06233	0.07373	0.08925	0.05760	
7	0.04888	0.05905	0.06554	0.08925		
8	0.04522	0.05905	0.06554	0.04462		
9	0.04462	0.05905	0.06554			
10	0.04462	0.05905	0.06554			
11	0.04462	0.05905	0.03277			
12	0.04462	0.05905				
13	0.04462	0.05905				
14	0.04462	0.05905				
15	0.04462	0.05905				
16	0.04462	0.02952				
17	0.04462					
18	0.04462					
19	0.04462					
20	0.04462					
21	0.02231					

TABLE E e^{-x}

x	0	.01	.02	.03	.04
0	1.000000	.990050	.980199	.970446	.960789
.10	.904837	.895834	.886920	.878095	.869358
.20	.818731	.810584	.802519	.794534	.786628
.30	.740818	.733447	.726149	.718924	.711770
.40	.670320	.663650	.657047	.650509	.644036
.50	.606531	.600496	.594521	.588605	.582748
.60	.548812	.543351	.537944	.532592	.527292
.70	.496585	.491644	.486752	.481909	.477114
.80	.449329	.444858	.440432	.436049	.431711
.90	.406570	.402524	.398519	.394554	.390628
1.00	.367879	.364219	.360595	.357007	.353455
1.10	.332871	.329559	.326280	.323033	.319819
1.20	.301194	.298197	.295230	.292293	.289384
1.30	.272532	.269820	.267135	.264477	.261846
1.40	.246497	.244143	.241714	.239309	.236928
1.50	.223130	.220910	.218712	.216536	.214381
1.60	.201897	.199888	.197899	.195930	.193980
1.70	.182684	.180866	.179066	.177284	.175520
1.80	.165299	.163654	.162026	.160414	.158817
1.90	.149569	.148080	.146607	.145148	.143704
2.00	.135335	.133989	.132655	.131336	.130029
2.10	.122456	.121238	.120032	.118837	.117655
2.20	.110803	.109701	.108609	.107528	.106459
2.30	.100259	.099261	.098274	.097296	.096328
2.40	.090718	.089815	.088922	.088037	.087161
2.50	.082085	.081268	.080460	.079659	.078866
2.60	.074274	.073535	.072803	.072078	.071361
2.70	.067206	.066537	.065875	.065219	.064570
2.80	.060810	.060205	.059606	.059013	.058426
2.90	.055023	.054476	.053934	.053397	.052866
3.00	.049787	.049292	.048801	.048316	.047835
3.10	.045049	.044601	.044157	.043718	.043283
3.20	.040762	.040357	.039955	.039557	.039164
3.30	.036883	.036516	.036153	.035793	.035437
3.40	.033373	.033041	.032712	.032387	.032065
3.50	.030197	.029897	.029599	.029305	.029013
3.60	.027324	.027052	.026783	.026516	.026252
3.70	.024724	.024478	.024234	.023993	.023754
3.80	.022371	.022148	.021928	.021710	.021494
3.90	.020242	.020041	.019841	.019644	.019448
4.00	.018316	.018133	.017953	.017774	.017597
4.10	.016573	.016408	.016245	.016083	.015923
4.20	.014996	.014846	.014699	.014552	.014408
4.30	.013569	.013434	.013300	.013168	.013037
4.40	.012277	.012155	.012034	.011914	.011796
4.50	.011109	.010998	.010889	.010781	.010673
4.60	.010052	.009952	.009853	.009755	.009658
4.70	.009095	.009005	.008915	.008826	.008799
4.80	.008230	.008148	.008067	.007987	.007907
4.90	.007447	.007372	.007299	.007227	.007155

TABLE E   e^{−x} (cont'd)

x	.05	.06	.07	.08	.09
0	.951229	.941765	.932394	.923116	.913931
.10	.860708	.852144	.843665	.835270	.826959
.20	.778801	.771052	.763379	.755784	.748264
.30	.704688	.697676	.690734	.683861	.677057
.40	.637628	.631284	.625002	.618783	.612626
.50	.576950	.571209	.565525	.559898	.554327
.60	.522046	.516851	.511709	.506617	.501576
.70	.472367	.467666	.463013	.458406	.453845
.80	.427415	.423162	.418952	.414783	.410656
.90	.386741	.382893	.379083	.375311	.371577
1.00	.349938	.346456	.343009	.339596	.336216
1.10	.316637	.313486	.310367	.307279	.304221
1.20	.286505	.283654	.280832	.278037	.275271
1.30	.259240	.256661	.254107	.251579	.249075
1.40	.234570	.232236	.229925	.227638	.225373
1.50	.212248	.210136	.208045	.205975	.203926
1.60	.192050	.190139	.188247	.186374	.184520
1.70	.173774	.172045	.170333	.168638	.166960
1.80	.157237	.155673	.154124	.152590	.151072
1.90	.142274	.140858	.139457	.138069	.136695
2.00	.128735	.127454	.126186	.124930	.123687
2.10	.116484	.115325	.114178	.113042	.111917
2.20	.105399	.104350	.103312	.102284	.101266
2.30	.095369	.094420	.093481	.092551	.091630
2.40	.086294	.085435	.084585	.083743	.082910
2.50	.078082	.077305	.076536	.075774	.075020
2.60	.070651	.069948	.069252	.068563	.067881
2.70	.063928	.063292	.062662	.062039	.061421
2.80	.057844	.057269	.056699	.056135	.055576
2.90	.052340	.051819	.051303	.050793	.050287
3.00	.047359	.046888	.046421	.045959	.045502
3.10	.042852	.042426	.042004	.041586	.041172
3.20	.038774	.038388	.038006	.037628	.037254
3.30	.035084	.034735	.034390	.034047	.033709
3.40	.031746	.031430	.031117	.030807	.030501
3.50	.028725	.028439	.028156	.027876	.027598
3.60	.025991	.025733	.025476	.025223	.024972
3.70	.023518	.023284	.023052	.022823	.022596
3.80	.021280	.021068	.020858	.020651	.020445
3.90	.019255	.019063	.018873	.018686	.018500
4.00	.017422	.017249	.017077	.016907	.016739
4.10	.015764	.015608	.015452	.015299	.015146
4.20	.014264	.014122	.013982	.013843	.013705
4.30	.012907	.012778	.012651	.012525	.012401
4.40	.011679	.011562	.011447	.011333	.011221
4.50	.010567	.010462	.010358	.010255	.010153
4.60	.009562	.009466	.009372	.009279	.009187
4.70	.008652	.008566	.008480	.008396	.008312
4.80	.007828	.007750	.007673	.007597	.007521
4.90	.007083	.007013	.006943	.006874	.006806

Index